The Filioque

OXFORD STUDIES IN HISTORICAL THEOLOGY

The Filioque

History of a Doctrinal Controversy

A. EDWARD SIECIENSKI

OXFORD
UNIVERSITY PRESS

OXFORD
UNIVERSITY PRESS

Oxford University Press is a department of the University of Oxford.
It furthers the University's objective of excellence in research, scholarship,
and education by publishing worldwide.

Oxford   New York
Auckland   Cape Town   Dar es Salaam   Hong Kong   Karachi
Kuala Lumpur   Madrid   Melbourne   Mexico City   Nairobi
New Delhi   Shanghai   Taipei   Toronto

With offices in
Argentina   Austria   Brazil   Chile   Czech Republic   France   Greece
Guatemala   Hungary   Italy   Japan   Poland   Portugal   Singapore
South Korea   Switzerland   Thailand   Turkey   Ukraine   Vietnam

Oxford is a registered trade mark of Oxford University Press
in the UK and certain other countries.

Published in the United States of America by
Oxford University Press
198 Madison Avenue, New York, NY 10016

© Oxford University Press 2010

First issued as an Oxford University Press paperback, 2013.

Library of Congress Cataloging-in-Publication Data
Siecienski, A. Edward (Anthony Edward)
The filioque : history of a doctrinal controversy / by A. Edward Siecienski.
   p. cm.
Includes bibliographical references.
ISBN 978-0-19-537204-5 (hardcover); 978-0-19-997186-2 (paperback)
1. Holy Spirit—Procession—History of doctrines. I. Title.
BT123.S54 2009
231'.3—dc22   2009019674

Printed in the United States of America
on acid-free paper

Preface

Jaroslav Pelikan, the famed historian of dogma, once wrote:

> If there is a special circle of the inferno described by Dante
> reserved for historians of theology, the principal homework
> assigned to that subdivision of Hell for at least the first
> several eons of eternity may well be a thorough study of all
> the treatises . . . devoted to the inquiry: Does the Holy Spirit
> proceed from the Father only, as Eastern Christendom
> contends, or from both the Father and the Son as the Latin
> Church teaches?[1]

I remember reading this early in my graduate studies, and realize
now that I should have taken it as a warning of what lay ahead should
I pursue my interest in the history of the *filioque*. Yet despite Pelikan's
admonition, I voluntarily confined myself to this "Hell" for the better
part of the next decade in the hopes of understanding one of Christianity's longest and most acrimonious debates.

Why? The historian Barbara Tuchman once said that there is no
trick in getting someone interested in history—all one needs to do is
to tell a good story. The history of the *filioque* is perhaps one of the
most interesting stories in all of Christendom. It is, ultimately, a tragic
tale insomuch as the *filioque* became the source and focus of a schism
between East and West that has endured for well over a millennium.
And yet it is also a story filled with characters and events that would
make even the best dramatists envious. For to tell the story of the *filioque* one must tell of the rise and fall of empires, of crusades launched

and repelled, of holy men willing to die for the faith, and of worldly men willing to use it for their own political ends.

To say that there is no shortage of material for such a study would be something of an understatement, since both Greeks and Latins have spent the better part of the last eleven centuries writing in order to justify their respective views on the procession of the Holy Spirit. There are dozens of Latin tracts written "Against the Errors of the Greeks" (*Contra Errores Graecorum*), not to mention the numerous Byzantine "lists" of Latin errors (e.g., *Opusculum Contra Francos*). Although most are highly polemical, aimed at nothing more than demonstrating the heretical nature of the religious other, other works were learned and elegant treatises by some of Christianity's foremost theologians. From the East there was Photius, Nicephorus Blemmydes, Gregory of Cyprus, Nilus Cabasilas, and Gregory Palamas, while the West was represented by such luminaries as Alcuin of York, Anselm of Canterbury, Bonaventure, and Thomas Aquinas.

The second reason why studying the *filioque* is a task worth undertaking, then, is that it involves a critical engagement with Christendom's greatest minds, all debating that most sublime of topics, God's very mode of being as Trinity. For the Christian this is not simply an academic matter. To receive mystically the Trinity, and share in God's own triune life by following the commands of Christ, was for the Church fathers the very purpose of human existence.[2] Although Karl Rahner once argued (correctly) that for modern Christians, theologians included, the Trinity had become little more than a footnote following the treatise *De Deo Uno* in the handbooks of dogma, this was not always the case. Post-Kantians may scratch their heads at the metaphysical speculation intrinsic to trinitarian theology, but coming to understand God's mode of subsistence was (and indeed is) for Christians ultimately an existential concern. If controversies about the procession of the Holy Spirit seem to us akin to the medieval debates over "how many angels can dance on the head of a pin," this is so perhaps because the Trinity no longer plays as central a role in our theological thinking.

This brings me to the third reason for studying the *filioque* and that is the very question of truth itself. I remember being asked at my dissertation defense whether my work had any practical value, since most theologians on both sides of the East–West divide now saw the *filioque* more as a nuisance than as a genuinely Church-dividing issue. Admittedly there is some truth here, since the consensus seems to be that the power and jurisdiction of the Bishop of Rome has long since supplanted the *filioque* as *the* issue separating the Orthodox from their Catholic bretheren. And yet even the most irenic of churchmen would not deny that the continued use of the *filioque* in the Western version of the Nicene-Constantinopolitan Creed remains an obstacle to ecclesial unity. Why? Because whatever their disagreements on individual doctrines, both Catholics and Orthodox maintain that truth can never be sacrificed for cheap ecumenical gain. Catholics profess the Spirit's procession from the Son because they believe it to be true. The Orthodox cannot accept that profession of faith because they believe the Western doctrine to be in error. While relativism has become the order of the day for a good part of the post-Enlightenment world, for the Church truth (especially theological truth) still matters. Therefore, if there is genuine (or perceived) disagreement about the faith, especially on so central a matter as God's trinitarian nature, it must be examined and addressed before the restoration of full communion can take place.

This is, in fact, what I have attempted to do in this book. When I was writing my dissertation on Maximus the Confessor's theology of the procession and its use at the Council of Ferrara-Florence, I noticed several things about existing works on the *filioque*. First, that despite the importance of the doctrine, I could not find a modern English language history of either the dogma or its inclusion in the creed. The 2001 publication of Bernd Oberdorfer's *Filioque: Geschichte und Theologie eines ökumenischen Problems* was significant, but the work was in German and its claim that the Protestant Reformation changed the dynamics of the debate was (to my thinking) highly suspect. Although several excellent studies have appeared in recent years discussing the *filioque* during specific historical periods (e.g., Papadakis's *Crisis in Byzantium: The Filioque Controversy in the Patriarchate of Gregory II of Cyprus*, Ngien's *Apologetic for Filioque in Medieval Theology*, Gemeinhardt's *Filioque-Kontroverse Zwischen Ost- Und Westkirche Im Frühmittelalter*, Tia Kolbaba's *Inventing Latin Heretics: Byzantines and the Filioque in the Ninth Century*, Gamillscheg's *Die Kontroverse um das Filioque: Moglichkeiten einer Problemlosung auf Grund der Forschungen und Gesprache der letzten hundert Jahre*) none of them attempted to tell the whole story from beginning to end. That there was a need for a complete and balanced presentation of the history seemed clear to me and to others with whom I spoke, leading me to begin the present work.

What I have attempted to do in this book is to tell the story of a doctrine, or more properly speaking, of a doctrinal controversy. It is, first and foremost, a theological work. However, it is impossible to write the history of this particular doctrine without contextualizing it within the larger political, cultural, and religious environment. For example, the debates between Photius and the Carolingians about the orthodoxy of the *filioque* can be understood only within the context of the larger dispute over Charlemagne's imperial coronation and its meaning for East–West relations. The later Byzantine belief that acceptance of the *filioque* was tantamount to ethnic betrayal makes sense only when one comprehends the impact of the Fourth Crusade upon the populace of Constantinople, when the interpolation was forced upon the Greeks as part of the Latin occupation. And so, while this is not a complete account of the schism (for this see Henry Chadwick's *East and West: The Making of a Rift in the Church*), the history of the "estrangement" (as Yves Congar called it) will not be forgotten.

I have also tried to avoid the temptation, present in many of the nineteenth-century histories of the *filioque*, of simply collecting another *florilegium* supporting or refuting the doctrine. The reader will soon discover that there is already a plethora of such works, and I saw no reason to write another. That certain writers, and indeed, certain texts, have played a key role in the debate is unquestioned, and thus it will be necessary to examine them in some detail. However, what I have attempted to do in examining the biblical and patristic teaching on the procession (if such a thing even existed) is to discover the theological principles grounding them, contextualizing the prooftexts in order to understand their meaning. Of particular interest, especially in the case of the Greek fathers, will be the vocabulary used to describe the Spirit's relationship to the Son, and the exact meaning of terms like διά and ἐκ.

There are inherent limitations in a work such as this. As John Behr and others have noted, studies of individual doctrines made outside the context of the larger Christian undertaking of understanding Christ's life and meaning "according to the Scriptures" perpetuate an oversystematized view of theology that would have been foreign to the Early Church.[3] To extract the *filioque* from the larger pneumatological, Christological, and soteriological reflections of the fathers as they tried to understand the mystery of Christ is already to impose categories on the patristic corpus that the fathers themselves would never have recognized. Acknowledging this fact, we can proceed cautiously, constantly reminding ourselves that these debates about the *filioque* are ultimately part of a larger inquiry as to how Christians come to understand God, and their own destiny, as revealed to them in Jesus Christ.

To understand the biblical material, I have relied heavily on modern commentaries by (primarily German- and English-speaking) exegetes. Quotations from the Scriptures are from the NRSV unless otherwise noted. For the patristic and medieval sources, I have made use of modern critical editions whenever possible, although the reader will still note frequent references to Migne's *Patrologia Graeca* (PG) or *Patrologia Latina* (PL). Special mention should be made of the volumes recently completed by Ann Freeman and Harold Willjung for the *Monumenta Germaniae Historica*, which provide critical editions of many of the Carolingian documents. For the Council of Ferrara-Florence there is the invaluable multivolume collection of conciliar and postconciliar documents assembled and published by the Pontifical Oriental Institute between 1940 and 1977. When they are available, I have utilized and referenced English translations, including the original language if I thought it necessary to clarify the terms of the debate. All other translations are my own, although I should acknowledge Dr. Katherine Panagakos of the Richard Stockton College of New Jersey for her willingness to check some of the Greek and Latin passages.

Most of the research for this book was completed during the writing of my dissertation under Rev. Joseph Lienhard, S. J., and Dr. George Demacopoulos, both of whom also offered to read and comment upon portions of the manuscript. Their suggestions, questions, and even their criticisms were of inestimable value in the process of writing both the original work and the present volume. I would also like to thank my colleagues at Misericordia University, Drs. Stevan Davies and Allan Austin, who were gracious enough to read through early drafts and provide invaluable feedback. Fr. Oliver Herbel and Dr. Brian Matz sent along their (soon-to-be published) translations of ninth-century primary sources and offered suggestions about handling the material. Drs. Tia Kolbaba and Elizabeth Fisher sent along early proofs of works in progress (which have since become available) and kindly allowed me to make use of them. My gratitude also goes to Cynthia Read, Stephanie Attia, and the editors at Oxford University Press for taking an interest in the project and seeing it through to completion. The final stages of the project were completed thanks to a grant from the Pappas Professorship in Byzantine Civilization and Religion, part of the Interdisciplinary Center for Hellenic Studies at the Richard Stockton College of New Jersey. Thanks also to Joseph Everett, a student at Stockton, who assisted me with various tasks as I was completing the book.

David Shapiro and Meg Lord deserve some recognition for their willingness to host me in New York while I was doing research at Fordham. My mother (Terri Siecienski) and mother-in-law (Martha Matwijcow) unhesitatingly gave their time to help out with child care, allowing me to finish the project in a timely manner. Last, I want to thank my wife, Kiev, a true *mulier fortis*. It can truly be said that without her love and support none of this would have been possible.

A wife is her husband's richest treasure, a helpmate, a steadying column.
—(Sir 36:24)

Contents

The Filioque

Introduction

On June 29, 1995, in a service attended by both pious worshippers and curious onlookers, Ecumenical Patriarch Bartholomew I joined Pope John Paul II in Rome for the solemn celebration of the feast of Sts. Peter and Paul. While the meeting of pope and patriarch is always a matter of some ecclesial import, garnering a fair amount of press attention, this particular moment was noteworthy for another reason. Although it was a Roman Catholic (i.e., Latin Rite) service, when time came for recitation of the Nicene-Constantinopolitan Creed, it was sung not in Latin but in Greek, and in its original form.[1] There were no interpolations. The *filioque*, a part of the Roman liturgical creed since the eleventh century, and part of the Latin theological tradition for several centuries before that, was conspicuously absent.

Most of those in attendance that day did not immediately grasp the significance of what had just happened. For almost fourteen centuries the presence of the *filioque* in the creeds of the Western Church had been the source of an ongoing and increasingly acrimonious debate. The addition of this one word in the creed of the Roman Church in 1014 was once famously described by Alexei Khomiakov as an act of "moral fratricide,"[2] and Vladimir Lossky went so far as to call the Latin doctrine of the *filioque* the "sole dogmatic grounds for the separation of East and West."[3] Almost a millennium after its first use in Rome, the *filioque* was being omitted by the Pope of Rome in the hope of reanimating the Catholic-Orthodox dialogue and hastening that day when the Church could once again "breathe with both lungs."[4]

The significance of this gesture was not lost on the Orthodox themselves, causing some to speculate that perhaps this was a sign of Rome's willingness to adhere to the recommendations of the 1979 Klingenthal Memorandum, which had urged that "the original form of the third article of the Creed, without the *filioque*, should everywhere be recognized as the normative one and restored."[5] While this view might have been overly optimistic, Rome was, in fact, already moving toward a reexamination of the doctrine and its meaning within the Latin theological tradition. This was apparent when, in September of that same year, the Vatican published "The Greek and Latin Traditions Regarding the Procession of the Holy Spirit," a statement aimed at clarifying the Western teaching on the *filioque* in light of the historic Orthodox objections.[6] The document was warmly received in the Christian East, although many were quick to point out that while it moved the two sides closer on the issue, further work was still required to bring about genuine agreement and the eventual restoration of ecclesial communion.

The question most would ask is how this one word could have become such a problem in the first place. Could the simple addition or omission of *one word*, even in this day and age, truly have the power to divide or unite the Christian world? Does it really matter whether the Spirit proceeds "from the Father" or "from the Father alone" or "from the Father and Son" or even "from the Father through the Son"? We no longer live in the time of Gregory of Nyssa, when individuals came to blows in the marketplace over words like *homoousios* or *homoiousios*, and thus it is often difficult for us to grasp why our forebears fought so tenaciously over doctrinal subtleties.[7] This is especially true since the *filioque* is meant to describe the inner workings of the trinitarian God, a matter beyond the comprehension of most Christians and one often relegated to the metaphysical backwaters by modern theologians more concerned with Christianity's waning influence on an increasingly secularized world. Perhaps in order to understand the significance of the *filioque* for ecumenical relations, we are first required to reexamine what was (and is) at stake in the debate and why both East and West have attacked the other so vehemently for their refusal to adhere to the "orthodox" position.

The Issues

It has long been recognized that there are, in fact, two distinct, albeit related issues at stake in the *filioque* debate—the truth of the doctrine itself and the liceity of the interpolation (or, more specifically, the right of the Pope of Rome to alter a creed composed and accepted by an ecumenical council). As far back as the ninth century, during the very early stages of the debate, Pope Leo III acknowledged this distinction, clearly separating his own acceptance of the Western teaching from his inability (or at least unwillingness) to add the *filioque* to the Nicene-Constantinopolitan Creed. However, once the *filioque* became part of the creed at Rome in the eleventh century, the issues of the interpolation's liceity and the doctrine's orthodoxy were irrevocably joined. The West argued that the *filioque* was not, in fact, an addition, but rather a clarification added to defend the faith against error, something never prohibited by the fathers. If the *filioque* was orthodox, then its use in the creed to clarify the Church's teaching on the matter of the Spirit's procession was therefore not a violation of the canons. As for the pope's right to alter the creed in this way, this was something (according to the Latins) that was granted to him by Christ himself.[8]

The Eastern position was quite different; they maintained that even if the *filioque* was orthodox (which it was not), its addition to the creed was prohibited by Canon 7 of the Council of Ephesus, which forbade anyone "to produce or write or compose any other creed except the one which was defined by the holy fathers who were gathered together in the Holy Spirit at Nicea."[9] Thus, according to the Byzantines, not only was it beyond the power of the Roman Pope to change the creed, but it was even beyond the power of another ecumenical council.

Because the East, much more than the West, recognized the interpolation as a separate issue, often it was treated without reference to the orthodoxy of the doctrine itself (although they believed its removal would have also been a *de facto* admission of the teaching's heretical nature). The Greeks maintained that any treatment of the *filioque* required that it be addressed both as a theological problem (properly speaking) and as an ecclesiological problem. Ultimately what was at stake was not only God's trinitarian nature, but also the nature of the Church, its teaching authority, and the distribution of power among its leaders. During the twentieth century it was very common to view the debate solely in terms of the latter—that is, the *filioque* as nothing more than another weapon in the power struggle between Rome and Constantinople. While this was occasionally the case (the exchange between Cardinal Humbert and Patriarch Michael Cerularius in 1054 being a perfect example), such a view does an injustice to those involved. Certainly the ecclesiological ramifications were never far from the minds of the theologians and hierarchs who spoke to the issue. Everyone knew that to challenge the truth of the *filioque* was to challenge the orthodoxy of Old Rome, and by extension any claims to power or legitimacy made by the pope. And if the pope seemed determined that the East should accept the doctrine, he was so, in part, because he knew that such an act was the tacit recognition of his own role as pastor and shepherd of all Christians.

Yet for many (if not most) of those involved in the debate, the theological issues at stake far outweighed the ecclesiological concerns. This was so because both Latins and Greeks knew that ultimately they were arguing over God's mode of subsistence as Trinity, so central a Christian doctrine that to deny the orthodox position (whatever that may be) placed one outside the community of faith. At issue were rather key questions about the monarchy of the Father, the eternal relationship between Son and Spirit, the transferable (or nontransferable) nature of hypostatic qualities, and the exact relationship between the economy (οἰκονομία) and theology (θεολογία). This last issue was particularly vexing, since the Greeks were more hesitant about blurring the lines between the two, while the Latins insisted that the economy revealed truths about the immanent Trinity, including the sending of the Spirit by/through/from the Son.

Perhaps the deeper question raised by the *filioque* debate was whether the two halves of Christendom, in their diverse approaches to the trinitarian mystery, had come to differing, and ultimately incompatible, teachings about the nature of God. It was over a century ago that Théodore de Régnon famously contrasted the approaches of Christian East and West: "Latin philosophy first considers the nature in itself and proceeds to the agent; Greek philosophy first considers the agent and afterwards passes through to find the nature."[10] Most scholars today argue that the lines are too clearly drawn here, with the subtleties of both Latin and Greek thought on the subject not being taken into account, Yet there is some validity to the claim that the approaches taken by East and West were distinct and that this difference has implications for their respective views on the Trinity and thus for the *filioque* debate.

Whether the trinitarian views of East and West were genuinely incompatible is almost secondary to the fact that beginning in the eighth or ninth century people began to think that they were. This was especially true in the East, where the link between orthodoxy and orthopraxis was much stronger, and the West's use of an interpolated creed signaled to many a substantively different faith. From the Latins' perspective, the Eastern rejection of the *filioque* was considered not only sinful disobedience to Peter's legitimate successor, but also a denial of the consubstantiality of the Father and Son, and thus a form of crypto-Arianism. As the centuries passed, and dialogue degenerated into polemics, Latins and Greeks could no longer see the possibility that the other's view was orthodox, and thus to preserve the integrity of the faith they attacked heterodoxy where they believed it to exist. Power and authority were key questions in the *filioque* dispute—of this there is no doubt—but the hatred manifested in this debate stems from something deeper—the belief that the other had destroyed the purity of the faith and refused to accept the clear teachings of the fathers on the Spirit's procession.

The Role of Authorities

From the very first mention of the *filioque* debate in Maximus's *Letter to Marinus* (c. 645/646) we have evidence that recourse was made to patristic testimony in order to support the Western teaching. This was only natural, as both East and West knew that novelty, when it came to matters of the faith, was something to be shunned at all costs. The dictim of Vincent of Lerins held true for all: the true faith was "what has been believed everywhere, always, and by everyone (*quod ubique, quod semper, quod ab omnibus creditum est*), meaning that the introduction of "new" doctrines was not the work of orthodox believers, but that of heretics.[11] This is why Maximus the Confessor, in defending the Latin's use of the *filioque*, immediately countered the charge that the teaching was novel, since the Romans "had produced the unanimous evidence of the Roman Fathers, and also of Cyril of Alexandria, from the study he made of the gospel of St. John."[12]

As the debate became more contentious in the ninth century, each side began assembling *florilegia* of biblical and patristic prooftexts in the hope of demonstrating to the other the antiquity and orthodoxy of their own position. This process continued unabated for several hundred years, with Latins and Greeks finding both explicit and implicit support for and against the doctrine in the writings of the Church's greatest luminaries. While both sides could agree that the writings of these fathers were the criteria *sine qua non* for determining the orthodox faith, there were several methodological problems in utilizing the patristic witness in this manner.

There was, of course, the question of ecumenicity, since by the ninth century the Greeks' knowledge of the Western fathers (and the Latins' knowledge of the East) was, on the whole, rather poor. For this reason the West relied quite heavily on the Latin fathers (especially Augustine) while the Byzantines depended almost solely on Greek-speaking authors. By the fifteenth century the Greek delegates at Florence were (on several occasions) forced to admit a total ignorance of the Latin patristic tradition.[13] And although the Latins and their unionist supporters in the East increasingly used Greek sources to prove their case, to claim that they utilized the Greek fathers is not to say that they understood them. As John Erickson has noted, "the Latins were oblivious to the basic intuitions and concerns of the Greek patristic tradition. . . . Misjudging the weight and consistency of their sometimes questionable sources, they sought to fit the theology of others into their own narrow system."[14] Part of this approach can be explained by the fact that most of what they understood of the Greek tradition was gained through *florilegia* in translations, not by firsthand knowledge of the sources themselves. This, of course, made understanding the referenced quotations extremely difficult, since they were always read outside of the context of the original work and the author's corpus as a whole.

The issue of ecumenicity was compounded by the problem of translation. As the centuries passed, fewer participants in the debate were bilingual, so Greeks and Latins alike were forced to rely on works received in translation. This process frequently fostered misunderstanding, for as the Christological controversies of the fourth and fifth centuries had demonstrated, some terms did not have an exact Greek or Latin equivalent.[15] This was particularly true of the Greek word ἐκπορεύεσθαι ("to proceed"), which was used in the Scripture (Jn 15:26) and the Nicene-Constantinopolitan Creed to describe the procession of the Holy Spirit. In the West this word was translated by the Latin verb, *procedere*, which was understood more broadly and used to translate a number of terms denoting origin, none of which had the same unique force that ἐκπορεύεσθαι had attained. For this reason, by the thirteenth century the Latins had little trouble finding Greek prooftexts (in Latin translation) referring to the Spirit's "procession" from or through the Son, since *procedere* had been so broadly employed for this purpose.

A third problem was the authenticity of the texts themselves, since it was recognized that forged or corrupted texts had been a problem in the Church for several centuries.[16] Eventually it became common practice in both the East and West, when challenged by a text that supported the position of the other, simply to cast doubt on its authenticity.[17] When confronted with Jerome and Augustine's writings on the *filioque*, Photius immediately questioned whether they were authentic. The Latins too employed this tactic, rejecting the authenticity of Maximus's *Letter to Marinus*, which had explicitly denied the teaching that the Son was "cause" of the Spirit's procession. As a point of fact, modern patristic scholarship has since proven that many of the texts employed in the debate were either corrupted or inauthentic. This problem holds true especially for the *Quicumque Vult*, or the "Athanasian Creed," long used as a key prooftext in support of the *filioque*. Most of the quotations used by Thomas Aquinas in the *Contra Errores Graecorum*, which had been taken from the *Libellus de fide ss. Trinitatis* of Nicholas of Cotrone, have since proven to be spurious, and the version of Basil's *Contra Eunomium* employed by the Latins at Florence is now known to include sections of Eunomius's own work, added later by an ancient editor.

Yet the methodological question that was the most perplexing was the hermeneutical one: should the Greek fathers, who wrote ambiguously of the Spirit's procession διὰ τοῦ Υἱοῦ, be interpreted in light of the Western fathers (who had spoken more explicitly about procession *ex filio*), or should the Latin patristic witness be read through the Greek lens, since their testimony was the more ancient? The working premise of the Latins and the Greek unionists (e.g., John Beccus and Bessarion) was that the former option made more sense, since "it is logical that the words of those who spoke more obscurely should be interpreted by the clearer utterances of the others, which in the present case means to explain the Greek fathers by the Latin."[18]

The Greek anti-unionists clearly rejected this argument. They believed that the Latin writers should be both explained and judged by the Greek fathers, who were not only the "teachers" of the Western saints, but also the key figures in the fourth- and fifth-century trinitarian debates from which much of the debated literature had originated. If later Western saints were shown to have deviated from the faith of the early Church (i.e., the Greek fathers), then one should either reject the texts as corrupted (the option preferred by Mark of Ephesus at the Council of Florence) or simply pass over their writings in silence, refusing to "imitate the sin of Ham by uncovering the nakedness of the fathers."[19]

Yet despite the hundreds of texts collected over the centuries either proving or disproving the orthodoxy of the *filioque*, there were few efforts made to understand the fathers or their writings on their own terms. As John Erickson wrote about the Council of Florence, "All agreed that we must look to the fathers, but in the absence of a common living tradition, this meant looking to the words of the fathers rather than to their message. . . . At the council both sides relied on assembling prooftexts, claiming for these isolated words the full message and authority of the fathers. This hardly is the mark of success."[20] The fathers thus became weapons, or "soldiers" mustered in support of a particular position already taken.[21] It would not be until the twentieth century, when Catholic and Orthodox scholars in Europe began to study the sources together, that serious dialogue on the meaning of these patristic texts finally started. The increasing availability of critical editions and modern translations addressed many of the methodological concerns that had hindered discussion of the *filioque* in the past. With the era of prooftexting over, the possibility of a new stage in the *filioque* debates finally started to emerge.

Dynamics of the Debate

The *filioque* doctrine itself, understood as an *explicit* affirmation of the Spirit's procession from both the Father and the Son, goes back to at least the fifth century in the West. Augustine of Hippo clearly affirmed it in his *De Trinitate*, and by the early sixth century Fulgentius of Ruspe (d. 533) taught the doctrine as genuinely apostolic. As early as the Council of Toledo (589) the *filioque* was accepted as a normative part of the Nicene-Constantinopolitan Creed, and evidence exists that several popes included the phrase in their synodal letters centuries before it became part of the Roman liturgical creed in 1014.

Yet Eastern sources make no mention of the *filioque* until the seventh century, when monothelites in Constantinople first raised the issue as a pretext for questioning the orthodoxy of Pope Theodore. It would be another two hundred years before Photius and Nicetas formulated the first Eastern theological responses to the *filioque*, and a further two centuries before Pope Sergius IV was stricken from the diptychs for using it. By the time the "novel teaching" of the *filioque* was listed among the reasons for breaking communion with the Frankish West, the doctrine had been part of the Latin theological tradition for almost six hundred years.

Even this brief glance at the history forces one to recognize the dynamic that characterized the *filioque* debate for several centuries—that is, that the East found itself consistently *reacting* to the West, addressing themselves to positions centuries after they had first been articulated and long after they had become established teaching. This delay put the Byzantines at a distinct tactical disadvantage, since their Latin counterparts almost always came to the table better prepared and with the benefit of doctrinal unaminity. Thus while the Latins entered the *filioque* debates of the ninth century supported by centuries of tradition and a commonly accepted trinitarian model, the Greeks relied on little more than an almost instinctual conviction that the West's teaching was in error. The *filioque* certainly sounded like an innovation (καινοτομία) to Photius and the Byzantines, and to the extent that they had only become aware of it quite recently they were correct. Yet the West continued to present patristic evidence to the contrary, later augmented by the scholastic arguments of Anselm, Lombard, and Aquinas. The Byzantines, most of whom were unfamiliar with and unsympathetic to the language and methodology of scholastic theology, had difficulty keeping up on such foreign ground. This dynamic, in large part, explains why both the Councils of Lyons (1274) and Ferrara-Florence (1438–39) were such unqualified victories for the Latins. It was not, as Joseph Gill and others have claimed, that the Greek delegates at Florence were theologically unsophisticated or intellectually lacking. Rather, it was that the Byzantines, bitterly divided among themselves and faced with over a millennium of Latin writing supporting the *filioque*, could not overcome the natural disadvantages enjoyed by the West.

This action-reaction dynamic should also be kept in mind when one is studying Eastern trinitarian theology, since it forces one to recognize that the Greeks never had the opportunity of explicating a theology of the procession outside the context of their conflict with the West. Even if one maintains (as I would) that the principles governing Eastern trinitarian theology were already well established by the seventh century, the Byzantines' position on the Spirit's procession was, in large part, worked out only in opposition to the Latin doctrine. The *Mystagogy*, the "founding document" of Byzantine teaching on the procession, was nothing more than a response to the Carolingians' (allegedly heretical) affirmation that the Spirit came forth from both the Father and the Son. Gregory of Cyprus and John Beccus developed their unique, albeit diverse, contributions to Eastern trinitarian thought only as responses to the Council of Lyons, when the imperial representatives to the gathering accepted the orthodoxy of the *filioque* in the name of the entire Eastern Church. Placed in the position of constantly having to prove the negative (i.e., that the Holy Spirit did *not* proceed from the Father and Son), the Greeks emphasized only certain aspects of the Eastern tradition while totally ignoring others. This approach explains why, in his struggles against the Carolingians, Photius never explored the deeper meaning behind the formula "through the Son" (διὰ τοῦ Υἱοῦ), or the necessary eternal relationship between the Son and the Spirit, "even though it was a traditional teaching of the previous Greek fathers."[22] This omission is understandable given Photius's intent, and yet his emphasis on the Spirit's procession from the Father alone (ἐκ μόνου τοῦ Πατρός), without reference to the Son, created an imbalance that later Byzantine theologians had to address.[23] In fact, it would not be until the mid-twentieth century that the Orthodox finally began to develop a theology of the procession outside of their polemical battle with the West, placing the Western Church in the unusual (but ultimately rewarding) position of having to engage in a genuine dialogue with Eastern trinitarian thought.

Maximus the Confessor

Among the hundreds of figures involved in the *filioque* debates throughout the centuries, Maximus the Confessor enjoys a privileged position. His *Letter to Marinus*, written in 645 or 646, is the earliest witness to the East's knowledge of, and hostility to, the Latin teaching on the procession. Maximus himself was the first Greek father to specifically address the procession of the Holy Spirit in light of the Latin teaching (which, by the mid-seventh century, was already well established). However, unlike the case of later Eastern responses to the *filioque*, Maximus's intention was not to refute the doctrine, but rather to understand it in light of the tradition. Maximus certainly was in a unique position to accomplish this task. As a Greek living in North Africa, and aligned with Rome against monothelites in Constantinople, Maximus often acted as a "mediator between East and West."[24] And while questions remain about Maximus's knowledge of Latin and the Latin fathers (esp. Augustine), he nevertheless demonstrates a genuinely ecumenical nature that would be sorely lacking in future generations.

It was this ecumenical spirit that allowed Maximus to reconcile the Western teaching on the *filioque* with the writings of the Greek fathers as he understood them. Yet he did not accomplish this harmony by making the Greek fathers closet filioquists (as later Byzantine unionists would do), nor did he ignore those Eastern principles that served as the basis for orthodox trinitarian teaching (e.g., the Father as "sole cause" [μία αἰτία]). Rather, what Maximus was able to do was express the *consensus patrum* on the Spirit's procession while concurrently affirming the theological concerns of both East and West. If this fact was lost to generations of Christians, the reason was that in their polemical fervor, entangled in the dialectic established in the ninth century, neither side was capable of reading Maximus correctly. The *Letter to Marinus* was not only the clearest explication of the patristic mind on the subject of the procession, but also a testament to how both East and West lost the ability to understand the fullness of the tradition, expressed so well by Maximus in the seventh century.

Because the *Letter to Marinus* played such a central role in the history of the *filioque* controversy, a separate chapter of this book is devoted to discussing Maximus and his theology of the procession. His writings on the procession of the Holy Spirit, especially the *Letter to Marinus* and *Quaestiones ad Thalassium* 63, reappear throughout the story, used by both Latins and Greeks to support their respective positions on the *filioque*. What I expect will become apparent is my own conviction, supported by the history itself, that Maximus's interpretation of the *filioque* provides modern theology with the most promising tool for bringing East and West closer together on this most divisive issue.

Council of Ferrara-Florence

By any standard the "reunion council" of Ferrara-Florence in 1438–39 was a disaster. However, the question that has intrigued (and divided) historians over the centuries is whether the Greek and Latin delegates at Florence even had a chance of succeeding given the longstanding enmity between them. Despite the fraternal rhetoric and the genuine desire of all for church union (each, of course, for his/her own reasons), John Meyendorff and others have asked whether or not real dialogue was ever possible at Ferrara-Florence.[25] Lacking a shared *sensus ecclesiae*, it is not surprising that the Council spent days quibbling over the authenticity of texts and repeating the same old arguments that had marked the *filioque* debate since the time of Photius. This was not "ecumenical dialogue" as it is currently understood, but rather "the meeting of two brothers who had lived together and grown up together, and moved apart and went their separate ways. When after many years they met again they neither recognized each other nor could they agree upon the manner of their former life together. Although they had met and had determined to resume fraternal relations, they separated and found themselves even greater strangers than before."[26]

This position is contrasted with that of Joseph Gill, who maintained that Florence had all the necessary ingredients for a successful reunion council: substantive debate, freedom of expression, and (unlike Lyons) full representation of the Eastern patriarchates.[27] According to Gill, the sole stumbling block to union was the stubbornness of one man (Mark of Ephesus), who simply refused to bow to the superior arguments of the Latins. Had Mark been silenced by the emperor, or punished for refusing to accept the decisions of an ecumenical council, the history of Christendom might well have been different.

Whether a success that failed or a failure that almost succeeded, the Council of Florence warrants a special place in our study of the *filioque* debates. All the evidence was brought forward—biblical, patristic, scholastic—and all the arguments either proving or disproving the orthodoxy of the doctrine were repeated. It was as if Photius and Cabasilas were meeting Ratramnus and Aquinas in open debate. Unwilling to bend or compromise, and convinced that the other was in error, Latins and Greeks argued back and forth for months without result. It was, in many ways, the history of the debate in miniature.

Especially interesting for our purposes was the use of Maximus's *Letter to Marinus*, a document that both sides seemed unable to understand completely, each using it simply as another prooftext for their respective positions on the procession. Perhaps no event better proves my earlier point about the loss of Maximus's trinitarian vision, and the inability of both East and West to extricate themselves from the dialectic established in the ninth century between procession "from the Father and the Son" and procession "from the Father alone." For this reason, particular attention will be given to both the Council of Florence and the use of Maximus the Confessor's theology of the procession as interpreted by the delegates. When contrasted with modern theology's grasp of Maximus and his trinitarian corpus, the flawed understanding of the Florentine delegates stands in sharp relief, forcing one to ask "what might have been" had they only been able to read the *Letter to Marinus* correctly.

The Twentieth Century

Beginning with the Bonn Conference in 1875, a new era of dialogue between East and West began, although the Roman Catholic Church would not become a participant for several more decades. By the mid-twentieth century the ecumenical movement was gaining momentum and was complimented by the initiation of formal theological dialogues between the churches, many of which focused on the theology of the procession. It is perhaps providential that during this period of intense ecumenical activity there also occurred a renewed interest in the works of Maximus the Confessor. This was especially true in the Western world, where Maximus's writings received scant academic attention until the 1941 publication of Hans Urs von Balthasar's *Kosmische Liturgie: Das Weltbild Maximus des Bekenners*.[28] Of particular interest have been the studies of Maximus's theology of the Trinity and his teaching on the *filioque* as contained in the *Letter to Marinus*.[29] The writings of Maximus, overlooked by Rome at the Council of Florence, have increasingly become Catholicism's chief hermeneutical tool for understanding and interpreting its own teaching on the *filioque*.

Even more encouraging is the fact that this last stage of the dialogue has been characterized by genuine Christian charity, a component conspicuously absent from previous East–West encounters. While it is true that important issues remain unresolved, and that the presence of the *filioque* in the creed remains a visible obstacle to unity, at no point since the seventh century have East and West been so close to resolving the dispute, or so determined to "speak the truth (together) in love."

However, in order for this new dialogue to succeed where so many others have failed, participants must first come to understand the history of the *filioque*, lest they simply repeat the mistakes of the past. It is here that the work of twentieth-century historical theologians has proved invaluable, providing both the texts and context of the debate in books (largely) free of denominational bias.[30] Each in its own way has added immensely to the dialogue between East and West, providing the historical tools necessary to understand both the doctrine and its significance for previous generations of Christians.

The Present Work

It is with this in mind that I offer the present volume and my own (small) contribution to *filioque* scholarship. Beginning with the biblical foundations of the doctrine, and moving through the patristic period, I hope to draw out those principles that shaped both Eastern and Western trinitarian theology. Maximus the Confessor, as was already mentioned, receives special attention, as will those figures throughout the centuries whose writings on the procession shaped subsequent debate. It will become vital for our study to understand the dialectic that was established in the ninth century, when the *filioque* became a *casus belli* separating East and West. It was during this period when both Latins and Greeks, each in their own way, lost important aspects of the patristic teaching on the procession and created an imbalance which is only now being addressed.

The work continues with a look at those post-schism figures on both sides whose writings contributed to the increasingly divergent views on the procession of the Holy Spirit. Anselm of Canterbury and Thomas Aquinas are significant in this regard, as are Theophylact of Ohrid and Nicetas of Nicomedia, whose twelfth-century debate with Anselm of Havelberg in 1136 demonstrated that consensus on the *filioque* (albeit strained) was still possible as late as the twelfth century. Central to an understanding of the Byzantine view(s) on the procession is the Council of Lyons and the three distinct "schools" of trinitarian theology that took shape in the years following the council. While the stances of the unionists and anti-unionists are the most familiar, the mediating position of Gregory of Cyprus (later taken up by Gregory Palamas) is by far the most interesting, in that it attempts to retrieve the authentic intuition and fullness of Maximus's own trinitarian vision.

As was stated earlier, a separate chapter is devoted to the Council of Ferrara-Florence, where Greeks and Latins demonstrated quite clearly how far apart the two traditions had grown. After examining the council and its impact upon post-Florentine theology, our study picks up with modern ecumenical dialogues, beginning in 1875 with the Bonn Conference between the Orthodox and Old Catholic Churches. Attention will be paid both to the official dialogues and to the work of those theologians, East and West, whose writings offered to modern theology new ways of understanding the doctrine and resolving the dispute. It is not an accident that many of these writers made explicit references to the work of Maximus, his trinitarian principles, and the *Letter to Marinus*, which has increasingly been seen as *the* key text for reconciling East and West on the subject of the procession. Its importance was particularly true in the Vatican's 1995 statement, "The Greek and Latin Traditions Regarding the Procession of the Holy Spirit," a clarification that received a generally warm reception in the Orthodox world.

Before proceeding with our study, it is important to note that the present work makes no claim to be a complete history of the *filioque* or the doctrinal controversy surrounding it. The reason is simple—at present the centuries-long debate over the theology and place of the *filioque* does not appear to be at an end. Despite the remarkable progress made over the last few decades, a great deal of work needs to be done before East and West can finally remove the *filioque* from the list of issues that divide them. There are, so to speak, chapters that have yet to be written, covering that period of time (hopefully in the not-too-distant future) when the *filioque* is no longer a stumbling block on the road to unity. I can only hope that I will still be around to read them.

I

The Procession of the Holy Spirit in the New Testament

Perhaps the best way to begin is to recognize that the New Testament does not explicitly address the subject of the Spirit's procession as later theology would understand the doctrine. According to Henry Swete, "there is no explicit teaching upon this point (i.e., the eternal relation of the Holy Spirit to the Son) in the apostolic writings. Even the statement that the Holy Spirit proceeds from the Father does not explicitly teach the doctrine of an eternal procession as it is conveyed in the modified terms of the creed."[1] There are, to be sure, certain principles established in the New Testament that shaped later Trinitarian theology, and particular texts that both Latins and Greeks exploited to support their respective positions vis-à-vis the *filioque*, but to claim more than that is already an exercise in eisegesis—reading into the text far more than the biblical authors themselves intended.

In fact, most biblical scholars today doubt that the New Testament authors even thought in trinitarian terms (i.e., with Father, Son, and Spirit each understood as distinct "persons" within God).[2] While post-Nicene writers would find the Scriptures littered with texts demonstrating Jesus' divine origin, modern exegetes question whether the New Testament ever explicitly refers to Jesus as "God" or whether Jesus thought of himself as such.[3] There are many verses that might be references to the persons or activity of the Trinity (Luke 1:35, 3:22, 4:1–14; Matt 1:18–23, 3:16–17, 28:19; Acts 1:1–6, 2:33, 38–39), but one must be careful about imposing later categories upon the biblical witness. Even Paul's frequent allusions to the activity of Father, Son, and Spirit (Eph 4:4–6 Gal 4:4–6, Tit 3:4–6, 1Cor 12:4–6) do not necessarily prove an explicit understanding of God's triune nature.[4]

Yet even if the New Testament lacks an explicit awareness of Trinity as post-Nicene Christianity understood it, it is still possible to recognize that the biblical authors, each in their own way, established relationships between God (the Father), Jesus Christ, and the Spirit that later became the basis for the Church's trinitarian teaching. This is particularly true of the relationship between the Son and the Spirit, both of whom are irrevocably linked to each other, and to the Father, in the biblical understanding of the work of salvation.

The Synoptics

The Infancy Narratives

Both the infancy narratives of Matthew and Luke affirm that Jesus' conception took place by the Holy Spirit (Luke 1:35, Matthew 1:18), yet this does not mean that the Holy Spirit was thought to be the father of Jesus, or that he took "the husband's role in the begetting."[5] In fact, Raymond Brown points out that no definite article is provided in Matthew's account (i.e., "she was found with child through *a* holy spirit"), which suggests that he understands the Holy Spirit not as a divine person but rather as an agent of divine activity.[6] Matthew's purpose is simply to make clear to the reader that the birth of Jesus is the work of God, not the result of any improper behavior on Mary's part.

Brown links the Lucan reference to the Holy Spirit (Luke 1:35) to the understanding of Jesus' sonship as found in Romans 1:3–4, where there is a clear contrast drawn between being born a son of David in the flesh and being born the Son of God according to the Spirit (an event that occurs for Paul in the resurrection). For Luke there is no such juxtaposition, no hint of "divine adoption," since here, even at his conception, Jesus is called the Son of God and Son of the Most High.[7] As in Matthew, there is no definite article provided, leading Joseph Fitzmeyer to suggest that "holy spirit" is used here simply as a parallelism to "power of the Most High" and thus is best understood "in the Old Testament sense of God's creative and active power present to human beings."[8]

According to Louis Bouyer, Luke also seems to suggest in his infancy narrative that the "spirit" mentioned here is the same one that is operative throughout the history of Israel. Before Jesus' birth the Spirit overshadowed Mary "just as the *Shekinah* (the Divine Presence) once descended on Sinai at the time of the first Covenant."[9] This same Spirit filled John the Baptist in his mother's womb (Luke 1:15), just as he spoke through figures such as David (Acts 1:16, 4:25) and Isaiah (Acts 28:26). All of this, according to Bouyer "testifies that the terrestrial birth of Jesus amounts to a descent of the Spirit on the earth. For the Spirit is shown at work everywhere and in everything."[10]

The Baptism of Jesus

It is at the baptism of Jesus that the Synoptics describe what will later become known in theology and iconography as "the Theophany" (i.e., the revelation of God as Trinity). In Mark 1:10–11 we read that "when he came up from the water, immediately he saw the heavens opened, and the Spirit descended upon him like a dove; and a voice came from heaven, 'Thou art my beloved Son with thee I am well pleased.'" Both Matthew and Luke draw heavily from Mark's account in their own retellings of the scene, although Matthew adds "Spirit of God" (Matt 3:16) and Luke refers to "the Holy Spirit" who "descended upon him in bodily form, as a dove" (Luke 3: 22). Scholars disagree about how to understand "dove" in this context, some arguing that it is best understood as a representative of Israel,[11] while others see it simply as a harbinger of good news or divine grace.[12]

While there is no direct evidence that Mark intended this event to be read in an adoptionist sense (i.e., that Jesus was here being adopted as God's Son through the power of the Spirit), it must also be admitted that there is also nothing in his account that precludes this reading. Certainly Matthew and Luke, both of whom had earlier affirmed Jesus' conception by God's Spirit, cannot be understood this way. For them, Jesus was already Son of God and filled with the Spirit from the moment of his conception. And yet the baptism "opens up an entirely new chapter. . . . A new communication or mission was initiated in the event of his baptism, when he was declared the Messiah, the one on whom the Spirit rests, who will act through the Spirit and who, once he has become the glorified Lord, will give the Spirit."[13]

Some modern scholars now talk about the baptism, especially as related in Luke, in terms of a "spirit Christology," whereby Jesus is given the power of the Spirit to exercise his ministry in the world.[14] According to Roger Haight, "the Holy Spirit is God's own power; Jesus' ministry of healing and exorcism is made possible by God's being with him and working within him. Thus the promise in Isaiah 42:1 is fulfilled. . . . In this way the anointing at Jesus' baptism equips Jesus with God's power for his ministry.[15]

Some have even gone so far as to speak of Jesus' "possession" by the Spirit—indicating that the historical Jesus thought of himself as possessed by the Spirit of God in such a way that he became its very incarnation.[16] James D. G. Dunn argues in favor of a "consciousness of inspiration, a sense of divine commissioning behind his preaching and of divine power in his ministry of healing," that would have placed Jesus well within the prophetic tradition.[17] However one wants to understand the material, the Synoptics unanimously testify to the role that the Spirit plays at the beginning of Jesus' public ministry. It is upon Jesus that God's Spirit rests, and it will be in his ministry that one will see the activity of the Spirit operative in the world.

The Ministry of Jesus

In the gospel of Luke, the Holy Spirit is not only the agent of Jesus' miraculous conception (1:35), but the power that fills him and then leads him into the desert to be tempted by the devil (4:1).[18] According to Joseph Fitzmeyer, Jesus conquers the devil because he is filled with the Spirit, the temptation itself being "under the aegis of God's Spirit."[19] When he returns, he does so "armed with the power of the Spirit" (4:14), showing that "the *dynamis* that Jesus possesses is not limited to a miraculous power (for healing and exorcising, as chiefly in Mark); it is closely associated with the Spirit under whose guidance he teaches and interprets Scripture."[20] "Having interpreted his baptism as the Spirit's anointing for his mission, he then outlines his mission as God's son," using the words of the prophet Isaiah.[21]

> "The Spirit of the Lord is upon me
> Because he has anointed me
> To bring glad tidings to the poor.
> He has sent me to proclaim liberty to the captives
> And recovery of sight to the blind
> To let the oppressed go free
> And to proclaim a year acceptable to the Lord."

Following the return of the seventy-two, Jesus rejoices in the Holy Spirit (10:21), "understood as the source and inspiration of Jesus' joy and praise of the Father."[22] He promises that those who pray to the Father will receive the Holy Spirit as a gift from the Father (11:13), and echoing Mark (3:28–30), he warns against blaspheming the Holy Spirit, since it is he who will teach the disciples what to say when they are dragged before the authorities (12:10–12). This picture is consistent with Dunn's assertion that "Jesus is presented consistently as a man of the Spirit during his life and ministry; not yet as the one who could freely dispense the Spirit."[23] The Spirit to come upon the disciples is still a future reality, even while presently active in their midst.

It is noteworthy that Matthew's version of the "Beelzebub controversy" as found in Mark 3:23–30 includes the (presumably Q) saying that "if it is by the Spirit of God that I cast out demons, then the Kingdom of God has come among you."[24] Matthew 12:28 is one of only four occasions where Matthew speaks about the Kingdom of God, a term that is usually reserved for the coming reign of the Father following the end times.[25] And yet here we have a clear reference both to the power of the Spirit alive in the person of Jesus, and to the presence of the Kingdom of God as demonstrated through the actions of that Spirit.[26] Later, when Jesus "yields up his spirit" (ἀφῆκεν τὸ πνεῦμα) on the cross (27:50) Matthew may be making a connection between the death and resurrection of Christ and the gift of this same Spirit to the community of believers.[27] According to Dunn, "He who was on earth was a man inspired by the Spirit by his resurrection becomes the man who dispenses the Spirit."[28]

The "Great Commissioning"

The conclusion of Matthew's gospel contains one of the clearest references to the Trinity in the entire New Testament (28:19).[29] Unlike Luke, where the commissioning takes place before the coming of the Holy Spirit at Pentecost, Matthew's gospel assumes that the Spirit is already known and active among the followers of the resurrected Jesus. According to R. T. France, having "drawn attention to the close links between himself and the Holy Spirit, . . . 'the Son' takes his place as the middle member, between the Father and the Holy Spirit"[30] imparting to others the gift of the Spirit that comes from the Messiah.[31]

Luke's version of the great commissioning has Jesus telling his apostles to stay in Jerusalem to "await the Father's promise" when they will be "invested with power from on high" (24:49). While the Holy Spirit is not specifically mentioned here, according to Fitzmeyer, "the word *dynamis* (power) . . . rings a bell for the careful reader of the Lucan gospel. For it was 'with the power of the Spirit' that Jesus himself withdrew to Galilee after his encounter in the desert with the devil (4:14). Moreover, it was with 'the power of the Lord' that he healed people. And the 'power that went forth from him' (6:19) is precisely the 'power' with which his disciples are now to be invested (see Acts 2:32–33)."[32]

John

Unlike the Synoptics, which clearly link the ministry of Jesus with the activity of the Spirit, John's gospel speaks of the Paraclete almost exclusively in the future tense.[33] The reason for his doing so is made clear in John 7:39: "As yet the Spirit had not been given because Jesus was not yet glorified." Jesus tells his disciples that the Spirit is the one "I will send" (πέμψω) (15:26, 16:7) from the Father, or the one that the Father will send in his name (14:26). The Father will give him (14:16) and he will teach them all things and remind them of everything Jesus said (14:26). He will convict the world of guilt in regard to sin (16:8), guide the disciples in all truth (16:13), and bring glory to Jesus by taking what is his and making it known (16:14–15). This understanding of Paraclete as a future reality, according to Raymond Brown, supports the idea of "a tandem relationship (between Jesus and the Spirit) whereby a second figure, patterned on the first, continues the work of the first."[34] The Spirit in John is seen as "the personal presence of Jesus in the Christian while Jesus is with the Father," and thus it is not coincidental that "everything that has been said about the Paraclete has been said elsewhere in the gospel about Jesus."[35]

What then is the relationship of the Paraclete to the Father? Ultimately the Paraclete, like Jesus himself, is an emissary of the Father. According to Brown, "In declaring or interpreting what belongs to Jesus, the Paraclete is really interpreting the Father to men; for the Father and Jesus possess all things in common. . . . In Johannine thought it would be unintelligible that the Paraclete has anything from Jesus that is not from the Father, but all that he has (for men) is from Jesus."[36]

It is with this understanding that one can better understand those statements that refer to the Spirit's origin, and to the fact that, according to John, he is given by (14:16), sent by (14:26), and proceeds from (15:26) the Father, but that he is also sent by the Son (15:26, 16:7) and receives what is his (16:14).[37] Insomuch as the death and glorification of Christ is a precondition for the coming of the Spirit, he is sent by the Son, but he is also sent by the Father, whose emissary he ultimately is. It is this reality that verse 15:26 tries to convey, as the Comforter "whom I will send you from the Father" becomes also "the Spirit of Truth who proceeds from the Father."

Important here is the meaning of ἐκπορεύεσθαι. The verb ἐκπορεύω in the middle and passive voices is usually translated as "to go forth," "proceed out of," "depart from," or simply "to leave" and occurs several times in the New Testament. It is seen in Mark 6:11 ("shake the dust from your feet when you leave" [ἐκπορευόμενοι]). In the middle voice it most often has the force of "to come forth," "to come out of," or "proceed out of" as in Mark 7:15–23, where the verb is used several times to teach that it is what comes out of [ἐκπορευόμενα] a man that makes him unclean, and John 5:29, where Jesus tells his followers that the hour is coming when the dead will hear the voice of the Son of Man and come out [ἐκπορεύσονται] from their tombs.

There are several occurrences of ἐκπορεύεσθαι or ἐκπορεύω in Matthew, including Matthew 3:5, describing how the people went out (ἐξεπορεύετο) to see John, Matthew 4:4, where there is a clear allusion to Jeremiah 44:17 ("one does not live by bread alone but by every word proceeding [ἐκπορευομένῳ]) from the mouth of God"), and Matthew 20:29 ("As Jesus and his disciples were leaving [ἐκπορευομένων] Jericho"). The verb also occurs twice in Matthew 15:10–20, which is the Matthean interpretation of Mark 7:15–23. Luke uses it in 4:22 to describe the gracious words that came forth [ἐκπορευομένοις] from Jesus' lips, and Ephesians 4:29 condemns unwholesome talk that comes out (ἐκπορευέσθω) of the mouth. In Acts it is used to describe the movement of both individuals and demons (19:12: "the evil spirits left [ἐκπορεύεσθαι] them").

The Book of Revelation uses the verb several times, to describe the sharp double-edged sword that came forth (ἐκπορευομένη) from the Son of Man (1:16), lightning coming (ἐκπορεύονται) from the throne (4:5), the fire, smoke, and sulfur that came forth (ἐκπορεύεται) from the horses (9:17–18), and fire coming from (ἐκπορεύεται) the mouth of the two witnesses (11:5). In the vision of John evil spirits go forth (ἐκπορεύεται) throughout the world (16:4), are struck down by the sword coming out (ἐκπορεύεται) of the Lord's mouth (19:15), and in the New Jerusalem the water of life flows (ἐκπορευόμενον) from the throne of God through the middle of the city (22:1).

Although Gregory Nazianzus and others later attached a specific theological significance to ἐκπορεύεσθαι (i.e., to speak about the unique manner of the Spirit's coming-to-be from the Father), there appears little reason to believe that John conveys that meaning in 15:26, or that he is deliberately trying to differentiate his ἐκπορεύεσθαι from the Father from his sending from the Son. As Rudolf Schnackenburg writes:

> The double statement, that is, that Jesus will send him and that he proceeds from the Father, is a synonymous parallelism, expressing the same idea in variation. Although this interpretation is in itself possible (i.e., ἐκπορεύεσθαι in an internally Trinitarian sense) it did not come within the Johannine vision. The Johannine Jesus having been sent by the Father can also be expressed by the formula 'I came forth (ἐξῆλθον) from God (or the Father)' (8:42, 13:3, 16:27,17:8) and we have already seen (7:29 and 8:42 above) that this does not have a different meaning, ἐκπορεύεσθαι being merely a stylistic variant of ἐξέρχεσθαι."[38]

For Schnackenburg, Brown, Barrett, and most other scholars, ἐκπορεύεσθαι simply describes the mission of the Spirit, who like Jesus comes forth from the Father and is sent by the Son into the world to continue his work of revealing God to humanity.[39] In this context, they argue, it is used not to describe the hypostatic origin of the Spirit (as later theology will contend) but rather it should be seen "in parallelism with the 'I shall send' in the next line and refers to the mission of the Paraclete Spirit to men. The writer is not speculating about the interior life of God, he is concerned with the disciples in the world."[40]

John 16:14 ("he will receive what is mine and make it known to you"), which later Latin theology will interpret as the Spirit's "receiving existence" from the Son, is more likely a restatement of verse 16:13 that the Spirit offers no new revelation (i.e., "that he will speak only what he hears"). According to Brown, this verse does not intend to describe the hypostatic origin of the Spirit, but rather wants to challenge the idea that the Spirit offers truths not already available in Christ.[41] Rudolf Bultmann agrees, concluding that the passage's intent is to confirm that "the Spirit's word is not something new, to be contrasted with what Jesus said. . . . The Spirit will bring no new illumination, or disclose new mysteries; on the contrary, in the proclamation effected by him, the word that Jesus spoke continues to be efficacious."[42]

Rudolf Schnackenburg sees the passage's purpose as Christological, affirming that since Jesus has received all from the Father, he is already in full "possession" of the revelation to be imparted by the Spirit. What the Paraclete will make known already belongs to Jesus, from whom he will receive it. "Jesus is therefore confirmed by the Paraclete as the one to whom everything is entrusted."[43] The next verse ("All that the Father has is mine") would seem to reinforce this notion, since it confirms that Jesus possesses the full revelation of the Father. Although this will later become a powerful prooftext in favor of the *filioque* (i.e., the Father's power to spirate the Holy Spirit must then also belong to the Son), the evidence suggests that the evangelist's intent was far different. For Bultmann and others it is simply a clear reminder of the unity of Father and Son; that if "the Spirit continues the proclamation of the word of *Jesus* it means it is the word of God, that is, revelation."[44]

Several Church fathers, in their exegesis on the passion, attempted to tie in the gift of the Spirit with Jesus' death on the cross, where he "gave up his spirit" (παρέδωκεν τὸ πνεῦμα) so that it could be bestowed upon the Church (represented underneath the cross by Mary and John). While such an interpretation "would not be inappropriate" given John's theological concerns, Brown reminds us that such a reference must be considered proleptic, since the "actual giving of the Spirit does not come now but in 20:22 after the resurrection."[45] More likely the use of παρέδωκεν is simply an allusion to Isaiah 53:12, where the same verb is used to describe the Suffering Servant and his voluntary "handing over" of his soul for the sins of many.[46]

Although scholars remain divided about the origins of verse 20:22 ("Receive the Holy Spirit"), its intent is clear—Jesus' promise in the farewell discourse about the coming Paraclete is fulfilled by his breathing of the Spirit upon the disciples. While Matthew had Jesus yield his spirit on the cross, and Luke described the descent of the Spirit on Pentecost, John clearly connects the reception of the Holy Spirit with the resurrection event. This is "the Johannine Pentecost" whereby the risen and ascended Lord gives the Spirit to his disciples.[47] By breathing on them (echoing, perhaps, the creation in Genesis 2:7, where God breathed life into Adam), John is "symbolically proclaiming that, just as in the first creation God breathed a living spirit into man, so now in the moment of the new creation Jesus breathes his own Holy Spirit into the disciples, giving them eternal life."[48] In fulfillment of not only his promises of the farewell discourse but the words spoken in 3:5 ("No one can enter the kingdom unless he be born again of water and the Spirit"), his followers are "baptized" so that now "they are truly Jesus' brothers and can call his Father their Father (20:17)."[49]

Alongside the gospel, the Johannine epistles contain references to the Spirit that both compliment and challenge the portrait of the Paraclete as given by the evangelist. This is particularly true of 1 John 2:1, where Christ himself is described as the Paraclete ("We have a Paraclete in the Father's presence, Jesus Christ, the one who is just"). This description should not be surprising, since the gospel had already portrayed the Spirit/Paraclete as "Jesus' ongoing presence," and Christ himself had spoken of the Spirit as "another Paraclete" (implying, perhaps, that Jesus was the first "advocate").[50] The epistle never addresses the Holy Spirit as Paraclete or speaks of him as a personal being, calling him only "the Spirit of God" and the "Spirit of Truth."[51] That being said, many of the functions given to the Paraclete in the farewell discourse (e.g., teacher, witness) do reappear in the epistles' thinking about the role of the Spirit in the community (e.g., 1 John 2:27).

The gift of the Spirit, which is mentioned in both 1 John 3:24 and 4:13, is referred to here as a gift from God rather than of Jesus, although the gospel had previously made it clear that the Spirit is ultimately a gift of both. The implication, according to Brown, is that "the same God, who gave the commandment [to love one another, also] gave the Spirit that enables us to live out the commandment."[52] According to Strecker, this gift is something the Christian possesses by virtue of baptism, although Bultmann denies this sacramental link.[53]

Acts of the Apostles

The Acts of the Apostles, written sometime between 80 and 100, continues the gospel of Luke and tells the story of the early Church from the Ascension to Paul's imprisonment in Rome circa 63 A.D. From the very beginning the Spirit plays a prominent role, since it is "through the Spirit" that Jesus instructs his apostles (1:2), commanding them after the resurrection to wait in Jerusalem, where they would receive the promised gift of the Father (1:4–5, 8).[54] In fact, there are sixty-two references to the Holy Spirit in Acts, some of which portray the Holy Spirit as "a dynamic force, the charismatic spirit of the Old Testament," while other passages speak "in terms which suggest that he is a person who speaks (1:16; 8:29), forbids (16:6), thinks good (15:28), appoints (20:28), sends (13:4), bears witness (5:32), snatches (8:39), prevents (16:7), is lied to (5:3), tempted (5:9), and resisted (7:51)."[55]

It is in chapter 2 that the Holy Spirit receives the most attention, for it is there that his descent upon the apostles is recalled.[56] This Spirit is symbolized as "the sound like the rush of a violent wind" appearing as "tongues of fire that separated and came to rest on them" (2:2–3). Filled with the Holy Spirit, the apostles began to speak in other tongues "as the Spirit enabled them" (2:4). According to Joseph Fitzmyer, "This is the moment when the apostolate becomes pneumatic or Spirit graced; from this point on all the apostles do will be under the guidance of the Spirit."[57] They begin to preach Jesus Christ as the revealed Lord, but this confession is made possible only in and through the gift of the Holy Spirit.

According to Fitzmeyer, there is a connection between the baptism of Jesus and the Pentecost event, since in both the Spirit has "an initiatory role, a function that launched not only the mission of Jesus but that of testimony to be given about him by commissioned apostles."[58] The same Spirit that Jesus received in the Jordan is now given to the apostles, so that "the Spirit's previous activity in Jesus can be reproduced on a wider scale in the apostles and their converts until its operation reaches the heart of the Gentile world."[59]

Peter's speech on this occasion three times addresses the coming of the Holy Spirit upon the apostles, and then by extension upon all those who believe. Refuting the accusation that the apostles are drunk ("It's only nine o'clock in the morning!"), Peter attributes the gift of tongues to the outpouring of the Holy Spirit as was described by the Prophet Joel (Joel 2:28–32).[60] The first two references, in 2:17–18 ("I will pour out my Spirit upon all flesh" and "I will pour out some of my spirit in those days"), come from Joel and show the Spirit as a gift from God (i.e., the Father). However, the third reference, in 2:33 ("Exalted to God's right hand, he has received from the Father the promised Holy Spirit and poured it forth."), attributes the gift of the Spirit to Jesus himself. The reason, according to Yves Congar, is simple: "For Luke the Holy Spirit is making present and spreading the salvation that has been gained in and through Christ. . . . This salvation is always attributed to Christ. It is communicated in the name of Christ, that is, in his power. . . . (it is) a transmission of his prophetic mission (in the full sense of the word) which consists of being the one who proclaims the message of God."[61]

Because Jesus is not dead but has been raised by the Father, "Jesus the man empowered by the Spirit becomes Lord of the Spirit; the one whose ministry was uniquely empowered by the eschatological Spirit became by his resurrection the one who bestowed the Spirit on others; or, more precisely, by his resurrection he began to share in God's prerogative as the giver of the Spirit."[62] For the Orthodox scholar Boris Bobrinskoy, the Pentecost story, and especially Peter's speech, clarifies the Trinitarian dynamic (or "knot") that undergirds both Luke's gospel and the Acts of the Apostles.

> God has borne witness to Jesus during his earthly life . . . and has anointed him with the Holy Spirit; He has raised him from the dead and has exalted him to his right hand. . . . And Jesus, who has been anointed by the Spirit of God who has been raised and exalted by the right hand of God (in Luke, a term indicating the work of the Spirit) henceforth pours out the Holy Spirit on all creation."[63]

Paul

Biblical exegetes have long noted the pivotal role played by τὸ πνεῦμα in the Pauline corpus, and yet there appears to be some disagreement among them as to whether Paul ever thought of the Spirit as a "person."[64] Joseph Fitzmeyer is among those who have argued that the idea of divine personhood is not a concept Paul would have recognized.

> In speaking of τὸ πνεῦμα, "the Spirit" Paul tends to treat it as it
> appears in the OT (see Ezk 36:26, "a new Spirit"; Isa 44:3). There it is
> a mode of expressing God's ongoing activity and presence in the
> world and his people in a creative, prophetic, quickening, or renovat-
> ing way (recall Gen 1:2; Pss 51:11; 139:7; Isa 11:2; Ezk 37:1–14). This is
> also the basic meaning Paul attributes to τό (ἅγιον) πνεῦμα, which is
> not yet understood as a personal being, distinct from the Father and
> the Son. . . . He may, indeed, personify the Spirit, that is to say,
> personify the activity of the Spirit and presence in the OT sense, but
> it is not yet conceived of as a person in his theology.[65]

Yet there are passages where it appears that Paul attributes some degree of personhood to the Spirit, since he "leads" (Romans 8:14), "intercedes" (Romans 8:26–27), "cries out" (Galatians 4:6), "chooses" (1 Cor 12:11), "witnesses" (Romans 8:16), "searches" (1 Cor 2:10–11), and allots" the gifts of grace as (1Cor 12:11). For this reason Viktor Warnach and others argue in favor of the Spirit's "personality" even if Paul does not develop this line of thought fully.[66]

Concerning the origin of the Spirit, Paul does not speak in terms of the resurrected Christ giving or sending the Spirit. Paul does on several occasions speak of the Spirit as the gift of God (e.g., 1 Cor 2:12: "We have not received the spirit of this world but the Spirit who is from God"; Romans 5:5: "God has poured out his love into our hearts by the Holy Spirit, whom he has given us"), but more often than not he simply states that the Spirit is something that is given to the Christian without specifying its source (e.g., 1 Cor 12:7–8, Galatians 3:2, Romans 8:15). As for the Spirit's relationship to Jesus, for Paul the believer's experience of the Spirit and his/her experience of the risen Christ appear to be the same thing.[67] In many passages Paul actually attributes the same functions to both Christ and Spirit, as is seen in this comparison by Edmund Fortmann.

> The Holy Spirit is the dispenser of the charismata and yet these are
> conferred "according to the measure of the gift of Christ" (1 Cor 12:11,
> Eph 4:9). By Jesus Christ we receive the adoption as sons, yet the
> Holy Spirit is the Spirit of adoption (Eph 1:5, Romans 8:15). We are
> justified in the Spirit and justified in the Lord (1 Cor 6:11, Gal 2:17),
> sanctified in the Spirit and sanctified in Christ (1 Cor 1:2, 6:11). The
> love of God comes to us from the Spirit and is given us through the
> Lord (Rom 5:5, 8:39). It is the same with peace (Rom 14:17, Phil 4:7),
> liberty (2 Cor 3:17, Gal 2:4), life (2 Cor 3:6, Rom 8:2), and glory (2 Cor
> 3:8, Phil 4:19).[68]

Despite assigning Christ and the Spirit similar roles, Paul is careful about preserving the unique part played by Christ in the salvific drama—that is, it is not the Spirit who became flesh, was crucified, and was raised by the Father. Yet Paul also makes it clear that it is only through the Spirit that we can know, recognize, and confess this Christ ("No one can say 'Jesus is Lord' except by the Holy Spirit" 1 Cor 12:2). He not only witnesses to this truth and makes our confession of it possible, but ultimately serves as the way in which the Lordship of Christ is exercised and present in the community. According to Brendan Byrne, "All this shows how tenuous for Paul is any distinction between the Spirit and the ongoing impact of Jesus as risen Lord."[69]

It is with this understanding of the Spirit's role for Paul that we can begin to make sense of those texts that speak of the Spirit as the "Spirit of the Son." This phrase (or some variant of it) appears several times in Paul, most notably in Romans 8:9 and Galatians 4:6, which later became the two key Pauline texts supporting the Latin teaching on the procession.[70] Romans 8:9 ("And if anyone does not have the *Spirit of Christ* he does not belong to Christ") occurs in the middle of an extended meditation on the role of the Spirit in the life of the Christian.[71] According to Dunn, Paul is here trying to answer the question of how one can "distinguish the spirit of God from other (less wholesome) spirits. No firm criteria were ever achieved within Judaism. But the first Christians in effect resolved the issue by making Jesus himself the criterion. The Spirit for them was now recognized as the Spirit of Jesus, the Spirit of the Son. The πνεῦμα Θεοῦ was more clearly defined as the πνεῦμα Χριστοῦ.[72]

The Greek phrase πνεῦμα Χριστοῦ can be interpreted several ways: it can be understood as an objective genitive (the Spirit that brings us to Christ), a possessive genitive (the Spirit that belongs to Christ), a genitive of origin (the Spirit that comes from Christ), or a genitive of identity (the Spirit who is Christ).[73] For Ernst Kasemann it is another affirmation of the close linking in Pauline theology between Christology and pneumatology, because, "in the Spirit the risen Lord manifests his presence and Lordship on earth."[74] By allowing this Spirit to live within us, we achieve a union with Christ and a new way of being. However, Paul immediately reminds readers that this Spirit is also the Spirit "of him who raised Jesus from the dead" (8:11) so that "the power vivifying the Christian is traced to its ultimate source, for the Spirit is the manifestation of the Father's presence and life-giving power in the world."[75] God's "Spirit" is also for Paul "Christ's Spirit," and "although such expressions may seem confusing at first because they are not clearly distinguished from one another," they do bring to the fore that "the Christian is, indeed, related not only to Christ, but to the Father and the Spirit as well"[76] Although not an explicitly trinitarian text, the verse contains a clear triadic structure, "which becomes a basis in later trinitarian theology for the indwelling of the three persons of the Trinity."[77]

Galatians 4:6 ("Because you are sons, God has sent the Spirit of his Son into our hearts, the Spirit who calls out 'Abba,' Father") is a problematic text in many respects. There are issues of translation (e.g., is the ὅτι clause meant to suggest that the Spirit comes as a result of being sons ["Because you are sons"] or as indication that the Spirit himself grants sonship ["the proof you are sons"]),of textual variation (e.g., the term τοῦ υἱοῦ is not present in some early manuscripts), and of origin (i.e., is this verse part of a pre-Pauline baptismal formula).[78] Scholars generally agree that while the ὅτι clause is causal, Paul does not establish a chronological process by which we become sons (since receipt of the Spirit and our adoption come about simultaneously at the moment of baptism). Having received the Spirit of the Son, the believer is conformed to him who was Son, allowing us to cry out (as Christ himself did) "Abba, Father." As in Romans, Paul speaks of the Spirit as Christ active in the present world, albeit in a different form. The crucified and risen one is no longer in the flesh but is sent into the human heart (καρδία), where (evoking Ezek 36:26–27 and Jer 31:31–34) the Spirit refashions us in his image.

Although later Latin theology will understand Romans 8:9 and Galatians 4:6 as references to the Spirit's hypostatic origin from the Son, the evidence does not appear to support this reading. Paul is not engaging in metaphysical speculation, but rather meditating on the existential impact of "life in the Spirit." Paul, just as he was with Christ, "is more concerned about the work . . . than the person."[79] If Paul occasionally failed to carefully distinguish between Christ and the Spirit, it is only because our experience of the latter is Christ made present here and now.

Concluding Thoughts

Even if we recognize that the Scriptures do not contain a "theology of the procession," as it will later be understood, the biblical witness is still the foundation upon which both Latins and Greeks built their respective theologies. That their thinking on the procession eventually came to differ is explained (at least in part) by the fact that, according to Boris Bobrinskoy, there are at least three distinct "movements" of trinitarian revelation that one can discern throughout the New Testament, movements "that complement one another, and all seem to have their inevitability."[80] When read without reference to the others, each "movement" easily lends itself to diverse, and even incompatible, understandings of relationships within the Trinity.

The first is the Father—Spirit—Christ schema, in which "the Father is at the origin, the Spirit is the mediator who descends and rests on the Son, who permits his incarnation and sends him. Christ appears then as the term in whom the fullness of the Divinity rests, the Spirit of grace and holiness."[81] This pattern is seen clearly in the synoptics, where Jesus' birth comes about through the agency of the Spirit (Matthew and Luke) and his ministry takes place through the power of the Spirit (Matthew, Mark, and Luke). Christ is filled with the Spirit and, following his baptism, even appears to be its sole possessor, until that time when, upon his death, the Spirit is once again released into the community of believers.

The second model is the Christ—Father—Spirit schema seen most clearly in John and in certain texts of Paul (e.g., 2 Cor 13:13: "The grace of the Lord Jesus Christ and the love of God [the Father] and the communion [koinonia] of the Holy Spirit). Here Christ is seen as the one who reveals the Father, and who will, with the Father, grant "the personal fullness of the Holy Spirit," as the gift of himself to those who believe.[82] For both John and Paul the Spirit is not the one who empowered Jesus during his ministry (as in the synoptics), but rather the ongoing presence of Jesus himself in the community. He is the "other paraclete" and the "Spirit of Christ" who continues to bind us to the Father through our adoption as his children.

The third schema, which Bobrinskoy claims "best completes the first" is the Father—Christ—Holy Spirit sequence seen most clearly in the Acts of the Apostles.[83] Here the Father and the glorified Lord together send the Spirit into the world so that Jesus the "man of the Spirit" also becomes the one who dispenses the Spirit. The Holy Spirit who empowered Jesus is now active in the community of believers and is given so that "the proper mission of the Holy Spirit" can begin— "to be active in the world, to be not merely the 'Giver of Life' but properly the Gift of the Son and of the Father (and of the Holy Spirit himself, the bond of love).[84]

Our examination of the biblical witness allows us to draw certain conclusions about those passages that were later used as prooftexts for or against the doctrine of the filioque. Although ἐκπορεύεσθαι will later take on a very specific theological meaning in Greek patristic thought (i.e., denoting the Spirit's mode of coming-to-be from the Father), it does not appear exegetically sound to read John 15:26 as proof of the Spirit's "eternal procession" from the Father alone. On the other hand, neither does the term "Spirit of Christ" (πνεῦμα Χριστοῦ) as used in Romans 8:9 and Galatians 4:6 appear to denote a relationship of eternal origin as Latin theology historically claimed. John 20:22 is the fulfillment of Jesus' promise that he would send his disciples "another Paraclete" in his absence; it is not the evangelist's attempt at metaphysical speculation on the hypostatic origin of the Holy Spirit. In short, we must conclude that the prooftexts prove nothing.

Yet the biblical material does allow us to make certain positive conclusions about the relationship of the Spirit to the Son and their common relationship to the Father. First, that the Father appears to have a unique role as the chief author of the salvific drama, for it is the Father who empowers Jesus through the Spirit in the Synoptics, who sends both the Son and the Spirit in John, and who grants us the Spirit of sonship in Paul. Without denying that all three persons of the Trinity are active at every stage of salvation history, the New Testament testifies to a certain "priority" of the Father, from whom the Son and Spirit come and to whom all things on earth are drawn. It is thus not surprising that later theology will also assign a certain metaphysical priority to the Father as "source" and "principle" within the godhead, responsible for both the generation of the Son and the procession of the Holy Spirit.

Second, that there appears to be a consensus among the biblical authors that the death and resurrection of Christ is somehow a precondition for the sending of the Spirit upon the Church. One can even go further and claim that there is a causal relationship at work—Christ is able to send the Spirit (i.e., his Spirit) as a gift from the Father only once he has been raised from the dead and seated at God's right hand. Thus even if the Spirit is ultimately the Father's gift, the Scriptures testify that he is also a gift that comes to us through the person and work of Christ. The question, ultimately unanswered by the biblical witness, is whether this same dynamic applies to life within the Trinity, and whether the Spirit also depends upon the Son for his eternal coming forth. Over the next several centuries the answer to that question would literally tear the Christian world in half.

If each side in that debate managed to find support in the Scriptures for their respective positions, it is partly due to the fact that very often the authors of the New Testament did not express themselves with a great deal of precision, especially when it came to the Trinity. For example, the Spirit is at times described as being sent by the Father, and elsewhere he is called a gift of the Son, sometimes within the same sentence (e.g., John 15:26). This lack of clarity is especially apparent in John and Paul, where Christ and the Spirit are often assigned similar functions and even given the same name (e.g., Christ as "Paraclete" in 1 John, the Holy Spirit as "Spirit of Christ" in Galatians and Romans). It should thus not surprise us that later theologians, searching the Scriptures for clear answers to complex trinitarian questions (e.g., "Who sends the Spirit?" or "Whose Spirit is it?") would be frustrated in their attempt at unanimity.

2

The Greek Fathers

As with the biblical material, it would be inaccurate to claim that the Greek patristic corpus explicitly addressed the procession of the Spirit from the Son (positively or negatively) as later theology would understand it. The pneumatological concerns of the Greek fathers (e.g., establishing the full divinity of the Holy Spirit) did not include a detailed exploration of exactly how the Son was (or was not) involved in the hypostatic coming-into-being of the third person of the Trinity. For that reason the claim, made by both Greeks and Latins throughout the centuries, that the Eastern fathers *explicitly* advocated or condemned the *filioque*, cannot be sustained given the evidence we possess.

And yet the writings of the Greek fathers do contain important trinitarian principles, later used by both East and West in their respective theologies of the procession. Particularly important in this regard were the anti-Eunomian writings of the Cappadocian fathers (which expressed a hesitancy about confusing theology and economy), the Council of Constantinople's creedal affirmation that the Spirit proceeded (ἐκπορεύεσθαι) from the Father, and the anti-Sabellian polemic (which made the protection of each person's unique hypostatic properties, especially the Father's role as one cause within the godhead, a special concern for the East).

Yet alongside these traditional themes there was also in the Greek fathers, particularly in the works of Gregory of Nyssa and Cyril of Alexandria, an effort to establish an eternal relationship between the Son and the Spirit, recognizing that the persons of the Trinity, while distinct, cannot be separated. For this reason there appears in the fathers an increasing awareness that both the mission of the Spirit and his eternal "flowing forth" (προϊέναι) from the Father take place "through the Son" (διὰ τοῦ Υἱοῦ). While not equivalent to the belief that the Spirit eternally "proceeds" (ἐκπορεύεσθαι) from the Son, this teaching remained an important part of Eastern trinitarian theology for centuries to come.

Origen (d. 254)

Although Origen of Alexandria was later listed (alongside Judas Iscariot and Pontius Pilate) among those whose damnation was all but assured, he remains one of the most significant Christian writers of the pre-Nicene period.[1] While his writings on the Trinity were rarely referenced during the *filioque* debates (a result of his reputation as a notorious heretic), Origen's trinitarian language shaped Greek patristic thought and influenced later authors (especially the Cappadocian fathers) in their own reflections on the mystery.[2]

Origen's theology of the Trinity has traditionally been considered subordinationist, a result of his appropriation of Platonic philosophy and his "substitution" of "Christian personalistic theology" for the "impersonalistic system of Neoplatonism."[3] According to Sergius Bulgakov, "he did this . . . simply by putting the hypostasis of the Father in place of the Neoplatonic One, the hypostasis of the Son in place of the Neoplatonic Mind, and the hypostasis of the Holy Spirit in place of the World Soul."[4] Without denying the consubstantiality of the Son, Origen is clear that the Father alone is "God" (ὁ θεός) while the Son and Spirit remain (relative to him) secondary and tertiary hypostases, "who possessed the godhead only by participation or derivation."[5] While Origen readily affirmed that the Son is eternally begotten and thus not a creature (as later Arian theology maintained), his language concerning the Spirit is less precise, at times questioning whether he was begotten like the Son, created, or brought forth in some other manner.

In several passages in the *Commentary on John* Origen speaks in terms of the Spirit's origin through the Son—that is, receiving divinity and life from the Father through the Son.

> We admit, as more pious and true, that the Holy Spirit is the most honored of all things made through the Word, and that he is [first] in rank of all the things which have been made by the Father through Christ. Perhaps this is the reason the Spirit too is not called son of God, since only the begotten alone is by nature a son from the beginning. The Holy Spirit seems to have need of the Son ministering to his hypostasis, not only for it to exist, but also for it to be wise, and

rational, and just, and whatever else other things we ought to understand it to be by participation in the aspects of Christ.[6]

At times Origen even spoke of the Spirit being "made" (ἐγένετο) through the Son, postulating that if "all things were made through Him," one must accept "the consequence that the Spirit, having an origin, has been made through the Word."[7] While elsewhere denying that the Spirit was a "creature," Origen in these passages implies that the Spirit is dependent upon the Son for his existence.[8] This idea comes forward again in Origen's reading of Romans 8:9, where he concluded "that the Spirit of God and the Spirit of Christ are one and the same," since "the Savior says 'he proceeds from the Father' and 'he will take from what is mine'; and [when I notice] the explanation of this word that he adds in what follows, 'Father all things that are mine are yours and that are yours are mine and therefore I have said, that he will take from what is mine.'"[9]

In his De Principiis Origen balanced these subordinationist tendencies with affirmations of the full equality of the three persons, since, "nothing in the Trinity can be called greater or less. . . . [and] we are most clearly shown that there is no separation in the Trinity, but that this which is called the gift of the Spirit is ministered through the Son, and worked by God the Father."[10] Yet Origen still maintained that "the original goodness must be believed to reside in God the Father, and from him both the Son and the Holy Spirit undoubtedly draw into themselves the nature of that goodness existing in the fount from which the one is born and the other proceeds."[11] In this Origen seems to anticipate the language of the Cappadocian fathers, who wanted to deny that the Spirit was a "second Son" yet also wanted to affirm a relationship of origin to the Father. Whether Origen would have accepted that this unique procession takes place "through the Son" is unclear, although the Commentary on John and Commentary on Romans do seem to point in this direction.

Gregory Thaumaturgus (d. 270)

Perhaps the best known of Origen's students was Gregory Thaumaturgus ("the Wonderworker"), who once claimed that his departure from the great teacher was akin to Adam's expulsion from the Garden of Eden.[12] According to the Vitae of Gregory of Nyssa, prior to his consecration as a bishop, the Theotokos appeared to Gregory and revealed the true faith to him in a vision, which he immediately wrote down in the form of a creed. Although its authenticity has recently come into question (some believing it to be the work of Gregory of Nyssa himself), this Confessio fidei was long accepted as genuine and quoted often in later florilegia.[13] Concerning the Holy Spirit, the Confession stated its belief in

one Holy Spirit, holding existence from God (ἐκ θεοῦ τὴν ὕπαρξιν ἔχον), and manifested through the Son (καὶ διὰ Υἱοῦ πεφηνὸς [δηλαδὴ τοῖς ἀνθρωπώποις]) (namely, to human beings); perfect image of the perfect Son; life, the Cause of living things; holiness who makes sanctification possible; by whom is manifested God the Father, who is over all and in all, and God the Son, who is through all. Perfect Trinity, in glory and eternity and sovereignty neither divided nor estranged.[14]

The bracketed phrase ("namely, to human beings") has long been thought to be the addition of a later editor hoping to clarify Gregory's position and keep it within the confines of post-Photian Byzantine orthodoxy (i.e., that the manifestation of the Holy Spirit through the Son is only on the level of the economy and does not concern his eternal procession).[15] How exactly Gregory intended πεφηνὸς to be understood cannot be answered with any certainty, even if one chooses to argue that his relationship to Origen would have made him think in terms of an eternal dependence.

Didymus the Blind (d. 398)

Among the Greek fathers, few figures were as important as Didymus the Blind in shaping Western trinitarian thinking. Ambrose of Milan was greatly influenced by Didymus's writings and borrowed freely from him when composing his own book on the Trinity. The irascible Jerome then translated Didymus's *De Spiritu Sancto* into Latin to embarrass Ambrose by demonstrating his complete dependence upon Greek sources.[16] This translation allowed Didymus's work to circulate in the West, where it survived only in Latin. While Jerome's Latin translation was undoubtedly the work of Didymus, scholars have long questioned whether it was completely faithful to the original Greek, or if later editors added to or edited the text.[17] Most agree that there is clearly "reason to fear that later hands have tampered with his work" and that "it is probable that the weight of this testimony would be much reduced by the recovery of the Greek treatise."[18] As traditionally received, the *De Spiritu Sancto* contains several passages long used to support the later Western teaching on the procession. It states, for example:

> the Holy Spirit receives from the Son that which he was of his own nature. . . . So too the Son is said to receive from the Father the very things by which he subsists. For neither has the Son anything else except those things given him by the Father, nor has the Holy Spirit any other substance than that given him by the Son (*neque alia substantia est Spiritus Sancti praeter id quod datur ei a Filio*).[19]

Elsewhere it claims that "Our Lord teaches that the being of the Spirit is derived not from the Spirit himself, but from the Father and the Son (*sed ex patre et me est)*"[20] and that "He goes forth from the Son, proceeding from the truth (*profertur a filio, id est procedens a veritate*)."[21]

There is another work, the *De Trinitate*, which was long credited to Didymus, although modern scholars have increasingly questioned its attribution.[22] The *De Trinitate* clearly ascribes the procession of the Holy Spirit to the Father, who breathes forth the Spirit and begets the Son in coeternal and corresponding actions.[23] According to the *De Trinitate*, the Spirit proceeds from God the Father (ἐξ αὐτοῦ ἐκπορευθὲν κατὰ φύσιν)[24] but, while eternally proceeding from the Father, eternally abides in the Son (τὸ πνεῦμα ἐκπορεύεται παρὰ τοῦ Πατρὸς καὶ μένει παρὰ τῷ Υἱῷ θεϊκῶς).[25] While allowing that the risen Christ pours out the Spirit upon the disciples "since he in fact poured it out like water coming substantially from him," this is a clear reference to the activity of the Spirit and not to the idea of eternal procession.[26]

The language of these texts, whether authentically Didymus's or not, later became powerful prooftexts for generations of Latin theologians seeking the support of Eastern patristic authors. There is certainly an emphasis in Didymus on the unity of substance and operation within the Trinity, so much so that one can say that the grace of both the Father and Son are communicated to the believer through the activity of the Spirit. However, to say that Didymus ascribed a role to the Son in the Spirit's eternal procession, especially on the basis of a few passages of dubious authenticity, appears unwarranted by the evidence.

Athanasius (d. 373)

The story of Athanasius is a fascinating one, whether one chooses to see it in terms of the ecclesiastical politics of the day (e.g., Athanasius was exiled five times during his forty-six–year episcopacy) or in terms of his contributions in defense of Nicene orthodoxy.[27] His early work, *De Incarnatione Verbi Dei*, has (rightly) become a classic Christian text, although John Behr and others have often lamented the fact that it is often read incorrectly (i.e., "as the first in a long line of works attempting to explain why God became man, the Eastern equivalent of Anselm's *Cur Deus homo*").[28] While his authentic writings focus mostly on christology, defending the consubstantiality of the Father and Son against the Arians, Athanasius also addressed the divinity of the Holy Spirit and the unique place of the Spirit in the life of the believer.[29] As with his Christology, Athanasius's overriding concern is not metaphysical but soteriological; that is, humanity's ultimate destiny in God was of far more interest to him than questions about the Son's role in the eternal procession.

The two works that give us Athanasius's teaching on the procession (such as it is) are the *Contra Arianos*, written during his exile in Rome (c. 339/346), and the *Epistula ad Serapionem*, composed over a decade later (c. 357/358).[30] The *Epistula* was written against the so-called Tropici, whose selective use of the

Scriptures (i.e.,"troping) led them to conclude that the Holy Spirit was not divine but rather a created being. Athanasius countered their charge, claiming that a creature could not sanctify creatures, and thus on soteriological grounds the Holy Spirit must be divine. For "if the Holy Spirit were a creature, there would not be for us any of God in the Spirit. . . . But if we become sharers in the divine nature through participation in the Spirit, one would have to be crazy to say that the Spirit is of a created nature and not the nature of God."[31]

When speaking of relationships within the Trinity, Athanasius claimed that the Spirit has the same relation of nature and order with respect to the Son that the Son has with respect to the Father.[32] Therefore he maintained that "the Spirit, who is said to be from God, belongs (ἴδιον) to the being of the Son . . . (just as) the Son belongs (ἴδιος) to the being of the Father because he is from the Father."[33] This linear schemata had the effect of making the Son a sort of "intermediary" between the Spirit and the Father, an impression reinforced at times by Athanasius's language. While avoiding some of the subordinationist tendencies seen in Origen, in the *Contra Arianos* he wrote that "the Spirit receives from the Word . . . for He, as has been said, gives to the Spirit, and whatever the Spirit hath he hath from the Word."[34] This Spirit is "in the image of the Son,"[35] and although "said to proceed from the Father . . . [He] shines forth (ἐκλάμπει) and is sent and given by the Word" from whom he receives.[36]

The question that will later be asked is whether the "shining forth" of the Spirit is a reference to his activity in this world (i.e., the economy) or to some sort of eternal relationship (in terms of either "eternal manifestation" or hypostatic origin). Later Latin theology tended to read Athanasius as a clear advocate of the *filioque*, an interpretation still found as late as the twentieth century (e.g., J. Lebon). Swete concluded that "it seems impossible to regard this ἔκλαμψις of the Spirit from the Word as implying less than an eternal derivation" and thus "the *filioque* is . . . substantially present" in the theology of Athanasius."[37]

However, Athanasius never explicitly attributed the procession (ἐκπόρευσις) of the Spirit to the Son, nor did he ever question the monarchical principle.[38] What Athanasius appears to advocate is the procession of the Spirit from the Father, while at the same time affirming that the Spirit is nevertheless the image of the Son who comes forth as his gift upon humanity—his emphasis here being soteriological rather than metaphysical. References to the Spirit coming "through the Son" thus concern only the communication of the divine life to the believer, since (according to Yves Congar, voicing the opinion of the majority of scholars) "Athanasius does not speculate about the eternal intradivine relationships but only speaks about them in the context of the activities of the divine persons within the economy of salvation."[39] Thus whatever the Son's role in the eternal origin of the Spirit, he is essential in our experience of the Spirit, since it is only through him that the Spirit's gifts flow forth, like a river, to the believer.

Basil the Great (d. 364)

Basil of Caesarea ("the Great"), whose defense of the Spirit's divinity against the *Pneumatomachoi* ("Spirit fighters") earned him the title of "Doctor of the Holy Spirit," authored several works (*De Spiritu Sancto* and *Contra Eunomium*) that later became key sources for those seeking prooftexts for and against the *filioque*.[40] Basil's polemics against the *Pneumatomachoi* had led him to stress the unity and equality of the divine persons, both in the economy of salvation and in our doxological confession of the Trinity. It was only by the Spirit that we could (as Paul claimed in 1 Cor 2:3) claim Jesus as Lord, and only "from the one Spirit through the one Son to the one Father" that we gained divine knowledge.[41] Following in many ways the arguments of Athanasius, Basil established the equality of the Spirit with the other persons of the Trinity through his unique relationship to the Son. This is why if "the Spirit is ranked with the Son and the Son with the Father, then the Spirit is obviously ranked with the Father also."[42]

Having established the equality of the Holy Spirit in this manner, it is not surprising that Basil (like Athanasius) appeared at times to place the Son in the role of "intermediary" between the Spirit and the Father, even as he went to great pains to acknowledge the Father as the one source of the Spirit's being. The "pious doctrine of the (Father's) monarchy" had to be upheld.[43] However, Basil wrote that "through the one Son, He (i.e., the Holy Spirit) is joined to the Father"[44] and that the "natural goodness, inherent holiness, and royal dignity reaches from the Father through the only-begotten (διὰ τοῦ Μονογενοῦς) to the Spirit."[45]

This twofold confession of the Spirit's necessary relationship to the Son and a unique relationship to the Father (as the font of divinity within the godhead) later made it possible for both Greeks and Latins to read Basil as an advocate of their respective positions vis-à-vis the *filioque*. Particularly troublesome in this regard was Basil's *Contra Eunomium*, which not only included statements capable of diverse interpretation, but also contained several passages of dubious authenticity.[46] Eunomius himself had claimed that the Spirit was third in nature and order within the Trinity, a created being "brought into existence at the command of the Father by the action of the Son."[47] Although Basil admitted that the Spirit is numbered third (since the baptismal formula places him after the Father and Son), he defended his equality and divinity, since "He (i.e., the Holy Spirit) himself *is* sanctification."[48] In Book Five, now known to be spurious, Basil allegedly maintained that the Spirit was related to the source of the divinity through the Son, who as the Word of the Father brought forth the utterance (ῥῆμα) of the Spirit.[49]

Yet if one uses Basil's authentic works as a basis, it is difficult (if not impossible) to find support for the position that he taught that the Son had any role in the Spirit's hypostatic origin. Basil, basing himself on John 15:26, clearly taught that the Holy Spirit proceeds from the Father, and he established the Spirit's uniqueness (i.e., that he is not a "second son") by the Spirit's procession from the Father (as distinguished from the Son's generation). While Basil employed the διὰ τοῦ Υἱοῦ formula to speak of our coming to know God (and conversely, of God's revelation of himself in the economy of salvation), he never ascribed any role to the Son in the Spirit's ἐκπόρευσις, nor demanded from his opponents anything more than the confession that "the Spirit of Truth proceeds from the Father."[50] As in Athanasius, there are passages in Basil that are certainly capable of being read as advocating something like the *filioque*, but to do so would be to misunderstand the inherently soteriological thrust of his work.

Gregory of Nazianzus (d. 391)

Gregory of Nazianzus ("the Theologian") occupies a special place in the development of Eastern trinitarian thinking, and the encomium granted to him testifies to his unique status among the great fathers of antiquity. Maximus the Confessor often referred to him simply as "the great teacher" (τὸν μέγαν διδάσκαλον), and even the cantankerous Jerome could not help but admire the genius of the man.[51] Along with Basil of Caesarea and Gregory of Nyssa (the other "Cappadocian fathers"), Gregory shaped the language and limits of the Church's trinitarian theology, often in opposition to those (like Eunomius) whose teachings denied the divinity, equality, or unity of the three hypostases within the godhead.[52]

It was against Eunomius that Gregory clearly affirmed the divinity of the Holy Spirit, unafraid (like Basil) to proclaim the Holy Spirit both "God" and *homoousios* with the Father and the Son.[53] Although Basil had been a firm defender of the divinity of the Spirit and paved the way for later thinking on the consubstantiality of the Spirit, the fourth-century Cappadocian father had famously hesitated calling the Spirit θεός, a fact Gregory of Nazianzus deftly handled in his panegyric to Basil given years after his death.[54] Gregory claimed that while Basil had not explicitly taught the consubstantiality of the Holy Spirit with the Father and Son, nevertheless he fervently believed it, even though this point "was unknown to the majority . . . and might well have been news to Basil's own followers."[55]

According to Gregory, the "one Holy Spirit . . . proceeds (προελθόν) or goes forth (προϊόν) from the Father" and is thus "'God' (Θεόν) to those who understand things properly."[56] In *Oration* 31 he spoke about the three persons of the Trinity as "light"—at one time stressing their essential unity even while maintaining their hypostatic distinctiveness.

"He was the true Light that enlightens every man coming into the world"—yes, the Father. "He was the true Light that enlightens every man coming into the world"—yes, the Son. "He was the true Light that enlightens every man coming into the world"—yes, the Comforter. These are three subjects and three verbs—he was and he was and he was. But a single reality *was*. There are three predicates—light and light and light. But the light is one, God is one.[57]

It was also against Eunomius that Gregory tried to maintain the distinction between the economy (οἰκονομία) and the theology (θεολογία), emphasizing the importance of the *via negativa* against the Eunomian claim that God was readily knowable since "all one needed to know for a true theological understanding was that ingenerateness was the supreme quality of God."[58] For Gregory, God's revelation in history (i.e., the economy) allowed us to make certain affirmations about God (e.g., *that* he is), but it was a mistake to apply these indiscriminately to the divine nature (i.e., describing *what* he is).[59] This was so because "Theology proper, the knowledge of God in Himself is impossible for all creatures, even for the most elect . . . or even for the highest ranks of the angelicals."[60] Yet while maintaining the necessity for apophaticism vis-à-vis God's nature, Gregory did affirm that God left reflections of himself in the world, like "shadowy reflections of the Sun in water, reflections which display to eyes too weak, because [we are] too impotent to gaze at it, the Sun overmastering perception in the purity of its light."[61] These reflections permit us only a limited understanding of God's trinitarian nature as it is revealed to us in history (i.e., the economic Trinity) yet make us incapable of adequately describing God's intratrinitarian life (the immanent Trinity).[62]

The irony is that Gregory, to counter the arguments of his opponents, did find it necessary to speak about the relationships between Father, Son, and Spirit within the godhead, even if he continued to acknowledge the limits both of his understanding and of language capable of describing the mystery.[63] For example, the Arians had maintained that the biblical affirmation "The Father is greater than the Son" denied the Nicene teaching on the consubstantiality of the persons. Like Athanasius and Basil, Gregory wanted to affirm the Father's unique role as the "source of divinity" (πηγὴ τῆς Θεότητος) and "the principle/origin of divinity" (τῆς Θεότητος ἀρχὴ) without denying the equality of the persons, which is why Gregory was quick to point out that while the Father was greater in that he is the cause (αἰτία) of the Son, "greater by causality" did not equal "greater by nature."[64]

Causality thus became an important concept for Gregory (and by extension for the entire Eastern tradition), since it was the Father's unique role as unbegotten cause within the godhead that both grounded the unity of the Trinity and distinguished the Father's hypostasis from that of the Son and the Spirit. The Father became the reference point for the entire godhead, since it was "the

Father from whom and towards whom everything else is referred."[65] According to John McGuckin, "the Gregorian doctrine of causality was fundamentally important to him. . . . The causation is synonymous with the Father's dynamic communication of the divine nature to the Son . . . (and) the Father's greatness is particularly and properly the fact that he is the source and origin of the self-same divine being which he communicates to the Son and the Spirit."[66]

In fact, causality became *the* distinguishing characteristic of the Father's hypostasis, since "All that the Father has belongs likewise to the Son except causality."[67] As "the one without beginning," the Father was distinguished from the Son and the Spirit, who, while still coeternal and coequal, each came forth from him, each in his unique manner.[68] McGuckin states, "Both of these generated and processed hypostases are God of God and, even though distinct (hypostatically), each hypostases relates to the others in a manner that ontologically flows back to union."[69]

It was in distinguishing between the unique hypostatic origination of the Son and the Spirit that Gregory made his most significant contribution to the doctrine of the procession, as he attempted to ward off the idea that the Spirit came forth from the unbegotten Father in the same way as the Son (thus making the Spirit a "second son"). The Eunomians had claimed that "the Holy Spirit must be either ingenerate or begotten. If he is ingenerate, there are two unoriginate beings. If he is begotten, we again have alternatives: begotten either from the Father or from the Son. If from the Father, there will be two sons who are brothers."[70] Gregory's response was: "The Holy Spirit is truly Spirit, coming forth (προϊεον) from the Father, but not in the manner of a Son or by generation but by procession (ἐκπόρευσις), if one must create new terminology for the sake of clarity."[71]

The word "procession" (ἐκπόρευσις), found in John 15:26, is here distinguished from the more generalized "coming forth" (προϊεον) of both the Spirit and the Son, and from the unique generation of the Son as only-begotten of the Father. For Gregory the Spirit's ἐκπόρευσις from the Father became his identifying hypostatic quality, just as causality was the Father's and begottenness was the Son's. Yet even here Gregory was forced to bow to the mystery, unable to explain the exact nature of the difference: "What then is 'proceeding'? You explain the ingeneracy of the Father and I will give you a biological account of the Son's begetting and the Spirit's proceeding—and let us go mad the pair of us for prying into God's secrets."[72]

Gregory's trinitarian schema, including the language of procession introduced to identify the unique coming-into-being of the Holy Spirit, exercised great influence over subsequent generations of Eastern theologians. In fact, Gregory's emphasis on the Father's unique role as cause within the godhead later became *the* theological foundation upon which the East's rejection of the *filioque* was built (since by the councils of Lyons and Florence the Latins also spoke of the Son as "cause" of the Spirit). It is therefore not surprising that

Gregory's writings became a chief source for Orthodox Christians looking to refute the Latin teaching on the procession, and why, with a few exceptions, he was rarely found in Latin *florilegia* in support of the doctrine.

Gregory of Nyssa (d. 395)

Gregory of Nyssa, often referred to as the most "speculative" of the Cappadocian fathers, has also been called "the most gifted" of the three, in terms of both "originality and intellectual ability."[73] The Seventh Ecumenical Council (787) went as far as to refer to him as "the father of fathers," even though several of his writings on the preexistence of souls and apocatastasis were considered "tainted" with the Origenist heresy.[74] His trinitarian writings built upon the insights already found in Basil and Gregory of Nazianzus, emphasizing the Father's unique role within the godhead as cause, and yet Nyssa acknowledged, more clearly than the others, some intermediary role for the Son in the procession of the Holy Spirit.

Gregory compared the "epistemological order" through which we come to a knowledge of the Trinity ("we are led by the Spirit to a knowledge of the Son, who reveals to us the Father") with the "ontological order" where, according to John Behr, "the Father alone is ingenerate and without beginning, while the Son derives from the Father, and the Spirit, who also derives from the Father, is always contemplated together with the Son."[75] As was the case with Athanasius and Basil, Gregory at times places the Son between the Spirit and the Father as some sort of intermediary, the difference being that in Nyssa this role seems to apply not only to the economy of salvation, but to the eternal relationships existing among the three persons. "The Holy Spirit, from whom all the abundance of good things gushes up to creation, depends (ἤρτηται) on the Son, with whom he is indivisibly apprehended. (He is) made known after the Son and with him and subsists from the Father."[76]

This idea, that the Spirit comes forth (in both the economy and theology) through the Son (διὰ τοῦ Υἱοῦ) is seen most clearly in his *Ad Ablabium quod non sint tres dii*. Like Gregory of Nazianzus, Nyssa used causality to distinguish the Father within the Trinity, since "we believe one to be a Cause, and the other to be from the Cause" (τῷ τὸ μὲν αἴτιον πιστεύειν εἶναι τὸ δὲ ἐκ τοῦ αἰτίου).[77] However, in differentiating between the Son and the Spirit he maintained that

> the one (i.e., the Son) is directly from the First and the other (i.e., the Spirit) is through the one who is directly from the First (τὸ δὲ διὰ τοῦ προσεχῶς ἐκ τοῦ πρώτου) with the result that the Only-begotten remains the Son and does not negate the Spirit's being from the Father since the middle position of the Son both protects His distinction as Only-begotten and does not exclude the Spirit from His natural relation to the Father.[78]

Elsewhere he used the image of a flame to explain this same reality, arguing that the divinity of the Spirit is in no way lessened because he comes forth from the first (i.e., the Father) through the second (i.e., the Son).

> It is as if a man were to see a separate flame burning on three torches (and we will suppose that the third flame is caused by that of the first being transmitted to the middle, and then kindling the end torch). . . . But if there is really no hindrance to the third torch being fire, though it has been kindled from a previous flame, what is the philosophy of these men, who profanely think that they can slight the dignity of the Holy Spirit because He is named by the Divine lips after the Father and the Son?[79]

Here and in other passages Gregory relied upon the idea of trinitarian ordering (τάξις), which claimed that the Holy Spirit, while eternally coequal with Father and Son, was third in the τάξις. He was emphatic that this concept neither was subordinationalist nor did it introduce the idea of temporality (i.e., that the Holy Spirit came forth after the Son). In the *Adversus Eunomium* he wrote:

> the difference (with the Holy Spirit) is only in the place assigned in order (τάξις). For as the Son is bound to the Father, and, while deriving existence from Him, is not substantially after Him, so again the Holy Spirit is in touch with the Only-begotten, who is conceived of as before the Spirit's subsistence only in the theoretical light of a cause.[80]

Gregory's intent appears to be the affirmation of the Father's role as unique source of the divinity (as αἰτία), while simultaneously allowing for an eternal relationship between the Son and the Spirit because in the trinitarian order (τάξις), the Spirit proceeds from the Father who is already acknowledged as Father of the Son. The Spirit "has his being attached to the Father, as a cause, from whom he also proceeds"[81] but is also attached to the Son "since the Spirit proceeds not simply from God, but from the Father of the Son, and therefore always in relation to the Son."[82] Thus while the Spirit's existence is not caused by the Son, "Gregory clearly affirmed the Son's mediation in the procession of the Spirit," since he becomes the presupposition for the Spirit's manifestation, not only in the economy, but in eternity.[83]

Because of the eternal relationship he established between the Son and the Spirit, one that seemed to imply a dependence of the latter upon the former, Gregory of Nyssa was often employed by the West as an Eastern witness to the development of the doctrine of the double procession. However, it should be noted that Gregory, even while affirming "that the Son played a part in the intradivine existence of the Spirit," never spoke "of the Father and Son as forming a single principle of active spiration" nor claimed that the Son's role "was of a causal nature."[84] It is thus doubtful that Gregory of Nyssa would have accepted the *filioque* as it was later understood in the West, although he witnesses to the important truth (often ignored in the East) that there is an eternal, and not simply economic, relationship of the Spirit to the Son.

Epiphanius of Salamis (d. 403)

Aside from his polemics against Origen, Epiphanius is best remembered for his two great works, the *Ancoratus* (on the fundamentals of the faith) and *Panarion omnium haeresium* (a catalogue of heresies), both of which earned him a well-deserved reputation for orthodoxy. In these books Epiphanius used language that often found their way into later Latin *florilegia*, especially since (unlike many of the other Eastern fathers) Epiphanius commonly spoke of the Spirit coming not only "through the Son," but also "from the Son," a rarity among the Eastern fathers.[85]

While, like Gregory of Nazianzus unafraid to proclaim the Holy Spirit both God and *homoousias* with the Father and Son, Epiphanius (allegedly) went further than the great Cappadocian in teaching the Spirit's origin from both, proclaiming that the Spirit is God "from the Father and the Son" (ἐκ Πατρὸς καὶ Υἱοῦ τὸ Πνεῦμα).[86] He is "the third light from the Father and the Son," being from the Father "from whom he proceeds and the Son from whom he receives."[87] "No one," Epiphanus wrote, "has seen the Son and the Father, except the Holy Spirit . . . who is from the Father and the Son" (ὃ παρὰ τοῦ Πατρὸς καὶ ἐκ τοῦ Υἱοῦ).[88] In the *Panarion*, Epiphanius also spoke of the Spirit having his personal subsistence "from the Father through the Son," which appears to reference an eternal dependence upon the Son.[89]

However, it should be noted that Epiphanius never spoke of the Spirit's procession (ἐκπόρευσις) from or through the Son, restricting himself instead to the scriptural affirmations that the Spirit proceeded from the Father (τὸ ἐκ Πατρὸς ἐκπορευόμενον) and received from the Son (καὶ ἐκ τοῦ Υἱοῦ λαμβανόμενον). Whether he thought in terms of the Spirit receiving existence, consubstantiality, or temporal mission "from the Son" has been debated for centuries—the Latin West seeing in Epiphanius a clear witness to the *filioque*, the East preferring to read these texts as references to the Spirit's *missio* (which he receives from Christ himself).[90] It must be admitted that Epiphanius's language allows for either reading, with scholars still divided over his precise meaning.[91]

Second Ecumenical Council at Constantinople (381)

Because none of the *acta* of the council have survived, what we know about the Council of Constantinople and its proceedings has to be reconstructed from the writings Gregory of Nazianzus (who was, for a time, the presiding bishop) and contemporary historians (Socrates and Sozemenus).[92] "We do possess . . . the synodal letter addressed to (Emperor) Theodosius, the list of members of the council, and the canons which were issued," as well as references to the council found in a letter written to Pope Damasus by a council in 382.[93] Of course the most important "product" of the council is the so-called Nicene-Constantinopolitan Creed, which J. N. D. Kelly has described as the only creed "for which ecumenicity, or universal acceptance, can be plausibly claimed" and thus "one of the few threads by which the tattered fragments of the divided robes of Christendom are held together."[94] John Behr went even further, claiming that the Nicene-Constantinopolitan Creed is "the most important text, after Scripture itself, for the Christian tradition."[95]

In 380 the Emperor Theodosius, who was selected to replace the pro-Arian Valens, expressed his desire to restore Nicene orthodoxy in the imperial capital. For that reason he called a council, selected Melitius of Antioch as its president, and confirmed Gregory of Nazianzus as bishop of the city. Present in Constantinople at the time were some of Christianity's greatest luminaries: Gregory of Nazianzus, Gregory of Nyssa, Jerome, Diodore of Tarsus, Evagrius Ponticus, John Chrysostom (who had recently been ordained deacon by Melitus), and Cyril of Jerusalem. When Melitus died suddenly, Gregory became the council's president, pressing the bishops to affirm both the Nicene faith and the Spirit's full divinity (i.e., his consubstantiality with both the Father and the Son). Thirty-six bishops who were followers of Macedonias left the council because Gregory introduced this "untraditional" teaching, and the remaining 150 became increasingly resistant to Gregory's leadership, reluctant to call the Holy Spirit *homoousios* with the Father and Son.[96]

Following Gregory's resignation, the council (allegedly) issued a creed that restated the teachings of Nicea, affirmed the full humanity of Christ against Appolinarus, and expressed the Church's mind on the subject of the Holy Spirit.[97] It was, according to McGuckin, "a wonderful mixture of specific Nicene thought and Pneumatomachian ambivalence."[98] The council (in what Gregory later called a fatal compromise) deliberately avoided calling the Holy Spirit "God" and *homoouisos* with the Father and the Son. Rather they contented themselves with the scriptural affirmations that the Spirit was "Lord" (2 Cor 3:17) and "Giver of Life" (John 6:63) "who spoke by the prophets" (2 Peter 1:21). The nonscriptural claim that the Spirit was "worshipped and glorified" alongside both the Father and Son came from Basil, who had earlier detailed the reasons why it was absurd not to glorify the Spirit.[99] Thus while such a claim was not an unambiguous affirmation of the Spirit's divinity, most bishops (Gregory of Nazianzus excepted) believed the issue settled.

However it is the confession that the Spirit "proceeds from the Father" that later became the subject of so much debate, and what the council intended to affirm (and deny) by the use of this term ἐκπορεύεσθαι. Although the statement itself is rooted in the Scripture (John 15:26), implicit in it also is the Cappadocian teaching that the persons of the Trinity are distinguished only in terms of being unbegotten, begotten, and procession. Thus the council's affirmation that the Spirit proceeds from the Father is primarily a matter of distinguishing his hypostatic existence from that of the other persons of the Trinity—the Father who is unbegotten cause and the Son who was "begotten of the Father before all ages." According to John Zizioulas, the council's purpose in affirming the procession *from the Father* was

> not simply to keep the traditional idea of the *monarchia*. . . . It was rather to safeguard the faith that the person precedes substance and "causes" it to be. The Spirit, therefore, is not simply a power issuing from divine substance; he is another personal identity standing vis-à-vis the Father. He is a product of love and freedom and not of substantial necessity. The Spirit by proceeding from the Father— and not from divine substance as such—is a person in the truest sense. And this seems to be the most important implication of the phrase "from the Father"[100]

If we accept that the conciliar teaching that the Spirit proceeds from the *person* of the Father, who is *cause* of the Spirit's being, did that negate (at least in the minds of the fathers gathered at Constantinople) any role for the Son in the coming-into-being of the Holy Spirit? For the next several centuries Greeks (following Photius) maintained that implicit in the creed was the belief that the procession of the Holy Spirit was from the Father *alone*, the ability to generate the Spirit (i.e., being *cause* of the Spirit's hypostatic existence) being a unique hypostatic quality of the person of the Father and thus not transferable to the Son. The Latins later claimed that the council's teaching in no way intended to exclude the possibility of the Son's having a place in the procession, and that the *filioque* only clarified a teaching long present in the Church, even if it was not explicitly included in the creed as originally composed. Zizioulas, examining the council's doctrine of the Holy Spirit in light of the Cappadocian teaching that inspired it, wrote that the idea of procession from the Father as defined at Constantinople neither "exclude[s] a mediating role of the Son in the principle of the Spirit" nor "allow[s] for the Son to acquire the role of αἰτία by being a mediator,"[101] an assessment that challenges, on some level, both the later Greek and Latin readings of the conciliar text.

Cyril of Alexandria (d. 444)

Among the Greek fathers the one who appears most frequently in Latin (and Greek unionist) *florilegia* in support of the *filioque* is Cyril of Alexandria, a figure more often remembered for his Christological writings against Nestorius and those who denied the title *Theotokos*.[102] As early as the seventh century Maximus the Confessor specifically named Cyril's *Commentary on John* as a witness to the orthodoxy of the *filioque*, most likely because selections of this work had already found their way into an early Latin *florilegium*. According to Hubert du Manoir de Juaye, for centuries "Cyril of Alexandria has been considered one of the most authoritative defenders of the *filioque*. . . . Catholic polemicists who were forced to refute the theories of Photius frequently had recourse to Cyril."[103]

While Cyril is often seen as an advocate of the later Latin teaching, his writings on the procession are, in fact, far more nuanced and must be read in light of his overriding christological and soteriological concerns.[104] Boris Bobrinskoy rightly claims:

> a study of St. Cyril of Alexandria, as much as of St. Athanasius, his spiritual father, should start from the doctrine of salvation and of sanctification . . . The unfolding of the common work of the divine hypostases (in creation and redemption) is specified in the constant use of the formula "From the Father, through the Son, in the Holy Spirit" . . . the mediation of the Son between the Father and the Holy Spirit . . . not signify[ing] in the least an ontological subordination of the hypostases.[105]

There is certainly no question that Cyril accepted the consubstantiality of the Spirit, who comes to us through the Son (διὰ τοῦ Υἱοῦ) since the Spirit "is of the essence of the Son, existing from him according to the nature (ἐξ αὐτοῦ κατὰ φύσιν) coming from him (παρ' αὐτοῦ) to the creature in order to accomplish his renewal."[106] He often used analogies to discuss this relationship, writing that the Spirit comes from the Son like sweetness from honey[107] or heat from light.[108] According to George Berthold, the question is whether "this pattern obtains in the realm of theology itself; can we speak in the manner of the internal processions within the godhead?"[109] Berthold argues that we can, maintaining that Cyril speaks "of the movement of the divine processions in the same line as the movement of grace beginning with the Father, going through the Son, in the Holy Spirit."[110] In support of this claim there are a host of quotations that seemingly speak of the Spirit's "procession" from both the Father and the Son:

> [The Holy Spirit] is the Spirit of God the Father as well as of the Son, and comes forth [προχεόμενον] substantially from both [ἐξ ἀμφοῖν], that is, from the Father through the Son.[111]

> Since the Holy Spirit when He is in us effects our being conformed to God, and He actually progresses from the Father and Son [πρόεισι δὲ καὶ ἐκ Πατρὸς καὶ Υἱοῦ], it is clear that He is of the divine

essence, progressing substantially in it and from it [οὐσιωδῶς προϊόν]. [112]

The Spirit is named the Spirit of truth, and Christ is the truth, and thus the Spirit flows forth [προχεῖται] from him as from God and Father. [113]

Yet in none of these passages, or anywhere in his writings, does Cyril say that the Spirit *proceeds* (ἐκπορεύεσθαι) from the Father and the Son. Rather he consistently maintains that the Spirit *progresses* or *flows forth* (προϊέναι, προχεῖται) from the Son, which is something rather different. That Cyril intends to retain an important distinction between the two concepts becomes clear in his exegesis of John 15:26, where he writes:

Jesus calls the Paraclete "the Spirit of Truth," that is to say, his consoling Spirit, and at the same time he says that He proceeds from the Father [παρὰ τοῦ πατρὸς ἐκπορεύεσθαι]. Thus as the Spirit is naturally proper to the Son, who exists in Him and progresses through him [δι αὐτοῦ προϊὸν], yet he is at the same time the Spirit of the Father.[114]

This distinction between ἐκπορεύεσθαι and προϊέναι allows Cyril, like Gregory of Nyssa before him and Maximus after him, to establish both a temporal and eternal relationship between the Son and the Spirit, yet one that does not involve the Son in the Spirit's ἐκπόρευσις. In Cyril's theology the Spirit proceeds from the Father [ἐκπορεύεται ἐκ τοῦ Πατρός] but "is not a stranger to the essence of the only Son because he progresses naturally from him [πρόεισι δὲ φυσικῶς ἐξ αὐτῆς]."[115] Even if he never fully explicates the exact nature of this progression, Cyril is clear that the Spirit does not derive his ἐκπόρευσις or personal existence from the Son, a fact that becomes apparent in his debate with Theodoret of Cyrus.[116]

Cyril, in his ninth anathema against Nestorius, had stated that the Spirit was Christ's own Spirit, which led Theodoret to question whether Cyril was advocating the idea that "the Spirit has his subsistence from the Son or through the Son" (ἐξ Υἱοῦ ἢ δὶ Υἱοῦ τὴν ὕπαρξιν ἔχον).[117] For Theodoret this idea was both "blasphemous and impious . . . for we believe the Lord who has said: 'the Spirit of Truth who proceeds from the Father.'" [118] Cyril denied that he held this teaching, leading Theodoret to confirm the orthodoxy of Cyril's trinitarian theology, since the Church had always taught that "the Holy Spirit does not receive existence from or through the Son, but proceeds from the Father and is called the *proprium* of the Son because of his consubstantiality."[119]

Thus while Cyril maintained a role for the Son in the eternal flowing forth of the Spirit, this belief did not necessarily make him, as the Latins later claimed, an advocate of the *filioque*. For Cyril and the East, procession (ἐκπόρευσις) had attained a rather specific meaning, describing a unique relationship between the Spirit and the Father. Yet Cyril did speak to an eternal relationship between the Son and the Spirit—a teaching that was already part of the Eastern tradition. The fathers prior to Cyril had used various formulas to speak of the Spirit's relationship to the Son, and this lack of uniformity explains why it remains impossible, even today, to give a quick and easy explanation of Greek patristic teaching on the procession. In Cyril, however, we begin to see a degree of clarity previously unknown, distinguishing between the Spirit's ἐκπόρευσις from the Father, and his eternal προϊέναι through or from the Son. Although questions remained (e.g., what exactly is the nature of this "flowing forth"), the Greek tradition was slowly moving toward consensus, with Cyril leading the way.

While the Greek fathers were still striving to find language capable of expressing the mysterious nature of the Son's relationship to the Spirit, Latin theologians, even during Cyril's lifetime, had already found their answer—the Holy Spirit proceeds from the Father and the Son (*ex Patre et Filio procedentem*). The degree to which this teaching was compatible with, or contradictory to, the emerging Greek tradition remains, sixteen centuries later, subject to debate.

3

The Latin West

At some point between the second and fifth centuries the belief that the Spirit proceeded from both the Father and the Son became an important part of Latin trinitarian thinking. By the sixth century the doctrine had achieved widespread acceptance in the West, taught not only by great saints and local councils, but by the Bishop of Rome, who (following the lead of Leo the Great) increasingly came to see himself as a the unique guarantor of orthodox teaching.[1]

Although a few important elements remain shrouded in mystery (e.g., exactly how the words "and the Son" first came to be included in the Nicene–Constantinopolitan Creed), the history of the *filioque* in the West is a relatively well-documented phenomenon. Although there are a few scattered references to the relationship of Son and Spirit in the writings of the apologists, Novatian, and Irenaeus of Lyons (e.g., the two "hands of God"), the story of *filioque* begins with Tertullian.[2] It was in his writings that the idea of Spirit's procession "through the Son" was made explicit, and it was following Tertullian that Latin theology began to link our understanding of God's very nature (i.e., the theology) and the biblical revelation (i.e., the economy), leading many of the fathers to read certain texts (e.g., John 20:22) as descriptions of life within the godhead. While the Greek fathers (following Gregory Nazianzus) were usually very careful about blurring the lines between economy and theology because of the heresy of Eunomius, Latin theology was unencumbered by such concerns. Rather, it was the continuing presence of Arianism that threatened the West, leading the fathers to stress the biblical truth (John 16:15) that all that the Father has belongs also to the Son, and that this must include some role in the procession of the Holy Spirit.

Tertullian (d. 220)

Tertullian occupies a special place in Latin trinitarian theology, since it was he who first provided the vocabulary (*una substantia, tres personae*) to describe the mystery of God's triunity.[3] Tertullian's writings on the Trinity were firmly grounded in the revelation of the three persons in the economy, with the Father understood as the one who sent the Son, the Son as the one who bestows the Spirit (or, more properly, the one through whom the Spirit is sent by the Father). Thus Tertullian, in his work *Adversus Praxeam*, can clearly affirm that the Spirit proceeds from the Father through the Son (*Hoc mihi et in tertium gradum dictum sit quia Spiritum non aliunde puto, quam a Patre per Filium*).[4]

The unanswered question is how closely Tertullian is linking God's revelation in history with God's inner being, and to what degree the Spirit's place as third in the order of revelation is indicative of his place in the Trinity itself. Although it would be anachronistic to speak of Tertullian's advocacy of the *filioque*, there is a case to be made for establishing a link in his theology between the economic and immanent Trinities.[5] Just as the Spirit is manifested third in the economy, a manifestation made possible through the Son, so too is the divine substance communicated from the Father to the Son and then through the Son to the Holy Spirit. The Son, as the one through whom the divine substance flows from the Father (since Tertullian was careful to protect the divine monarchy), thus becomes a necessary precondition not only for the manifestation of the Spirit but for his existence as a person. He writes: "The Spirit, then, is third from God and the Son, just as the third from the root is the fruit from the stem, and third from the fountain is the stream from the river, and third from the sun is the apex of the ray."[6]

Tertullian's influence on Latin trinitarian thinking, even after his lapse into heresy, was immense. The direction he set for Western theology, especially in equating the immanent and economic Trinities, shaped the thinking of later figures such as Marius Victorinus and Augustine and set the stage for the acceptance of the *filioque* in the West. Although it would be inaccurate to describe Tertullian himself as a "filioquist" or an advocate of a "double procession," his writings remain among the oldest witnesses to the idea of procession *from* or *through the Son*, providing the foundation upon which the *filioque* will be built.

Hilary of Poitiers (d. 367)

Hilary of Poitiers, the "Athanasius of the West," is often listed, along with Augustine of Hippo, as the chief patristic source for the Latin teaching on the *filioque*.[7] Hilary was certainly an influence on the trinitarian thinking of Augustine and was the only Church father quoted by name in Augustine's *De Trinitate*. Like the Bishop of Hippo, Hilary maintained that the unity of God is grounded in the divine nature (as opposed to the person of the Father), and he taught that the Spirit, understood as the mutual "gift" (*donum*) of Father and Son, comes to us from both. Echoing Romans 8:9, Hilary clearly affirmed that the "Spirit of God is the Spirit also of Christ. And since the Spirit of Christ is in us, the Spirit of Him also who raised Christ from the dead is in us."[8] Yet there is also reason for questioning Hilary's alleged support for the *filioque* as later theology will understand it, especially given the ambiguous nature of his language as it concerns the procession.

Hilary's major trinitarian work, *De Trinitate*, was composed during his exile in Constantinople (356–59) although books 1–3 seem to have been written earlier (possibly while he was still in Gaul) and then joined with books 4–12 to form the work as we know it. Although Hilary's primary theological concern, both here and elsewhere, was to stress the consubstantiality of the Father and Son in order to combat the Arian heresy, he is also careful to stress the divinity of the Holy Spirit. In book 2 of *De Trinitate*, for example, Hilary spoke of the Spirit, *qui Patre et Filio auctoribus confitendus est*, which has been understood by generations of Latin writers as an endorsement of the *filioque*.[9] The problem is that while this text can be understood to mean that "we are bound to confess Him, proceeding, as he does, from Father and Son," a better reading might be "confess him on the evidence of the Father and the Son."[10]

Later in *De Trinitate* Hilary spoke more explicitly to the issue of the procession, asserting:

> Nor will I infringe upon any one's liberty of thought in this matter, whether they may regard the Paraclete Spirit as coming from the Father or from the Son [*utrum ex Patre an ex Filio Spiritum paracletum putent esse*]. The Lord has left nothing uncertain. . . . Consequently, He receives [*accipit*] from the Son who has been sent by Him and proceeds from the Father [*A Filio igitur accipit qui et ab eo mittitur et a Patre procedit*]. . . . The Spirit of truth proceeds from the Father, but He is sent by the Son from the Father [*A Patre enim procedit Spiritus veritatis, sed a Filio a Patre mittitur*].[11]

Was there a difference between receiving and proceeding? Hilary addressed this question directly when he wrote:

And I ask the question whether it is the same to receive from the Son as to proceed from the Father? But, if we must hold that there is a difference between receiving from the Son and proceeding from the Father, then, certainly, we shall have to admit that it is one and the same to receive from the Son as it is to receive from the Father. . . . For, since He asserts that everything that the Father has is his, and has, therefore, said that they must be received from him, he likewise teaches that what is to be received from the Father must still be received from Him, because everything that belongs to the Father is his.[12]

Although Hilary appears here to equate the ideas of receiving and proceeding, it is interesting to note that he reserves the verb *procedere* for the activity of the Father, while affirming that the Spirit is both sent by (*mittere*) and receives from (*accipere*) the Son. Whether Hilary was attempting to communicate the uniqueness of the Spirit's eternal relation to the Father by ἐκπόρευσις, differentiating his procession *a Patre* from his temporal sending/receiving from the Father through the Son is still open to question. He is careful to protect the monarchy of the Father, affirming elsewhere that "there is one source [*auctor unus*] of all. God the Father is one from whom are all things [*ex quo omnia*]; and our Lord Jesus Christ is one through whom are all things [*per quem omnia*]; and the Holy Spirit is one, the gift in all things [*donum in omnibus*]."[13] Yet in the end Hilary is simply forced to surrender himself to the ineffable nature of the divine life, "assert[ing] nothing else about the Holy Spirit that is above the judgment of the human mind except that He is Your Spirit. And I pledge myself not to a futile contest of words, but to the persevering profession of an unquestioning faith."[14]

Although later Latin theology regarded Hilary, especially in his frequent use of the *per filium* formula (e.g., "who is from You [i.e., the Father] through the Only-begotten") as an advocate of the *filioque*, it remains unclear whether Hilary himself would have accepted the teaching.[15] While it is easy to see how Hilary's language later lent itself to the development of filioquist thinking, the degree to which the great anti-Arian can be credited (or blamed) for this development is still open to debate.

Marius Victorinus (d. 365)

One the one hand, it can legitimately be argued that the writings of the great rhetor and Platonist Marius Victorinus did not play a significant role during the *filioque* debates, in that later Latin theologians rarely used them to support their teaching on the procession.[16] On the other hand, the possible influence of Victorinus on Augustine, and the fact that many of the trinitarian images used by the Bishop of Hippo are also found in his works (especially his four books *Against Arius* written in 361–62), make a study of Victorinus integral for under-standing the development Western thinking on the procession.[17] Augustine certainly regarded him as an important figure, writing in the *Confessions* that after learning of Victorinus's conversion he "burned to imitate him."[18]

Early in his work *Against Arius*, Victorinus explicitly affirmed the full con-substantiality of the three persons, unafraid to describe them as *homoousioi*, for "just as the Son is from the bosom of the Father and in the bosom of the Father, so the Spirit is from within the Son [*sic a ventre filii spiritus*]."[19] It was this emphasis on the unity of God that led him to utilize the neo-Platonic image of the One, whereby the Father is the unknowable and transcendent One who makes himself known through the "form" (*Logos*).[20] Victorinus's writing on the Trinity also focused on its likeness to the human soul (formed in the *imago dei*), where the triad of "being" (*esse*), "living" (*vivere*), and "understanding" (*intel-ligere*) coexisted just as Father, Son, and Holy Spirit exist in the one *substantia* or *essentia* of God.

> For as the soul in its "to be" gives both life and knowledge, possess-ing these together, *homoousia*, in unity, before understanding; and yet these three are individuated in their own substance without being separated by sectioning, division or overflowing, extension or reproduction; but they are always three, each existing really in the other which truly and substantially exist. Therefore the soul is "according to the image."[21]

In God the "three subsistences of the one substance"[22] eternally exist and coexist, although there are times when the language of Victorinus seems to imply a temporal and hierarchical ordering of Father, Son, and Spirit. He claimed that the Father was "older" than the Son (who is "younger"), yet main-tained against the Arians that "both the Father and the Son are *homoousian* and that they are always such, and from eternity and for eternity."[23] Victorinus clear-ly affirmed the Father's monarchy, since he is source and principle of the divine life, yet while both the Son and Spirit come forth by a unique movement of the Father, "because all that the Father has he has given to the Son . . . the Son also, who is movement, gave all to the Holy Spirit."[24] Victorinus referred to the Holy Spirit as "the utterance of the voice"[25] and said that "just as from the Father comes the Son . . . from the Son [comes] the Holy Spirit."[26] In fact, several times in *Against Arius* he stated that the Holy Spirit *is* Jesus, but in another mode "united to the Father through the Son."[27] Victorinus claimed that this is why only the risen Christ can send the Spirit because "while the Logos was in pres-ence, that is, Christ, the Logos in hiding, that is, the Holy Spirit, could not come. . . . Therefore these are also two, one coming from the other, the Holy Spirit from the Son just as the Son comes from God and, as a logical conse-quence, the Holy Spirit also comes from the Father."[28]

In his trinitarian hymns Victorinus put forward another image which was later used by Augustine and which became the chief paradigm for understanding the Spirit's role within the Trinity—that is, as the bond of love between the Father and Son.

> Holy Spirit assist us!
> The bond between Father and Son!
> In repose you are Father, in your procession, Son,
> And binding all in one, you are the Holy Spirit.[29]

Victorinus maintained that the Spirit, as the bond of love, was "third" in the Trinity, even as he insisted on the coequality and consubstantiality of the three persons.

> You, Holy Spirit, are a bond, but a bond is whatever unites two
> In order to unite all, you first unite the two.
> You, the third, are the embrace of the two:
> An embrace identified with the one, since you make the
>   two one.[30]

The question later asked (especially by critics of the *filioque*) is whether Victorinus, in introducing this image, gave a priority to the Father–Son dyad over the Spirit and allowed the Holy Spirit to be both depersonalized and deemphasized. Victorinus certainly would have rebuffed the allegation, especially given his frequent affirmations of the Spirit's being *homoousias* and equal to both the Father and Son.[31] And while Victorinus himself never explicitly advocated the *filioque*, elements of his thinking provided the foundation upon which the Latin doctrine would later be built. When these same ideas were put forward by Augustine (who may or may not have received them from Victorinus), they had a profound impact upon the debates to come.

Pope Damasus I (d. 384)

Among the earliest known references to the *filioque* in the Roman Church is the so-called creed of Pope Damasus (sometimes known as the twenty-four *Anathematisms*).[32] Scholars have traditionally been divided on its origins, some believing it was composed by Damasus himself in reply to a treatise by Priscillian of Avila, while Künstle argued that it was the work of the Synod of Saragossa held in 380, an anti-Priscillian gathering whose work was sent to the pope for approval.[33] Modern scholarship has argued for an earlier dating (late 377 or early 378) and that it was probably a "compiled work" based on the proceedings of a Roman council.[34] Regardless of its origins, its apparent purpose was to refute certain christological and trinitarian errors, including the belief that the Spirit was somehow a work or creation of the Son. It stated, "We believe . . . in the Holy Spirit, not begotten nor unbegotten, not created nor made, but proceeding from the Father and the Son, always co-eternal with the Father and the Son."[35] Here the intention was simply to acknowledge the equality of the Spirit rather than to delve into the question of the procession proper.

The *Decretum Gelasianum* (*Explanatio fidei*), or at least the first three chapters, is thought by some to be the work of the Roman Synod of 382 also held under Damasus. Others, including Bernd Oberdorfer, think that the trinitarian language (which reflects Augustine's thinking in the *Tractates on the Gospel of John*) argues for a later dating or the recognition that some portions of the work were added by a later editor.[36] The disputed section includes the teaching that:

> The Holy Spirit is not only the Spirit of the Father, or not only the Spirit of the Son, but the Spirit of the Father and the Son. For it is written, "If anyone loves the world, the Spirit of the Father is not in him" (1 John 2:15). Likewise it is written, "If anyone, however, does not have the Spirit of Christ, he is none of His (Romans 8:9)." When the Father and the Son are mentioned in this way, the Holy Spirit is understood, of whom the Son himself says in the Gospel, that the Holy Spirit "proceedeth from the Father (John 15:26)," and "He shall receive of mine and shall announce it to you (John 16:14)."[37]

Whether this passage is genuinely the work of Pope Damasus or a later interpolation, it became an important prooftext in later pro-*filioque florilegia*, especially given its (alleged) acceptance by a Roman synod. Authentic or not, it provides evidence that Latin theology already by the late fourth century was moving toward a particular way of understanding the biblical truth that the Holy Spirit was "Spirit of the Son."

Ambrose of Milan (d. 397)

Ambrose of Milan probably composed his *De Spiritu Sancto* in 381 in an attempt to combat the heresy of Macedonius, who had claimed that the Holy Spirit was merely a "minister or servant" of God and thus not divine. Ambrose, fluent in Greek and already familiar with the arguments presented on this matter by Basil the Great, Didymus, and Athanasius, freely borrowed from their writings in composing his own treatise on the Holy Spirit.[38] Yet while firmly rooted in the Eastern tradition, Ambrose is also one of the earliest Latin witnesses to the explicit affirmation of the Spirit's procession from the Father *and* the Son.

Ambrose, like Hilary, often employed the *per filium* formula favored by the Greeks, paraphrasing Basil's own *De Spiritu Sancto* when he wrote that "from one Spirit through one Son into one Father does our knowledge proceed, and from the one Father through one Son and into one Holy Spirit is goodness and sanctification and imperial right of eternal power handed down."[39] Yet Ambrose also stated that the Spirit "proceeds from the Father and the Son" (*procedit a Patre et a Filio*) and that "when the Holy Spirit proceeds from the Father and the Son, He is not separated from the Father, nor is he separated from the Son."[40] In that same work Ambrose described the Father and the Son as the fountains of life, "that is, the fountain of the Holy Spirit, since the Spirit is Life."[41] Yet in both passages it should be noted that most scholars have traditionally maintained that Ambrose is speaking of the Spirit's activity in the economy of salvation and not speculating about the inner-trinitarian life. Ambrose, like Basil before him, simply wanted to affirm that since the persons of the Trinity share a common nature and will, their activity in salvation history can never be separated.[42] Ambrose also taught that the Son is both sent and given by the Father *and* by the Holy Spirit, who anoints and empowers him for his mission, without ever implying that the Son has his eternal origin from the Spirit.[43]

However, the question remains whether for Ambrose the Spirit's procession from both Father and Son signified not only a temporal, but also an eternal, relationship. Ambrose certainly affirmed that the Holy Spirit was also the Spirit of the Son, but although later Latin theology equated being "of the Son" with the idea of being "from the Son," it is impossible to read this view into Ambrose's theology. Perhaps the most that can be legitimately claimed is that Ambrose's writings leave open the possibility of a pro-*filioque* interpretation, and that his affirmation of the Spirit's procession *a Patre et a Filio* set the stage for what was to come. Whether Ambrose himself would have accepted the doctrinal content implied by the later Latin teaching on the *filioque* remains unknown.

Jerome (d. 420)

Jerome's views on the procession of the Holy Spirit defy easy categorization. His name regularly appears in later Latin *florilegia* as a supporter of the *filioque*, and in the ninth century Photius felt the need to defend Jerome's reputation against those who used him to support the doctrine. However John Meyendorff and others have claimed that Jerome "could hardly be regarded as [a] proponent of the *filioque*," in that his work contains few references to the teaching and even these are far from unambiguous affirmations of a double procession.[44]

The most quoted writing of Jerome in later *florilegia* was not his own, but the *Interpretatio libri Didymi De Spiritu Sancto*, a translation of Didymus's work completed in 387.[45] Debate remains as to how much of Jerome's own thinking is reflected in this translation, especially given the fact that the original Greek text is no longer extant. Jerome himself usually expressed a reserve toward "speculative theology," leading him to take a very conservative stance vis-à-vis trinitarian thought, even going so far as to reject the "one *ousia*, three *hypostases*" formula as inconsistent with Nicene orthodoxy. Yet while Jerome was in

Constantinople during the council of 381, he met Gregory Nazianzus, who "opened Jerome's prejudiced eyes to its [the formula's] essential orthodoxy."[46] Gregory, whom Jerome often described as "my teacher," was very influential in his theological development, especially as it pertained to trinitarian doctrine. It was Gregory who introduced Jerome to Gregory of Nyssa and Amphilochius of Iconium, from whom he absorbed the arguments for the Spirit's divinity and the anti-Eunomian thrust of the great Cappadocian fathers.

But perhaps Jerome's most significant contribution to the *filioque* debate was his translation of the Bible and his decision to use the Latin verb *procedere* to translate not only ἐκπορεύεσθαι (sixteen times, including John 15:26) but also ἔρχεσθαι, προέρχεσθαι, προσέρχεσθαι, ἐξέρχεσθαι, and προβαίνω (four times).[47] While ἐκπορεύεσθαι was beginning to take on a particular meaning in Greek theology designating the Spirit's unique mode of coming-to-be as opposed to the generation (γέννησις) of the Son, *procedere* had no such connotations. For Jerome and subsequent generations of Latin theologians, *procedere* was a broader term that could be used to describe both the Spirit's and the Son's coming from the Father (e.g., John 8:42: *Ego enim ex Deo processi et veni*).

Augustine of Hippo (d. 430)

To call Augustine the greatest of the Latin fathers is a commonplace. Many would go even further, echoing Jaroslav Pelikan's belief that Augustine was "perhaps not the greatest of Latin writers, but almost certainly the greatest man who ever wrote Latin."[48] His impact upon the Western world is incalculable, for Augustine was not only the author of *The Confessions* and *City of God* (which are regularly listed among Western civilization's greatest literary achievements), but also the chief patristic source for many of the central teachings of the Latin Church. This was especially true of Augustine's writings on the Trinity, which became the foundation for subsequent Latin trinitarian theology and later served as the basis for the doctrine of the *filioque*.[49]

However, the idea that his trinitarian theology was "new," or that he was introducing something "novel" in proposing the *filioque*, would have been anathema to Augustine. While he recognized the speculative nature of his *De Trinitate*, Augustine believed his conclusions to have a solid foundation in both Scripture and the Tradition, beginning his reflections with recourse to both.[50] Using language and categories borrowed from the neo-Platonists (and perhaps Marius Victorinus himself), Augustine tried to make sense of the biblical affirmation that the Holy Spirit "who proceeded from the Father" was also "Spirit of the Son." Thus Augustine was not trying to solve a "metaphysical problem" but instead trying to make sense of the biblical witness and the teachings of the Church using the tools available to him.[51]

Although Augustine of Hippo would eventually become the most quoted Latin father supporting the *filioque*, it should be noted that his earliest writings on the creed make no mention of the doctrine. In his work *De Fide et Symbolo*, composed in 393, Augustine claimed that "the learned and eminent exponents of sacred scripture . . . have not yet applied themselves to the subject of the Holy Spirit."[52] Yet it had been established that "the Holy Spirit is not begotten, as they assert of the Son, from the Father, for Christ is the only-begotten Son, nor is he begotten from the Son, the grandson, as it were of the almighty Father. . . . [T]he Holy Spirit owes his existence to the Father, from whom everything comes, lest we should find ourselves postulating two principles of origin without an origin, an assertion that would be totally false, utterly absurd, and contrary to the Catholic faith."[53]

Yet by the time Augustine wrote his *De Trinitate* (begun in 399 and finished in 420) his view seems to have shifted considerably. This move was in large part made possible by Augustine's trinitarian model, which (like that of Victorinus) spoke of the Trinity's likeness to the human mind, where the triad of "memory" (*memoria*), "understanding" (*intelligentia*), and "will" (*voluntas*) coexisted just as Father, Son, and Holy Spirit exist in the one *substantia* of God. He wrote: "These three then, memory, understanding, and will, are not three lives but one life, not three minds but one mind. So it follows, of course that they are not three substances but one substance."[54]

Augustine employed other models throughout the work, but perhaps the most influential was the triad of "lover" (*amans*), "beloved" (*amatus*), and "love" (*amor*).[55] In this model the Spirit becomes, as it was for Victorinus, the bond of love joining lover (Father) and beloved (Son). "For whether he is the unity of both the others or their holiness, or their charity, whether he is their unity because their charity and their charity because their holiness, it is clear that he is not one of the two, since he is that by which the two are joined each to the other, by which the begotten is loved by the one who begets him and in turn loves the begetter."[56]

Not only was the Holy Spirit the mutual love of Father and Son, but their mutual gift (*donum*) of this love poured out upon humanity. Since "the Holy Spirit is something common to Father and Son" and thus "the gift of both," Augustine can affirm that, "according to the Holy Scriptures this Holy Spirit is not just the Father's alone, nor the Son's alone, but the Spirit of them both." (*Qui spiritus sanctus secundum scripturas sanctas nec patris est solius nec filii solius sed amborum*).[57] Since he is the Spirit of both, it logically followed for Augustine that the Holy Spirit must proceed from both.

> And just as for the Holy Spirit his being the gift of God means his proceeding from the Father, so his being sent means being known to proceed from him. Nor, by the way, can we say that the Holy Spirit

does not proceed from the Son as well; it is not without point that the same Spirit is called the Spirit of the Father and of the Son.[58]

Augustine justified this position from the Scriptures, grounding the procession of the Spirit from the Son in the frequent biblical affirmations that the Holy Spirit is the Spirit of the Son who is sent by him into the hearts of believers. Because "Augustine does not distinguish between eternal procession and mission in time, nor between the immanent Trinity and the economic Trinity,"[59] these passages were read as revelations of God's interior life. This was especially true in his *Tractates on the Gospel of John*, where he wrote:

> Why, therefore, should we not believe that the Holy Spirit also proceeds from the Son [*de Filio procedat Spiritus sanctus*], since he is also the Spirit of the Son? For if he did not proceed from him [Jesus], after the resurrection, showing himself anew to his disciples, he would not have breathed upon them, saying, "Receive the Holy Spirit." For what else did that insufflations signify except that the Holy Spirit also proceeds from him [*nisi quod procedat Spiritus sanctus et de ipso*]?[60]

Augustine, keenly aware of the monarchical principle, went out of his way to affirm that this teaching in no way violated the unique role of the Father within the divinity, since "the source of all godhead or, if you prefer it, of all deity, is the Father [*videlicet ostendens quod totius divinitatis, vel, si melius dicitur, deitatis, principium Pater est*]. So the Spirit who proceeds from the Father and the Son is traced back, on both counts, to him of whom the Son is born."[61]

Yet while "only the Father is called the one from whom the Word is born and from whom the Holy Spirit principally proceeds [*procedit principaliter*]," Augustine immediately clarified this statement, saying, "I added 'principally,' because we have found that the Holy Spirit also proceeds from the Son [*quia et de filio spiritus sanctus procedere reperitur*]. . . . He [i.e., the Father] so begot him then that their common gift would proceed from him too, and the Holy Spirit would be the Spirit of them both."[62]

For Augustine, the ability to bring forth the Spirit is not something inherently belonging to the Son, but rather his by a gift of the Father, since "If the Son has everything that he has from the Father, he clearly has it from the Father that the Holy Spirit should proceed from him. . . . The Son is born of the Father and the Holy Spirit proceeds from the Father principally, and by the Father's wholly timeless gift from both of them jointly."[63]

Augustine was forced to address the charge that in affirming the Spirit's procession from both the Father and Son, he was postulating two principles within the godhead (the "absurd and false" notion he had earlier denounced in *De Fide et Symbolo*). He stated:

> If, therefore, what is given also has him it is given by as its origin, because it did not receive its proceeding from him from anywhere

else, we must confess that the Father and the Son are the origin of
the Holy Spirit; not two origins, but just as Father and Son are one
God and with reference to creation one creator and one lord, so with
reference to the Holy Spirit, they are one origin; but with reference to
creation Father and Son, and Holy Spirit are one origin, just as they
are one creator and one lord.[64]

The one aspect of Augustine's trinitarian thought that later Latin theologians (especially Anselm and Aquinas) adopted and adapted was the teaching
that "Father," "Son," and "Spirit" were not absolute, but rather relative terms
denoting relationships within the Trinity. Augustine had written that "Although
being Father is different from being the Son, there is no difference in substance,
because they are not called these things substance-wise but relationship-
wise."[65] For that reason, according to Augustine, the Father "is not anything
with reference to himself, and that not only his being Father but also his simply
being is said with reference to the Son."[66] According to Joseph Ratzinger (later
Pope Benedict XVI):

> Here the decisive point comes beautifully to light. "Father" is purely a
> concept of relationship. Only in being—for the other is the Father; in
> his own being-in-himself he is simply God. Person is the pure relation
> of being related, nothing else. Relationship is not something extra
> added to the person, as it is with us; it only exists at all as relatedness.[67]

While this schema works well in describing the Father–Son dyad, it
has long been recognized (especially among Augustine's critics) that the Holy
Spirit does not fit neatly into the system. As Yves Congar described it:

> This theory of the relationships which make the Persons different
> within the substance or essence without dividing the latter is simple,
> grand and satisfactory. Nonetheless it does involve a difficulty in char-
> acterizing the Holy Spirit. "Father" and "Son" are correlative, terms
> which comprise an opposition in a reciprocal relationship. . . . What
> correlative term has the Spirit from which he proceeds and which
> points to a hypostasis?[68]

For Augustine the answer was simple—the Son is the Son because he comes
from the Father; the Spirit, who is the mutual love of Father and Son, has his
origin, that is, he proceeds, from both and is the gift of both. In this way is
the person of the Spirit defined and differentiated in terms of his relational
opposition to both Father and Son.

While there are literally dozens of passages, chiefly from *De Trinitate*, the
Tractates on the Gospel of John, and the *Contra Maximinum*, that could be adduced
to demonstrate Augustine's support for a double procession, a few important

qualifications should be made. First, the phrase *a Patre filioque procedit* never actually appears in Augustine's writings.[69] Second, Augustine (while affirming the Spirit's procession from the Son) is not clear himself as to what procession is. In a passage that echoes Gregory of Nazianzus's *Oration* 31 Augustine wrote:

> What the distinction is between being born and proceeding, who can explain, when speaking of that most excellent nature? Not everything that proceeds is born, although everything that is born proceeds. . . . This I know; but how to distinguish between the former, begetting, and the latter, procession, I do not know, I am not able, I do not suffice [*nescio, non valeo, non sufficio*]. And that both the one and the other are ineffable is clear from this, as the prophet said speaking of the Son: "Who will tell of his generation?" (Isa 53:8), so too is it said most truly about the Holy Spirit, "Who will tell of his procession?"[70]

Last, and perhaps most important, is Augustine's own awareness of his limitations, especially as they relate to speaking about the Deity. For although he believed his teachings to be solidly grounded in the faith of the Church ("This is also my faith inasmuch as it is the Catholic faith"),[71] Augustine recognized the possibility of introducing error. For this reason his *De Trinitate* began with an invitation for his readers to correct him if they could (as long as they did so "charitably and truthfully"),[72] and it concluded with a prayer: "O Lord the one God, God the Trinity, whatsoever I have said in these books that is of you, may those that are yours acknowledge; whatsoever of myself alone, do you and yours forgive. Amen."[73]

Whether Augustine had actually erred in advocating the procession of the Spirit from the Son is a question that would occupy Christianity's greatest minds for the next several centuries. While largely unknown in the East (at least until the fourteenth century), Augustine's writings in the West took on the role of a "second canon," with his *De Trinitate* viewed as the criterion *sine qua non* for orthodox trinitarian theology. The *filioque* came to be seen not as a theological opinion but as doctrine, and "the Augustinian version of the trinitarian dogma . . . as the universal faith of the church."[74] While he was not necessarily the point of division between East and West, or the individual responsible for the schism that came to divide the Christian world, it is difficult to escape the conclusion that Augustine himself provided the language and theology that future generations used to justify that schism. One cannot help but think that the idea would have grieved Augustine greatly.

Pope Leo I (d. 461)

Pope Leo I ("the Great") became bishop of Rome in 440, just a few years after Augustine's death. On the subject of the procession Leo is a sword that cuts both ways, in that his writings were later used by both Latins and Greeks to support their respective positions. Some believe that Leo's relationship to Prosper of Aquitaine, who was his secretary and the great defender of the Augustinian legacy, explains to some degree the few references to the teaching found in his sermons and letters.[75] For example, in Sermon 75, on the feast of Pentecost, Leo had written:

> If indeed the Son is the only-begotten from the Father, and the Holy Spirit is the Spirit of the Father and the Son, he is not like any created being which belongs to the Father and the Son, but is with each, living and powerful [*cum utroque vivens et potens*] and subsisting eternally from that which is the Father and the Son [*ex eo quod est Pater filiusque subsistens*].[76]

In a letter to Turribius, Bishop of Astorga (*Epistle 15*), Leo allegedly affirmed the doctrine of the *filioque* in no uncertain terms, although there remain doubts about the authenticity of the letter itself.[77] While preserving the common Western belief that "it is the same essence, not the persons, which explains the unity in the Trinity" (*quia unitatem in Trinitate non eadem persona, sed eadem implet essentia*), Leo attacked the modalism of the Priscillianists by upholding the distinctiveness of the persons.[78]

> They hold impiously as to the Divine Trinity who assert that Father, Son and Holy Spirit are one person, as if the same God is called at one time the Father, at another the Son, and another the Holy Spirit, and there is not one who begat, another who is begotten, another who proceeded from both [*alius qui de utroque processerit*].[79]

Although these texts have long been used in the West to claim Leo's support for the doctrine, since the time of Photius the East has been quick to point out that Leo accepted the canons of Chalcedon (canon 28 excepted), including its reaffirmation of the Nicene-Constantinopolitan Creed in its original form (i.e., without the *filioque*).[80] Whatever Leo's stance may have been, given his other, more pressing concerns, it does not seem to be a matter to which he dedicated a great deal of thought. What can be stated with some assurance is that in the years that followed Leo's pontificate the *filioque* began to appear more frequently in the West, and nothing suggests that this development was ever questioned by Leo's successors in Rome.

Africa, Gaul, and Beyond

During the mid-fifth century, as Augustine's thought came to exert an increasing influence upon Western theology, references to the *filioque* proliferated, especially in Africa and Gaul, where his work was more widely disseminated. [81] Even those who were inclined to argue with the Bishop of Hippo about other matters (e.g., predestination and the will) seemed to accept his teaching on the procession without hesitation. Whereas Augustine felt the need to explain the procession of the Holy Spirit from the Son, authors in the fifth and sixth centuries simply stated it as a given. Even if one discounts those passages that modern scholarship has shown to be interpolated or spurious, the passages that follow clearly demonstrate that by the late sixth century the *filioque* achieved a level of acceptance in the West bordering on unanimity.

Among those who followed Augustine on the procession was Eucherius of Lyons (d. 450), the great advocate of asceticism to whom John Cassian (d. 430) dedicated part two of the *Conlationes*.[82] In his *Instructiones ad Salonium* he wrote:

> [T]he Father is unbegotten, the Son begotten, the Holy Spirit neither begotten or unbegotten. If we should say, "unbegotten," we might seem to be speaking of two fathers and if begotten, of two Sons, but rather who proceeds from the Father and the Son [*qui ex Patre et Filio procedat*], as a sort of concord of the Father and Son [*velut quaedam Patris Filioque concordia*].[83]

Gennadius of Marseilles (d. 495), an opponent of Augustine on predestination and the will, clearly stated his belief "that there is one God, Father, Son, and Holy Spirit; Father, in that he has a Son; Son, in that he has a Father; Holy Spirit in that he proceeds from the Father and the Son [*ex Patre et Filio procedens*]."[84] Julianus Pomerius (d. 498) said that all the faithful should be taught "of the Father, how he alone is to be unbegotten; of the Son, how he is begotten of him; of the Holy Spirit, how proceeding from the Father and Son [*quomodo ex Patre et Filio procedens*] cannot be called either unbegotten or begotten."[85] Avitus of Vienne (d. 523) affirmed against the Arian Goths "that we say the Holy Spirit proceeds from the Son and the Father [*a Filio et Patre procedere*] . . . [and] it is the property of the Holy Spirit to proceed from the Father and the Son [*ut sicut est proprium Spiritui sancto a Patre Filioque procedere*]."[86]

Pope Hormisdas (d. 523), who is best remembered for ending the Acacian schism, allegedly authored a confession of faith to the Emperor Justin, which taught that "it is characteristic of the Spirit to proceed from the Father and the Son in one substance of deity" (*proprium est Spiritus, ut de Patre et Filio procederet sub una substantia Deitatis*).[87] Although the passage had long used as a prooftext by the Latins (especially as it was a papal statement that implied Eastern acceptance of the *filioque*), most scholars now doubt its authenticity.[88]

The philosopher Boethius (d. 524), following the example of Augustine, wrote in his *De Trinitate* that the terms "Father," "Son," and "Spirit" were predicates of relation, and thus while the Father was always the Father (as the one who eternally begot the Son), the predicate "Father" was still a relative one. This fact, he argued, established an "otherness of persons" but not plurality within the godhead. Thus:

> We shall admit that God the Son proceeded from God the Father and the Holy Ghost from both [et ex utrisque Spiritum Sanctum] . . . But since the Father is God, the Son is God, and the Holy Spirit is God, and since there are in God no points of difference distinguishing Him from God, He differs from none of the others.[89]

Agnellus (d. 569), the anti-Arian Bishop of Ravenna, defended the Church's trinitarian faith in his *Epistola ad Armenum de ratione fidei*, writing that "the Son is from the Father, from the Father and the Son proceeds the Holy Spirit. . . . How great is the omnipotence of God, that he should be Almighty Father, the Begetter of the Son, and Virtue proceeding from the Father and the Son, which is the Holy Spirit."[90] Cassiodorus (d. 580) claimed that the creed of "holy, spotless, perfect mother Church, from which nothing could be added or taken away" professed "the unbegotten Father, the begotten Son, and the Holy Spirit, proceeding from the Father and Son" (*de Patre et Filio procedentem*).[91] Gregory of Tours (d. 594), in his *History of the Franks*, included the confession that the Holy Spirit proceeded from the Father and the Son.[92]

Among the Latins, Rusticus, who was a deacon at Rome and the nephew of Pope Vigilius, appears alone in expressing any reservations about the *filioque*. Rusticus's doubts may have arisen during his two extended stays in Constantinople (both before and after his uncle excommunicated him for supporting the "Three Chapters"). However, for Rusticus the question was not about the doctrine itself (which he accepted) but about its meaning (i.e., whether procession from the Son is exactly the same as procession from the Father). He wrote:

> just as the Spirit does not eternally beget the Son with the Father, so neither does the Spirit proceed from the Son in the same way as from the Father [*nec procedit Spiritus a Filio sicut a Patre*]; truly I confess that the Spirit is not eternally begotten (neither, in fact, do we say there are two Fathers); whether he truly proceeds from the Son in the same way as he proceeds from the Father, I have not yet been perfectly satisfied [*utrum vero a Filio eodem modo quo a Patre procedit, nondum perfecte satisfactum habeo*].[93]

While Rusticus raised an important question, he failed to answer it, busied as he was with more immediate ecclesiological concerns. By the time Latin theology finally concerned itself with addressing the issue of *how* the Spirit proceeds from the Son, the idea *that* he proceeded from the Son was already firmly established as part of the (Western) Church's faith. Within a few short years the fifth- and sixth-century fathers would themselves become authoritative witnesses to the orthodoxy of the *filioque*, providing dozens of prooftexts in support of the Latin teaching. While Western theology was hardly monolithic, the evidence clearly suggests that on this one matter a hitherto unknown level of consensus was reached, and reached so quickly that by the mid-sixth century the *filioque* was simply assumed to be part of the ancient faith.

Fulgentius of Ruspe (d.533)

Fulgentius of Ruspe has a unique place in the history of the *filioque* debates, becoming the most quoted Western father (besides Augustine himself) in later *florilegia* supporting the teaching. Fulgentius himself spent most of his life either in exile or in transit, moving from monastery to monastery and defending Nicene orthodoxy against the Arians in Germany. Thought by many to be the most talented theologian of his age, Fulgentius was a great defender of the Augustinian legacy, including the Bishop of Hippo's teaching on the procession of the Holy Spirit.

He wrote that the Spirit's procession from the Son was the same as his procession from the Father, since he was "given by the Son just as it is given by the Father . . . it is completely of the Son because by nature it is the one Spirit of the Father and the Son."[94] Like Augustine, he admitted that the procession of the Spirit still takes place *principaliter de Patre*, since it proceeds from the Son by virtue of the Son's consubstantiality with the Father, yet "as a whole, it has proceeded from the Father and the Son, it remains completely in the Father and the Son, because it remains in such a way that it proceeds, it proceeds in such a way that it remains."[95] Fulgentius went so far as to describe the Spirit's procession from the Father and the Son as one of its "hypostatic properties," so that "it is the property of the Father alone that he was not born but begot; it is the property of the Son that he did not beget but was born; it is the property of the Holy Spirit that he neither begot nor was born but proceeded from the begetter and the begotten."[96]

Yet perhaps the clearest exposition of Fulgentius's teaching on the procession is found in his *De Fide ad Petrum*, a summary of the faith prepared for pilgrims traveling to Jerusalem (where reaction to Chalcedon continued to divide Christians). Heavily influenced by the *De ecclesiasticis dogmatibus* of Gennadius of Marseilles, Fulgentius presented the faith of the Church as he understood it. Early in the work he spoke of the Spirit "who is eternal and without beginning, because the Holy Spirit proceeds from the nature of the Father and the Son,"[97] later enjoining pilgrims to "hold most firmly and never doubt in the least that the same Holy Spirit, who is the one Spirit of the Father and the Son, proceeds from the Father and the Son. For, the Son says, 'when the spirit of Truth comes, who has proceeded from the Father,' where he taught that the Spirit was his since he is the truth."[98] For Fulgentius the *filioque* was not a novelty introduced by Augustine, but rather a doctrine that "the prophetic and apostolic teaching shows us."[99] The *filioque* was now so widely embraced that it was simply assumed to be apostolic, a notion soon reinforced by its appearance in the creed.

The *Quicumque Vult*

The Athanasian Creed, or the *Quicumque Vult* (a title taken from its opening words, "Whoever wishes to be saved"), was for centuries believed to be the work of Athanasius, although modern scholarship now recognizes that it was composed somewhere in the Latin West during the late fifth or early sixth century.[100] It was first mentioned in 542 by Caesarius of Arles and later became an important (if not the chief) prooftext for the *filioque* among the Latins, especially given its alleged origin from an early Eastern father. By the ninth century it was included (with the Apostles' Creed and Lord's Prayer) in many psalters, and by the thirteenth century it was considered (along with the Nicene-Constantinopolitan and Apostles' Creed) to be a binding confession of the faith. Concerning the Holy Spirit it read:

> The Father was made by no one, neither created nor begotten. The
> Son is from the Father alone, not made, nor created, but begotten
> The Holy Spirit is from the Father and the Son, not made, neither
> created nor begotten, but proceeding [*Spiritus sanctus a Patre et Filio,*
> *non factus nec creatus nec genitus sed procedens*]. Therefore there is one
> Father, not three fathers, one Son, not three sons, one Holy Spirit,
> not three holy spirits.[101]

The *filioque* had now achieved both apostolicity and, through the alleged writings of Athanasius, ecumenicity.

The Third Council of Toledo (589)

For centuries the Council of Toledo has been used to date the first use of the *filioque* in the Western version of the Nicene-Constantinopolitan Creed. It was at Toledo, under the presidency of Archbishop Leander (the older brother of Isidore of Seville), that King Reccard and the Visigoths accepted the Catholic faith and renounced both Arianism and Priscilianism, pledging their acceptance of the ancient councils of Nicea, Constantinople, Ephesus, and Chalcedon. Since the acts of these councils were read out, those assembled at Toledo were very much aware of the prohibitions of Ephesus regarding "producing, editing, or composing another faith other than that set out by the Holy Fathers gathered at Nicea with the Holy Spirit."[102] In order to maintain continuity with the faith of these councils, King Reccard mandated that the symbol of faith of the

Council of Constantinople (i.e., "of the 150 bishops") should be recited at the celebration of every Eucharist in all the churches of Spain and Gallacia "according to the form of the Eastern Church."[103] It is thus clear that the Council of Toledo had no intention of adding anything to the creed, or no consciousness that they were introducing something novel.

Yet in his opening speech at the council, King Reccard professed his belief that "in equal degree must the Holy Spirit be confessed by us and we must preach that he proceeds from the Father and the Son" (*a Patre et a Filio procedere*).[104] In its third anathema, the council condemned "whoever does not believe in the Holy Spirit, or does not believe that he proceeds from the Father and the Son [*a Patre et Filio procedere*], and denies that he is coeternal and coequal with the Father and the Son."[105] Even the Nicene-Constantinopolitan Creed, as it was allegedly recited at Toledo, taught that the "Holy Spirit, Lord and giver of life, proceeds from the Father and the Son [*ex Patre et Filio procedentem*]."[106] In the mind of Reccard and those assembled at Toledo, this was the creed "in its Eastern form," demonstrating again a lack of awareness that any alteration or addition was being made in the faith of the universal church.

Here we must assume that either the council was using an already interpolated creed, one that "had made its way from Church to Church . . . and established so firm a footing that no suspicion of its genuineness was entertained," or that the acts of the council had themselves been altered and the *et Filio* added by the hand of a later editor.[107] This latter (and more probable) theory was first advanced in 1908 by A. E. Burn, who pointed out that in many early copies of the councils acts the phrase was either missing or obviously in another hand.[108] However, regardless of its exact origin, it is clear that within a few short years of the council the interpolated creed was firmly established in both the liturgy and theology of the Spanish Church.

Isidore of Seville (d. 636), younger brother of Leander, in the *De Ecclesiae Officiis* clearly affirmed the "Holy Spirit [to be] not begotten nor unbegotten, but proceeds from the Father and the Son."[109] In 633 he presided over the Fourth Council of Toledo, which also declared its belief in the Holy Spirit who is "neither created nor begotten but proceeds from the Father and the Son [*sed procedentem ex Patre et Filio*]."[110] Nine subsequent councils held at Toledo during the seventh century reaffirmed the teaching, including the sixth (638), eighth (655), eleventh (675), twelfth (681), thirteenth (683), fourteenth (688), fifteenth (688), sixteenth (693), and seventeenth (694).[111] Liturgical texts in the Gothic breviary and the Mozarabic Liturgy are addressed to the Holy Spirit "who proceeds from the Father and the Son."[112] By the end of seventh century in Spain, in large part because of the work begun at the Council of Toledo in 589, "the *filioque* had taken such firm root that its excision from the creed would have seemed nothing less than the abandonment of the faith itself."[113]

Gregory the Great (d. 604)

Pope Gregory the Great (or "Dialogos," as he is often referred to in the Eastern Church) is usually included among those who taught the Spirit's procession from the Son, despite the fact that he was also included by Photius and later Byzantine theologians as a witness against the doctrine. This seeming inconsistency can be attributed to two factors. The first is Gregory's "loose and unguarded language" about the procession, which, depending on the context, could be read by both Latins and Greeks "as favoring their views."[114] For example, the lengthy *Moralia in Job* (originally written at Leander of Seville's urging while Gregory was in Constantinople as *apocrisiarius*) affirmed that "the Holy Spirit proceeds from the Father" (*qui de Patre procedens*)," and "the Spirit which proceeds from the Father before all ages (*idem Spiritus qui de Patre ante saecula procedit*)."[115] Yet elsewhere in the same work Gregory claimed that "the Spirit, even in substance, flows [*profertur*] from the Son"[116] and "a sound proceeds from the mouth of the Lord, when his consubstantial Spirit comes to us through his Son."[117] In Book 30 of the *Moralia* he even wrote that "the Spirit of the Father and the Son who issues from both . . . proceeds ever from the Father," a statement easily capable of diverse interpretations.[118]

A second reason why Gregory's position on the *filioque* is still debated concerns Pope Zacharias's Greek translation of the *Dialogues*. The Latin version clearly affirmed the *filioque* ("*cum enim constet quia Paracletus Spiritus a Patre simper procedat et Filio*"), while Zacharias's translation reads "ἐκ τοῦ Πατρὸς προέρχεται καὶ ἐν τῷ Υἱῷ διαμένει" (i.e., speaking not of the Spirit's "procession from," but of his "abiding in," the Son).[119] This Greek version of the *Dialogues*, which earned Gregory his fame in the East, became the basis for the later Byzantine assertion that Gregory did not support the double procession, regardless of what the Carolingians claimed.

The most often quoted selection demonstrating Gregory's alleged support of the Latin position is from Homily 28 on John 20:21, in which Gregory (following the Augustinian logic) related the economic manifestation of the Spirit with his eternal procession:

> We can also understand his [i.e., the Son's] being sent in terms of his divine nature. The Son is said to be sent from the Father from the fact that he is begotten of the Father. The Son relates that he sends the Holy Spirit. . . .. The sending of the Spirit is that procession by which it proceeds from the Father and the Son. Accordingly, as the Spirit is said to be sent because it proceeds, so too it is not inappropriate to say that the Son is sent because he is begotten.[120]

Gregory's true views on the procession are difficult, if not impossible, to discern, especially given the variety of ways in which he described the mysterious nature of the Spirit's relationship to the Son. However, given the widespread acceptance of the *filioque* by the beginning of the seventh century, it would in fact be strange if Gregory had not in some fashion advocated the teaching, even if he did not understand the *filioque* as later Latin theology would—that is, in terms of a "double procession." This view was also most likely true of Pope Gregory's successor, the Greek-speaking Theodore, who included the *filioque* in his synodical letter to the imperial capital, occasioning the first Eastern reaction to the teaching. Ironically, it would not be a Latin, but a Greek refugee living in Africa, who explained and defended the Western doctrine in this initial encounter—Maximus the Confessor, "probably the most remarkable genius of the late patristic period."[121] What the *filioque* meant, and more important, what it did not mean, was about to be made clear.

4

Maximus the Confessor

Life and Work of Maximus

According to information provided in the *Vita Sancti Maximi* and the *Relatio Motionis*, Maximus the Confessor was born in 580 to a prominent Constantinopolitan family.[1] In the introduction to the *Mystagogia*, he claimed that he was privately educated, without "experience in the power and practice of discourse," although the *Vita* states that Maximus received the ἐγκύκλιος παίδευσις, which would have been a formal training in rhetoric and grammar lasting until his twenty-first year.[2] Maximus entered the imperial service under the Emperor Heraclius, eventually becoming head of the chancellery, where he remained until 613–14, when he entered the monastery in Chrysopolis in order to pursue a life of prayer (ἡσυχία). The *Vita* notes that because of his great piety, Maximus was soon chosen abbot of the monastery at Chrysopolis, although by 624–25 Maximus departed Chrysopolis for the monastery of St. George at Cyzicus, where he wrote both the *Liber Asceticus* and *Centuriae de Caritate*. It was also during his time in Cyzicus that Maximus, in conversation with the local bishop, began the *Ambigua*, originally conceived as an attempt to explain some controversial passages in the work of Gregory Nazianzus and Pseudo-Dionysius.

In 626 the advancing Persian army forced the evacuation of St. George's monastery, and Maximus and his companions traveled West, settling in North Africa sometime between 628 and 630.[3] It was at the monastery of Euchratas that Maximus came under the tutelage of Sophronius, the first great opponent of monothelitism (the belief that Christ had only one operative will).[4] When Sophronius became Patriarch of Jerusalem in 633, Maximus remained at Euchretas, writing copiously and earning for himself a reputation as both a great theologian and spiritual figure. It was at this time that he finished the *Ambigua*, the *Mystagogia*, and the *Quaestiones ad Thalassium*, as well his first explicitly antimonothelite work, *Epistle 29* to Patriarch Pyrrhus of Constantinople.[5]

In 645 the exiled Pyrrhus came to Carthage, where Maximus publicly debated the former patriarch, convincing Pyrrhus to travel to Rome and reconcile with Pope Theodore (642–49).[6] Maximus himself went to Rome shortly afterward, where he was asked by Theodore's successor Martin I (649–55) to participate in the antimonothelite Lateran Synod.[7] The Synod condemned Pyrrhus and his predecessor Sergius, something that angered the Emperor Constans, whose 648 *Typos* had prohibited further debate about the wills and operations of Christ. In 652 he had Pope Martin arrested and brought for trial to Constantinople; he was found guilty of treason and sent into exile at Cherson, where he died as a martyr in 655.

Maximus was also arrested and brought "naked and shoeless" to the imperial capital, where he too was accused of treason.[8] Although under great pressure from the emperor and the monothelite hierarchy, Maximus maintained his innocence and refused to retract his views. Subsequently he was exiled to Bizya in Thrace and then to Perveris, where he remained for six years before being summoned again to Constantinople for a second trial in 662. Maximus, now over 80 years old and in ill health, remained steadfast in his refusal to enter into communion with the Constantinopolitan patriarch as long as the *Typos* remained in force. Before he was exiled to Lazica on the Black Sea, his tongue and right hand were removed so that he could no longer spread, in word or writing, his alleged "heresy." He was later taken to a fort called Schemaris, where he died on August 13, 662. Although the Sixth Ecumenical Council at Constantinople (680–81) would vindicate the cause for which he gave his life, no mention was made of Maximus for fear of embarrassing the imperial family. He is celebrated as a confessor for the orthodox faith, his feast being celebrated in both the Eastern and Western Churches, on January 21 and August 13 respectively.

Maximus's Trinitarian Thought

Although the Trinity played an important role in his theology, and trinitarian "creeds" are found in several of his works, Maximus had little need to engage in metaphysical speculation on the nature of the Deity.[9] For the most part, he simply assumes the trinitarian faith of the early councils and concerns himself with the existential—that is, not how Christians define the inner workings of the trinitarian God, but how we came to participate in the divine life revealed in the person of the Word made flesh (i.e., θέωσις). Although he was an original and speculative thinker, his theology of the Trinity remains firmly grounded in the mystery of the incarnation, for it is "in becoming incarnate [that] the Word of God teaches us theology" (θεολογίαν μὲν γὰρ διδάσκει σαρκούμενος ὁ τοῦ Θεοῦ Λόγος).[10] As Felix Heinzer noted, Maximus, more than most, "is profoundly aware of the intimate and inseparable link between what the Greek fathers called theology and economy, between the mystery of the trinitarian God and the mystery of the incarnation and redemption."[11]

This thinking was certainly not new to Maximus, and it clearly manifests his reliance on the Cappadocian tradition, despite Gregory of Nazianzus's hesitations about blurring the lines between economy (οἰκονομία) and theology (θεολογία) because of the heresy of Eunomius.[12] Maximus, writing long after Gregory's Eunomian opponents had been quieted, adopts and adapts his position so that "this distinction between theology and economy is strictly upheld . . . but at the same time he relates them intimately so that a correspondence is established."[13] While, like Gregory, Maximus was hesitant to develop what later generations would call "natural theology," he allowed the eyes of faith to discern certain "adumbrations" of the Trinity within the natural order.[14] As he wrote in *Quaestiones ad Thalassium* 13, "from beings we believe in God who is, that he exists . . . from the wise contemplation of creation receiving the idea of the Holy Trinity of the Father and the Son and the Holy Spirit."[15]

Maximus even perceived these "adumbrations" in the constitution of humanity, where the Trinity was seen as the archetype of mind (νοῦς), reason (λόγος), and spirit (ψυχή), as well as in the triadic structure of the human soul.[16] Yet this perception was possible only because of the incarnation of the Word, who remained the "lynchpin" in humanity's ability to accept the paradox that is Trinity. To utilize the language of later theology, in Maximus's program there can be no *analogia entis* without the *analogia fidei*.

For Maximus this revelation of God in Christ was not simply an "economic accommodation of the godhead to the world's condition. It *is* the only God himself," revealed as Father Son and Spirit.[17] While he did not collapse the two realms (economy and theology), neither did he differentiate them in such a way that one could not learn about God's trinitarian nature (θεολογία) from his revelation in history. As he stated in the *Orationis dominicae expositio*:

> In becoming incarnate the Word of God teaches us the mystical
> knowledge of God [Θεολογίαν] because he shows us in himself
> the Father and the Holy Spirit. For the full Father and full Holy Spirit
> are essentially and completely in the full Son, even the incarnate Son,
> without being themselves incarnate. Rather, the Father gives approval
> and the Spirit cooperates in the incarnation of the Son who effected it.[18]

He repeated this formula almost verbatim in *Quaestiones ad Thalassium* 60, demonstrating that the incarnation itself was an essentially trinitarian act revealing not only the Word, but also God's mode of subsisting (τρόπος τῆς ὑπάρξεως) in three hypostases. The fact that "no one of them [the hypostases] is able to exist or to be conceived without the others" precluded any notion that one could isolate the action of any of the persons, on the level of either economy or theology.[19] They must always be co-indicated—always be in relation to one another. Even the "Our Father" for Maximus points to the essential unity of the three persons, since "the words of the prayer point out the Father, the Father's name, and the Father's kingdom to help us learn from the source himself to honor, to invoke, and to adore the one Trinity. For the name of God the Father who subsists essentially is the only-begotten Son, and the kingdom of God the Father who subsists essentially is the Holy Spirit."[20]

Christ's very being allowed humanity to point to the Trinity as the source of salvation and invited us to participate in God's own triune life. It was here that the idea of περιχώρησις (interpenetration) became central for Maximus. For just as there was in Maximus a περιχώρησις between the divine and human natures in Christ (i.e., union without confusion), we were invited to penetrate into the divine nature, becoming one with the divinity. This was accomplished when, having retrained the gnomic will (θέλημα γνωμικόν) and rid it of self-love (φιλαυτία) through prayer, self-mastery (ἐγκράτεια), and love of neighbor (ἀγάπη), we followed the example and command of Christ. For "he who receives the Logos through the commandments also receives through Him the Father who is by nature present in him, and the Spirit who likewise is by nature in Him. . . . In this way, he who receives a commandment and carries it out receives mystically the Holy Trinity."[21] Thus not only do we come to know the τρόπος τῆς ὑπάρξεως of God through Christ, but through περιχώρησις we come to share something of the trinitarian life itself.[22]

This notion raised the question of inner-trinitarian relationships in Maximus's theology. In both *Ambigua* 24 and 26 Maximus addressed the begetting of the Son and his eternal relationship to the Father in an attempt to ward off an Arian interpretation of the Son's generation. Equating willer, willed, and will within the divinity, Maximus wrote that the Father and Son, sharing the same nature, also shared a single will so that the Father's willing presupposed the existence of the Son. Maximus wrote: "In our example the begotten Son is therefore at the same time the Father that generates, and is thus eternally, without the smallest interval being introduced between him and the begetting Father, for the Son is not the Son of a will but of the begetting Father. . . . The Son is not separated from the Father by a will . . . having from the beginning a single will, simple and indivisible, therefore a single essence and nature."[23]

Maximus argued that the Father, as unoriginate cause of the Son, was greater (as Father) but that he was not greater by nature, since the nature of Father and Son was one and the same.[24] This situation did not make the Son a passive subject vis-à-vis the Father (as if he were simply begotten of another's operation, like a child from a parent). Rather, because the Son is in eternal relation to the Father ("simultaneously with him and in him"), the Son was understood as "an essentially subsistent activity" whose relationship to the Father as only-begotten determined the hypostatic identities of both.[25]

This last point becomes important in discussing the relationship of the Son and Spirit in Maximus's thought, since the Father who spirates is always the Father of the Son (with whom he is in eternal relation). In the "trinitarian order" (τάξις), the Spirit, being third, proceeds from the First Cause (i.e., the Father) in such a way that he comprehends the Father's eternal relation to the only-begotten Son. Thus while he does not derive hypostatic origination from the Son, his procession from the Father does presuppose the Son's existence. This important truth allows us to understand better *Quaestiones ad Thalassium* 63, later a pivotal text in the *filioque* debate. In an exegesis of Zechariah 4:2–3, Maximus spoke to the role of the Holy Spirit in the Church.[26] In Zechariah's vision:

> The Church of God, worthy of all praise, is a lampstand wholly of gold, pure and without stain, undefiled and without blemish, receptacle of the true light that never dims. . . . The lamp above her is the true light of the Father which lights up every man coming into this world, our Lord Jesus Christ, become light and called such. . . . And if Christ is the head of the Church according to human understanding, then he is the one who by his nature has the Spirit and has bestowed the charisms of the Spirit on the Church. . . . *For the Holy Spirit, just as he belongs to the nature of God the Father according to his essence so he also belongs to the nature of the Son according to his essence, since he proceeds inexpressibly from the Father through his begotten Son* [Τὸ γὰρ Πνεῦμα τὸ ἅγιον, . . . οὕτως καὶ τοῦ Υἱοῦ φύσει κατ᾽ οὐσίαν ἐστίν, ὡς ἐκ τοῦ Πατρὸς οὐσιωδῶς δὶ Υἱοῦ γεννηθέντος ἀφράστως ἐκπορευόμενον] and bestows on the lampstand—the church—his energies as through a lantern.[27]

In this text one notes the central mediatory role of the incarnate Logos, who not only illumes humanity but also pours forth the gifts of the Spirit upon the Church. In this sense it can be said that the Spirit, like a light, flows from the Father through the Son. This passage clearly echoes Gregory Nazianzus and Gregory of Nyssa, both of whom had utilized the image of light and flame to show the flow from the unoriginate source (the Father) through another (the Son) to shine forth in another (the Spirit).[28] Yet in context all three fathers appear to be referencing the economic manifestation of the Trinity and the way Christians come to experience, in time, the gifts of the Spirit.

However, in speaking about "the Holy Spirit . . . belong[ing] to the nature of the Son according to his essence, since he proceeds inexpressibly from the Father through his begotten Son," scholars have long wondered (and often debated) whether Maximus is describing not merely the temporal manifestation of the Spirit, but also his eternal relationship to the Son. This concept brings us back to the idea of "trinitarian order" (τάξις) and the recognition found in Maximus and the Eastern fathers that although "originated from the Father, the Spirit comprehends, in his relation to the Father, the relationship between the Father and the Son."[29] Thus while the Father remains unoriginate cause of the Spirit, he is always Father of the Son, and thus the Spirit comes forth from him in such a way that this eternal relationship to the Son is not excluded. How is this eternal relationship between Spirit and Son then expressed? For Maximus, as it was for many of the Greek fathers, it is in speaking of the Spirit's procession/progression "through the Son" (διὰ τοῦ Υἱοῦ). This can be seen not only in Maximus's *Quaestiones ad Thalassium* 63, but in *Quaestiones et dubia* 34, where he wrote: "Just as the mind [i.e., the Father] is cause of the Word, so is he also [cause] of the Spirit through the Word. And, just as one cannot say that the Word is of the voice, so too one cannot say that the Son is of the Spirit."[30]

Thus while the Father remained the sole cause of the Spirit's hypostasis (as the one who spirates him), the Spirit, intimately aware of the Father's begetting of the Son, comes forth from the begetter through the begotten as the Spirit eternally manifesting their common nature. This was the important theological truth that both Cyril and Gregory of Nyssa had both hinted at in their writings, and this was the concept that Maximus's *Letter to Marinus* tried to express with even greater clarity.

The Beginnings of the *Filioque* Debate—*The Letter to Marinus*

According to Polycarp Sherwood, Maximus composed the *Letter to Marinus* (preserved in *Opusculum* 10) in 645 or 646, sometime shortly before his journey to Rome.[31] Apparently word had reached Maximus that the monothelites in Constantinople were attacking the orthodoxy of Pope Theodore on the basis of the contents of his recent synodal letter.[32] Maximus wrote to the priest Marinus in Cyprus that:

> the men of the Queen of cities [Constantinople] have attacked the
> synodal letter of the present most holy Pope, not in all the chapters
> you have written about, but only two of them. One relates to the
> theology and makes the statement that "The Holy Spirit proceeds
> from the Son." The other deals with the divine incarnation.[33]

According to John Meyendorff, by 646 Pope Theodore was already infamous in Constantinople, having signed the excommunication of the monothelite Patriarch Pyrrhus "with a pen dipped in the Eucharistic chalice."[34] The Constantinopolitan See under his successor, Paul II (also a monothelite), would certainly have looked for every opportunity to impugn Theodore's orthodoxy in order to strengthen the case against the dyothelites in the West. If Theodore expressed heretical views on the Trinity, so the argument runs, certainly his views on the wills of Christ must be equally heterodox.

Maximus understood the logic behind this argument and knew that his own position vis-à-vis the monothelites would be weakened if the orthodoxy of "Old Rome" was put into question. For this reason he differentiated between the trinitarian faith of the Romans, which while couched in strange language, was still orthodox, and the obvious impiety of the monothelites in the imperial capital. "The latter [i.e., the Romans] were therefore accused of precisely those things of which it would be unfair to accuse them, whereas the former [the Byzantines] were accused of those things that it was quite just to accuse them [i.e., monothelitism] and for which they have offered, even now, not the least defense."[35]

For centuries there have been doubts about the authenticity of the *Letter to Marinus* and about whether Maximus is actually the first witness to a debate between East and West on the procession of the Holy Spirit. Among the chief reasons given for questioning its authenticity is the fact that the first mention of the *Letter* does not occur until 874, in Anastasius Bibliothecarius's letter to John the Deacon, which was written during the so-called Photian Schism, when the *filioque* was already a hotly debated issue.[36] Also Maximus, in another epistle to Marinus, spoke of a letter that was falsely attributed to him, which may or may not be a reference to *Opusculum* 10.[37] Vasilios Karayiannis, in his book *Maxime le Confesseur: Essence et Energies de Dieu*, argued that while elements of the letter may be authentic, the section concerning the *filioque* is certainly an interpolation from a later Latin author hoping to bridge the gap between the positions of Photius and the West. For him, "the question of the *filioque* as it is treated in this text is premature for the era of Maximus" and it was silly to believe that Maximus was in a position to settle a theological debate that had not yet begun.[38]

However none of these arguments, individually or collectively, provides sufficient grounds for rejecting the authenticity of the *Letter to Marinus* as we have received it. Both Polycarp Sherwood and Alexander Alexakis, who have done textual analyses of the *Letter*, conclude that "stylistic and other internal evidence excludes the possibility of a ninth-century fabrication."[39] While the precise terms of the *filioque* dispute would not be clarified until the ninth century during the so-called Photian Schism, there is certainly enough *prima facie* evidence to argue that even by the time of Pope Theodore the language of Western trinitarian theology would have sounded suspicious to Byzantine ears. By the seventh century many of the Latin fathers had, to one degree or another, spoken of the Spirit's procession from (*ex*) or through (*per*) the Son, and the *filioque* already included in the creedal statements of the Third and Fourth Councils of Toledo. Thus although we do not possess Pope Theodore's synodal letter, it is certainly possible (indeed, probable) that the *filioque* would have appeared in some form.[40] Given the ninth-century Byzantine reaction to the interpolation, and to the *filioque* in general, there is little doubt that had they become aware of these developments two centuries earlier (especially in the synodical of a reigning pope), they would have raised some serious doubts about his orthodoxy.

However, the best argument for the authenticity of the *Letter to Marinus* is the argument from theological consistency, for although textual questions continue to exist (e.g., its fragmentary nature), the case for Maximus's authorship is made much stronger by the fact that the trinitarian principles put forward are undoubtedly his.[41] Thus we are able to see in the *Letter to Marinus* not only the "opening salvo" of the *filioque* debate, but a clear explication of Maximus's (and indeed, Rome's) theology of the procession as it existed in the seventh century.

Maximus began the *Letter* by addressing the accusations made against Pope Theodore's confession that "The Holy Spirit proceeds from the Son" (ἐκπορεύεσθαι κἀκ τοῦ Υἱοῦ τὸ Πνεῦμα τὸ ἅγιον), starting with the charge that the teaching was novel: "In the first place they [the Romans] produced the unanimous evidence of the Roman Fathers, and also of Cyril of Alexandria, from the study he made of the gospel of St. John."[42]

The unresolved issue raised by this statement is the exact nature of the patristic testimony that Maximus is referring to, especially as it pertains to the Latin fathers. It is difficult to determine how much of the Latin theological tradition Maximus had been exposed to during his years in Carthage.[43] Certainly, as we have seen, by the mid-seventh century there were more than a few Latin writers who had utilized some variant of the *procedere ex Filio* or *per Filium* formula. However, if Alexander Alexakis is correct and Maximus is referencing a preexisting pro-*filioque* florilegium (edited around 645/6), then his knowledge of the Western teaching on the procession might have been limited to just a few select quotations.[44]

While we cannot establish how well acquainted Maximus was with Augustine and the trinitarian theology of the Latin West, in the *Letter to Marinus* he referred also to the teaching of the Greek fathers (with whom he was more familiar), and specifically to Cyril of Alexandria's *Commentary on the Gospel of St. John*. Many of these fathers (especially Gregory of Nyssa and Cyril), had spoken of the Son's possessing some mediatory role in the Spirit's eternal progression (προϊέναι), even if they had been clear that this did not involve the Spirit's unique ἐκπορεύεσθαι (procession) from the Father, nor in any way compromised the Father's role as μία αἰτία within the godhead.[45] It was with this teaching in mind that Maximus detailed the Roman position as he understood it.

> From this [the writings of the fathers] they showed that they themselves do not make the Son the cause of the Spirit for they know that the Father is the one cause of the Son and the Spirit, the one by

begetting and the other by procession, but they show the progression through him and thus the unity of the essence.[46]

Maximus affirmed that the Latin teaching in no way violated the monarchy of the Father, who remained the sole cause (μία αἰτία) of both the Son and the Spirit. This idea had been a point of emphasis in Eastern trinitarian theology since the time of Gregory Nazianzus, who had posited the Father's unique role as cause as the source of unity and the means of distinguishing the individual hypostases within the Trinity (the Father alone being cause, the Spirit and Son being caused, one by begetting and the other by procession).[47]

As for Maximus himself, it is clear from his other writings that he was fully in agreement with the Cappadocian teaching on the matter, upholding the Father as both the source of divinity and principle of unity. He wrote: "There is one God, because the Father is the begetter of the unique Son and the fount of the Holy Spirit: one without confusion and three without division. The Father is the unoriginate intellect, the unique essential Begetter of the unique Logos, also unoriginate, and the fount of the unique everlasting life, the Holy Spirit."[48] According to Emmanuel Ponsoye, the monarchical principle was one "that for Maximus was the criterion of orthodoxy concerning the procession of the Holy Spirit. If the pope considered the Son as a cause of the procession of the Holy Spirit (or believed that the Son was sort of a second cause, or even with the Father a unique cause), Maximus would not have considered such an opinion acceptable."[49]

One could maintain that Maximus was deliberately misrepresenting the Romans' position on this matter (ignoring their heresy in order to fight another), but that possibility seems unlikely given Maximus's commitment to, and ultimate sacrifice for, doctrinal orthodoxy. It seems more logical to maintain that Maximus genuinely believed that the Latins held the Father to be the unique cause of the Son and Spirit because in the seventh century that *is* what the Latins themselves believed. In other words, if Western theology did later attribute causality to the Son, then this must be regarded as a post-patristic phenomenon and not a part of the Latin tradition as it existed in Maximus's time.

Yet protecting the monarchical principle did not mean that Maximus contemplated any person of the Trinity's being treated in isolation or envisioned without the others. One had to protect the uniqueness of the Father, yet one also had to account for both the essential unity and eternal relationship shared between the Son and the Spirit. Maximus, like Cyril and Gregory of Nyssa before him, chose to communicate this reality utilizing a terminological distinction between ἐκπορεύεσθαι and προϊέναι, speaking not only of the Spirit's procession from the Father, but also of his eternal progression through Son with whom the Father is in eternal relationship. Jean-Claude Larchet, in his book *Maxime le Confesseur, médiateur entre l'Orient et l'Occident*, summarized this distinction.

For the most part the Greek fathers use the verb ἐκπορεύεσθαι when they want to affirm that the Spirit receives his personal existence from the Father (proceeding from him in the strict sense) and they use the verb προϊέναι in those cases when they want to affirm that the Holy Spirit comes from the Father through the Son (i.e., is manifested through him, either eternally or temporally in the world where he is sent or given).[50]

Juan Miguel Garrigues discusses the importance of this distinction in chapter 2 of his book *L'Esprit qui dit "Pere": Le problème du Filioque.*[51] The verb ἐκπορεύεσθαι, Garrigues argued, was used both in Scripture (John 15:26) and in the Greek version of the creed to speak about the coming forth of the Spirit (ὃ παρὰ τοῦ πατρὸς ἐκπορεύεται), although in other contexts it was used simply to signify a "coming out" or even a "going away" whereby the subject of the verb appears to leave its point of origin as a distinct entity. In the Septuagent version of the Old Testament, for example, it was applied to a word coming forth from the mouth (Prov, 3:16) and water coming forth from the temple (Ezek. 47:1, 8, 12).[52] Although in Greek patristic thought it was usually reserved to the procession of the Holy Spirit, Pseudo-Athanasius and John of Damascus also applied it to the creation of Eve, who came forth out of Adam's rib.[53]

On the other hand, προϊέναι, as distinct from ἐκπορεύεσθαι, had the force of "progression" or "advance" whereby the subject flowed from its source but retained an element of continuity (or, in the case of the Trinity, consubstantiality).[54] For example, in Thucydides the word was often used to describe the advance of armies, and in Herodotus time itself was described as moving forward (προϊόντος τοῦ χρόνου).[55] Unlike the term ἐκπορεύεσθαι, which in patristic literature referred only to the hypostatic origin of the Holy Spirit, προϊέναι was used more generally and applied to both the Spirit and the Son, in terms not only of their economic manifestation, but also of the eternal communication of the divine nature, which flowed from the Father through the begotten Son to the Spirit.

This theory is supported by much of the patristic witness. Gregory of Nazianzus had differentiated between the Spirit's unique relationship to the Father (by ἐκπόρευσις) and that enjoyed by both the Spirit and the Son (both having "progressed from" the Father).[56] Although Cyril would on occasion apply ἐκπορεύεσθαι to the Son's generation from the Father, he never used it to describe the relationship of the Spirit to the Son.[57] As a general rule in Greek trinitarian thought, ἐκπόρευσις can only characterize one's relationship to the source of the Trinity, the Father.

Garrigues's theory cannot be applied universally, since there was still a lack of linguistic rigidity in the Greek fathers that allowed them at times to use ἐκπορεύεσθαι and προϊέναι synonymously. For example, several fathers (including Gregory Nazianzus and Cyril) used προϊέναι to designate the Spirit's hypostatic origination.[58] Maximus's own *Quaestiones ad Thalassium* 63 spoke of the Spirit's coming forth (ἐκπορευόμενον) from the Father through the Son. While these examples prevent an absolute differentiation between the two terms, this fact does not necessarily invalidate Garrigues's theory. It has long been noted that the patristic doctrine of the procession (where it existed at all) remained ambiguous, in terms of both content and form. For centuries there existed a fluidity of language that defied rigid categorization, even if one recognizes that ἐκπόρευσις increasingly came to have a very specific meaning (referring to the Spirit's hypostatic origin from the Father).[59] In the *Letter to Marinus* Maximus simply offered a clarification, differentiating the Spirit's unique hypostatic coming-to-be (ἐκπόρευσις) from his προϊέναι from the Father through the Son, applied here to their relationship both in the economy and in eternity (in the trinitarian τάξις).

The fact that the Latin language could not adequately reproduce this subtlety is probably what Maximus refers to when he wrote:

> At your request, I asked the Romans to translate what is unique to
> them in order to avoid such obscurities. But since the practice of
> writing and sending letters has already been observed, I do not know
> if they will comply. Especially, they might not be able to express their
> thought with the same exactness in another language as they might
> in their mother tongue, just as we could not do.[60]

Maximus recognized that Theodore's use of "ἐκπορεύεσθαι κἀκ τοῦ Υἱοῦ τὸ Πνεῦμα τὸ ἅγιον" (which was apparently how the expression *Spiritum sanctum etiam ex Filio procedere* was translated), though not unorthodox, was a poor rendering of the Latins' intent and was easily capable of misinterpretation. This occurred in large part because the West did not possess an exact equivalent to ἐκπορεύεσθαι, and *procedere* did not communicate the idea of the Spirit's "unique hypostatic coming-to-be" from the Father, being instead a better translation of προϊέναι.

Juan Miguel Garrigues traced the roots of the problem back to Tertullian's writings against Praxeas, where his use of *procedere* served to translate, not the idea of ἐκπορεύεσθαι, but the Greek notion of προβεβλήσθαι as used by Irenaeus and the other Greek fathers.[61] As was noted earlier, Jerome, in his rendition of the Gospel of John, then translated προέρχεσθαι and ἐκπορεύεσθαι with the verb *procedere*, which now came to encompass both the temporal manifestation of the Spirit and his hypostatic origination.[62] The uniqueness of ἐκπορεύεσθαι was lost in Latin translation. However, Garrigues argued that there were those in the West, such as Hilary of Poitiers, who continued to acknowledge the uniqueness of ἐκπορεύεσθαι, reserving *procedere* for the activity of the Father while using *mittere* and *accipere* to speak about the Spirit's eternal relationship to the Son.[63] According to Garrigues, even Augustine followed Hilary in recognizing the unique ἐκπόρευσις of the Spirit from the

Father, choosing to express this concept in the Latin adverbially, writing that the Spirit proceeds from the Son but principally proceeds (*procedit principaliter*) from the Father."[64] By protecting the distinctiveness of *procedere* with the adverb *principaliter*, Augustine was deliberately attempting to ward off any idea of a "double procession" or the idea (embraced by later Latin theology) that the Spirit derived his ἐκπόρευσις from the Son.

If this was how Maximus understood the Western fathers, then he can certainly make the good-faith affirmation that the Romans did not confess the Spirit's ἐκπόρευσις (i.e., his hypostatic existence) from the Son. If the synodal letter received by the Constantinopolitans contained the phrase ἐκπορεύεσθαι κἀκ τοῦ Υἱοῦ τὸ Πνεῦμα τὸ ἅγιον, then this must not be understood as a denial of the Father's unique role within the godhead, but as a poor translation of their (shared) belief in the Spirit's eternal progression (προϊέναι) from the Father through the consubstantial Son (διὰ τοῦ Υἱοῦ), an idea with a long history in Byzantine thought. According to Maximus, Latins and Greeks together affirmed both the monarchy of the Father (as sole cause of the Son and the Spirit) and the Spirit's comprehension of the Father's unique relationship to the Son, as he flows from the begetter through the begotten, manifesting the common nature of both. If the Constantinopolitans perceived differences between their faith and that of Latins, these must be regarded not as substantive but as linguistic.

The Significance of the *Letter to Marinus* and Maximus's Trinitarian Thought

Although his theology of the Trinity, and especially his thoughts on the procession of the Holy Spirit, are never set forth systematically, from our study of Maximus's trinitarian writings one can still discern certain theological principles that undergird his thinking on the subject:

1. There is an intimate relationship between the economy (οἰκονομία) and theology (θεολογία), which while recognizing a distinction, acknowledges that God's very mode of subsistence as Trinity is revealed to us in Christ.
2. The mystery of the incarnate Word not only reveals God's mode of subsistence as Trinity (θεολογίαν μὲν γὰρ διδάσκει σαρκούμενος ὁ τοῦ Θεοῦ Λόγος) but also invites us into the mystery of the trinitarian communion (περιχώρησις).
3. The Father is the source of life and unity within the godhead and greater as the one cause (μία αἰτία) of the Son's generation and the Spirit's procession, but not greater by nature.
4. Because the Father is always Father of the Son, this eternal relationship determines the hypostatic identities of both.

5. The Holy Spirit, who comes forth (ἐκπορεύεσθαι) from the Father, comprehends this eternal relationship, and this reality is expressed by one's speaking of the Spirit's flowing forth (προϊέναι) from the Father through the Son.
6. This progression through the Son not only applies to the level of economy, but expresses something of the theology and the place of the Spirit in the τάξις.

These important principles, present throughout his corpus and clarified in the *Letter to Marinus*, must guide any attempt to understand Maximus's theology of the procession and the place (if any) of the *filioque*. In many ways it can be said that they challenge both the traditional Eastern and Western understandings of the legitimacy of the doctrine. On one hand the *Letter to Marinus* is not (as later Latin theology contended) a wholehearted endorsement of "filioquism," despite Maximus's defense of the *filioque*'s orthodoxy. Yet neither can one disassociate economy (οἰκονομία) and theology (θεολογία) in Maximus's thinking such that one cannot speak about God's mode of subsisting based on his revelation as Trinity in history. Although its purpose was irenic, even today the *Letter to Marinus* challenges both East and West by presenting those principles (e.g., the Father's role as μία αἰτία within the godhead, the eternal relationship between Son and Spirit) that Maximus believed to be "non-negotiables" for orthodox theology.

Perhaps his greatest contribution to the discussion was in distinguishing between the Spirit's ἐκπορεύεσθαι from the Father and his προϊέναι through the Son, explicating a theological principle that he believed to have been part of the *consensus patrum*, and which he himself held to be true. There is an eternal relationship between the Son and the Spirit, the latter flowing from the Father through the consubstantial Son, with whom he enjoys an eternal relationship as Father. Maximus's understanding of the godhead as revealed by the incarnate Word, whereby the three hypostases of the Trinity were "co-indicated" in every action of each person, made it impossible to speak of any of them in isolation. The Father was unique among the persons of Trinity as sole cause, but he was always the Father of the Son. Thus while the procession of the Holy Spirit is a distinguishing characteristic of the Father's hypostasis, one cannot isolate the Father from the Son with whom he shares a common nature and will. Maximus, like Gregory of Nyssa and Cyril, chose to express this reality by speaking of the eternal flowing forth (προϊέναι) of the Spirit from the Father through the only-begotten Son. This relationship applied not only to the gifts of the Spirit poured out upon the Church in the economy of salvation, but to the eternal manifestation of the Spirit as both the Spirit of God and Spirit of Christ.

While willing to accept the *filioque* as an orthodox expression of this reality, one must be careful not to read into Maximus's position an endorsement of the later Latin teaching, especially as it was explicated by the Carolingians and

Scholastics. Maximus did not allow for an understanding of the *filioque* that attributed a transference of the Father's hypostatic properties to the Son, making him, even in a secondary way, responsible for the Spirit's ἐκπόρευσις. While there was περιχώρησις among the persons of the Trinity, there could never be confusion or exchange of their hypostatic properties. The Father remained the sole cause (μία αἰτία) of the Son and the Spirit, and to the extent that later Latin theology attributed causality to the Son (a unique property of the Father's hypostasis), it deviated from the tradition of the Church as Maximus understood it. The *filioque* was an orthodox (albeit clumsy) way of articulating an important theological truth—the προϊέναι of the Spirit through the Son in the trinitarian order [τάξις]. However, the teaching that the ἐκπόρευσις (hypostatic origin) of the Spirit comes from both from the Father and the Son as from a single principle finds no support in the trinitarian program of Maximus, whether it be in the *Quaestiones ad Thalassium* 63 or in the *Letter to Marinus*.

5

The *Filioque* from the Seventh to the Eleventh Century

Following the death of Maximus the Confessor in 662 there is a centuries-long silence about the *filioque* from Eastern sources, although the West continued to embrace and teach the doctrine as an integral part of the orthodox faith. However, with the beginning of the iconoclastic controversy in the eighth century, tension between Byzantium and the West increased (exacerbated by the political and cultural divisions created by Charlemagne's imperial coronation), and the *filioque* was quickly catapulted from the obscure theological backwaters to become a *casus belli*. By the beginning of the second millennium, Christian East and West were on the verge of a formal schism, each side claiming that the other's acceptance or rejection of the *filioque* was the chief theological reason for the break. While both Latins and Greeks claimed to base their respective positions on the Scriptures and the tradition of the ancient Church, what became painfully obvious rather quickly was that by the ninth century their differing readings of those sources had led them to embrace two separate, if not contradictory, understandings of the Spirit's procession. Maximus's irenic efforts went largely forgotten (although they briefly reappear in the works of Anastasius Bibliothecarius and John Scotus Erigena) and instead the terms of the debate were framed as a simple choice— either the Spirit proceeded from the Father alone (as Photius and the East maintained) or he proceeded from the Father and the Son (according to the Carolingian teaching). It was this dynamic, established in the ninth century, that characterized the *filioque* debates for the next several centuries.

The Late Seventh Century

With the resolution of the monothelite controversy at the Sixth Ecumenical Council in 680, tensions between East and West temporarily subsided, a phenomenon partially explained by the emperor's growing need for Western support against the invading Muslim armies. Pope Agatho (678–81), for his part, avoided using the *filioque* in his syndoal letter to the Council, perhaps cognizant that Theodore's earlier inclusion of the term had precipitated such consternation in the imperial capital. In the letter, written on behalf of 125 Western bishops who had gathered in Rome, there is simply the stated belief in "the Holy Spirit who proceeds from the Father [*ex Patre procedentem*]."[1] Although the canons of the Council in Trullo (held from 691–92) briefly reignited tension between East and West (over issues such as priestly celibacy and the status of Constantinople vis-à-vis Rome), the *filioque* was not among the disputed points and no sign exists that it remained a source of disagreement.[2]

While Pope Agatho shunned the interpolation in his correspondence with the East, local gatherings in the West continued to teach the *filioque* without compunction, including the sixth (638), eighth (655), eleventh (675), twelfth (681), thirteenth (683), fourteenth (688), fifteenth (688), sixteenth (693), and seventeenth (694) Councils of Toledo, as well as the Synod of Merida in 666 and the Fourth Synod of Braga in 675.[3] Among the seventh-century councils that taught the double procession, the Council of Hatfield (680) is perhaps the most interesting, especially as its president was a Greek, Theodore of Tarsus (602–90).

According to Bede, when Pope Vitalian (657–72) appointed Theodore to Canterbury, he sent the monk Hadrian with him "to prevent Theodore from introducing into the Church over which he presided any Greek customs."[4] Despite these misgivings, Theodore was a sound choice whose antimonothelite credentials were impeccable (he had probably been at the Lateran Synod with Maximus the Confessor in 649).[5] Although Bede claimed that Theodore convoked the Council of Hatfield "to preserve the churches from the heresy of Eutyches," there is some evidence that he also used the gathering to respond to Bishop Wilfrid of York, who had been in Rome complaining about Theodore's governance of the English Church.[6] The Council's statement of faith, which apparently assured Pope Agatho of Theodore's orthodoxy, affirmed the faith of Nicea, Constantinople, Ephesus, Chalcedon, Constantinople II, and the Lateran Synod of 649, and included belief in "the Holy Spirit, ineffably proceeding from the Father and the Son, as proclaimed by all whom we have mentioned above, holy apostles, and prophets, and doctors."[7]

The two questions raised by this confession of faith were how Theodore would have interpreted this teaching, and how long the *filioque* had been part of the creed in England. While it is possible that Augustine of Canterbury (d. 609) might have taught the *filioque* during his mission to England (given his connection with Pope Gregory I), there is also a chance that it was introduced by Theodore's companion Hadrian, an African by birth whose study of Augustine and Fulgentius would likely have included their teaching on the procession. As for Theodore himself, it is possible that he understood the *filioque* in accord with the principles Maximus had enunciated years earlier in the *Letter to Marinus*, especially if (as is likely) the two knew each other in Rome. What is clear is that Pope Agatho, although busy preparing his own statement of faith for the Constantinopolitans (without the *filioque*), happily received the proceedings of Hatfield, including its confession in the procession of the Holy Spirit from both the Father and the Son.

The Franks and the Council of Gentilly

Among the kingdoms that grew up in Europe following the dissolution of the Western Empire in 475, the Franks occupy a unique place. According to Gregory of Tours, in 496 Clovis (d. 511) and some 3,000 soldiers accepted baptism at Reims, creating a link between the Frankish kingdom and the Catholic faith that would last for the next several centuries.[8] As the Merovingian dynasty weakened in the eighth century, Charles Martel (d. 741) rose from the ranks to fill the growing power vacuum, expanding the Frankish kingdom beyond its original borders.[9] It was Martel ("the Hammer") who defeated the Muslim armies at Tours/Poitiers in 732, stopping the advance of Islam in Western Europe, and it was Martel's son Pippin (d. 768) who was anointed King of the Franks and *patricius Romanorum* by Pope Steven II (752–57).[10] Steven's reasons for recognizing Pippin's kingship were largely practical—the Lombards were moving closer to Rome, and the emperor, Constantine V (d. 775), had neither the troops nor the inclination to assist. Pippin quite happily offered his services against King Aistulff and the Lombards, who were quickly forced by Pippin to cede Ravenna and other territories to the pope (establishing the so-called "Donation of Pippin"). The alliance between the Franks and the papacy was cemented, although this bond would soon be tested by the imperial campaign to end the use of images in the Church (iconoclasm).

Iconoclasm, which had shaken the East since the reign of Emperor Leo III (d. 741), had long been opposed in the West despite the pressure for Pippin to adapt himself to the prevailing Eastern view.[11] In 754 Emperor Constantine V convoked an iconoclast council at Hiereia, calling it ecumenical despite Rome's noninvolvement. Pope Paul I (757–67) urged Pippin to hold firm, although in 767 Pippin did permit a delegation from Constantinople to discuss the veneration of icons at Gentilly (near Paris). Although this Synod of Gentilly initially gathered to settle the question of iconoclasm, it was here that the *filioque* was again raised, although there is no way to know which side (Latin or Greek) broached the issue. The *Acta* of the Synod are lost, and the scant references to the proceedings tell us only that the procession of the Spirit was among the issues discussed (*et quaestio ventilata inter Graecos et Romanos de Trinitate, et utrum Spiritus sanctus sicut procedit a Patre, ita procedat a Filio*).[12]

Having long since accepted the theology behind the *filioque*, the Franks might very well have brought up the issue, especially as it seems unlikely that the iconoclast Byzantines would have introduced another contentious topic during a meeting designed to sway Pippin to their cause. While we do not know the context, what is known is that for the second time in history the *filioque* was raised as a side issue in a much larger debate, and that at Gentilly "the first spark of a fire was kindled" that neither East nor West would be able to extinguish.[13]

John of Damascus (d. 749)

In the East, the battle against iconoclasm was led by John of Damascus, author of the *Three Treatises on the Divine Images*.[14] Among the fathers that subsequent generations of Eastern polemicists and theologians used to support their understanding of the procession, few would play as central a role as John of Damascus, whose *De fide orthodoxa* proved a rich source for prooftexts explicitly denying that the Son was "cause" of the Spirit's being. Utilizing the concept of περιχώρησις that Maximus had applied to the two natures of Christ, John spoke of the "unity without confusion" existing among the three hypostases of the Trinity, each one sharing the same essence but each one retaining the distinctive properties of his respective person. Echoing Gregory of Nazianzus, John claimed that "the Father and the Son and the Holy Ghost are one in all things save in the being unbegotten [ἀγέννητος], the being begotten [γεννητός], and the procession [ἐκπορευόμενον]."[15] John, like Gregory, was unable to clarify the exact nature of this difference between generation and procession, saying only that procession "is another manner of existence and is just as incomprehensible and unknowable as is the begetting of the Son."[16] Adhering to the Eastern tradition, John affirmed (as Maximus had a century earlier) that "the Father alone is cause [αἴτιος]" of both the Son and the Spirit, and thus "we do not say that the Son is a cause or a father, but we do say that He is from the Father, and is the Son of the Father."[17] While Christians deny the claim "that the Spirit is from the Son," nevertheless they "call Him the Spirit of the Son" since "he was manifested and communicated to us through the Son . . . like the brightness [of the sun] is communicated to us through the rays."[18]

While this last quotation is clearly a reference to the Spirit's action in the economy, John of Damascus also followed the Confessor in establishing an

eternal relationship between the Son and Spirit using language similar to Maximus's *Quaestiones ad Thalassium* 63. John wrote that the Spirit should not be
thought "as being from him [the Son] but as proceeding through him from the
Father [δι αὐτοῦ ἐκ τοῦ Πατρὸς ἐκπορευόμενον]—for the Father alone is
Cause."[19] Thus we witness here the same dynamic that was operative in the
thought of Maximus: while one cannot speak of the Son as a cause of the Spirit's hypostatic being (the Father being the μία αἰτία), there is an eternal relationship between the Father and the Son (since "the Father could not be so
called without a Son,") that demands that one uphold the Son as a condition of
the Spirit's coming forth from the Father both in time and on the level of the
theology.[20]

The Council of Nicea (787) and the *Opus Caroli Regis*

King Pippin died in 768 and was succeeded by his son Charles "the Great,"
better known to history as Charlemagne (742–814).[21] Like his father, Charlemagne continued to oppose the iconoclast tendencies of the Constantinopolitan emperors, whom he increasingly came to see as both heretical and corrupt.[22]
Yet at the same time neither was Charlemagne sympathetic to the arguments
of the iconodules (i.e., defenders of images), believing them to advocate a form
of idol worship specifically prohibited by the first commandment.[23] It was for
this reason (among others) that Charlemagne rejected the decisions of the Seventh Ecumenical Council, held at Nicea and presided over by Patriarch Tarasius
(784–806), despite the fact that Pope Hadrian (772–95) had supported the
council's conclusions.[24] Hadrian issued a response to Charlemagne's objections (the *Hadrianum*), occasioning a formal refutation of the council under-
taken at the king's request by Theodulf of Orleans (750–821). This work (the
Capitulare adversus synodum), written sometime between 791 and 793, was later
expanded and became known as the *Liber Carolini*, although more recently the
preferred title is the *Opus Caroli Regis contra synodum*.[25]

Among the so-called heresies of the Council specifically repudiated in the
Opus Caroli Regis was Patriarch Tarasius's confession that "the Holy Spirit is
not from the Father and the Son according to the most true and holy rule of
faith but proceeds from the Father through the Son" (*Spiritum sanctum non ex
Patre et Filio secundum verissimam sanctae fidei regulam, sed 'ex Patre per Filium
procedentem*).[26] In his defense of the council, Pope Hadrian claimed that "Tarsius had not pronounced this dogma by himself but has confessed it by the
doctrine of the holy fathers," warning his readers (particularly Charlemagne)
that rejection of this teaching was tantamount to rejection of the ecumenical
councils.[27]

Unlike later Carolingian works defending the Western teaching, the *Opus
Caroli Regis* was not a patristic *florilegia* (although over thirty biblical texts are

brought forward as witnesses to the doctrine), but rather an attack upon the idea that procession *ex Patre per Filium* (διὰ τοῦ Υἱοῦ) was equivalent to procession *ex Patre et Filio* (ἐκ Πατρὸς καὶ Υἱοῦ)—ironically the same argument later employed by Greek anti-unionists in the period following the Council of Lyons.[28] According to Theodulf, it was improper to say that the Spirit proceeded from the Father *per Filium*, since this formula was both ambiguous (and "definitions of faith should be clear and understandable without any ambiguity or intricacy")[29] and led one to account the Spirit as a creature (since John 1:3 had also spoken of the creation of all things δι αὐτοῦ).

> And for that reason it can be asked whether it can correctly be said
> that the Holy Spirit proceeds from the Father "through the Son"
> [*Spiritus sanctus a Patre 'per Filium' procedure*] while at the same time
> this preposition "through" is placed recklessly in the profession of
> the great mysteries by those, serving up their fetid cup of Arian
> errors, who blaspheme and claim the Holy Spirit is a creature created
> through the Son just like everything else and who in their baptisms
> do not baptize according to the gospel command, "In the name of the
> Father and the Son and the Holy Spirit, but, "In the name of the
> Father through the Son in the Holy Spirit."[30]

Theodulf then argued that the *per Filium* formula was forbidden because it was not included in either the creeds of Nicea or Chalcedon, and that the alteration of the creed (which he apparently assumes to have contained the *filioque*) is wrong. "The whole Church universally confesses and believes" that the Spirit proceeds from the Father and the Son, a fact testified to by both the Scriptures and the writings of the fathers (i.e., Augustine and Isidore).[31] While acknowledging the nature of the procession from the Son was "inscrutable and incomprehensible to our frail human understanding," Theodulf maintained that the ancient faith (i.e., the confession of the Spirit's procession *ex Patre filioque*) must be maintained.[32]

While the chief purpose of the *Opus Caroli Regis* was to address the theological differences between East and West, it can also be read as a "declaration of independence"—that is, that the Frankish kingdom no longer considered itself dependant upon Constantinople, either politically or religiously.[33] Charlemagne was insulted that Nicea had claimed ecumenicity for itself despite the fact that no Frankish bishops had attended, and its "heretical" conclusions only proved that the Byzantines, now ruled by a woman and a filicide, no longer had legitimate claim to govern a Christian Empire.[34]

As Charlemagne and his court theologians increasingly came to define the orthodox faith in opposition to the prevailing Byzantine view, they were faced with a new heresy gaining popularity in Spain—Adoptionism. Adoptionism, usually associated with such figures as Elipandus of Toledo (d. 802) and Felix of Urgel (d. 818), is the "term used by historians of doctrine . . . to designate the idea that Jesus was a human being uniquely chosen to exercise the function or role of divine sovereignty and Sonship."[35] To counter the heresy's Arian presuppositions, anti-Adoptionist writers stressed the consubstantiality of the Father and the Son, emphasizing the scriptural truth that the Son shared all that the Father had, which must (so it was argued) include a role in the procession of the Spirit. It was for this reason that the *filioque* increasingly became an important criterion for christological orthodoxy in the West, and the East's rejection of the doctrine was seen as another manifestation of their heterodox ways.

The Councils of Frankfurt (794) and Friuli (797)

It was against the Adoptionists that the Council (or Synod) of Frankfurt met in 794 and that the *Opus Caroli Regis* was received as part of Church's faith. Although the *acta* are no longer extant, we know that the *Libellus* against Elipandus, written by Paulinus of Aquileia (d. 802), was read out (asserting belief in the Holy Spirit, *a Patre filioque procedit*), as was Charlemagne's letter to the Spanish bishops (confessing the Spirit, *procedentem ex Patre et Filio*).[36] Pope Hadrian was represented at the Council by his legates, and although tension between Charlemagne and the pope still lingered over the Council of Nicea, they are both alleged to have subscribed to the acts. Hadrian's own letter to the bishops of Spain professed the *filioque* (*Spiritum Sanctum . . . ex Patre filioque essentialiter procedat*), although he remained unhappy with the continued Carolingians' attack on Tarasius.[37] When Hadrian died in 795, succeeded by Pope Leo III (795–816), relations between Rome and Aachen (the Frankish capital) finally improved, although the interpolation continued to remain an area of contention.

In 797 the Council of Friuli met under Paulinus of Aquileia and issued an extended defense of the *filioque*'s addition to the creed, one that would be used by the Latins for the next several centuries.[38] Paulinus was well aware of the canons of Ephesus and the prohibitions against teaching another faith or composing another creed, safeguards (he maintained) against the errors of Nestorius and Eutyches.[39] Yet for Paulinus there was an important distinction between that which was added to the creed legitimately and that which was added or subtracted "craftily . . . contrary to the sacred intentions of the fathers" (*sed addere vel minuare est subdole contra sacrosanctum eorum sensum*).[40] For example, Paulinus argued that the Council of Constantinople had legitimately added to the Nicene Creed and that such actions were sometimes necessary in order to clarify the faith and remove "the thorns of deceptions [i.e., heresies] when they arise."[41] Thus additions were permissible as long as they could be shown to be in accordance with the intentions of the fathers and consistent with the faith of the ancient Church.

What occasioned the interpolation? According to Paulinus, the *filioque* was added to combat those "manifest heretics who whisper [that] the Holy Spirit exists from the Father alone and proceeds from the Father *alone*" (*qui sussurant Sanctum Spiritum solus esse Patris et a solo procedere Patre*). [42] For that reason "these holy Fathers were not culpable as though they had added something or subtracted [something] from the faith of the 318 Fathers because they did not think contrary to the intentions of the fathers, but strove to supplement their pure understanding with sound usage."[43]

Paulinus witnesses here that the teaching so often associated with Photius of Constantinople (i.e., that "the Holy Spirit proceeds from the Father *alone*") appears to have been in circulation for some time already. It was against this position, according to Paulinus, that the *filioque* was added, and it was to maintain the pure faith against such heresies that the interpolated creed must be learned by Christians of every age, sex, and condition of life.[44] Alcuin of York (d. 804) agreed, and it was probably for this reason that he introduced the interpolated creed into the liturgy at Aachen, which was coming to be seen as "a second Rome," with Charlemagne in the role as "the new Aeneas."

The Coronation of Charlemagne (800)

The ecclesiastical ramifications of the imperial coronation of Charlemagne at the hands of Pope Leo III cannot be overstated, for it destroyed the old order, replacing "the axis between Old Rome and New Rome with the one between the papacy and Northern Europe."[45] As early as the thirteenth century Humbert of Romans, in preparing for the Reunion Council of Lyons (1274), listed the division of the empire as the chief underlying cause of division between the Eastern and Western Churches.[46] Charlemagne, already *patristicus Romanorum* and *rex Francorum et Langobardorum*, had become emperor of the West in all but name by 800 A.D.—Alcuin writing about the *imperium christianum* long before Charlemagne's famous trip to Rome.[47] In Constantinople the Empress Irene ruled in violation of Salic law (operative in the West since the time of Clovis), thus negating her claims to legitimacy and leaving the imperial throne vacant.[48]

Charlemagne's opportunity came in 799 when the Roman aristocracy deposed and imprisoned Pope Leo. Leo escaped and fled to Charlemagne, who knew that while he could not sit in judgment of the pope (Alcuin had reminded him of that fact), neither could he allow the situation to continue. Charlemagne went to Rome, where he was received with all the pomp due an emperor.[49] Accepting Leo's oath of innocence on December 23, 800 (and thus confirming him in his office), Charlemagne attended Christmas mass two days later, where Leo formally crowned him "Roman Emperor and Augustus," anointing Charlemagne with oil and making his formal obeisance to him (as was the Byzantine custom). Einhard would later claim that Charlemagne was "far from wanting this [and] made it clear that he would not have entered the cathedral that day at all . . . if he had known in advance what the pope was planning to do."[50] However, once the deed was done, Charlemagne settled into his new role as emperor, hoping to consolidate his power by marriage to the very woman whose title he had just usurped—Irene.

The Byzantine reaction to Constantine's coronation was, according to contemporary sources, rather muted.[51] While such an act would have been seen by the Greeks as the height of presumption, it does not appear that they saw it as a direct challenge to their own imperial claims. Charlemagne was eventually recognized as Βασιλεύς of his own people but never referred to as Emperor of the Romans, a title reserved for the emperor in Constantinople.[52] Irene herself was said to be considering marriage to Charlemagne when a palace coup removed her and exiled her to the island of Lesbos, where she died in 803.[53] Deprived of this opportunity of uniting East and West under his rule, Charlemagne continued to enhance the prestige of his own imperium, presiding over a great "renaissance" of learning in Western Europe, in large part led by his tutor and friend Alcuin of York.

Alcuin of York (d. 804)

Alcuin of York had come to Aachen in 782 to serve as a tutor in Charlemagne's court, becoming in a very short time one of the king's closest advisors and friends.[54] Aside from his contributions to education and liturgical reform, Alcuin played a key role in the debate about the procession, introducing the interpolated creed at the imperial chapel in Aachen and composing the *De Fide sanctae et individuae Trinitatis* in defense of the *filioque* in 802. The book was intended to be a means of maintaining the "Catholic peace" (*catholica pax*) throughout the newly established empire, summarizing the faith and explaining those points (like the *filioque*) that had come into dispute.[55] Although Alcuin does not always cite his sources, John Cavadini claims that the *De Fide sanctae et individuae Trinitatis* is "highly derivative, in which whole chapters are liable to consist of a single *verbatim* citation from an earlier source" (the two most common being Augustine and Fulgentius of Ruspe).[56]

Alcuin's trinitarian theology accepted as its basic premise the Augustinian teaching that the Spirit is the bond of communion between Father and Son. While fully "equal, co-eternal, and consubstantial" (*aequalis, coaeternus, et consubstantialis*), the Spirit, "who proceeds equally from the Father and Son, is ineffably the communion between them" (*qui de Patre et Filio aequaliter procedit, ineffabilis quaedam Patris Filiique communio est*).[57] Unlike the Cappadocian understanding, in this schema the Son and the Spirit are distinguished not by the manner of their coming-into-being (one being begotten while the other proceeded), but in the Son's coming from the Father *alone* while the Spirit proceeded from *both*.

If, in fact, the Holy Spirit, is said nowhere to be either unbegotten nor begotten, this is so that if he should be called unbegotten like the Father there might not be thought that there would be two Fathers in the Holy Trinity, and in the same way if he should be called begotten like the Son there would not be judged that there were two Sons in the same Holy Trinity, but rather he alone ought to be said in safe fidelity to proceed from the Father and the Son [sed tantummodo procedere de Patre et Filio, salva fide dicendus est]."[58]

As was common for the Carolingians, the emphasis was always on the substantial unity of the three persons, most likely as guard against the Adoptionist threat. Alcuin's stress on the unity of the godhead led him to attribute certain properties (e.g., being "first principle," which in Eastern thought was reserved solely to the hypostasis of the Father) to all three persons within the Trinity. Thus for Alcuin, while the Father was rightly called "first principle, and the Son first principle; yet there are not two first principles . . . the Holy Spirit is also the first principle, yet there are not three first principles, Father, Son, and Holy Spirit, but one first principle."[59] Alcuin's language would certainly have sounded heretical to Greek ears, as it seemed to replace the monarchy of the Father with many principles (πολυαρχία) within the godhead—a charge that was to be hurled against the Latins for the next several centuries.

Pope Leo III and the Jerusalem Controversy

Once the interpolated creed became part of the liturgy at Aachen in 799, it soon spread throughout the Empire. In 806 Abbott Georg Egilbald and his companions were at the imperial chapel, where they first heard the *filioque* sung as part of the liturgy. Upon returning to their community on the Mount of Olives in Jerusalem, they introduced the custom so that their community could conform to the imperial (and, it was erroneously believed, the Roman) practice. Soon after, in 807, a controversy erupted when some monks from St. Sabbas heard the interpolated creed and protested the novelty of the addition, accusing the Franks of heresy.[60] The monks of St. Sabbas even tried to eject the community from the Church of the Nativity during their Christmas celebrations and continued to accuse them of the worst kinds of heresies despite their exoneration by the Jerusalem clergy. The Latin monks wrote to Pope Leo III, since it was their belief that these monks had, by extension, also imputed the orthodoxy of the Throne of Peter.[61]

There is little doubt that Leo himself accepted the Augustinian triadic model and the theology of the double procession as it had been explicated in the West. For that reason he wrote a *Letter to the Eastern Churches*, which was unambiguous in its support for the doctrine:

We believe the Holy Spirit proceeds equally from the Father and the Son and is consubstantial and co-eternal with the Father and the Son. . . . The Holy Spirit, proceeding from the Father and Son, is fully God.[62]

Leo, however, was silent on the liceity of the addition, only stating that "all must hold the correct and inviolate faith according to the Holy Roman Catholic and Apostolic Church."[63] Rather than taking a position, he forwarded the matter to Charlemagne for his judgment (since Charlemagne was not only emperor but also Christian protector of the Holy Land), along with the monks' request for a *florilegium* to support their position. Charlemagne seized the opportunity, beginning preparations for a council to meet at Aachen to discuss the issue and commissioning Theodulf of Orleans (among others) to compose *florilegia* for use at the gathering.[64]

Theodulf of Orleans's *Libellus de Processione Spiritus Sancti*

Theodulf's *Libellus de Processione Spiritus Sancti* was among the more influential collections of patristic texts used to support the Carolingian teaching on the *filioque*. The work itself had a dual purpose—while primarily meant to support the Carolingian teaching against the accusations of the Jerusalem monks, it had the more polemical intent of "accus[ing] the East, which could boast a continuous link to its patristic past, of distorting the heritage of the fathers."[65] By bringing together the great fathers of antiquity as witnesses to the Carolingian teaching, Theodulf was implicitly contrasting the Franks' adherence to the patristic witness with the "novelty" of the Greeks, who (as with their advocacy of "icon worship") had abandoned the tradition of the Church and ceded to the West the role of defender of the faith.

While a majority of the quotations come from the Augustinian corpus and the post-Augustinian West, Theodulf also included several selections from the Greek fathers, including Didymus, Pseudo-Athanasius, and Cyril of Alexandria.[66] According to Richard Haugh, all of the quotations chosen by Theodulf support the premise that the starting point for trinitarian theology is "the idea of the absolute oneness of God. . . . [This] leads to the stress on the inseparability of the nature of the Trinity . . . [and] ultimately this leads to the conclusion that the Holy Spirit proceeds from the nature or substance of the Deity."[67] Theodulf used Pseudo-Athanasius to uphold the notion that the Holy Spirit proceeded from the divine nature rather than from the person of the Father (*quod spiritus sanctus nec pater sit nec filius, sed de unita natura existens*).[68] References to Christ's sending (*mittere*) of the Spirit were read as demonstrations of the Spirit's dependence upon the Son for his very being (i.e., his procession). This interpretation allowed Theodulf to read several passages from Ambrose's *Letter* to *Gratian* as prooftexts for the Western doctrine because they spoke of the sending of the Spirit from the Son "where 'sending' is understood as 'procession'" (*ubi missio processio intelligitur*).[69] Cyril's *Letter to Nestorius* also appeared ("The Spirit is named the Spirit of truth, and Christ is the truth, and thus the Spirit procedes [Latin: *procedit*, in Cyril's original Greek: προχεῖται] from him as from God and Father"), adding a further Eastern witness to the Western teaching.[70]

The Council of Aachen (809) and Leo's Response

When the Council of Aachen finally met in November of 809, it was actually the document provided by Arn(o) of Salzburg (d. 821) that was used as the basis for the council's teaching on the procession.[71] The text demonstrated "the procession and mission of the Holy Spirit from the Father and the Son" (*de processione et missione spiritus sancti a patre et filio*) and established that many authorities had called "the Holy Spirit the Spirit of the Father and the Son" (*spiritus sanctus patris et filii . . . vocatur spiritus*).[72] Conciliar weight was added to the argument, since the Second Council of Constantinople (553) had embraced the theology of Ambrose, Hilary, and Augustine, all of whom (allegedly) taught the *filioque*.

> Most Blessed Augustine, whose authority and doctrine was confirmed
> by the holy Church at the Synod of Constantinople, [taught] that the
> Holy Spirit proceeds from the Son [*Spiritum sanctum a Filio procedere*].[73]

Ephesus recognized the orthodoxy of Cyril's *Letter to Nestorius* (with its seemingly pro-filioquist language) and Pope Leo's *Tome to Flavian*, which spoke about the gift of the Spirit coming from the Son (*et flatu suo dabet Spiritum sanctum*). Both Cyril and Leo's orthodoxy had been affirmed at Chalcedon, when the assembled fathers cried out: "This is the faith of the fathers, this is the faith of the Apostles! So we believe, so all the orthodox believe! Anathema to him who does not thus believe. Peter has spoken through Leo! So taught the Apostles! Piously and truly did Leo teach, so taught Cyril. Everlasting be the memory of Cyril. Leo and Cyril taught the same thing, anathema to him who does not so believe."[74]

Thus, according to the council, the *filioque* not only was orthodox and *could* be included in the creed, but as "a central teaching of the Catholic faith . . . [it] must be firmly believed and professed without doubt with a pure and sincere heart . . . by all the orthodox and faithful."[75] In other words, it was not simply that the West acted correctly in adding it, but also that the East was in error by omitting it.

At the conclusion of the council Charlemagne sent three representatives (including Smaragdus of St. Mihiel) to Rome in the hopes of having Pope Leo ratify its decisions. Smaragdus's introductory letter to Leo described the whole controversy as a God-given opportunity to bring to light the long-neglected question of the Spirit's procession.[76] He believed that the East would soon recognize the truth of the Carolingians' position, especially given all "the statements of the divine books . . . [and] the weight of so many Orthodox witnesses" produced at Aachen.[77] Leo was in a rather awkward position—on the one hand it is clear that he accepted without question the theology of the double procession as it had come to be understood in the West. And yet the addition of the *filioque* by imperial fiat seemed a direct challenge to Leo's authority as head of the Church.[78] Aside from the difficulties it might cause in the East, the pope knew that altering the creed was not something a local council was authorized to do, even if it did so with the emperor's blessing. Like Hadrian before him, Leo was caught between Constantinople and Aachen, determined to thwart Charlemagne's meddling in ecclesiastical affairs despite his own strong belief in the Spirit's procession from the Son.

It was for this reason that, in a two-day meeting with Smaragdus in 810, the pope stated his position clearly: the *filioque* is undoubtedly orthodox, and it is among those truths necessary for salvation, for "it is forbidden not to believe such a great mystery of the faith." [79] Yet Leo was clear that "we do not presume in our reading or teaching to add anything to the creed by insertion" since that was forbidden by the councils.[80] Leo was content to leave the work of the conciliar fathers untouched, since "they acted upon divine illumination rather than by human wisdom . . . and far be it from me to count myself their equal."[81] This last comment was clearly aimed at the Carolingians' presumption, a fact immediately recognized by Smaragdus. He replied:

> If we presume not only to prefer ourselves to the Fathers, but even to
> equate ourselves to them, it is only because of the way of our
> times. . . . Since the end of the world is coming, . . . [and] we are
> eager to restore the faithful in the Lord to the mysteries of faith; and,
> therefore, since we have found that the Creed was sung in such a
> manner by some, and since we feel that it touches the faith of the
> Church. . . . it seemed better to us to teach men by singing rather
> than silently to leave them untaught.[82]

Leo replied that many things necessary for salvation are not included in the creed and, while he gave permission for the singing of the creed, he never allowed "for the adding, subtracting, or altering of the Creed while it is sung."[83] He concluded the audience by ordering the *filioque*'s removal and recommending "that gradually in the Palace the custom of singing the Creed be dispensed with."[84] Leo's hope was that if the creed were no longer sung in Aachen, soon "all will dispense with it" and the issue of the interpolation would resolve itself.[85]

It was at this time that Pope Leo, "out of the love he bore for the orthodox faith," placed two silver shields in Rome with the uninterpolated creed in both

Greek and Latin.[86] While Leo undoubtedly loved the faith, there is little doubt that his true purpose was to remind Charlemagne who was ultimately responsible for the governance of the Church. Rome, not Aachen, was where the catholic faith was both defined and preserved. The author of the *Mystagogia* later appealed to "the God-inspired foresight" of Pope Leo in producing these shields, although he mistakenly believed that both shields had been written in Greek since (he claimed) Leo knew that "the meagerness of the [Latin] language could not match the breadth of Greek."[87] As for the Franks, undeterred by papal opposition, they continued to sing the interpolated creed during their liturgies, bringing this practice with them as they competed with the Byzantines for the souls of the Bulgars under King Boris.[88] It was there that the *filioque* first came to the attention of the Patriarch of Constantinople, Photius.

Photius of Constantinople (d. 895) and the So-Called Photian Schism

Photius of Constantinople was "one of the most prolific writers of the [ninth] century" and an intellectual whose varied interests included "philosophy, history, mathematics, astronomy, geography, medicine, music, poetry, and even law."[89] In 858, amid a flurry of political and ecclesiastical intrigues involving the return of iconoclasm and the Emperor Michael's deposition of his mother Theodora, Photius was chosen to replace Ignatius as patriarch.[90] Although the pope's legates in Constantinople recognized the legitimacy of Photius's election, Pope Nicholas (858–67) himself did not, believing it to have been uncanonical. Nicholas objected to the fact that Photius had been a layman before his elevation by Michael III, receiving over the course of five days the offices of lector, subdeacon, and priest before his episcopal ordination on Christmas Day in 858. Also, anti-Photian partisans in Rome (e.g., Theognostos) had little difficulty in convincing Nicholas that Ignatius had been unjustly denied his See and that, should the papacy restore him, a grateful Ignatius would concede to papal demands for Roman jurisdiction in Illyricum.[91] It was for this reason, among others, that in 863 Pope Nicholas held a synod at the Lateran deposing Photius and restoring Ignatius to the See of Constantinople.[92]

King Boris I of the Bulgars (d. 907), who had been baptized by Photius with the Emperor Michael as his godfather, decided to exploit the growing conflict between Rome and Constantinople for his own ends.[93] Several years earlier Boris had flirted with a Frankish alliance, but a coordinated Byzantine–Moravian invasion in 864 convinced him of the wisdom of accepting Christianity in its Byzantine form. Photius wrote to Boris instructing him on the faith and sent missionaries from Constantinople to convert his subjects, reinforcing (at least in Boris's mind) the growing reality of Byzantine ecclesiastical and political hegemony.[94] Fearing for his independence, Boris wrote to Nicholas in the hopes that the pope would grant the Bulgarian church a greater degree of autonomy (perhaps even a patriarch) in return for recognizing Rome's claims to jurisdiction. In his letter, Boris asked a series of questions about Latin Christianity, dealing mostly with ritual and practice, although his questions about the pentarchy and Constantinople's standing vis-à-vis Rome were probably more to the point.[95] Nicholas's reply, which he sent along with the bishops Paul of Populonia and Formosos of Porto, was apparently enough to convince Boris to eject the Byzantines and invite Frankish missionaries to take their place. When these Byzantine missionaries returned to the imperial capital, they told Photius about the strange practices being introduced by the Franks, among which was their use of an interpolated creed.[96]

Although Photius was a man of great learning, his knowledge of Latin theology appears to have been rather limited.[97] For this reason his attacks on the *filioque*, contained in both the *Encyclical to the Eastern Patriarchs* (Epistle 2) and the *Letter to the Patriarch of Aquileia* (Epistle 291), are attempts not to refute the Latins' patristic evidence, but rather to attack the logical consequences of a "double procession" from both Father and Son.[98] Photius's chief arguments, which became the foundation upon which the Orthodox case against the *filioque* was built, can be summarized as follows:

1. If "the Father is one source of the Son and the Holy Spirit, and the Son another source of the Holy Spirit, the monarchy of the Holy Trinity is transformed into a dual divinity."[99]

2. "If his [i.e., the Spirit's] procession from the Father is perfect and complete—and it is perfect, because he is perfect God from perfect God—then why is there also procession from the Son?"[100]

3. "If the Son participates in the quality or property of the Father's own person, then the Son and the Spirit lose their own personal distinctions. Here one falls into semi-Sabellianism."[101]

4. "Because the Father is the principle and source, not because of the nature of the divinity but because of the property of his own hypostasis . . . the Son cannot be a principle or source."[102]

5. "By the teaching of the procession from the Son also, the Father and the Son end up being closer to each other than the Father and the Spirit, since the Son possesses not only the Father's nature but also the property of his person [i.e., of being a principle or source of the Spirit]."[103]

6. The procession of the Spirit from the Son makes the Son a father of the Spirit's being; thus "it is impossible to see why the Holy Spirit could not be called a grandson!"[104]

Similar arguments are found in the work of one of Photius's contemporaries, Niketas Byzantinos, known primarily for his anti-Islamic writings (e.g., *Confutatio Dogmatum Mahomedes*), but also as author of one of the earliest works against the *filioque*, the *Syllogistic Chapters*.[105] Of particular import for

Niketas is the idea that there can be only one principle within the godhead, an idea that (according to Tia Kolbaba) came not only from his understanding of the patristic material, but "directly from his knowledge of Muslim anti-Christian polemic. The Muslims, confronted by the Christian doctrine of a Trinity, accused the Christians of polytheism. Against them, Niketas argued that Christians recognized three persons in the Godhead, but only one principle."[106]

Niketas's arguments, like Photius's, attacked the flawed logic of the Franks using the kind of syllogistic reasoning that the Byzantines would later associate with Latin scholasticism. For example, Niketas maintained that since our

> opponents say that the Son is also sender-forth of the Spirit, let us ask them . . . if the Son is both caused by the Father and a cause of the Spirit, is he sender-forth of the Spirit as a cause or sender-forth of the Spirit as a caused being? If they say he is sender-forth of the Spirit as a cause, then they have posited two causes in the Godhead . . . and we have already established that that is blasphemy of the worst sort. If they say that he is sender-forth of the Spirit as a caused being . . . then they are saying that the Spirit is caused by the Son . . . which makes the Spirit a grandson. We need not say more.[107]

Later he wrote:

> the sending-forth of the Spirit can be a characteristic of only one person. Otherwise, if the Son shares with the Father the character of sender-forth and the characteristic of sending-forth, then the Father and the Son will share a characteristic that the Spirit does not have. Unless, of course, you are ready to say that the Spirit, too, is a sender-forth. But see the absurdity of that position: is the Spirit the sender-forth of itself? Or is the Spirit the sender-forth of some other person, which would then render the Trinity a Quaternity?[108]

This last argument was later picked up in the *Mystagogia*, when the author (who may or may not have been Photius) claimed that the Latins had erroneously posited the procession of the Holy Spirit not from the person of the Father, but from his substance.[109] He maintained that this claim would then make the Holy Spirit (being consubstantial with both Father and Son) responsible for his own procession, "in part producer and in part be produced, in part the cause and in part the caused."[110] If the ability to spirate a person within the godhead was a property of the divine nature, then the Holy Spirit would, by necessity, have to spirate a fourth person, and this person would then produce a fifth and so on, "until they would surpass even pagan polytheism."[111]

The *Mystagogia* also dealt with the Frankish interpretation of the biblical witness, and especially with the claim that the expression "the Spirit of the Son" referred to the eternal procession. For centuries Latin theology had used both Romans 8:9 and Galatians 4:6 as support for the *filioque*, which the author of the *Mystagogia* believed was a perversion of the Pauline witness. According to the author, Paul was not here speaking of the Spirit's procession from the Son, but of "his consubstantiality with each [i.e., the Father and the Son]."[112] Thus the Frankish interpretation was confused, for "the Spirit of the Son" means one thing, while "the Spirit proceeding of the Father" teaches something else. "Let not the similarity of the grammatical case make your case hopeless."[113]

Refuting the Latin's patristic testimony was more difficult for the author of the *Mystagogia*, as he was apparently aware (probably through the *florilegia* produced by the Franks) that several Latin fathers had, in fact, used language amenable to filioquism.[114] While he did not discount the possibility that the Latins' writings had been corrupted or interpolated (for "how can one trust or vouch with confidence that their writings have not been maliciously altered after the passage of so much time"),[115] the author accepted that Augustine and Ambrose may have spoken of the Spirit's procession from the Son, either "through ignorance or through negligence" or because "of necessity of attacking the madness of the pagans or of refuting another heretical opinion or of condescending to the weakness of their hearers."[116] This being the case, rather than dishonoring the memory of these fathers by "publishing abroad the[ir] shame," what the Franks should do is to pass over these errors in silence rather than become "parricides," imitating the sin of Ham.[117] For the author of the *Mystagogia*, the overwhelming patristic consensus, including that of the bishops of Rome (e.g., Leo, Gregory, Vigilius, Agatho) supported the belief that the Spirit proceeds from the Father alone, as did the ecumenical councils and John of Damascus.

In 867 Photius summoned a council in Constantinople that anathematized Pope Nicholas and condemned the Franks for their heretical practices, chief among them being the introduction of the *filioque*.[118] However, imperial politics soon complicated matters as Michael III was murdered by his co-emperor Basil, who decided to consolidate his power by restoring Ignatius as patriarch and reestablishing relations with the pope. Another council was convoked in Constantinople in 869 (called the eighth ecumenical in the West), which annulled the acts of the earlier synod in 867 and sent Photius ("who, like a dangerous wolf, leapt into the sheepfold of Christ . . . and filled the world with a thousand upheavals and disturbances") into exile, where he remained until 873.[119] By that time Ignatius and Photius had reconciled, and Photius was allowed to return to Constantinople as tutor for the emperor's children. It was Ignatius himself who recommended that Photius be named his successor, and upon his death in 877 Photius once again became patriarch.

Soon afterward in 879 the emperor called for another council to meet in Constantinople in the hopes that the new pope, John VIII (872–82), would recognize the validity of Photius's claim upon the patriarchate. This council, sometimes called the eighth ecumenical in the East, was attended by the papal legates (who had brought with them a gift from the pope—a pallium for Photius) and by over 400 bishops, and who immediately confirmed Photius as rightful patriarch.[120] The acts of the anti-Photian synods of 863 and 869 were "completely rejected and annulled, and not to be included or numbered with the holy councils."[121] In the *Horos* of the council, the Creed (without the *filioque*) was read out and a condemnation pronounced against those who "impose on it their own invented phrases [ἰδίας εὑρεσιολογίαις] and put this forth as a common lesson to the faithful or to those who return from some kind of heresy and display the audacity to falsify completely [κατακιβδηλεῦσαι ἀποθρασυνθείη] the antiquity of this sacred and venerable *Horos* [Rule] with illegitimate words, or additions, or subtractions."[122]

This conciliar condemnation of the interpolation played a large role in later Byzantine polemics and seemed a complete vindication of the position of Photius.[123] Johan A. Meijer, in his study of the council, points out that this condemnation was aimed not so much at Rome itself (since Photius knew that the Roman Church had not approved of the interpolation), but at those Frankish missionaries and theologians who had introduced the teaching among the Bulgarians.[124] Pope John VIII, for his part, gave his qualified assent to the acts chiefly because, like Leo III before him, he resented Aachen's grow-ing influence on ecclesiastical policy, which he believed was his alone to decide.

Despite his victory at the Council of Constantinople, Photius was again deposed in 886, dying in exile in 895. However, centuries later his arguments against the Latin teaching on the procession were revived, forming the basis for subsequent Eastern reflection on the issue of the *filioque*.[125] However, it should be noted that Photius's work (which may or may not include the *Mystagogia*) was never intended to be a complete explication of Eastern trinitarian thought— it was only a reaction to the perceived heresies of the Latin missionaries in Bulgaria. It is for this reason that Photius never explored the patristic tradition behind the διὰ τοῦ Υἱοῦ formula or the necessary eternal relationship between the Son and the Spirit, "even though it was a traditional teaching of the previ-ous Greek fathers."[126] While this is understandable given Photius's intent, the emphasis on the Spirit's procession from the Father alone (ἐκ μόνου τοῦ Πατρὸς) helped to create a dialectical tension between procession ἐκ μόνου τοῦ Πατρὸς and procession *filioque*, now claimed by men such as Aeneas of Paris, Hincmar of Reims, and Ratramnus of Corbie to be the faith of the universal Church.

Aeneas of Paris (d. 870) and the Council of Worms (868)

When Pope Nicholas first became aware of the Eastern attack upon the *filioque* and other Western practices, he regarded it as a "ridiculous and utterly abomi-nable disgrace" that "the Holy Church of God" should be so accused.[127] This was an attack not only upon the pope, but upon Latin Christianity as a whole, and thus Nicholas called Christians throughout the West to "advance together in concerted battle" against those he believed responsible for this impiety—the Emperor Michael and the false Patriarch Photius.[128] Nicholas wrote to Hincmar of Reims (d. 882) and Liutbert of Mainz (d. 889) and asked them to forward "divinely inspired writings . . . to confound their madness," calling upon them to gather the bishops of Germany so that a conciliar response to the Greeks could be issued.[129]

Among the first to respond to the pope's call for writings against the Greeks was Aeneas of Paris, author of the *Liber adversus Graecos*.[130] Like the works earlier prepared for the Council at Aachen in 809, Aeneas's work is largely a *florilegia* intended to ground the *filioque* in biblical and patristic testimony. Although Augustine is the chief witness to the doctrine, what is interesting is that Aeneas also used Alcuin's *De Fide sanctae et individuae Trinitatis* as patristic support for the double procession, the assumption being that Alcuin had already come to be considered "a father of the Church." Among the Greek fathers, Cyril and Athanasius were the most prominent witnesses, the *Quicumque Vult* still believed to be a genuine work of the great bishop of Alexandria (which, he emphasized, "is second only to the See of Rome").[131]

What one notices almost immediately about the *Liber adversus Graecos* is the rabidly anti-Byzantine tone that pervades the entire work. Aeneas claimed that whereas Rome had kept the true faith untainted, Constantinople had always been the breeding ground of heresy from which many "great and dangerous errors had arisen."[132] The testimony of the fathers and the canons of the councils all opposed the "foolish stupidities" of the Greeks, whose "dialectical subtleties" once again stood opposed to the true faith as defined by the "Father of the whole Church," the Roman Pontiff.[133] And yet Peter Gemeinhardt points out that the real "achievement" of the *Liber* was its emphasis on the idea (found in Augustine and then again in Alcuin) that Father, Son, and Holy Spirit are relative (as opposed to absolute) terms denoting relationships within the Trinity.[134]

This stress on the inherently relational nature of the predicates Father, Son, and Holy Spirit is also seen in the acts of the Council of Worms, which met in 868.[135] The subject of the *filioque* occupies only a few columns in the *acta*, and only one father, Augustine, is used to provide patristic support for the doctrine. While clearly affirming the monarchy of the Father, who remained "fountain and origin of the whole Trinity" (*fons et origo totius Trinitatis*),[136] so too is the Latin teaching that:

> The Holy Spirit, neither begotten nor created but proceeding from the Father and the Son, is the Spirit of them both. For neither does he proceed from the Father upon the Son nor does he proceed from the Son alone to sanctify all creation; but rather he is shown to proceed from both because he is the love and holiness of both.[137]

Ratramnus of Corbie (d. 868)

The most comprehensive Carolingian response to the Byzantines was the *Contra Graecorum Opposita Romanam Ecclesiam Infamantium* of Ratramnus of Corbie.[138] Ratramnus addressed not only the thorny issue of the *filioque*, but also the other liturgical and disciplinary differences between Constantinople and Rome that had come into dispute (e.g., the celibacy of the Latin clergy and the fasting practices of the Western Church). Anti-Byzantine to the core, Ratramnus began this highly polemical tome accusing the emperors Michael and Basil of heresy, blasphemy, and outright stupidity (*vel falsa, vel haeretica, vel superstitiosa, vel irreligiosa*) for their opposition to the teaching authority of the Roman See.[139]

Ratramnus upheld the *filioque* on biblical, patristic, and conciliar grounds, maintaining that the doctrine was a sure defense against the Arians and their denial of the Son's consubstantiality with the Father. Following Paulinus of Aquilla, Ratramnus defended the Latins' use of the *filioque* as a clarification of the Nicene Creed (as opposed to an addition to it) meant to defend the Church against heresies, no different than what the Council of Constantinople had done in 381. He also argued that the Greeks' had similarly "added" to the creed, since they now apparently maintained procession from the Father *alone*, an erroneous teaching never affirmed by the councils.[140]

According to Ratramnus, the Latin doctrine is clearly taught by the Scriptures themselves, since Jesus possesses "all that the Father has" (John 16:15), which must include the Father's ability to generate the Spirit. As in Theodulf, procession is viewed as a property not of the Father's hypostasis but of the divine substance. Thus:

> The Holy Spirit proceeds from the Father because he flows from his substance [*Procedit Spiritus sanctus a Patre, illius quia de substantia manat*] . . . and just as the Son received his substance from the Father by being begotten, so also he received from the Father the ability to send the Spirit of Truth from himself through proceeding. . . . For just as the Father and the Son are of one substance, so too by procession from both did the Holy Spirit receive his consubstantial existence [*sic et de utroque procedendo Spiritus sanctus accepit consubstantialitatis existentiam*].[141]

The *Contra Graecorum* also repeated Alcuin's stance in *De Fide*, maintaining that the distinction between the Son and Spirit was not, as the Greeks believed, in the manner of their coming to be from the Father (one being begotten while the other proceeded), but in the Son's coming from the Father *alone* while the Spirit proceeded from *both*. Ratramnus based this argument on the fact that the Latin translation of John 8:42 had also used the term "procession" to refer to the *Son* ("*Ego ex Deo processi, et veni*"). Thus for Ratramnus, "if the Son proceeds from God the Father and the Holy Spirit also proceeds, what will keep the Arians silent, not blaspheming that the Holy Spirit is also the Son of the Father?"[142]

Ratramnus's use of the fathers (including Athanasius, Ambrose, Didymus, Augustine, Paschasius, Gennadius, and Fulgentius) was extensive and included detailed commentary for many of the selections. Even Gregory of Nazianzus was enlisted, since Ratramnus believed that Gregory's reflections of the Pentecost mystery led him to advocate procession *ex filio*.[143]

> Let us hear what Gregory Bishop of Nazianzus says, in his homily on the Holy Spirit that he gave in the Church of Constantinople on the day of Pentecost: ". . . it is not suitable for either the Son to have ever been absent from the Father or the Spirit to have ever been absent from the Son." By professing the Son never to have been less than the Father, nor the Spirit less than the Son, you are refuted. . . . For if, according to your opinion, he had wanted the Holy Spirit to proceed from the Father alone, he should have said neither the Son *nor* the Holy Spirit had at any time been less than the Father: but now . . . he clearly said the Son to have been born concerning the Father without any time, and the Spirit to have proceeded from the Son before all time.[144]

Anastasius Bibliothecarius (d. 878) and John Scotus Erigena (d. 877)

Despite the apparent consensus achieved by Ratramnus, Aeneas, and the other Carolingians on the issue of the procession, at least two writers, Anastasius Bibliothecarius and John Scotus Erigena, argued for the possibility of rapprochement with the East. Not coincidentally, both men were fluent in Greek and both were translators of the works of Maximus the Confessor. Erigena had translated both the *Quaestiones ad Thalassium* and *Ambigua* of Maximus (the latter at the specific request of Charles the Bald), while Anastasius corrected some of Erigena's earlier translations of Dionysius, adding to it Maximus's own commentary, becoming "the basis . . . for all, or almost all, subsequent Western scholarly work on Dionysius and, thereafter, for subsequent knowledge of Maximus as well."[145]

John Scotus Erigena was deeply influenced by the works of Maximus, an indebtedness he acknowledged in the preface to his translation of the *Ambigua*.[146] While a majority of Latin writers maintained that the *ex Patre per Filium* formula was both ambiguous and inadequate (echoing the argument of the *Opus Caroli Regis*), Erigena advocated its use, believing it to have solid patristic support (specifically in the works of Maximus and Gregory of Nyssa).[147] He unambiguously affirmed only one causal principle in the godhead, and demon-strated that Latin theology in no way contradicted the Greek teaching that "it is from the substance of Father that the Son is born and the Holy Spirit proceeds" (*ex substantia Patris et Filius nascitur, et Spiritus sanctus procedit*).[148]

Anastasius Bibliothecarius had been papal librarian under Pope Nicholas and was legate to the Council of Constantinople that condemned Photius in 869.[149] In his *Letter to John the Deacon*, Anastasius produced the *Letter to Marinus* to justify the Roman position on the *filioque* and its conformity with Eastern trinitarian thought:

> Moreover, we have from the letter written by the same Saint Maximus to the priest Marinus concerning the procession of the Holy Spirit, where he implies that the Greeks tried, in vain, to make a case against us, since we do not say that the Son is a cause or principle of the Holy Spirit, as they assert. But, not incognizant of the unity of substance between the Father and the Son, as he proceeds from the Father, we confess that he proceeds from the Son, understanding *processionem*, of course, as "mission" [*Sed, unitatem substantiae Patris ac Filii non nescientes, sicut procedit ex Patre, ita eum procedere fateamur ex Filio, missionem nimirum processionem intelligentes*]. Interpreting piously, he instructs those skilled in both languages to peace, while he teaches both us and the Greeks that in one sense the Holy Spirit proceeds from the Son and in another sense he does not proceed, showing the difficulty of expressing the idiosyncrasies of one lan-guage in another.[150]

This explanation by Anastasius is significant for several reasons. Not only did he reintroduce the witness and theology of Maximus the Confessor, but he also repeated Maximus's explicit denial that the Son is a cause or principle (*non causam vel principium*) of the Spirit, refuting the charge that Photius had lev-eled against the Carolingians. Interestingly, Anastasius interpreted ἵνα τὸ δι᾽ αὐτοῦ προϊέναι δηλώσωσι καὶ ταύτῃ τὸ συναφὲς τῆς οὐσίας κὰι ἀπαράλλακτον παραστήσωσι as reference to the "mission" (*missionem*) of the Spirit. If this referred only to the temporal mission of the Spirit, Anastasius's reading of the *Letter to Marinus* would certainly have been amenable to Photius and his follow-ers. If Anastasius was aware of another interpretation of Maximus's use of προϊέναι (i.e., the eternal flowing forth or emission of the Spirit), he does not indicate so here.

The Aftermath

Following the resolution of the so-called Photian Schism, the Eastern and Western Churches remained in communion for over a century despite the unresolved theological differences that had been raised during the debate. Francis Dvornik long ago debunked the myth of the so-called "second Photian Schism" and argued rather conclusively that Photius, despite his polemics against the *filioque*, ultimately died in communion with the Roman Church. [151] For most of the tenth century very little was said by either side about the issue of the Spirit's procession, and the uneasy peace between Rome and Constantinople was maintained.[152] Steven Runciman attributes this to the fact that for most of the tenth century (904–62) Rome was governed by the pro-Byzantine Theophylact family, "whose puppet-Popes were not permitted to endanger the alliance."[153] However, the growing influence of the Saxons under Otto I ("the Great") was about to shift the dynamics of power in Europe, eventually causing Rome to contemplate that which it had for so long rejected—the acceptance and use of the interpolated creed.

6

The *Filioque* from the Eleventh to the Thirteenth Century

Although an uneasy peace was maintained in the years after Photius, during the tenth and eleventh centuries political, cultural, and religious factors were rapidly driving East and West further part. Of course, each side was quite aware of the dissimilarities in their respective discipline and worship, and while some were willing to write these off as unimportant, increased contact (and conflict) during the crusades led both sides to the conclusion that these practices (the first of which was usually the use or omission of the *filioque*) were manifestations of a substantively different faith. The mutual excommunications of Cardinal Humbert and Patriarch Michael Cerularius in 1054, often called the beginning of the "Great Schism" between East and West, was thus only one marker, albeit a significant one, in a long process of "estrangement" that actually took centuries to ripen into genuine schism.[1]

In the debate over the *filioque*, while the Greek-speaking East continued to rely heavily on the claims put forward in the *Mystagogia*, the rise of scholasticism in the West enabled Latin theologians to advance an entirely new series of arguments in favor of the doctrine. Although theological encounters between the two sides (e.g., Bari in 1098, or the lecture of Peter Grossolanus to the people of Constantinople in 1112) often proved frustrating and demonstrated how far East and West had grown apart, some (Anselm of Havelberg and Nicetas of Nicomedia in 1136) demonstrated that consensus was possible even as late as the mid-twelfth century. Yet political developments continued to frustrate attempts at resolving the theological debate, and theologians on both sides of the East–West divide increasingly found themselves defending (in rather polemical terms) the positions of their respective churches against the "heresies" put forward by their "Frankish" or "Greek" opponents.

The Ottonians and the Acceptance of the *Filioque* in Rome

In 962 Otto I ("the Great") was crowned and anointed as emperor of the West by Pope John XII, who recognized *de jure* what had become evident to all—Otto not only had become the most powerful monarch in Europe but had reconstituted Charlemagne's empire.[2] Otto declared himself protector of the papal states, confirming the rights given the papacy by the Carolingians and in return exacting the promise that future popes would swear allegiance to the emperor (the so-called "Ottonian privilege"). Otto energetically involved himself in papal politics (which at this time in history was largely a "Roman" affair), bringing about the deposition of both the treasonous John XII (955–64) and his successor, Benedict V (964), and forcing the cardinals to elect (and then reconfirm) a layman, Leo VIII (964–65), as pope.[3] Otto quickly turned the papacy into an imperial "gift" to be bestowed upon those whose loyalty was proved, paving the way for increased Germanic influence in the practice and theology of the Roman Church.

Yet Otto also had reason to look East, which is why in 968 he sent Bishop Liutprand of Cremona (d. 972) to Constantinople to arrange a marriage between his son (Otto II) and a Byzantine princess (most likely Anna, daughter of Romanos II, who later married Vladimir of Kiev). Liutprand was appalled by the pretensions of the Byzantine court, the effeminate toadying of the court eunuchs, the horrible food and *retsina* (which he claimed gave him diarrhea), and the emperor Nicephorus himself, a "monstrosity of a man, a pygmy and fat-headed . . . [whom] it would not be pleasant to meet in the middle of the night."[4] From the Byzantine perspective, Liutprand had been sent by a barbarian "clothed in furs and skins," whose imperial title had been bestowed by a degenerate and a simoniac (John XII).[5] Although the Byzantines harangued him about a number of "Frankish" beliefs and practices (e.g., the numbering of the councils), Liutprand nowhere mentions the *filioque* among them, although the Germans had long since accepted the doctrine as their own.[6] Ultimately Liutprand returned to the West resentful and empty-handed, since the Byzantines were unwilling to marry a "woman born in the purple" to an imperial pretender, although eventually Otto II was betrothed to the niece of the Emperor John Tzimiskes, Theophano.[7]

Chartophylax Nicetas (of Maronea) claimed that in 1009 there was a "schism between the two Sergii" (Patriarch Sergius and Pope Sergius IV), which may have resulted from Pope Sergius's inclusion of the *filioque* in his synodal letter to Constantinople, although the exact reason for the break remains unknown.[8] It is possible that earlier popes had not been commemorated in Constantinople because of their use of the *filioque* (Pope Gregory V in 996, Sylvester II in 999) but the schism between the two Sergii was significant—after 1009 the popes were never again commemorated in the diptychs at Constantinople (except during the Latin occupation and brief periods of *unia* following Lyons and Florence).[9]

The first recorded use of the interpolated creed in Rome occurred on February 14, 1014, at the insistence of Emperor Henry II (d. 1024). Berno of Reichenau, who was present at the ceremony, testified that prior to this occasion the creed had not been chanted in Rome but that the emperor had insisted that the Saxon custom be upheld.[10] For over two centuries the popes had refused to bow to imperial pressure on the use of the interpolated creed, but with Pope Benedict VIII (1012–24) the *filioque* finally received papal sanction and became part of the Roman liturgy for Sundays and feasts. Although there is no record that this inclusion caused an immediate uproar in the East, Benedict's decision was significant because it had the effect of linking the *filioque* with the pope's right to define the faith of the universal Church. Eastern attacks upon the use of the interpolated creed henceforth became *de facto* attacks upon the powers of the pope, who (thanks to the Cluniac reformers) was increasingly becoming aware of his universal role as pastor and teacher of all Christians.[11]

Humbert (d. 1061), Cerularius (d. 1059), and the Beginning of the "Great Schism"

The event that turned the *filioque* debate into a genuinely Church-dividing issue was the exchange of anathemas in 1054 between Cardinal Humbert of Silva Candida and Patriarch Michael Cerularius.[12] Humbert had come to Constantinople at the request of Pope Leo IX to secure the emperor's help against the Normans (whose conquests in Italy were troubling both the Byzantines and papacy) and to deal with recent Eastern complaints about the Western use of unleavened bread (azymes), and in particular with the charges raised in Leo of Ohrid's letter to John of Trani.[13] The *filioque* was not originally among the issues to be discussed, although the subject had been raised at a disputation held at Bari in 1053. Thus Humbert (who later authored the *Rationes de sancti spiritus processione a patre et filio*, in part based upon the proceedings of Bari) was acutely aware of the difference in the Greek and Latin creeds, even if his understanding of how this difference came about was rather faulty.[14]

It has long been noted that both Humbert and Cerularius were "intolerant and overbearing," neither being "the man to promote conciliation and understanding."[15] Humbert (whom Berengar had once called a "stupid Burgandian") was a firm believer in the primacy of Rome and had recently been archbishop in Sicily, where his contacts with Eastern Christians had led him to the conclusion that Greek churchmen were both devious and inherently untrustworthy. "Confrontation without concession or discussion was the chosen method of Humbert."[16] Cerularius's volatile nature had long been noted even by his fellow Byzantines, who saw in his self-proclaimed right to wear purple clear manifestations of his political ambitions (he had earlier been implicated in a plot against the Paphlagonian Michael IV, which had brought about his entry into monastic life).[17] Cerularius, "an ambitious man, fussy about secondary matters,"[18] also had an exalted view of his own position, possessing an "understanding of patriarchal power . . . not all that different from what the reform movement claimed about the papacy."[19] That an encounter between two such men should end acrimoniously is not surprising.

Although the papal representatives dealt chiefly with the emperor (refusing at times even to acknowledge the patriarch's presence), Humbert also wanted Cerularius to retract the accusations that had recently been raised by Leo of Ohrid and Nicetas Pectoratus and to accept the Roman practices as both orthodox *and* universally binding. Humbert himself raised the *filioque* as an issue, claiming that the East's *omission* of the word from the Nicene Creed had brought them into serious heresy.[20] On July 16 Humbert and his party entered *Hagia Sophia* just as the liturgy was to begin and placed the bull of excommunication against Patriarch Michael, Leo of Ohrid, and "all their followers in the aforesaid errors and presumptions" on the altar.[21] While careful to note that "with respect to the pillars of the empire and its wise and honored citizens, the city is most Christian and orthodox," the bull took direct aim at "Michael, false neophyte patriarch, who only out of human fear assumed the monastic habit, now known notoriously to many because of his extremely wicked crimes."[22] Among these crimes (and there were many) was the charge that Michael and his followers, "like Pneumatomachians or Theoumachians, have *deleted* from the creed the procession of the Holy Spirit from the Son."[23]

Although the subdeacons made feverish attempts to return the bull to Humbert, he and his companions literally shook the dust from their feet (in accordance with the biblical command) and left both the Church and the city before the emperor even knew what had occurred.[24] Hopes of recalling them soon collapsed, and the emperor, now under pressure from both the clergy and the populace, abandoned his hoped-for alliance with Rome and gave Cerularius permission to respond accordingly. A synod was summoned, and a response to the excommunication (which had been translated into Greek) was issued. The edict of the Synod attempted to show how the Latins, in attacking the Greek Church, had demonstrated their own heterodox nature, especially when it came to the matter of the creed. Unlike the Latins, the Synod claimed that "we do not wish to tamper with the sacred and holy creed, which holds its authority inviolate from synodal and ecumenical decrees, by the use of wrongful arguments, illegal reasoning, and extreme boldness. And unlike them, we do not wish to say that the Holy Spirit proceeds from the Father and the Son—O what artifice of the devil!—but rather we say that the Holy Spirit proceeds from the Father."[25]

Drawing upon the arguments presented during the ninth-century debates, the edict then connected this "blasphemy against holy doctrine," added without "evidence from the evangelists nor from the ecumenical councils" with the faulty theology that undergirded it.[26] The origin of this "new impiety," it went on, stemmed from the heresy of Macedonius, since by professing the *filioque*, the Latins maintained that "the Son [is] closer to the essence of the Father than the Spirit."[27] Unlike orthodox believers, the Latins would not accept that "the procession of the Holy Spirit is not common to all three [persons, but] is the property of one of the three."[28]

Cerularius clearly maintained that procession was an act of the Father's hypostasis rather than the divine nature, and that if one posited procession from the Son as well, one not only fell into Sabellianism but put into question the universally held belief that the Father alone was principle or cause within the Trinity. He later wrote, "O Latin, cease and desist from saying that there are many principles and many causes, and acknowledge that the Father is the one cause."[29]

For their various heresies, these "impious men coming out of darkness [i.e., the West]" and "all who had something to do with [the bull] either in will or act" were to be anathematized and the document itself deposited in the archives as testament to their evil.[30] Scholars today debate the actual canonical consequences of this exchange of anathemas, most regarding the events of 1054 "more symptomatic of a state of mind than a primary cause" of the Great Schism between East and West.[31] By the eleventh century Greeks and Latins were finding it increasingly difficult to recognize the other as a member of the same church, although some continued to see the possibility of rapprochement even in the midst of this power struggle between Christendom's two most powerful sees.

Peter III of Antioch and Theophylact of Ohrid (d. 1107)

Soon after Humbert's departure from Constantinople, Cerularius wrote to the other Eastern patriarchs to enlist their help in resisting both the heresies and pretensions of the Latin Church. Among the recipients was Peter III of Antioch, whose earlier letter to Dominic, Bishop of Grado, had affirmed the orthodoxy of Rome on all matters (except the use of azymes). Peter quickly realized that many items on Cerularius's list of Latin "errors" either were manifestly untrue or concerned trivial matters of ritual and discipline that should not affect the maintenance of ecclesial communion. However, Peter considered the addition to the creed to be on a different level than the eating of lard and the use of silken vestments. The interpolation was "an evil, even the most evil of evils," probably caused by the fact that the Latins had for too long been under the control of the barbarian Vandals and consequently had lost their copies of the Acts of Nicea.[32] Even the use of azymes (which Peter had earlier condemned) and the prohibition against married clergy could be forgiven if the Latins would only correct the addition to the symbol. Peter thus urged Cerularius to tolerance, asking him to differentiate between the trivial, those errors that required only fraternal correction, and those (like the *filioque*) that must be resisted. Besides, the Latins were "our brothers, even if from rusticity or ignorance they often lapse from what is right. . . . we ought not to expect barbarian races to attain the same level of accuracy that we ask of our own people."[33] Peter himself refused to break communion with Rome, regarding the events of 1054 as a private matter between the two patriarchs and not, as later history would remember it, a church-dividing schism.

Another irenic figure was Archbishop Theophylact of Ohrid, who, like Peter of Antioch, maintained that the so-called "errors" of the Latins were few and insignificant.[34] He railed against those zealots who "through unmeasured zeal . . . and lack of humility" accused the West of all sorts of heresies, despite the fact that many of the charges were either laughable or obviously false.[35] The addition to the symbol was another matter, since Theophylact believed not only that the *filioque* was theologically incorrect, but that its introduction into the creed was an unauthorized Frankish "innovation" (καινοτομία).[36] It was an error that touched the core of the patristic faith and must be resisted.

Yet while clearly regarding the *filioque* as an error, Theophylact maintained that it was an error due "less to wickedness than to ignorance."[37] The Latins, he argued, had confused the Spirit's eternal procession (τὸ ἐκπορεύεσθαι) with his sending and economic manifestation (τὸ πέμπεσθαι), something attributable to the poverty of the Latin language and its inability to convey the necessary theological subtleties. The West, he claimed, had used one verb (*procedere*) to translate a variety of Greek terms, erroneously supposing "that proceeding (ἐκπορεύεσθαι) is identical with being imparted (χεῖσθαι) and being conferred (διαδίδοσθαι)." Therefore, because the Church confessed "that that the Spirit was sent, imparted, and conferred by the Son," the Latins thought that they "committed no error even if [they] say that he proceeds from the Son."[38] Believing the difference to be linguistic rather than substantive, he urged the East to charity, allowing the Latins to express the faith in their own way—as long as they accepted the uninterpolated creed.

Peter Damien (d. 1072) and Anselm of Canterbury (1033–1109)

In 1061 the monk Peter Damien, without being "requested . . . nor ordered by the Roman Pontiff," sent a short letter to the new patriarch of Constantinople,

Constantine III Lichoudes, responding to his (alleged) request that the Latins produce biblical evidence for their teaching on the procession.[39] Damien claimed that the error of the Greeks ("and some Latins") on this issue stemmed from their overreliance on those biblical texts (e.g., John 15:26, Matthew 10:20) that spoke of the Holy Spirit's being from the Father. Damien reminded the patriarch of the many other passages that (from the Latins' perspective) also affirmed the *filioque* (e.g., John 14:26, John 16:14, Romans 8:9, Acts 2:33), even interpreting the power that went forth from Jesus in Luke 8:46 (the woman with the hemorrhage) as a reference to the Holy Spirit's "procession" from the Son. As for the fathers, Damien supported his position using Ambrose, Jerome, Augustine, Fulgentius, and Gregory the Great, adding selections from Pseudo-Athanasius and Cyril in case "those knowing only Greek . . . object that a demonstration based on the Roman Doctors will only be convincing when we make use of the Greek fathers."[40]

In 1089 Pope Urban II (1088–99), in an effort to secure Eastern recognition of his claims to the papacy against his rival, (anti)Pope Clement III, held a council at Melfi to discuss Greek–Latin relations. Although the proceedings do not survive, we know that Urban (apparently unaware of the events of 1054, or choosing to ignore them) wrote to Emperor Alexios I in Constantinople asking why the Roman popes were no longer commemorated in the diptychs there.[41] The emperor, in consultation with the patriarch, responded that, indeed, no reason could be found for the omission of the pope's name, although the patriarchal synod did request that Urban revive the custom of sending a letter announcing his election and including his profession of faith, before any changes were made.[42] Despite his dreams of a joint crusade against the Turk, Urban never complied, nor did he ever accept the emperor's invitation to come to Constantinople.[43]

Possibly as a response to Emperor Alexios's pleas for aid, in 1095 Urban issued his famous call for a crusade at Clermont.[44] Although many of the knights who went East did so, in part, to assist the Byzantines in their ongoing struggles against the forces of Islam, not everyone in the imperial capital was happy to welcome their Frankish rescuers.[45] Increased contact between Latins and Greeks soon led to tension about their divergent beliefs and practices, and although often a *modus vivandi* was established in those places where the crusaders established themselves, Urban's dream of a united front (and a united church) required more than strained toleration. For this reason in 1098 the pope convoked a synod to meet at Bari (where the tomb of St. Nicholas of Myra had recently been moved) to discuss those issues still in dispute. Among the Latin representatives was Anselm of Canterbury, considered one of the most influential figures in Western theology and a person regarded by Urban as "pope of another world."[46]

Although we do not possess the proceedings of Bari, we do have Anselm's *De Processione Spiritus Sancti*, which is a summary of the arguments he presented there.[47] Unlike the Carolingians, Anselm does not support the *filioque* with prooftexts gleaned from the writings of the fathers. Rather, *De Processione Spiritus Sancti* is an attempt to argue the logic of the Latin position given the shared assumptions of both Greeks and Latins on the subject of the Trinity. Although the work is nonpolemical in tone, Anselm clearly believed the Greeks to be in error, maintaining that the *filioque* was a logical necessity if one was to hold simultaneously both the unity of substance within God and the distinctiveness of the persons,[48] each of whom can be understood only in terms of their "relational opposition."[49]

Unlike the Greeks, who distinguished the Spirit and the Son by their unique forms of coming-into-being from the Father (the one by begetting the other by procession), Anselm argued that distinctions in the godhead were found chiefly in their relations of origin.[50] For Anselm "unity should never lose its consequence except when a relational opposition stands in the way."[51] The Father was the origin of both the Son and the Spirit, but what then was the distinction between the Spirit and the Son, both of whom came forth from the Father? For Anselm, either the Son was from the Holy Spirit (which neither Greeks nor Latins maintained, since this was both logically impossible and foreign to the universal faith of the Church) or the Holy Spirit was from the Son. Therefore "by universal and irrefutable logic" Anselm demonstrated the Spirit's origin from the Son, a fact that the Greeks should now come to accept.[52]

Perhaps the most intriguing aspect of Anselm's work was his answer to the Greek charge (undoubtedly encountered at Bari) that in speaking of the Spirit's procession from the Father and the Son, the Latins necessarily posited two causes or sources within the godhead. Anselm argued that just as Christians say that God is the one cause of creation although there are three persons (Father, Son, and Holy Spirit), "when we say that he is from the Father and the Son, [it] is not from two sources but one, which is the Father and the Son, as the Spirit is from God, who is Father and Son."[53] Thus while Anselm did not hold the Son to be *a* separate cause of the Holy Spirit, he did maintain that, with the Father, he is *the* single cause or source. This assertion did not introduce two causes within the godhead (i.e., the Father as cause of the Son, the Father and Son as cause of the Holy Spirit), "but one cause, just as there are not two Gods but one God, from whom the Son and Holy Spirit are."[54] Here Anselm accepted the Latin premise that procession was not necessarily a property of the Father's hypostasis but came from the divine substance shared by all three persons (*secundum eandem deitatis unitatem*) and here applied only to the Father and the Son (since the Spirit was not the cause of his own existence).[55] If the creed professed that the Spirit proceeded from the Father, and the Father is God, Anselm argued that the *filioque* is "clearly demonstrated [since] the creed says that the Holy Spirit proceeds from God, since the Son is God."[56] If some (e.g., Augustine) argue that the Son proceeds principally from the Father, "we signify only that the Son himself from whom the Spirit is, has from the Father the very fact that the Holy Spirit is from the Son since he has his substance from the Father."[57]

Peter Lombard (d. 1160) and Richard of St. Victor (d. 1173)

The *Sentences* of Peter Lombard became, after the Scriptures, one of the most commented upon, and thus significant, theological works of the Middle Ages.[58] In Book I, Lombard dealt with the procession of the Holy Spirit from both the Father and the Son, a teaching "proved by many testimonies of divine utterances . . . [but] which many heretics [i.e., the Greeks] have denied."[59] The reasons given by the Greeks to support their erroneous teaching, as Lombard summarizes them, are threefold:

1. "In the Gospel, which contains the whole of faith, speaking of the procession of the Holy Spirit (John 15:26), names the Father alone."[60]
2. "In the principal councils . . . Creeds were approved, to which were appended anathemas [i.e., Canon 7 of Ephesus], declaring it unlawful for anyone to teach or preach concerning faith in the Trinity anything other than what was there contained [*nulli de Trinitatis fide aliud*]."[61]
3. "In accordance with the tradition of the said Councils, Leo III had transcribed at Rome on a silver tablet, that was placed behind the altar of blessed Paul, and which he left to posterity, as he says 'for the sake of love and the safeguarding of the orthodox faith.' In that Creed the Father alone is mentioned in regard to the procession of the Holy Spirit."[62]

Lombard first addressed the liceity of the interpolation, distinguishing between an alteration in the creed and an addition to it, claiming that "we determine the words . . . 'whoever should teach or preach otherwise' . . . just as the Apostle [Paul] did in the Epistle to the Galatians: 'If anyone should evangelize otherwise' [*aliud evangelizaverit*], that is, to the contrary, 'let him be anathema.' He does not say: 'If anyone should add anything else.'"[63]

Lombard argued that the Greeks, like the Latins, also "confess the Holy Spirit to be of the Son, just as he is of the Father, because the Apostle too says 'the Spirit of the Son,' and Truth affirms in the Gospel: 'the Spirit of truth.'"[64] Since the Greeks agree with the substance of the Latin doctrine (because being "Spirit of the Father and of the Son is not other than being from the Father and the Son"), the dispute over the *filioque* was really a matter of words.[65] Lombard then produced the patristic evidence for the doctrine, although much of it has since been shown to be spurious (e.g., the *Quicumque Vult*, Pseudo-Chrysostom). He concluded his treatment on the procession with the admonition, "Let every tongue confess that the Holy Spirit proceeds from the Father and the Son."[66]

Richard of St. Victor's *De Trinitate*, unlike so many other Latin works composed during this period, was not aimed at refuting Greek objections to the Western teaching on the procession.[67] Instead, Richard was a speculative and mystical writer who attempted to examine the Trinity utilizing the understanding of God as both the highest good (*summum bonum*) and perfect charity. He did not so much defend the *filioque* as presume it, viewing the Holy Spirit as the *condilectus* (co-beloved) sharing the love of both Father and Son—a third person within the godhead being necessary if God were to be understood as perfect charity.

Like the Greek fathers, Richard began his examination of the Trinity with the person of the Father rather than with the divine essence, arguing that for the Father's love to be perfect it cannot be self-love but must be directed outward, since "no one has perfect charity because of the exclusively personal love he has for himself."[68] The Son, who shares divinity and alone is capable of true reciprocity, thus becomes the object of the Father's love, returning love with love. Yet for Richard this is not yet perfect love, since perfect love would require that it move outside itself and be shared with another (forming a *consortium amoris*), thus necessitating a third divine person.

> When one person gives love to another and he alone loves only the other, there certainly is love, but it is not shared love. When the two love each other mutually and give to each other the affection of supreme longing . . . in this case there certainly is love on both sides but not shared love. Shared love is properly said to exist when a third person is loved by two persons harmoniously and in community, and the affection of the two persons is fused into one affection by the flame of love for the third. From these things it is evident that shared love would have no place in Divinity itself if a third person were lacking.[69]

Unlike Augustine, where the Holy Spirit was viewed as the bond of love existing between Father and Son, the Holy Spirit becomes for Richard their "common friend" who is the focus of this shared love. According to Dennis Ngien, this shift "allows the distinctiveness of the Holy Spirit to come through far more clearly and strongly than Augustine's mutual love theory," since the Spirit is now a person rather than an impersonal "bond."[70] Richard then argues that the Spirit, as the "gift" of love, does not bring forth another person, but rather "is sent to us, the mission is given to us at the same time and in the same way by the Father and the Son. After all, it is from the one and from the other that the Spirit has everything that he has. And because it is from the one and the other that he has his being, power, and will, it is proper to say that it is they who send and give him."[71]

Anselm of Havelberg (d. 1158) and Nicetas of Nicomedia

In 1136 the Emperor John II invited Bishop Anselm of Havelberg (who was in Constantinople on a diplomatic mission) to debate Nicetas of Nicomedia on the most controversial issues of the day: the use of unleavened bread, the primacy of Rome, and the procession of the Holy Spirit.[72] Unlike in the disastrous 1112 visit of Peter Grossolanus of Milan (whose acrimonious debate with John Phournes, Nicetas of Seides, and Eustratius of Nicea only served to inspire further hatred of the Latins), the proceedings were carried out in an atmosphere of genuine ecumenical understanding.[73] Although both participants were convinced of the truth of their own position, one discerns in the debates a genuine willingness to avoid the "pride and eagerness for victory" that so often characterized such encounters. Nicetas himself was impressed by Anselm's cordiality (e.g., Anselm referred to Nicetas as *frater charissime*) and his willingness to embrace the witness of the Greek fathers, something that many of his Latin co-religionists seemed unwilling to do.[74]

Nicetas's chief complaint was that this doctrine was proposed by the Latins "while no rational thought, no authority of the canonical Scriptures, and finally no general council says or teaches it" (*Praesertim cum nulla ratio, nulla auctoritas canonicarum Scripturarum, nullum denique generale concilium hoc dicat vel doceat*).[75] Taking up the argument of Photius, Nicetas argued that the *filioque* was contrary to reason because it introduced many principles (πολυαρχία or *multa principia*) into the godhead.

> For if we were to say that the Holy Spirit proceeds from the Father and the Son, then the Father would be a principle of the Holy Spirit and similarly the Son would be a principle of the Holy Spirit, it would immediately follow for us that there are two principles, and we would fall into πολυαρχίαν, that is, many principles, which is against all reason. Therefore we believe and teach that the Father is the principle of the Son whom he begot, and the same Father alone is the principle of the Holy Spirit, who from himself alone proceeds [*eumdem Patrem solum esse principium Spiritus sancti, qui ab ipso solo procedit*].[76]

Anselm was well aware of this objection to the Latin position and went to great lengths to convince Nicetas that the *filioque* did not create two principles in God. Anselm believed *principium* was a relative term, difficult to apply univocally. Thus, in one sense, while the Father alone was without principle (*sine principio*), the Son and the Spirit were also without principle since they were consubstantial and coeternal with the Father and thus did not have a beginning. However, in another sense, the Son and Holy Spirit were both *de principio*—one by begetting from the Father the other from procession from the Father and Son. In a similar manner, while the Trinity was "a simple omnipotent *principatus*," "the Father is the principle of the Son as cause, and the Father simultaneously with the Son is the principle of the Holy Spirit as cause" (*Est itaque Pater principium Filii ut causa, et est Pater simul et Filius principium Spiritus sancti ut causa*).[77] This concept did not, in Anselm's thinking, lead to there being simultaneous principles, or co-principles, in the Trinity but one principle, who is God. Nicetas then asked,

> What, or rather, what sort of thing do you think is that procession of which we speak? Does it seem true to you that the Holy Spirit should be said to proceed according to the common substance or according to a separate and individual person [*secundum communem substantiam, an secundum discretam et propriam personam*]?[78]

Anselm realized that this question was something of a trap. If he said that procession was from the divine substance, he would have to address the critique of Photius (i.e., that the Spirit, being consubstantial with the Father and the Son, must then cause not only his own existence but the procession of another person). If he claimed that procession was the property of a hypostasis, he then excluded the possibility of both the Father's and the Son's being involved without falling into the error of Sabellius. Anselm, basing himself on the Augustinian trinitarian model, claimed that as the bond of love between Father and Son, the Spirit proceeded, not from their persons or substance, but according to their mutual relation and "is the one sent by both sending, a gift from both giving, a love from both loving" (*missus ab utroque mittente, donum ab utroque donante, amor ab utroque amante*).[79]

Nicetas recognized that some of the Greek fathers had spoken of procession from or through the Son, but he gave his own interpretation of their meaning:

> The wisest of the Greeks ascribe the first cause of procession properly to the Father, from whom the Son is properly by generation, and from whom the Holy Spirit is by procession. They moreover ascribe the procession of the same Holy Spirit to the Son, but not properly, because the Son is neither from his own self, nor is he the cause of his own self . . . nor is he the primary cause of the Holy Spirit . . . and therefore I concede that the Holy Spirit proceeds properly from the Father, who is from no one; from the Son, however, because the Son is also from the Father, he does not proceed properly [*et ita concedo Spiritum sanctum a Patre, qui a nullo est, proprie procedere; a Filio autem, quia et ipse a Patre est, non ita proprie procedere*].[80]

Anselm agreed completely, claiming that the Latins also affirmed that the Father is "principal author and causal principle both of the generation in relation to the Son and of the procession in relation to the Holy Spirit" (*Est itaque Pater principalis auctor et causale principium tam generationis ad Filium, quam processionis ad Spiritum sanctum*).[81] The encounter ended on this note of agreement, Nicetas allowing that the Son had a role in the procession of the Spirit, Anselm affirming that the Father remained the principal source (ἀρχή) of the divinity. Yet despite the significance of the gathering, events conspired against future exchanges building upon the consensus reached.[82]

Brief mention should be made of two other figures: Nicetas of Maroneia (d. 1145) and Hugo Etherianus (d. 1182). Nicetas, briefly Archbishop of Thessalonica, deplored the rabid anti-Latinism of his countrymen and penned his *Six Dialogues between a Latin and a Greek* to support the unionist policies of Manual I Comnenus (d. 1180).[83] Most of the first dialogue is a detailed refutation of the Eastern charge that the Latin teaching is Sabellian, and the sixth dialogue contains the Greek explanation of the expression διὰ τοῦ Υἱοῦ (which the East confessed, although they did not and could not add it to the creed).[84] If the Latin position was in accord with this teaching (i.e., if procession "from the Son" was substantially equivalent to procession "through the Son"), then agreement between the two sides was possible.[85] However, Nicetas never accepted Roman claims to primacy and joined Theophylact of Ohrid in arguing that the creed must remain in its original form for religious peace to be maintained.

A second figure was Hugo Etherianus, a Pisan who lived in Constantinople and was respected by the Byzantines for his abilities as both a translator and a theologian. At the request of Emperor Manuel, who had asked him if the Latins had "any authorities or saints who say that the Holy Spirit proceeds from the Son," Etherianus wrote his *De haeresibus quos graeci in latinos devolvunt*, later sending copies to both Patriarch Aimerikos of Antioch and Pope Alexander III.[86] Written in both Greek and Latin, Etherianus's work contained not only patristic prooftexts (from Athanasius, Cyril, Basil, Augustine, and others) but detailed refutations of more recent Eastern authors, such as Photius, Nicetas of Maroneia, and Theophylact of Ohrid. The purpose of the work, aside from grounding the Western teaching on the procession in the patristic corpus, was to answer the Eastern charge that the *filioque* necessitated two principles in the godhead. As the debate between Nicetas and Anselm had made clear some years earlier, this issue was, and continued to be, a chief concern of Eastern theology vis-à-vis the Latin teaching on the procession.

The Fourth Crusade (1204) and Its Aftermath

Although Pope Urban had hoped that a crusade against a common foe would draw the Eastern and Western churches closer together, the resulting tensions, both political and religious, only served to consummate the schism that had grown up between them.[87] The Latins who had been living in the East came to despise that "brood of vipers . . . the perfidious Greek nation"[88] who, because of their heresies "concerning the treatment of the holy Eucharist and concerning the procession of the Holy Spirit . . ., were judged not to be Christian."[89] The

Byzantines felt very much the same about the "barbarian" Latins, rebaptizing Westerners who married Greek women and purifying any altar upon which a Latin mass had been celebrated "as if they had been defiled."[90] By 1182 anti-Latin sentiment had already reached such heights that the Latin quarter of Constantinople was burned to the ground and its inhabitants indiscriminately put to the sword (the only difference allegedly being that "greater fury was displayed toward those who wore the honorable habits of high office or religion").[91] Three years later the Normans matched brutality for brutality, sacking Thessalonica and "committing such impieties as to provoke divine reaction."[92] According to some accounts, women (including nuns) were raped and killed ("used, by all, like a urinal"), while others were decapitated as they shouted the *Kyrie Eleison*.[93] Yet nothing matched the significance of the Fourth Crusade (1204) and the subsequent establishment of a Latin empire in Byzantium, which many historians today mark as a more accurate dating of the division between East and West.[94]

The crusaders, many of whom began the venture with the noblest of intentions, had agreed to pay the Venetians 85,000 marks for ships and supplies, but they were 35,000 marks short of their goal when the crusade began, in large part because many of those who were expected to come never arrived. Although their attack on the city of Zara (which had rebelled against Venetian authority) was partial payment of the debt, the continued need for funds made the offer of the exiled Byzantine prince, Alexius, rather attractive—help reclaim the imperial throne in exchange for enough money and supplies to continue the crusade. The crusaders and their Venetian allies (led by the aged and blind Doge, Enrico Dandolo) then made their way to Constantinople, where Alexius was quickly restored to the throne. However, financial considerations and internal politics made the now-Emperor Alexius hesitant about rewarding his former allies, whose continued loitering in and around Constantinople fostered anti-Latin feelings among the inhabitants. Eager for payment, the crusaders laid siege to the city, and by April 13 the sack of Constantinople had begun.[95]

Even by the standards of the day (remembering that medieval warfare was often a bloody business), the sack of Constantinople remains singular in its excesses. Violating their crusader oaths, drunken soldiers raped "pious matrons, girls of marriageable age, . . . and maidens who, having chosen a life of chastity, were consecrated to God."[96] Others "breathing murder . . . pillaged the holy places, trampled upon divine things, ran riot and cast down holy images of Christ and his holy mother."[97] Constantinople's relics were looted, jewels pried from the altars of churches, and a prostitute seated on the patriarch's throne, where she sang bawdy songs to the cheers of her Latin audience. To the occupants of Constantinople the Latins had become "forerunners of the Anti-Christ, the agents and harbingers of his anticipated ungodliness."[98]

Although Pope Innocent III (1198–1216) immediately condemned the actions of the crusaders, with the imperial coronation of Baldwin of Flanders and the election of a Venetian patriarch, he soon reconciled himself to the situation, seeing it as a God-given opportunity to end the schism and reestablish the authority of the Roman See.[99] In 1205 he issued a call for the *reductio Graecorum*, claiming that the crusade, which had finally put an end to the Byzantines' disobedience, was "the Lord's doing, and it is wonderful in our eyes."[100] In 1215 the Fourth Lateran Council called by Innocent affirmed without hesitation that "the Holy Spirit is from both [the Father and the Son] equally, eternally without beginning or end."[101] Noting that "the Greeks in our day are returning to the obedience of the apostolic see," the council allowed for the maintenance of their customs and rites ("as much as we can in the Lord"), yet demanded that they "conform themselves like obedient sons to the holy Roman Church, their mother."[102] As a result, during the half-century of occupation, the Latin hierarchy forced the Byzantines to accept various Western ecclesial practices, including the recitation of the interpolated creed. In the Byzantine consciousness, acceptance of the *filioque* soon became equated with the imposition of a foreign rite and culture, and thus was considered not only heretical, but an act of ethnic betrayal.

With "Byzantine xenophobia, anti-Latin sentiment, and hostility"[103] at a new high, Eastern polemicists began compiling lists of Latin errors, outlining the various customs (e.g., improper Lenten fasting, the use of azymes) that clearly demonstrated the heretical nature of Western Christianity.[104] As with those lists produced in the eleventh century, almost all included the addition of the *filioque* to the creed, although few dealt with the theological issues involved in the debate. The reason, most likely, is that these lists were in large part addressed to the uneducated, who had little understanding of the theological subtleties involved.[105] When theological reasons were given (as in the *Opusculum contra Francos*), recourse was made to the criticisms of Theophlact and Peter of Antioch, and the idea that "because of the deficiency of their language they [the Franks] think that procession from the Father and the mission of the Holy Spirit through the Son are the same thing. And they reason barbarously and without education that mission is in no way different from procession."[106]

Nicephorus Blemmydes (d. 1272) and Attempts at Union

While the Latins occupied Constantinople, the Byzantine court in exile at Nicea continued its efforts to regain the capital, occasionally dangling before Rome the prospect of church union in exchange for an end to Latin rule in the East. In 1232 the patriarch-in-exile, Germanus II, sent letters to Pope Gregory IX suggesting such a scheme.[107] The pope's response was cool, but he was willing to send a delegation of Dominicans and Franciscans to Nicea, where in January of 1234 they debated the patriarch and his two representatives, Demetrios Karykes and Nicephorus Blemmydes.[108] This first encounter between the Greeks and

Latin scholasticism did not go well; Emperor John III Ducas Vatatzes upbraided the Latin delegation for its continued use of syllogistic reasoning, and Blemmydes took issue with their reading of Cyril of Alexandria.[109] He pointed out that the Spirit's indwelling in the Son (which Cyril had maintained as a doctrine of the faith) did not imply (as the West held) the Spirit's procession from him. When the emperor suggested a compromise—that the Greeks accept the use of azymes and the Latins accept the Greek teaching on the procession—the friars left, claiming, "The Lord Pope and the Roman Church will never abandon a single iota of their faith!"[110] The Greeks shouted back "It is you who are the heretics!" and the debate was at an end.[111]

Several years later, in 1250, Blemmydes once again found himself publicly debating the Latins on the subject of the procession, this time with John of Parma at Nymphaion.[112] This debate focused on the Greek patristic texts that spoke of the Spirit's acting "through the Son," which John argued was substantially the same as the Spirit's procession "from the Son"—the prepositions διά ("through") and ἐκ ("from") in this context being interchangeable. Blemmydes claimed that the formula διὰ τοῦ Υἱοῦ ("through the Son") was never meant to attribute causality to the Son (since this was a hypostatic property belonging only to the Father), but rather was used by the fathers to show the unity of the divine essence.

The debates had a profound effect on Blemmydes and caused him not only to become a strong advocate for Church union but also to explore the meaning of the "through the Son" formula in patristic thought. In two short treatises written after 1253 (addressed to Jacob, Archbishop of Ohrid, and Emperor Theodore II Lascaris), Blemmydes collected those patristic texts that utilized the formula "through the Son," attacking those who, because of their anti-Latin zeal, refused to grant them more significance.[113] He argued that the Son did participate in some way in the eternal procession of the Spirit and that he was a necessary intermediary not only in the Spirit's temporal mission but also in his eternal coming-into-being. While some scholars argue that Blemmydes therefore accepted the Latin teaching on the procession, others are quick to point out that he never went so far as to accept the *ex filio* or *filioque* formulae, since the language seemed to make the Son a separate principle of the Spirit's hypostasis, destroying the doctrine of the monarchy as Greek theology had traditionally understood it.[114]

Bonaventure (1221–74)

Bonaventure's views on the *filioque* can be found in a number of places, including his *Disputed Questions on the Trinity, Breviloquium, Itinerarium,* and the *Collations on the Hexaemeron,* although his most explicit treatment of the subject is found in one of his earliest works, the *Commentary on the Sentences.*[115]

Bonaventure recognized that the Byzantines' objections to the *filioque* were based in part upon the "argument from silence"—that is, that because the *filioque* was not explicitly mentioned in the Scriptures nor in the original version of the creed, it could not be taught as a doctrine of the Church. These "scurrilous progeny" of the Greek fathers then attempted to "fortify their error" through false reason and the patristic witness, which is why the Roman Church had rightly condemned them as both "heretics and schismatics."[116]

In his defense of the *filioque*, Bonaventure included many of the arguments that had become common by the thirteenth century: that the Holy Spirit proceeded as the mutual gift and love of both Father and Son, and that persons in the Trinity can be distinguished from one another only by virtue of their origin. Thus Bonaventure maintained that since "every distinction of persons among the divine is according to relation and origin, therefore if the Holy Spirit does not proceed from the Son, nor the other way around, there is no origin there, thus no mutual relation or distinction [*ergo si Spiritus sanctus non procedit a Filio, nec e converso, nulla est ibi origo: ergo nulla est ibi mutua relatio, ergo nec distinctio*]."[117]

In advocating the *filioque*, Bonaventure was careful to protect to monarchy of the Father, affirming that the "Father is properly the One without an originator, . . . the Principle who proceeds from no other; the Father as such."[118] He is "principle of the whole deity" (*principium totius divinitatis*), whose "fontal plentitude" (*fontalem plenitudinem*) leads him to beget the Son and (with the Son) spirate the Spirit.[119] Because the Son received from the Father the ability to bring forth the Holy Spirit, one can say that the Son "principally produces the Holy Spirit [but]the Father does so *more principally*, since in Him there is only authorship, not sub-authorship [*quia in eo est tantum auctoritas, non subauctoritas*]."[120]

For Bonaventure the divine life is not communicated to the Spirit by nature (*per modem naturae*), but rather through the will (*per modum voluntatis*)—coming forth as the freely given and received love of the Father and the Son, and "proceeding from the Father and Son not insofar as they are distinct persons, but insofar as there is in them one fruitfulness of the will, or one active spiration."[121] "This love that is the Holy Spirit does not proceed from the Father insofar as he loves himself, nor from the Son insofar as he loves himself, but proceeds insofar as the one loves the other, because he is the nexus (a bond of unity). Therefore the Holy Spirit is the Love, by which the one loving tends to the other."[122]

Bonaventure upbraided the East for their lack of theological sophistication, claiming that while "the Greeks have compared the Spirit to the spiration of the exterior breath, the Latins [compared it] to the spiration of interior love . . . [understanding it] in a more spiritual and more fitting manner; for that reason they were elevated by their reckoning."[123] He then claimed that the Greeks' refusal to profess the *filioque* stemmed from their "ignorance, pride and pertinacity" (*ex ignorantia, ex superbia et pertinacia*), especially since it was added to the creed "from the truth of the Faith, from the necessity of danger, and from the authority of the Church."[124] The Byzantine belief that the addition required the authority of an ecumenical council (with representation from the other patriarchal sees) was easily handled by Bonaventure, who argued "that it was not opportune to call them, because the Church could [do this] without them; it was laborious, on account of the distance; it was not unfruitful, because there was no longer the great wisdom among the Greeks [as there once was] since it had passed over to the Latins; it was dangerous, because it was dangerous to put into doubt what was already held certain."[125]

Thomas Aquinas (1225–74)

Negotiations between Nicea and Rome continued apace throughout the 1250s and 1260s, which explains why only two years after recovering the Constantinople from the Latins in 1261, Emperor Michael VIII Palaeologus (1258–82) was once again willing to discuss the possibility of ecclesiastical reunion.[126] Keenly aware of the theological differences that had kept East and West apart, Pope Urban IV asked the Dominican Thomas Aquinas to prepare a statement on the beliefs of the Latin Church concerning the most important issues under discussion—the primacy of the pope, azymes, purgatory, and the procession of the Holy Spirit.[127]

Thomas's arguments in favor of the Spirit's procession from the Son appear in several of his works—including his *Commentaries on the Sentences*, *De Potentia Dei*, *Summa Theologiae*, and the *Summa Contra Gentiles*—and presume the Augustinian understanding of the Trinity (i.e., the Holy Spirit as the bond of love between Father and Son). Therefore "because the Holy Spirit is the mutual love and bond of two he needs be spirated by two," coming forth as the mutual love and gift of both the Father and the Son, then imparted to us through Jesus Christ in the economy of salvation.[128]

"Since articles of faith should be confirmed not only by reason but by authorities," Thomas supported his case by employing those biblical texts that spoke of the "Spirit of Christ" (Rom. 8:9, Gal. 4:6, Acts 16:7), concluding from this phrase that "the Son must exercise authority over the Holy Ghost."[129] Since there can be "no slavery or subjection" in God, the authority must be in respect to origin.[130] He then argued that if the Holy Spirit "receives from the Son" (John 16:14), he must also eternally proceed from him "since he could not receive anything that was not from him eternally."[131]

However, like Anselm before him, Thomas's main argument for the *filioque* is the argument from relations. Beginning with the divine essence (a common starting point for scholastic theology, since unity logically preceded differentiation), Thomas then asked how one could distinguish persons within the godhead. Since all three enjoyed a common essence, the only possible distinction was in their relation to one another, and these were, out of necessity, relations of opposition. Since "there cannot be in God any relation opposed to each other except relations of origin"[132] in order to establish an eternal relation between the Son and the Spirit (which was necessary to distinguish them), "we must conclude that it is necessary to say that either the Son is from the Holy Ghost; which no one says; or that the Holy Ghost is from the Son, as we confess."[133]

Like Bonaventure, Thomas unambiguously affirmed the Father as *principium totius deitatis* within the godhead, since he alone was the principle without principle.[134] However, that assertion did not keep Thomas from explicitly affirming that the Son was *auctor* (author), *principium* (principle), and *fons* (source) of the Holy Spirit. [135] This was so because the Son has "the same spirative power [that] belongs to the Father," which he possesses as a gift from the Father.[136] "Therefore the Holy Ghost proceeds equally from both, although sometimes He is said to proceed principally or properly from the Father because the Son has this power from the Father."[137] The Greeks themselves appeared to Thomas to accept this fact (since they accepted procession "through the Son, or his flowing forth "from the Son"), although they refused to acknowledge it "out of ignorance or obstinacy."[138] Thomas countered the Greek charge that the Latin teaching necessitated two principles, maintaining that there was only a single spiration and a single spirative power (i.e., the Father and Son). For this reason it was better to say that "the Father and Son are two spirating . . . but not two spirators;" not two principles or causes, but one.[139]

In 1264, in answer to Pope Urban's request, Thomas wrote his most detailed defense of the *filioque*. Known today as the *Contra Errores Graecorum* (Thomas, it should be noted, was not responsible for its rather polemical title), the work itself shows a genuine effort toward both ecumenicity and conciliation. For example, Thomas pointed out that the Greeks' use of certain theological concepts (e.g., their preference for αἰτία or *causa* rather than *principium*), while unfamiliar and even suspicious to the Latins, did not denote a substantially different faith. "And, doubtless," he continued, "there are many similar instances,"[140] since "many things which sound well enough in Greek do not perhaps sound well in Latin. Hence, Latins and Greeks professing the same faith do so with different words. . . . When anything expressed in one language is translated merely word for word into another, it will be no surprise if perplexity concerning the meaning of the original sometimes occurs."[141]

Believing this was the case with the *filioque*, Thomas, unlike the Carolingians, was willing to accept the Greeks' acceptance of the διὰ τοῦ Υἱοῦ formula as substantially equivalent to the Latin doctrine of procession *ex filio*, which, he believed, "has the same meaning."[142] According to Aquinas "whenever one is said to act through another, this preposition *through* points out . . . some cause of principle of that act."[143] Thus the Greeks' use of the διὰ τοῦ Υἱοῦ formula meant that they too recognized that the Son was a cause (albeit a mediate cause) of the Holy Spirit, for "the Holy Spirit proceeds from the Father immediately, as from Him, and mediately, as from the Son and thus He is said to proceed from the Father through the Son."[144] Aquinas compared this to the generation of Abel, who proceeded immediately from Adam and mediately from Eve (who came from Adam's rib), "although the example of material procession is inept to signify the immaterial procession of the divine persons."[145]

Thomas's handling of the patristic material in the *Contra Errores Graeco-rum* presents two distinct problems.[146] The first is the recognition that many of the patristic quotations cited in the work (especially from the Greek fathers) have since proved to be either corrupted or spurious.[147] The second concerns the very problem Thomas had hoped to avoid—confusion due to mistranslation. In reading the patristic corpus, Thomas was convinced that many fathers had advocated procession from or through the Son in large part because of their (mis)understanding of the Latin notion of *processio* and its relation to the Greek verb ἐκπορεύεσθαι. According to Aquinas:

> the word procession [*processio*] is the one most commonly applied to all [terms] that denote origin of any kind. For we use the term to describe any kind of origin; as when we say a line proceeds from a point, a ray from the sun, a stream from a source, and likewise in everything else. Hence, granted that the Holy Ghost originates in any way from the Son, we can conclude that the Holy Ghost proceeds from the Son.[148]

For this reason, Thomas argued that any mention in Greek patristic litera-ture of the Spirit's coming from the Son (by either procession proper [ἐκπορεύεσθαι], progression [προϊέναι], or going forth [προέρχομαι]) should be read as proof of his eternal *processio*, "for, if anything is in any way at all from something we say it proceeds from that thing."[149] It should be noted that Tho-mas was not being disingenuous. As Theophylact of Ohrid had already noted, Latin theology had for centuries used *procedere* to translate a host of Greek verbs denoting origin.[150] Unable to read Greek and having received most of his proof-texts in translation from the *Libellus* of Nicholas of Cotrone, Thomas would almost certainly have been unaware of how these verbs were used in their orig-inal contexts. This was especially the case with ἐκπορεύεσθαι, for as Michael Torre has noted "while it may be true that the Latin '*procedere*' refers to originat-ing 'in any way at all' this is just what ἐκπορεύω does not mean in Greek!"[151]

The *Contra Errores Graecorum* also dealt with the Latin understanding of the Roman primacy, including the pope's right to define the faith of the Church. As the Spirit's procession from the Son was a doctrine "necessary for faith and salvation,"[152] the pope was correct to defend the honor of Christ against those (i.e. the Greeks) who, by denying the *filioque*, "diminish his dignity as far as this lies in their power."[153] That the pope had the power to alter the creed was, for

Thomas, beyond doubt, since as "successor of Peter and Vicar of Christ [he] is the first and greatest of all the bishops," possessing "fullness of power over the whole Church of Christ."[154]

Thomas Aquinas was on his way to the reunion council at Lyons, carrying with him his *Contra Errores Graecorum*, when he died on March 7, 1274.[155] In the centuries that followed, the writings of the "Angelic Doctor" achieved a level of authority in the West unknown since Augustine, and his arguments in favor of the *filioque* became an important part of the Latin theological tradition.[156] Thomas's position on the *filioque*, like his opinion on so many subjects, became the position of the Church itself. As events would soon show, the Byzantines did not possess that kind of doctrinal unity, a fact that put them at a distinct tactical disadvantage when they were engaging their counterparts in the West.

7

The Council of Lyons to the Eve of Ferrara-Florence

Despite the hope that the schism between Rome and Constantinople could be healed by a reunion council, by the thirteenth century more than theology separated the Churches of East and West. Embittered by the fourth crusade and the subsequent occupation, many Byzantines speculated that it would be better to wear the turban of the sultan than to bow to Rome and wear the cardinal's hat.[1] Yet the Palaeologan emperors, who ruled in Constantinople from 1261 to 1453, continued to negotiate religious union in the hopes of thwarting the ambitions of not only the Turks, but Western adventurers like Charles of Anjou. While each attempt at union only proved how far the two sides had grown apart, these encounters did provide the East with the opportunity to debate and refine their own thinking on the *filioque*'s place (if any) in the theology of the Church. This was especially true of the gathering at Lyons, when three distinct "schools" of thought emerged from the aftermath of the council, each laying claim to being a faithful interpreter of the patristic mind on the procession of the Holy Spirit.

The first was the unionist position of John Beccus, which accepted the premise that procession διὰ τοῦ Υἱοῦ was substantially the same as procession ἐκ τοῦ Υἱοῦ. Since the former formula had been used by so many of the Greek fathers, the orthodoxy of the Latin position (to them) appeared clear. The second (and certainly the most popular among the three) was the anti-unionist position, repeating Photius's insistence on procession from the Father alone (ἐκ μόνου τοῦ Πατρὸς) in order to uphold the monarchy of the Father and defend against the (perceived) Sabellianism of the Latins. Perhaps the most interesting of the three schools, however, was the third. Although it never achieved widespread acceptance in Greek ecclesiastical circles, the position established by Gregory of Cyprus and Gregory Palamas allowed for an orthodox interpretation of the *filioque* (as an expression of the Spirit's eternal [or energetic] "flowing forth" through or from the Son) while simultaneously denying the Son any causal role in the Spirit's hypostatic origin. They alone seemed able to establish an eternal (not merely economic) relationship between the Son and Spirit without compromising the historic Eastern emphasis on the Father's role as μία αἰτία within the godhead.

While the Greeks were at odds among themselves on the place of the *filioque*, Latin Christianity suffered no such handicap. Although divided by the Great Western Schism (1378–1417) and the ensuing conciliarist debates, the Latins nevertheless came to Ferrara-Florence with a unified voice on the matter of the Spirit's procession from both the Father and the Son. It is perhaps for this reason that theologians in the West produced few significant works on the procession in the period between Lyons and Florence, except for the occasional polemical tract.[2] Among the Byzantines, however, the debate was just beginning.

The Second Council of Lyons (1274)

Preparations for a reunion council had begun within months of Michael VIII Palaeologus's recapture of Constantinople and imperial coronation in 1261.[3] Although Michael was now emperor, his "position was precarious.... He faced the ambitious Balkan kingdoms, the Latin principalities by now firmly rooted in Greek soil, the new Western claimants to the Latin Empire of Baldwin II ... in addition to [the] disquieting uncertainties in the Asian world caused by Mongol turmoils and rising Turkish powers. Like his Lascari predecessors, Michael VIII saw his best hope in coming to terms with the papacy."[4]

Michael wrote to Pope Urban in 1262 and then again in 1263, offering terms so favorable to the papacy that Urban immediately began preparations for a council to consummate the union. However, Urban died in 1264 and the demands of his successor, Clement IV (1265–68), were so great (e.g., the imposition of Roman doctrine and customs) that Michael's enthusiasm for union soon dimmed. Hope was renewed with the election of Pope Gregory X (1271–76), a deeply spiritual man whose desire for a crusade to recapture Jerusalem led him to embrace the cause of Church unity.[5] The terms he offered Michael were substantively the same as those offered by Clement, although Gregory seems to have been more sensitive to the emperor's delicate position vis-à-vis the quite powerful and increasingly anti-Latin Byzantine clergy.

In preparation for the council, Gregory issued two bulls (*Salvator Noster* in 1272 and *Dudum super generalem* in 1273) asking for reports on the causes of the schism and suggesting ways they might be addressed at the upcoming council. In response to the pope's request, Humbert of Romans wrote the *Opusculum tripartitum*, whose second part details his understanding of the history and nature of the separation.[6] The schism, he argued, was caused by the Greeks' refusal to maintain communion with the Bishop of Rome, although he recognized that the Latins' scandalous behavior during the occupation had needlessly prolonged it.[7] Recognizing the many liturgical, cultural, and political differences that were in large part responsible for the estrangement, Humbert also included the addition of the *filioque* to the creed without Eastern consent, which the Greeks had interpreted as an affront.[8] The Greeks, he argued, may be both schismatics and "manifest heretics," yet they were also Christians whose misguided understanding of the procession was caused by their exclusive reliance on the Greek fathers ("which they hold to pertinaciously").[9] He therefore suggested that Byzantine scholars come to the West for study and that translations of the Latin fathers be made for the Greeks, which, he hoped, would correct this imbalance. Yet Humbert also urged his co-religionists in the West to study Greek so that they could better understand and aid their ailing brother.[10]

In preparation for the hoped-for reconciliation of the churches, Pope Gregory sent the Greek-born and very popular Franciscan John Parastron to instruct Emperor Michael in the Latin faith.[11] Parastron was an irenic figure who had often acted as an intermediary between Constantinople and the West, praying publicly with the Byzantine clergy and even receiving the antidoron (blessed bread) following the divine liturgy.[12] However, it would be Jerome Ascoli, rather than the more popular Parastron, who received the profession of faith written for the emperor and his son and co-emperor, Andronicus.[13] It stated:

> We believe also that the Holy Spirit is complete and perfect and true
> God, proceeding from the Father and the Son [*ex Patre Filioque
> procedentem*], co-equal and consubstantial, co-omnipotent, and
> co-eternal through all things with the Father and the Son.[14]

Michael was keenly aware that union with the Latin Church had little support among the Greek clergy and populace. In an effort to ensure their cooperation, he promised the clergy that the upcoming union would leave the Church "untouched by innovation" (e.g., the recitation of *filioque*), the only exception being the inclusion of the pope's name in the dyptichs. The anti-unionist majority balked, openly proclaiming that the Latins were heretics who must be avoided like mad dogs. Patriarch Joseph I, while holding that the Latins were indeed heretics, nevertheless urged the anti-unionists to charity, writing:

After all, they were formerly our brothers, reborn brothers of the same font of holy baptism; if they are sick, if they are eccentric, they nevertheless merit more pity than hate. We need to be merciful, to love them, to pray for them.[15]

Joseph himself refused to participate in the upcoming council, since he believed it to lack the qualities necessary for ecumenicity—that is, the participation of the five patriarchal sees and freedom to discuss all questions in dispute. Most of the clergy followed suit, signing an anti-unionist oath that pledged to "keep inviolate the teachings of the Savior" regardless of what might be decided at Lyons.[16]

The emperor issued a *Tomos* (since lost) demonstrating the Latin's orthodoxy, but his arguments were refuted in the *Apologia* authored by the monk Job Jascites.[17] Frustrated by their continued opposition, Michael bullied the clergy into submission, issuing a chrysobull on Christmas Day 1273 defining the terms of the union—acknowledgement of Roman primacy and the commemoration of the pope in the dyptichs.[18] The *filioque* was nowhere mentioned, although the emperor continued to guarantee that the rites and doctrines of the Church would remain unchanged. The clergy's response, which "fell far short of constituting a profession of faith in the manner required by Rome," was signed by less than one-third of the Eastern bishops.[19] In the letter they acknowledged that in the matter of Church union "we have come to the same conclusion as our God-crowned and mighty holy and Lord Emperor."[20] However, the *filioque* was not even mentioned, let alone affirmed.

Jerome Ascoli, armed with this letter and the emperor's profession of faith, arrived in Lyons before the council's scheduled opening on May 1, 1274.[21] When the council began on May 7, there were already some 300 bishops and clergy present, along with King James of Aragon and delegations from France, Germany, England, and Sicily. Also in attendance were some of Western Christianity's greatest luminaries, Albert Magnus and Bonaventure, although there is no evidence that they ever entered into formal debate on the procession of the Spirit or the other issues under dispute.[22] The reason was simple—there was no formal debate. In fact, the statement on the procession of the Holy Spirit, the chief dogmatic issue between East and West, was formulated at the second session of the council, weeks before the Byzantine delegation arrived in Lyons. A complete restatement of the historic Latin position, it read:

> We profess faithfully and devoutly that the Holy Spirit proceeds eternally from the Father and the Son, not as from two principles, but as from one principle [*tantum ab uno principio*]; not by two spirations, but by one single spiration . . . this is the unchangeable and true belief of the orthodox fathers and doctors, Latin and Greek alike.
> . . . [W]ith the approval of the sacred council, [we] condemn and reprove all who presume to deny that the Holy Spirit proceeds eternally from

the Father and the Son, or rashly to assert that the Holy Spirit proceeds from the Father and the Son as from two principles and not as from one.[23]

Included in this definition, but not present in the earlier confession of Emperor Michael, is the affirmation that in God there was only one principle and one spiration [uno principio . . . unica spiratione]. The Latins were well aware of the Greek charge, echoed in one form or another since the time of Photius, that the filioque had destroyed the monarchy of the Father and introduced many principles (πολυαρχία) into the godhead. It had, in fact, been among the chief critiques of the doctrine made in the Apologia of Job Jascites. For the Latins, two principles meant two natures, and in God there was only one divine nature (shared by Father, Son, and Holy Spirit), and thus one principle.[24] The Greeks therefore were to be condemned on two counts—not only for refusing to admit the Spirit's procession from the Son, but also for their denial of the consubstantiality of the three persons by their "rash assertion" that the filioque introduced two principles (and therefore two natures) into the godhead.[25]

The Greek delegation (including George Acropolites, the former patriarch Germanus III, and Theophanes of Nicea) finally arrived in Lyons on June 24, delayed by a storm that had destroyed one of their ships and sent most of its passengers to their deaths.[26] Ironically, Acropolites, charged with securing union with Rome on the emperor's behalf, had once written a tract against the filioque, arguing that the creed should be recited in its original form even in the West.[27] And yet, at the solemn mass celebrated on June 29, at which the gospel was read in both Latin and Greek, Acropolites and the other delegates were made to sing the creed with the interpolation, repeating the filioque no less than three times (ter cantaverunt).[28]

When the fourth session began on July 6, the emperor's confession (along with that of his son, Andronicus) was read out in Latin translation, as was the letter signed by the forty-one bishops responding to Michael's chrysobull. Following his profession, the emperor included a request that "the Greek Church be permitted to recite the creed as it had been before the schism up to our time. . . . This is not crucial to your holiness but for us it is a matter of vital importance because of the immense multitude of our people."[29] Michael, it should be remembered, had already assured the clergy that union would not affect the practices of the Eastern Church, knowing that the introduction of foreign rites (i.e., the filioque) would be met with firm resistance. Yet despite the emperor's plea, it is significant that after the Greek delegates read his profession of faith, they were not only forced to recite the creed with the interpolation, but to repeat the filioque clause twice.[30]

Although there was some question as to whether Michael's delegates possessed the right to swear on the emperor's behalf (Acropolites had a letter

allegedly giving him the authority to do so), at the end of proceedings they formally subscribed to the union and the schism was proclaimed ended.[31] The
council issued several more documents in the days that followed, but these
dealt largely with particular issues in the Western Church (such as the future
of the mendicant orders and the method of papal elections) and were of little
interest to the Greeks. The Byzantine delegation left Lyons days after the
council's final session on July 17, knowing full well that the union would not
be popular in the East, a fact immediately confirmed upon their arrival in
Constantinople. According to George Metochites, one of the lay delegates at
the council, the charges leveled against them included not only heresy, but
ethnic betrayal.

> Instead of refutative proof, instead of arguments from the Scriptures,
> what we envoys constantly hear is φράγκος καθέσθηκας [You have
> become a Frank]. Should we who are pro-unionists, simply because
> we favor union with Rome, be subjected to being called supporters of
> a foreign nation [ἀλλοεθνεῖς] and not Byzantine patriots?[32]

When the union was formally proclaimed in Constantinople on January
16, 1275, it was celebrated in the imperial chapel at Blachernae rather than
Hagia Sophia, and the *filioque* was not included in the creed (although Pope
Gregory was commemorated).[33] Michael's own sisters aligned themselves
with the growing anti-unionist majority, and Patriarch Joseph resigned rather
than submit. Among the few supporters of the emperor's unionist policies
was the man chosen to replace him as patriarch, the former chartophylax
John Beccus.

John XI Beccus (1275–82)

John Beccus is usually listed among the so-called "Latin-minded" theologians
of the late Byzantine period, despite the fact that he was "passionately attached
to the Byzantine way of life" and completely unconvinced by the arguments of
Western scholasticism.[34] He had originally been a vocal opponent of Michael's
unionist agenda, openly referring to the "Italians" as heretics despite his self-
admitted ignorance of theological matters.[35] In 1273 the emperor imprisoned
him for his intransigence, sending him the writings of Nicephorus Blemmydes
and Nicetas of Maroneia in the hopes of converting him to the unionist cause.
Beccus, whose theological training was up to this point rather limited, was
completely won over by their arguments, claiming that the patristic teaching on
procession διὰ τοῦ Υἱοῦ spoke to the Son's necessary intermediary role in the
Spirit's eternal coming-into-being. His conversion complete, on May 27, 1275,
Beccus succeeded Joseph as patriarch and was entrusted by the emperor with
enforcing the unpopular union.[36]

Beccus's defense of the *filioque* rested on his understanding of the prepositions διά ("through") and ἐκ ("from"), which, he argued, were often used synonymously in the theological language of the fathers. Beccus held that just as
the phrases "born through a woman" and "born from a woman" were identical
in meaning, so references in the Greek patristic corpus to procession ἐκ τοῦ
Πατρὸς δι Yἱοῦ should be understood as identical to the Latin teaching of procession *ex filio* ("from the Son"). If the teaching of the two churches is the same
despite these linguistic differences, then there was no reason to "quibble over
little words" since "it is not in words, but in idea that the Church of Rome demonstrates its attachment to orthodoxy."[37] According to Beccus, "we know that
the apostolic Church of Rome is orthodox and that we are in agreement with it
so far as it concerns thought and idea. We believe, in fact, . . . in the Spirit who
proceeds from the Father through the Son. He comes forth from the Father in
nature and in essence, he comes forth from the Son in the same manner as
from God the Father."[38]

As for the addition, he argued that since "in its tenor, [it] causes no injury
Despite this seeming agreement, Beccus clearly denied that the Son was in
any way a "cause" within the godhead, issuing anathemas against those who
asserted "that the Son is the cause of the Spirit [or] who think that the Son is
co-cause of the Spirit."[39] He claimed that "the Italians, when they add to the
reading of the Creed the phrase, 'and from the Son,' do not say that there are
two causes of the one Spirit, since they do not assert the Spirit to be from the
Father and the Son in any dyarchic, dualistic way."[40]

As for the addition, he argued that since "in its tenor, [it] causes no injury
to our traditional faith. . . . I pardon my brothers for this; I overlook the addition
of the word . . . as a true disciple of those teachers who overlooked verbal disagreement so that they might embrace peace."[41] Beccus believed that while there
was no problem with the Latin version of the creed—"since it is in conformity
with piety, with Orthodoxy, and with truth"—the East need not adopt the Western practice.[42] For while "there exists no difference in faith between those who
read the creed of the first council of Nicaea, those who recite the creed of the
second council of Constantinople, and those who revere this same creed such
as it is read by the Roman Church, with the addition, . . . we ourselves should
preserve without change the customs which have flourished in our Church
since its origins.[43]

Although Beccus wrote several works defending his unionist views, most
of which dealt specifically with the question of the procession, by far the most
influential was the *Epigraphae*, a *florilegia* designed to support his main argument: that the expressions ἐκ τοῦ Πατρὸς δι Yἱοῦ and ἐκ τοῦ Πατρὸς καὶ Yἱοῦ
were identical in meaning.[44] The *Epigraphae* contained over 123 quotations
from Cyril of Alexandria alone, with other key texts from Gregory of Nyssa,
Maximus the Confessor, and John of Damascus. All the quotations were specifically chosen not only to demonstrate the frequent use of the διὰ τοῦ Yἱοῦ
formula in Greek patristic thought, but also to illustrate the other ways that the

fathers spoke of the Spirit's eternal relationship to the Father (e.g.,"The Father is projector [προβολεύς], through the Word, of the manifesting Spirit").[45]

Despite all their efforts, administrative and theological, to overcome the hostility of the clergy and consummate the union, Michael VIII and Beccus never achieved their goal. In 1278 Pope Nicholas III sent legates to Constantinople, demanding the personal submission of every cleric in the empire and the adoption of the *filioque* throughout the East (since "unity of faith does not permit diversity in its confessors or in confession . . . especially in the chanting of the creed").[46] Although the emperor had dutifully tried to enforce the union (e.g., by imprisoning anti-unionist leaders), he thought the terms excessive and tried his best to ameliorate them. When the papal envoys were eventually given the signatures of the bishops who submitted themselves, Pachymeres reports, it was full of forged names from fictitious sees.[47] Michael's efforts, however, brought him few rewards; for his failure to secure the union he was excommunicated by Pope Martin IV as an alleged "supporter of heretics" and when he died in 1282 he was denied the usual imperial funerary rites for his betrayal of the Orthodox faith.[48] Within days Beccus was forced to resign by the new emperor, Andronicus II, who quickly repudiated the unionist policies of his father.[49] Both at his trial and later from his exile, Beccus continued to defend his views, attacking not only the strict Photian understanding of the procession, but also the theological innovations of his successor on the patriarchal throne, Gregory II.

Gregory II of Cyprus (1283–89)

According to Aristedes Papadakis, Gregory of Cyprus was not only a "highly gifted patriarch" whose contributions to the *filioque* debate have for too long remained unappreciated, but also "a major figure in Byzantine literature [who] like Photius belongs as much to the history of scholarship as to ecclesiastical history."[50] Born in Latin-occupied Cyprus, Gregory seems to have originally been a supporter of the emperor's unionist policy, although questions remain about his motives.[51] What is known is that by 1283, upon the death of Patriarch Joseph (who briefly occupied the throne following the deposition of Beccus), Gregory's anti-unionist credentials were sound enough that he was selected to replace him. Within days, Gregory began a campaign against the unionists, beginning with Beccus and his theology of the procession.

Gregory once again brought forward the traditional arguments against the *filioque*, arguing that Beccus had made the Son a cause within the godhead (a charge Beccus himself continued to deny) and had compromised the unique hypostatic identity of the Father, who alone was cause, source, and principle of both the Son and the Holy Spirit. The Latin doctrine, Gregory maintained, implied that the Father was incapable of spirating the Spirit without help, making him, in some way, imperfect. As Theodore Mouzalon (a student and staunch supporter of the Patriarch) argued at Blachernae "Is the Father such an imperfect cause that he needs the Son as joint helper and joint cause?"[52]

At the Synod of Blachernae in 1285, which was called to refute the "fabrications" of Beccus and his allies ("men who are filled with blasphemy, malice, and fall short of all ecclesiastical prudence"), Gregory dealt with the main argument of the unionists—the alleged equivalence between διά ("through") and ἐκ ("from").[53] Gregory recognized that many patristic texts spoke of the Spirit's procession διὰ τοῦ Υἱοῦ ("through the Son")' and that these passages were capable of being read in a pro-Latin manner. What was necessary, he argued, was for the orthodox fathers to receive an orthodox interpretation, since all texts, including the Scriptures, were capable of distortion by enemies of the true faith (e.g., the Arian use of John 14:28: "The Father is greater than I"). Beccus's error was to misread the patristic witness and (wrongly) interpret passages speaking of the Spirit's procession διὰ τοῦ Υἱοῦ as references to his hypostatic coming-into-being. This interpretation was foreign, novel, and heterodox (perhaps the three most damning criticisms one can make in the Byzantine tradition). However, Gregory was also aware that one could not relegate all references to the Spirit's coming "through the Son" to his economic manifestation.[54] To find a way out of this impasse, Gregory introduced an important terminological distinction (believed implicit in the works of the fathers) between:

1. Eternal existence: the hypostatic existence of the Spirit is from the Father *alone*, who is the θεογόνος θεότης.
2. Eternal manifestation: the Spirit's eternal illumination or manifestation (ἀΐδιον ἔκφανσιν) is *through* the Son, but NOT his hypostatic existence.
3. Temporal manifestation: in the economy of salvation, the Spirit can be said to proceed from the Father *and* the Son.[55]

According to Aristedes Papadakis, Gregory based this distinction on his belief that there is a "difference between existing [ὑπάρχει] and having existence [ὕπαρξιν ἔχειν] . . . [for while] the Spirit exists from or through the Son [this] did not mean, however, that it also had its existence from or through him."[56] Thus, *contra* Beccus, Gregory argued that "in the phrase 'from the Father through the Son,' the first 'from' denotes existence-procession, while the second 'through' denotes eternal manifestation and splendor, not existence-procession . . . 'through' then, denotes eternal manifestation in contradistinction to eternal procession."[57]

For Gregory, according to the mind of the Church, the Spirit obtained his hypostatic existence immediately from the Father alone, but it eternally shines forth and is manifested through the Son like the light of the sun through a ray.

In his *Tomus*, and then later in his *Apologia pro tomo suo* and *De Processione Spiritus sancti*, Gregory outlined his position:

> According to the common mind of the Church and the aforemen-
> tioned saints, the Father is the foundation and the source of the Son
> and Spirit, and the only source of divinity, and the only cause. If, in
> fact, it is also said by some of the saints that the Spirit proceeds
> [ἐκπορούεσθαι] through the Son, what is meant here is the eternal
> manifestation [ἔκφανσιν] of the Spirit by the Son, not the purely
> personal emanation [πρόοδον] into being of the Spirit, which has
> existence [ὕπαρξιν ἔχοντος] from the Father alone.[58]

This schema allowed Gregory to establish an eternal relationship between the Son and the Spirit without making the Son a cause (either immediate or proximate) of the Spirit's being. He was simultaneously able to uphold the monarchy of the Father (as sole source and cause of the divinity) while allowing for an orthodox reading of the διὰ τοῦ Υἱοῦ formula as used by the fathers, particularly those, like Maximus the Confessor and John of Damascus, who had been employed by Beccus to support the Latin teaching.

> The great Maximus, the holy Tarasius, and even the saintly John
> knew that the Holy Spirit proceeds from the Father, from whom it
> subsists with respect to both its hypostasis and cause of its being [τὸ
> Πνεῦμα τὸ ἅγιον ἐκ Πατρὸς ἐκπορευόμενον, ἐξ οὗπερ ὑφέστηκε,
> καὶ τὴν τῆς ὑποστάσεως, καὶ τὴν τοῦ εἶναι αἰτίαν]. And at the same
> time, they acknowledge that the Spirit flows forth, is manifested,
> shines forth, appears, and is made known through the Son
> ['Ηιδεσαν δὲ τοῦτο ἅμα καὶ διὰ τοῦ Υἱοῦ προϊὸν καὶ
> φανερούμενον καὶ ἐκλάμπον, καὶ πεφηνὸς, καὶ ἦκον, καὶ
> γνωριζόμενον].[59]

While Gregory's theology initially found acceptance at Blachernae, its perceived "novelty" was soon attacked by both Beccus and the anti-unionists. Beccus,
who thought Gregory's distinctions amounted to little more than a tacit acceptance of the unionist position, wondered "where this subtle and wonderful
theologian contrives to distinguish the origination of the Spirit through the
Son into shining forth from his origination simply into being? . . . What else
can the origination of the Spirit through the Son into eternal shining forth
be except the origination of his hypostasis from the Father through the Son?"[60]

The anti-unionists, including Gregory's former disciple Mark, agreed with
Beccus on this count, seeing in the theology of the *Tomos* a pale reflection of the
Latin teaching.[61] In 1289 Gregory was forced to resign in order to maintain the
peace, and his name was eventually omitted from the list of patriarchs remembered in the *Synodicon*. And yet the Synod of Blachernae, whose decisions were
never overturned, became (and remain) *the* official Orthodox response to the

Latin doctrine of the procession as defined at Lyons, and Gregory's teaching on the procession the *de facto* teaching of the Orthodox Church.

Maximus Planudes (d. 1305), Demetrius Cydones (d. 1397), and Barlaam of Calabria (d. 1350)

During the thirteenth and fourteenth centuries there occurred in Byzantium an intellectual rebirth—the so-called "Palaeologan Renaissance"—that saw a renewed interest in Western learning and the scholastic retrieval of Greek philosophy.[62] It was during this time that Augustine's *De Trinitate* first became available in Greek translation, thanks to the work of Maximus Planudes.[63] Planudes, however, rejected the bishop of Hippo's arguments in favor of the *filioque*, although Bessarion (quoting Demetrius Cydones) later claimed that this "unnatural behavior" from a "foster child and admirer" of Augustine was only "to escape prison and chains."[64] The translation itself was not without detractors, Latin polemicists claiming that the "venerable [ha!] monk passed over in silence and suppressed the procession of the Holy Spirit from the Son . . . thus operating as a forger and not a translator, telling a lie not only to mankind but even to God."[65] George Scholarius later criticized Planudes's translation, arguing that he had misrepresented Augustine in translating every instance of *procedere* with ἐκπορεύεσθαι, instead of recognizing that

> when *procedere* is applied to the Father alone it should be translated with ἐκπορεύεσθαι and when applied to the Son, or to the Father and the Son, with προϊέναι. . . . For the assemblage of our teachers proclaims aloud that the Spirit both is of the Son and goes forth [προϊέναι] from the Son . . . [and] Augustine speaks very well in agreeing with them in respect to this understanding . . . except if *procedere* is always translated with ἐκπορεύεσθαι. . . . Either [he] was inept in our theology and for this reason held to the teacher's single expression, or he had the Latins' understanding [of the question] and corrupted his translation.[66]

Among the others busying themselves translating Latin theological texts were the Cydones brothers, Demetrius and Prochorus (d. 1369).[67] Encouraged by the Emperor John Cantacuzenos (1347–54), who saw knowledge of Latin texts as an essential precondition for dialogue with the West, Demetrius Cydones translated the *Summa contra Gentiles* and parts of the *Summa Theologiae* of Thomas Aquinas. In the process, he became so enamored with the work of the great scholastic that he eventually entered into communion with Rome.[68] In the *Apology* for his conversion, Cydones bemoaned the fact that while the Byzantines continued to view Westerners as "oxen and asses [who] could not be credited as being capable of anything worthy of human beings [except] . . .

a dubious skill in trade and running taverns," it was the Latins who had achieved superiority in both philosophy and theology.[69] Concerning the *filioque* ("the weightiest and most debated problem which had divided our peoples and plunged the world into irreconcilable conflict") Cydones believed "that the Latins were far more thorough in the investigation of the subject" and that by "the sheer force of their logic" they had overcome the Byzantines, whose writings, he said, contained only "evil slander . . . anger, enormous tension, great bitterness, and enormous hatred."[70]

Because he was a staunch advocate for union and eventually entered into communion with Rome, Barlaam of Calabria is usually listed alongside the Cydones brothers among the so-called "Latin-minded." However, Barlaam had little sympathy for the syllogisms of scholastic theology and in 1333–34, while negotiating for the reunion of the churches with a delegation of French and English Dominicans, he wrote treatises against both the *filioque* and papal primacy from which later authors (such as Nilus Cabasilas and Doethius of Jerusalem) borrowed in their own anti-Latin writings.[71] Interestingly, among Barlaam's witnesses against the *filioque* was Augustine, whom he had come to know through the translations of Planudes. For Barlaam, the teaching that the Spirit proceeded κυρίως καὶ ἰδίως from the Father was based on Augustine's teaching that the Spirit "principally proceeded" (Planudes's translation: ἐκπορεύεται ἀρχοειδῶς) from him, thus affirming the Father's monarchy and denying the Son any causal role within the godhead.[72]

However, Barlaam's chief argument against the Western teaching came from his reading of Pseudo-Dionysius, and the belief that because all theological discourse was limited by the apophatic principle (i.e., our inability to know God's intra-trinitarian life), the Latins were wrong to claim that the *filioque* was demonstrably true.[73] It was arrogance to believe that one could apodictically prove the procession of the Holy Spirit from the Son. Since syllogistic reasoning offered no proof for or against the doctrine, Barlaam maintained that both Greeks and Latins should content themselves with the language of the creed (*without* the interpolation), leaving all talk about the Son's role in the procession to the realm of theological speculation. Once both sides agreed that the *filioque* was not a dogmatic stumbling block, the union of the Churches could take place. In 1339 Barlaam went to Avignon and proposed a plan for union along these lines.[74] He told Pope Benedict XII that the intellectuals of Byzantium would easily be won over by the logic of his position but that the only way to guarantee popular support was to convoke an ecumenical council in the East at which all the patriarchates would be represented. Otherwise, "when the scholars return home they will be able to do nothing with the people. Some men will arise who, either from jealousy or from vainglory and perhaps believing they act rightly, will teach exactly the opposite of what you have defined. They will say to the Greeks, 'Do not let yourselves be seduced by these men who have sold themselves for gold and are swelled up with pride.' "[75]

Barlaam's arguments against the *filioque*, based as they were on the unknowability of God, raised serious concerns on Mount Athos, where (according to John Meyendorff) Barlaam's theological agnosticism was thought to lead to a dangerous form of "dogmatic relativism."[76] Barlaam had also been critical of those monks on Athos who practiced ἡσυχία—a form of prayer that claimed to give the practitioner a direct experience of the divine. Barlaam's highly apophatic sensibilities led him to deride these hesychasts as ὀμφαλόψωχοι ("men with their souls in their navel") and to doubt their claim that God could be both known and experienced in prayer.

Gregory Palamas (1296–1359)

For Palamas,[77] Barlaam's critique of hesychasm touched the very heart of orthodox life and spirituality. While accepting the basic premise that God (in His essence) was unknowable, Gregory felt that the doctrine of θέωσις (divinization) demanded a real knowledge and experience of the Divine. We could (and did) know something about God's trinitarian life because God has revealed it to us in Christ and invited us to participate in it. He therefore rejected the dogmatic relativism implicit in Barlaam's writings, believing that "the Orthodox position [on the procession] . . . seemed perfectly demonstrable and it coincided, in his view, with the opinions expressed fifty years earlier by the Patriarch Gregory of Cyprus."[78]

According to Meyendorff's dating, Gregory Palamas's first work on the procession of the Holy Spirit (*Logoi Apodeiktikoi*) was written in 1336, several years before the advent of the hesychast controversy. The work contained the usual criticism that Western trinitarian teaching introduced two principles or causes into the godhead. Because procession was the property of a hypostasis and not the act of the divine nature, the attribution of procession to two distinct hypostases (Father and Son) logically forced one to admit two principles. The other alternative, just as dangerous for Palamas, was to allow a distinct hypostatic property of the Father (i.e., causality) to be given to the Son, therefore confusing their persons and making them, in the manner of Sabellius, the same hypostasis (ὁμουπόστατος).[79]

Palamas maintained that the Father alone is principle within the godhead, even if, in other contexts, the Son could also be described as the principle through which creation takes place (e.g., Col. 1:16).[80] This is so because for Palamas there is a clear difference between the "fatherly principle" (πατρικὴ ἀρχὴ) that governs intra-trinitarian relations and the "triadic principle" (τριαδικὴ ἀρχὴ) that applied when all three persons act in concert (e.g., in the act of creation).[81] For Palamas, the unity of the Trinity is founded upon the person of the Father because (paraphrasing Nazianzus in *Oration* 42) "God is one not only because there is a single nature, but also because what is from his person [i.e., the Father] returns to him as cause and sole principle" (ἀλλ' ὅτι καὶ εἰς ἓν πρόσωπον τὴν ἀναφορὰν ἔχει τὰ ἐξ αὐτοῦ, καὶ εἰς ἓν αἴτιον καὶ μίαν ἀρχὴν τὰ ἐξ ἀρχῆς ἀναφέρεται).[82] The Latins, in positing procession as an act of the divine essence, not only destroyed the monarchical principle upon which the unity of the Trinity was established, but made the Holy Spirit, who is con-substantial with the Father and Son, responsible for his own being. For these reasons Palamas vehemently maintained that the Latin teaching on the *filioque* was in error.

However, Palamas too recognized that many of the fathers (including Cyril of Alexandria and Maximus) had spoken about the Spirit's procession "through the Son" and even "from the Son." It was here that Palamas made use of the distinction between the divine *essence* (which was unknowable) and God's uncreated *energies* (which can be experienced in the economy of salvation) in order to provide an orthodox reading of these texts.[83] Palamas argued that the fathers' use of "procession through/from the Son" applied not to the Spirit's hypostatic existence, which came forth from the Father alone, but rather to his energetic procession. In a passage examining Maximus's *Quaestiones ad Tha-lassium* Palamas wrote:

> whenever you hear him say that the Holy Spirit proceeds from both,
> because it comes from the Father essentially through the Son,
> understand reverently that he is teaching that the natural powers
> and energies of God are poured forth [Ὅταν οὖν ἀκούσῃς αὐτὸν ἐξ
> ἀμφοῖν, ὡς ἐκ πατρὸς οὐσιωδῶς δὶ υἱοῦ προχεόμενον τὸ πνεῦμα τὸ
> ἅγιον λέγοντα, τὴν τῶν φυσικῶν τούτων δυνάμεών τε καὶ
> ἐνεργειῶν τοῦ Θεοῦ μετάδοσιν] but not the Spirit's divine
> hypostasis.[84]

This energetic procession of the Holy Spirit from the Father through the Son is an eternal act, which is then manifested and experienced by us in time when the Father and Son will it. This is the meaning of such biblical texts as John 20:22, where Jesus poured forth the energies of the Spirit upon the apos-tles and demonstrated the common will of the Father and the Son in giving the Spirit to those who are worthy.

Palamas's trinitarian theology even found a place for Augustine's "love" analogy, which had described the Spirit as the bond of love between Father and Son.[85] Unlike Augustine, however, Palamas applied this analogy not to the hypostasis of the Spirit, but rather to "common energy which is the love of the Triune God."[86] It was this same love, eternally coming forth from the Father through the Son, which drew the believer closer to the Trinity in communion and allowed him or her an experience of the uncreated energies in the depths of ἡσυχία. This is why one could legitimately speak of the Spirit being eter-nally from Christ (ἐξ αὐτοῦ) as long as this was properly applied to the uncre-ated energies. Elsewhere he summarized his argument:

Thus the Holy Spirit is of Christ, as of God, both in essence and in energy. According to essence and hypostasis he is of him, but not from him; according to energy, he is both of him and from him [Οὕτω καὶ τὸ πνεῦμα τὸ ἅγιον τοῦ Χριστοῦ ἐστιν ὡς Θεοῦ καὶ κατ' οὐσίαν καὶ κατ' ἐνέργειαν. Ἀλλὰ κατὰ μὲν τὴν οὐσίαν καὶ τὴν ὑπόστασιν αὐτου ἐστιν, ἀλλ' οὐκ ἐξ αὐτοῦ, κατὰ δὲ τὴν ἐνέργειαν καὶ αὐτοῦ ἐστιν καὶ ἐξ αὐτοῦ].[87]

While the Latin doctrine remained heterodox, there was thus a sense in which the *filioque* could be interpreted in an orthodox manner and not simply in reference to the economy. Palamas thus offered the Byzantines a constructive alternative to the prevailing unionist and conservative tendencies of his contemporaries, keeping alive the *via media* established by Maximus the Confessor and Gregory of Cyprus. However, while Gregory's theology was accepted by no fewer than three local councils (often referred to as the Palamite councils of 1341, 1347, and 1351), it remained controversial enough that at Ferrara-Florence its introduction was forbidden by the emperor.[88]

Nilus Cabasilas (1298–1363)

Nilus Cabasilas, like his student Demetrius Cydones, had been a great admirer of Thomas Aquinas and was familiar with (and originally sympathetic to) the Western arguments in favor of the *filioque*.[89] Yet Cabasilas later broke with the unionists and wrote several treatises against the Latins, including a point-by-point refutation of fifteen Thomistic syllogisms used to support the *filioque*.[90] In this he borrowed heavily from the anti-Latin tracts of Barlaam the Calabrian, rejecting the scholastic syllogisms that claimed to prove from reason truths that were explicitly denied by both Scripture and patristic tradition. Cabasilas even attacked Palamas's use of Augustine's love analogy, despite having succeeded Gregory as Bishop of Thessalonica, believing it to subordinate the Spirit to the Father-Son dyad.

In his *De processione Spiritus Sancti* Cabasilas later assembled patristic evidence against the *filioque*, using Maximus the Confessor's *Letter to Marinus* as a prooftext against the Western teaching on the procession.[91] Cabasilas conceded the fact that during the seventh century East and West were of one mind on the matter of the Spirit's procession. As the *Letter to Marinus* attested, the Romans once held the "orthodox" view, acknowledging "that the Father is the cause of the Son and the Holy Spirit, one by generation, the other by procession, but that the Son is not the cause of the Spirit. . . . Moreover, if formerly some heard the Roman fathers say that the Spirit proceeds also from the Son, one must not believe that the Son is the cause, but rather believe that they are expressing his flowing forth through the Son [μὴ τὸν Υἱὸν ἡγεῖσθαι αἰτίαν, ἀλλὰ τὸ λεγόμενον βούλεσθαι τὸ δι' αὐτοῦ τοῦ Υἱοῦ προϊέναι]."[92]

The fact that the Latins currently maintained that the Son *was* a cause of the Spirit clearly demonstrated for Cabasilas how far they had strayed from the patristic teaching. Beccus and the unionists were thus wrong to claim that Photius caused the current schism, since it was the Latins who had deviated from the patristic faith, and now, to protect themselves, cast aspersions on the authenticity of the *Letter to Marinus*.

> But it is completely ridiculous for the Latins to be at war against
> themselves, sometimes not being ashamed to bring it forth against
> us and declaring that this letter of the divine Maximus is genuine . . .
> and other times, when we defend ourselves from this letter in a way
> that seems best to us, they maintain the opposite, ashamed to agree
> with their earlier position.[93]

Cabasilas believed that denying the *Letter*'s authenticity was easier for the Latins than reconciling its teaching with current Western belief and practice. For if the Latins affirmed both the Father and Son as cause of the Spirit, they could not help but recognize that, contrary to Maximus's teaching, they introduced two principles (Father and Son) into the godhead.[94] For his part, Cabasilas had no doubts about the authenticity of the *Letter*, "preserving the ancient constructions and same style as the other writings of the divine Maximus, his stay in Rome, and his association with Marinus, as well as his just reproof against our Church."[95] It was, both for Cabasilas and then for the anti-unionists at Ferrara-Florence, the perfect prooftext for the position of Photius.

The Road to Ferrara-Florence

Sylvester Syropoulus actually begins his account of the Council of Ferrara-Florence during the reign of Emperor Manuel II Palaeologus (1391–1425), almost two decades before the Byzantines' arrival in Italy.[96] Manuel, like many of his predecessors, was keenly aware both of the need for Western aid against the growing Turkish threat to Constantinople and of the price for such assistance—willingness to negotiate religious union with Rome.[97] According to the Byzantine historian Sphrantzes, Manuel had told his son John how best to deal with the growing Turkish threat:

> Our last resource against the Turks is their fear of our union with the
> Latins. . . . As often as you are threatened by the miscreants, present
> this danger before their eyes. Propose a council; consult on the
> means; but ever delay and avoid the convocation of the assembly. . . .
> The Latins are proud; the Greeks are obstinate; neither party will
> recede or retract; and the attempts at perfect union will confirm the
> schism and alienate the churches.[98]

However, negotiation with the Latin Church was difficult given the confused ecclesiastical situation in the West after the election of two popes in 1378 (Urban VI and Clement VII), and then a third (Alexander V) after the Council of Pisa in 1409. When the Great Western Schism finally ended in November 1417 with the election of Pope Martin V, the Byzantine representatives were already in Rome prepared to negotiate on the emperor's behalf. By 1420 both parties had agreed to hold a council in Constantinople, although in 1422 the advancing Turkish armies made this meeting impossible. Pope Martin then suggested that the Byzantines should travel to Italy and expressed his willingness to provide transport for the delegation.[99] The patriarch chafed at the idea, claiming that this would make the Greeks his "hireling slaves."[100] However, before any agreement could be reached, Pope Martin died, leaving all hopes for reunion in the hands of his successor, Eugene IV.

Pope Eugene IV (1431–47) had his own reasons for achieving union with the East. Aside from a genuine desire to end the schism, Eugene knew that a successful reunion council under his presidency would consolidate his position over both the conciliarists and all those (Greek and Latin) who questioned the universal jurisdiction of the Bishop of Rome.[101] However, Eugene's ongoing struggle with the Council of Basel complicated his task, as the Byzantines weighed separate offers from both the pope and the conciliarists, each hoping to strengthen their own position through a union with the East.[102] When the papal and conciliarist fleets docked in Constantinople hoping to escort the Greeks to the proposed reunion council, only the emperor's personal intervention prevented them from firing upon one another. Finally, after much discussion, the emperor and the patriarch left with Eugene's representatives, although the Greeks did not exclude the possibility of future contact with the fathers at Basel.[103]

Before leaving with the papal envoys in November 1437, the Byzantines had certain preparations to make for the council. The first was to ensure its ecumenicity, and doing this meant securing the participation of the other patriarchal sees (Alexandria, Antioch, and Jerusalem) and the representatives of the various Slavic churches. Although none of the patriarchs could attend because of the Turkish occupation, they did appoint proxies to act in their stead: Anthony of Heraclea and Mark Eugenicus for Alexandria, Joasaph of Ephesus and Gregory (the emperor's confessor) for Antioch, and Dionysius of Sardis and Isidore for Jerusalem.[104] Isidore was soon made Archbishop of Kiev, while Dionysius and Bessarion were named Metropolitans.

With the delegation set, the theological preparation for the council began in earnest. The most important question to be decided was the focus of the upcoming conciliar debate: should the Greeks first discuss the legitimacy of the addition or the theology behind the dogma? The majority, led by Mark Eugenicus, maintained that the first subject discussed must be the interpolation, since it was the primary cause of the schism.[105] This position was generally accepted, although

Scholarius and Eugenicus were assigned the task of studying the works of Nilus Cabasilas in preparation for the dogmatic discussions, should they become necessary.[106]

As they left Constantinople, both Patriarch Joseph II and the emperor were optimistic that a face-to-face to meeting with the pope would end the sad division of the churches and bring needed military aid to their besieged city. The elderly patriarch was particularly keen to meet the pope, which is why, despite the obvious risks to his health, he boarded the ship for a prolonged journey to the West. Many of the delegates were equally optimistic, believing that the Latin case would quickly collapse under the weight of the patristic evidence, and convinced that the council itself would last only a few short weeks. Events, however, would prove that their collective optimism was completely unjustified.

8

The Council of
Ferrara-Florence (1438–39)

The Ethos of the Council

Christian East and West were about to come together in council to discuss the restoration of full ecclesial communion, and yet the reality was that after centuries of estrangement the two halves of Christendom knew very little about the theological ethos of the other and neither side (with few exceptions) was particularly eager to change the situation.[1] Almost immediately after the Byzantines' arrival in Italy, the long-simmering cultural and ecclesiastical differences that had separated the two halves of Christendom manifested themselves, quickly dispelling any hopes that either side might have had for a speedy reconciliation.[2]

The Byzantines were welcomed to Italy by the Venetians with lavishly prepared banquets, their hosts apparently unaware that the Greeks had already started their pre-Lenten fast.[3] While the Greeks were awed by the impressive display of Venetian pomp and wealth, they could not help but notice that many of the icons and artifacts on display at St. Mark's had been "appropriated" from Hagia Sophia during the Fourth Crusade.[4] The patriarch offended many of his Venetian hosts by referring to Eugene as his "brother," and he was genuinely shocked when, in a not-so-fraternal gesture, the papal envoys informed him that he was expected to conform to the Latin custom of kissing the pope's foot.[5] Joseph immediately rejected the proposal and threatened to return immediately to Constantinople if the protocol was not changed.

Whence has the pope this right? Which synod gave it to him? Show me from what source he derives this privilege and where it is written? . . . This is an innovation and I will not follow it. . . . If the pope wants a brotherly embrace in accordance with ancient ecclesiastical custom, I will be happy to embrace him, but if he refuses, I will abandon everything and return to Constantinople.[6]

While Eugene consented to dispense with the custom as long as the welcoming ceremony was done privately, other matters of protocol soon caused consternation among the Greeks. Adding to the atmosphere of distrust that had begun to take shape, the Bishop of Ferrara refused permission for the Greek clergy to use his churches for the divine liturgy.[7] To put it simply, Greeks and Latins no longer recognized each other as members of the same church.[8] A poignant reminder of this reality is found in the words of a Greek prelate at the Council:

When I enter a Latin church, I do not revere any of the [images of the] saints that are there because I do not recognize them. At the most I may recognize Christ, but I do not revere him either since I do not know in what terms he is inscribed. So I make the sign of the cross and I revere the sign that I have made myself and not anything that I see there.[9]

Ferrara and the Addition

After the formal opening of the council on April 9, 1438, the emperor pushed for a four-month delay since he was still hoping for representatives from the Western powers to make their way to Ferrara. While they waited, the pope requested that informal discussions take place between small delegations chosen from each side.[10] By May a committee of ten delegates from each side (or sixteen, if the *Acta latina* are to be believed) was appointed to discuss the contested issues. Among the Greek delegates were Bessarion of Nicea and Mark Eugenicus of Ephesus, while the Latins were represented by Cardinal Julian Cesarini, Andrew of Rhodes, and John of Torquemada.

Bessarion of Nicea (1403–72), student of the great humanist and Platonist George Gemistus (Pletho), was generally considered among the best orators and most learned of the Byzantine delegates.[11] While some have suggested that he arrived in Italy predisposed toward the union,[12] Syropoulus and the other anti-unionists attributed Bessarion's change of heart to jealousy, ambition, or desire for reward (since he, like Isidore, was later named a cardinal of the Roman Church).[13] Joseph Gill has proposed the most credible explanation— that "the more the Metropolitan of Nicea studied the question of the procession of the Holy Spirit, the deeper was his understanding of the Latin doctrine and the firmer his conviction of its orthodoxy."[14]

Unpersuaded by the Latin case, and leader of the anti-unionists at the council, was Bessarion's counterpart, Mark Eugenicus of Ephesus (1392–1445).[15] Although it is often maintained that Mark was almost instinctually anti-Latin, the evidence suggests that he came to Ferrara-Florence with a genuine hope of reestablishing ecclesial communion, his only condition being the removal of the *filioque* from the creed. As Mark stated in his opening address to Pope Eugene:

> this Symbol, this noble heritage of our Fathers, we demand back
> from you. Restore it then as you received it. . . . The addition of a
> word seems to you a small matter and of no great consequence. So
> then to remove it would cost you nothing; indeed it would be of the
> greatest profit, for it would bind together all Christians. . . . It [the
> *filioque*] was added in the exercise of mercy; in the exercise of mercy
> remove it again so that you may receive to your bosoms brethren torn
> apart who value fraternal love so highly.[16]

When it became apparent that the Latins had no intention of altering their creed, Mark increasingly became an outright opponent to union with the West. He claimed that the Latins were both schismatics and heretics who used corrupted and spurious texts to prove their case.[17] For this reason he alone among the Greek delegates refused to sign the decree of union, allegedly prompting Pope Eugene to comment, "Then we accomplished nothing" (Λοιπὸν ἐποιήσαμεν οὐδέν).[18]

The formal debate on the liceity of the addition demonstrated how difficult the achievement of union was going to be. The Greek case was primarily based on their reading of Canon 7 of Ephesus (431), a prohibition against any alterations or additions to the creed, that applied not only to the pope but even to an ecumenical council. Bessarion told the pope:

> We wish your Reverence to know that we withhold this permission
> from every Church and synod even oecumenical and not from the
> Roman Church alone, since no matter how great is the Roman
> Church, it is notwithstanding less than an Oecumenical Synod and
> the universal Church: and we withhold it from the whole Church,
> much more so then from the Roman Church do we withhold it. But
> we withhold it not as by ourselves, but we consider that this has been
> forbidden by the decrees of the Fathers.[19]

The Latins countered with the argument (based in large measure on Aristotle's *De generatione et corruptione*) that the *filioque* was not an addition but rather a clarification. According to Andrew of Rhodes: "[A]n exposition or development is not an addition; . . . the *filioque* is a development being contained in *ex Patre*—therefore it is not an addition. . . . Every addition is from without . . . but a development or clarification is not from without—therefore it is not an addition."[20]

The Latins maintained that the prohibitions of Ephesus had only meant to exclude heterodox teaching, and so as long as the orthodoxy of the *filioque* was established there was no reason to protest its inclusion. Therefore Cesarini argued "that if you can show that the Holy Spirit does not proceed also from the Son, I will say that in no way was it permitted for the Roman Church to add it to the symbol. If you cannot do this, but instead the contrary is demonstrated, then I am persuaded that you will make no controversy about it."[21]

The Latins did try to introduce patristic evidence testifying to the liceity of the addition, but this proved counterproductive. Cardinal Cesarini produced an allegedly ancient codex containing the acts of the seventh council, but with the phrase *et ex Filio* apparently added to the creed.[22] The Greeks knew that this text had been interpolated, and it was Pletho who happily pointed out this fact to the Latins.

> If the testimonies of your copy and your historian were just, or at
> least had been known long ago to the Church of Rome, then no
> doubt your Thomas Aquinas and divines preceding would not have
> made use of so many other arguments to prove the validity of the
> addition. Instead of this, they might have simply referred to the
> addition made to the creed by the seventh ecumenical council. But
> your divines are silent about this.[23]

It was also at this point, during the sixth session, that Andrew of Rhodes tried to introduce the testimony of Maximus the Confessor's *Letter to Marinus*.[24] Although the Greeks disputed both Andrew's translation and his contention that it attested to the early nature of the addition, now that the Latins had introduced Maximus's *Letter* (a text they had formerly rejected), the Byzantines realized that a "window of opportunity" had opened and that it could (and should) be exploited.[25]

According to Syropoulus, it was immediately after Andrew's speech that a private conference took place in the sacristy of St. Francis at which the Greeks formally proposed the *Letter to Marinus* as a means to reunion. "If this letter is accepted gladly on your part," the Byzantines told the Romans, "the union will happily proceed."[26] The rest of the Latin delegates, unwilling at this point to compromise or surrender, were forced to publicly repudiate Andrew's use and interpretation of Maximus's text. According to the *Memoirs*, the Latins claimed, "We chided the Bishop of Rhodes on this account, that contrary to our will he has produced it. We do not admit it, because it is not found to be complete."[27] While Andrew's introduction of the *Letter to Marinus* might have proved his point vis-à-vis the ancient nature of the addition, his co-religionists were aware that Maximus's testimony cut both ways. Even if their doubts about the *Letter*'s authenticity were genuine, theologically the position of Maximus was too far removed from the fifteenth-century Western understanding to serve as the starting point for negotiation.

Florence and the Theology of the Procession

Debate on the orthodoxy of the *filioque* did not begin until March 2, 1438 (the second session at Florence),[28] after the council had left Ferrara because of an outbreak of plague.[29] After sixteen months in the West the Greeks were tired, homesick, and wearied by the prolonged debates that had marked the discussions both on purgatory and on the addition to the creed.[30] Frustrated by the seemingly endless public sessions, they began to express their desire to return home.[31]

John of Montenero began the presentation of the Latin case with an attempt to clarify the terms of the debate. He asked the Byzantines to explain the meaning of the Greek word ἐκπόρευσις since the Vulgate of Jerome had applied the Latin *processio/procedere* both to the Holy Spirit and to the Son.[32] Mark then differentiated between the Spirit's "going forth" (πρόοδος) and his ἐκπόρευσις, a term used exclusively to express the hypostatic coming-to-be of the Spirit, and distinguished in Greek theology from the generation (γέννησις) of the Son. As proof of his position Mark cited the *De Fide orthodoxa* of John of Damascus, where John made the distinction between the Spirit's manner of existence (τρόπος τῆς ὑπάρξεως) and the generation of the Son, a difference whose nature "is beyond understanding."[33]

Montenero, who understood *processio/procedere* more generically, equated the idea of procession with the notion of "receiving existence" (λαμβάνει τὸ εἶναι), which permitted him to maintain that "the Holy Spirit's receiving being from the Father is the same as proceeding from him. . . .. but it is said that the Spirit receives being from the Son. . . . From whom he receives being, he also proceeds. Therefore, he proceeds also from the Son."[34]

To prove his point Montenero quoted the *Ancoratus* of Epiphanius, translated by Ambrogio Traversari, to support this conclusion, maintaining that the expressions "to be from" (εἰμί παρὰ) and "receiving" (λαμβάνει) also meant "receiving existence" (λαμβάνει τὸ εἶναι) and thus also "procession" (ἐκπόρευσις).[35] Mark Eugenicus did not accept Montenero's logic, claiming that "the blessed Epiphanius did not say that the Holy Spirit receives being from the Son, but simply that he receives. . . . [Rather] he intends something different than "to proceed" from [his use of] λαμβάνειν—ἐκπορεύεσθαι displays the existence of the Holy Spirit from the Father, while λαμβάνειν displays the agreement and concord of the Holy Spirit in regard to the Father and the Son according to which the Holy Spirit announces to the disciples the things that are necessary to teach them, receiving the subject matter from the Son himself."[36]

Mark then asked the Latins the question Nicetas of Nicodemia had posed to Anselm of Havelberg centuries earlier: when they said the Holy Spirit had his being (τὸ εἶναι) from the Father and the Son, did they mean that he came from the individual hypostases (ἐκ τῆς ὑποστάσεως) or from the substance common to both.[37] Montenero explained:

> [We] speak in such a way that the Spirit is from one principle because the procession of the Holy Spirit is in common from the Father and is in the Son. . . . as many times as we say "to be from the Father," we say from his hypostasis; and as often [as we say] "from the Son," we mean from his hypostasis. Since the substance of the Father and the Son is the same, and he comes out of the Father, he also comes out of the Son, the Holy Spirit comes out as from one.[38]

Mark maintained that the fathers had always taught procession to be a hypostatic property of the Father alone,[39] while Montenero claimed that the Greek fathers did speak of the Spirit's coming forth (i.e., procession) from the hypostasis of the Son.[40] Mark reiterated that this was not the Byzantine understanding, which differentiated the eternal procession of the Spirit from the Father alone and his temporal manifestation through or from the Son. According to Mark: "On the one hand, the Spirit proceeds from the Father, that is, has existence [from him] but on the other hand he is given from the Son and is received by those who believe in him."[41] What the Latins had done, he argued, was fail to make the necessary distinction between the eternal and temporal missions, accounting for their misreading of the patristic witness.

The second session, on March 5, renewed the debate over the meaning of Basil of Caesarea's *Adversus Eunomium*. Mark continued to maintain that the phrase "the Spirit is from the Father himself and not from elsewhere" must be seen as an affirmation that the Spirit did not come forth from another hypostasis, but from the Father alone.[42] If the Latins claimed that the Spirit came forth from the substance of the Father (ἐκ τῆς φύσεως αὐτοῦ), they must then accept that he comes from the divine substance shared also by the consubstantial Son. "Therefore you are saying that the substance of the Father and of the Son [and not their individual hypostases] is the cause of the Holy Spirit."[43] John denied that this was the Latin view, explaining how "the substance [itself] does not generate but, and I have said this many times and I say it again, whenever we hear that the Spirit [is] from the substance of the Father, we understand him as from the one underlying person, and from the Son as the underlying person."[44]

Eugenicus thought this idea illogical and concluded that for the Latins there must be two substances within the godhead, the substance that causes (i.e., the common nature of the Father and Son) and that which is caused (i.e., the Holy Spirit).[45] He asked the Latins "if it is true to say that the Holy Spirit comes forth hypostatically from the common substance of the three Persons?"[46] Even Bessarion thought the Latin position confused and he asked them how they understood the phrase "[the] substance of Father, Son, and Holy Spirit."[47] Frustrated by the lack of progress, Cardinal Cesarini simply ended the session before the terms of the debate could be clarified.

The next session (March 7) and the three that followed (March 10, 11, and 14) were concerned almost exclusively with the authenticity and meaning of the third book of Basil's *Adversus Eunomium*. Montenero had wanted to examine this book during the previous session only to have Mark Eugenicus demand that the debate over the meaning of "substance" be concluded first.[48] Montenero kept insisting that since the work of the fathers and the ancient councils was accepted by both Greeks and Latins as normative, it would be more productive (and less time-consuming) to return to the patristic witness. Although in favor of continuing the debate from the third session, Eugenicus reluctantly assented.[49]

During the second session significant textual variations had been discovered in the codices of Basils' *Adversus Eunomium*. The differences, reconstructed by Joseph Gill, are seen below:[50]

Latin version	*Greek version*
Even if the Spirit is third in dignity and order, why need he also be third in nature? For that he is second to the Son, having his being from him and receiving from him and announcing to us and being completely dependent upon him, pious tradition recounts; but that his nature is third we are not taught by the saints nor can we conclude logically from what has been said.	Even if the Holy Spirit is third in dignity and order, why need he also be third in nature? For that he is second pious tradition perhaps recounts; but that his nature is third we are not taught by the saints nor can we conclude from what has been said
so that, although the Holy Spirit is behind the Son in order and dignity, all the same he would not be considered as of another nature,	that, although he is subordinated to the Son, let us make this supposition, still it does not follow that he is of another nature
so, namely although the Holy Spirit is below in dignity and order, for we have received	so, therefore, although the Holy Spirit is below in dignity and order, as they say, for we have received and hold

Eugenicus admitted that four or five codices in Constantinople had the Latin reading but that there were a thousand others, including the most ancient, that did not.[51] He speculated that Montenero's codex had probably been interpolated by some later supporter of the Latin doctrine.[52] The Latin text, written on parchment rather than paper and obviously ancient, had recently been brought from Constantinople by Nicholas of Cusa and showed no signs of having been amended.[53] Montenero, in an attempt to demonstrate that Mark's text had been altered, quoted St. Cyril of Alexandria's warning about the interpolation and corruption of texts in the Eastern Church.[54] Mark responded that the corruption of texts was not a uniquely Eastern phenomenon, citing the case of Pope Zosimus to prove his point.[55]

Debate then turned to the meaning of the text in the context of Eunomius's teaching and Basil's other writings. Mark insisted that Basil was making a concession for the sake of argument: even if one were to admit Eunomius's premise that the Holy Spirit is third in dignity and order (which Basil did not), one need not admit the conclusion that he is third in nature.[56] Montenero held that Basil, like Eunomius, did admit that the Spirit was third both in order and in dignity, but that he challenged Eunomius's conclusion that he was also third in nature.[57] According to the Latin interpretation, the Son was second in order and dignity and the Holy Spirit third—this order being also the order of their procession. The Son comes after the Father because the Father is the cause of the Son; likewise the Holy Spirit comes third because he is caused by the Father and the Son and thus proceeds from both. "Therefore if there is an order of nature of the Holy Spirit in relation to the Son, it must follow that the Spirit has his being and receives nature from the Son."[58]

In the exchange that followed, Mark challenged John to show where Basil or any of the saints held the opinion that the Spirit was third in order and dignity. This, he suggested, was the teaching of the Pneumatomachoi against which the fathers had struggled, not the teaching of the Church. For Eugenicus, Basil taught that the Spirit "depends" upon the Son only in the sense that he is made known "through him and with him"—not because he is caused by him.[59] Following the example of Photius, references to the Spirit being "through the Son" were applied only to the economic manifestation of the Spirit's gifts, not to the Spirit's hypostatic coming-to-be.

It was at this point that Montenero asked whether the gifts of the Spirit were created or uncreated, that is, whether we receive the Spirit himself or something else.[60] Here Mark might naturally have explained the position of Gregory Palamas on the distinction between God's essence and the uncreated energies, but he was prevented from doing so by a direct command from the emperor.[61] Eugenicus, in obedience to the imperial will, simply refused to answer Montenero's question and remained silent.[62] Although they continued to press Mark for an answer, it was the emperor himself who finally intervened, twice reminding the Latins that the created/uncreated distinction was both off topic and closed to discussion. Robert Haddad has quite accurately noted the opportunity that was missed:

> Palamas's teaching at least held out hope of resolving the question
> that had bedeviled relations between the two Churches since the
> ninth century . . . [and yet it was] intentionally avoided at the Council
> of Ferrara-Florence. Theologically, this deliberate evasion of Palamite
> teaching may have represented the point of no return.[63]

By the sixth session, on March 17, Eugenicus and the Greeks (including the emperor) had become frustrated over the lack of progress and decided to abandon the question-and-answer format in favor of a complete explication of their position. When the Latins objected, Eugenicus complained that five days had been wasted debating a few dubious or corrupted texts and that the time had come to demonstrate, from the authentic and undisputed works of the fathers, the truth of the Greek position.[64] After some grumbling, the Latins reluctantly consented.

Beginning with the Scriptures, especially John 15:26, Mark explained how Christ himself taught procession from the Father alone, "for when he says 'who proceeds from the Father' he shows the cause of the Spirit from which he takes his existence. . . . He undoubtedly would have said 'who proceeds from us' if he had avowed the procession of the Holy Spirit from himself also."[65] St. Paul agreed when he called the Holy Spirit "the Spirit which is of God" (1 Cor. 2:12), the term "God" used here to refer exclusively to the Father ("for otherwise he would not have said, 'and appearing to men through the Son'").[66] Mark then cited both Dionysius and Athanasius, who had both called the Father "the one source of the pre-essential godhead . . . [and] the only source of the Divinity."[67] The first and second ecumenical councils had also taught that the Spirit proceeds from the Father, "for if the Council had admitted the Spirit's procession from the Father and the Son, why then did it not in speaking of the Father and Son say, 'who proceeds from the Father and the Son'?"[68] Gregory Nazianzus had spoken clearly enough when he said: "Everything the Father has belongs to the Son with the exception of causality."[69] The council of Ephesus had approved certain portions of the Nestorian creed presented by the priest Charisius, including the statement that "the Holy Spirit is not the Son, neither does he take his existence through the Son."[70] Cyril of Alexandria clearly rejected the accusation, once thrown at him by Theodoret, that he taught that "the Spirit receives his existence from the Son or through the Son" (ἐξ Υἱοῦ ἢ δι Υἱοῦ τὴν ὕπαρξιν ἔχον).[71] Upon receipt of this denial, Theodoret had even confirmed the orthodoxy of Cyril's trinitarian theology, since the Church had always taught that "the Holy Spirit does not receive existence from or through the Son, but proceeds from the Father and is proper to the Son."[72] Mark concluded his presentation with the hope that, now that the unadulterated teaching of the fathers had been made clear, his Latin counterparts would neither "recite nor receive in the Church anything beyond what they have said."[73]

Montenero concluded the session by trying to assuage any fears the Byzantines might have had about the Latin teaching on causality within the godhead:

> We follow the apostolic see and affirm one cause of the Son and the Spirit, the Father. . . . it does not confess two principles or two causes but one principle and one cause. We anathematize all those who assert two principles or two causes.[74]

This affirmation, more than the six sessions of debate that preceded it, made a deep impression on the Greeks.[75] The emperor, desirous of consummating the union, was ready to believe that if the Latins confessed the Father as the μία αἰτία, then they would have no hesitation in accepting the testimony of Maximus as a basis for reunion, regardless of their doubts about the text's authenticity. Thus at a meeting of the Greek delegation immediately following Montenero's presentation, he again put forward the *Letter to Marinus* as a reunion formula. Both the *Acta graeca* and the *Memoirs* are clear that this was an imperial initiative, although they diverge on its reception among the Greeks. The *Acta* describe how, after the reading of the *Letter*, the delegation expressed their desire that the text immediately be brought to the pope, nothing more being required for union than his acceptance of Maximus's testimony. "And everyone together said, 'If the Latins are persuaded by this epistle, then nothing else is required for us to unite with them.' Therefore the synod designated the emperor to go to the pope and ask if he received the epistle and confession of St. Maximus."[76]

However, the *Memoirs*—in a more likely scenario, given the tension that would characterize intra-Byzantine debates for the remainder of the council—present the reintroduction of the *Letter* as a cause of division among the Greeks. According to Syropoulus, once the elderly Patriarch absented himself from the room, the emperor polled the remaining delegates. He asked them, "If we should discover that the Latins gladly accept whatever Holy Maximus relates in his *Letter to Marinus* on the subject of the Holy Spirit, does it not seem good to you that we should unite through it?"[77]

Bessarion and Isidore of Kiev quickly voted in the affirmative, although they were opposed by Mark of Ephesus and Anthony of Heraclea, who claimed that it would mean little if the Latins accepted the testimony of Maximus yet twisted his words in such a way that they contradicted the orthodox position. Eugenicus's objections are recorded by Syropoulus: "How can we unite with them when they accept, in word alone, the statement of Holy Maximus while among themselves they opine the opposite, even proclaiming it openly in their churches! No, they must first confess our teaching—clearly and without ambiguity. Only in this way will we consummate the union with them."[78]

The emperor told Eugenicus that he was asking the impossible—monitoring not only what the Latins confessed in their churches, but also the contents of their hearts.[79] Mark responded that if there were substantive differences in how the two sides thought about the faith, then reunion was indeed impossible.[80] Both Mark and Anthony continued to argue against a union based solely on the text of Maximus unless the Latins were willing to make the necessary clarifications. The emperor, supported by the majority (who voted with Bessarion), thus brought the *Letter to Marinus* to the pope as a means to reunion.

The pope, however, insisted that it was not yet possible to settle the issue, since the Latins had not yet been given the opportunity to respond to Mark's presentation. John of Montenero, like Mark of Ephesus (who was conspicuously absent during these sessions), began his address on March 21 with the

Scriptures.[81] Countering the historical Byzantine criticism that the Latin reading of the Bible confused the Spirit's temporal mission with his eternal procession, Montenero maintained that "temporal mission necessarily presupposes
origin from a person . . . and that this is according to reason, founded on the
text of Scripture and many testimonies of the holy doctors, both Greek and
Latin."[82] Nevertheless Rome affirmed that the Father is still the "first principle
and source of all divinity" since Augustine was clear that the Spirit still "proceeds principally" from him. Yet the Latins recognized that this spirative power
is received by the consubstantial Son, who, with the Father, is the one cause and
principle of the Spirit's being.

The Montenero then mustered the witness of the Latin fathers, especially those
whose orthodoxy was well established in the East (e.g. Leo, Hilary, Jerome,
Ambrose), in order to demonstrate that the *filioque* was taught for centuries
before the schism.[83] Of course the most explicit testimony to the *filioque's*
orthodoxy came from Augustine, whose *De Trinitate* and *In Joannis Evangelium
Tractatus* provided a firm patristic basis for the Roman teaching.[84] Next came
the testimonies of the councils and of Popes Hormisdas[85] and Gregory the
Great.[86] There were numerous other Western witnesses, Montenero claimed,
but he decided the time had come to introduce the writings of the Eastern
fathers, "who declare this truth like bolts of lightning" (*qui ut fulmina hanc
veritatem declarant*).[87]

The Dominican provincial began his presentation of the Greek fathers on
March 24 with the two fathers whose works had been the subject of so much
earlier debate, Basil of Caesarea and Epiphanius.[88] Didymus the Blind and
Athanasius were also cited,[89] although the most quoted Greek father, by far, was
Cyril of Alexandria. For example, Cyril had written that "the Spirit flows from
[*profluit*/προχεῖται] from him [the Son] as from God the Father," which Montenero read as a direct reference to Spirit's eternal procession, unafraid to
equate *profluit*/προχεῖται with *procedit*/ἐκπορεύεται.[90] John maintained that
Cyril himself equated these terms when elsewhere he wrote that "the Spirit is
consubstantial and flows forth [*profluit*/προχεῖται], that is, proceeds
[*procedit*/ἐκπορεύεται], as from a source from God and Father."[91] "Therefore he
[Cyril] declares that to proceed and to flow from are the same and that when he
says 'to flow from the Son' it is necessary to say . . . that the Spirit proceeds from
the Son just as he does from the Father."[92]

The fourth part of Montenero's presentation was a direct refutation of
Eugenicus's use of the patristic witness. "Not one Greek or Latin ever dared to
say" (*quin ymmo nullus nec Grecus nec Latinus ausus est dicere*) that the Nicene-
Constantinopolitan creed meant to exclude the teaching of the Spirit's procession from the Son.[93] And while Eugenicus was correct to maintain the Father
as the source and principle of the divinity, the Church had also taught that the
spirative power was given to the Son, so that together Father and Son "are not
two fonts (of the Holy Spirit) but one" (*nec sunt duo fontes, sed unus*).[94] Finally,

eight hours after he began, Montenero concluded his case and the last public session at Florence came to an end.

Although most of the gatherings had been spent in heated (and ultimately fruitless) debate, two solid days of patristic testimony had a significant effect on the Byzantine delegation. Most important, Bessarion of Nicea, Isidore of Kiev, and George Scholarius all came to accept the orthodoxy of the *filioque*, becoming the strongest advocates for the union among the Greeks. As Bessarion later wrote in his *De Spiritus Sancti processione ad Alexium Lascarin Philanthropinum*:

> It was not the syllogisms . . . or the force of arguments that lead me to believe this [i.e., the Latin position], but the plain words of the doctors. For when I saw and heard them, straightway I put aside all contention and controversy and yielded to the authority of those whose words they were. . . . For I judged that the holy fathers, speaking as they did in the Holy Spirit, could not have departed from the truth and I was grieved that I had not heard their words before.[95]

The Final Negotiations

The Greek delegation was now bitterly divided. The only thing they could agree upon was the futility of further public sessions—the unionists claiming that the Latins had adequately proved their case, the anti-unionists convinced that continued disputation with the "heretics" was pointless. The time had come to either unite with the West or return home to Constantinople, where a Turkish attack was now rumored to be imminent. Dositheus of Monembasia, voicing the sentiments of the anti-unionist majority, claimed that he would rather die than Latinize (ἐγώ φησί, βούλομαι ἀποθανεῖν ἢ λατινίσαι ποτέ).[96] The unionists argued that, lacking an effective response to Montenero's presentation—except to say that their quotations were false, which was unreasonable, or to reply with lies, which was unbefitting—the union must be consummated.[97] Although the emperor was eager for Western aid, he was unwilling to silence Mark of Ephesus and Anthony of Heraclea for fear that he, like Michael VIII before him, would die excommunicate for enforcing an unpopular union. It appeared that an impasse had been reached and that the months of debate had all been for nothing.

With the public sessions at an end, Bessarion and George Scholarius decided to address the Greek delegation.[98] The first to speak was Bessarion, who was now firmly committed to the unionist cause. His argument, found in the *Oratio Dogmatica*, was both simple and persuasive:[99]

1. The fathers East and West, inspired by the same Spirit, could not contradict one another. This was the universally accepted principle that there existed a "symphony of the saints."

2. Methodologically, one had to interpret the more obscure passages in the fathers in light of the clearer.
3. If the Latin fathers unanimously taught procession *ex patre et filio*, which Montenero had demonstrated quite clearly, then passages in the Greek fathers in which they spoke of procession διὰ τοῦ Υἱοῦ (which were also plentiful) must have referred to this same truth.
4. This "flowing forth" or "coming forth" of the Spirit referred to by the fathers concerned not merely the economy but the theology. Here it is obvious that Bessarion followed Beccus in accepting the equivalence not only between διά and ἐκ, but between ἐκπορεύεσθαι and προϊέναι.
5. This teaching neither denied the monarchy of the Father (who remained principal cause) nor did it imply two causes, since the Latins affirmed that the Son is, with the Father, a single spirating principle.
6. Since the weight of the patristic evidence clearly supported this position, the Greeks had no legitimate reason to withhold their consent to the union.

In order to prove this last point, Bessarion found it necessary to deal with two fathers that the Greeks had traditionally used to counter the Latin understanding of the Spirit's procession: John of Damascus and Maximus the Confessor. Bessarion produced *Quaestiones ad Thalassium* 63 as proof that that the Confessor did not intend to deny all causality to the Son, since he clearly taught that the Spirit's eternal procession (ἐκπορεύεσθαι) took place through him. "For, as he says, the Spirit is substantially of the Son, not newly acquired and from without, nor has the Son received it temporally, but rather he possesses it eternally and substantially just like the Father. And thus he is the cause, because the Spirit proceeds substantially from the Father through him."[100] Basil the Great spoke of the same reality when he wrote of the Spirit's manifestation through the Son (δι᾽ αὐτοῦ πεφηνέναι), which Bessarion interpreted as a reference to his eternal manifestation.[101] Thus, according to Bessarion's reading of the fathers, the Son must be a cause of the Spirit, since the Spirit's eternal manifestation, procession, and hypostatic existence all took place δι᾽ αὐτοῦ.[102] For this reason Bessarion claimed that Basil and Maximus substantively agreed with the Western doctrine, since all spoke of the same reality (the procession of the Spirit from or through the Son) with only subtle differences in language: "It signifies nothing other than that he is manifested through the Son according to Basil the Great, and proceeds through the Son according to Maximus, and proceeds from the Son and has essence from Him according to the Western doctors . . . here it is seen that the three terms are equivalent."[103]

Bessarion knew that the Greeks would never accept the Western teaching unless it could be reconciled with the affirmation, found in both John of Damascus and the *Letter to Marinus*, that the Father alone was cause (Μόνος γὰρ αἴτος ὁ πατήρ).[104] Like his Latin hosts, Bessarion was not convinced of the authenticity of Maximus's *Letter*, "since it was not found in the ancient codices nor discovered among his works."[105] Yet even if one conceded its authenticity (as he did here for the sake of argument), Bessarion believed that the *Letter to Marinus* was not the clear condemnation of the Latin position that Mark and the anti-unionists had supposed.

Bessarion explained that, following the Greek usage, John of Damascus and Maximus were hesitant about using the preposition ἐκ to speak about the Spirit's procession from the Son, since ἐκ more often than not denoted a relation to the first and principal cause, that is, the Father.[106] For this reason both chose instead to speak of procession διὰ τοῦ Υἱοῦ, allowing the Son to be a cause of the Spirit, although not in a primordial way since this role was reserved to the Father alone, who remained μία αἰτία. To deny that Maximus or John intended to reject the attribution of all causality to the Son was, for Bessarion, to misunderstand their thought and the Greek theological tradition as a whole. For the Greeks, the Father "alone is the first and principal cause," yet the Son, who is neither the first nor the principal cause, is still cause or principle of the Spirit, one and the same with the Father.[107] Thus Bessarion accepted Maximus's teaching as contained in the *Letter*, writing in his post-conciliar work, *Refutatio Capitum Syllogisticorum Marci Ephesii*: "That the Son is not the cause of the Spirit we can also say, for we understand the meaning of cause in the strictest sense, as used in the Greek idiom, whereby cause always is understood as the primordial first cause."[108]

Bessarion's presentation employed a plethora of quotations (from such works as Gregory of Nyssa's *Letter to Ablabius* and the *Confession* of Patriarch Tarsius) to support the premise that διά and ἐκ were substantially equivalent. Drawn directly from the *Epigraphae* of John Beccus, when coupled with the testimony of the Latin fathers produced by Montenero (which the Latins happily made available in writing) the anti-unionist opposition began to crumble under the weight of the patristic evidence.

Next to speak was George (Gennadius) Scholarius (1405–72), a committed Thomist and a staunch advocate of the Florentine union.[109] Scholarius's presentation, unlike Bessarion's, was not an elaborate theological treatise (which he certainly would have been capable of undertaking) but a heartfelt appeal to his listeners' emotions. At once a critique of his fellow delegates' inability to muster a defense against the Latins and an impassioned plea for Christian unity against the Turkish foe, Scholarius's *On the Need for Aiding Constantinople* played both to the patriotism of the Byzantines and their deep longing to return home.[110] If the Greeks could muster no defense against the Latins except to claim that their sources were corrupt (which he called the "height of stupidity"), then the bonds of friendship should be renewed so that the emperor could return home and undertake the defense of the Great City.

The cumulative effect of these two addresses was enough to persuade the Greeks to return to the negotiating table, where ten members from each side were chosen to discuss the possibility of union.[111] Mark was still insistent that any reunion scheme must include the removal of the *filioque*, although this was for the Latins a nonstarter.[112] It was Bessarion, according to Syropoulus, who at the very first gathering suggested the *Letter to Marinus* as a formula for reunion.[113] While the *Memoirs* simply say that the Latins rejected this offer (οἱ δὲ Λατῖνοι οὐδόλως κατεδέξαντο τοῦτο), the *Acta* detail the Latin response:

> For even we ourselves would say that the Son is not the primary
> cause of the Spirit: we assert one cause of the Son and the Spirit, the
> Father, the one according to generation and the other according to
> procession; but in order to signify the communion and the equality
> of the essence we also assert the procession through the Son and
> clearly confess the inseparability of the substance. For the Son is
> substantially the Son of the Father and the Holy Spirit substantially is
> of the Father and the Son. Since he is substantially of the Father and
> the Son, and the substance of the hypostasis is inseparable, therefore
> the Holy Spirit is also from the hypostasis of the Son. Maximus states
> that the pronouncements of the holy Roman fathers do not say
> otherwise, not only Augustine, Jerome, and Ambrose but the rest
> whose books manifestly assert the Holy Spirit is from the Father and
> the Son.[114]

The Latins here repeated the understanding of the *Letter* that Bessarion had given only days earlier—Maximus had only intended to deny the Son's role as principal cause of the Spirit, not to deny the procession from the Father and the Son *ab tantum uno principio*. They maintained, as the West had for centuries, that there were not two causes of the Spirit (Father and Son), but they did not hesitate to attribute some causal role to the Son, since he was (with the Father) the one spirating principle. Thus they could affirm (as Montenero had done) with Maximus that the Son is not *the* cause (i.e., the primordial first cause) of the Spirit, since the Spirit still principally proceeded from the Father, yet they could not affirm that the Son in no way constitutes *a* cause of the Spirit's procession. Given their desire that the Byzantines clearly recognize and affirm the Roman doctrine, it was not surprising that the Latins rejected Bessarion's reintroduction of Maximus as a reunion formula.

After five sessions with no result, the Latins sent the Greeks a formula they believed (or more precisely, hoped) summarized the position of both Churches:

> In the name of the Holy Trinity . . . we profess that the Holy Spirit is
> eternally from the Father and the Son, and proceeds eternally from
> both as from one principle and one spiration, declaring that what the
> holy doctors and fathers say, namely that the Holy Spirit proceeds
> from the Father through the Son, is directed to this sense that by it is
> meant that the Son, like the Father, is according to the Greeks the

cause, but according to the Latins the principle, of the subsistence of the Holy Spirit.[115]

This formula immediately split the Greek delegation once again. While Bessarion, Isidore, and the unionists urged the delegates to accept the Latin formula, Mark insisted that the statement was utterly contrary to the Greek patristic tradition as he understood it. Particularly upsetting to the anti-unionist majority was the affirmation that the Son was also a cause of the Spirit, something that both John of Damascus and Maximus had explicitly denied. When Mark tried to bring forward the *Letter to Marinus* as testimony on his behalf, Bessarion (who had suggested the *Letter* as a reunion formula only a few days before) simply refused to accept its authenticity.[116] If Eugenicus refused to read Maximus correctly, (i.e., as supporting the Latin position), Bessarion, following the example of his Latin hosts, simply denied it a hearing. This situation left the Damascene as the only father who had explicitly denied causality to the Son. Bessarion, echoing the position of Scholarius, expressed the view that one witness could not, and should not, stand against the weight of the patristic consensus.[117] If there was an apparent contradiction, John's writings should simply be made to conform.

Charged with responding to the Roman proposal was Scholarius, who composed a statement of faith that both Latins and Greeks considered vague and inadequate. It stated:

> We Greeks confess and believe that the Holy Spirit proceeds [ἐκπορεύεσθαι] from the Father, is proper to the Son and gushes forth [ἀναβλύζειν] from him, and we affirm and believe that he flows forth[προχεῖσθαι] substantially from both, namely from the Father through the Son.[118]

While Scholarius's purpose may in fact have been to present an equivocal statement open to various interpretations, there is also reason to believe that he was trying to introduce the language and theology of the "third school" of Byzantine trinitarian thought, represented by Gregory of Cyprus and Gregory Palamas. Scholarius himself later claimed Blachernae to be a *de facto* ecumenical gathering and called Gregory of Cyprus a figure "in no way inferior to the greatest of the ancient writers on the subject of the procession."[119] And yet, like the work of Gregory himself, Scholarius's statement of faith was rejected by both sides of the argument—Eugenicus believing it too vague and capable of misinterpretation ("like an actor's boot"), the Latins afraid that verbs such as προχεῖσθαι and ἀναβλύζειν would be understood by the Greeks as reference to the Spirit's temporal procession alone. Although it was approved by the Byzantine delegation by a vote of 21–12 with the consent of the aging patriarch (whose physical condition began to deteriorate rapidly), the Latins refused to accept it.

Following their rejection of the Scholarius's statement, the Latins presented the Greeks with twelve questions in the hopes of clarifying their position, especially how they understood such terms as ἐκπορεύεσθαι, ἀναβλύζειν and διὰ τοῦ Υἱοῦ in terms of causality.[120] When the Byzantines failed to respond, the Latins continued their demands for a clearer statement of the Greeks' trinitarian theology, one that explicitly affirmed the orthodoxy of the Latin teaching.

By May 1439 the Byzantine delegates, increasingly frustrated both with the progress of the discussions and with their irregular payments from the papal treasury, renewed their demands to return home. Even the emperor, who was unambiguously in favor of union, began to feel dissatisfied with the continued Latin demands and poured out his frustrations to the pope: "[Verbs like] 'gush forth' [ἀναβλύζειν] 'pour forth' [προχεῖσθαι] and the rest attribute cause to the Son even if they [the writers] do not state it clearly owing to the ignorance of individuals. You profess the Son is a cause of the Spirit; we do not deny it; what else do you want?"[121]

On May 21 the emperor finally told Cesarini that the Latins could either accept Scholarius's original statement or simply let the Greeks go home.[122]

Pope Eugene, now fearful that his efforts had all been in vain, called together the Greeks for a solemn session on May 27 so that he could make one last urgent plea for unity. Although he certainly presented a heartfelt appeal for the unity of the Church, Eugene also dangled before the Byzantines the promise of Western aid against the Turks, which would be forthcoming only if the union were consummated.[123] So powerful was his presentation that Bessarion, Isidore, and some of the other unionists told the emperor that they were prepared to unite with Rome even if the rest of the delegation were not. The emperor, now under tremendous pressure from both the Latins and the unionists within his own ranks, began a "forced march" toward union that eventually brought the Byzantines, however reluctantly, back to the negotiating table. Those, like Mark Eugenicus and Anthony of Heraclea, who continued to stand in the way were now labeled by the increasingly unionist delegation as "traitors and Judases" who were preventing both the unity of Christ's Church and the salvation of the Great City. However, Eugenicus remained unmoved, especially since he had continued doubts about the authenticity of the codices employed by the Romans.[124] The emperor, in an effort to end the intra-Byzantine debate about the legitimacy of the Latin texts, polled the delegates for their opinion of the Western saints and the authenticity of their writings. According to Mark's account, while most of the Greeks accepted the Latin codices, they continued to reject the teaching that the Son was cause of the Spirit. Both of these positions, he says, were based on their adherence to the testimony of Maximus.

Adducing passages from the works of the Western teachers and the great St. Cyril, apparently favorable to Latinism, and after having before this attacked me one by one with their sophistries, they then

asked the members present at the council what they thought of the
adduced passages, and whether they avow the Son as a cause of the
Holy Ghost. The members answered that they did not doubt the
authenticity of these passages, relying on the Epistle of the divine
Maximus; but most of the members refused to admit the Son as a
cause of the Spirit according to these passages because the wise
Maximus also gives the same opinion of these passages.[125]

As for Mark himself, he had little doubt that the Latin codices had been
falsified by upholders of the Roman doctrine. Citing several examples from the
public debates, including the introduction of the falsified version of the seventh
ecumenical council, Mark demonstrated how the Latins had continually
attempted to use spurious or corrupted texts to prove their argument. Which
writings did Mark accept? "I receive as authentic only those texts that are in
accord with the letter of the divine Maximus and the writings of St. Cyril. All
those that are contrary I reject as false."[126] This attitude left the unionists
speechless: "Who would dare suggest such a thing—complete homilies, commentaries on the gospels, whole theological treatises—why, if we remove these
from their books, nothing would remain but blank pages!"[127]

When a vote on the orthodoxy of the *filioque* was taken the next day, May 30,
the Latin teaching was rejected by a 17–10 majority. Patriarch Joseph, now close
to death, invited members of the delegation for private meetings at which he
asked them to support the union, reminding them both of their collective theological ignorance and of their debt to him personally.[128] Three days later, on
June 3, when a second vote was taken, the delegates (excluding Eugenicus,
Anthony of Heraclea, Dositheus of Monemvasia, and Sophronius of Anchiaus)
unambiguously embraced the position of the unionists and accepted the argument that the Son was, in fact, a cause of the Holy Spirit (according to Mark "an
idea not even mentioned in the Latin quotations").[129] Eugenicus later claimed
that he kept his own opinion hidden, even while he continued to maintain that
his position alone was capable of conforming to the witness of Maximus and
the Eastern saints.

> But I boldly explained my opinion in words, and showed that the
> words of the Eastern and Western fathers can only be reconciled to
> each other by means of the explanation given them in the epistle of
> Maximus, that is, that the Son must not be thought to be the cause of
> the Spirit.[130]

The Byzantines then drafted a confession to be sent to Latins as a basis for
reunion. It stated:

> [the Holy Spirit] proceeds from the Father and the Son as from one
> principle and one substance. He proceeds through the Son as

connatural and consubstantial; proceeding from the Father and from the Son as from one spiration and procession.[131]

While Mark viewed the statement as a complete capitulation to the Latins and a betrayal of the true faith, the Romans still remained unsatisfied. According to Cesarini, nothing short of complete acceptance of both the Latin doctrine and language (i.e., the *ex filio* formula) would do, believing as he did that any reference to procession διὰ τοῦ Υἱοῦ might be open to misinterpretation. Besides, "the delegates of our most Holy Father and of your paternities always stood fast that the question should be defined in accordance with the dogmas of the Holy Roman Church."[132] When the Greeks finally conceded the point two days later, a new statement was drawn up and translated into Latin. On the morning of June 8, when the parties gathered to hear the statement read publicly, there was such joy over the impending union that the delegates embraced one another, exchanging the kiss of peace.[133]

Union of the Churches

The Byzantines had hoped that agreement on the *filioque* would be enough to satisfy the Romans and bring an end to the schism, but the pope insisted that the other disputed points— purgatory, the use of azymes, the consecratory formula, and most important, the primacy of Rome—needed to be settled first. The situation of the Greeks worsened two days later when Patriarch Joseph died, leaving the Greeks without an ecclesiastical leader.[134] The emperor, although desirous that the union should be consummated as soon as possible, was outraged by the continued Latin demands and threatened to return home.[135]

Despite the emperor's reluctance to provide the West with an unqualified victory, the statements on the remaining issues, very much like the one on the *filioque*, were little more than summaries of the Latin positions with some concessions made to Greek sensibilities.[136] According to Syropoulus, the only subject that occasioned intense debate was the order of the signatures on the union decree, the Latins demanding that the pope should go first and the emperor insisting that, following the example of the ancient councils, his name should be prefixed.[137] Although it was hoped that the decree might be ready for the feast of Peter and Paul on June 29, continued bickering postponed the ceremony for another week.

Finally, on July 5, the union decree (*Laetentur Caeli*) was sent to the delegates for their signature. The following day, amidst the pomp and pageantry of a pontifical liturgy, it was publicly proclaimed, first in Latin by Cardinal Cesarini and then in Greek by Bessarion.[138] Both Latins and Greeks expressed their consent (*Placet!*), and the ceremony concluded with a solemn *Te Deum* sung by Pope Eugene himself. According to Syropoulus, despite the pretense of unity, not a single Greek ecclesiastic took an active part in the liturgy (which was celebrated according to the Latin rite) or accepted the unleavened host.[139]

Concerning the procession of the Holy Spirit, the chief theological issue dividing the two Churches, the union decree stated:

> The Holy Spirit is eternally from the Father and the Son, and has his essence and his subsistent being from the Father together with the Son, and proceeds from both eternally as from one principle and a single spiration. We declare that when holy doctors and fathers say that the Holy Spirit proceeds from the Father through the Son, this bears the sense that thereby also the Son should be signified, according to the Greeks indeed as cause, and according to the Latins as principle of the subsistence of the Holy Spirit, just like the Father. We define also that the explanation of those words "and from the Son" was licitly and reasonably added to the creed for the sake of declaring the truth and from imminent need.[140]

The one notable absence from the proceedings was Mark of Ephesus, who later, in an interview with the pope, detailed the reasons for his refusal to sign:

> I express not my own opinions, I introduce nothing new into the Church, neither do I defend any errors. But I steadfastly preserve the doctrine which the Church, having received from Christ the Savior, has ever kept and keeps. This doctrine was also adhered to by the Church of Rome unanimously with that of the East until the beginning of the division.[141]

This reference to the Roman teaching prior to Photius is a clear allusion to the *Letter to Marinus*, whose testimony Mark regarded as a defense for his refusal to bow to the "novelties" of the Latins. Rome had once clearly denied all causality to the Son, affirming with Maximus and the Eastern tradition that the father was the μία αἰτία. Now that the Roman faith had changed, was it just for Eugene and the Latins to condemn him for defending their former (and genuinely orthodox) opinion? The pope, after having failed to convince Mark to sign, demanded that he be punished for his obstinacy. The emperor claimed that he had already guaranteed Mark safe passage back to Constantinople and that, as an Eastern metropolitan, he would not allow Mark to be judged in Rome.[142]

The Aftermath

Within days of the signing, the Byzantine delegation began their preparations to leave Florence and journey back to Constantinople. While waiting in Venice for the emperor's arrival, the Doge invited them to serve the Byzantine liturgy at St. Mark's, but the Greeks were hesitant. According to Syropoulus, when Anthony of Heraclea and the Greeks finally acquiesced, they used their own antimensia (altar cloth) and vessels, omitted the pope's name from the diptychs, and recited the creed without the *filioque*.[143] After two years of prolonged debate and the solemn proclamation of ecclesiastical union, absolutely nothing had changed.

By the time the Greeks finally arrived back in Constantinople in February of 1440, their rejection of the union was complete. As the chronicler Doukas explained:

> As soon as the hierarchs came ashore, the Constantinopolitans . . . embraced them and asked, "How are you? What news do you bring from the synod? Have we gained the victory?" They replied, "No, we have betrayed our faith. We have exchanged piety for impiety. We have renounced the pure sacrifice and become azymites."[144]

The unionist Patriarch Metrophanes, who was chosen by lot after both Eugenicus and Anthony of Heraclea withdrew their names from consideration, was immediately denounced when, at the Pentecost liturgy, he included Pope Eugene's name in the diptychs. His successor, Gregory Mammas (Melissenus), was equally unsuccessful, retreating to Rome in 1451 when Emperor Constantine XI opened a dialogue with the anti-unionist leadership. Bessarion, who was made a cardinal in December 1439, returned to Italy in 1440, where he spent the remaining thirty years of his life embroiled in the affairs of the papal court. He wrote several works in defense of the Florentine union, aided Greek refugees after the fall of Constantinople, and was even appointed patriarch by the pope in 1463.[145] Isidore of Kiev (also made a cardinal) was imprisoned in 1441 after an unsuccessful attempt to promulgate the union in Poland, Lithuania, and Russia.[146] After his escape, Isidore became papal envoy to Constantinople, where he witnessed the formal proclamation of the union in December 1452, only five months before the city was taken by Sultan Mehmet II. The last Christian liturgy in Hagia Sophia, at which Isidore was present, was the union's last (perhaps only) bright shining moment.

> For on that evening the bitterness was ended. . . . Priests who held union with Rome to be a mortal sin came to serve at the altar with their Unionist brethren. The Cardinal was there, and beside him bishops who would never acknowledge his authority; all the people came to make confession and take communion, not caring whether Catholic or Orthodox administered it. . . . At that moment there was union in the Church of Constantinople.[147]

George Scholarius, who accepted leadership of the anti-unionist cause after the death of Mark Eugenicus in 1445, became the first patriarch under the Turkish rule (under the name of Gennadius II), convinced that the Greeks' betrayal of the faith at Florence had been the cause of the city's misfortunes.[148] In 1484 the Florentine union was officially repudiated in Constantinople, bringing the story of the council to a sad, if not inevitable, conclusion.

9

From Florence to the Modern Era

The Council of Ferrara-Florence accomplished exactly what Emperor Manuel II Palaeologus had predicted—rather than healing the schism, it confirmed it, separating East and West for the next several centuries. Roman Catholicism embraced Ferrara-Florence as an ecumenical gathering, giving the teachings of *Laetentur Caeli* on the *filioque* (not to mention the primacy of the pope) the force of dogma. Although the Reformation soon split the Latin-speaking world into a host of competing churches and ecclesial communities, the *filioque* was not among those issues challenged by the Protestant critique and it remained an integral part of Western belief. While some of the Reformers made overtures to the East in an effort to enlist their support against Rome, on the subject of the *filioque* the dialogue rarely progressed beyond the usual polemical exchanges. In the seventeenth century, as Catholics and Protestants made their way into traditionally Orthodox territory, the Christian East continued to reject the Latin theology of the procession despite the increased influence of Western thought in other areas. Orthodox confessions issued during this time clearly reaffirm the rejection of the *filioque*, just as Roman Catholic documents of the era made clear that acceptance of the Florentine decrees was a nonnegotiable condition for future reconciliation.

However, a new period of rapprochement started in 1874, when a group of Anglicans and Old Catholics (those who had rejected the decrees of the First Vatican Council) began an exchange with the

Orthodox at Bonn. Although many of the old arguments were brought forward, for the first time in centuries polemics were replaced by genuine dialogue and a willingness to engage, rather than overcome, the religious other. By the beginning of the twentieth century men like Boris Bolotov would go so far as to claim that the *filioque* was no longer an impediment to Church unity. If not itself a period of great ecumenical achievement, the nineteenth century nevertheless paved the way for what was to come and allowed the twentieth century to become a time of immense progress on the road to unity.

Martin Luther (1483–1546), Philip Melanchthon (1497–1560), and Martin Chemnitz (1522–86)

In 1517 Martin Luther, protesting the sale of indulgences in order to finance the rebuilding of St. Peter's, nailed his *Ninety-five Theses* to the church door in Wittenburg. While challenging several aspects of the Catholic system, Luther never questioned the legitimacy of the Nicene-Constantinopolitan creed or Rome's decision to include the *filioque*, a fact explained in large part by his acceptance of the Augustinian trinitarian model and the ecumenicity of the *Quicumque vult.*[1] Although Luther was sympathetic to several teachings of the Greek Church and used them to oppose the Roman view (on papal primacy, private masses, and communion under both kinds), his trinitarian teaching was clearly Western.[2] The Smalcald Articles, written by Luther, affirm "that the Father is begotten of no one; the Son was begotten by the Father; the Holy Spirit proceeded from the Father and the Son."[3] Elsewhere he wrote:

> The distinction of the Father, as we have heard, is this, that He derived His deity from no one, but gave it from eternity, through the eternal birth, to the Son. . . . And the fact that Father and Son are God and Creator they do not owe to the Holy Spirit; but the Holy Spirit owes the fact that He is God and Creator *to the Father and the Son.* . . . Namely, that the Father is the source, or the fountainhead (if we may use that term as the fathers do) of the Godhead, that the Son derives it from Him and that the Holy Spirit derives it *from Him and the Son,* and not vice versa.[4]

Luther had little reason to explore interpersonal relationships within the Trinity, choosing instead to emphasize the soteriological rather than the metaphysical.[5] The job of the Spirit, he claimed, was to sanctify us and bring us to Christ, for "neither you nor I could ever know anything of Christ or believe in him, and take him as our Lord, unless these were first offered to us and bestowed on our hearts through the preaching of the Gospel by the Holy Spirit."[6] "It is he who has called me to the Gospel, enlightened me with his gifts, and sanctified and preserved me in true faith, just as he calls, gathers, enlightens, and sanctifies the whole Christian church."[7]

Concerning the Trinity, Luther's friend and disciple Philip Melanchthon wrote that the Reformers had maintained the traditional faith of the (Western) Church.[8] Yet Melanchthon himself was sensitive to the ecumenical implications of the *filioque*—in 1559 he had written to Ecumenical Patriarch Joasaph II and for six months hosted his representative, Deacon Demetrius Mysos.[9] But despite his desire for better relations with the East, Melanchthon clearly affirmed the *filioque*, teaching that the Spirit "proceeds from the Father and the Son and is sent into the regenerated hearts by the word of the gospel."[10] Upholding the personhood of the Holy Spirit against the radical reformers, Melanchthon brought forward the testimony of the ancient councils, including the Council of Constantinople, which had "defended the article that the Holy Spirit is a person proceeding from the Father *and the Son*."[11] Elsewhere he distinguished between the persons in the godhead:

> The Father is a person, unbegotten . . . the Son is the image of the
> Father, begotten from eternity by the Father . . . the Holy Spirit sets
> things in motion. He proceeds from the Father and Son and is sent
> to sanctify our minds.[12]

Among the Reformers, few understood the "long and acrimonious" debate "between the later Greek theologians and the Latin Church" better than Martin Chemnitz.[13] Chemnitz knew the fathers well, and he believed that there was a *consensus patrum* on the procession of the Holy Spirit, although the Greek and Latin fathers often used different prepositions to describe the reality. He wrote:

> Both parties confessed that the Spirit is of the Son as well as of the
> Father; but the Greeks said that He is "from the Father through the
> Son," and the Latins said "from the Father and the Son." They each
> had reasons for speaking the way they did. . . . Therefore, the Greeks
> said that the Holy Spirit proceeds from [*ek, ex*] the Father through
> [*dia*] the Son, so that the property of each nature (or person) is
> preserved. Nor did the Latins take offense at this formula for
> describing the matter. For Jerome and Augustine both say that the
> Holy Spirit properly and principally proceeds from the Father, and
> they explain this by saying that the Son in being begotten of the
> Father receives that which proceeds from the Father, namely, the
> Holy Spirit.[14]

Eventually "when major distractions arose, the Greeks spoke anathemas against those who confessed that the Holy Spirit proceeds from the Son . . . and the Latins in turn condemned those who say the Holy Spirit proceeds from the Father through the Son."[15] However, Chemnitz was unwilling to write the debate off as "some inane argument over words," since for him it concerned the very truth of the gospel.[16] Believing somewhat erroneously that the issue had been settled at Florence, Chemnitz defended the traditional Western belief rather than "destroy the consubstantiality of the Father and Son;" unafraid to "speak the language of the Church" simply to "avoid unpleasant and dangerous arguments."[17]

Of particular interest is Chemnitz's understanding of the vocabulary of the debate. Because he knew Greek, Chemnitz was well aware of the difference between ἐκπορεύεσθαι and other verbs used in the Scriptures to describe the coming of Christ or the Spirit (e.g., ἐξῆλθεν in John 13:3, or ἐπελεύσεται in Luke 1:35). He recognized that although many of these terms were often translated by the same Latin word (*procedere/processi*), in Greek "the word ἐκπορεύεσθαι is reserved for, and peculiar to, the eternal procession when it is used with reference to the Holy Spirit."[18] This distinction, he argued, is important in differentiating the unique procession of the Spirit from the begottenness of the Son, who also comes forth from the Father, but not by means of procession proper (i.e., ἐκπορεύεσθαι). Although Chemnitz accepted the uniqueness of ἐκπορεύεσθαι in denoting the procession, he refused to sacrifice the Latin teaching despite the fact that the Scriptures nowhere spoke of the Spirit's ἐκπορεύεσθαι from the Son. Both in his *Loci Theologici*, and then later in the *Formula of Concord*, Chemnitz simply repeated the traditional Latin teaching that "the Holy Spirit proceeds from him (Christ) as well as from the Father and therefore he is and remains, to all eternity, his and the Father's own Spirit."[19]

John Calvin (1509–64)

Despite his reputation as a reformer, John Calvin spent a great deal of time vigorously and even violently defending the traditional teaching of the Church, especially as it pertained to the Trinity.[20] As with Augustine and the scholastics, Calvin confessed that God was one, but within the Trinity a distinction of persons is established by their mutual relationships, for "ecclesiastical writers do not concede that the one is separated from the other by any difference of essence. 'By these appellations which set forth the distinction [says Augustine] is signified their mutual relationships and not the very substance by which they are one.'"[21] Regarding the procession of the Spirit, Calvin maintained the traditional Western view that

> the Son is said to come forth from the Father alone; the Spirit from
> the Father and the Son at the same time. This appears in many
> passages, but nowhere more clearly than in chapter 8 of Romans,
> where the same Spirit is indifferently called sometimes the Spirit of
> Christ, sometimes the Spirit of him who raised up Christ . . . from

the dead—and not without justification. For Peter also testifies that it was by the Spirit of Christ that the prophets testified (2 Peter 1:21) even though Scripture often teaches that it was the Spirit of God the Father.[22]

As with Luther, there was an emphasis on the soteriological and on the Spirit's role in bringing us to Christ.[23] He is "the bond by which Christ effectually unites us to himself,"[24] and "our inner teacher" through whom we come to understand the promise of salvation.[25] This is why the Holy Spirit is called the "Spirit of Sanctification" that "God the Father gives us . . . for his Son's sake."[26] Yet because the Father has also "bestowed the whole fullness of the Spirit upon the Son to be minister and steward of his liberality. . . . the Spirit is sometimes called the 'Spirit of the Father,' sometimes the 'Spirit of the Son.'"[27] It was this intimate link between Christ's work and that of the Spirit that led Calvin, in both the *Institutes of the Christian Religion* and the *French Confession of Faith* (1559), to defend the traditional Western view of the procession as found in the Scriptures, the fathers, and the pronouncements of the councils.

> The Father [is] first cause, principle, and origin of all things [*Le Père, première cause et principe et origine de toutes choses*]. The Son, his Word and eternal wisdom. The Holy Spirit, his virtue, power, and efficacy. The Son begotten from eternity by the Father; the Holy Spirit proceeding eternally from them both [*Le Saint-Esprit procédant éternellement de tous deux*]; the three persons not confused, but distinct, and yet not separate, but of the same essence, equal in eternity and power. And thus we confess that which has been established by the ancient councils, and we detest all sects and heresies which were rejected by the holy doctors, such as St. Hilary, St. Athanasius, St. Ambrose, and St. Cyril.[28]

Patriarch Jeremiah II (1572–79, 1580–84, 1586–95) and the Tübingen Theologians

Despite their clear reaffirmation of the *filioque* in their confessional statements, many of the reformers were nevertheless convinced that their understanding of the gospel would be warmly received in the East, particularly in Constantinople.[29] The Lutherans, following Melanchthon and Chemnitz, believed not only that their theology was firmly grounded in the apostolic and patristic tradition, but also that the Patriarchate's historic antipathy to Rome would make it sympathetic to Protestantism's critiques of the papal system. For this reason in 1574 Jacob Andreae and Martin Crusius of Tübingen began a correspondence with Patriarch Jeremiah II, sending him a Greek translation of the Augsburg Confession.[30] The patriarch responded to these "wise German men and spiritual sons" by reminding them of the words of Nicea, "which clearly reveal that the Holy Spirit proceeds from the Father."[31] This creed, he argued, should be left untouched so that "unscathed and unadulterated" this "most sacred and most perfect credo of our piety" could be professed and preserved.[32] After a lengthy, and at times critical, response to the other articles of the confession (e.g., those dealing with original sin, justification, faith and works, the sacraments, ministries in the Church) the patriarch concluded by accepting the "love and friendliness" of Andrae and Crusius, whom he called "beloved children of our humble self."[33]

The response of the Tübingen theologians (Lucas Osiander writing in behalf of Andreae) expressed great satisfaction that there were so many areas of agreement. There was also the hope that the patriarch might eventually come to accept the orthodoxy of the reformers' positions in those areas where disagreement remained (e.g., the *filioque*, where they recognized that "the Greek churches reject that which we positively assert).[34] Osiander and Crusius knew that the creed of Nicea did not contain the *filioque*, but they nevertheless argued that "for this article we firmly stand on the testimony of the Scriptures."[35] They argued that the Greeks, in maintaining that "the Spirit is from the Father alone and through the Son but does not proceed from the Son ... , think the impossible for these things clearly oppose one another and contradict one another."[36] The Latin position was the correct one, they argued, as can be shown not only from the Scriptures, but also from the writings of the very fathers the patriarch claimed to revere—Cyril, Athanasius, and Epiphanius.[37]

This critique of the Eastern position, although by this time quite familiar to the Byzantines, reopened an ancient wound and solicited a lengthy response from the patriarch. The bulk of his letter simply reiterated the traditional Eastern position—there was a difference between eternal procession and temporal mission, a difference between διά and ἐκ, a difference between the bestowal of the Spirit's gifts and the Spirit's eternal coming-into-being. There was also, the patriarch reminded them, an important distinction in the Trinity, apparently forgotten by the Latins, between personal hypostatic qualities and the shared divine nature, which is why the West erred in attributing causality (which was a property of the Father alone) to the Son from their misreading of certain biblical texts (e.g., John 17:10).

After reminding the Lutheran theologians of the dire theological consequences of filioquism ("See how many absurd conclusions from every side trail those who say that the Spirit proceeds from both the Father and the Son!"), Patriarch Jeremiah brought forward the patristic witnesses to the Eastern teaching.[38] For if the Latins, that is, the Church of Rome, and others can produce witnesses who are acceptable such as Augustine, Ambrose, Jerome, and others, we can also produce many more *and even more trustworthy* Fathers to speak up for the truth."[39]

Jeremiah then enlisted not only the Eastern fathers but also the Roman popes—including Sylvester, Damasus, Agatho, Gregory the Great, Zacharias, Leo III, and Benedict III— to establish both the ecumenicity of the Eastern teaching and longstanding prohibition against creedal alterations. The patriarch concluded his treatment of the procession by invoking "the Paraclete himself, the Spirit who proceeds from the Father," so that his Lutheran friends would "cease to utter words about that which are remote from the truth . . . keeping the confession of faith unfragmented, unshakable, and steadfast."[40]

The Lutheran response, while cordial, nevertheless contained a vigorous defense against the charges the patriarch had made. The Latins did distinguish between procession and mission but believed, following Augustine, that "the one . . . is the preparation for the other . . . presupposed and induced by the other because it is caused by it."[41] Like the East, the West also acknowledged that the Father is "origin, source, and cause" within the Trinity, but they believed that "by reason of origin" the Son is second (i.e. to the Father) and the Holy Spirit third ("being posterior to both by reason of origin").[42] If the Spirit "receives" from the Son (John 16:14), this fact clearly means he receives existence, which is why the Son can truly be said to be "origin, source, cause, and emitter of the Holy Spirit since He is the one who breathes him."[43] This power, which belongs to the Father (who remains "the prime origin and source") "is granted the Son necessarily through the begetting" so that he truly proceeds from both.[44] Regarding the patriarch's reading of the patristic corpus, the Tübingen theologians acknowledged that the fathers often spoke of the Spirit's procession from the Father (a doctrine "we have never denied"), but that "it is one thing to say that the Spirit proceeds from the Father and another to say that he does not proceed from the Son also. The above-mentioned fathers and hierarchs say the first part, but they do not say the second—far from it. Consequently they do not oppose our position . . . [but] rather they agree with us."[45]

Patriarch Jeremiah had originally intended to remain silent, but fearing that "by silence it might appear that we agree with you," he wrote back to the Lutherans, focusing only on the (alleged) Latin confusion between procession and mission.[46] There was, he argued, an important difference between nature and mission, a difference long recognized by the fathers, that the West continued to ignore at its peril. Obviously frustrated, Jeremiah concluded the correspondence:

Therefore, we request that from henceforth you do not cause us more grief, nor write to us on the same subject if you should wish to treat these luminaries and theologians of the Church in a different manner. You honor and exalt them in words, but you reject them in deeds. For you try to prove our weapons which are their holy and divine discourses as unsuitable. And it is with these documents that we would have to write and contradict you. Thus, as for you, please release us from these cares. Therefore, going about your own ways, write no longer concerning dogmas; but if you do, write only for friendship's sake. Farewell.[47]

The *Sigillion* of 1583 and Maximos Margounios (1549–1602)

As Catholic and Protestant theology increasingly came to exert an influence in the East, the Orthodox response, more often than not, was to reject these "foreign" beliefs and those Christians who erroneously accepted them as orthodox. In 1583, only two years after his last exchange with the Tübingen theologians, Patriarch Jeremiah issued a *Sigillion* (signed also by Sylvester of Alexandria and Sophronius of Jerusalem) formally repudiating "the newly invented Paschalion and Menologion of the Pope's atheist astronomers" (i.e., the Gregorian calendar), condemning any as "rotten members" who accepted the various teachings and practices of the Roman Church.[48] Singled out for particular condemnation were those who did "not confess with heart and mouth that he is a child of the Eastern Church baptized in Orthodox style, and that the Holy Spirit proceeds out of only the Father, essentially and hypostatically, as Christ says in the Gospel."[49]

There were, however, still a few figures in the East who remained open to dialogue with the Latins. Among them was Maximos Margounios, "the most outstanding figure in the intellectual and theological history of the Greek Orthodox Church during the later sixteenth century."[50] In 1577 Patriarch Jeremiah invited Margounios, who was born in Crete and educated in Padua, to come to Constantinople to reorganize the patriarchal school. Although Margounios initially had to decline the offer, in 1583 he dedicated *Three Books on the Procession of the Holy Spirit* to Jeremiah, penned as an attempt to reconcile East and West on the issue of the *filioque*. On the basis of his reading of both the Eastern and Western fathers, with whom he was equally familiar, Maximos believed that there were two processions in the godhead—one eternal and one temporal—and that the *filioque*, when applied to the second, was perfectly orthodox.

Margounios's irenicism was not appreciated so soon after the disaster of Ferrara-Florence, and his views quickly came under attack, first from the Orthodox, who thought that anyone "who exhibited or even suggested any tolerance of the Latin view was suspect"[51] and then from Rome, where they requested that he be tried by the Inquisition.[52] Gabriel Severus, who had studied with Margounios in Padua, claimed that he had deviated from the true faith by compromising the monarchy of the Father, and although Patriarch Jeremiah tried to make peace between the two, the debate became increasingly bitter. After the publication of Maximos's (allegedly) pro-Latin views in Germany, the Holy Synod in Constantinople asked him to clarify his position by letter, which he then sent to the patriarch for review. Despite their continued reservations, the Synod formally recognized Maximos's orthodoxy, and in 1593 even his long-time rival Severus was reconciled. Forced to give up his dream of reuniting East and West, Margounios nevertheless represented "the first and only significant attempt on the part of a Greek theologian to bring about a closer understanding between the two churches after the failure of the famous Council of Florence."[53]

The Synod of Brest

In July 1569 the Union of Lublin united the kingdom of Poland with the grand duchy of Lithuania, creating one of the largest nation-states in Europe. Predominately Roman Catholic, the new kingdom also had a significant Protestant population (especially in the cities of Danzig, Thorn, and Elbing) as well as a large number of Orthodox Christians (concentrated in Lv'iv and Kiev). The Kyvian Church had long been in an anomalous position vis-a-vis the schism—they were technically in communion with the churches of both Constantinople and Rome.[54] However, Polish Catholics renewed their efforts to convert the Ruthenians to Latin Christianity, judging their beliefs and practices to be at odds with the Roman Catholic faith. The famous Jesuit orator Piotr Skarga (1536–1612) attacked these "schismatics," claiming that only within the Roman Catholic Church could the Ruthenians find the true faith and spiritual renewal.[55] And yet the Church of Kiev continued to recognize the authority of the Ecumenical Patriarch, whose historic rights over the Ruthenian Church were reaffirmed as late as 1589 by King Sigismund III (1566–1632).

However, a combination of factors, both political and theological, began to make union with Rome more attractive in the eyes of the Kyvian hierarchy.[56] By 1595 Metropolitan Michael and the hierarchs of the Church drafted the "Articles for which We Need Guarantees from the Lord Romans before We Enter into Unity with the Roman Church," stating the conditions under which they would accept the union. The very first condition concerned the *filioque*:

> Firstly, since among the Romans and the Greeks there is a dispute as to the procession of the H[oly] Spirit, which is a considerable obstacle to unification and which probably endures for no other reason than that we do not understand each other, we, therefore, request that we not be constrained to a different confession [of faith], but that we remain with the one that we find expressed in the S[acred] Scriptures, in the Gospels, and also in the writings of the H[oly] Greek Doctors [i.e., Church Fathers], namely that the H[oly] Spirit does not have two

origins, nor a double procession, but that He proceeds from one origin, as from a source—from the Father through the Son.[57]

The union was approved by King Sigismund in August, and the terms were then brought to Pope Clement VIII (1592–1605) for final approval. The Ruthenian delegates (Bishops Ipatii and Kyryll) were warmly received by the pope, and on December 23, 1595, the Union of Brest-Litovsk, as it has become known, was formally promulgated in the constitution *Magnus Dominus*. At the ceremonies Bishops Ipatii and Kyryll professed the creed with the *filioque*, acknowledging, among other things, the primacy of the pope and the Roman teaching on purgatory. The Roman commission that examined the Ruthenians' *Articles* (led by the Spanish Dominican, Juan Saragoza de Heredia) rejected them, arguing that one could not impose preconditions for union with the one true Church. Nevertheless, *Magnus Dominus* "benignly permit[ed], concede[d], and grant[ed]" the Ruthenians the right to their own customs and traditions, including the recitation of the creed in its original form.[58]

Metrophanes Kritopoulos (1589–1639), Cyril Lukaris (1572–1637), and the Age of the Orthodox Confessions

Metrophanes Kritopoulos first traveled to England in 1617 at the request of his friend Cyril Lukaris (who was then Patriarch of Alexandria), where he studied theology and literature at Balliol College, Oxford.[59] His years in the West included stays in London, Germany, Switzerland, and Venice, returning East to be consecrated Bishop of Memphis in 1633 and then Patriarch of Alexandria in 1636. In 1625 he authored a private *Confessio*, called by modern scholars "the most original, independent, and the most free from heterodox influence of the four confessions of faith produced in the seventeenth century by Orthodox writers."[60]

The *Confessio* of Kritopoulos contains a detailed treatment of the procession, teaching that the Holy Spirit is "naturally produced by the hypostasis of the Father" who is the "one source and one cause."[61] This statement, he knew, contradicted the "unreasonable" teaching of the Latins, who professed "two sources and two causes in the one God (for this conclusion certainly follows from the assertion that the Holy Spirit proceeds from both)."[62] Orthodox trinitarian theology must preserve the unique characteristics of the three hypostases within the godhead, which can occur only "if to the Father alone we attribute the begetting of the Son and the projection of the Holy Spirit."[63] As so many had done before, Kritopoulos differentiated between "procession" and "mission," acknowledging that the Spirit is sent to us through or from the Son, but this does not (as the Latins erroneously insist) refer to the Spirit's eternal origin, since "not everything that is from a man also derives its being from him."[64]

Although the Latins claimed to avoid "giv[ing)] to the Son the property of begetting and being a Father" ("which is well ... for it is truly terrible and dangerous"),
to Kritopoulos it seemed that they could not escape the Sabellian conclusion
that followed from their position.[65]

Cyril Lukaris, the so-called "Protestant Patriarch," was born in Crete in
1572 and educated by Maximos Margounios in Padua.[66] In 1596 he participated
in the Constantinopolitan Synod that condemned the Union of Brest, traveling
to Poland–Lithuania to communicate the Synod's decision to King Sigismund.
Confronted there with the increasing success of the Jesuit missionary effort,
Lukaris took the stance that an Orthodox-Protestant alliance was the only possible recourse against Roman hegemony. Elected as Patriarch of Alexandria in
1601 and Ecumenical Patriarch in 1620, Lukaris actively worked to establish
relations with both the Anglicans (corresponding with two Archbishops of Canterbury, George Abbott and William Laud), and the Calvinists, whose influence
upon him can clearly be seen in his 1629 *Eastern Confession of the Christian
Faith.*[67]

Although there is continued scholarly debate about its authorship, the *Confessio* was likely composed by Lukaris with the intent of achieving "a synthesis of
Eastern Orthodox dogma and mildly Calvinist theology," in order to articulate
"the genius of each tradition . . . without doing violence to the other."[68] On the
filioque, the *Confessio* affirmed the Nicene Creed without the addition, teaching
that the "Holy Spirit comes forth from the Father through the Son [*Spiritus Sanctus a Patre per Filium procedens*] and is consubstantial with the Father and the
Son."[69] While this teaching conformed in large part to the Orthodox understanding, the *Confessio*'s teachings on predestination, the relationship of Tradition to
Scripture, Eucharist, free will, and justification by faith were all heavily influenced by Calvinist thought. For this reason the *Confession* was condemned by
several Constantinopolitan Synods (including the 1638 gathering at which Kritopoulos was present), the Synod of Jassy (1642), and the Synod of Jerusalem
(1672). As for Lukaris himself, despite frequent affirmations of his orthodoxy
from the other patriarchs, he was deposed and reinstated several times for his
alleged Calvinism and eventually was executed by the sultan for high treason.[70]

Among the most significant responses to the Lukaris's *Confessio* was the
Orthodox Confession of the Catholic and Apostolic Eastern Church written by the
Metropolitan of Kiev, Peter Mogila (d. 1647).[71] Similar in style to the catechisms
of Peter Canisius and other Catholic authors of the post-Tridentine period, it
has been called "the most Latin document ever to be adopted by an official
council of the Orthodox Church."[72] Mogila's *Confession* was accepted by the
Synod of Jassy in 1642, endorsed by the four major patriarchates (Constantinople, Jerusalem, Alexandria, and Antioch) in 1643,[73] and adopted by the Synod
of Jerusalem in 1672 as an authoritative exposition of the Orthodox faith.[74]
Despite its markedly Western style, the *Confession*'s teaching on the procession
was thoroughly Eastern, affirming that "the Father is the cause of the Son and

the Holy Ghost, insomuch as both these persons have their origin from him . . .
the Son, begotten before all worlds by the Father and consubstantial with him,
the Holy Ghost, proceeding from the Father from all eternity."[75] Later Moglia
addressed the *filioque* more directly:

> 69. What is the eighth article of faith?
> "I believe in the Holy Ghost, the Lord and Giver of life, who
> proceedeth from the Father, who with the Father and the Son
> together is worshipped and glorified, who spoke through the
> prophets."[76]
> 71. What is the second thing taught by this article?
> That the Holy Spirit proceeds from the Father only, as from the
> fountain and origin of his divinity. . . . Let it, therefore, suffice us that
> we hold what Christ himself taught; what the Catholic and Orthodox
> Eastern Church believes and altogether professed in the Second
> Ecumenical Council, and let us hold the faith without the addition
> "and from the Son," as the Church has commanded. No, not only the
> Orthodox and Catholic Eastern Church has passed a heavy censure
> on those who add these words, but also the Western Roman Church.
> This is evident from the two silver tables . . . which were by order of
> Leo III, Pope of Rome, affixed up in St. Peter's Church, in the Year of
> our Lord 809.[77]

Along with the *Confession* of Mogila and the earlier letters of Jeremiah II to
the Tübingen theologians, the Synod of Jerusalem also approved the *Confession*
of Patriarch Dositheus, who had presided over the gathering. Unlike Moglia's
work, Dositheus's *Confession* did not explicitly treat the *filioque* but simply stated its belief in "the Holy Spirit proceeding from the Father, and consubstantial
with the Father and the Son."[78] The rest of Dositheus's work was devoted to
refuting the *Confessio* of Lukaris, which it followed "article by article and question by question."[79]

Because of its alleged "Westernizing" tendencies, the *Longer Catechism of
the Orthodox, Catholic, Eastern Church,* issued by Philaret of Moscow in 1823,
never achieved the same status as many of the earlier confessions of faith.
On the subject of the procession, however, Philaret firmly grounded himself
in the traditional Eastern arguments against both the *filioque* and the creedal
interpolation.

> Whence know we that the Holy Ghost proceedeth from the Father?
> This we know from the following words of Jesus Christ himself: But
> when the Comforter is come, whom I will send unto you from the
> Father, even the Spirit of truth, which proceedeth from the Father, he
> shall testify of me. (John 15: 26)

Does the doctrine of the procession of the Holy Ghost from the
Father admit of any change or supplement?

No. First, because the Orthodox Church, in this doctrine, repeats the
very words of Jesus Christ; and his words, without doubt, are an exact
and perfect expression of the truth. Secondly, because the second
ecumenical Council, whose chief object was to establish the true
doctrine respecting the Holy Ghost, has without doubt sufficiently
set forth the same in the Creed; and the Catholic Church has
acknowledged this so decidedly, that the third ecumenical Council
in its seventh canon forbade the composition of any new Creed.[80]

The *Catechism of Nicholas Bulgaris* (1861) spoke little on the procession,
although he brought forward the shields of Pope Leo III to witness that even
Rome had once recognized its inviolability.[81] Yet by the eighteenth and nineteenth centuries Rome's position on the addition was far different from Leo's,
especially as it pertained to the Churches of the East and their profession of the
Catholic faith.

Rome and the Eastern Catholic Churches

In the centuries following the Union of Brest, other churches entered into
communion with Rome, including (but not limited to) portions of the Syrian
Church in 1662, most of the Antiochene Church under Patriarch Cyril VI in
1724, and the Armenian Catholic Church in 1742. As early as 1575 Pope Gregory
XIII had prescribed the specific creed to be used by Eastern Christians wishing
full communion, including the affirmation of:

> all the things the holy ecumenical synod of Florence defined and
> declared concerning the union of the western and eastern church,
> namely that the Holy Spirit is eternally from the Father and the Son;
> and that he has his essence and His subsistent being from the Father
> and the Son together [*et essentiam suam suumque esse subsistens habet
> ex Patre simul et Filio*]; and that he proceeds from both eternally as
> from one principle and by a single procession. . . . and that the Son,
> according to the Greeks, is also the cause [*secundum Graecos quidem
> causam*] . . . and that the explanation of these words, *filioque* for the
> sake of declaring the truth and because of immanent necessity, has
> been lawfully and reasonably added to the creed.[82]

In 1642 Pope Urban VIII promulgated a similar statement of faith for Eastern Christians, and in 1743 Benedict XIV issued *Nuper ad nos*, which contained
a profession for the Maronites explicitly affirming the teachings of the first
eight ecumenical councils (the eighth being the anti-Photian synod, at which
"Photius was rightfully condemned").[83] Also to be embraced by the Maronites

were the later councils, "especially the Synod of Florence" and its teachings on the procession, which it repeated verbatim.[84] However, Pope Benedict had earlier made it clear in his 1742 bull, *Etsi Pastoralis*, that while "the Greeks are bound to believe that the Holy Ghost proceeds from the Son . . . they are not bound to proclaim it in the Creed."[85] Later, in the encyclical *Allatae Sunt* (promulgated in 1755) Benedict explained the Roman policy in more detail. He maintained that "there is no room for doubting that this procession is a dogma of the Faith and that every true Catholic accepts and professes this."[86] Yet when dealing with the necessity of professing the *filioque* liturgically, Benedict recognized that the Catholic Church has

> sometimes allowed the Orientals and Greeks to say the Creed without this addition . . . [and] at other times this See has insisted on Greeks and Orientals using the addition. It has done this when it had grounds to suspect that they were unwilling to include the addition in the Creed because they shared the false view that the Holy Spirit does not proceed from the Father and the Son or that the Church had no power to add the phrase "and from the Son."[87]

Benedict used historical examples to prove his point—the Council of Lyons had allowed the Greeks to recite the creed without the addition, but Pope Nicholas II later insisted on the use of the *filioque* when "he realized that Emperor Michael was not acting in good faith."[88] The Greeks at Ferrara-Florence were allowed to recite the unaltered creed, but the Armenians were obliged to use it "perhaps because he [Pope Eugene IV] had learned that the Armenians were less averse to the addition then were the Greeks."[89] At present Benedict desired that the Eastern Catholics "should not be ordered to say the Creed with the addition of the phrase 'and from the Son,' provided that they confess that the Holy Spirit proceeds from the Father and the Son and that they recognize the Church's power of making this addition."[90] The only time Greek Catholics "should be obliged to say the additional phrase" is when "its omission would cause scandal, if this particular custom of reciting the Creed with its addition prevailed in their locality, or it were thought necessary to obtain unambiguous proof of the correctness of their faith."[91]

The Bonn Conferences (1874–76)

Dr. Johann Joseph Ignaz von Döllinger (1799–1890), the great Catholic historian of doctrine, was excommunicated in 1871 for his refusal to acknowledge the teachings of the First Vatican Council on the universal jurisdiction and infallibility of the Pope.[92] He spent the remaining years of his life working to reunite those churches that he believed shared the proper understanding of doctrine and history—primarily the "Old Catholic," Anglican, and Orthodox. For this purpose, in September 1874 he organized a reunion conference in Bonn,[93] attended by approximately forty representatives, who within two days accepted fourteen articles that they believed (or rather hoped) provided the foundation for future communion between them. One article dealing with the addition, written by Döllinger himself, was not among the fourteen articles accepted, because many of Western delegates thought the wording too strong. It stated: "The way in which the *filioque* was inserted in the Nicene Creed was illegal, and that, with a view to future peace and unity, it ought to be restored to its primitive form, as put forth by the general councils of the undivided Church."[94]

The following year a second union conference met to discuss the *filioque* in more detail, covering not only the interpolation but also the theology behind it. Döllinger's view was that in adding to the creed, "a fault had been committed" and that the *filioque* should be removed in order for the Western Church to "rectify, as far as lies in our power, an old wrong."[95] Some of the Western delegates (e.g., Canon H. P. Liddon of St. Paul's, to whom Edward Pusey later addressed his famous letter against the conference) took exception to Döllinger's scheme, fearing that the *filioque*'s removal "would prove a stumbling block to believing souls in the West, as giving the impression that God has not actually revealed a relation of the Son to the eternal procession of the Holy Spirit from the Father."[96] The final statement of the conference, "being the fruit of longer and more anxious deliberation," acknowledged only the shared reception of the original creed and the recognition that the addition "did not take place in an ecclesiastically legitimate way."[97]

Concerning the theology of the procession, Döllinger recognized that "it appeared bold—almost foolhardy—at all events hopeless, to attempt, in so short a time, to solve a question which for centuries has occasioned such great division in Christendom."[98] Among the first topics discussed was the precise meaning of *procedere*, which both sides recognized was a poor translation of ἐκπορεύεσθαι. Bishop Gennadius maintained that "the Greek language is richer than the Latin. We have two expressions, ἐκπορεύεσθαι and προϊέναι; to the last *procedere* corresponds."[99] Thus the Holy Spirit proceeds [ἐκπορεύεσθαι] from the Father alone, from whom he has his existence [τὸ εἶναι, τὴν ὕπορξιν ἔχει]. However, as the conference progressed, many of the Greeks acknowledged that in speaking of the Spirit's προϊέναι from or through the Son, the Fathers (particularly Maximus the Confessor, whose *Letter to Marinus* was cited frequently) did intend to give the Son a role both in the temporal and in the eternal ἔκλαμψις or ἔκφανσις of the Spirit.[100] Thus while the Spirit did not receive his ὕπαρξις from the Son ("because there is in the Godhead but one beginning [ἀρχή], cause [αἰτία], and source [πηγή])," the Son and the Spirit did enjoy an eternal relationship, often expressed (as it was by John of Damascus) by the idea of the Spirit coming δι αὐτοῦ."[101]

Many of the delegates left Bonn convinced that they had succeeded where all before them had failed. Döllinger proclaimed that "the question of the

Holy Ghost is therefore exhausted . . . [and] the result . . . is an agreement which far exceeds my hopes. . . . With regard to the main matter we are one. . . . The Orientals here present partake for themselves this conviction, and we are permitted to hope that the authorities of their churches will agree with them."[102]

Unfortunately Döllinger's hopes were never realized—the articles of the Bonn Conference were not accepted by the authorities of the Eastern Churches, and future conferences became impossible to organize because of Russian–English tensions in the Crimea. The Russian Church in 1892 established a commission to study the work of the Bonn Conference (the St. Petersburg Commission), which in turn communicated its findings to the Old Catholic Church, who subsequently established a commission (the Rotterdam Commission) to respond.[103] Ultimately the Russian Church reached the conclusion that, despite protests to the contrary, Bonn had made the Son a "cause" or "co-cause" of the Holy Spirit. In the West, the Old Catholic Church did not drop the *filioque* from its creed until 1969, and the Anglicans waited until the 1978 Lambeth Conference before recommending its deletion. Despite the collective optimism of the Bonn delegates, the subject of the *filioque* was not exhausted, and the union of East and West was not yet to be.

Papal Encyclicals on Unity and the Orthodox Response

In January 1848, soon after his election, Pope Pius IX (1846–78) issued the apostolic letter *In Suprema Petri Apostoli Sede* addressed to the East on the subject of Christian unity.[104] The Eastern patriarchs vehemently rejected the pope's overtures, seeing it "as an attempt to mix the clear streams of orthodox doctrine with the deleterious dregs of heresy."[105] How, they wondered, could the East unite with those who professed the *filioque*, which had been "condemned by many Holy Councils" and "subjected to anathema . . . by the eighth Ecumenical Council."[106] The doctrine was "novel" (perhaps the most damning criticism the East had to offer), contrary to Scripture and "the universal Confession of the Catholic Church."[107] It also "introduced diverse and unequal relations [in the Trinity], with a confusion or commingling of them," and "destroyed the oneness from the one cause [i.e., the Father]."[108] The *filioque*, they claimed, had crept into the creed "like a wolf in sheep's clothing"[109] and was originally rejected by the popes, but "enticed by the antisynodical privileges offered them for the oppression of the Churches of God . . . [the popes] changed the ancient worship at will, separating themselves by novelties from the old received Christian Polity."[110] The status of Christians, or churches, who accepted the doctrine was clear:

> The novel doctrine of the Holy Ghost proceeding from the Father and the Son is essentially heresy, and its maintainers, whoever they be,

are heretics, according to the sentence of Pope St. Damasus
("If anyone rightly holds concerning the Father and the Son, yet
holds not rightly of the Holy Ghost, he is a heretic"),[111] and that the
congregations of such are also heretical, and that all spiritual
communion in worship of the orthodox sons of the Catholic Church
with such is unlawful.[112]

In 1894 Pope Leo XIII (1878–1903), who took a particular interest in the
Churches of the East (both in and out of communion with Rome), published an
apostolic letter on Christian Unity (*Praeclara Gratulationis Publicae*) urging the
Orthodox to "return to the fold they have abandoned" and embrace the true
Church.[113] Leo implored them:

> Our mouth is open to you, to you all of Greek or other Oriental Rites
> who are separated from the Catholic Church . . . There [is no] reason
> for you to fear . . . that We or any of Our Successors will ever dimin-
> ish your rights, the privileges of your Patriarchs, *or the established
> Ritual* of any one of your Churches.[114]

In response to the pope's letter, Patriarch Anthimos VII of Constantinople (1895–97) wrote his *Reply to the Papal Encyclical of Pope Leo XIII on Reunion* (1895).[115] He was "astonished and perplexed" by the Rome's protestations
of friendship when in the Ukraine and elsewhere "traps are laid for the conscience of the more simple orthodox Christians by means of deceitful work-
ers transformed into apostles of Christ, sending into the East clerics with the
dress and headcovering of orthodox priests."[116] Although the primacy, particularly as it was defined by *Pastor Aeternus*, took up a good portion of the
letter, Anthimos also spoke directly to the *filioque* and Rome's claims to
orthodoxy.

Central to Anthimos's argument was the relative novelty of the addition.
He wrote: "If the Westerners prove from the teaching of the holy Fathers and
the divinely assembled Ecumenical Councils that the then orthodox Roman
Church . . . before the ninth century read the Creed with the addition. . . . we
have no more to say."[117] However, Anthimos believed that the opposite was true
and that the pope himself knew it—that "the one holy, catholic and apostolic
Church of the seven Ecumenical Councils believed and taught . . . that the Holy
Ghost proceeds from the Father."[118]

> Certainly Pope Leo XIII is not ignorant that his orthodox predecessor
> and namesake, the defender of orthodoxy, Leo III, in the year 809
> denounced synodically this anti-evangelical and utterly lawless
> addition. . . . Likewise he is by no means ignorant that . . . this
> anti-evangelical and lawless addition was with difficulty inserted
> officially into the holy Creed at Rome . . . and that consequently the

Roman Church . . . renders herself fully responsible before the one holy, catholic and apostolic Church of Christ.[119]

Boris Bolotov

Attempting to build on the consensus reached at Bonn, in 1898 the Russian theologian Boris Bolotov anonymously put forward his famous "Twenty-seven Theses on the *Filioque*."[120] Bolotov addressed the *filioque* as both a theological and an ecumenical issue, providing what he believed to be a mutually acceptable theology of the Spirit's procession and a way of resolving the historical conflict surrounding it. He first claimed that there were numerous references in the patristic corpus to the Spirit proceeding, or progressing, or shining forth (ἐκπορεύεσθαι, προϊέναι, ἔκλαμψις) through the Son.[121] These references were so frequent that one "cannot simply regard [them] as the private opinion of a father . . . but are bound to accord [them] the value of an ecumenical *theologoumenon*."[122] To claim (as many Orthodox did) that these references "imply nothing but a temporal mission of the Holy Spirit . . . led to violent distortions of some patristic texts."[123] Instead, the διὰ τοῦ Υἰοῦ formula must be understood as "containing an indication of the mysterious aspect in the life and the eternal relationships of the Holy Spirit with the Father and the Son" even if the exact nature of that relationship remained an "incomprehensible truth."[124] However, Bolotov was clear that the relationship established by this expression should not be confused with the Spirit's unique procession (ἐκπόρευσις) from the Father alone (ἐκπόρευσις understood here "in the strict sense"), a *theologoumenon*, but not a dogma, that had long standing in the Eastern Church.[125]

This thesis led to Bolotov's second argument—"that the formula *ex Patre filioque*, as found in the writings of St. Augustine, is *not* identical in its terminology, nor even in its meaning, with the teaching of the Eastern fathers. . . . This idea is unknown in the Eastern fathers [and] even as a private opinion cannot be recognized . . . as equivalent to the Eastern διά Υἰοῦ.[126] Unlike earlier figures (e.g., Beccus and Bessarion) who tried to harmonize the Eastern and Western approaches, Bolotov simply recognized them as diverse, yet equally legitimate, approaches to the describing the trinitarian mystery. He suggested that the Eastern belief in procession from the Father alone (ἐκ μόνου τοῦ Πατρὸς) and the Latin belief in procession from the Father and the Son (*filioque*) both be accorded the status as *theologoumena* and that neither belief be imposed upon the other side as a universal (and binding) dogma of the Church.[127] After all, for centuries East and West were united despite their different understandings of the procession—even Photius, he argued, agreed to communion with Rome without an explicit rejection of the *filioque*. "Therefore it was not the question of the *filioque* which caused the division of the Church," which is why it should not today "constitute an *impedimentum dirimens* for the reestablishment of communion."[128]

While some in Russia (e.g. Alexander Kireev and Rev. John Leont'evich Janyshev) embraced Bolotov's theses and wanted the Orthodox Church to recognize the Old Catholics under the terms proposed, others (e.g., Professor Dimitri Gusev) still believed the Western teaching on the *filioque* to be incompatible with the Orthodox faith.[129] Against Bolotov, Gusev maintained that the *filioque* was, in fact, a Church-dividing issue and that the Spirit's procession "from the Father alone" was a nonnegotiable dogma of the Orthodox Church.[130] The debate between the two sides became increasingly acrimonious, and it continued until it was silenced by the Revolution. The twentieth century was about to bring great changes to Russia, and the *filioque* debate was about to enter an entirely new phase of its own.

10

The Twentieth and Twenty-first Centuries

The progress that was made during the nineteenth century began to bear fruit in the twentieth, as theologians and hierarchs worked toward resolving the *filioque* debate—putting aside the polemics of the past in order to clarify (in terms acceptable to both East and West) the faith of the ancient Church as it concerned the procession of the Holy Spirit. A number of factors explain this transformation. In the first half of the century Orthodoxy began a constructive reengagement with the West after the Bolshevik Revolution, as Russian émigrés in Paris began discussing (rather than debating) theology with their Catholic and Protestant colleagues. At the same time, Roman Catholic theology was enjoying a renaissance of biblical and patristic studies, coupled with a renewed interest in pneumatology and the place of the Spirit in the life of the Church. Individual theologians of all denominations (e.g., Karl Rahner, Yves Congar, Vladimir Lossky, Oliver Clément, Jurgen Moltmann, Karl Barth) were writing on the role of the Spirit and the theology of the procession—even in their disagreements adding much to the ongoing dialogue. The nascent ecumenical movement, with the early participation of the Orthodox and Protestant churches (and the eventual involvement of the Catholic Church), brought theologians and hierarchs together for formal dialogues, all aimed at healing the divisions that had grown up between them.

The twentieth century dialogues, both bilateral (e.g., between the Catholic and Orthodox) and multilateral (e.g., those meetings sponsored by the World Council of Churches), were remarkable in the level of consensus reached on the theology of the *filioque*. Official statements of the Catholic Church, for example, went further than ever before in acknowledging traditional Eastern concerns about the doctrine, leading some in the Orthodox world to wonder aloud if the *filioque*, as a theological matter, was still a separating issue. Even the status of the creedal interpolation and the pope's right to have added the *filioque*, which have not yet been explicitly addressed in the Catholic-Orthodox dialogue, may soon come under discussion as both Churches explore the implications of the Ravenna Statement (2007) and its understanding of the Roman primacy. The doctrinal controversy surrounding the *filioque* is not yet resolved, but the past century does provide reason to hope that a resolution is not far off.

Orthodox Ecumenism and the Old Catholic-Anglican Dialogues

In 1902 Patriarch Joachim III (1878–84, 1901–12) sent a letter to the Orthodox bishops of the world for their thoughts on "our present and future relations with the two great growths of Christianity, viz. the western Church and the Church of the Protestants."[1] Of particular interest to the Patriarch were the Anglicans and Old Catholics, for although "a clear and agreed opinion as to their professed confession of faith does not yet prevail among us,"[2] "one would not be wrong to say that of the Christians of the West they are the closest to the Orthodox Church."[3]

Relations between Anglicans and Orthodox, especially in the West, remained warm throughout the first part of the century and provided several opportunities for exchange about the theology of the *filioque*.[4] In 1918 an unofficial conference on unity between members of the Episcopal Church in America and Metropolitan of Athens Meletios Metaxakis quickly came to a mutual understanding of the procession (based on the findings of the Bonn Conference), although disagreement remained about its place in the creed. The Metropolitan said that union demanded the *filioque*'s removal, otherwise "the question that will be placed before us by many over there [Greece] is: 'If the Anglican Church accepts that as we do, and puts the same interpretation on it as we do, how is it that in her spirit of protest against the Roman Church, she still keeps these words?'"[5] The Episcopalians insisted that the *filioque* was not of Roman origin but was placed in the creed to protect the deity of Christ against the Arians. While its insertion might have "violated the letter of the Council of Ephesus's decisions [regarding alterations to the creed], it kept the spirit of it" since it was used to defend the true faith.[6] Even now the *filioque* was important in order "to protect the Godhead of the Son against modern Unitarian attacks" and could not be removed without (minimally) approval of the entire Anglican Church or (optimally) the sanction of an ecumenical council.[7]

In 1920 the Ecumenical Patriarchate issued an encyclical, "Unto the Churches of Christ Everywhere," calling for practical steps, including the establishment of a "league" of churches, to increase rapprochement and fellowship among Christians.[8] Soon after, the Archbishop of Canterbury, Randall Davidson, invited the Ecumenical Patriarchate to send a delegation to the upcoming Lambeth Conference in order to discuss the dogmatic questions that continued to separate them. As with previous discussions, while agreement on the theology of the procession was easily reached, the Anglicans continued to oppose the removal of the *filioque* from the creed. They suggested that in assemblies of Eastern and Western Christians the unaltered creed be recited, while the creed with the *filioque* could still be used in Anglican services provided it was understood in an orthodox manner, that is, according to the interpretation of John of Damascus.[9]

The 1930 Lambeth Conference, at which a sizable Orthodox delegation was present, asked both the Archbishop of Canterbury and the Ecumenical Patriarch "to appoint representatives ... to a doctrinal commission. ... [to] prepare a joint statement on the theological points about which there is difference and agreement between the Anglican and the Eastern Churches."[10] This led to the first meeting of the Joint Doctrinal Commission in 1931, which once again used the Bonn Conference as a basis for agreement.[11] The Anglicans affirmed that the *filioque* did not imply two principles or causes in God but simply expressed the teaching (found in John of Damascus and many of the Greek fathers) that the Holy Spirit comes from the Father through the Son. This clarification, they hoped, would ally the East's fears enough to allow the Anglicans continued use of the interpolated creed. The Orthodox delegates, however, insisted on the excision of the *filioque*, claiming that "we are of the opinion that on this point no concession is possible, because in the Creed of Nicea it is the eternal procession of the Spirit from the Father alone which is taught and confessed, and not the temporal mission which comes through the Son."[12]

In July of that same year, at Bonn, a Union Conference was held at which the Anglican and Old Catholic Churches formally established intercommunion, each recognizing "the catholicity and independence of the other."[13] The Old Catholics, led by Bishop Kenninck of Utrecht, met with the Orthodox at Bonn three months later in the hopes of negotiating a similar arrangement. Unlike the Anglicans, the Old Catholics were more open to the removal of the *filioque*, and they pointed out to Metropolitan Germanos and the Orthodox delegates that it had already been deleted by the Churches in Holland and Switzerland.[14] The Orthodox expressed their joy, and the conference concluded with both sides agreeing that there appeared to be no dogmatic obstacles to the establishment of communion between them.[15]

Orthodox Theology: Sergius Bulgakov (1871–1944), Vladimir Lossky (1903–58), and the Neo-Palamites

Sergius Bulgakov, philosopher and theologian, was among the most brilliant—and the most controversial—of the Russian émigrés who made their way West following the October Revolution.[16] Exiled by the Bolsheviks in 1922, Bulgakov went on to found *l'Institut de Théologie Orthodoxe Saint-Serge* (St. Sergius Orthodox Theological Institute), where he taught until his death in 1944. The middle volume of his trilogy *On Divine Humanity* was dedicated to the Holy Spirit, with a sizable portion of the work devoted to the issue of the procession, which he called "the sole problem . . . in pneumatology in the course of the last millennium. It is as if no other problem exists."[17]

After reviewing the history of the *filioque* debate, Bulgakov came to the conclusion that until the ninth century there was a mutual recognition of the "incompleteness" of the Nicene-Constantinopolitan Creed as it concerned the Holy Spirit—that is, it failed to mention not only the Holy Spirit's divinity but also his eternal relationship to the Son. Various opinions about the exact nature of this relationship (e.g., that the Spirit proceeded through/from the Son) peacefully coexisted for several centuries until East–West "relations were . . . poisoned by rivalry and lust for power."[18] The East, following Photius (upon whom Bulgakov placed a good deal of blame), wrongly insisted that "proceeds from the Father" was prohibitive or limiting, just as in their "arrogance" the West wrongly dogmatized a legitimate *theologoumenon* and turned the *filioque* into a Church-dividing issue.

Bulgakov rejected the Anselmic-Thomistic idea of "necessary relational opposition" within the Trinity, calling it a "theological absurdity."[19] Relations are predicates, not subjects, for "a relation arises and exists only where the things that are related exist; it is grounded by them and arises between them. It does not ground them."[20] The West had "abolished the existence of the hypostases as such," which is why it found it so easy to "leap" from the individual hypostases of the Father and the Son to their "shared divine nature" when speaking about the procession of the Holy Spirit from both "as from a single principle."[21]

Bulgakov claimed that the *filioque* was an "imaginary dogma which derives from an imaginary problem," since both the Photian and Latin positions on the procession were premised on the causal origination of the hypostases within the eternal godhead, an idea neither scriptural nor patristic.[22] The fathers wanted to speak about the essential triunity of God, which is why, beginning with the Father, they spoke about the persons in terms of their relationship with the other two hypostases. Only later was the nature of this relationship defined (or distorted) in terms of hypostatic origination—whether in terms of the Spirit's origination "from the Father alone" or "from the Father and the Son." In their attempts to clarify what had remained obscure (i.e., how the Spirit and his procession related him to the other persons), later theologians destroyed not only the mystery of the Trinity, but the unity of the Church.

Bulgakov followed Bolotov in suggesting that the various opinions about the exact nature of the Spirit's procession be regarded as legitimate *theologoumena* that do not represent an *impedimentum dirimens* to unity. Even the liturgical use of the *filioque* in the Western churches could be tolerated, since "by virtue of its antiquity [it] has acquired a sacred character and a kind of inviolability."[23] Since "in practice, the two sides, East and West, do not differ in their veneration of the Holy Spirit despite their divergence over the procession" and since the "spirit of un-love and active schism" that fueled the debate was now subsiding, Bulgakov believed it the perfect time to recognize the controversy for what it was—a "sterile and empty" debate needlessly prolonged and, he hoped, soon ended.[24]

Among those who took issue with Bulgakov's irenicism was fellow émigré Vladimir Lossky, who saw in the *filioque* the "root" of all subsequent Latin errors. He famously wrote:

> By the dogma of the *filioque*, the God of the philosophers and
> savants is introduced into the heart of the Living God, taking the
> place of the *Deus absconditus, qui posuit tenebras latibulum suum.* The
> unknowable essence of the Father, Son, and Holy Spirit receives
> positive qualifications. It becomes the object of natural theology: we
> get 'God in general,' who could be the god of Descartes, or the god of
> Leibnitz, or even perhaps, to some extent, the god of Voltaire and of
> the dechristianized Deists of the eighteenth century.[25]

Lossky believed that while one could "admit the possibility of the *filioque* as it first appeared at Toledo, for example,"[26] the Orthodox were right to refuse "to admit a relation of origin which opposes the Holy Spirit to the Father and the Son, taken as a single principle."[27] For Lossky (as for Bulgakov) "relations only serve to express the hypostatic diversity of the three, they are not the basis for it."[28] The position of Anselm and Thomas (despite its "logical clarity") had the effect of relativizing and depersonalizing the hypostases and was rightly rejected by the East.[29]

Lossky firmly defended the Eastern teaching of the Spirit's procession ἐκ μόνου τοῦ Πατρὸς—a formula that "may seem novel [but] represents in its doctrinal tenor nothing more than the plain affirmation of the traditional teaching of the monarchy of the Father."[30] The Father is "the cause of the consubstantial hypostases of the Son and Holy Spirit and also presides over the external manifestation of the unity of the Trinity," although there was an important distinction between these categories of eternal causality and economic manifestation that the West had historically failed to recognize.[31] The East, however, knew there to be a difference between "the hypostatic procession of the Holy

Spirit—His personal existence ἐκ μόνου τοῦ Πατρὸς—and the manifesting natural procession of the common Godhead *ad extra* in the Holy Spirit διὰ τοῦ Yίοῦ."[32] However, Lossky acknowledged that one could not relegate, "as some Orthodox polemicists have," all references to procession διὰ Yίοῦ "solely to the temporal mission of the Holy Spirit."[33] There was also the category of *eternal* manifestation, something once recognized by the Western fathers although the teaching seems to have gotten distorted by the "theologically rude and uneducated minds of Western Christians of the Carolingian period."[34] Once Latin theology, "frozen so long in dogmatic isolation," rediscovered this category with all its palamite implications, the issue of the *filioque* would no longer be a stumbling block to unity.[35]

Other Orthodox theologians followed Lossky in the attempt to interpret the *filioque* according to the categories explicated by Gregory of Cyprus and Gregory Palamas—that is, utilizing the distinction between God's unknowable essence and His eternal/energetic manifestation.[36] Among them was the Romanian author Dimitru Staniloae (1903–93), who even followed Palamas in accepting Augustine's understanding of the Spirit as "the Life creating a bond between the two Living Ones, and hence also as Love."[37] However Staniloae grounded this teaching not in the works of Augustine, but in the writings of Maximus the Confessor, who had described the Spirit as "incomprehensible Life . . . springing up wholly from that which, while itself without beginning, is nevertheless the beginning of all, the Father."[38] For this reason, Staniloae maintained that the Spirit came forth as a person (i.e., received his hypostatic existence) from the Father as the incomprehensible love of the Father for the Son, but proceeds "towards the Son" and comes to abide in him as his goal, thus creating an eternal relationship between the Word and the Spirit.[39] This resting or abiding in the Son is answered by the eternal "shining forth" of the Spirit from the Son, which is nothing less than "the joyful response of the Son's love when confronted with this loving initiative of the Father."[40] This is what the Eastern fathers (e.g., Maximus, Gregory of Cyprus, Gregory Palamas) intended to convey when they differentiated between the Spirit's unique procession (ἐκπόρευσις) from the Father and his eternal "progression" or "shining forth" from the Son (i.e., his προϊέναι or ἔκλαμψις).[41]

Staniloae rejected the *filioque* (i.e., the procession of the Spirit from the Father and the Son as from a single principle) as unacceptable to the Orthodox, since it "confuses the Persons and makes the divine essence a source of personal being."[42] Procession from the Father alone, he argued, "is not a mere *theologoumenon*, but a point of faith."[43] Like Lossky, he blamed the *filioque* for subsequent Latin errors, including the fact that "in the West ecclesiology has become an impersonal, juridical system, while theology, and in the same way the whole of Western culture with it, has become strictly rational."[44] As the Spirit became less important in the West, Christ's abiding presence came to be seen "in the Pope, and bishops, and priests [who] occupied the place of the absent Christ . . . [not] through the Spirit in the hearts of the faithful . . . as it is in Orthodoxy."[45]

Oliver Clément, a student of Lossky, went further than his mentor in order to discover what he called "the authentic intuitions of filioquism."[46] Clément criticized Eastern polemicists who "thought against [the Latins] . . . without understanding or pinning down the truth of the other."[47] The Orthodox needed to recognize that "the double affirmation that the Spirit proceeds from the Father alone, and that his sending by the Son concerns only his temporal mission, cannot account, it seems, for either the richness of the Revelation or for all the expressions of the Fathers."[48]

Clément began his own treatment of the *filioque* with the patristic principle (seen especially in Maximus and John of Damascus) that the inseparability of the persons within the godhead made it impossible to isolate the activities of any one of them. Therefore he asked "whether the subsequent controversies did not arise because people partly forgot the divine 'logic' which is always simultaneously one and threefold. . . . To say that the Spirit 'proceeds' from the Father is necessarily to name the Son, since from all eternity the Father puts his Other in unity; so when he causes the Spirit to 'proceed' he remains Father *of the Son*."[49]

Distinguishing between the person/essence of the Spirit (τὸ Πνεῦμα) and his energy (πνεῦμα), Clément tried "go beyond filioquism by integrating it" into the Orthodox (i.e. palamite) trinitarian model.[50] He wrote: "as person, one could say, on the level of essence, the Spirit proceeds from the Father alone, since the Father is the one 'cause' in the Trinity. He proceeds 'conjointly' with the Son on whom he rests. But the 'spirit' as divine energy pours forth from the Father through the Son, or, if one prefers, from the Son."[51] On this level, he argued, the *filioque* was completely orthodox.

Boris Bobrinskoy echoed Clément's irenicism, even claiming to see certain "positive" elements of the doctrine, which the East would do well to recognize. He argued that the Western teaching emphasized:

1. The Holy Spirit is the mutual love and the bond of love between the Father and Son.
2. The Spirit is the common gift of the Father and the Son.
3. The eternal Son is not extraneous to the procession of the Holy Spirit (although Orthodox theology adds that this occurs in an ineffable manner and without bringing in the idea of causality).[52]

Bobrinskoy also noted the christocentrism inherent in the Latin model of the Trinity, which led many in the West to postulate in the eternal procession "the same dynamic of the Church's experience of the Spirit . . . [i.e.,] as the gift of the Father and the Son."[53] While not inaccurate, he pointed out the other "movements" of trinitarian revelation as found in the Scripture, and the necessity of balancing them in order to achieve theological truth.[54] The Spirit sent by

Christ, he reminded his readers, is also the Spirit sent by the Father who rests on Christ and empowers him for his mission.

Bobrinskoy also discussed the "negative" elements of the *filioque*—those aspects of the doctrine that the Orthodox rightly reject. The *filioque*, he argued, is wrong because:

1. It wrongly introduced, "even [in a] purely conceptual and speculative" manner, the idea of "anteriority in the generation of the Son relative to the procession of the Spirit." This concept "contributes to the unbalancing of the trinitarian mystery" by failing to recognize the "concomitant and simultaneous" character of the hypostases.
2. The Father "does not transmit hypostatic properties even to the Son"; the idea of procession *tamquam ab uno principio* is "radically unacceptable."
3. Although there is an orthodox interpretation of the *per filium* formula, historically the attempts to equate it with the *filioque* have led to ambiguities and problems.[55]

Ultimately Bobrinskoy was optimistic that "an essential convergence between the most creative patristic intuitions of Byzantine theology [St. Gregory of Cyprus and St. Gregory Palamas] and contemporary theological research" could lead to both a revival of pneumatology (East and West) and the resolution of the ancient controversy surrounding the *filioque*.[56] Others in the Orthodox world remained, and still remain, unconvinced. Among them was John Romanides (1928–2001), who believed that Western theology had strayed too far from the orthodox teaching of the Church fathers, especially as it concerned its non-recognition of the essence–energy distinction. Filioquism, he argued, was as bad a heresy as Arianism, and it, along with its progenitor, Augustine, must be firmly rejected if the West was to return to the Orthodox fold.[57] More recently the same view was upheld by Michael Azkoul[58] and Joseph Farrell,[59] although increasingly (at least among theologians) a more irenic spirit has prevailed. And yet, even among the most ecumenically minded, there remains among the Orthodox the insistence that for theological dialogue to succeed, the Nicene-Constantinopolitan Creed must "recover its primitive form . . . [so that] the *filioque* will cease to be seen as a sin against unity and love."[60]

Catholic Theology: Karl Rahner (1904–84), Yves Congar (1904–95), and the *Filioque* in France

Although Karl Rahner wrote little on the *filioque* itself, his advocacy of a revival of trinitarian studies was particularly influential among Western Christians, especially Roman Catholics.[61] His *grundaxiom*, that "the 'economic' Trinity is the 'immanent' Trinity and the 'immanent' Trinity is the 'economic' Trinity" was originally conceived as an attempt to recapture the experiential aspect of trinitarian theology, saving it from the metaphysical and speculative backwaters that kept it isolated and untouched.[62] Rahner was afraid that for most Christians, theologians included, the Trinity had become little more than a footnote following the treatise *De Deo Uno* in the handbooks of dogma, and he stated that "Christians are, in their practical life, almost mere monotheists. We must be willing to admit that, should the doctrine of the Trinity have to be dropped as false, the major part of religious literature could well remain virtually unchanged."[63]

Rahner's attempt was lauded by many, especially those in the Christian East, who saw in his project the possibility for a renewal in Western pneumatology.[64] John Zizioulas (later Metropolitan John of Pergamon) looked quite favorably on Rahner's thought, especially his decision to ground the understanding of God on the person of the Father, as opposed to the unity of the divine substance.[65] Although, as Gregory Havrilak makes clear, "one would search long and hard for direct references to Eastern luminaries in Rahner's trinitarian works," there is an obvious sympathy with the insights of Cappadocian theology and, by extension, with the teaching of the Orthodox Church.[66]

Alongside the pneumatological revival occasioned by Rahner's writings, in France the *nouvelle théologie* brought about a renewal in patristic studies, led by such figures as Henri de Lubac and Jean Danielou. New critical editions of patristic works (e.g., in the *Sources chrétiennes* series) allowed Catholic and Orthodox scholars to examine the fathers without the methodological issues that had plagued earlier generations.[67] Of particular importance was the 1941 publication of Hans Urs von Balthasar's *Kosmische Liturgie: Das Weltbild Maximus des Bekenners*, which ushered in a new era of Maximus studies.[68] Since that time, critical editions and translations of Maximus's works have proliferated in the West, complemented by hundreds of books and articles on the Confessor's unique contributions to theology and the spiritual life. Among these works have been the studies by French Roman Catholics on Maximus's theology of the Trinity, allowing his writings (particularly as found in the *Letter to Marinus*) to become an important hermeneutical tool in understanding the mind of the fathers on the subject of the procession.

Juan Miguel Garrigues, in his 1981 work *L'Esprit qui dit 'Pere': Le Problème du Filioque*, attempted to trace the roots of the *filioque* debate, which he believed to be largely linguistic, and to propose some solutions.[69] Garrigues argued that the translation of ἐκπορεύεσθαι with *procedere* in the Latin version of the Nicene-Constantinopolitan Creed accounted for much of the difficulty, maintaining that *qui ex Patre exportat* ("who goes forth out of the Father") would have been a far better way to describe the Spirit's unique coming-into-being. *Processio* is a translation of προϊέναι or προχωρεῖν, terms that were used in the patristic corpus to refer to the Spirit's consubstantial existence (which "proceeds or "flows forth" from the Father through the Son).[70]

According to Garrigues, the fathers were attempting to balance several important theological truths in their trinitarian writings, including the monarchy of the Father (who remained unique cause within the godhead), the consubstantiality of the Trinity, and the idea of a trinitarian τάξις. This last idea, seen especially in Gregory of Nyssa and Maximus the Confessor, was crucial, since the procession (ἐκπόρευσις) of the Spirit from the Father presupposed the begetting of the Son (for "as soon as God . . . is named Father He is thought of as having a Son").[71] Without introducing any temporality, the fathers gave a certain "logical prius" to the Son, which explained, in large part, the various formulas used to express the "strictly dogmatic content of the *filioque* . . . that the Holy Spirit goes forth [ἐκπορευόμενον] from the Father *as Father*, i.e., as begetter of the unique Son."[72] Both the Augustinian (*qui ex Patre filioque procedit*) and Eastern (ἐκ μόνου τοῦ Πατρὸς διὰ τοῦ Υἱοῦ ἐκπορευόμενον) formulas should thus both be considered *theologoumena* expressing (albeit with different emphases) the same theological truths—the first stressing the Son as a positive condition of the Spirit's consubstantial procession, the second affirming that the ἐκπόρευσις of the Spirit is from the Father (of the Son) as from a unique cause.

Borrowing heavily from Maximus the Confessor's *Quaestiones ad Thalassium* 63 and the *Letter to Marinus*, Garrigues suggested several reunion formulas, which he believed summed up the mind of the undivided Church on the procession. Among them was the idea that "the Holy Spirit, by going forth [ἐκπορευόμενον /exportans] out of the one Father who begets the unique Son, proceeds [προχωρῶν /procedit] in origin from both."[73] Creedally this could also be expressed with the formula: "I believe in the Holy Spirit, the Lord the giver of life, who issued forth from the Father [ἐκ τοῦ Πατρὸς ἐκπορευόμενον] and proceeds from the Father and the Son [ἐκ τοῦ Πατρὸς καὶ τοῦ Υἱοῦ προϊόν]."[74]

André Halleux proposed a far less complicated solution: rather than introducing another statement of faith, the Roman Catholic Church should simply drop the *filioque* and "receive" the unaltered creed of 381 as the basis for reunion.[75] However, Halleux was clear that this did not and should not necessitate the rejection of the Latin teaching on the procession, but rather should lead to its reinterpretation. Halleux believed that the Councils of Lyons and Florence failed, in large part, because they imposed upon the East an unabashedly Western interpretation of the διὰ τοῦ Υἱοῦ formula (i.e., one in keeping with post-Carolingian Latin theology). He then asked whether modern dialogue might be more productive if it were to reverse this hermeneutic, reading the Latin teaching on the *filioque* in light of the East's traditional understanding of the διὰ τοῦ Υἱοῦ. This modification would allow the West to "acknowledge the radical truth of monopatrism" while the Orthodox themselves could come to appreciate the authentic intuitions of the *filioque*, which Halleux believed were well grounded in patristic tradition.[76]

Perhaps no Catholic author in the twentieth century concerned himself more with the history and theology of the *filioque* debate than Yves Cardinal Congar. The third volume of Congar's magisterial *I Believe in the Holy Spirit* dealt almost exclusively with the *filioque*, and concluded with several proposals for resolving the debate. Congar recognized the historical problems caused by the (mis)translation of ἐκπορεύεσθαι and προϊέναι, recognizing that in the Greek trinitarian theology these verbs were not synonymous. However, Congar did not follow Garrigues in giving these terms a palamite reading—that is, denoting a real difference between hypostatic existence and consubstantial existence. While accepting the legitimacy of this paradigm within the Greek trinitarian system, Congar did not think it was possible to transpose this teaching onto the Latin model.[77]

For Congar, resolution of the *filioque* required both East and West to recognize that, despite a legitimate diversity in trinitarian thinking, both sides confessed the same central truths: the consubstantiality of the third person within the Trinity, the notion that the Son was "not unrelated" to the Father in the production of the Spirit, and the monarchy of the Father (who remained "principle without principle, or beginning, of the whole divinity").[78] Historically the West adopted the *filioque* in its attempt to affirm the first two truths, the East rejected it in order to preserve the third. Yet Congar noted that the Greek fathers too, in their use of the διὰ τοῦ Υἱοῦ formula, "claimed that the Word, the Son, has a share in the production of the Holy Spirit, which cannot be reduced to the economic order," just as the Latin fathers continued to affirm the monarchy of the Father (e.g., from whom, in the words of Augustine, the Spirit "principally proceeds" [*procedit principaliter*]).[79] That neither side completely succeeded in balancing all of these truths can be explained, in large part, both by inadequacies of language and by the mutual lack of charity that characterized the debate (with "each side being certain of itself . . . only wanting to reduce [the other's views] to its own ideas and formulas").[80]

Congar suggested a few concrete steps for moving beyond the historical impasse. First, following Halleux, he proposed a new hermeneutic, asking the West "after having affirmed for such a long time that the διὰ τοῦ Υἱοῦ was the equivalent of the *filioque*, [whether] it would be possible to agree in return that the *filioque* goes back to the διὰ τοῦ Υἱοῦ . . . [and] recognize the fundamental authenticity of monopatrism?"[81] Second, Congar suggested calling a new council so that both sides could "combine the truths invested in the two formulae by showing they are complementary . . . re-using the terms of John 15:16 and 16:14–15 . . . [and] avoiding all ambiguity."[82] Lastly, Congar, who described himself as "categorically in favor of suppression," argued that Rome "as a gesture of humility and brotherhood" should remove the *filioque* from the creed.[83] It had been "introduced in a canonically irregular way" in the first place, and its suppression "if it was welcomed in a really 'genuine' sense by the Orthodox Church, could create a new situation which would be favorable to the reestablishment of full communion."[84]

While Congar's views on the *filioque* have been incredibly influential among Roman Catholic scholars, there are still those who maintain the necessity of keeping the Western creed in its present form. Among them is Aidan Nichols, who has argued that while Rome could acknowledge the *filioque*'s introduction as "gravely imprudent" and suppress it "as an act of ecclesiastical charity and reconciliation . . . the pastoral ill-consequences of removing an article from the creed may be quite high."[85] He concluded:

> The solution for the Roman see is clear: to insist on the *filioque* in the Latin Church . . . both as doctrine and as clause, and to require it as doctrine for the Eastern churches but not as clause. It is simply unthinkable that the Catholic Church should abandon the *filioque* as doctrine. . . . What is possible is that the see of Rome could legislate that on occasions when different rites are represented the creed will always be said or sung without the *filioque* clause. But whether such a modest measure will satisfy Orthodox intransigence . . . is open to every possible question.[86]

Thomas Weinandy offered a defense of the *filioque* from a very different perspective, trying to understand the "active" roles of both the Son and the Spirit in intratrinitarian life. The Eastern view, he argued, rightly stressed the monarchy of the Father but had the effect of making the Son and the Spirit merely passive recipients of the Father's divine life. The traditional Western view was also inadequate, because it assigned the Son an active role in the origin of the Spirit but not vice versa, despite the biblical affirmations of the Spirit's agency in the life and ministry of Jesus. Weinandy therefore attempted to balance the *filioque* with a *spiritque*, seeing the Spirit as an active participant in trinitarian *perichoresis*. For Weinandy "the Son is begotten by the Father *in the Spirit* and thus the Spirit simultaneously proceeds from the Father as the one in whom the Son is begotten. The Son, being begotten in the Spirit, simultaneously loves the Father in the same Spirit by which he himself is begotten."[87] Here, he believes, both the Eastern view (on the monarchy) and the Western tradition (on the *filioque*) are maintained, as the Spirit comes forth from the Father, but as the Spirit intimately involved in the Son's response to the Father's love.

Protestant Theology: Karl Barth (1886–1968) and Jürgen Moltmann

Karl Barth, author of the *Epistle to the Romans* and the *Church Dogmatics*, is considered by many to be the most influential Protestant theologian of the twentieth century.[88] Upholding the "infinite qualitative gap" between humanity and God, bridgeable only by the Word made flesh, Barth's theology exhibited a radical christocentrism that found an important place for the *filioque*. Barth began by acknowledging that the exact nature of the "procession" is impossible for us to know, and he contented himself with what can be known: that the Holy Spirit is God (for "what proceeds from God can only be God once again") and yet is, by his unique mode of coming into being, differentiated from the Son.[89] Barth was clear that this procession takes place from the Father and the Son, and although he recognized the East's continued objections, he believed that while "the Greek view . . . was not to be regarded as a heresy . . . the Western view was simply to be regarded as better."[90]

Barth's reasons for championing the Latin position stemmed from the rule, "which we regard as basic, that statements about the divine mode of being antecedently in themselves cannot be different in content from those that are made about their reality in revelation."[91] Even the most hardened opponents of the *filioque* admitted that "in their *opus ad extra* . . . the Holy Spirit is to be understood as the Spirit of both the Father and the Son."[92] If this is how God revealed Himself, then this view applied "not just in his work *ad extra*" but also in eternity.[93] The East's error was to establish truths about the divine mode of being independent of biblical revelation, using one passage (John 15:26) to negate "the many others which equally plainly call Him the Spirit of the Son."[94]

Barth's chief concern in defending the Western view was the centrality of Christ, who is *the* point of contact between God and humanity. "'And the Son' means that not merely for us, but in God himself, there is no possibility of an opening and readiness and capacity for God in man . . . unless it comes from Him."[95] He wondered aloud whether the Eastern position inevitably led to the belief that the "Spirit of the Father" can be obtained in "a direct and immediate relation, a mystical union with *the principium et fons Deitatis* . . . [setting aside] the Mediator of revelation, the Son or Word."[96] Barth even found the διὰ τοῦ Υἱοῦ (as traditionally interpreted by the East) inadequate for expressing the "logical and necessary" teaching that the Spirit comes to us, eternally and temporally, only from the Word.[97] For Barth, the Son, as Son of the Father, is truly *spirator Spiritus*, the Spirit coming forth from Father and Son as from "a common origin."[98]

Jürgen Moltmann is among those Protestant theologians who differed with Barth on the *filioque*, believing that its continued presence in the creed was not only an ecumenical stumbling block, but also a barrier to renewed pneumatological and trinitarian studies.[99] The addition "contributes nothing new to the statement about the procession of the Spirit from the Father. It is superfluous, is not required, and can consequently be struck out."[100] "By withdrawing the *filioque* a schism in the Church can be ended; but a common discussion about the doctrine of the Trinity must begin at the same time. The one is impossible without the other."[101]

Moltmann did not challenge the orthodoxy of the *filioque*, but instead maintained that as originally conceived it was simply an interpretation meant to address the "incompleteness" of the Nicene-Constantinopolitan Creed vis-à-vis the exact nature of the Son's participation in the procession of the Holy Spirit from the Father. The Father was indeed sole cause within the godhead and origin of both the Son and the Spirit, yet his Fatherhood did not derive from his causality (as if he were simply "universal Father like Zeus, Jupiter, Vishnu, or Wotan . . . merely because he is the unique cause on whom all things depend").[102] He is Father because he is the eternal Father of the eternal Son, and thus even the procession of the Spirit from the Father has as its premise the "generation . . . [and] existence of the Son . . . [and] the mutual relationship of the Father and Son."[103] The *filioque* is an attempt to express this truth, which is why Moltmann offered a more precise formulation: *The Holy Spirit who proceeds from the Father of the Son.*[104]

Moltmann then attempted to understand the procession by asking what exactly the Spirit receives from the Son. If he did not receive his being from the Son (his ὑπόστασις or ὕπαρξις), since he received this from the Father alone, then Moltmann postulates that he must have received from Him his "inner-trinitarian, interpersonal, perichoretic form" (his πρόσωπον or εἶδος).[105] Acknowledging that some Western readers may be surprised by this distinction, Moltmann believed it both valid and worthwhile, especially as it tried to communicate what the East traditionally meant by the Spirit's eternal or energetic manifestation. Moltmann then offered a clarification of his earlier formula, which he believed summed up the truth of the *filioque* in a manner acceptable to both traditions: *The Holy Spirit who proceeds from the Father of the Son, and receives his form from the Father and from the Son.*[106] Remove the *filioque* from the creed, Moltmann argued, and theological agreement on its meaning would soon follow.

Bilateral and Multilateral Dialogues

After the Second World War, formal theological dialogues between the churches became a regular and important part of the burgeoning ecumenical movement. The Old Catholics and Anglicans were still the most active dialogue partners with the Orthodox, as they attempted to build on the level of consensus reached before the war. In 1969 the position of Bishop Urs Küry, son of Bishop Adolf Küry, became the basis for the Old Catholics' decision to officially remove the *filioque* from the creed.[107] In their statement the addition was "entirely rejected as uncanonical . . . and an offense against love as the bond of unity."[108] Furthermore the Old Catholics "firmly rejected any theological doctrine which makes the Son a joint cause of the Spirit," affirming that "there is only one principle and source, namely the Father . . . [and that] the Holy Spirit proceeds from the Father alone."[109] In their 1975 conversation with the Orthodox at Cambésy, the Old Catholics repeated this position, relegating all references to procession διὰ τοῦ Υἱοῦ "to his temporal revelation and sending into the world" which takes place "through the Son or even from both the Father and Son."[110] It was as close as any Western church has come to rejecting the *filioque*, both as a creedal statement and as a doctrine.

Orthodox dialogue with the Anglicans continued in 1956 with the Moscow Conference, which was far less optimistic than previous gatherings.[111] Delegates from the Moscow Patriarchate clearly labeled the *filioque* "a heresy condemned by the whole Oecumenical Orthodox Church," and they demanded as "an absolute condition of union . . . the exclusion of the *filioque* from the creed and the condemnation of the teaching of the *filioque*."[112] The Anglicans balked and assured the Orthodox that their understanding of the *filioque* was fully in keeping with patristic tradition (i.e., that it did not allow for two principles or causes in God), even as the Orthodox insisted that this interpretation was impossible—that "to use the *filioque* was to accept two origins of the godhead."[113] While agreeing that "the word *filioque* has been irregularly introduced into the creed," the Anglican delegates nevertheless hoped that they would be permitted "in view of twelve hundred years of traditional use . . . to continue to recite in our liturgy the creed in the form to which we are accustomed," understanding the *filioque* "in a wholly orthodox sense."[114]

Twenty years later, in 1976, the Anglicans met again with the Orthodox in Moscow and finally conceded that because it had been "introduced into the creed without the authority of an ecumenical council and without due regard for Catholic assent . . . the *filioque* clause should not be included in the creed."[115] While "some [Anglican delegates] seemed willing to abandon the *filioque* doctrine altogether. . . . others urged that no condemnation be passed on the Augustinian teaching about the double procession."[116] It is interesting to note that in their discussions, the delegates differentiated eternal procession from temporal mission but deliberately avoided "the suggestion advanced by Greek theologians of the thirteenth and fourteenth centuries . . . that there is also an "eternal manifestation of the Spirit by both Father and Son."[117] For this reason the conference "left it as an open question whether the *filioque* could, in some cases, legitimately be affirmed as a *theologoumenon*" as long as it lost its dogmatic and creedal character.[118] The Athens Statement of 1978 (which was, in part, a response to the decisions of the 1976 General Convention of the Episcopal Church to permit the ordination of women) repeated the findings of the Moscow Commission, calling upon the Anglicans to remove the *filioque* "as soon as it is pastorally and constitutionally possible."[119] This took place later that year, when the Lambeth Conference formally requested "that all member Churches of the Anglican Communion . . . consider omitting the *filioque* from the Nicene Creed."[120]

Concerning the theology of the procession, the Dublin Agreed Statement of 1984 was a significant step forward, the Orthodox on one hand stating that the doctrine of the *filioque* remained unacceptable," yet recognizing that "it was capable of an Orthodox interpretation . . . [as long as] the Son is not considered a cause or co-cause of the existence of the Holy Spirit."[121] This position was based on their reading of Maximus's *Letter to Marinus*, which had acknowledged a distinction "between two senses of procession, one by which the Father causes the existence of the Spirit [ἐκπόρευσις] and the other by which the Spirit shines forth [ἔκφανσις] from the Father *and* the Son."[122] In terms of this latter concept (the eternal shining forth of the Spirit), the *filioque* could potentially be regarded as a legitimate *theologoumenon* of the Western Church.[123] For their part the Anglicans affirmed that the Father was sole "fount of deity," and that even though Western theology often associated the Son with the Father as principle (*principium*) of the Spirit, "the Anglicans on the Commission put on record that they do not wish to defend the use of the term 'cause' [*causa*] in this context."[124]

Perhaps the single most significant dialogue on the *filioque* was organized by the Faith and Order Commission of the World Council of Churches, which had been established in 1948. Meeting at Schloss Klingenthal near Strasbourg, first in October 1978 and the again in May 1979, this multilateral commission—composed of Orthodox, Protestants, and Roman Catholics—published its findings along with a report (the "Klingenthal Memorandum") detailing their results and recommendations.[125] At stake, they believed, were not only diverse approaches to the Trinity and the addition of a word, but also the ecumenical significance of the creed itself and its ability to serve as a "shared statement of the Christian faith."[126]

The Klingenthal Memorandum begins with a history of the debate and the biblical texts that detail the Spirit's relationship to both Christ and the believer, pointing out the important truth that the Holy Spirit is active before and during the ministry of Jesus, so that "it would be insufficient and indeed illegitimate to 'read back' into the Trinity only those New Testament passages which refer to the sending of the Spirit by Jesus Christ."[127] They then ask whether the *filioque*, which is grounded in this temporal sending of the Spirit by the Son, "involves the unbiblical subordination of the Spirit to the Son . . . [and perhaps is] inadequate as an articulation of a full and balanced doctrine of the Trinity."[128]

Noting the different approaches to the Trinity as found in the Augustine and the Cappadocians, the Klingenthal Memorandum nevertheless recognized that communion between East and West was maintained until the eleventh century, and that Maximus the Confessor demonstrated that "though divergent and at times in friction with one another . . . the two traditions of trinitarian teaching . . . were not considered to be mutually exclusive."[129] The two issues that had since become the focus of debate, and were as yet unresolved, were the unique role of the Father in the Trinity (hence the East's insistence on procession "from the Father alone") and the place of the Son (if any) in the procession of the Spirit.

Concerning the first issue, the commission examined the East's insistence that the Father's hypostatic properties (those that differentiated him from the

Son and the Spirit) could not be transferred without introducing confusion within the godhead. Since chief among these properties was being "the bringer forth" of the other persons, and thus "only cause of the being of the Son and of the Holy Spirit," the East had traditionally rejected the *filioque* as a danger to the monarchy of the Father and his unique place within the godhead.[130] The West continued to affirm this monarchy, even if "in describing the Son as 'secondary cause' . . . the *filioque* gave the impression of introducing two principles . . . and treating the Son in his consubstantiality and unity with the Father as the origin of the person of the Holy Spirit."[131]

According to the commission, what the West was (and is) attempting to convey in the *filioque* was the truth that the Father is always Father of the Son, and even the East affirms that while the Spirit proceeds from the Father alone, he does not proceed "in isolation from the Son."[132] How then should this unique relationship between the Son and the Spirit be expressed? The commission first suggested that the traditional Western formula ("the Spirit proceeds from the Father and the Son") should *not* be used, "for this would efface the difference in the relationship to the Father and to the Son."[133] As an alternative they proposed several expressions, which "well deserve to be given attention and consideration in future discussion."[134] These included:

- The Spirit proceeds from the Father of the Son
- The Spirit proceeds from the Father through the Son
- The Spirit proceeds from the Father and receives from the Son
- The Spirit proceeds from the Father and rests on the Son
- The Spirit proceeds from the Father and shines out through the Son.

The West had originally embraced the *filioque* to underline the truth that "the Holy Spirit is none other than the Spirit of Jesus Christ," although this had the unfortunate side effect of depersonalizing the Spirit "as if he were a mere 'instrument' or 'power.'"[135] In order that Christians might again "confess their common faith in the Holy Spirit" who is "the one who in his fullness both rests upon Jesus Christ and is a gift of Christ to the Church," the Klingenthal Memorandum concluded by recommending that "the original form of the third article of the creed, without the *filioque*, should everywhere be recognized as the normative one and restored."[136]

Catholic-Orthodox Dialogues and Statements: 1995–2003

Although relations between the Roman Catholic and Orthodox Churches remained cold in the first part of the twentieth century, a thaw began to take place in the 1950s. In 1948 Aristocles Spyrou (who had enjoyed cordial relation with Roman Catholics in Bitolj, Corfu, and New York) ascended the patriarchal throne as Athenagoras I (1948–72), and in 1958 Angelo Roncalli (former Apostolic representative in Bulgaria and Turkey) was elected Pope John XXIII (1958–63).[137] Pope and patriarch soon began a "dialogue of love" that blossomed during and after the Second Vatican Council (1962–65), leading not only to the 1964 meeting of Athenagoras with Paul VI (1963–78) on the Mount of Olives, but to the mutual "lifting of anathemas" in 1965.[138] Pope John Paul II (1978–2005) made union with the East a particular theme of his pontificate, especially as he prepared for the jubilee year with the encyclicals *Ut Unum Sint* and *Orientale Lumen.* The promising theological exchange that began in 1980 produced extraordinary results, although it was sidetracked in 1989 by the reemergence of the Eastern Catholic churches (especially in the Ukraine) and the problem of "Uniatism."[139] Six years later, perhaps as a way of revitalizing the stalled dialogue, the Vatican issued "The Greek and Latin Traditions Regarding the Procession of the Holy Spirit," a document aimed at explicating the Roman position on the *filioque.*[140] Although the 1992 *Catechism of the Catholic Church* had briefly (but clearly) reaffirmed the doctrine, the 1995 statement attempted to clarify the teaching, especially in light of historic Orthodox concerns. [141]

The document began with a clear affirmation that "the Father alone is the principle without principle [ἀρχὴ ἄναρχος] of the two other persons of the Trinity, the sole source [πηγή] of the Son and of the Holy Spirit . . . [who] takes his origin from the Father alone in a principal, proper, and immediate manner."[142] The Father is thus "the sole trinitarian cause [αἰτία] or principle [*principium*] of the Son and of the Holy Spirit."[143] The Roman Catholic Church affirmed that the doctrine of the *filioque* must never contradict this truth, "nor the fact that he is the sole origin [μία αἰτία] of the ἐκπόρευσις of the Spirit."[144] The Vatican recognized that in the language of the fathers, especially Gregory Nazianzus and Cyril of Alexandria, there was an important difference between ἐκπορεύεσθαι ("which can only characterize a relationship of origin to the principle without principle of the Trinity: the Father") and προϊέναι/*procedere.* Rome knew that problems of translation and the vagaries of history had conspired to create "a false equivalence" between the two concepts, which, it believed, had fueled the controversy. However, Maximus the Confessor (whose *Letter to Marinus* is quoted at length) clarified the Roman teaching that "the *filioque* does not concern the ἐκπόρευσις of the Spirit issued from the Father as source of the Trinity, but manifests his προϊέναι [*processio*] in the consubstantial communion of the Father and the Son."[145] "This does not mean that it is the divine essence or substance" that brings forth the Spirit, but instead that it comes from the hypostases of "the Father and the Son who have it in common."[146]

The East has "given a happy expression" to this same reality with the formula διὰ τοῦ Υἱοῦ ἐκπορευόμενον, which tells how "the spiration of the Spirit from the Father takes place by and through . . . the generation of the Son."[147] This is so because "in the trinitarian order [τάξις] the Holy Spirit is consecutive to the relation between the Father and the Son, since he takes his origin from the Father as Father of the only Son."[148] Thus, according to the Vatican statement, the approaches of East and West reflect a "legitimate complementarity" in the profession of the "same mystery," which, purged of a potentially subordinationist reading and linguistic misunderstanding, allow for a perfectly orthodox interpretation of the *filioque*.[149]

Reaction to the Roman document was, on the whole, very positive.[150] Several Orthodox theologians applauded the Vatican's clarification, especially in recognizing the distinction between ἐκπορεύεσθαι and προϊέναι as it had been made by Maximus in the *Letter to Marinus*. Metropolitan John Zizioulas wrote that for the fathers προϊέναι "was used to denote the Holy Spirit's dependence on the Son owing to the common substance or οὐσία which the Spirit in deriving from the Father alone as Person or ὑπόστασις receives from the Son, too, as οὐσιωδῶς, that is, with regard to the one οὐσία common to all three persons."[151] This is why for Maximus "the *filioque* was not heretical because its intention was to denote not the ἐκπορεύεσθαι but the προϊέναι of the Spirit."[152] Zizioulas urged Rome to move even closer to Maximus's position as outlined in the *Letter to Marinus* and claimed that the "single cause" (μία αἰτία) principle should be the basis for further discussion on the *filioque*, for "as St. Maximus the Confessor insisted . . . the decisive thing . . . lies precisely in the point that in using the *filioque* the Romans do not imply a 'cause' other than the Father. . . . If Roman Catholic theology would be ready to admit that the Son in no way constitutes a 'cause' [αἰτία] in the procession of the Spirit, this would bring the two traditions much closer to each other with regard to the *filioque*."[153] However, although the clarification was certainly helpful on a theological level, he concluded his observations by asking: "Is this enough? Or should we still insist that the *filioque* be removed also from the Latin text of the Creed?"[154] For Zizioulas, and indeed most Orthodox, it remained "difficult to imagine a situation whereby Greek and Latin Christians would recite the Creed together without using a common text."[155]

Building upon the Vatican's 1995 clarification, the North American Orthodox–Catholic Theological Consultation began its own dialogue in 1999 to address the question of the *filioque*, issuing its findings in October of 2003.[156] The Agreed Statement offered a brief but comprehensive summary of the historical debate, noting the long-unrecognized contributions of Gregory of Cyprus and the recent uses of the uninterpolated creed by Rome, which seemed to suggest "a new awareness on the Catholic side of the unique character of the original Greek text of the Creed as the most authentic formulation of the faith that unifies Eastern and Western Christianity."[157]

Theologically, the Agreed Statement began with a recognition of the apophatic principle, stating that in theological dialogues concerning the Trinity "the first habit of mind to be cultivated is doubtless a reverent modesty. . . . [because] our speculations always risk claiming a degree of clarity and certainty that is more than their due."[158] That said, there are certain affirmations that both Catholic and Orthodox Christians can make concerning the Trinity, including "that the Father is the primordial source [ἀρχὴ] and ultimate cause [αἰτία] of the divine being . . . [and] that the three hypostases or persons in God are constituted in their hypostatic existence and distinguished from one another solely by their relationships of origin, and not by any other characteristics or activities."[159] Like the Vatican clarification, the Agreed Statement recognized the uniqueness of ἐκπορεύεσθαι in Greek patristic literature and the inability of *procedere* (which had a broader meaning) to capture its essence. Referencing the *Letter to Marinus*, the document was clear that while "the difference between the Greek and the Latin traditions . . . is more than simply a verbal one, much of the original concern in the Greek Church over the insertion of the word *filioque* . . . may well have been due—as Maximus the Confessor explained—to a misunderstanding on both sides of the different ranges of meaning implied in the Greek and Latin terms for 'procession.'"[160]

The substantive issues generated by the debate, which continue to remain divisive, fell into two categories: theological and ecclesiological. The first concerned the precise nature of the Son's role in the procession. Both the Greek and Latin patristic traditions acknowledged "that the 'mission' of the Spirit in the world also involves the Son, who receives the Spirit into his own humanity at his baptism, breathes the Spirit forth onto the Twelve on the evening of the resurrection, and sends the Spirit in power into the world."[161] The Latins (applying *procedere* to both the eternal and temporal sendings) tended to speak of this "procession" occurring through or from the Son, even while recognizing, in their use of the phrase, "a somewhat different relationship from his 'procession' from the Father."[162]

The Greeks too "struggled to find ways of expressing a sense that the Son . . . also plays a mediating role of some kind in the Spirit's eternal being and activity."[163] Here the Agreed Statement recalled two of the most significant contributions: by Gregory of Cyprus and Gregory Palamas. It was the *Tomos* of Gregory of Cyprus that had insisted that while "the Holy Spirit receives his existence and hypostatic identity solely from the Father, who is the single cause of the divine Being, he shines from and is manifested eternally through the Son, in the way that light shines forth and is manifest through the intermediary of the sun's rays. In the following century Gregory Palamas proposed a similar interpretation that—in terms of the transcendent divine energy, although not in terms of substance or hypostatic being—'the Spirit pours itself out from the Father through the Son, and, if you like, from the Son over all those worthy of it,' a communication which may even be broadly called 'procession' (ἐκπόρευσις)."[164]

That the two traditions "remain in some tension with each other" was clear; "the differences, though subtle, are substantial, and the very weight of theological tradition behind both of them makes them all the more difficult to

reconcile theologically with each other."[165] This problem was further complicated by the second substantive issue dividing East and West: "pastoral and
teaching authority in the Church—more precisely, the issue of the authority of
the Bishop of Rome to resolve dogmatic questions in a final way, simply in
virtue of his office."[166] The Orthodox saw the insertion of the *filioque* "as a
usurpation of the dogmatic authority proper to ecumenical Council. . . . [while]
Catholic theology has seen it as a legitimate exercise of his primatial authority
to proclaim and clarify the Church's faith."[167] Thus the root issue, which
should be kept "methodologically separate" from the properly theological discussion concerning the procession, was the exercise of papal primacy "with all
its implications."[168]

The Agreed Statement concluded with some recommendations, including
a plea for "a new and earnest dialogue concerning the origin and person of the
Holy Spirit," where both "Orthodox and Catholics refrain from labeling as
heretical the traditions of the other side on the subject of the procession of the
Holy Spirit."[169] In trying to determine the manner of the Spirit's origin, a matter "which still awaits full and final ecumenical resolution," theologians should
examine the "theological traditions of both our Churches . . . giv[ing] careful
consideration to the status of later councils held in both our Churches after
those seven generally received as ecumenical."[170] The Catholic Church, which
had recognized the "normative and irrevocable dogmatic value of the Creed of
381" in the 1995 Clarification, was asked in future to use the uninterpolated
creed in both catechetical and liturgical settings."[171] This way "the ancient
Creed of Constantinople . . . by our uniform practice and our new attempts at
mutual understanding [could become] the basis for a more conscious unity in
the one faith."[172] This conviction was "based on our own intense study and
discussion, that our traditions' different ways of understanding the procession
of the Holy Spirit need no longer divide us."[173]

Epilogue

As I mentioned in the introduction, this book is not a complete history of the *filioque* because such a book cannot yet be written. At present the *filioque* debate remains unresolved, a subject of disputation not only in internet chat rooms (and there are more than a few!), but also among the clergy and hierarchs of the various churches. Admittedly recent dialogues have demonstrated a level of consensus undreamed of only a century ago, and most theologians, East and West, would be hesitant to regard the *filioque* in itself as an insurmountable obstacle to unity. And yet it remains an issue, perhaps because its continued presence in the creed of the Western churches is a constant reminder to the Orthodox of a centuries-old wound.

I do not pretend to know where the debate goes from here. The optimist in me believes that a resolution is possible, and I am firmly convinced that Maximus's *Letter to Marinus* offers a theologically sound hermeneutic capable of bringing together the East and West on the issue of the procession. However, a sober analysis of the history also demonstrates that optimism, as it concerns the *filioque*, is often unwarranted. For centuries hierarchs and theologians have (all too prematurely) proclaimed that the debate was over. *Te Deums* were sung at Lyons and Florence, and yet the schism persists. Döllinger proclaimed the question exhausted, and yet the *filioque* remains unresolved. Perhaps the most that one can say at present is that the potential for resolution is there. "How," "when," or "if" that potential is realized is beyond my competency to say.

Notes

ABBREVIATIONS

ACW = *Ancient Christian Writers*
ANF = *Ante-Nicene Fathers*
CCG = *Corpus Christianorum Series Graeca*
CCL = *Corpus Christianorum Series Latina*
CF = *Concilium Florentinum: Documenta et Scriptores*
FC = *Fathers of the Church*
MGH = *Monumenta Germaniae Historica*
NPNF = *Nicene and Post-Nicene Fathers*
PG = *Patrologia Graeca*
PL = *Patrologia Latina*
SC = *Sources chrétiennes*

NOTES TO PREFACE

1. Jaroslav Pelikan, *The Melody of Theology: A Philosophical Dictionary* (Cambridge: Harvard University Press, 1988), 90.

2. See, for example, Maximus the Confessor: "He who receives the Logos through the commandments also receives through Him the Father who is by nature present in him, and the Spirit who likewise is by nature in Him. . . . In this way, he who receives a commandment and carries it out receives mystically the Holy Trinity" *Capita theologica et oeconomica* §71 (Eng. trans: G. E. H. Palmer, Philip Sherrard, and Kallistos Ware, *The Philokalia* 2 [London: Faber and Faber, 1981], 154–55).

3. See, for example, the opinions of John Behr, *The Mystery of Christ: Life in Death* (Crestwood: St. Vladimir's Seminary Press, 2006).

NOTES TO INTRODUCTION

1. This had also been done for the 1987 visit of Ecumenical Patriarch Demetrius and was later repeated during the Patriarch's visit to Pope Benedict XVI in 2008.

2. Alexei Khomiakov, quoted in A. Gratieux, *A. S. Khomiakov et le Mouvement Slavophile* 2 (Paris: Editions du Cerf, 1939), 8.

3. Vladimir Lossky, "The Procession of the Holy Spirit in Orthodox Trinitarian Doctrine," in *In the Image and Likeness of God* (Crestwood, N.Y.: St. Vladimir's Seminary Press, 1985), 71.

4. A favorite expression of the late Pope John Paul II.

5. Lukas Vischer, ed., *Spirit of God, Spirit of Christ: Ecumenical Reflections on the Filioque Controversy* (London: SPCK, 1981), 18.

6. English translation found in "The Greek and Latin Traditions Regarding the Procession of the Holy Spirit," *Catholic International* 7 (1996): 36–43.

7. "In this city, when you ask someone for change, he will discuss with you whether the Son is begotten or unbegotten. If you ask about the quality of bread you will receive the answer that 'the Father is greater, the Son is less.' If you suggest that you require a bath you will be told that 'there was nothing before the Son was created,'" Gregory of Nyssa, *De deitate Filii et Spiritus Sancti* (PG 46, 557).

8. According to Thomas Aquinas, "It is also demonstrated that to the aforementioned pontiff belongs the right of deciding what pertains to the faith. For Cyril, in his *Thesaurus*, says, 'Let us remain members in our head on the apostolic throne of the Roman Pontiffs, from whom it is our duty to seek what we must believe and what we must hold.' And Maximus in the Letter addressed to the Orientals says: 'All the ends of the earth which have sincerely received the Lord and Catholics everywhere professing the true faith look to the Church of the Romans as to the sun, and receive from it the light of the Catholic and Apostolic faith'" *Contra Errores Graecorum* 36 (Eng. trans: James Likoudis, *Ending the Byzantine Greek Schism* [New Rochelle, N.Y.: Catholics United for the Faith, 1992], 184).

9. *Canons of the Council of Ephesus* (Eng trans: Norman Tanner, ed., *Decrees of the Ecumenical Councils*, 1 [Washington D.C.: Georgetown University Press, 1990], 65). Peter L'Huillier acknowledges this as the basis for later Orthodox objections against the *filioque*, but he cautions that "it is materially impossible to base this condemnation on Canon 7 of Ephesus, which did not directly envision some addition but rather the composition of another formula of faith and furthermore concerned the definition of Nicaea." Peter L'Huillier, *The Church of the Ancient Councils: The Disciplinary Work of the First Four Ecumenical Councils* (Crestwood, N.Y.: St. Vladimir's Seminary Press, 1996), 163.

10. Théodore de Régnon, *Etudes de théologie positive sur la Sainte Trinité* (Paris: Retaux, 1892), 309.

11. Vincent of Lerins, *Commonitorium* 2.3 (Eng trans: NPNF 2.11.132).

12. Maximus the Confessor, *Opusculum* 10 (PG 91, 136).

13. "If we cannot discern in certain of our own manuscripts of Chrysostom, which we read from infancy to old age, the false or true, what will it be regarding the Western saints, of which we have never known or read the writings?" Mark of Ephesus: "I am not even certain whether these words really are those of the holy Fathers. We have none of their writings," V. Laurent ed., *Les "Mémoires" du Grand*

Ecclésiarque de l'Église de Constantinople Sylvestre Syropoulos sur le Concile de Florence *(1438–1439)*, CF 9 (Rome: Pontificium Institutum Orientalium Studiorum, 1971), 440. "Till now we have never known the Latin saints nor read them," Joseph Gill, ed., *Quae supersunt Actorum Graecorum Concilii Florentini: ResFlorentinae gestae*, CF 5.2.2 (Rome: Pontifical Oriental Institute, 1953), 427.

14. John Erickson, "*Filioque* and the Fathers at the Council of Florence," in *The Challenge of Our Past* (Crestwood, N.Y.: St. Vladimir's Seminary Press, 1991), 163.

15. For example, "the trinitarian quarrels of the fourth century had already shown what misunderstandings could result from the parallelisms *persona* (πρόσωπον) and *substantia-natura* (οὐσία-φύσις)," John Meyendorff, *Christ in Eastern Christian Thought* (Crestwood, N.Y.: St. Vladimir's Seminary Press, 1987), 25.

16. See, for example, the warnings of Cyril of Alexandria in *Epistula* 39 (PG 77, 181) and *Epistula* 40 (PG 77, 200–201).

17. See A. Edward Siecienski, "Avoiding the Sin of Ham: Dealing with Errors in the Works of the Fathers," *Studia Patristica* 45, ed. J. Baun, A. Cameron, M. Edwards, and M. Vinzent (Leuven, Belgium: Peeters, 2010) 175–79.

18. Emmanuel Candal, ed., *Bessarion Nicaenus, Oratio dogmatica de unione*, CF 7.1 (Rome: Pontifical Oriental Institute, 1958), 18–19 (Eng. trans: Joseph Gill, *The Council of Florence* [Cambridge: Cambridge University Press, 1959], 240).

19. *Mystagogia*, 70 (Eng. trans: Photius of Constantinople, *The Mystagogy of the Holy Spirit*, trans. Holy Transfiguration Monastery [Astoria, N.Y.: Studion Publishers, 1983], 100).

20. John Erickson, "*Filioque* and the Fathers at the Council of Florence," 162, 166.

21. An expression I "borrowed" (with permission) from Brian Matz's soon-to-be published paper, "Marshalling Patristic Soldiers in the Ninth-Century *Filioque* Dispute."

22. Markos Orpanos, "The Procession of the Holy Spirit according to Certain Later Greek Fathers," in Lukas Vischer, ed., *Spirit of God, Spirit of Christ*, 25.

23. For this reason, one needs to exercise caution when reading works such as the *Mystagogia*, which should not be understood as complete statements of Eastern trinitarian theology (although far too many Orthodox have done so).

24. See Jean-Claude Larchet, *Maxime le Confesseur, médiateur entre l'Orient et l'Occident* (Paris: Les Editions du Cerf, 1998).

25. See John Meyendorff, "Was There an Encounter between East and West at Florence?" in *Rome, Constantinople, and Moscow: Historical and Theological Studies* (Crestwood, N.Y.: St. Vladimir's Seminary Press, 1996), 87–111.

26. James Jorgenson, "The Debate Over Patristic Texts on Purgatory," in Giuseppe Alberigo, ed., *Christian Unity: The Council of Ferrara-Florence 1438/9* (Louvain: University Press, 1991), 333–34.

27. While Gill's position may be overly sanguine, he did successfully challenge the position of Syropoulus, whose account had been uncritically accepted throughout most of the Orthodox world. If Syropoulus is to be believed, the Greeks were starved into submission and signed the union decree only under a combination of imperial, financial, and psychological pressure (except for those apostates, like Bessarion and Isidore, whose orthodoxy was simply bought). Gill's work clearly proved that the anti-unionists enjoyed full freedom of speech (witnessed by the fact that Mark

remained the Greeks' spokesman until the very end) and that the privations endured by the Greeks (which were genuine) were not part of a plot to extort them, but rather were caused by the pope's inability to meet the ever-increasing costs of indefinitely maintaining the Byzantine delegates. See Gill, "The Council of Florence: A Success that Failed," in *Personalities of the Council of Florence* (Oxford: Basil Blackwell, 1964), 1–14; idem, "The Freedom of the Greeks in the Council of Florence," in *Church Union: Rome and Byzantium 1204–1453* (London: Variorum Reprints, 1979).

28. English trans.: Hans Urs von Balthasar, *Cosmic Liturgy: The Universe According to Maximus the Confessor*, trans. Brian Daley (San Francisco: Ignatius Press, 2003).

29. These works include: Juan Miguel Garrigues, *L'Esprit qui dit 'Père': Le Problème du Filioque* (Paris: Tequi, 1981); Jean-Claude Larchet, *Maxime le Confesseur, médiateur entre l'Orient et l'Occident*; Pierre Piret, *Le Christ et la Trinité selon Maxime le Confesseur* (Paris: Beauchesne, 1983).

30. Among the more notable contributions have been Frances Dvornik's *The Photian Schism* (1948), Joseph Gill's *The Council of Florence* (1959), Richard Haugh's *Photius and the Carolingians: The Trinitarian Controversy* (1975), Maria-Helene Gamillscheg's *Die Kontroverse um das Filioque: Moglichkeiten einer Problemlosung auf Grund der Forschungen und Gespräche der letzten hundert Jahre* (1996), and Aristeides Papadakis's *Crisis in Byzantium: The Filioque Controversy in the Patriarchate of Gregory II of Cyprus* (1996). More recent additions to *filioque* scholarship have been the publication of Dennis Ngien's *Apologetic for Filioque in Medieval Theology* (2005), Peter Gemeinhardt's *Filioque-Kontroverse Zwischen Ost-Und Westkirche Im Frühmittelalter* (2002), Bernd Oberdorfer's *Filioque: Geschichte und Theologie eines ökumenischen Problems* (2001), and Tia Kolbaba's *Inventing Latin Heretics: Byzantines and the Filioque in the Ninth Century* (2008).

NOTES TO CHAPTER I

1. H. B. Swete, *The Holy Spirit in the New Testament* (Eugene, Ore.: Wipf and Stock Publishers, 1999), 304.

2. "The New Testament contains no doctrine of the Trinity," Donald Juel, "The Trinity in the New Testament," *Theology Today* 54 (1997): 313. See also Arthur Wainwright, *The Trinity in the New Testament* (London: SPCK, 1967); G. S. Hendry, *The Holy Spirit in Christian Theology* (Philadelphia: Westminster, 1965); C. K. Barrett, *The Holy Spirit in the Gospel Tradition* (New York: Macmillan, 1947); G. T. Montague, *The Holy Spirit: Growth of a Biblical Tradition* (New York: Paulist Press, 1976); E. Schweitzer, *The Holy Spirit* (Philadelphia: Fortress Press, 1980); Raymond Brown, "Diverse Views of the Spirit in the New Testament: A Preliminary Contribution of Exegesis to Doctrinal Reflection," chapter in *Biblical Exegesis and Church Doctrine* (New York: Paulist Press, 1985), 101–13.

3. See, for example, Raymond Brown, "Does the New Testament Call Jesus God?" in *Jesus: God and Man* (New York: Macmillian Publishing, 1967), 1–38; Murray Harris, *Jesus as God: The New Testament Use of Theos in Reference to Jesus* (Grand Rapids, Mich.: Baker Academic, 1998).

4. For example, Edmund Fortman argued that while "he (i.e., Paul) accepted a threefold pattern of Father, Son, and Spirit to describe the activity of God, . . . he showed no clear awareness of a threefold problem within the godhead." Edmund

Fortman, *The Triune God: A Historical Study of the Doctrine of the Trinity* (Eugene, Ore.: Wipf and Stock Publishers, 1999), 22.

5. Raymond Brown, *The Birth of the Messiah* (New York: Doubleday, 1977), 124.

6. Ibid.

7. Ibid., 311–16. Brown linked this to the "backward development of Christology."

8. Joseph Fitzmyer, *The Gospel According to Luke I-IX*, Anchor Bible Series 28 (New York: Doubleday, 1981), 350.

9. Louis Bouyer, *The Eternal Son: A Theology of the Word of God and Christology*, trans. Simone Inkel and John Laughlin (Huntington, Ind.: Our Sunday Visitor, 1978), 257.

10. Ibid., 256.

11. William Foxwell Albright and C. S. Mann, *The Gospel According to Matthew*, Anchor Bible Series 26 (New York: Doubleday, 1971), 30. Yves Congar agreed, suggesting that the dove "may be a representation or the symbolic presence of that people and of the perennial movement with which Jesus wanted to be at one, since he was the new Adam and represented and embodied the new people of God (Mt 3:14–15)" Yves Congar, *I Believe in the Holy Spirit* 1 (New York: Crossroad Publishing, 1997), 16.

12. Thierry Maertens made the connection between Jesus' baptism and the flood based on his reading of 1 Peter 3:20–4:6, with the dove seen in both cases as the bringer of good news. Thierry Maertens, *The Spirit of God in Scripture* (Baltimore: Helicon, 1966), 101–2. Fred Craddock suggested that the dove is simply used here as a harbinger of divine grace, as was often the case in Hellenic literature. Fred Craddock, *Luke*, Interpretation Commentaries (Louisville: John Knox Press, 1990), 51.

13. Yves Congar, *I Believe in the Holy Spirit* 1, 16.

14. See especially the work of James D. G. Dunn: *The Christ and the Spirit 1: Christology* (Grand Rapids, Ind., Eerdmans, 1998); idem, *The Christ and the Spirit 2: Pneumatology* (Grand Rapids, Ind.: Eerdmans, 1998); idem, *Jesus and the Spirit: A Study of the Religious and Charismatic Experience of Jesus and the First Christians as Reflected in the New Testament* (Grand Rapids, Ind.: Eerdmans, 1997).

15. Roger Haight, *Jesus: Symbol of God* (New York: Orbis Books, 1999), 164.

16. See G.W.H. Lampe, "The Holy Spirit and the Person of Christ," in *Christ, Faith, and History: Cambridge Studies in Christology*, ed. S. W. Sykes and J. P. Clayton (Cambridge: Cambridge University Press, 1972), 117; Stevan Davies, *Jesus the Healer: Possession, Trance, and the Origins of Christianity* (New York: Continuum Publishing Company, 1995).

17. James D. G. Dunn, *Christology in the Making: A New Testament Inquiry into the Origins of the Doctrine of the Incarnation* (Grand Rapids, Ind.: Eerdmans, 2003), 137. According to John Nolland, there is debate as to whether Luke considered the baptism an anointing for a prophetic or a messianic role. After surveying the debate, he concluded that "Luke thinks in both prophetic and messianic terms, though . . . the prophetic thought is predominant." John Nolland, *Luke 1–9:20*, Word Biblical Commentary 35a (Dallas: Thomas Nelson, 1989), 196.

18. Among the Synoptics, Luke refers to the Spirit (17) more often than either Mark (6) or Matthew (12).

19. Joseph Fitzmyer, *The Gospel According to Luke I-IX*, 513.

20. Ibid., 523.

21. Joel Green, *The Gospel of Luke*, New International Commentary on the New Testament (Grand Rapids, Ind.: Eerdmans, 1997), 207.

22. Joseph Fitzmyer, *The Gospel According to Luke X–XXIV*, 871.

23. James D. G. Dunn, *Christology in the Making*, 141.

24. Luke's version (11:20) has "finger of God."

25. William Foxwell Albright and C. S. Mann, *The Gospel According to Matthew*, 155. See also Alexander Sand, *Das Evangelium nach Matthäus*, Regensburger Neues Testament (Regensburg: Verlag Friedrich Pustet, 1986).

26. "Jesus' healings and exorcisms are signs of the advent of God's reign and the guarantee of Jesus' messianic identity." Donald Senior, *Matthew*, Abbington New Testament Commentaries (Nashville: Abbington Press, 1998), 142.

27. C. S. Mann, "Pentecost, Spirit, and John," *Theology* 62 (1959): 188. The NRSV has translated this same passage as "breathed his last," understanding πνεῦμα in this context quite differently. This stance is supported by Senior, who sees the language here as simply a Jewish way of understanding death, whereby the individual "yields back to God the life breath originally given." Donald Senior, *Matthew*, 333. The NIV and NAB opt for "gave up his spirit," viewing this as Matthew's deliberate alteration of the Marcan parallel (Mk 15:37) where he uses ἐξέπνευσεν.

28. James D. G. Dunn, *Christology in the Making*, 142.

29. See J. Schaberg. *The Father, the Son, and the Holy Spirit* (Chico, Cal.: Scholars Press, 1982). Also B. J. Hubbard, *The Matthean Redaction of the Primitive Apostolic Commissioning* (Missoula, Mont.: Scholars Press, 1974); Raymond Brown, *An Introduction to the New Testament* (New York: Doubleday, 1997), 203.

30. R. T. France, *The Gospel of Matthew*, New International Commentary on the New Testament (Grand Rapids, Ind.: Eerdmans, 2007), 1118.

31. William Foxwell Albright and C. S. Mann, *The Gospel According to Matthew*, 27.

32. Joseph Fitzmyer, *The Gospel According to Luke X–XXIV*, 1580.

33. The exceptions include John 6:63 ("The Spirit gives life; the flesh counts for nothings. The words I have spoken to you are spirit and they are life") and 14:13 ("This is the Spirit of Truth. . . . You know him because he abides in you and he will be in you"). According to C. K. Barrett, explicit references to the power of the Spirit working through Jesus are absent because "Jesus himself is the bearer of the Spirit. . . . The Spirit descends on him and—a Johannine addition—abides upon him. It is unnecessary for John to record the numerous ecstatic features of the synoptic narratives: the Spirit rests permanently, not occasionally, upon Jesus." C. K. Barrett, *The Gospel According to St. John* (London SPCK, 1967), 74.

34. Raymond Brown, *The Gospel According to John XIII–XXI*, Anchor Bible Series 29a (New York: Doubleday, 1970), 1139.

35. Ibid., 1140. See especially Günther Bornkamm "Der Paraklet im Johannes-Evangelium," in *Geschichte und Glaube Erster Teil* (Munich: Kaiser,1968), 68–89. Here Bornkamm parallels statements made about the Paraclete with those already made about Jesus.

36. Raymond Brown, *The Gospel According to John XIII–XXI*, 716–17.

37. See F. Porsch, *Pneuma und Wort* (Frankfurt am Main: J. Knecht, 1974); Andreas Köstenberger and Scott Swain, *Father, Son, and Spirit: The Trinity and John's Gospel* (Downers Grove, Ill.: Intervarsity Press, 2008).

38. Rudolf Schnackenburg, *The Gospel According to St. John 3*, trans. David Smith and G. A. Kon (New York: Crossroad, 1982), 118–19.

39. "It is doubtful whether John intended any difference between the two statements." C. K. Barrett, *The Gospel According to St. John*, 402.

40. Raymond Brown, *The Gospel According to John XIII–XXI*, 689.

41. Ibid., 716.

42. Rudolf Bultmann, *The Gospel of John: A Commentary* (Louisville: Westminster John Knox Press, 1971), 575.

43. Rudolf Schnackenburg, *The Gospel According to St. John 3*, 136.

44. Rudolf Bultmann, *The Gospel of John: A Commentary*, 576.

45. Raymond Brown, *The Gospel According to John XIII–XXI*, 931. Barrett agrees: "It is possible that in John's mind πνεῦμα was not the human spirit of Jesus, given up when his body died, but the Holy Spirit, which, when he died, he was able to hand over (παραδιδόναι) to the few representative believers who stood by the cross. This suggestion is attractive because it corresponds to the undoubted fact that it was precisely at this moment, according to John, that the gift of the Spirit became possible." C. K. Barrett, *The Gospel According to St. John*, 460.

46. Raymond Brown, *The Gospel According to John XIII–XXI*, 910.

47. Köstenberger and Swain argue against both Brown and Barrett on this point, believing that, at best, this is only an "anticipatory sign" of the Pentecost to come. See Andreas Köstenberger and Scott Swain, *Father, Son, and Spirit: The Trinity and John's Gospel*, 101.

48. Raymond Brown, *The Gospel According to John XIII–XXI*, 1037.

49. Ibid., 1038.

50. Raymond Brown, *The Epistles of John*, Anchor Bible Series 30 (New York: Doubleday, 1982), 216. See also John Painter, *1,2,and 3 John*, Sacra Pagina Series 18 (Collegeville, Minn.: Liturgical Press, 2002); I. Howard Marshall, *Epistles of John*, New International Commentary on the New Testament (Grand Rapids, Ind.: Eerdmans, 1994).

51. Georg Strecker claims that this "crucial difference" between the portrayal of the Paraclete in the gospel (where he "clearly represents the eschatological helper who will be active in the disciples' future lives") and his portrayal in the epistles provides a "further argument for different authors of the gospel and the letter." Georg Strecker, *The Johannine Letters*, Hermeneia Series, trans. Linda Maloney (Minneapolis: Fortress Press, 1996), 38.

52. Raymond Brown, *The Epistles of John*, 482.

53. Georg Strecker, *The Johannine Letters*, 129. For Bultmann's views see Rudolf Bultmann, *The Johannine Epistles*, Hermeneia Series (Minneapolis: Fortress Press, 1973), 60 n.84.

54. For a description of the Spirit's role in Acts see J. H. E. Hull, *The Holy Spirit in the Acts of the Apostles* (London: Lutterworth, 1967); James D. G. Dunn, *Jesus and the Spirit: A Study in the Religious and Charismatic Experience in the New Testament*; R, P. Menzies, *The Development of Early Christian Pneumatology with Special Reference to*

Luke-Acts (Sheffield: JSOT Press, 1991); Rudolf Pesch, *Die Apostelgeschichte*, Evangelisch-Katholischer Kommentar zum Neuen Testament (Zürich: Benzinger Verlag, 1986); Josef Zmijewski, *Die Apostelgeschichte*, Regensburger Neues Testament (Regensburg: Verlag Friedrich Pustet, 1994).

55. A. W. Wainwright, *The Trinity in the New Testament* (London: SPCK, 1962), 200–201.

56. The historicity of this event has long been a question, especially given the witness of Matthew and John, who seem to date the reception of the Holy Spirit quite differently. Fitzmyer contends that the description of Pentecost is a dramatization of the events leading to Peter's first proclamation of the risen Lord in Jerusalem (an event that appears to have some historical basis). Luke's working assumption is that this occurs only because of the presence of the Spirit among the apostles, a gift that must have been given them at some point beforehand. See Joseph Fitzmyer, "The Ascension of Christ and Pentecost," *Theological Studies* 45 (1984): 409–40. Ernst Haenchen agrees, claiming that the purpose here is to vividly depict . . . one of the most important incidents since the departure of Jesus: the coming of the Spirit . . . so that it will rise unforgettably before the eyes of his readers." Ernst Haenchen, *The Acts of the Apostles: A Commentary* (Philadelphia: Westminster Press, 1971), 173.

57. Joseph Fitzmyer, *Acts of the Apostles*, Anchor Bible Series 31 (New York: Doubleday, 1998), 235.

58. Ibid., 236.

59. G. W. H. Lampe, *The Holy Spirit* (Oxford: SLG Press, 1974), 193.

60. Luke Timothy Johnson notes that the citation from Joel is altered "in several important ways, making the Spirit's outpouring an eschatological, and above all a prophetic event." See Luke Timothy Johnson, *Acts of the Apostles*, Sacra Pagina 5 (Collegeville, Minn.: Liturgical Press, 1992), 54. Haenchen argues that the crowd's ability to understand Peter allows Luke to "provide the theological meaning" of the event—that is, on this day "the Spirit of Christ heals the division of mankind and the confusion of Babel is abolished." Ernst Haenchen, *The Acts of the Apostles: A Commentary*, 174.

61. Yves Congar, *I Believe in the Holy Spirit* 1, 45.

62. James D. G. Dunn, *Christology in the Making*, 142.

63. Boris Bobrinskoy, *The Mystery of the Trinity: Trinitarian Experience and Vision in the Biblical and Patristic Tradition*, trans. Anthony Gythiel (Crestwood, N.Y.: St. Vladimir's Seminary Press, 1999), 103.

64. See Gordon Fee, "Paul and the Trinity: The Experience of Christ and the Spirit for Paul's Understanding of God," in *The Trinity: An Interdisciplinary Symposium on the Trinity* ed. Steven Davies, Daniel Kendall, and Gerald O'Collins (Oxford: Oxford University Press, 1999): 49–72; idem, *Paul, the Spirit and the People of God* (Peabody, Mass.: Hendrickson, 1996); James D. G. Dunn, *The Theology of Paul the Apostle* (Grand Rapids, Mich.: Eerdmans, 1998): 413–41.

65. Joseph Fitzmyer, *Romans*, Anchor Bible Series 33 (New York: Doubleday, 1993), 480.

66. Viktor Warnach, "Das Wirken des Hl. Geistes in den Gläubigen nach Paulus," in *Pro Veritate: Ein theologischer Dialog. Festgabe L. Jaeger und W. Stählin*, ed. E. Schlink and H. Volk (Münster and Kassel, Aschendorff, 1963), 156–202.

67. James D. G. Dunn, *Christology in the Making*, 146.

68. Edmund Fortman, *The Triune God*, 20.

69. Brendan Byrne, *Romans*, Sacra Pagina 6 (Collegeville, Minn.: Liturgical Press, 1996), 240. C.K. Barrett agrees, arguing that "it is idle to seek a distinction between the two . . . (for) it is only through Christ that the Spirit is known and received" C. K. Barrett, *Epistle to the Romans*, 2nd ed, Black's New Testament Commentaries (London: A & C Black, 1991), 149.

70. See also Romans 8:15 (πνεῦμα υἱοθεσίας); 2 Cor 3:17 (τὸ πνεῦμα κυρίου), Phil1:19 (πνεύματος Ἰησοῦ Χριστοῦ)

71. Paul mentions the Spirit nineteen times in chapter 8 alone.

72. James D.G. Dunn, *Romans 1–8*, Word Biblical Commentary 38a (Dallas: Thomas Nelson, 1988), 429.

73. Gerald O'Collins, *The Tripersonal God: Understanding and Interpreting the Trinity* (New York: Paulist Press, 1999), 63.

74. Ernst Käsemann, *Commentary on Romans* (Grand Rapids: Eerdmans, 1980), 213.

75. Joseph Fitzmyer, *Romans*, 491.

76. Ibid., 481.

77. Ibid.

78. For a discussion of these various issues see Hans Dieter Betz, *Galatians: A Commentary on Paul's Letter to the Churches of Galatia*, Hermeneia Series (Minneapolis: Fortress Press, 1979), 209–11 and Frank Matera, *Galatians*, Sacra Pagina 9 (Collegville: Liturgical Press, 1992), 151. See also F.F. Bruce, *The Epistle to the Galatians*, New International Greek New Testament Commentary (Grand Rapids: Eerdmans, 1982); Richard Longenecker, *Galatians*, Word Biblical Commentary 41 (Dallas: Thomas Nelson, 1990).

79. Edmund Fortman, *The Triune God*, 23.

80. Boris Bobrinskoy, *The Mystery of the Trinity*, 65.

81. Ibid., 65–66.

82. Ibid., 68.

83. Ibid.

84. Ibid.

NOTES TO CHAPTER 2

1. For Origen's theological legacy see Rowan Williams, "Origen: Between Orthodoxy and Heresy," in *Origeniana Septima: Origenes in den Auseinandersetzungen des 4. Jahrhunderts*, ed. W. A. Bienert and U. Kühneweg (Leuven: Peeters, 1999); Henri Crouzel, *Origen* (San Francisco: Harper and Row Publishers, 1989); idem, *Bibliographie Critique D'Origèn* (Hagae Comitis: Nejhoff, 1971); G. L. Prestige, *Fathers and Heretics: Six Studies in Dogmatic Faith with Prologue and Epilogue* (London: SPCK, 1968); Jean Danielou, *Origen* (New York: Sheed and Ward, 1955); Henri de Lubac, *Histoire et Esprit: L'intelligence de l'Écriture d'après Origène* (Paris: Éditiones Montaigne, 1950).

2. See A. Logan, "Origen and the Development of Trinitarian Theology," in L. Lies, ed., *Origeniana Quarta* (Innsbruck-Vienna: Tyrolia, 1987): 424–29.

3. Sergius Bulgakov, *The Comforter* trans. Boris Jackim (Grand Rapids, Ind.: Eerdmans, 2004), 18. Theodore de Régnon defended Origen against the charge of subordinationism in his *Etudes de Theologie positive sur La Sainte Trinite* (Paris: Victor Retaux et Fils, 1898), 8.

4. Ibid.

5. Edmund Fortman, *The Triune God* (Eugene, Ore.: Wipf and Stock), 56. John Behr also notes that according to Origen's reading of the Scripture "it is the Father alone who is 'the one true God' (Jn 17:3) and 'the God of all gods' (Ps 49:1 LXX) and is referred to as '*the* God' (ὁ θεός). All other beings called 'god' in Scripture, designated by the noun without the article, are made god by participation in his divinity." John Behr, *The Way to Nicea* (Crestwood, N.Y.: St. Vladimir's Seminary Press, 2001), 188.

6. Origen, *Commentary on John* 2.75–76 (Eng. trans.: Origen, *Commentary on the Gospel According to St. John Books 1–10*, trans. Ronald Heine, FC 80 [Washington, D.C.: Catholic University of America Press, 1990], 114).

7. Origen, *Commentary on John* 2.79 (Eng. trans.: Origen, *Commentary on the Gospel According to St. John*, 114).

8. "Up to the present have been able to find no passage in the Holy Scriptures which would warrant us in saying that the Holy Spirit was a being made or created." Origen, *De Principiis* 1.3.3 (Eng. trans.: Origen, *On First Principles*, trans. G. W. Butterworth [New York: Harper and Row, 1973], 31).

9. Origen, *Commentary on Romans* 6.13.3 (Eng. trans.: Origen, *Commentary on the Epistle to the Romans Books 6–10*, trans. T. P. Schek, FC 104 [Washington, D.C.: Catholic University of America Press, 2001–2002], 54).

10. Origen, *De Principiis* 1.3.7 (Eng. trans.: Origen, *On First Principles*, 37–38).

11. Origen, *De Principiis* 1.2.13 (Eng. trans.: Origen, *On First Principles*, 28).

12. Gregory Thaumaturgus, *Address of Thanksgiving to Origen* 16 (Eng trans: *St. Gregory Thaumaturgus: Life and Works*, trans. Michael Slusser [Washington, D.C.: Catholic University of America Press, 1998], 122).

13. See L. Abramowski, "Das Bekenntnis des G bei Gregor v. Nyssa u. das Problem seiner Echtheit," *Zeitschrift für Kirchengeschichte* 87 (1976): 145–66.

14. Gregory Thaumaturgus, *Confessio fidei* (Eng. trans.: "Life of Gregory the Wonderworker" in *Gregory Thaumaturgus: Life and Works*, 54).

15. A. Arunde, "El Espíritu Santo en la Exposición de fe de S Gregorio Taumaturgo," *Scripta Teol* 10 (1978): 373–407.

16. Critical edition found in Didymus, *Traité du Saint-Esprit*, SC 386, ed. Louis Doutreleau (Paris: Éditions du Cerf, 1992). The introduction to the work (128–31) discusses Didymus's role as an authority during the *filioque* debates.

17. Yves Congar claimed that "there is little doubt that Jerome left his mark on the text and was probably responsible for such expressions as *a Patre et me illi est* and *procedens a Veritate* or *neque alia substantia est Spiritus Sancti praeter id quod datur ei a Filio.*" Yves Congar, *I Believe in the Holy Spirit* 3, 26. Many of these phrases have been omitted from the *Sources Chrétiennes* critical edition.

18. H. B. Swete, *On the History of the Doctrine of the Procession of the Holy Spirit from the Apostolic Age to the Death of Charlemagne* (Eugene, Ore.: Wipf and Stock, 2004), 94–95.

19. Didymus, *De Spiritu Sancto* 37 (PG 39, 1065–66).

20. Didymus, *De Spiritu Sancto* 34 (PG 39, 1063–64).

21. Didymus, *De Spiritu Sancto* 36 (PG 39, 1064).

22. Alasdair Heron, *Studies in the Trinitarian writings of Didymus the Blind his authorship of the Adversus Eunomium IV-V and the De Trinitate* (University of Tübingen, 1972). The text with German translation is found in Jürgen Hönscheid and Ingrid Seiler, *De Trinitate* (Meisenheim: Hain, 1975).

23. Didymus, *De Trinitate* 2.2 (PG 39, 460).

24. Didymus, *De Trinitate* 2.2 (PG 39, 456).

25. Didymus, *De Trinitate* 1.31 (PG 39, 425).

26. Didymus, *De Trinitate* 2.2 (PG 39, 456).

27. Secondary literature on Athanasius is extensive. For his writings on the Spirit, see C. R. B. Shapland, *The Letters of Saint Athanasius Concerning the Holy Spirit* (London: Epworth Press, 1951); Theodore Campbell, "The Doctrine of the Holy Spirit in the Theology of Athanasius," *Scottish Journal of Theology* 27 (1974): 408–43; J. MacIntyre, "The Holy Spirit in Greek Patristic Thought," *Scottish Journal of Theology* 7 (1954): 353–75; R. P. G. Hanson, "The Divinity of the Holy Spirit" *Church Quarterly* 1 (1969): 298–306; M. Damaskinos, "La disponbilité au Saint Esprit et la fidelité aux origins d' après les Pères grecs," *Istinia* 19 (1974): 49–64; Charles Kannengieser, "Athanasius of Alexandria and the Holy Spirit between Nicea I and Constantinople I," *Irish Theological Quarterly* 48 (1981): 166–80; Joost van Rossum, "Athanasius and the *Filioque*: Ad Serapionem 1.20 in Nikephorus Blemmydes and Gregory of Cyprus," *Studia Patristica* 22, ed. Elizabeth Livingstone (Leuven: Peeters, 1997), 53–58.

28. John Behr, *The Nicene Faith* 1 (Crestwood, N.Y.: St. Vladimir's Seminary Press, 2004), 169.

29. We leave aside those works that later authors attributed to Athanasius, including the *De Incarnatione contra Apollinarem, Sermo mair de fide, Expositio fidei, Interpretatio in Symbolum, Dialogi contra Macedonianos,* and the so-called Athanasian Creed (*Quicumque Vult*) (which will be discussed in the next chapter). Many of these works were often quoted in later debates, despite the fact that all are now known to be spurious. See Johannes Quasten, *Patrology 3: The Golden Age of Greek Patristic Literature* (Westminster, Md.: Christian Classics, 1990), 29–34.

30. Critical Edition found in Athanasius, *Athanase D'Alexandrie: Lettres a Sérapion,* SC 15, ed. Joseph Lebron (Paris: Éditions du Cerf, 1947).

31. Athanasius, *Epistola ad Serapionem* 1.24 (Eng. trans.: Khaled Anatolios, *Anthanasius,* The Early Church Fathers [New York: Routledge, 2002], 223).

32. Athanasius, *Epistola ad Serapionem* 1.21 (Eng. trans.: Khaled Anatolios, *Anthanasius,* 220).

33. Athanasius, *Epistola ad Serapionem* 1.25 (Eng. trans.: Khaled Anatolios, *Anthanasius,* 224).

34. Athanasius, *Contra Arianos,* 3.24 (Eng. trans.: NPNF 2.4.407).

35. Athanasius, *Epistola ad Serapionem* 1.24 (Eng. trans.: Khaled Anatolios, *Anthanasius,* 224).

36. Athanasius, *Epistola ad Serapionem* 1.20 (Eng. trans.: Khaled Anatolios, *Anthanasius,* 220).

37. H. B. Swete, *On the History of the Doctrine of the Procession of the Holy Spirit,* 92.

38. A quotation long attributed to Athanasius, and used frequently in later debates, claimed that the Father "alone is unbegotten and alone is the only source of the Divinity" (μόνος ἀγέννητος καὶ μόνος πηγὴ θεότητος). (Pseudo) Athanasius, *Contra Sabellianos* (PG 28, 97).

39. Yves Congar, *I Believe in the Holy Spirit* 3, 25.

40. For an analysis of Basil's contributions to pneumatology see Volker Henning Drecoll, *Die Entwicklung der Trinitätslehre des Basilius von Cäsarea* (Göttinggen, Germany: Vanderhoeck & Ruprecht, 1996); Stephen Hildebrand, *The Trinitarian Theology of Basil of Caesarea* (Washington, D.C.: Catholic University of America Press, 2007).

41. Basil of Caesarea, *De Spiritu Sancto* 18.47 (Eng. trans.: Basil the Great, *On the Holy Spirit*, trans. David Anderson [Crestwood, N.Y.: St. Vladimir's Seminary Press, 2001], 74–75).

42. Basil of Caesarea, *De Spiritu Sancto* 17.43 (Eng. trans.: Basil the Great, *On the Holy Spirit*, 70).

43. Basil of Caesarea, *De Spiritu Sancto* 18.47 (Eng. trans.: *Basil the Great, On the Holy Spirit*, 75).

44. Basil of Caesarea, *De Spiritu Sancto* 18.45 (Eng. trans.: *Basil the Great, On the Holy Spirit*, 72).

45. Basil of Caesarea, *De Spiritu Sancto* 18.47 (Eng. trans.: Basil the Great, *On the Holy Spirit*, 75).

46. This was a particularly vexing problem at the Council of Florence. Books 4 and 5 of *Adversus Eunomium* are now known to have been authored by someone other than Basil. See Bernard Sesboüé, ed., *Basile de Césarée: Contre Eunome*, SC 305 (Paris: Les Éditions du Cerf, 1983), 146–47, n. 1. See also M. Van Pays, "Quelques remarques à propos d'un texte controversé de Saint Basile au Concile de Florence," *Irenikon* 40 (1967): 6–14.

47. John Behr, *The Nicene Faith* 2 (Crestwood, N.Y.: St. Vladimir's Seminary Press, 2004), 281.

48. Basil of Caesarea, *Contra Eunomium* 3.2 (Basile de Césarée, *Contre Eunome*, 152).

49. Basil of Caesarea, *Contra Eunomium* 5 (PG 29, 731).

50. This was part of a creed submitted to test the orthodoxy of Eustathius of Sebasteia. See Basil of Caesarea, *Letter 125* (Eng. trans.: St. Basil, *Letters 1–185*, FC 13, trans. Agnes Clare Way [Washington, D.C.: Catholic University of America Press, 1951], 259).

51. Maximus the Confessor, *Ambiguum 4* (Bart Janssens, ed., *Ambigua ad Thomam una cum Epistula Secunda ad Eundem*, CCG 48 [Turnhout: Brepols, 2002], 15).

52. See the recent work by Christopher Beeley, *Gregory of Nazianzus on the Trinity and the Knowledge of God* (Oxford: Oxford University Press, 2008).

53. "What then? Is the Spirit God? Certainly. Is he consubstantial? Yes, if he is God." Gregory of Nazianzus, *Oration* 31.10 (Eng. trans.: Gregory of Nazianzus, *On God and Christ: The Five Theological Orations and Two Letters to Cledonius*, ed. and trans. Lionel Wickham and Frederick Williams [Crestwood, N.Y.: St. Vladimir's Seminary Press, 2002], 123).

54. See Gregory of Nazianzus, *Oration* 43 (Eng. trans.: Leo P. Mccauley, John J. Sullivan, Martin R. P. Mcguire, Roy J. Deferrari, eds., *Funeral Orations by Saint Gregory*

Nazianzen and Saint Ambrose, FC 22 [Washington, D.C.: Catholic University of America Press, 1968], 27–100).

55. John McGuckin, *Saint Gregory of Nazianzus: An Intellectual Biography* (Crestwood, N.Y.: St. Vladimir's Seminary Press, 2001), 374.

56. Gregory of Nazianzus, *Oration* 25.15–18 (Eng. trans.: Christopher Beeley, *Gregory of Nazianzus on the Trinity and the Knowledge of God*, 202).

57. Gregory of Nazianzus, *Oration* 31.3 (Eng. trans.: Gregory of Nazianzus, *On God and Christ*, 118).

58. John McGuckin, *Saint Gregory of Nazianzus*, 283.

59. Basil had already pointed this out to Eunomius, who had read statements such as "made Lord and Christ" (Acts 2:36) as an affirmation that the Word was a created being. Basil claimed instead that this statement "is not given in the manner of theology, but clarifies the principles of the economy." Basil of Caesarea, *Contra Eunomium* 2.3 (Basile de Césarée, *Contre Eunome*, 16–19).

60. John McGuckin, *Saint Gregory of Nazianzus*, 285.

61. Gregory of Nazianzus, *Oration* 28.3 (Eng. trans.: Gregory of Nazianzus, *On God and Christ:* 39).

62. Although the distinction between the "economic" or "immanent" Trinity later became quite common in theological discourse, John Behr has questioned whether this idea truly has its roots in the Gregory's theology. He writes: "It is doubtful that the distinction, drawn in the manner, between 'immanent' and 'economic' trinitarian theology really corresponds, as is often asserted, to the patristic usage of '*theologia*' and '*economia*.'" John Behr, *The Nicene Faith* 1, 7.

63. "In these questions [i.e., the soul, the resurrection, the sufferings of Christ], to hit the mark is not useless, to miss it is not dangerous. But of God himself the knowledge we shall have in this life will be little, though soon after it will perhaps be more perfect, in the same Jesus Christ our Lord, to whom be glory forever and ever." Gregory of Nazianzus, *Oration* 27.10 (Eng. trans.: Gregory of Nazianzus, *On God and Christ*, 33–34).

64. Both John Behr (*The Nicene Faith* 2, 361 n. 49) and John McGuckin (*Saint Gregory of Nazianzus*, 294 n. 352) discuss whether Gregory is logically inconsistent on this point. See also E. P. Meijering, "The Doctrine of the Will and of the Trinity in the Orations of Gregory of Nazianzus," *Nederlands Theologisch Tijdschrift* 27 (1973): 224–34.

65. Gregory of Nazianzus, *Oration* 42.15 (Eng. trans.: Brian Daley, ed., *Gregory of Nazianzus*, Early Church Fathers [New York: Routledge, 2006], 147).

66. John McGuckin, *Saint Gregory of Nazianzus*, 295.

67. Gregory of Nazianzus, *Oration* 34 (Eng. trans.: NPNF 2.7.337).

68. Gregory of Nazianzus, *Oration* 42.15 (Eng. trans.: Brian Daley, ed., *Gregory of Nazianzus*, 147).

69. John McGuckin, *Saint Gregory of Nazianzus*, 307.

70. Gregory of Nazianzus, *Oration* 31.7 (Eng. trans.: Gregory of Nazianzus, *On God and Christ*, 121).

71. Gregory of Nazianzus, *Oration* 39.12 (Eng. trans: Brian Daley, ed., *Gregory of Nazianzus*, 133).

72. Gregory of Nazianzus, *Oration* 31.8 (Eng. trans.: Gregory of Nazianzus, *On God and Christ*, 122).

73. Stanley Burgess, *The Holy Spirit: Ancient Christian Traditions* (Peabody, Mass.: Hendrickson, 1984), 144.

74. John Behr, *The Nicene Faith* 2, 414

75. Ibid., 419.

76. Gregory of Nyssa, *Letter to Peter*, 4 (Eng. trans.: John Behr, *The Nicene Faith* 2, 419). This letter was long thought to be the work of Basil (as Letter 38 to his brother Gregory) and was included in the English translation of his correspondence (Basil of Caesarea, *Letters 1–185*, FC 13, trans. Agnes Clare Way [Washington, D.C.: Catholic University of America Press, 1951]).

77. Gregory of Nyssa, *Ad Ablabium* (Fridericus Mueller, ed., *Gregorii Nysseni opera dogmatica minora*, vol 3.1, Gregorii Nysseni opera [Leiden: Brill, 1958], 56).

78. Ibid.

79. Gregory of Nyssa, *De Spiritu Sancto adversus Pneumatomachos Macedonianos* (Eng. trans.: NPNF 2.5.317).

80. Gregory of Nyssa, *Adversus Eunomium* 1.42 (Eng. trans.: NPNF 2.5.100).

81. Gregory of Nyssa, *Letter to Peter*, 4 (Eng. trans.: John Behr, *The Nicene Faith* 2, 419).

82. John Behr, *The Nicene Faith* 2, 434.

83. Ibid.

84. Yves Congar, *I Believe in the Holy Spirit* 3, 32.

85. See Oliver Kösters, *Die Trinitätslehre des Epiphanus von Salamis* (Göttingen, Germany: Vanderhoeck & Ruprecht, 2003).

86. Epiphanius, *Ancoratus* 9 (PG 43, 32).

87. Epiphanius, *Ancoratus* 73 (PG 43, 153).

88. Ibid.

89. Epiphanius, *Panarion* 73.16 (Epiphanius, *Epiphanius* 3: *Panarion Haer 65–80*, ed. Karl Holl, Die Griechischen Christlichen Schrift Steller der Ersten Jahrhunderte (Berlin: Akademie-Verlag, 1985), 288.

90. See in particular Mark of Ephesus's interpretation of Epiphanius at the Council of Ferrara-Florence.

91. For Orthodox scholar Boris Bobrinskoy, Epiphanius's intention was to maintain that "Christ truly sends the Spirit who proceeds from the Father, the Son (being) not only the One on whom the Spirit rests, but the One who gives the Spirit." Boris Brobrinkoy, *The Mystery of the Trinity*, 70. Yves Congar, while recognizing that Epiphanius "neither speculates nor suggests any explanation concerning the procession of the Spirit," does believe that he is referring to the "intra divine being" when he refers in the *Panarion* to the idea of receiving subsistence from the Son. Yves Congar, *I Believe in the Holy Spirit* 3, 27.

92. For Gregory's view of the council, and the "quacking of angry geese" that forced his resignation, see particularly his *De Vita Sua* vv.1506–1904 (PG 37, 1133–62). Socrates's account is found in his *Ecclesiastical History* (1.5.8), Sozomen's in *Ecclesiastical History* 1.7.7.

93. See Peter L'Huillier, *The Church of the Ancient Councils* (Crestwood, N.Y.: St. Vladimir's Seminary Press, 1996), 105.

94. J. N. D. Kelly, *Early Christian Creeds*, 3rd ed. (New York: Longman, 1972), 296. It is thus a sad irony that this same text is also partly responsible for the schism that divided Christendom.

95. John Behr, *The Nicene Faith* 2, 379.

96. This was due not only to Gregory's theological program, but also to the rather complicated political machinations involved in choosing a successor for Melitus at Antioch. As for their unwillingness to proclaim the Holy Spirit *homoousias*, Gregory lamented: "I stood by and watched as the sweet and pristine spring of our ancient faith, which had joined that sacred and adorable nature of the Trinity in one, as formerly professed at Nicea, was now wretchedly polluted by the flooding in of the brine of men of dubious faith." *De Vita Sua*, 1704–08 (Eng. trans.: John McGuckin, *Saint Gregory of Nazianzus*, 355).

97. It is still an open question whether the Nicene-Constantinopolitan Creed was actually issued by the council. A.M. Ritter in his *Das Konzil von Konstantinopel und sein Symbol* (Göttingen, Germany: Vandenhoek and Ruprecht, 1965) and J. N. D. Kelly, in his *Early Christian Creeds*, argue that the creed was, in fact, promulgated by the council, originally as a "compromise" text meant to placate the Macedonians. It may also have been an adaptation of the baptismal creed used by Cyril at Jerusalem (von Harnack), or the creed used in the baptism and consecration of Nectarius, who succeeded Gregory Nazianzus as the council's president, thus becoming associated with the proceedings of the council. (the explanation accepted by L'Hullier).

98. John McGuckin, *Saint Gregory of Nazianzus*, 367.

99. See Basil of Caesarea, *De Spiritu Sancto* 23–24 (Eng. trans.: Basil the Great, *On the Holy Spirit*, 85–89).

100. John Zizioulas, "The Teaching of the Second Ecumenical Council on the Holy Spirit in Historical and Ecumenical Perspective," in *Credo in Spiritum Sanctum: Atti del Congresso teologico internazionale di pneumatologia in occasione del 1600 anniversario del I Concilio di Costantinopoli e del 1550 anniversario del Concilio di Efeso : Roma, 22–26 marzo, 1982* (Rome: Libreria Editrice Vaticana, 1982), 42–43.

101. Ibid., 44.

102. Cyril's formula "the one nature of God the Word incarnate" (μία φύσις τοῦ Θεοῦ Λόγου σεσαρκωμένη) later became the criterion *sine qua non* for orthodox christology, and was used by the (so-called) monophysite churches as reason for rejecting the Council of Chalcedon (451).

103. Hubert du Manoir de Juaye, *Dogme et Spiritualité chez Saint Cyrille d'Alexandrie* (Paris, 1944), 225 (cited in Richard Haugh, *Photius and the Carolingians: The Trinitarian Controversy* [Belmont, Mass.: Nordland Publishing, 1975], 191).

104. For a more detailed exposition of Cyril's views on the *filioque*, see Marie-Odile Boulnois, *La paradoxe trinitaire chez Cyrille d'Alexandrie: Herméneutique, analyses philosophiques et argumentation théologique* (Paris: Institut d'Études Augustiniennes, 1994); John Meyendorff, "La Procession du Saint-Esprit chez les Pères orientaux," *Russie et chrétienté* 2 (1950): 158–78; Thomas Weinandy and Daniel Keating, eds., *The Theology of Cyril of Alexandria: A Critical Appreciation* (New York: T & T Clark, 2003).

105. Boris Bobrinskoy, *The Mystery of the Trinity*, 251–52.

106. Cyril of Alexandria, *Thesaurus de sancta et consubstantiali trinitate* 34 (PG 75, 608).

107. Cyril of Alexandria, *Thesaurus de sancta et consubstantiali trinitate* 34 (PG 75, 588).

108. Cyril of Alexandria, *Thesaurus de sancta et consubstantiali trinitate* 34 (PG 75, 589).

109. George Berthold, "Cyril of Alexandria and the *Filioque*," *Studia Patristica* 19 (1989): 144.

110. Ibid., 144–45.

111. Cyril of Alexandria, *De Adoratione in Spiritu et Veritate* 1 (PG 68, 148).

112. Cyril of Alexandria, *Thesaurus de sancta et consubstantiali trinitate* 34 (PG 75, 585).

113. Cyril of Alexandria, *De Fide sanctae et individuae Trinitatis* (PG 77, 105–22).

114. Cyril of Alexandria, *Commentariorum in Joannem* 10.15.26–27 (PG 74, 417). In *Epistula* 55 Cyril seemingly did equate the two terms, but only in reference to the Spirit's relationship to the Father, since "the Spirit is poured forth (προχεῖται), that is, proceeds (ἐκπορεύεται), as from the fountain of God the Father and is bestowed on creation through the Son." Cyril of Alexandria, *Epistula* 55.40 (Eng. trans.: Cyril of Alexandria, *Letters 51–110*, ed. John McEnerney, FC 77 [Washington, D.C.: Catholic University of America Press, 1985], 34).

115. Cyril of Alexandria, *Commentariorum in Joannem* 10.16.12–13 (PG 74, 444).

116. See André de Halleux, "Cyrille, Théodoret et le *Filioque*," *Revue d'histoire eclésiastique* 74 (1979): 597–625. This essay was later collected with others and published in André de Halleux, *Patrologie et Œcuménisme: Recueil d'Études* (Leuven, Belgium: Leuven University Press, 1990).

117. Cyril of Alexandria, *Apologeticus contra Thedoretum* (PG 76, 432).

118. Ibid.

119. Theodoret, *Epistula* 171 (PG 83, 1484).

NOTES TO CHAPTER 3

1. Pope Gelasius (492–96) seems to have been the first pope to assert that not only had Rome never erred with regard to doctrinal decisions, but the Apostolic See *could not err.* For recent histories of the development of the papal teaching office, see Bernhard Schimmelpfennig, *The Papacy* (New York: Columbia University Press, 1992);William La Due, *The Chair of St. Peter: A History of the Papacy* (New York: Orbis Books, 1999); Klaus Schatz, *Papal Primacy: from Its Origins to the Present* (Collegeville, Minn.: Litugucal Press, 1996); Robert Eno, *The Rise of the Papacy* (Wilmington. Del.: Michael Glazier, 1990); Brian Tierny, *The Origins of Papal Infallibility* (Leiden: Brill Academic Press, 1972).

2. See, for example, Novatian's *De Trinitate* 29 (Eng. trans.: Novatian, *The Trinity, The Spectacles, Jewish Foods, In Praise of Purity, Letters*, trans. Russell Desimone, FC 67 [Washington, D.C.: Catholic University of America Press, 1972], 99–104).

3. See Joseph Moingt, *Théologie Trinitaire de Tertullien*, 3 vols. (Paris: Aubier, 1966).

4. Tertullian, *Adversus Praxeam* 4 (PL 2, 182).

5. Bertrand de Margerie (in *The Christian Trinity in History*, trans. Edmund Fortman [Still River, Mass.: St. Bede's Publications, 1981]) agreed with Swete, who had claimed that Tertullian's writings contained "the first distant approximation to the Western doctrine of the procession" (H. B. Swete, *On the History of the Doctrine of the Procession of the Holy Spirit* [Eugene, Ore.: Wipf and Stock, 2004], 54). Joseph Moingt was wary of making such a claim (Joseph Moingt, *Théologie Trinitaire de Tertullien*, vol 3, 1067).

6. Tertullian, *Adversus Praxeam* 8 (PL 2, 187).

7. For a full discussion of Hilary's trinitarian teaching see P. Smulders, *La Doctrine trinitaire de S. Hilaire de Poitiers* (Rome: Pontificia Universitas Gregoriana, 1944); L F Ladaria, *El Espiritu Santo en San Hiliarie de Poitiers* (Madrid: Eapsa, 1977); C. Kaiser, "The Development of the Johannine Motifs in Hilary's Doctrine of the Trinity" in *Scottish Journal of Theology* 29 (1976): 237–47; P. Löffler, "Die Trinitätslehre des Bischofs Hilarius zwischen Ost und West," *ZKG* 71 (1960): 26–36; E. P. Meijering, *Hilary on the Trinity* (Leiden, Brill Academic Press, 1982); Mark Weedman, *The Trinitarian Theology of Hilary of Poitiers*, Supplements to Virgiliae Christianae (Leiden: Brill, 2007), 89. Published too late to be included in this work is also Carl Beckwith, *Hilary of Poitiers on the Trinity: From De Fide to De Trinitate* (Oxford: Oxford University Press, 2008).

8. Hilary of Poitiers, *De Trinitate* 8, 20 (Eng. trans.: Hilary of Poitiers, *The Trinity*, trans. Stephen McKenna, FC 25 [Washington, D.C.: Catholic University of America Press, 1954], 290).

9. Hilary of Poitiers, *De Trinitate* 2, 29 (Eng. trans.: Hilary of Poitiers, *The Trinity*, 57–58).

10. The translation in the *Fathers of the Church* series has "Him in whom we must believe together with the Father and the Son who begot Him" (Eng. trans.: Hilary of Poitiers, *The Trinity*, 57–58). The English translation in the NPNF is, "we are bound to confess Him, proceeding, as he does, from Father and Son," although the attached footnote indicates the possibility of the translation above (NPNF 2.9.60).

11. Hilary of Poitiers, *De Trinitate* 8, 20 (Eng. trans.: Hilary, *The Trinity*, 289–90).

12. Hilary of Poitiers, *De Trinitate* 8, 20(Eng. trans.: Hilary, *The Trinity*, 290).

13. Hilary of Poitiers, *De Trinitate* 2, 1 (Eng. trans.: Hilary, *The Trinity*, 35).

14. Hilary of Poitiers, *De Trinitate* 12.56 (Eng. trans.: Hilary, *The Trinity*, 542).

15. Hilary of Poitiers, *De Trinitate* 12, 57 (Eng. trans.: Hilary, *The Trinity*, 543).

16. It seems that posterity, in large part, agreed with Jerome's assessment of Victorinus's work: (It is) "written in dialectic style and very obscure language, which can only be understood by the learned." Jerome, *Lives of Illustrious Men*, 101 (Eng trans.: NPNF 2.3.381).

17. Scholarly opinion is divided over the exact nature of Victorinus's influence on Augustine. Some argue that there is no direct connection between the two fathers (i.e., Augustine never read Victorinus's exegetical or dogmatic works) other than their common Neoplatonist background. Others (e.g., Nello Cipriani)

see Augustine's use of certain trinitarian terms as evidence that he was familiar with Victorinus's writings on the subject. See Nello Cipriani, "Marius Victorinus," in Allan Fitzgerald, ed., *Augustine through the Ages: An Encyclopedia* (Grand Rapids, Mich.: William Eerdmans Publishing, 1999), 533–35. For Victorinus see Paul Henry, "The Adversus Arium of Marius Victorinus, the First Systematic Exposition of the Doctrine of the Trinity," *Journal of Theological Studies* ns1 (1950): 42–55; John Voelker, "Marius Victorinus: Early Latin Witness of the Filioque," *Studia Patristica* 46, ed. J. Baun, A. Cameron, M. Edwards, and M. Vinzent (Leuven, Belgium: Peeters, 2010) 125–30.

18. Augustine of Hippo, *Confessions* 8.5 (Eng. trans.: Augustine of Hippo, *The Confessions*, trans. Maria Boulding, *The Works of St. Augustine: A Translation for the 21st Century* [Brooklyn, N.Y.: New City Press, 1996], 186). It is not surprising that Victorinus had such an impact, since his fame as a rhetor was so great that while he was still living, a statue of him was erected in the Forum of Trajan.

19. Marius Victorinus, *Adversus Arium* 1.8 (Eng. trans.: Marius Victorinus, *Theological Treatises on the Trinity*, ed. Mary Clark, FC 69 [Washington, D.C.: Catholic University of America Press, 1981], 99–100).

20. Marius Victorinus, *Adversus Arium* 4.20 (Eng. trans.: Marius Victorinus, *Theological Treatises on the Trinity*, 281–83).

21. Marius Victorinus, *Adversus Arium* 1.63 (Eng. trans.: Marius Victorinus, *Theological Treatises on the Trinity*, 192).

22. Marius Victorinus, *Adversus Arium* 2.24 (Eng. trans.: Marius Victorinus, *Theological Treatises on the Trinity*, 205).

23. Marius Victorinus, *Adversus Arium* 1.34 (Eng. trans.: Marius Victorinus, *Theological Treatises on the Trinity*, 147).

24. Marius Victorinus, *Adversus Arium* 3.8 (Eng. trans.: Marius Victorinus, *Theological Treatises on the Trinity*, 234).

25. Marius Victorinus, *Adversus Arium* 3.16 (Eng. trans.: Marius Victorinus, *Theological Treatises on the Trinity*, 247).

26. Marius Victorinus, *Adversus Arium* 4.16 (Eng. trans.: Marius Victorinus, *Theological Treatises on the Trinity*, 303).

27. Marius Victorinus, *Adversus Arium* 4.33 (Eng. trans.: Marius Victorinus, *Theological Treatises on the Trinity*, 106).

28. Marius Victorinus, *Adversus Arium* 1.13 (Eng. trans.: Marius Victorinus, *Theological Treatises on the Trinity*, 106).

29. Marius Victorinus, Hymn 1 (Eng. trans.: Marius Victorinus, *Theological Treatises on the Trinity*, 315).

30. Marius Victorinus, Hymn 3 (Eng. trans.: Marius Victorinus, *Theological Treatises on the Trinity*, 333).

31. It is, according to Voelker, "a point he makes relentlessly throughout the treatise as well in smaller, summary treatises that followed." John Voelker, "Marius Victorinus: Early Latin Witness of the Filioque."

32. Damasus, *Tomus Damasi: Confessio fidei* (PL 13, 558–64).

33. Karl Künstle, *Antipriscilliana* (Freiburg im Breisgau: Herder, 1905), 46.

34. Charles Piétri, *Roma Christiana* 1 (Rome: École Française de Rome, 1976), 873–80.

35. Text in August Hahn, *Bibliothek der Symbole und Glaubensregeln der Alten Kirche* (Hildesheim, Germany: Georg Olms, 1962), 271–75.

36. Bernd Oberdorfer, *Filioque: Geschichte und Theologie eines ökumenischen Problems* (Göttingen,Germany: Vandenhoeck and Ruprecht, 2001), 132. The fact that the biblical citations used were particular favorites of the Carolingians adds weight to Oberdorfer's case.

37. *Decretum Gelasianum* (Eng. trans.: Roy Deferrari, ed., *Sources of Catholic Dogma* [St. Louis: Herder, 1955], 33).

38. Rufinus later defended Ambrose against Jerome's claim that in plagiarizing the Greeks (especially Didymus) he had become a "jackdraw who decks himself in other birds' showy feathers." Rufinus, *Apology* 2.23–25 (Eng. trans.: NPNF 2.3.470–71).

39. Ambrose, *De Spiritu Sancto* 2.12.130 (Eng. trans.: Ambrose of Milan, *Theological and Dogmatic Works*, trans. Roy Deferrari, FC 44 [Washington, D.C.: Catholic University of America Press, 1963], 141); Basil of Caesarea, *De Spiritu Sancto* 18, 47 (Eng. trans.: Basil of Caesarea, *On the Holy Spirit*, 75).

40. Ambrose, *De Spiritu Sancto* 1, 11, 120 (Eng. trans.: Ambrose of Milan, *Theological and Dogmatic Works*, 79).

41. Ambrose, *De Spiritu Sancto* 1, 15, 152 (Eng. trans.: Ambrose, *Theological and Dogmatic Works*, 90).

42. "But if the Holy Spirit is both of one will and operation with God the Father, he is also of one substance, since the creator is known from His works. . . . Not the same, so that He Himself is Father, Himself Son, Himself Spirit" Ambrose, *De Spiritu Sancto* 2.12.142 (Eng. trans.: Ambrose, *Theological and Dogmatic Works*, 146).

43. "That the Holy Spirit also sent the Son of God. For the Son of God said 'The Spirit of the Lord is upon me because the Lord has anointed me. . . . For as the Son of Man he was both anointed and sent to preach the gospel." Ambrose, *De Spiritu Sancto* 3.1 (Eng. trans.: Ambrose, *Theological and Dogmatic Works*, 153–54).

44. John Meyendorff, *Byzantine Theology: Historical Trends & Doctrinal Themes* (New York: Fordham University Press, 1974), 60.

45. For a discussion of this work and Jerome's translation see pp. 36–37.

46. J. N. D. Kelly, *Jerome: His Life, Writings, and Controversies* (Peabody, Mass.: Hendrickson, 1998), 71.

47. According to H. B. Swete, the Latin translation known to Novatian, Hilary, and Ambrose had also translated ἐκπορεύεσθαι with *procedere*. Jerome also used several other Latin verbs to translate ἐκπορεύεσθαι, including *ejicior, divulgor, proficiscor, egredior*, and *exeo*. H. B. Swete, *On the History of the Doctrine of the Procession of the Holy Spirit*, 7.

48. Jaroslav Pelikan, *The Melody of Theology* (Cambridge: Harvard University Press, 1988), 14.

49. See Joseph Lienhard, "Augustine and the Filioque" in *Festschrift for Roland Teske* (forthcoming); Ferdinand Cavallera, "La doctrine de Saint Augustin sur l'Esprit-Saint à propos du 'De Trinitate,'" *Recherches de théologie ancienne et médiévale* 2 (1930): 365–87; 3 (1931): 5–19; Gerald Bonner, "St. Augustine's Doctrine of the Holy Spirit," *Sobornost* 2 (1960): 51–66; François Bourassa, "Communion du Père et du Fils," *Gregorianum* 48 (1967): 657–707; idem, "Théologie trinitaire chez saint Augustin I-II," *Gregorianum* 58 (1977): 675–775; 59 (1978): 375–412; Emile Bailleux, "L'Esprit du Père

et du Fils selon saint Augustin," *Revue thomiste* 7 (1977): 5–29; M.-F. Berrouard, "La théologie du Saint-Esprit dans les *Tractates*," *Homélies sur l'Evangile de saint Jean LXXX-CIII*, Bibliothèque Augustinienne 74B (Paris: Institut d'études augustiniennes, 1998), 9–64; Michel René Barnes, "Rereading Augustine's Theology of the Trinity" in *The Trinity: An Interdisciplinary Symposium on the Trinity*, 145–76.

50. "First we must establish by the authority of the holy scriptures whether the faith is in fact like that. . . ." "The purpose of all the Catholic commentators I have been able to read on the divine books of both testaments who have written before me on the trinity which God is. . . ." Augustine of Hippo, *De Trinitate* 1.1.4.7 (Eng. trans.: Augustine of Hippo, *The Trinity*, trans. Edmund Hill, *The Works of St. Augustine: A Translation for the 21st Century* [Brooklyn, N.Y.: New City Press, 1991], 67,69).

51. Theodore Stylianopoulos maintained that "the crucial difference seems to be that despite his own repeated reservations, Augustine seems to explain the Trinity as a metaphysical problem. . . . By contrast Athanasius and the Cappadocians . . . are concerned about defending [against the Arians] the uncreated nature of the Son and the Spirit deriving their very being from God. . . . These differences in theological approach signal, at least for many Orthodox theologians, tremendous implications regarding the way of Western theology and the way of Eastern theology." Theodore Stylianopoulos, "The Filioque: Dogma, Theologoumenon or Error," in *Spirit of Truth: Ecumenical Perspectives on the Holy Spirit*, ed. Theodore Stylianopoulos and S. Mark Heim (Brookline, Mass.: Holy Cross Orthodox Press, 1986), 29–30.

52. Augustine of Hippo, *De Fide et Symbolo*, 19 (Eng. trans.: Augustine of Hippo, *On Christian Belief*, ed. Boniface Ramsey, *The Works of St. Augustine: A Translation for the 21st Century* [Brooklyn, N.Y.: New City Press, 2005], 168). Although John Romanides later claimed that this statement is both "unbelievably naive and inaccurate," especially in light of the pneumatological debates of the mid-fourth century, the fact that Augustine did not understand Greek explains it to some degree. In *De Trinitate* he had written that "the fact . . . is that sufficient works on this subject have not been published in Latin, or at least they are not all that easy to find; and as for Greek . . . most of us are hardly well enough acquainted with that language to be able to read Greek books on the subject with any real understanding" (Augustine, *De Trinitate* 3.1 [Eng. trans.: Augustine of Hippo, *The Trinity*, 127]). As for Augustine's knowledge of the Cappadocians, according to Lewis Ayres, "The specific question of Cappadocian influence on Augustine has been the subject of debate throughout the century. T. De Regnon rejected the influence of Nazianzen's account of 'relationship' on Augustine while I. Chevalier argued strongly in favor of this influence via the translation of some of Gregory's *Orations* by Rufinus of Aquileia." Lewis Ayres, "Cappadocians," in Allan Fitzgerald, ed., *Augustine through the Ages: An Encyclopedia* (Grand Rapids, Mich.: William Eerdmans Publishing, 1999), 121–24. Joseph Lienhard examined Augustine's corpus for direct and indirect references to the Cappadocians in "Augustine of Hippo, Basil of Caesarea, and Gregory Nazianzen," in George Demacopoulos and Aristotle Papanikolaou eds., *Orthodox Readings of Augustine* (Crestwood, N.Y.: St. Vladimir's Seminary Press, 2008), 81–99.

53. Augustine of Hippo, *De Fide et Symbolo*, 19 (Eng. trans.: Augustine of Hippo, *On Christian Belief*, 168–69).

54. Augustine of Hippo, *De Trinitate* 10.4.18 (Eng. trans: Augustine of Hippo, *The Trinity*, 298).

55. Other models found in De Trinitate include: *mens, notitia, amor* (9.3.3), *res, visio, intentio* (11.2.2), *memoria, visio, volitio* (11.3.6–9), *memoria, scientia, voluntas* (12.15.25), *scientia, cogitatio, amor* (13.20.26), *memoria Dei, intelligentia Dei, amor Dei* (14.12.15).

56. Augustine of Hippo, *De Trinitate* 6.5.7 (Eng. trans.: Augustine of Hippo, *The Trinity*, 209).

57. Augustine of Hippo, *De Trinitate* 15.17.27 (Eng. trans.: Augustine of Hippo, *The Trinity*, 418).

58. Augustine of Hippo, *De Trinitate* 4.20.29 (Eng. trans.: Augustine of Hippo, *The Trinity*, 174).

59. Joseph Lienhard, "Augustine and the Filioque" in *Festschrift for Roland Teske* (forthcoming). See also Joseph Moingt, "Procession et mission du Saint-Esprit," in *La trinité: livres VIII–XV*, Bibliothèque Augustinienne 16 (Paris: Études Augustiniennes, 1991), 659.

60. Augustine of Hippo, *In Joannis Evangelium Tractatus* 99, 16, 7 (Eng. trans.: Augustine of Hippo, *Tractates on the Gospel of John 55–111*, trans. John Rettig, FC 90 [Washington, D.C.: Catholic University of America Press, 1994], 226). A similar argument is found in *De Trinitate* 4.20.29.

61. Augustine of Hippo, *De Trinitate* 4.20.29 (Eng. trans.: Augustine of Hippo, *The Trinity*, 174).

62. Augustine of Hippo, *De Trinitate* 15.17.29 (Eng. trans: Augustine of Hippo, *The Trinity*, 419).

63. Augustine of Hippo, *De Trinitate* 15.26.47 (Eng. trans: Augustine of Hippo, *The Trinity*, 432–33).

64. Augustine of Hippo, *De Trinitate* 5.14.15 (Eng. trans: Augustine of Hippo, *The Trinity*, 199).

65. Augustine of Hippo, *De Trinitate* 5.5.6 (Eng. trans: Augustine of Hippo, *The Trinity*, 192). See also *De civitate Dei* 11.10.1. This idea was not unknown in Greek theology. See M. William Ury, *Trinitarian Personhood: Investigating the Implications of Relational Definition* (Eugene, Ore.: Wipf and Stock Publishers, 2002).

66. Augustine of Hippo, *De Trinitate* 7.1.2 (Eng. trans: Augustine of Hippo, *The Trinity*, 219).

67. Joseph Ratzinger, *Introduction to Christianity*, trans. J. R. Foster (New York: Seabury, 1969), 131.

68. Yves Congar, *I Believe in the Holy Spirit* 3 (New York: Crossroad Publishing, 1997), 84.

69. The only exception is Letter 170, which might contain the phrase, although the editor of the CSEL decided against its inclusion (A. Goldbacher, ed., *S. Avreli Augustini Hipponiensis Episcopi Epistulae*, CSEL 44, 625). Roland Teske chose to include it in the recent English translation of this work, although he notes its omission in the CSEL. See Augustine of Hippo, *Letters 156–210*, trans. Roland Teske, The Works of St. Augustine: A Translation for the 21st Century 2.3 (Brooklyn, N.Y.: New City Press, 2005), 116 n. 3.

70. *Contra Maximinum* 2.14.1 (PL 42, 770). (Eng. trans. in Joseph Lienhard, "Augustine and the Filioque," in *Festschrift for Roland Teske* [forthcoming]).

71. Augustine of Hippo, *De Trinitate* 1.1.7 (Eng. trans.: Augustine of Hippo, *The Trinity*, 70).

72. Augustine of Hippo, *De Trinitate* 1.1.5 (Eng. trans.: Augustine of Hippo, *The Trinity*, 68).

73. Augustine of Hippo, *De Trinitate*, 15.28.51 (Eng. trans.: Augustine of Hippo, *The Trinity*, 437).

74. Jaroslav Pelikan, *The Christian Tradition 3: The Growth of Medieval Theology* (Chicago: University of Chicago Press, 1978), 22.

75. Although it should be noted that Prosper, occupied as he was in his ongoing struggle against the (so-called) "Semi-Pelagians," wrote little on the procession. This dearth can be explained, in large part, by the widespread acceptance of Augustine's trinitarian theology—there was no need to defend what had never been challenged. As for Proper's influence upon Leo, see N. W. James, "Leo the Great and Prosper of Aquitaine: A Fifth Century Pope and His Advisor," JTS 44 (1993): 554–84; Alexander Hwang, *Intrepid Lover of Perfect Grace: The Life and Thought of Prosper of Aquitaine* (Washington, D.C.: Catholic University of America Press, 2009); R. A. Markus, "Chronicle and Theology: Prosper of Aquitaine" in *The Inheritance of Historiography 350–900*, ed. Christopher Holdsworth and T. P. Wiseman (Exeter: Exeter University Press, 1986), 31–43; Philip Barclift, "Predestination and Divine Foreknowledge in the Sermons of Pope Leo the Great," *Church History* 62 (1993): 5–21; idem, "Shifting Tones of Pope Leo the Great's Christological Vocabulary." *Church History* 66 (1997): 221–22.

76. Leo the Great, Sermon 75. 3 (Eng. trans.: Leo the Great, *Sermons*, trans. Jane Patricia Freeland and Agnes Josephine Conway, FC 93 [Washington, D,C,: Catholic University Press, 1996], 332). See also sermon 76.2 (PL 54, 404).

77. J. A. de Aldama accepts its authenticity in his *El simbolo Toledano I Su texto, su origin, su posición en la historia de los simbolos* (Rome: Pontificia Universitas Gregoriana, 1934), 54, n. 34. Künstle claims it as a forgery made after the Synod of Braga in 563. See *Antipriscilliana* (Freiburg, Germany: Herder, 1905), 117–26. It was not included in the English translation of Leo's letters found in Leo the Great, *Letters*, trans. Edmund Hunt, FC 34 (Washington, D.C.: Catholic University Press, 1957).

78. Leo the Great, *Epistle 15 to Turribius, Bishop of Astorga* (PL 54, 681).

79. Leo the Great, *Epistle 15 to Turribius, Bishop of Astorga* (PL 54, 680–81).

80. The same argument was later used to enlist Pope Vigilius (who accepted the Fifth Ecumenical Council at Constantinople in 553) and Pope Agatho (who accepted the Sixth Ecumenical Council at Constantinople in 680–81).

81. The exception here appears to be Nicetas, Bishop of Remesiana (d. 414), whose *De Spiritus Sancti Potentia*, 3, spoke only of the Spirit's procession from the Father (*sed hoc solum quia de Patre procedit*) (PL 52, 854). See also his *Explanatio Symboli*, 7: "*Hic Spiritus Sanctus unus est, sanctificans omnia; qui de Patre procedit solus scrutans mysteria et profunda Dei*" (PL 52, 870).

82. See John Cassian, *The Conferences*, trans. Boniface Ramsey, ACW 57 (New York: Paulist Press, 1997), 399–400.

83. Eucherius of Lyons, *Instructiones ad Salonium*, 1 (PL 50, 774).

84. Gennadius of Marseilles, *De ecclesiasticis dogmatibus* (PL 58, 980).

85. Julianus Pomerius, *De Vita Contemplativa* 1.18 (PL 59, 432–33).

86. Avitus of Vienne, *Fragmento libri de divinitate Spiritus Sancti* (PL 59, 385).

87. Hormisdas, *Epistula 79 ad Justinum Augustinum* (PL 63, 514).

88. In older manuscripts the disputed passage is found to have been added by a later hand. See the note in PL 63, 514. See also the O. Gunther, ed., *Collectio Avellana*, CSEL 35 (Vienna, 1898), 236.

89. Boethius, *De Trinitate* 5 (Eng. trans.: Boethius, *The Theological Tractates*, trans. H. F. Stewart and E. K. Rand, Loeb Classical Library [New York: Putnam and Sons, 1926], 27, 29).

90. Agnellus, *Epistola ad Armenium de ratione fidei* (PL 68, 383–84).

91. Cassiodorus, *In Psalterium Praefatio* (Eng. trans.: Cassiodorus, *Explanation of the Psalms* 1, trans. P. G. Walsh, ACW 51 [New York: Paulist Press, 1990], 41–42). In this, according to Swete, "the great Senator was doubtless wrong; the Church Catholic had not proclaimed the *filioque* . . . yet. Even Rome at this period had not learned to regard the procession from the Son as *de fide*. Nevertheless the time was close at hand" H. B. Swete, *On the History of the Doctrine of the Procession of the Holy Spirit*, 160.

92. Gregory of Tours, *Historica Francorum* (Eng. trans.: Gregory of Tours, *The History of the Franks*, trans. O. M. Dalton [Oxford: Clarendon, 1927], 5).

93. Rusticus, *Contra Acephalos Disputatio* (PL 67, 1237).

94. Fulgentius of Ruspe, *Epistula* 14.28 (Eng. trans.: Fulgentius of Ruspe, *Selected Works*, trans. Robert Eno, FC 95 [Washington, D.C.: Catholic University of America Press, 1997], 538). See also *Epistula* 10, 3 (*De Incarnatione Filii*): "It is the Father alone who begat the Son; only the Son who is born of the Father; it is only the Holy Spirit who is neither born of the Father nor begot the Son but proceeds from the Father and the Son" (Eng. trans.: Fulgentius of Ruspe, *Selected Works*, 427).

95. Fulgentius of Ruspe, *Epistula* 14.28 (Eng. trans.: Fulgentius of Ruspe, *Selected Works*, 538).

96. Fulgentius of Ruspe, *Epistula* 10.4 (Eng. trans.: Fulgentius of Ruspe, *Selected Works*, 427).

97. Fulgentius of Ruspe, *De Fide ad Petrum* 4 (Eng. trans.: Fulgentius of Ruspe, *Selected Works*, 62–63).

98. Fulgentius of Ruspe, *De Fide ad Petrum* 11.54 (Eng. trans.: Fulgentius of Ruspe, *Selected Works*, 93–94).

99. "The procession of the Holy Spirit is also of the Son, a doctrine commended to us by the prophets and apostles" (*De filio quoque procedere Spiritum Sanctum, prophetica atque apostolica nobis doctrina commendat*). Fulgentius of Ruspe, *Selected Works*, 93–94). Ibid.

100. See J. N. D. Kelly, *The Athanasian Creed* (London: Adam & Charles Black, 1964). Kelly suggested Vincent of Lerins as an author, but this possibility remains in doubt. Others suggested: Caesarius himself, Vigilius of Thapsus, Honoratus, and Fulgentius. See also G. Morris, "L'Origine du symbole d'Athanase," *Revue Bénédictine* 44 (1932): 207–19.

101. *The Athanasian Creed* (Eng. trans.: Jaroslav Pelikan and Valerie Hotchkiss, eds., *Creeds and Confessions of Faith in Christian Tradition* 1 [New Haven, Conn.: Yale University Press, 2003], 676–77).

102. *Canons of the Council of Ephesus* (Eng. trans.: Norman Tanner, ed., *Decrees of the Ecumenical Councils* 1, 65).

103. According to Theodore the Reader, the practice of reciting the creed at liturgy had been introduced in 471 at Antioch and then adopted at Constantinople in 511 by Patriarch Timothy in order to disparage Macedonius. See Theodore, *Ecclesiasticae Historiæ* 2.32 (PG 86, 201).

104. Mansi 9. 977–78 (Eng. trans.: J. N. D. Kelly, *Early Christian Creeds*, 3rd ed. [Essex: Longmans, 1973], 361).

105. Mansi 9. 985 (Eng. trans.: J. N. D. Kelly, *Early Christian Creeds*, 361–62).

106. Ibid.

107. H. B. Swete, *On the History of the Doctrine of the Procession of the Holy Spirit*, 170.

108. A. E. Burn, "Some Spanish MSS of the Constantinopolitan Creed," *Journal Theological Studies* 9 (1908): 301–3. See also José Orlandis and Domingo Ramos-Lisson, *Die Synoden auf der Iberischen Halbinsel bis zum Einbuch des Islam* (Paderborn, Germany: F. Schöningh, 1981), 109.

109. Isidore of Seville, *De Ecclesiasticis Officiis* 2.23 (Eng. trans.: Isidore of Seville, *De Ecclesiasticis Officiis*, trans. Thomas Knoebel, ACW 61 [New York: Paulist Press, 2008], 106). See also *Etymologiae* 7.3 (PL 82, 268): "The Holy Spirit, who proceeds from the Father and the Son [*quia ex Patre Filioque procedit*]."

110. Mansi 10.613.

111. The interpolated creed was also used at Merida (666) and the Synod of Braga (675).

112. *Missale Mixtum Secundum Regulum B. Isidori* Pars I (PL 85, 612) and *Breviarium Gothicum* (PL 86, 691). At matins for the same feast: "O Holy Spirit, who proceeds from the Father and the Son [*qui ex Patre Filioque procedis*]." Ibid.

113. H. B. Swete, *On the History of the Doctrine of the Procession of the Holy Spirit*, 175–76.

114. F. Homes Dudden, *Gregory the Great: His Place in History and Thought* 2 (London: Longmans, Green, and Co., 1905), 348. See also R. A. Markus, *Gregory the Great and His World* (Cambridge: Cambridge University Press, 1997); John Moorhead, ed., *Gregory the Great, The Early Church Fathers* (New York: Routledge, 2005).

115. Gregory the Great, *Moralia in Iob* 5.65 (PL 75, 419); 24.74 (PL 76, 19). While Gregory did spend time in Constantinople, the scholarly consensus is that he would not have known enough Greek to have grasped the nuances of Eastern trinitarian theology. See Joan Peterson, "Did Gregory the Great Know Greek," in D. Baker, ed., *The Orthodox Churches and the West*, Studies in Church History 13 (Oxford: Oxford University Press, 1976), 121–34; idem, "'Homo omnino Latinus'? The Theological and Cultural Background of Pope Gregory the Great," *Speculum* 62/63 (1987): 529–51; G. J. M. Bartelink, "Pope Gregory the Great's Knowledge of Greek," in *Gregory the Great: A Symposium* (Notre Dame, Ind.: University of Notre Dame Press, 1995), 117–36.

116. Gregory the Great, *Moralia in Iob* 2.92 (Grégoire le Grand, *Morales sur Job* 1–2, ed. Robert Gillet, SC 32 [Paris: Les Éditions du Cerf, 1950], 246).

117. Gregory the Great, *Moralia in Iob* 27.34 (PL 76, 419).

118. Gregory the Great, *Moralia in Iob* 30.17 (PL 76, 534).

119. Gregory the Great, *Dialogues* 2.38 (Grégoire le Grand, *Dialogues* 1–3, ed. Adalbert de Vogüé, SC 260 [Paris: Les Éditions du Cerf, 1979], 248).

120. Gregory the Great, *Homiliarum in Evangelia libri duo* 2.26 (Eng. trans.: Gregory the Great, *Forty Gospel Homilies*, trans. Dom David Hurst [Kalamazoo, Mich.: Cistercian Publications, 1990], 202).

121. John Meyendorff, *Imperial Unity and Christian Divisions*, The Church in History 2 (Crestwood, N.Y.: St. Vladimir's Seminary Press, 1989), 362.

NOTES TO CHAPTER 4

1. The date is based upon Maximus's claim that he was 75 at the time of his first trial in 655. See *Relatio Motionis*, 11 (Critical edition and English translation in Pauline Allen, ed., *Maximus the Confessor and His Companions: Documents from Exile* [Oxford: Oxford University Press, 2002], 70). For the *Vita* see Pauline Allen and Bronwen Neil, eds., *The Life of Maximus the Confessor Recension 3*, Early Christian Studies 6 (Stratford: St. Pauls, 2003). Although long thought to have been composed by his disciple Anastasius the Apocrisiarios, the *Vita* is now believed to have been put into its current form in the tenth century by the Studite monk Michael Exaboulites. However, the first redaction of the work may have been done as early as 680–81. See R. Devreesse, "La Vie de S. Maxime le Confesseur et ses récensions," *Analecta Bollandiana* 46 (1928): 5–49. There is an earlier account called the *Syriac Life*, written by an anonymous monothelite author of the seventh century (probably George Reš'aina), but its polemical tone and purpose cast serious doubts on its reliability as a source. See Sebastian Brock, "An Early Syriac Life of Maximus the Confessor," *Analecta Bollandiana* 85 (1967): 285–316. We also have some contemporary accounts of Maximus's trial and later years from the *Relatio Motionis, Disputatio Bizyae*, and letters written by his disciple Anastasius, also found in Allen's *Maximus the Confessor and His Companions*. However, the best source for understanding the life and thought of Maximus remains his own writings, especially the letters, from which we can contextualize and date many of his works. See Polycarp Sherwood, *An Annotated Date List of the Works of St. Maximus the Confessor* (Rome: Herder, 1952).

2. *Vita Sancti Maximi* 3 (Eng. trans.: Pauline Allen and Bronwen Neil, eds., *Life of Maximus the Confessor*, 43).

3. There remains the question of whether Maximus stopped at Crete and/or Cyprus on his way to Africa. Polycarp Sherwood points out that Maximus himself, in *Opuscula theologica et polemica* 3 (PG 91, 49), admits to a stay in Crete at some point where he held a dispute with the monophysites. As for a visit to Cyprus, Sherwood claims this can only be "inferred from the fact of his correspondence with the Cypriote Marinus and from a possible acquaintance with the bishop Arcadius." Polycarp Sherwood, *Annotated Date List*, 5.

4. Monothelitism, although not explicitly formulated until 634, had its roots in the lengthy and somewhat complicated debates surrounding the Council of Chalcedon. The Chalcedonian formula, adapted from the Tome of Pope Leo to Flavian, stated:

> So, following the saintly fathers, we all with one voice teach the confession of one and the same Son, our Lord Jesus Christ . . . acknowledged in two

natures [ἐν δύο φύσεσιν] which undergo no confusion, no change, no
division, no separation; at no point was the difference between the natures
taken away through the union [ἕνωσιν], but rather the property of both
natures is preserved and comes together into a single person and a single
subsistent being [ἓν πρόσωπον καὶ μίαν ὑπόστασιν]; he is not parted or
divided into two persons [οὐκ εἰς δύο πρόσωπα], but is one and the same
only-begotten Son, God, Word, Lord Jesus Christ. (Norman Tanner, ed.,
Decrees of the Ecumenical Councils 1, 86)

5. Several factors explain Maximus's opposition to the monothelitism. Certainly
his relationship to Sophronius accounts, in part, for his initial involvement in the
debate. The fall of Jerusalem in 638 to the Persians and Sophronius's death later that
year may have prompted Maximus to maintain the orthodoxy of his deceased *abba's*
position. Equally important was Maximus's firm belief in the truth of Chalcedon and
his unwillingness to see that position eroded by a kind of creeping monophysitism. As
he stated in his *Diputatio cum Pyrrho*:

And if he has two natures, then he surely must have two natural wills, the
wills and essential operations being equal in number to the natures. For just
as the number of natures of the one and the same Christ correctly understood and explained, do not divide Christ but rather preserve the distinction
of natures in the union, so likewise the number of essential attributes, wills,
and operations attached to those two natures do not divide Christ either.
(Maximus the Confessor, *Diputatio cum Pyrrho* [Eng. trans.: Joseph Farrell,
*The Disputation with Pyrrhus of our Father among the Saints Maximus the
Confessor* (South Canaan, Penn.: St. Tikhon's Seminary Press, 1990), 4].)

6. Pyrrhus would later flee to Ravenna and "returned like a dog to his own
vomit," again taking up the monothelite cause. *Vita Sancti Maximi* 16 (Eng. trans.:
Pauline Allen and Bronwen Neil, eds., *Life of Maximus the Confessor*, 69).

7. For a discussion of Maximus's role at the Synod see Rudolf Riedinger, "*Die
Lateransynode von 649 und Maximos der Bekenner*," in Felix Heinzer and Christoph
Schönborn, eds., *Maximus Confessor: Actes du Symposium sur Maxime le Confesseur,
Fribourg, 2–5 September 1980* (Fribourg-en-Suisse, Switzerland: Editions Universitar-
ires, 1982), 111–21.

8. He was accused of conspiring to hand over Egypt, Tripoli, and Africa to the
Saracens, and of "making sounds of contempt and derision" (μυττία ποιῶν καὶ
λαιμία), when the emperor's name was mentioned. When asked why he preferred the
Romans to his native people (the Byzantines), he replied, "I love the Romans because
we share the same faith, whereas I love the Greeks because we share the same
language" (Ἀγαπῶ τοὺς Ῥωμαίους ὡς ὁμοπίστους, τοὺς δὲ Γραικοὺς ὡς ὁμογλώσσους)
Relatio Motionis, 11 (Eng. trans.: Pauline Allen, ed., *Maximus the Confessor and His
Companions*, 70).

9. Such creeds can be found in the *Capita theologica et oeconomica* (2nd cent., 1)
and the *Expositio Orationis Dominicae*. Both works can be found in English translation
in George Berthold, ed., *Maximus the Confessor: Selected Writings* (Mahwah, N.J.: Paulist
Press, 1985).

10. Maximus the Confessor, *Expositio Orationis Dominicae* (P.Van Deun, ed., *Maximi Confessoris Opuscula exegetica duo*, CCG 23 [Turnhout, Belgium: Brepols: 1991], 31).

11. Felix Heinzer, "L'explication trinitaire de l'économie chez Maxime le Confesseur," in Felix Heinzer and Christoph Schönborn, eds., *Maximus Confessor*, 159.

12. Although Maximus was in many ways influenced by the Pseudo-Dionysian corpus, in dealing with the triune God it was largely to the Cappadocians that Maximus turned, since for Dionysius the "Trinity seems to be merely a Christian name of the superessential monad." George Berthold, "The Cappadocian Roots of Maximus the Confessor," in Felix Heinzer and Christoph Schönborn, eds., *Maximus Confessor*, 56.

13. Lars Thunberg, *Man and the Cosmos: The Vision of Maximus the Confessor* (Crestwood, N.Y.: St. Vladimir's Seminary Press, 1985), 40.

14. However, this idea needs to be balanced against other statements in Maximus where he explicitly affirms that

the holy Godhead is by essence beyond ineffability and unknowably and countlessly raised above infinity, leaving not the slightest trace [ἴχνος] of comprehension to those who are after it, nor disclosing any idea to any being as to how and how far the same is both monad and triad, since the uncreated is not naturally contained by the created, nor is the unlimited comprehended by what is limited. (Maximus the Confessor, *Ambiguum* 10 [Eng. trans.: Andrew Louth, ed., *Maximus the Confessor* (New York: Routledge, 1996), 132–33].)

15. Maximus the Confessor, *Quaestiones ad Thalassium* 13 (Carl Laga and Carlos Steel, eds., *Maximi Confessoris Quaestiones ad Thalassium*, CCG 7 [Turnhout, Belgium: Brepols, 1980], 95).

16. Maximus's thoughts on the Trinity as archetype can be found in both *Ambigua* 7 and 10. See Edward Jeanneau, ed., *Ambigua ad Iohannem*, CCG 18 (Turnhout, Belgium: Brepols, 1988). *Ambiguum* 7 in English translation can be found in Paul Blowers and Robert Wilken, eds., *The Cosmic Mystery of Jesus Christ* (Crestwood, N.Y.: St. Vladimir's Seminary Press, 2003), 45–78. *Ambiguum* 10 is in Andrew Louth, ed., *Maximus the Confessor*, 94–154.

17. Aidan Nichols, *Byzantine Gospel: Maximus the Confessor in Modern Scholarship* (Edinburgh: T&T Clark, 1993), 68.

18. Maximus the Confessor, *Expositio Orationis Dominicae* (Eng. trans.: George Berthold, *Maximus the Confessor*, 103).

19. Maximus the Confessor, *Capita theologica et oeconomica* §1 (Eng. trans.: G. E. H. Palmer and Kallistos Ware, eds., "Two Hundred Texts on Theology and the Incarnate Dispensation of the Son of God," in *The Philokalia* 2, 137).

20. Maximus the Confessor, *Expositio Orationis Dominicae* (Eng. trans.: George Berthold, *Maximus the Confessor*, 106).

21. Maximus the Confessor, *Capita theologica et oeconomica* §71 (Eng. trans.: G. E. H. Palmer and Kallistos Ware, eds., *The Philokalia* 2, 154–55).

22. See Verna Harrison, "Perichoresis in the Greek Fathers," *St. Vladimir's Theological Quarterly* 35 (1991): 53–65.

23. Maximus the Confessor, *Ambiguum* 24 (Edward Jeanneau, ed., *Ambigua ad Iohannem*, 149–51).

24. See John Behr, *The Nicene Faith* 2, 361 n. 49, and John McGuckin, *Gregory of Nazianzus* (Crestwood, N.Y.: St. Vladimir's Seminary Press, 2001), 294, n. 352.

25. "The name of the Father is neither the name of the essence nor a name of the energy but rather a name of a relationship [*schesis*] and it says how the Father is towards the Son and how the Son is towards the Father," Maximus the Confessor, *Ambiguum* 26 (Edward Jeanneau, ed., *Ambigua ad Iohannem*, 153).

26. "He said to me, 'What do you see?' And I said, 'I see a lampstand all of gold, with a bowl on the top of it; there are seven lamps on it, with seven lips on each of the lamps that are on the top of it. And by it there are two olive trees, one on the right of the bowl and the other on its left'" (Zech 4:2–3).

27. Maximus the Confessor, *Quaestiones ad Thalassium* 63 (Carl Laga and Carlos Steel, eds, *Quaestiones ad Thalassium*, 155).

28. See pp. 40–41, 44.

29. Pierre Piret, *Le Christ et la Trinité selon Maxime le Confesseur*, 99.

30. Maximus the Confessor, *Quaestiones et dubia* 34 (José Declerk, ed., *Quaestiones et dubia*, CCG 10 [Turnhout, Belgium: Brepols, 1982], 151).

31. Polycarp Sherwood, *Annotated Date List*, 54. Sherwood's dating is based on the fact that the letter was written from Carthage, and he believes it unlikely that Maximus traveled back to Africa after the Lateran Synod in 649.

32. Very often Martin I, rather than Theodore, is given as the author of the synodal letter, although Sherwood's dating would indicate otherwise. Since there are no extant synodal letters from either pope, it is impossible to verify which one authored the epistle in question. However there is no *prima facie* reason to reject Sherwood's conclusion since, as Jean-Claude Larchet has argued, both Theodore and Martin defended the orthodox position against the monenergists and monothelites, and thus either could have been responsible for the composition of the disputed text. Jean-Claude Larchet, *Maxime le Confesseur*, 11.

33. Maximus the Confessor, *Opusculum* 10 (PG 91, 136).

34. John Meyendorff, *Imperial Unity and Christian Divisions* (Crestwood, N.Y.: St. Vladimir's Seminary Press, 1989), 365.

35. Maximus the Confessor, *Opusculum* 10 (PG 91, 136).

36. Anastasius Bibliothecarius, *Ad Ioannem Diaconum* (PL 129, 567).

37. See PG 91, 129.

38. Vasilios Karayiannis, *Maxime le Confesseur: Essence et Energies de Dieu* (Paris: Beauchesne, 1993), 89; idem, "Ο ΑΓΙΟΣ ΜΑΞΙΜΟΣ Ο ΟΜΟΛΟΓΗΤΗΣ ΚΑΙ Η ΕΚΚΛΗΣΙΑ ΤΗΣ ΚΥΠΡΟΥ," *Apostolos Varnavas* 53 (1992): 379–98.

39. Polycarp Sherwood, *Annotated Date List*, 54; Alexander Alexakis, *Codex Parisinus Graecus 1115 and Its Archetypes* (Washington, D.C.: Dumbarton Oaks Research Library and Collection, 1996), 76.

40. The only surviving letters of Pope Theodore are to Patriarch Paul II (PL 129, 577–84) and to another bishop requesting Paul's removal from the diptychs (PL 87, 75–82).

41. See A. Edward Siecienski, "The Authenticity of Maximus the Confessor's *Letter to Marinus*: The Argument from Theological Consistency," *Vigiliae Christianae* 61 (2007): 189–227.

42. Maximus the Confessor, *Opusculum* 10 (PG 91, 136).

43. It is an open question whether Maximus, during his many years in North Africa, ever came to know the works of Augustine of Hippo and the other Latin fathers whose writings shaped Western trinitarian theology. Translations of Western writers into Greek were rare, and in Greek-speaking monasteries (like Euchratas) knowledge of Latin was often limited or nonexistent. In *Opusculum* 15 Maximus did make reference to Western authors such as Ambrose of Milan and Pope Leo I (ὁ τῆς μεγάλης Ῥωμαίων ἔξαρχος Ἐκκλησίας Λέων ὁ παναλκὴς καὶ πανίεπος), but both were already recognized in the East as great fathers of the Church. As for Augustine, although there is no direct evidence for a connection, the majority opinion is that his influence had become so widespread by the seventh century that such a connection cannot be excluded. Jaroslav Pelikan concludes that "a *prima facie* argument [can] be made for some knowledge of Augustine . . . but that only makes the absence of Augustinian references all the more fascinating" Jaroslav Pelikan, "Maximus in the History of Christian Thought," in Felix Heinzer and Christoph Schönborn, eds., *Maximus Confessor*, 399). See also George Berthold, "Did Maximus the Confessor Know Augustine?" *Studia Patristica* 7 (1982): 4–17.

44. See Alexander Alexakis, *Codex Parisinus Graecus 1115*, 74–85.

45. See pp. 43–45, 47–50.

46. Maximus the Confessor, *Opusculum* 10 (PG 91, 136).

47. See pp. 41–42.

48. Maximus the Confessor, *Diversa capita ad theologiam et oeconomiam spectantia deque virtute ac vitio* 4 (Eng. trans.: G. E. H. Palmer and Kallistos Ware, eds., *The Philokalia* 2, 165).

49. Emmanuel Ponsoye, ed., *Opuscules Théologiques et Polémiques* (Paris: Les Éditions du Cerf, 1998), 82.

50. Jean-Claude Larchet, *Maxime le Confesseur* (Paris: Les Editions du Cerf, 1998), 53.

51. See Juan Miguel Garrigues, *L'Esprit qui dit 'Pere': Le Problème du Filioque* (Paris: Tequi, 1981). The arguments here are largely based on his earlier article, "Procession et ekporèse du Saint Esprit: discernement de la tradition et reception oecuménique," *Istina* 17 (1972): 345–66.

52. For the New Testament use of ἐκπορεύεσθαι see pp. 22–23.

53. Pseudo-Athanasius, *Quaestiones Allae* 15 (PG 28, 785), John of Damascus, *De Fide orthodoxa* 1, 8 (PG 94, 817).

54. See Henry Liddell and Robert Scott, eds., *Greek English Lexicon*, rev. ed. with supplement (Oxford: Clarendon, 1996), 1145.

55. Thucydides, *Peloponnesian War* 1.61.5, 2.21.1, 4.13.2; Herodotus, *Histories* 3.96.

56. See pp. 41–42.

57. See pp. 48–49.

58. Gregory Nazianzus, *Oration* 20, 11 (SC 270, 78); Cyril of Alexandria, *Epistle* 4 (PG 77, 316).

59. See, for example, Sergius Bulgakov, *The Comforter*, 75–87.; Victor Rodzianko, "*Filioque* in Patristic Thought," *Studia Patristica* 2 (1957): 295–308.

60. Maximus the Confessor, *Opusculum* 10 (PG 91, 136).

61. Juan Miguel Garrigues, *L'Esprit qui dit "pere,"* 57–64.

62. See pp. V. Rodzianko has also pointed to the Latin translation (or mistranslation) of the Nicene Creed, which he has called "entirely wrong" since the Greek word ἐκπορεύεσθαι, the middle voice of ἐκπορεύω, does not have any of the connotations of passivity or derivation communicated by the Latin *processio*. Victor Rodzianko, "*Filioque* in Patristic Thought," 297.

63. See pp.

64. Juan Miguel Garrigues, *L'Esprit qui dit "pere,"* 73–74. Augustine of Hippo, *De Trinitate* 15.17. 29.

NOTES TO CHAPTER 5

1. Rudolf Riedinger, ed., *Acta Conciliorum Oecumenicorum, Series Secunda 2.1* (Berlin: Walter de Gruyter, 1990), 127.

2. For the Council in Trullo see G. Nedungatt and F. Featherstone, eds., *The Council in Trullo Revisited* (Rome: Pontifical Oriental Institute, 1995); J. Williams, "Use of Sources in the Canons of the Council in Trullo," *Byzantion* 66 (1996): 470–88; H. Ohme, *Das Concilium Quinisextum und seine Bischofsliste* (Berlin: Walter de Gruyter, 1990); Demetrius Constantelos, *Renewing the Church: The Significance of the Council in Trullo* (Brookline, Mass.: Holy Cross Press, 2007).

3. See pp. 68–69.

4. Bede, *Historia ecclesiastica gentis Anglorum* 4.1 (Eng. trans.: Bede, *Ecclesiastical History of the English People*, trans. Judith McClure and Roger Collins [Oxford: Oxford University Press, 1994], 171).

5. See M. Lapidge, *Archbishop Theodore, Commemorative Studies on His Life and Influence* (Cambridge: Cambridge University Press, 1995).

6. Bede, *Historia ecclesiastica gentis Anglorum* 4.17 (Eng. trans.: Bede, *Ecclesiastical History of the English People*, 199).

7. Bede, *Historia ecclesiastica gentis Anglorum* 4.17 (Eng. trans.: Bede, *Ecclesiastical History of the English People*, 200).

8. "And now the king first demanded to be baptized by the bishop. Like a new Constantine he moved forward to the water to blot out the former leprosy, to wash away in this new stream the foul stains borne from old days. . . . The king, therefore, confessing Almighty God, three in one, was baptized in the name of the Father, Son and Holy Ghost, and anointed with holy chrism with the sign of the cross of Christ. Of his army were baptized more than three thousand." (Gregory of Tours, *Historia Frankorum* 2.22. [Eng. trans.: Gregory of Tours, *History of the Franks*, trans. Lewis Thorpe (New York: Penguin, 1976), 69–70]). It should be remembered that Gregory himself confessed the *filioque*, which opens the possibility that the theology of the double procession had been part of the Frankish faith since the time of Clovis.

9. See Paul Fouracre, *The Age of Charles Martel* (New York: Longmans, 2000).

10. The historical importance of this battle has since become the subject of much scholarly debate. The view that Tours/Poitiers was one of the most decisive battles in

history was popularized in the eighteenth century by Edward Gibbon, who famously described the stakes for Christian Europe:

> A victorious line of march had been prolonged above a thousand miles from the rock of Gibraltar to the banks of the Loire; the repetition of an equal space would have carried the Saracens to the confines of Poland and the Highlands of Scotland; the Rhine is not more impassable than the Nile or Euphrates, and the Arabian fleet might have sailed without a naval combat into the mouth of the Thames. Perhaps the interpretation of the Koran would now be taught in the schools of Oxford, and her pulpits might demonstrate to a circumcised people the sanctity and truth of the revelation of Mahomet." (Edward Gibbon, *The History of the Decline and Fall of the Roman Empire* 3, vols. 5–6 [New York: Penguin, 1994], 336.)

For an opposing view see Franco Cardini, *Europe and Islam* (New York: Blackwell, 2001).

11. For more on the history of iconoclasm see Edward James Martin, *History of the Iconoclastic Controversy* (London: SPCK, 1930); Jaroslav Pelikan, *Imago Dei: The Byzantine Apologia for Icons* (Princeton, N.J.: Bollingen Foundation, 1990); Ambrosios Giakalis, *Images of the Divine: The Theology of Icons at the Seventh Ecumenical Council* (Leiden: E. J. Brill, 1994); Kenneth Parry, *Depicting the Word: Byzantine Iconophile Thought of the Eighth and Ninth Centuries* (Leiden: E. J. Brill, 1996).

12. Adonis Viennensis, *Chronicon in Aetates Sex Divisum* (PL 123, 125).

13. Richard Haugh, *Photius and the Carolingians* (Belmont: Nordland Publishing, 1975), 43.

14. John of Damascus, *Three Treatises on the Divine Images*, trans. Andrew Louth (Crestwood, N.Y.: St. Vladimir's Seminary Press, 2003).

15. John of Damascus, *De Fide orthodoxa* 1.2 (Eng. trans.: John of Damascus, *John of Damascus: Writings*, trans. Frederic Chase, FC 37 [Washington, D.C.: Catholic University of America Press, 1958], 167).

16. John of Damascus, *De Fide orthodoxa* 1.8 (Eng. trans.: John of Damascus, *Writings*, 181).

17. John of Damascus, *De Fide orthodoxa* 1.8 (Eng. trans.: John of Damascus, *Writings*, 188).

18. Ibid.

19. John of Damascus, *De Fide orthodoxa* 1.12 (Eng. trans.: John of Damascus, *Writings*, 196).

20. Ibid., 178.

21. Secondary works on Charlemagne have proliferated in recent years and include: Jeff Sypeck, *Becoming Charlemagne: Europe, Baghdad, and the Empires of AD 800* (New York: Harper Collins, 2006); Derek Williams, *Charlemagne* (New York: Doubleday, 2006); Roger Collins, *Charlemagne* (Toronto: University of Toronto Press, 1998); Matthias Becher, *Charlemagne*, trans. David Bachrach (New Haven, Conn.: Yale University Press, 2003); Alessandro Barbero, *Charlemagne: Father of a Continent*, trans. Allan Cameron (Berkeley: University of California Press, 2004); Johanna Story, ed., *Charlemagne: Empire and Society* (Manchester, England: Manchester University Press, 2005); Jean Favier, *Charlemagne* (Paris: Fayard, 1999); Rosamond McKitterick,

Charlemagne: The Formation of European Identity (Cambridge: Cambridge University Press, 2008); Christine Ratkowitsch, *Karolus Magnus—alter Aeneas, alter Martinus, alter Justinus* (Vienna: Verlag der Österreichischen Akademie der Wissenschaften, 997).

22. This was particularly true of the current Empress, Irene, who had arranged the murder of her own son. See Daniel Barone, *Irene of Byzantium. Woman, Empress and Fiancée of Charlemagne* (London: Francis Aldor, 1947); Lynda Garland, *Byzantine Empresses: Women and Power in Byzantium AD 527–1204* (New York: Routledge, 1999); Judith Herrin, *Women in Purple* (Princeton, N.J.: Princeton University Press, 2004).

23. It has long been recognized that Charlemagne's confusion on this point was caused by the poor translation of certain Greek texts (including the decrees of the Seventh Ecumenical Council in 767). According to Andrew Louth, this confusion was understandable since "the distinction that the iconodules had painstakingly drawn between a form of veneration expressing honor [*proskynesis*] and a form of veneration expressing worship [*laetria*] has no natural lexical equivalent [in Latin]." Andrew Louth, *Greek East and Latin West: The Church from 681–1071*, The Church in History 3 (Crestwood, N.Y.: St. Vladimir's Seminary Press, 2007), 86–87.

24. Hadrian was not completely satisfied with the Council of Nicea (since it did not address matters pertaining to the pope's jurisdiction in Illicum and Sicily), and he was put in the position of defending the council's iconodule theology against Charlemagne in the West while simultaneously claiming (against the Byzantines) that its job was not yet complete.

25. For the recent critical edition of the *Opus* see Ann Freeman, ed., MGH Leges 4 Concilia 2 Suppl. 1: *Opus Caroli regis contra synodum* (Hanover, Germany: Hahnsche Buchhandlung, 1998). Freeman's case for Theodulf's authorship (which few now doubt) is found on pages 12–23. The case against Theodulf's authorship is found in Luitpold Willach, *Diplomatic Studies in Latin and Greek Documents from the Carolingian Age* (Ithaca, N.Y.: Cornell University Press, 1977). For a textual history of the work see Ann Freeman, "Theodulf of Orleans and the Liber Carolini," *Speculum* 32 (1957): 663–705; idem, "Further Studies in the Liber Carolini," *Speculum* 40 (1965): 203-89; idem, "Further Studies in the Liber Carolini III," *Speculum* 46 (1971): 597–612. These and other of Freeman's articles were reprinted in idem, *Theodulf of Orleans: Charlemagne's Spokesman Against the Second Council of Nicaea*, Variorum Collected Studies Series, 772 (Aldershot: Ashgate, 2003). See also Thomas Noble, "From the *Liber Carolini* to the *Opus Caroli Regis*," *Journal of Medieval Latin* 9 (1999): 131–47.

26. *Opus Caroli regis contra synodum* 3.3 (Ann Freeman, Opus *Caroli regis contra synodum*, 345). See also Stephanos Efthymiades, trans., *The Life of the Patriarch Tarasios by Ignatios the Deacon* (Aldershot: Ashgate, 1998).

27. Hadrian, *Epistula Adriani Papae ad beatum Carolum Regum* (PL 98, 1249). In the same work Hadrian quoted a number of Eastern (Athanasius, Basil, Gregory of Nyssa, Gregory of Nazianzus, Cyril) and Western (Augustine, Hilary, Amborse, Leo, Gregory) fathers in his attempt to prove the orthodoxy of the "through the Son" (*per Filium*) formula. See PL 98, 1249–52.

28. This should not be taken to mean that the work discounted the patristic witness. For the use of the fathers in the *Opus Caroli Regis* see Willemien Otten, "The Texture of Tradition: The Role of the Church Fathers in Carolingian Theology," in *The*

Reception of the Church Fathers in the West from the Carolingians to the Maurists, vol. 1, Irena Backus, ed. (Leiden: Brill Academic Publishers, 2001), 3–50.

29. *Opus Caroli regis contra synodum* 3.3 (Ann Freeman, Opus *Caroli regis contra synodum*, 346).

30. *Opus Caroli regis contra synodum* 3.3 (Ann Freeman, Opus *Caroli regis contra synodum*, 346–47).

31. *Opus Caroli regis contra synodum* 3.3 (Ann Freeman, Opus *Caroli regis contra synodum*, 349). Theodulf's use of Isidore of Seville, who had claimed that the *filioque* was "contained in the apostolic symbol and handed down by the ancient doctors," explains this belief in part.

32. *Opus Caroli regis contra synodum* 3.3 (Ann Freeman, Opus *Caroli regis contra synodum*, 345).

33. It can also be argued that in their opposing Pope Hadrian there was a statement also being made about the Carolingians' independence vis-à-vis Rome.

34. Scholars have long noted the polemically anti-Byzantine tone of the *Opus* and other Carolingian theological works. According to Freeman, "Ambition, arrogance, and boastful pride are the sins of the Byzantine monarchs and their spokesmen at the council, lying at the root of all their excesses—this is a constant theme of the *Opus Caroli*," Ann Freeman, *Opus Caroli regis contra synodum*, 4.

35. Lionel Wickham, "Adoptionism," in *Encyclopedia of Early Christianity*, ed. Everett Ferguson (New York: Garland, 1998), 20. See also John Cavadini, *The Last Christology of the West: Adoptionism in Spain and Gaul 785–820* (Philadelphia: University of Pennsylvania Press, 1993).

36. Paulinus of Aquileia, *Libellus Sancrosyllabus Episcoporum Italiae* (Albert Werminghoff, ed., MGH Concilia 2 Tomos 2 Pars 1: *Concilia Aevi Karolini*, 136 [Hanover, Germany: Hahnsche Buchhandlung, 1906]); Charlemagne, *Epistula Karoli Magni ad Elipandum et Episcopos Hispaniae* (Albert Werminghoff, ed., *Concilia Aevi Karolini*, 163).

37. Hadrian, *Epistula Hadriani I Papae ad Episcopos Hispaniae Directa* (Albert Werminghoff, ed., *Concilia Aevi Karolini*, 128). Hadrian's use of *essentialiter* in this context might indicate that his theology of the procession, like his language (i.e., the preference for the *per Filium* formula), was more in sympathy with the traditional Eastern view.

38. See Carl Giannoni, *Paulinus II, Patriarch von Aquileia: Ein Beitrag zur Kirchengeschichte Österreichs im Zeitalter Karls des Grossen* (Wien, Austria, 1896).

39. *Concilium Foroiuliense* (Albert Werminghoff, ed., *Concilia Aevi Karolini*, 181).

40. *Concilium Foroiuliense* (Albert Werminghoff, ed., *Concilia Aevi Karolini*, 182).

41. Ibid.

42. Ibid.

43. Ibid.

44. The *Symbolum Fidei* attached to the acts of the council clearly stated its belief "in the Holy Spirit, Lord and giver of life, who proceeds from the Father and the Son," teaching that "the Holy Spirit is true God . . . neither begotten nor created, but proceeding atemporally and inseparably from the Father and the Son." *Concilium Foroiuliense* (Albert Werminghoff, ed., *Concilia Aevi Karolini*, 187).

45. Mark Whittow, *The Making of Byzantium 600–1025* (Berkeley: University of California Press, 1996), 304. See also Robert Folz, *The Coronation of Charlemagne*, trans. J. E.Anderson (London: Routledge, 1974).

46. See Charles Elliott, "The Schism and Its Elimination in Humbert of Rome's *Opusculum Tripartitum*," *Greek Orthodox Theological Review* 34 (1989): 71–83.

47. Henry Chadwick notes that the MGH Epistula 4 index contains several references to the *imperium* prior to 800. See Henry Chadwick, *East and West: The Making of a Rift in the Church* (Oxford: Oxford University Press, 2003), 87.

48. Salic law excluded females from inheriting lands or kingdoms ("But of Salic land no portion of the inheritance shall come to a woman: but the whole inheritance of the land shall come to the male sex"). According to John Julian Norwich, that "the empress was notorious for having blinded and murdered her own son was, in the minds of both Leo and Charles, almost immaterial; it was enough that she was a woman. The female sex was known to be incapable of governing and by old Salic tradition was debarred from doing so" John Julian Norwich, *Byzantium: The Early Centuries, History of Byzantium* 1 (London: Viking, 1988), 378.

49. According to Einhard, Charlemagne, who had long hair and wore Frankish clothes, had to be persuaded to adopt more "Roman" dress for the occasion. Einhard, *Vita Caroli* 23 (Eng. trans.: Einhard, "Life of Charlemagne" in *Einhard and Notker: Two Lives of Charlemagne*, trans. Lewis Thorpe [London: Penguin, 1969], 77–78).

50. Einhard, *Vita Caroli* 28 (Eng. trans.: Einhard, *Two Lives of Charlemagne*, 81).

51. The *Chronographia* of Theophanes simply stated that "In this year [800] the ninth indiction, on December 25 Charles the king of the Franks was crowned by Pope Leo." (Eng. trans.: Theophanes, *The Chronicle of Theophanes*, trans. Harry Turtledove [Philadelphia: University of Pennsylvania Press, 1982], 157).

52. This, in part, explains the Byzantine Emperor Michael's rather insulting greeting to Charlemagne's son Louis, as "glorious King of the Franks and Lombards, who is called *their* emperor." For their part, the Franks responded by referring to the Eastern emperor as "Emperor of the Greeks," which became a commonplace in Western writing. Louis claimed: "We have received the government of the Roman Empire for our orthodoxy while the Greeks have ceased to be emperors of the Romans for their cacodoxy. Not only have they deserted the city [Rome] and the capital of the Empire, but they have also abandoned Roman nationality and even the Latin language. They have migrated to another capital city and taken up a completely different nationality and language."

53. Theophanes, *Chronographia* (Eng. trans.: Theophanes, *The Chronicle of Theophanes*, 158–61).

54. For more on Alcuin see Stephen Allott, *Alcuin of York: His Life and Letters* (York: William Sessions, 1974); Eleanor Shipley Duckett, *Alcuin, Friend of Charlemagne* (New York: MacMillan, 1951); Donald Bullough, "Charlemagne's Men of God: Alcuin, Hildebrand, and Arn," in *Charlemagne: Empire and Society*, ed. Johanna Story (Manchester, England: Manchester University Press, 2005), 136–50. The *Vita Alcuini* is found in W. Arndt, ed., MGH Scriptores 15.1 (1887), 182–97.

55. See John Cavadini, "The Sources and Theology of Alcuin's *De Fide Sanctae et Individuae Trinitatis*," *Traditio* 46 (1991): 123–46.

56. Ibid., 132.

57. Alcuin, *De Fide sanctae et individuae Trinitatis* (PL 101, 17).

58. Alcuin, *De Fide sanctae et individuae Trinitatis* (PL 101, 22).

59. Alcuin, *Commentary on the Gospel of John* (Eng. trans.: Richard Haugh, *Photius and the Carolingians*, 43).

60. For more on the controversy see Claudia Sole, *Jerusalem-Konstantinopel-Rom: Die Vitan des Michael Synkellos und der Brüder Theodorus und Theophanes Graptoi* (Stuttgart, Germany: Steiner, 2001), 163–202; M. Borgolte, "Papst Leo III, Karl der Große und der Filioque-Strit von Jerusalem," *Byzantia* 10 (1980): 403–27.

61. A full English text of the letter is found in Haugh, *Photius and the Carolingians*, 64–67.

62. Leo III, *Epistula 15 seu symbolum orthodoxae fidei Leonis papae* (Eng. trans.: Haugh, *Photius and the Carolingians*, 68).

63. Ibid.

64. Others were prepared by Arn(o) of Salzburg, Smaragdus of St. Mihiel, Heito of Basel, and Adalwin of Regensburg. Recently these texts received a new critical edition, along with the council's final document, long thought lost and now believed to have been authored by Arno. See Harald Willjung, ed., MGH Concilia Tomus 2, Supplementum 2: *Das Konzil von Aachen 809* (Hanover, Germany: Hahnsche Buchhandlung, 1998).

65. Willemien Otten, "The Texture of Tradition: The Role of the Church Fathers in Carolingian Theology," 4.

66. A full list of the authorities quoted comprises Athanasius, Cyril, Hilary, Ambrose, Didymus, Augustine, Vigilius, Proclus, Agnellus, Gregory the Great, Isidore, Prosper, Fulgentius, Hormisdas, Leo the Great, Cassiodorus, and Prudentius.

67. Richard Haugh, *Photius and the Carolingians*, 70.

68. Theodulf of Orleans, *Libellus de Processione Spiritus Sancti* (Harald Willjung, ed., *Das Konzil von Aachen 809*, 325).

69. Ibid., 342.

70. Ibid., 335. This same quote was later used in the Decree of the Council of Aachen, although there the verb προχεῖται was translated with *profluit*. See *Decretum Aquisgranense* (Harald Willjung, ed., *Das Konzil von Aachen 809*, 238).

71. For Arn(o) of Salzburg see Meta Niederkorn-Bruck, Anton Scharer, Wilhelm Störmer, *Erzbischof Arn von Salzburg* (Wien, Austria: Oldenbourg, 2004); Donald Bullough, "Charlemagne's Men of God: Alcuin, Hildebrand, and Arn," in *Charlemagne: Empire and Society*, 136–50.

72. Arn of Satzburg, *Testimonia ex sacris voluminibus collecta* (Harald Willjung, ed., *Das Konzil von Aachen 809*, 254).

73. *Decretum Aquisgranense* (Harald Willjung, ed., *Das Konzil von Aachen 809*, 244).

74. Ibid., 240.

75. Ibid., 237.

76. Smaragdus of St. Michiel, *Epistula de processione spiritus sancti* (Harald Willjung, ed., *Das Konzil von Aachen 809*, 303) (Eng. trans.: Richard Haugh, *Photius and the Carolingians*, 80).

77. Smaragdus of St. Michiel, *Epistula de processione spiritus sancti* (Harald Willjung, ed., *Das Konzil von Aachen 809*, 312) (Eng. trans.: Richard Haugh, *Photius and the Carolingians*, 81).

78. For Pope Leo's motives see R. G. Heath, "Western Schism of the Franks and the *Filioque*," *Journal of Ecclesiastical History* 23 (1972): 97–113. See also Kevin Kennedy, "The Permanence of an Idea: Three Ninth Century Frankish Ecclesiastics and the Authority of the Roman See," in *Aus Kirche und Reich: Studion zu Theologie Politik und Recht im Mittelatter*, Hubert Mordek, ed. (Sigmaringen, Germany: J. Thorbecke, 1983), 105–16.

79. *Ratio de symbol fidei inter Leonem III papam et missos Caroli imperatoris* (Harald Willjung, ed., *Das Konzil von Aachen 809*, 289) (Eng. trans.: Richard Haugh, *Photius and the Carolingians*, 81–88).

80. *Ratio de symbol fidei inter Leonem III papam et missos Caroli imperatoris* (Harald Willjung, ed., *Das Konzil von Aachen 809*, 293) (Eng. trans.: Richard Haugh, *Photius and the Carolingians*, 87).

81. *Ratio de symbol fidei inter Leonem III papam et missos Caroli imperatoris* in Harald Willjung, ed., *Das Konzil von Aachen 809*, 289 (Eng. trans.: Richard Haugh, *Photius and the Carolingians*, 83–84).

82. *Ratio de symbol fidei inter Leonem III papam et missos Caroli imperatoris* in Harald Willjung, ed., *Das Konzil von Aachen 809*, 290 (Eng. trans.: Richard Haugh, *Photius and the Carolingians*, 84).

83. *Ratio de symbol fidei inter Leonem III papam et missos Caroli imperatoris* in Harald Willjung, ed., *Das Konzil von Aachen 809*, 293 (Eng. trans.: Richard Haugh, *Photius and the Carolingians*, 87).

84. *Ratio de symbol fidei inter Leonem III papam et missos Caroli imperatoris* in Harald Willjung, ed., *Das Konzil von Aachen 809*, 294 (Eng. trans.: Richard Haugh, *Photius and the Carolingians*, 88).

85. Ibid.

86. These shields remained in place for several centuries and were noted by Anastasius Bibliothecarius (PL 128, 1238), Peter Lombard (PL 142, 552), and Peter Abelard (PL 178, 629). See Vittorio Peri, "Il Simbolo Epigrafico di S. Leone III nelle Basiliche Romane dei SS. Pietro e Paolo," *Rivista di Archeologia Christiana* 45 (1969): 191–221.

87. *Mystagogia*, 88 (Photius of Constantinople, *The Mystagogy of the Holy Spirit*, 112). For this reason Photius also believed that Pope Leo had commanded the recitation of the Creed only in Greek.

88. See A. P. Vlasto, *The Entry of the Slavs into Christendom* (Cambridge: Cambridge University Press, 1970); Dimitri Obolensky, *The Byzantine Commonweaklth: Eastern Europe 500–1453* (London: Weidenfield and Nicolson, 1971).

89. Despina Stratoudaki White, "Patriarch Photios—A Christian Humanist," *Greek Orthodox Theological Review* 20 (1980): 195–96. Among Photius's best known works are the *Bibliotheca* (René Henry, ed., *Bibliothèque*, 9 vols [Paris: Société d' édition, 1959–91]), a review and summary of some 280 books many of which are now lost), the *Lexicon*, the *Amphilochia* and his *Epistles* (Johannes Baletta, ed., *Photios Patriarchos Constantinopolitanos: Epistolae* [New York: Georg Olms Verlag, 1978]).

90. For more on the circumstances of Photius's elevation see Francis Dvornik, *The Photian Schism: History and Legend* (Cambridge: Cambridge University Press, 1948), 1–69.

91. See Francis Dvornik, *The Photian Schism: History and Legend*, 100–101.

92. Although he believed the 863 synod was binding, Nicholas continued to suggest to the emperor that both Photius and Ignatius should send representatives to Rome so that the matter could be settled once and for all. Nicholas III, *Epistula 98 ad Michaelem Imperatorem* (PL 119, 1016–45).

93. Boris's decision to become a Christian was opposed by many of the nobility, who rose in open revolt. Boris put down the revolt, although hostility to Christianity continued. Boris retired to a monastery in 889 but returned to public life in 893 when his son Vladimir tried to return the country to paganism. Vladimir was blinded, and Boris's third son, Simeon, made tsar in his place.

94. Despina Stratoudaki White and Joseph R. Berrigan, eds., *The Patriarch and the Prince: The Letter of Patriarch Photios of Constantinople to Khan Boris of Bulgaria* (Brookline, Mass.: Holy Cross Orthodox Press, 1982).

95. Nicholas's reply on this last point was clear—without apostolic foundation, Constantinople's claims to equality with Rome were groundless. Nicholas even went so far as to doubt Constantinople's place within the pentarchy, for "only those should be regarded as true patriarchs who occupy apostolic sees in succession of pontiffs. . . . Such is the case of the Sees of Rome, Alexandria, and Antioch. . . . The bishops of Constantinople and of Jerusalem, although they are called patriarchs, are not of such importance as those mentioned above" Nicholas III, *Epistula 92 Responsa Nicholai ad consulta Bulgarorum* (PL 119, 1012).

96. Robert Haddad claimed that the *filioque* was already well known in Byzantium, but because "its defilement had never before spread so close to home. . . . Constantinople, imperial and patriarchal, had chosen to ignore the *filioque* as long as it was confined to the Latin west. . . . [However] the perceived Latin threat in Bulgaria ensured that the *filioque* would never again be ignored." Robert Haddad, "The Stations of the Filioque," *St. Vladimir's Theological Quarterly* 4 (2002): 228.

97. Photius did demonstrate some knowledge of Augustine's anti-Pelagian writings, although there is no evidence that he actually read them. See Bernard Altaner, "Augustinus in der griechischen Kirche bis auf Photius," *Historisches Jahrbuch* 71 (1951): 37–76.

98. Both Paul Speck and Tia Kolbaba maintain that Epistle 2 to the Eastern Patriarchs is a composite work, although its being so does not necessarily negate the possibility that Photius authored it. Paul Speck, "Die griechischen Quellen zur Bekehrung der Bulgaren und die zwei ersten Briefe des Photios," in *Polupleuros Nous. Miscellanea für Peter Schreiner zu Seinem 60, Geburtstag* (Munich: K.G. Saur, 2005), 342–59; Tia Kolbaba, *Inventing Latin Heretics: Byzantines and the Filioque in the Ninth Century* (Kalamazoo, Mich.: Medieval Institute Publications, 2008).

99. Photius, *Encyclical to the Eastern Patriarchs* (Eng. trans.: Photius, *The Mystagogy of the Holy Spirit*, 50–51).

100. Photius, *Encyclical to the Eastern Patriarchs* (Eng. trans.: Photius, *The Mystagogy of the Holy Spirit*, 51).

101. Photius, *Encyclical to the Eastern Patriarchs* (Eng. trans.: Photius, *The Mystagogy of the Holy Spirit*, 51).

102. Photius, *Encyclical to the Eastern Patriarchs* (Eng. trans.: Photius, *The Mystagogy of the Holy Spirit*, 51).

103. Photius, *Encyclical to the Eastern Patriarchs* (Eng. trans.: Photius, *The Mystagogy of the Holy Spirit*, 51).

104. Photius, *Encyclical to the Eastern Patriarchs* (Eng. trans.: Photius, *The Mystagogy of the Holy Spirit*, 52). This last criticism echoes Gregory Nazianzus in *Oration* 31: "If he [the Spirit] is begotten by the Son, our God apparently has a grandson, and what could be odder than that?" Gregory of Nazianzus, *Oration* 31.7 (Eng. trans.: Gregory of Nazianzus, *On God and Christ*: 121).

105. J. Hergenroether, *Monumenta graeca ad Photiumeiusque Historia Pertinentia* (Ratisbon, Germany, 1869), 84–138.

106. Tia Kolbaba, *Inventing Latin Heretics*, 125.

107. Niketas Byzantinos, *Syllogistic Chapters* (Eng. trans.: Tia Kolbaba, *Inventing Latin Heretics*, 126).

108. Niketas Byzantinos, *Syllogistic Chapters* (Eng. trans.: Tia Kolbaba, *Inventing Latin Heretics*, 130).

109. Recent scholarship has put Photius's authorship of the *Mystagogia* into question, arguing (among other things) that the earliest manuscripts attribute the work to Metrophanes of Smyrna. As late as the twelfth century, authors who invoked the arguments of the *Mystagogia* did not necessarily associate Photius with the work. For more see Tia Kolbaba, *Inventing Latin Heretics*.

110. *Mystagogia* 6 (Eng. trans.: Photius, *Mystagogy*, 72).

111. *Mystagogia* 37 (Eng. trans.: Photius, *Mystagogy*, 86).

112. *Mystagogia* 53 (Eng. trans.: Photius, *Mystagogy*, 92).

113. *Mystagogia* 54 (Eng. trans.: Photius, *Mystagogy*, 92).

114. "These fathers represented a special dilemma: on the one hand, it could not well be denied that they had actually asserted the *filioque*; on the other, it was difficult to deny that they must actually be ranked among the fathers. Thus, at one stroke both the usual expedients were eliminated." Richard Paul Vaggione, "'All These Were Honored in Their Generation'—The Problem of Conflicting Patristic Evidence in Photius," *Patristic and Byzantine Review* 2 (1983): 277.

115. *Mystagogia* 71 (Eng. trans.: Photius, *Mystagogy*, 100).

116. *Mystagogia* 68, 72 (Eng. trans.: Photius, *Mystagogy*, 98, 100).

117. *Mystagogia* 70 (Eng. trans.: Photius, *Mystagogy*, 100).

118. Although the acts of this council are lost, Cyril Mango claims that Photius's final homily from the council (Homily 18) is preserved. See Cyril Mango, *The Homilies of Photius of Constantinople: English Translation, Introduction, and Commentary* (Cambridge, Mass.: Harvard University Press, 1958), 306–15.

119. Among the decisions were Canon 4: "We declare that he [Photius] never was nor is now a bishop nor must those, who were consecrated or given advancement by him to any grade of the priesthood, remain in that state to which they were promoted," and Canon 6:

Photius, after the sentences and condemnations most justly pronounced against him by the most holy pope Nicholas for his criminal usurpation of the church of Constantinople, in addition to his other evil deeds, found some men of wicked and sycophantic character from the squares and streets of the city and proposed and designated them as vicars of the three most holy patriarchal sees of the East. He formed with these a church of evil-doers and a fraudulent council and set in motion accusations and charges entailing deposition against the most blessed pope Nicholas and repeatedly, impudently and boldly issued anathemas against him and all those in communion with him. The records of these things have been seen by us, records which were cobbled together by him with evil intent and lying words, and all of which have been burnt during this very synod. (Norman Tanner, *Decrees of the Ecumenical Councils*, 169, 171.)

120. See Johan A. Meijer, *A Successful Reunion Council: A Theological Analysis of the Photian Synod of 879–80* (Thessalonikē: Patriarchikon Hydrima Paterikōn Meletōn, 1975).

121. Francis Dvornik in *The Photian Schism*, details the complicated historical reasons why, in the West, the acts of this council were forgotten and the acts of the earlier anti-Photian synod became part of the Roman canonical tradition. Chief among them was the importance of Canon 22, "forbidding laymen to interfere with episcopal elections, 'discovered' by the canonists of the Gregorian period." This canon gave the Church of Rome support in their ongoing struggle against lay involvement in ecclesiastical affairs. Francis Dvornik, *The Photian Schism*, 330.

122. Trans. George Dragas, "The Eighth Ecumenical Council: Constantinople IV (879/880) and the Condemnation of the *Filioque* Addition and Doctrine," *Greek Orthodox Theological Review* 44 (1999): 364.

123. V. Grumel, "Le Filioque au concile photien de 879–880 et la témoignage de Michel dAnchialos" *Echos d'Orient* 29 (1930): 257–64; Martin Jugie, "Origine de la controverse sur l'addition du Filioque au Symbole," *Revue des sciences philosophiques et théologiques* 28 (1939): 369–85.

124. Both the *Letter to the Patriarch of Aquileia* and the *Mystagogia* assumed that the opponent was not the See of Rome (given Pope John's recognition of the Council of 879), but rather the Carolingians, who were thought to be both theologically unsound and disobedient to the teachings of their own patriarch.

125. It is interesting to note that although Photius would later be remembered as a great champion against the heresies of the Latins, there is nothing to indicate that this attribute was part of his reputation in the two centuries that followed his death. See Martin Jugie "Le culte de Photius dans l'Église byzantine," *Revue de l'orient chrétien* 3 (1922–23): 107.

126. Markos Orpanos, "The Procession of the Holy Spirit according to Certain Later Greek Fathers," 25.

127. Nicholas III, *Epistula 152 Ad Hincmarum et caertos episcopos in regno Caroli constitutos* (PL 119, 1153).

128. Nicholas III, *Epistula 152 Ad Hincmarum et caertos episcopos in regno Caroli constitutos* (PL 119, 1153).

129. Nicholas III, *Epistula 152 Ad Hincmarum et caertos episcopos in regno Caroli constitutos* (PL 119, 1160).

130. Aeneas of Paris, *Liber adversus Graecos* (PL 121, 683–721).

131. Ibid., 690. This last comment was meant to remind his readers that not only had the West never recognized Constantinople's claim to be "New Rome" and second within the pentarchy (Canon 28 of Chalcedon), but even Constantinople's claims to a patriarchal status were in doubt because of lack of apostolic foundation.

132. Ibid., 686.

133. Ibid., 686–90.

134. Peter Gemeinhardt, *Filioque-Kontroverse Zwischen Ost-Und Westkirche Im Frühmittelalter* (Berlin: Walter de Gruyter, 2002), 226.

135. "Truly, in a relative way do the names of the persons refer: Father to Son, Son to Father, Holy Spirit to both. And although they are called three persons relatively, yet only one nature and substance must be believed." *Repsonsio Episcoporum Germaniae Wormatiae coadunatorum de Fide Sante Trinitas contra Graecorum Haeresim* (PL 119, 1201–12).

136. Ibid.

137. Ibid.

138. Ratramnus of Corbie, *Contra Graecorum Opposita Romanam Ecclesiam Infamantium* (PL 121, 225–346). In translating passages of this work, I gratefully acknowledge the assistance of Dr. Brian Matz.

139. Ibid., 226. Photius's name appears nowhere in the work, so it is likely that Ratramnus was responding not to the *Encyclical to the Eastern Patriarchs*, but to the charges contained in the imperial letter given to the Pope through King Boris.

140. Ibid., 245.

141. Ibid., 229.

142. Ibid., 247.

143. Romans 8:9 had long been used by the Latins as a basis for the teaching on the procession, and Richard Haugh believes Ratramnus's interpretation of the passage is the hermeneutical key to the whole work. Richard Haugh, *Photius and the Carolingians*, 109.

144. Ratramnus of Corbie, *Contra Graecorum Opposita Romanam Ecclesiam Infamantium* 2.3 (PL 121, 248).

145. Deno John Geanakoplos, "Some Aspects of the Influence of the Byzantine Maximus the Confessor on the Theology of East and West," *Church History* 38 (1969): 151.

146. PL 122, 1193–96. See Edward Jeauneau, "Pseudo-Dionysius, Gregory of Nyssa and Maximus the Confessor in the Works of John Scotus Eriugena," in *Carolingian Essays*, Uta-Renate Blumenthal, ed. (Washington, D.C.: Catholic University of America Press, 1983), 137–49; idem, "Jean l'Érigène et las Ambigua ad Ioahannem de Maxime le Confesseur," in Felix Heinzer and Christoph Schönborn, eds., *Maximus Confessor*, 343–64.

147. See especially John Scotus Erigena, *De divisione naturae* 2.31–34 (PL 122, 601–14).

148. John Scotus Erigena, *De divisione naturae* 2.34 (PL 122, 613). It should be noted that Erigena, following Maximus and Nazianzus, assumes *substantia* to be the Latin equivalent of ὑπόστασις, which he differentiated from *essentia* or οὐσίας.

149. Anastasius had actually been "antipope" for a short time during the pontificate of Benedict III (855–58). Because of his great learning and knowledge of

Greek, he was given the post of papal librarian after his rehabilitation. Aside from his literary output (which was prodigious), Anastasius also supported Cyril and Methodius in their mission among the Slavs and represented Emperor Louis II to the Byzantines in his unsuccessful attempt to unite the Eastern and Western empires through marriage. It was during this time in Constantinople that he attended the council of 869–70.

150. Anastasius Bibliothecarius, *Ad Ioannem Diaconum* (PL 129, 560–61).

151. Francis Dvornik, *The Photian Schism*, 202–36.

152. K. Leyser, "The Tenth Century in Byzantine-Western Relationships," in Derek Baker, ed., *Relations between East and West in the Middle Ages* (Edinburgh: Edinburgh University Press, 1973).

153. Steven Runciman, *The Eastern Schism: A Study of the Papacy and the Eastern Churches during the Eleventh and Twelfth Centuries* (Oxford: Oxford University Press, 1955), 27.

NOTES TO CHAPTER 6

1. "Estrangement" is the term preferred by Yves Congar in his book *After Nine Hundred Years: The Background of the Schism between the Eastern and Western Churches* (New York: Fordham University Press, 1959).

2. The last emperor had been Berengar I of Friuli, who died in 924. From the beginning of his reign as King of the Germans in 936 Otto did all he could to associate himself with Charlemagne's imperial legacy, from being crowned at Aachen, to his use of the *dominica hasta*—a sacred lance, allegedly carried by the Emperor Constantine, containing one of the nails that had pierced Christ. See Howard Adelson, "The Holy Lance and the Hereditary German Monarchy," *The Art Bulletin* 48 (1966): 177–92. For Otto see John J. Gallagher, *Church and State in Germany under Otto the Great (936–973)* (Washington, D.C.: Catholic University of America, 1938).

3. According to tradition, John XII was not only politically ambitious, but amorous—legend has it that his death was a result of being thrown out of the window by a jealous husband who had discovered his wife with the pontiff *in flagrante delecto*. Otto's choice did not fare much better. Leo VIII allegedly died in bed with his mistress in 965.

4. Liutprand of Cremona, *Relatio de legatione Constantinopolitana* (Eng. trans.: Lynn Nelson and Melanie Veenbuer Shirk, eds., *Mission to Constantinople: Liutprand of Cremona* [Lawrence, Kan.: Coronado Press, 1972], 3).

5. Aside from their annoyance at Otto's preferred title as "Emperor of the Romans" and Liutprand's attempts to purchase purple (i.e., imperial) cloth when in Constantinople, the Byzantines were also insulted by the constant references to Nikephorus as "Emperor of the Greeks."

6. Liutprand of Cremona, *Relatio de legatione Constantinopolitana* (Eng. trans.: Lynn Nelson and Melanie Veenbuer Shirk, eds., *Mission to Constantinople*, 17–19).

7. Theophano assumed the role of regent for a time after her husband's death, because her son, Otto III, had not yet reached majority. See Adelbert Davids, *The Empress Theophano: Byzantium and the West at the Turn of the First Millennium* (Cambridge: Cambridge University Press, 1995). Otto III, in part because of his

mother's influence, introduced several Byzantine customs to the imperial court and was about to marry a Byzantine princess when in 1002 he died of malaria at age 21. See Gerdt Althoff, *Otto III* (Darmstadt: Wissenschaftliche Buchgellschaft, 1996).

8. While Runciman thinks it possible that this schism was due to the *filioque*, Martin Jugie (*Le Schisme Byzantin* [Paris: P. Lethielleux, 1941], 166–67) doubts it. Steven Runciman, *The Eastern Schism* (London: Oxford University Press, 1955), 33.

9. The evidence suggests, however, that the pope's name continued to be commemorated in both Antioch and Jerusalem.

10. Bernonis, *Libellus de quibusdam Rebus ad Missae Officium Pertinentibus* (PL 142, 1060–61).

11. In 1024 the Patriarch Eustathius of Constantinople suggested a formula to finally resolve the dispute over the respective powers of Rome and Constantinople— "Let the Church of Constantinople be called and accounted universal in its own sphere, as Rome is throughout the world." Rodulfus Glaber, *Historiarum libri quinque* 4.1 (PL 142, 671). Pope John XIX was initially in favor of accepting the formula, but he was reminded by the Abbot of Saint-Benignus at Dijon that while the imperial power could be distributed between East and West, Peter's power over the Church resided solely in his successor and could not be so divided.

12. See Richard Mayne, "East and West in 1054" *Cambridge Historical Journal* 11 (1954): 133–48; Axel Bayer, *Spaltung der Christenheit: Das sogenannte Morgenländische Schisma von 1054* (Cologne: Böhlau Vertag, 2002); V. Laurent, "Le schisme de Michel Cérulaire," *Echos d'Orient* 31 (1932): 97–110; Tia Kolbaba, "The Legacy of Humbert and Cerularius: Traditions of the Schism of 1054 in Byzantine Texts and Manuscripts of the Twelfth and Thirteenth Centuries," in Charalambos Dendrinos, Jonathan Harris, and Judith Herrin eds., *Porphyrogentia: Essays on the History and Literature of Byzantium and the Latin East in Honour of Julian Chrysostomides* (Aldershot: Ashgate, 2003), 47–62.

13. Leo of Ohrid, *Epistula ad Ioannem Tranensem* in Cornelius Will, ed., *Acta et Scripta quae de controversiis ecclesiae graecae et latinae saeculo undecimo composite extant* (Leipzig, 1861). See also John Erickson, "Leavened and Unleavened: Some Theological Implications of the Schism of 1054," in *The Challenge of Our Past* (Crestwood, N.Y.: St. Vladimir's Seminary Press, 1991), 133–55; Mahlon Smith, *And Taking Bread . . . Cerularius and the Azymite Controversy of 1054, Théologie Historique* 47 (Paris: Beauchesne, 1978).

14. Humbert, *Rationes de sancti spiritus processione a patre et filio* (Anton Michel, *Humbert und Kerularios: Quellen und Studien zum Schisma des XI. Jahrhunderts* 1 [Paderborn, Germany: Schöningh, 1924], 97–111).

15. J. M. Hussey, *The Orthodox Church in the Byzantine Empire*, Oxford History of the Christian Church (Oxford: Clarendon Press, 1986), 133.

16. Henry Chadwick, *East and West: The Making of a Rift in the Church* (Oxford: Oxford University Press, 2003), 210.

17. For contemporary views of Cerularius see John Skylitzes, *Synopsis Historion* (PG 122, 368–72). A modern portrait can be found in F. Tinnefeld, *Jahrbuch der österreichischen Byzantinistik* 39 (1989): 95–127.

18. Henry Chadwick, *East and West: The Making of a Rift in the Church*, 210.

19. Andrew Louth, *Greek East and Latin West* (Crestwood, N. Y.: St. Vladimir's Seminary Press, 2007), 309.

20. Humbert was not alone in this belief. William of Ockham also understood the Creed of Nicea to contain the *filioque*, its "removal" by the Greeks making them schismatics and heretics and thus incapable of governing a Christian empire. See his *Allegationes de potestate imperiali* in H. S. Offer, ed., *Opera Politica* 4 (Oxford: Oxford University Press, 1997).

21. *Excommunicatio qua feriuntur Michael Caerularius atque ejus sectatores* (Cornelius Will, ed., *Acta et scripta*, 153–54) (Eng. trans.: Deno John Geanakoplos, *Byzantium: Church, Society and Civilization Seen through Contemporary Eyes* [Chicago: University of Chicago Press, 1984], 208–9). Pope Leo's death in April (even before the legates arrived in Constantinople) calls into question the validity of their actions, since their mandate would have died with the pope. It is entirely possible that Humbert himself knew of the pope's death, and that is why he felt bound to act before it became known throughout the capital. By the time Cerularius issued his response days later, news of Leo's death had leaked out. See A. Herman, "I legati inviati da Leoni IX nel 1054 a Constantinopoli," *Orientalia Christiana Periodica* 8 (1942): 209–18.

22. Ibid. Among those specifically anathematized was also a certain Constantine, who had allegedly broken into the Latin churches and "with profane feet" trampled on the eucharist because it was consecrated with unleavened bread.

23. Ibid. The other complaints brought against the Greek Church included treating Latins as heretics (and subsequently rebaptizing them, like the Arians) and allowing priests to marry (like the Nicolaites). The bull also notes that, like the Nazarenes, they forbade baptism until the eighth day, forbade communion to menstruating women, and refused to be in communion with "those who, according to the custom of the Roman Church, cut their hair and shave their beards." Humbert also made sure to note Michael's personal rudeness to the pope's representatives (e.g., forbidding use of a church in which to celebrate mass), demonstrating his insolence to the Holy See, "in opposition to which he signed himself "ecumenical patriarch."

24. "If anyone will not welcome you or listen to your words, shake off the dust from your feet as you leave that house or town. Truly I tell you, it will be more tolerable for the land of Sodom and Gomorrah on the day of judgment than for that town" Matthew 10:14–15. See also Mark 6:11 and Luke 9:5.

25. *Edictum Synodi Constantinopolitanae* (Cornelius Will, *Acta et scripta*, 155–58) (Eng. trans.: Deno Geanakoplos, *Byzantium*, 209–12).

26. Ibid.

27. Ibid.

28. Ibid.

29. Ceruliarus, *Panoply* 62.1 (Anton Michel, ed., *Humbert und Kerularios* 2, 274) (Eng. trans.: Jaroslav Pelikan, *The Christian Tradition* 2: *The Spirit of Eastern Christendom* [Chicago: University of Chicago Press, 1974], 197).

30. *Edictum Synodi Constantinopolitanae* (Cornelius Will, *Acta et scripta*, 155–58) (Eng. trans.: Deno Geanakoplos, *Byzantium*, 209–12). The Greek translations were later publicly burned.

31. Henry Chadwick, *East and West: The Making of a Rift in the Church*, 218.

32. Peter of Antioch, *Petri Theopoleos totiusque Orientis patriarchae disertatio* (PG 120, 804).

33. Ibid., 805.

34. For more on Theophylact see Dimitri Obolensky, "Theophylact of Ohrid," in *Six Byzantine Portraits* (Oxford: Clarendon Press, 1988), 34–82; Margaret Mullett, *Theophylact of Ochrid: Reading the Letters of a Byzantine Archbishop*, Birmingham Byzantine and Ottoman Monographs 2 (London: Variorum, 1997).

35. Theophylact of Ohrid, Liber *de iis in quorum Latini incusantur* (PG 126, 224).

36. Ibid., 225.

37. Ibid., 228.

38. Ibid., 228–29.

39. Peter Damien, *Contra errorem Graecorum de Processione Spiritus sancti* (PL 145, 633–42) (Eng. trans.: James Likoudis, *Ending the Byzantine Greek Schism* [New Rochelle: Catholics United for the Faith, 1992], 191–203).

40. Peter Damien, *Contra errorem Graecorum de Processione Spiritus sancti* 5 (Eng. trans.: James Likoudis, *Ending the Byzantine Greek Schism*, 200). He does, however, testify that the shields of Leo bearing the uninterpolated creed can still be seen in Rome.

41. See W. Holtzman, "Die Unionsverhandlungen zwischen Kaiser Alexios I und Papst Urban II im Jahre 1089," *Byzantinische Zeitschrift* 28 (1928): 38–67.

42. It is interesting to note that there was no specific demand regarding the *filioque* (i.e., either its exclusion or some sort of explanation). Goffredo Malaterra's *Historia Sicula* claims that the only issue separating the Churches at this time was the Latins' continued use of azymes in the Eucharist. He wrote: "The emperor had requested that he [the pope] and other learned Catholic men should come to Constantinople where a council would be held at which there would be a discussion between the Greeks and Latins to secure a common definition in the Church of God, which had up to that time been torn apart by schism because the Greeks sacrificed with leavened and the Latins with unleavened bread." Goffredo Malaterra, *Historia Sicula* 4.13 (PL 149, 1192).

43. Chadwick speculates that the post-Gregorian understanding of papal primacy would have made answering such a request impossible, since it would have suggested that the pope had to defend his orthodoxy (and the orthodoxy of the Western Church) before being recognized. Henry Chadwick, *East and West: The Making of a Rift in the Church*, 223.

44. Urban's speech, as recorded by Robert the Monk:

O race of the Franks. . . . From the confines of Jerusalem and the city of Constantinople a horrible tale has gone forth and very frequently has been brought to our ears, namely, that a race from the kingdom of the Persians, an accursed race, a race utterly alienated from God, a generation forsooth which has not directed its heart and has not entrusted its spirit to God, has invaded the lands of those Christians and has depopulated them by the sword, pillage and fire . . . it has either entirely destroyed the churches of God or appropriated them for the rites of its own religion. . . . The kingdom of the Greeks is now dismembered by them and deprived of territory so vast in extent that it cannot be traversed in a march of two months. On whom therefore is the labor of avenging these wrongs and of recovering this territory incumbent, if not upon you? (Eng. trans.: Dana C. Munro, "Urban and the Crusaders,"

Translations and Reprints from the Original Sources of European History, vol 1.2 [Philadelphia: University of Pennsylvania, 1895], 5–8).

See also idem, "The Speech of Urban II at Clermont," *American Historical Review* 11 (1906): 231–40; idem, "Did the Emperor Alexius Ask for Aid at the Council of Piacenza 1095?" *American Historical Review* 27 (1922): 731–33.

45. See Jonathon Harris, *Byzantium and the Crusades* (New York: Palgrave, 2003); Angeliki Laiou and Roy Parviz Mottahedeh, eds., *The Crusades from the Perspective of Byzantium and the Muslim World* (Washington, D.C.: Dumbarton Oaks, 2001).

46. See George Berthold, "St. Anselm and the Filioque" in George Berthold, ed., *Faith Seeking Understanding: Learning and the Catholic Tradition* (Manchester, N.H.: St. Anselm College Press, 1991), 227–34; William Mann, "Anselm on the Trinity," in Brian Davies and Brian Leftow, eds., *Cambridge Companion to Anselm* (Cambridge: Cambridge University Press, 2004), 257–78.

47. Anselm of Canterbury, *De Processione Spiritus Sancti* (F. S. Schmitt, ed., *Anselmi Opera Omnia*, 6 vols. [Edinburgh: T. Nelson and Sons, 1938], 2:175–219) (Eng. trans.: Anselm of Canterbury, "On the Procession of the Holy Spirit," in *Anselm of Canterbury: The Major Works*, ed. Brian Davies [Oxford: Oxford University Press, 1998], 390–434.

48. Anselm was cautious about the use of "person" in reference to the godhead for fear that this term might indicate three individuals, and thus three gods. He uses the term but elsewhere refers to God as one, because of a unity of essence, Trinity because of "three I–do-not-know-whats" (tres *nescio quid*). Anselm of Canterbury, *Monologion* 79 (Eng. trans.: Brian Davies, *Anselm of Canterbury*, 79).

49. Anselm of Canterbury, *De Processione Spiritus Sancti* 1 (Eng. trans.: Brian Davies, *Anselm of Canterbury*, 393).

50. Although Anselm, unlike later Latin theologians who applied *procedere* to both the Son's and the Spirit's origin from the Father, did recognize the importance of the unique way each came into being. "The Son and the Holy Spirit, of course, have existence from the Father but in different ways, since one is from the Father by generation, the other from the Father by procession, so that the Son and the Holy Spirit are on that account distinct from one another, as I have said." Anselm of Canterbury, *De Processione Spiritus Sancti* 1 (Eng. trans.: Brian Davies, *Anselm of Canterbury*, 393).

51. Ibid.

52. *De Processione Spiritus Sancti* 1(Eng. trans.: Brian Davies, *Anselm of Canterbury*, 398).

53. *De Processione Spiritus Sancti* 10 (Eng. trans.: Brian Davies, *Anselm of Canterbury*, 420).

54. Ibid.

55. *De Processione Spiritus Sancti* 1 (Eng. trans.: Brian Davies, *Anselm of Canterbury*, 396).

56. *De Processione Spiritus Sancti* 2 (Eng. trans.: Brian Davies, *Anselm of Canterbury*, 403).

57. *De Processione Spiritus Sancti* 14 (Eng. trans.: Brian Davies, *Anselm of Canterbury*, 428).

58. See Phillip Rosemann, *Peter Lombard* (New York: Oxford University Press, 2004); idem, *The Story of a Great Medieval Book: Peter Lombard's "Sentences"* (Peterborough, Ontario: Broadview Press, 2007).

59. Peter Lombard, *Libri Quatuor Sententiarum* 1.11.1 (Eng trans: Peter Lombard, *The Sentences. Book 1: The Mystery of the Trinity*, trans. Giulio Silano. MST 42 [Toronto: Pontifical Institute for Medieval Studies, 2007], 62).

60. Ibid., 62–63.

61. Ibid., 63.

62. Ibid.

63. Ibid.

64. Ibid., 64.

65. This view was later echoed by Duns Scotus, who wrote:

[I]f two learned scholars, one Greek and the other Latin, both really loving the truth and not their own way of expressing it from their individual point of view, were to discuss the opposition, they would end by finding that it is not a real one, but only based on words. Otherwise, either the Greeks or ourselves, the Latins, are really heretical. . . . It is therefore probable that, despite their different modes of expression, there is no real disagreement between the thought of these Fathers [Greek and Latin] who are opposed to each other. There is more than one way of expressing oneself. . . . However, since the Catholic Church has declared it as having to be held as faith, it is necessary to maintain that the Holy Spirit proceeds *ab utroque* (Duns Scotus, *Ordinatio* 1.2.9 and *Sent.* 9.1 *Opera Omnia* 9 [Paris 1893], 325; New ed., *Opera Omnia* 5, 2–3.)

For more on Scotus and the *filioque* see Richard Cross, *Duns Scotus on God* (London: Ashgate, 2004), 203–22; Friedrich Wetter, *Die Trinitätslehre des Johannes Duns Scotus* (Münster, Germany: Aschendorff, 1967), 180–269.

66. Peter Lombard, *Libri Quatuor Sententiarum* 1.11.2 (Eng. trans.: Peter Lombard, *The Sentences*, 65).

67. Long noted has been Richard's reliance on the work of Achard of St. Victor. See A. M. Ethier, *Le "De Trinitate" de Richard de Saint-Victor* (Paris: J. Vrin, 1939); M. W. Blastic, *Condilectio: Personal Mysticism and Speculative Theology in the Works of Richard of St. Victor* (Ann Arbor: Mich.: UMI, 1991); N. Den Bok, *Communicating the Most High: a Systematic Study of Person and Trinity in the Theology of Richard of St. Victor* (Paris: Brepols, 1996). For his reliance on Achard see J. Bligh, "Richard of St Victor's *De Trinitate*: Augustinian or Abelardian?" *Heythrop Journal* 1:2 (1960): 126–31.

68. Richard of St. Victor, *De Trinitate* 3.2 (Richard de Saint-Victor, *La Trinité*, G. Salet, ed., SC 63 [Paris: Les Éditions du Cerf, 1959], 169) (Eng. trans.: Grover Zinn, ed., *Richard of St. Victor: The Book of the Patriarchs, The Mystical Ark, Book Three of the Trinity* [New York: Paulist Press, 1979], 374).

69. Richard of St. Victor, *De Trinitate* 3 (Eng. trans.: Grover Zinn, ed., *Richard of St. Victor*, 392).

70. Dennis Ngien, *Apologetic for Filioque in Medieval Theology* (Waynesboro, Ga.: Paternoster Press, 2005), 71.

71. Richard of St. Victor, *De Trinitate* 6.14 (Richard de Saint-Victor, *La Trinité*, 417).

72. Anselm was hoping to persuade the Byzantines to join Lothair III in his campaign against Roger II of Sicily. See Norman Russell, "Anselm of Havelberg and the Union of the Churches," *Sobornorst* 1 (1979): 19–41.

73. Describing the dynamics of this meeting, Steven Runcimann wrote, "Amongst the unhappy delusions of mankind is the belief that a dispute can be settled by a debate." Steven Runcimann, *The Eastern Schism*, 108. For Grossolanus see Alfredo Lucioni, "Grossolano," in *Dizionario della Chiesa Ambrosiana* 3 (Milan: NED, 1989), 1531–32.

74. Nicetas claimed, "I appear to have found a Latin who is catholic; if only Latins of such disposition would come to us in these times!" Anselm of Havelburg, *Dialogi* 2.1 (PL 188, 1165).

75. Ibid.

76. Ibid.

77. Anselm of Havelburg, *Dialogi* 2.3 (PL 188, 1168).

78. Anselm of Havelburg, *Dialogi* 2.4 (PL 188, 1171).

79. Anselm of Havelburg, *Dialogi* 2.10 (PL 188, 1179).

80. Anselm of Havelburg, *Dialogi* 2.24 (PL 188, 1204–5).

81. Anselm of Havelburg, *Dialogi* 2.25 (PL 188, 1206).

82. Even Anselm's later debate (1154) with Basil of Ohrid in Thessalonica did not end as happily as his encounter with Nicetas, primarily because of Basil's rejection of the papacy's claims to power.

83. Nicetas of Maroneia, *De Procession Spiritus Sancti* (PG 139 169–222).

84. Ibid., 221.

85. Anti-unionist Andronicus Camateros composed a similar dialogue around this time, using passages from the fathers to prove the error of the Latin teaching. John Beccus later wrote a detailed refutation of this work (John Beccus, *Adversus Andronicum Camaterum* [PG 141, 395–612]).

86. Hugo Etherianus, *De haeresibus quas Graeci in Latinos devolvunt, sive quod Spiritus Sanctus ex utroque Patre et Filio procedit* (PL 202, 227–396).

87. According to Aristeides Papadakis, "Before 1095, in both East and West, Christians still believed in a single undivided Christendom, whereas afterward very few did so." Aristedes Papadakis, *The Christian East and the Rise of the Papacy*, The Church in History 4 (Crestwood, N.Y.: St. Vladimir's Seminary Press, 1994), 105.

88. William of Tyre, *A History of Deeds Done beyond the Sea*, trans. E. Babcock and A. C. Krey (New York, Columbia University Press, 1943), 464–65.

89. Odo of Deuil, *De profectione Ludovici VII in orientem*, trans. V. Berry (New York: Columbia University Press, 1948), 57.

90. Ibid.

91. William of Tyre, *A History of Deeds Done beyond the Sea*, 464–65.

92. Eustathius of Thessalonika, *L'espugnazione de Thessalonica*, S. Kyriakedes, ed., (Palermo, Italy, 1961), 112–14.

93. Ibid.

94. See Geoffrey de Villehardouin, "Chronicles of the Fourth Crusade and the Conquest of Constantinople," in *Chronicles of the Crusades*, ed. and trans. Margaret

Shaw (New York: Penguin, 1972), 29–162; Alfred Andrea, *Contemporary Sources for the Fourth Crusade*, Medieval Mediterranean 29 (London: Brill, 2000). Secondary sources include Steven Runciman, *A History of the Crusades*, vol. 3: *The Kingdom of Acre and the Later Crusades* (Cambridge: Cambridge University Press, 1951); Donald Queller and Thomas Madden, *The Fourth Crusade: The Conquest of Constantinople* (Philadelphia: University of Pennsylvania Press, 1997); Thomas Madden, *The Fourth Crusade: Event, Aftermath, and Perceptions* (London: Ashgate, 2008); Michael Angold, *The Fourth Crusade: Event and Context* (Harlow, U.K.: Longman, 2003); Jonathan Phillips, *The Fourth Crusade and the Sack of Constantinople* (New York: Penguin, 2005).

95. Queller and Madden contrast the attitudes of Latins and Greeks on the morning of April 13. The Byzantines were busy lining the streets for the new emperor's arrival and went out to the crusaders' camp (in full ceremonial dress) to greet the new emperor (Boniface of Montferrat) and do him reverence, their view being that the city had not been conquered but merely was awaiting another in a long line of dynastic changes. The crusaders, however, saw things quite differently and were preparing for the traditional period of looting following the capture of a city. "Unaware of what was coming, the citizens [of Constantinople] still stood by the side of the roads with their precious vestments and rich icons. How little they understood the Latins! As the Westerners came in torrent down these streets, they found the Greeks had made the task of plunder, rape, and murder that much easier." Donald Queller and Thomas Madden, *The Fourth Crusade*, 192.

96. Nicetas Choniates, *The Sack of Constantinople*, trans. D. C. Munro, Trans. and reprs. from the Original Sources of European History Series 1, 3.1 (Philadelphia: University of Pennsylvania Press, 1912), 15–16.

97. Ibid.

98. Ibid.

99. Innocent had on several occasions warned the crusaders against attacking the imperial capital and using the Byzantines' disobedience to the Holy See as a religious pretext for their greed. For Innocent and his attitude see Kenneth Setton, *The Papacy and the Levant 1204–1571*, 1 (Philadelphia: American Philosophical Society, 1976), 1–26.

100. Innocent III, *Epistula* 7.154 (PL 215, 456).

101. *Constitutions of the Fourth Lateran Council* (Norman Tanner, ed., *Decrees of the Ecumenical Councils* 1, 230).

102. Ibid., 235–36.

103. Aristeides Papadakis, "Byzantine Perceptions of the Latin West," *Greek Orthodox Theological Review* 36 (1991): 234.

104. Already in the ninth century Photius, in his *Encyclical to the Eastern Patriarchs*, had pointed to four other problems with Latin Christianity alongside the use of the *filioque*:

1. The Latin fast on Saturdays
2. The Latin prohibition of clerical marriage (and their refusal to receive eucharist from married clergy)
3. The Latin practice breaking the Lenten fast
4. The Latin practice of allowing only bishops to confirm (chrismate)

Since in the Byzantine consciousness there often was a close connection between heterodoxy and heteropraxis, the unspoken assumption was that if the Latins had different liturgical and disciplinary practices, this difference must denote a substantively different (and therefore heretical) faith. Tia Kolbaba, in her study of the medieval "lists" of Latin errors, is careful to note that while many Byzantines did exhibit an openness toward other traditions, "such tolerance was far from universal and certainly not a feature of the lists." Tia Kolbaba, *The Byzantine Lists: Errors of the Latins* (Chicago: University of Illinois Press, 2000), 13. See also idem, "Byzantine Perceptions of Latin Religious 'Errors': Themes and Changes from 850 to 1350," in Angeliki Laiou and Roy Parviz Mottahedeh, eds., *The Crusades from the Perspective of Byzantium and the Muslim World*, 117–43.

105. See Tia Kolbaba, *The Byzantine Lists: Errors of the Latins*, 23–31.

106. *Opusculum Contra Francos* (J. Hergenroether, ed., *Monumenta graeca ad Photium eiusque Historiam Pertinentia* [Ratisbon, Germany, 1869], 62–71) (Eng. trans.: Tia Kolbaba, *The Byzantine Lists: Errors of the Latins*, 40).

107. See also Joseph Gill, "An Unpublished Letter of Germanos, Patriarch of Constantinople," *Byzantion* 44 (1974): 138–51. Here the patriarch called the introduction of the *filioque* "shameless and ill-omened, for in this way they [the Latins] infiltrate two causes and prepare the way to reopen in free debate the heresy of Mani, Marcion, and Simon," 145.

108. G. Golubovich, "Disputatio Latinorum et Graecorum," *Archivum Franciscanum Historicum* 12 (1919), 428–70; P. Canard, "Nicéphore Blemmyde et la mémoire adressé aux envoyés de Grégoire IX (Nicée, 1234)," *Orientalia Christiana Periodica* 25 (1959), 310–25; J. Munitiz, "A Reappraisal of Blemmydes First Discussion with the Latins" *Byzantinoslavica* 51 (1990): 20–26.

109. John Meyendorff explored the irony that "the formal renunciation in the eleventh century of the Greek philosophical inheritance in Greek-speaking Byzantium" coincided with "the almost simultaneous 'discovery' of Aristotle in the Latin West. . . . Paradoxically, in the Middle Ages the East was becoming less 'Greek' than the West." John Meyendorff, "Byzantium as the Center of Theological thought in the Christian East," in *Schools of Thought in the Christian Tradition* ed. P. Henry (Philadelphia: Fortress Press, 1984), 70. See also David Bradshaw, *Aristotle East and West: Metaphysics and the Division of Christendom* (Cambridge: Cambridge University Press, 2004).

110. G. Golubovich, "Disputatio Latinorum et Graecorum," 428–70.

111. Ibid.

112. Nicephorus Blemmydes, *Curriculum Vitae*, A. Heisenberg (Leipzig, 1896), 74–80.

113. Blemmydes's letters are found in *De Processione Spiritus sancti orationes duae* (PG 142, 553–84), although neither was ever meant to be published. See also V. Grumel, "Nicéphore Blemmyde et la procession du Saint-Esprit," *Revue des sciences philosophiques et théologiques* 18 (1929): 636–56.

114. For a summary of the views on Blemmydes see V. Barvinok, *Nikofor Vlemmid I ego sochineniia* (Kiev, 1911), 109–45 and Joseph Gill, *Byzantium and the Papacy 1198–1400* (New Brunswick, N.J.: Rutgers University Press, 1979),152–57.

115. Bonaventure, *Commentaria In Quatuor Libros Sententiarum* I d.11, a. 1, q. 1 in *Doctoris Seraphici S. Bonaventurae Opera omnia* 1 (Quaracchi, Italy, 1882), 209–14. See

also Jacques Guy Bougerol, *Introduction à saint Bonaventure* (Paris: Librairie Philos-ophique J. Vrin, 1988); Christopher M. Cullen, *Bonaventure* (Oxford: Oxford University Press, 2006); Zachary Hayes, "Introduction to Saint Bonaventure's *Disputed Questions on the Mystery of the Trinity*," in *Works of St. Bonaventure* 3 (New York: The Franciscan Institute, 1979), 3–40; Wilfred Royer, "The Trinity in the Thought of St. Bonaventure: An Eastern Orthodox *Perspective*" (PhD Thesis, Fordham University, 1994); Hanspeter Heinz, *Trinitarische Begegnungen bei Bonaventura : Fruchtbarkeit einer appropriativen Trinitaïstheologie* (Münster, Germany: Aschendorff, 1985).

116. Bonaventure, *Commentaria In Quatuor Libros Sententiarum* I d.11, a. 1, q. 1 (*Doctoris Seraphici S. Bonaventurae Opera omnia* 1, 213).

117. Ibid., 210.

118. Bonaventure, *Breviloquium* 1.3, trans. José de Vinck, The Works of Bonaven-ture 2 (Paterson, N.J.: St. Anthony Guild, 1963), 39.

119. Bonaventure, *Commentaria In Quatuor Libros Sententiarum* I d.27, pt. 1, a. 1, q. 2 (*Doctoris Seraphici S. Bonaventurae Opera omnia* 1, 470).

120. Bonaventure, *Commentaria In Quatuor Libros Sententiarum* I d.12, a. 1, q. 2 (*Doctoris Seraphici S. Bonaventurae Opera omnia* 1, 222).

121. Bonaventure, *Commentaria In Quatuor Libros Sententiarum* I d.10, a. 1, q. 2 (*Doctoris Seraphici S. Bonaventurae Opera omnia* 1, 195).

122. Bonaventure, *Commentaria In Quatuor Libros Sententiarum* I d.13, a. 1, q. 2 (*Doctoris Seraphici S. Bonaventurae Opera omnia* 1, 231).

123. Bonaventure, *Commentaria In Quatuor Libros Sententiarum* I d.11, a. 1, q. 1 (*Doctoris Seraphici S. Bonaventurae Opera omnia*, 1, 211).

124. Ibid., 212.

125. Ibid.

126. See Joseph Gill, *Byzantium and the Papacy 1198–1400*; Deno Geanakopolos, *Emperor Michael Palaeologus and the West* (Cambridge, Mass.: Harvard University Press, 1959).

127. Secondary literature on Thomas's views on the Trinty and the *filioque* include Michael Fahey and John Meyendorff, *Trinitarian Theology East and West: St. Thomas Aquinas and St. Gregory Palamas* (Brookline, Mass.: Holy Cross Orthodox Press, 1977); Reinhard Simon, *Das Filioque bei Thomas von Aquin: Eine Untersuchung zur dogmenges-chichtlichen Stellung, theologischen Struktur und ökumenischen Perspektive der thoma-nischen Gotteslehre* (Frankfurt: Peter Lang, 1994); Giles Emery, *Trinity in Aquinas* (Ypsilanti, Mich.: Sapientia Press, 2003); idem, *The Trinitarian Theology of St. Thomas Aquinas* (Oxford: Oxford University Press, 2007); Douglas Hall, *The Trinity: An Analysis of St. Thomas Aquinas' Expositio of the De Trinitate of Boethius* (Leiden: Brill, 1992); Michael Torre, "St. John Damascene and St. Thomas Aquinas on the Eternal Procession of the Holy Spirit," *St. Vladimir's Theological Quarterly* 38 (1994): 303–27.

128. Thomas Aquinas, *Quaestiones disputatae de potential dei* III, q. 10, art. 2 (Eng. trans.: Thomas Aquinas, *On the Power of God*, trans. English Dominican Fathers [Westminster, Md.: Newman Press, 1932], 189).

129. Thomas Aquinas, *Quaestiones disputatae de potential dei* III, q. 10, art. 4; (Eng. trans.: Thomas Aquinas, *On the Power of God*, 202).

130. Ibid.

131. Ibid., 203.

132. Thomas Aquinas, *Summa Theologiae* I, q.36, art.2 (Eng. trans.: Thomas Aquinas, *Summa Theologica* I, trans. English Dominican Fathers [Westminster, Md.: Christian Classics, 1981], 184).

133. Ibid.

134. Thomas Aquinas, *Summa Theologiae* I, q.33, art.1 (Eng. trans: Thomas Aquinas, *Summa Theologica*, 173). The chief disagreement between the two seems to have been the question as to whether the Father begets because he is Father, or is Father because he begets.

135. Thomas Aquinas, *Contra Errores Graecorum* 2.13–15 (Eng. trans: James Likoudis, *Ending the Byzantine Greek Schism*, 172–73).

136. Thomas Aquinas, *Summa Theologiae* I, q.36, art.3 (Eng. trans: Thomas Aquinas, *Summa Theologica*, 186).

137. Ibid.

138. Thomas Aquinas, *Summa Theologiae* I, q.36, art.2 (Eng. trans.: Thomas Aquinas, *Summa Theologica*, 185).

139. Thomas Aquinas, *Summa Theologiae* I, q.36, art.4 (Eng. trans.: Thomas Aquinas, *Summa Theologica*, 188).

140. Thomas Aquinas, *Contra Errores Graecorum* (Eng. trans.: James Likoudis, *Ending the Byzantine Greek Schism*, 126).

141. Ibid.

142. Thomas Aquinas, *Summa Theologiae* I, q.36, art.3 (Eng. trans.: Thomas Aquinas, *Summa Theologica*, 186).

143. Ibid.

144. Ibid.

145. Ibid.

146. Unlike other *florilegia*, which relied heavily on Western authors, the three most cited authorities in the *Contra Errores Graecorum* are Athanasius (60), Cyril of Alexandria (32), and Basil of Caesarea (24) with only 17 citations from Augustine of Hippo. Leo Elders, "Thomas Aquinas and the Fathers of the Church," in Backus, *The Reception of the Church Fathers in the West* (Leiden: Brill Academic Publishers, 2001), 347.

147. Most of the patristic quotations employed by Thomas were taken verbatim from the *Libellus de fide ss. Trinitatis* of Nicholas of Cotrone, a statement of the Latin position written for Michael Palaeologos. See Antoine Dondaine, "Nicolas de Cotrone et la sources du *Contra errores Graecorum* de Saint Thomas," *Divus Thomas* 29 (1950): 313–40; Mark Jordan, "Theological Exegesis and Aquinas' Treatise 'Against the Greeks,'" *Church History* 56 (1987): 445–56. See also Jaroslav Pelikan, "The Doctrine of the *Filioque* in Thomas Aquinas and Its Patristic Antecedents," in *St. Thomas Aquinas Commemorative Studies* 2 vols. (Toronto: Pontifical Institute of Medieval Studies, 1974), 1:315–36.

148. Thomas Aquinas, *Summa Theologiae* I, q.36, art.2 (Eng. trans.: Thomas Aquinas, *Summa Theologica*, 186).

149. Thomas Aquinas, *Summa Contra Gentiles* 4.24 (Eng. trans.: Thomas Aquinas, *Summa Contra Gentiles* 5, trans. Charles O'Neil [Notre Dame, Ind.: University of Notre Dame Press, 1975], 136).

150. See p. 116.

151. Michael Torre, "St. John Damascene and St. Thomas Aquinas on the Eternal Procession of the Holy Spirit," 312.

152. Thomas Aquinas, *Contra Errores Graecorum* 31 (Eng. trans.: James Likoudis, *Ending the Byzantine Greek Schism*, 180).

153. Ibid.

154. Thomas Aquinas, *Contra Errores Graecorum* 32 (Eng. trans.: James Likoudis, *Ending the Byzantine Greek Schism*, 181).

155. Thomas may have died of an internal hemorrhage caused by a blow he received from a tree branch while on the road from Teano. Another possibility is that he died from physical/mental exhaustion that began to affect him in early December of 1273, when he told his friend Reginald of Piperno that he was incapable of proceeding any further with work on the *Summa*. A popular rumor of the time even suggested that Thomas had been poisoned by agents of Charles of Anjou, longtime nemesis of Emperor Michael VIII Palaeologus. See Jean-Pierre Torrell, *St. Thomas Aquinas* 1: *The Person and His Work*, trans. Robert Royal (Washington, D.C.: Catholic University of America Press, 1996), 289–95.

156. At Ferrara-Florence, while the Latins called him "Blessed Thomas" (ὁ μακάριος Θωμᾶς), the Greeks simply referred to him as "Thomas the Latin teacher" (Θωμᾶς ὁ τῶν Λατίνων διδάσκαλος). For more on Thomas's reception in Byzantium see S. Papadopoulos, "Thomas in Byzanz: Thomas Rezeption und Thomas Kritik in Byzanz zwischen 1354 und 1435," *Theologie und Philosophie* 49 (1974): 274–304.

NOTES TO CHAPTER 7

1. A quotation attributed to Lucas Notaras.

2. Particularly active in this regard were the Dominicans and the other orders that had houses in and around Constantinople. See William Hyland, "John-Jerome of Prague (1368–1440) and the *Errores Graecorum*: Anatomy of a Polemic against Greek Christians," *Journal of Religious History* 21 (1997): 249–67.

3. Michael had been proclaimed co-emperor with John IV Lascaris on Christmas Day 1258 and was re-crowned in Constantinople after the capture of the city in July 1261. John IV, only eleven years old, was blinded and sent to Marmara, where he died almost fifty years later. See Deno John Geanokoplos, "The Byzantine Recovery of Constantinople from the Latins in 1261: A Chrysobull of Michael VIII Palaeologus in Favor of Hagia Sophia," in *Constantinople and the West* (Madison: University of Wisconsin Press, 1989), 173–88; idem, *Emperor Michael Palaeologus and the West*.

4. J. M. Hussey, *The Orthodox Church in the Byzantine Empire* (Oxford: Clarendon Press, 1986), 222.

5. See V. Laurent, "La croisade et la question d'Orient sous le pontificat de Grégoire X," *Revue historique du Sud-Est européen* 22 (1945): 105–37. According to Joseph Gill, "Union with the Greeks, good though it was in itself, was for him [Gregory] more a means than an end. It would enormously facilitate a grand crusade." Joseph Gill, *Byzantium and the Papacy*, 123. See also D. M. Nicol, "The Greeks and the Union of the Churches: The Preliminaries to the Second Council of Lyons 1261–1274,"

in *Byzantium: Its Ecclesiastical History and Relations with the Western World* (London: Variorum, 1972).

6. See Charles Elliott, "The Schism and Its Elimination in Humbert of Rome's *Opusculum Tripartitum*," 71–83; Edward Tracy Brett, *Humbert of Romans: His Life and Views of Thirteenth Century Society* (Toronto: Pontifical Institute for Medieval Studies, 1984).

7. Humbert of Romans, *Opusculum tripartitum* 2.10.

8. Humbert of Romans, *Opusculum tripartitum* 2.11.

9. Ibid.

10. "There are many Latins who, although they do not give occasion for the previously mentioned scandal, nevertheless care little or not at all about the sad state of the Greeks. The Greeks are Christians like themselves, and therefore the Latins are like the priest and the Levite who, meeting a wounded brother on the road, passed by caring nothing for him. . . . Those Latins, therefore, sin against nature who do not care that the Greeks, who are members of the same body as themselves, are in a sad state. The Greeks are less healthy in the faith than the Latins. Concerning such infirmity the apostle said, 'Assist those infirm in faith.' But where are the doctors?" Humbert of Romans, *Opusculum tripartitum* 2.15 (Eng. trans.: Edward Tracy Brett, *Humbert of Romans*, 189).

11. For Parastron see G. Golubovich, "Cenni storici su Fra Giovanni Parastron," *Bessarione* 10 (1906): 295ff.

12. His popularity was such that upon his death the Greek emperor and clergy allegedly petitioned the pope to proclaim him a saint. Nicholas Glassberger, *Chronica* (*Analecta franciscana* 2 [Quarracchi, Italy, 1887], 88).

13. The language was taken from the creed first proposed to Michael by Pope Clement in March 1267. It has been noted that the christological and trinitarian parts of this confession echo the language of Pope Leo IX's letter to Peter of Antioch, which itself was drawn from the *Statua Ecclesiae Antiqua*, a canonical collection made in Gaul during the fifth century. See C. Munier, ed., *Les Statua Ecclesiae Antiqua* (Paris:Presses universitaires de France, 1960).

14. Mansi 24, 70 (Eng. trans.: H. Denzinger, *Sources of Catholic Dogma* [St. Louis: Herder, 1957], 184).

15. V. Laurent and J. Darrouzès, eds., *Dossier Grec de l'Union de Lyon 1273–1277* (Paris, 1976), 299 (Eng. trans.: Aristeides Papadakis, *Crisis in Byzantium: The Filioque Controversy in the Patriarchate of Gregory II of Cyprus 1283–1289* [Crestwood,N.Y.: St. Vladimir's Press, 1996], 21).

16. V. Laurent and J. Darrouzès, eds., *Dossier Grec de l'Union de Lyon 1273–1277*, 134.

17. Text in V. Laurent and J. Darrouzès, eds., *Dossier Grec de l'Union de Lyon 1273–1277*.

18. Text in V. Laurent and J. Darrouzès, eds., *Dossier Grec de l'Union de Lyon 1273–1277*, 317–19; and Joseph Gill, "The Church Union of Lyons Portrayed in Greek Documents," *Orientalia christiana periodica* 40 (1974): 12–18.

19. Deno John Geanakoplos, "Bonaventura, Two Mendicant Orders and the Council of Lyons," in *Constantinople and the West*, 204. Fn. 41 on this page notes the debate about the exact number of signatures on the letter, Geanakoplos opting for H. Beck's choice of forty-four. Text in Burkhard Roberg, *Die Union zwischen der*

griechischen und der lateinischen Kirche auf dem II Konzil von Lyon, Bonner historische Forschungen 24 (Bonn, 1964), 235–39 and Joseph Gill, "The Church Union of Lyons Portrayed in Greek Documents," 28–33.

20. Joseph Gill, "The Church Union of Lyons Portrayed in Greek Documents," 33.

21. Aside from the works already mentioned, see also H. Wolter and H. Holstein, *Lyon I et Lyon II* (Paris: Éditions de l'Orante, 1966); Antonio Franchi, ed., *Il Concilio II di Lione (1274) secondo la ordinatio concilii generalis Lugdunensis,* Studi e Testi Francescani 33 (Rome: Edizioni Francescane, 1965).

22. Albert seems to have come to Lyons to press the imperial claim of Rudolf of Hapsburg. Although he had written on the procession, and later writers claimed he had confronted the "many errors" of the Greeks at Lyons (*in hoc concilio venerabilis frater Albertus plures errores destruxit praecipue Grecorum*), he does not seem to have been active in the council's formal deliberations. The only theological debate at Lyons that Albert is known to have engaged in was an informal discussion as to whether or not fornication was a mortal sin, which the Greeks had allegedly denied (*Graeci qui dicebant quod fornication non esset mortale peccatum, in concilio Lugdunensi coacti sunt hoc revocare*). A. Borgnet, ed., *Albertus Opera Omnia* 18 (Paris, 1890–99), 60. See Deno John Geanakoplos, "Bonaventura, Two Mendicant Orders and the Council of Lyons," 195–223.

23. *Constitutions of the Second Council of Lyons* (Norman Tanner, *Decrees of the Ecumenical Councils* [Washington DC: Georgetown University Press, 1990], 314).

24. Mary Ann Fatula has argued that the language of the council finds its closest parallels in the works of Anselm of Canturbury, who had denied the procession from two principles insofar as the Father and Son are one essence (and thus acting as one principle). See Mary Ann Fatula, "A Problematic Western Formula," *One in Christ* 17 (1981): 324–34.

25. Ibid., 331.

26. Aboard this ship was not only the official translator George Berroiotes, but also the gift that had been specially chosen for the pope—the altar cloth taken by the emperor himself from Hagia Sophia.

27. George Acropolites, "Λόγος δεύτερος περὶ τῆς ἐκ πατρὸς τοῦ ἁγίου πνεύματος ἐκ πορεύσεως" in *Georgii Acropolitae Opera* vol 2, A. Heisenberg, ed., (Stuttgart: Teubneri, 1978), 45–66.

28. Antonio Franchi, ed., *Il Concilio II di Lione,* 91–92.

29. Burkhard Roberg, *Die Union zwischen der griechischen und der lateinischen Kirche auf dem II Konzil von Lyon,* 227–28 (Eng. trans. Deno Geanakoplos, "Bonaventura and the Council of Lyons," 203).

30. Antonio Franchi, ed., *Il Concilio II di Lione,* 91–92.

31. This letter in Burkhard Roberg, *Die Union zwischen der griechischen und der lateinischen Kirche auf dem II Konzil von Lyon,* 148.

32. Report of Metochites in M.tt. Laurent, C. Giannelli, and L.B. Gillan, *Le bienheureux Innocent v et son temps* (Vatican City: Biblioteca apostolica vaticana, 1947) 419–43. (Eng. trans.: Deno Geanakoplos, *Byzantium,* 219).

33. George Pachymeres, *De Michaele et Andronico Palaeologis libri tredecim* 1 (Bonn: Corpus Scriptorum Historiae Byzantinae, 1835), 399.

34. J. M. Hussey, *The Orthodox Church in the Byzantine Empire,* 236. See also G. Hoffman, "Patriarch Johann Bekkos und die latienisch kultur," *Orientalia Christiana*

Periodica 11 (1945): 141–61; Joseph Gill, "John Beccus, Patriarch of Constantinople," *Byzantina* 7 (1975): 251–66.; R. Souarn, "Tentatives d'union avec Rome: un patriarche grec catholique au XIIIe siècle," *Echos d'Orient* 3 (1899/1900): 229–37, 351–70; V. Grumel, "Un ouvrage recent sur Jean Beccos, patriarche de Constantinople," *Echos d'Orient* 24 (1925): 229–37; J Gouillard, "Michel VIII et Jean Beccos devant l'Union," in *1274: Année charnière. Mutations et continuities* (Paris: CNRS, 1977), 179–90; Alexandra Riebe, *Rom in Gemeinschaft mit Konstantinopel: Patriarch Johannes XI. Bekkos als Verteidiger der Kirchenunion von Lyon (1274)* (Wiesbaden, Germany: Harrassowitz Verlag, 2005).

35. "Because he was truthful, he was not afraid to confess his ignorance [about the doctrine of the procession]. The reason was that he was occupied with secular studies; neither was he familiar with Holy Scripture nor had he studied it." George Pachymeres, *De Michaele et Andronico Palaeologis libri tredecim* 1, 38 (Eng. trans.: Aristeides Papadakis, *Crisis in Byzantium*, 23).

36. Although his motives have often been questioned, the evidence suggests that Beccus's conversion was the result of a sincere search for truth. According to Hussy, "He was not a man who could change from side to side as a matter of *oeconomia* or expediency" J. M. Hussey, *The Orthodox Church in the Byzantine Empire*, 236. Papadakis agrees, arguing "it is useless to deny (as is often done) either the sincerity or the reality of this moment in Beccus's religious evolution." Aristeides Papadakis, *Crisis in Byzantium*, 23.

37. John Beccus, *Refutatio photiani libri de processione Spiritus sancti* (PG 141, 741).

38. John Beccus, *Letter to Pope John XXI* (Joseph Gill,"The Church Union of Lyons Portrayed in Greek Documents," 40).

39. These anathemas are recorded by George Pachymeres, *De Michaele et Andronico Palaeologis libri tredecim* 1.32.

40. *John Beccus, De unione ecclesiarum* (PG 141, 24–28).

41. John Beccus, *De unione ecclesiarum* (PG 141, 52).

42. John Beccus, *Letter to Pope John XXI* (Joseph Gill, "The Church Union of Lyons Portrayed in Greek Documents," 40).

43. Ibid.

44. John Beuus, *Epigraphae* (PG 141, 613–724).

45. John Beccus, Epigraphae (PG 141, 625); John of Damascus, *De Fide orthodoxa* 1.8.

46. J. Gay, *Les Registres de Nicolas III* (Paris: Bibliothèque des Ecoles Françaises d'Athènes et de Rome, 1904), 128 (Eng. trans.: Deno John Geanokoplos, *Emperor Michael Palaeologus and the West, 1258–1282*, 313).

47. George Pachymeres, *De Michaele et Andronico Palaeologis libri tredecim* 1, 461.

48. Martin's motives were largely political. Three months before the emperor's excommunication the pope had accepted Charles of Anjou's plan for the restoration of a Latin Empire in Constantinople.

49. See Angeliki Laiou, *Constantinople and the Latins; The Foreign Policy of Andronicus II, 1282–1328* (Cambridge, Mass.:, Harvard University Press, 1972).

50. Aristeides Papadakis, *Crisis in Byzantium*, 37.

51. For Gregory, see also Bernhard Schultze, "Patriarch Gregorios von Cyprem über das Filioque," *Orientalia Christiana Periodica* 51 (1985): 163–87.

52. George Metochites, *Historia dogmatica* 2, ed. A. Mai (Rome, 1871), 155 (Eng. trans.: Aristeides Papadakis, *Crisis in Byzantium*, 89).

53. Gregory of Cyprus, *Expositio fidei contra Veccum* 11 (Eng. trans: Aristeides Papadakis, *Crisis in Byzantium*, 223). On top of the theological charges, ethnic betrayal was also added:

> They were originally members of our nation and of our doctrine and belonged to the Church. . . . [but] showed themselves blameworthy children, estranged sons, who had veered from their paths . . . [accepting] this alien doctrine . . . brought here like a foreign plague. . . . He [Beccus] nourished it, in my opinion, from the rivers of evil and lawlessness, or, as he falsely said, from Holy Scriptures, interpreting it wrongly, spreading babble from there, and committing sacrilege." (*Expositio fidei contra Veccum* [Eng. trans: Aristeides Papadakis, *Crisis in Byzantium*, 213,215])

54. According to John Meyendorff, "Instead of simply repeating Photius's formulas about 'eternal procession' of the Holy Spirit from the Father alone and the 'emission in time' by the Son, Gregory recognized the need to express the permanent relationship existing between the Son and the Holy Spirit as divine hypostases and he spoke of an; 'eternal manifestation' [ἔκφανσις ἀΐδιος] of the Spirit by the Son." John Meyendorff, *A Study of Gregory Palamas* (Crestwood, N.Y.: St. Vladimir's Seminary Press, 1998), 13.

55. Gregory of Cyprus, *De Processione Spiritus Sancti* (PG 142, 272).

56. Aristeides Papadakis, *Crisis in Byzantium*, 123.

57. From Gregory's speech at Blachernae as recorded by George Metochites, *Historia dogmatic* 2, 135 (Eng. trans.: Aristeides Papadakis, *Crisis in Byzantium*, 96).

58. Gregory of Cyprus, *Expositio fidei contra Veccum* (Eng. trans.: Papadakis, *Crisis in Byzantium*, 220).

59. Gregory of Cyprus, *Apologia pro tomo suo* (PG 142, 262).

60. John Beccus, *Refutatio libr Georgii Cyprii* (PG 141, 863–923) (Eng. trans.: Sergius Bulgakov, *The Comforter*, 106).

61. See Aristeides Papadakis, "Gregory of Cyprus and Mark's Report Again," *Greek Orthodox Theological Review* 21 (1976): 147–57.

62. See G. Podskalsky, *Theologie und Philosophie in Byzanz* (Munich: Beck, 1977), 173–80; Constantine Tsirpanlis, "Byzantine Forerunners of the Italian Renaissance: Plethon, Bessarion, George of Trebizond, John Argyropoulos, Manuel Chrysoloras, Demetrios Cydones, Barlaam of Calabria," *Patristic and Byzantine Review* 15 (1996-97): 23–57.

63. Critical edition with Augustine's Latin original in Manoles Papathomopoulos, Isabella Tsavari, and Gianpaolo Rigotti, eds., Αὐγουστίνου περὶ Τριάδος βιβλία πεντεκαίδεκα ἅπερ ἐκ τῆς Λατίνων διαλέκτου εἰς τὴν Ἑλλάδα μετήνεγκε Μάξιμος ὁ Πλανούδης (Athens: Kentron Ekdoseos Ergon Hellenon Syngrapheon, 1995). Planudes had also translated Cicero's *Somnium Scipionis*, Julius Caesar's *Gallic War*, Ovid's *Heroides* and *Metamorphoses*, and Boethius's *De consolatione philosophiae*.

64. Bessarion, *Against the Syllogisms of the Monk Maximus Planoudes concerning the Procession of the Holy Spirit according to the Latins* (PG 161, 312) (Eng. trans.: Elizabeth Fisher, "Planoudes' *De Trinitate*, the Art of Translation, and the Beholder's

Share," in George Demacopoulos and Aristotle Papanikolaou, eds., *Orthodox Readings of Augustine*, 56).

65. Text in Antoine Dondaine, "Contra Graecos: Premiers écrits polémiques des dominicains d'Orient," *Archivum Fratrum Praedicatorum* 21 (1951): 421–22 (Eng. trans.: Elizabeth Fisher, "Planoudes' *De Trinitate*, the Art of Translation, and the Beholder's Share," 58).

66. George (Gennadius) Scholarius, "Tractatus De processu spiritus sancti" in L. Petit and M. Jugie, eds., *Oeuvres completes de Georges (Gennadios) Scholarios* 2 (Paris: Bonne Presse, 1929), 228 (Eng. trans.: Elizabeth Fisher, "Planoudes' *De Trinitate*, the Art of Translation, and the Beholder's Share," 60).

67. For more on the Cydones brothers see Norman Russell, "Palamism and the Circle of Demetrius Cydones" in Charalambos Dendrinos, Jonathan Harris, and Judith Herrin, eds., *Porphyrogenita: Essays on the History and Literature of Byzantium and the Latin East in Honour of Julian Chrysostomides* (Aldershot: Ashgate, 2003), 153–74; Athanassia Glycofrydi-Leontsini, "Demetrius Cydones as a Translator of Latin Texts" in *Porphyrogenita*, 175–86; G. Podskalsky, *Theologie und Philosophie in Byzanz* (Munich: Beck, 1977), 195–210; Giovanni Mercati, *Notizie di Procoro e Demetrio Cidone Manuele Caleca e Teodoro Meliteniota ed altri appunti per la storia della teologia e della letteratura bizantina del secolo XIV*, Studi e testi 56 (Vatican City: Biblioteca Apostolica Vaticana, 1931); Giuseppe Cammelli, "Demetrio Cidonio al fratello Procoro," *Studi bizantini* 2 (1927): 49–55; Martin Jugie, "Démétrius Cydonès et la théologie latine à Byzance," *Echos d'Orient* 31 (1928), 385–402.

68. Several other Byzantine scholastics and anti-Palamites, such as Manuel Kalekas and Joannes Kypariossiotes, also entered into communion with Rome at this time.

69. Demetrius Cydones, *Apologia* (Eng. trans.: James Likoudis, *Ending the Byzantine Greek Schism*, 28).

70. Ibid.

71. Critical edition in Antonis Fyrigos, ed., *Barlaam Calabro: Opere contro I Latini: introduzione, storia dei testi, edizione critica, traduzione e indici*, 2 vols., Studi e testi 347–48 (Vatican City: Biblioteca apostolica vaticana, 1998). For Barlaam see also Tia Kolbaba, "Barlaam the Calabrian. Three treatises on papal primacy, introduction, edition and translation," *Revue des études byzantines* 53 (1995): 41–115; Reinhard Flogaus, "Palamas and Barlaam Revisited: A Reassessment of East and West in the Hesychast Controversy of 14th Century Byzantium," *St. Vladimir's Theological Quarterly* 42 (1998): 1–32; Robert Sinkewicz, "A New Interpretation for the First Episode in the Controversy between Barlaam the Calabrian and Gregory Palamas," *Journal of Theological Studies* n.s. 31 (1980): 489–500.

72. Barlaam of Calabria, *Syntagma* 45 (Antonis Fyrigos, ed., *Barlaam Calabro: Opere contro I Latini*, 664.387–89).

73. See, for example, Robert Sinkewicz, "The Doctrine of Knowledge of God in the Early Writings of Barlaam the Calabrian," *Medieval Studies* 44 (1982):181–242.

74. Ciro Giannelli, "Un progetto di Barlaam per l'unione delle chiese," in *Miscellanea Giovanni Mercati 3: Letteratura e storia bizantina*, Studi e Testi 123 (Vatican City: Biblioteca apostolica vaticana, 1946); John Meyendorff, "Un mauvais théologien de l'unité au quatorzième siècle: Barlaam le Calabrais," in *L'église et les églises*,

1054–1954: Etudes et travaux offerts a Dom Lambert Baudouin vol. 2 (Chevetogne, Belgium: Éditions de Chevetogne, 1955), 47–64.

75. Eng. trans.: Deno Geanakoplos, *Byzantium*, 221.

76. John Meyendorff, *A Study of Gregory Palamas*, 43.

77. For a full bibliography on Palamas and recent survey of secondary works on his contributions to Eastern theology, see Robert Sinkewicz, "Gregory Palamas," in *La théologie Byzantine et sa tradition* 2, Caremlo Conticello and Vassa Conticello, eds. (Turnhout, Belgium: Brepols, 2002), 131–88.

78. John Meyendorff, *A Study of Gregory Palamas*, 43. Despite Meyendorff's view, and the many similarities between Gregory of Cyprus and Palamas, it should be noted that Palamas never mentions the Cypriot's works (although he was critical of certain aspects of it) and was himself a disciple of Theoleptos of Philadelphia, one of Gregory's fiercest opponents. See Reinhard Flogaus, "Palamas and Barlaam Revisited," 17. For more on Theoleptos see Robert Sinkewicz, "Life and Work of Theoleptos," in *Theoleptos of Philadelphia: The Monastic Discourses* (Toronto: Pontifical Institute of Medieval Studies, 1992); Sévérien Salaville, "Une lettere et un discours inédits de Théolepte de Philadelphie," *Revue des études byzantines* 5 (1947), 101–15; V. Laurent, "Les crises réligieuses à Byzance: Le schisme anti-arsénite du métropolite Théolepte de Philadelphie," *Revue des études byzantines* 18 (1960): 45–54; Demetius Constantelos, "Mysticism and social involvement in the Later Byzantine Church. Theoleptus of Philadelphia: A Case Study," *Byzantines Studies* 6 (1979): 49–60.

79. Gregory Palamas, *Logos Apodeiktikos* 2.67 (Boris Bobrinsky, ed., *Logoi Apodeiktikoi*, in *Gregoriou tou Palama Syggrammata* vol.1, ed. Panagiotes Chrestou [Thessalonica, Greece, 1962], 138).

80. "For in him all things in heaven and on earth were created, things visible and invisible, whether thrones or dominions or rulers or powers—all things have been created through him and for him."

81. Gregory Palamas, Ἐπιστολὴ πρὸς Ἀκίνδυνον 1.5. See Markos Orpanos, "The Procession of the Holy Spirit According to Certain Later Greek Fathers," in Lukas Vischer, ed., *Spirit of God, Spirit of Christ: Ecumenical Reflections on the Filioque Controversy* (London: SPCK, 1981), 31.

82. Gregory Palamas, *Logos Apodeiktikos* 1.37 (Boris Bobrinsky, *Logoi Apodeiktikoi*, 68).

83. For an introduction to Gregory's thought on the subject and his sources see Edmund Hussey, "Palamite Trinitarian Models," *St. Vladimir's Theological Quarterly* 16 (1972): 83–89; idem, "The Person-Energy Structure in the Theology of St. Gregory Palamas," *St. Vladimir's Theological Quarterly* 18 (1974): 22–43; L. C. Contos, "The Essence-Energies Structure of St. Gregory Palamas with a Brief Examination of Its Patristic Foundations," *Greek Orthodox Theological Review* 12 (1967): 283–94; Vasilios Karayiannis, *Maxime le Confesseur: Essence et Energies de Dieu*; Christos Yannaras, "The Distinction Between Essence and Energies and Its Importance for Theology," *St. Vladimir's Theological Quarterly* 19 (1975): 232–45.

84. Gregory Palamas, *Logos Apodeiktikos* 2.20 (Boris Brobrinsky, *Logoi Apodeiktikoi*, 96).

85. Palamas's reliance on Augustine for this and other trinitarian images is still a debated question, although Reinhard Flogaus has argued rather convincingly that

Palamas had not only read Planudes's' translation of Augustine's *De Trinitate*, but lifted sections of it for his own work. See Reinhard Flogaus, "Inspiration-Exploitation-Distortion: The Use of Augustine in the Hesychast Controversy," in George Demacopoulos and Aristotle Papanikolaou, eds., *Orthodox Readings of Augustine* (Crestwood, N. Y.: St. Vladimir's Seminary Press, 2008), 63–80; idem, "Palamas and Barlaam Revisited: A Reassessment of East and West in the Hesychast Controversy of 14th Century Byzantium," *St. Vladimir's Theological Quarterly* 42 (1998): 1–32; idem, "Die Theologie des Gregorios Palamas—Hindernis oder Hilfe für die ökumenische Verstandigung?" *Ostkirchlichen Studien* 47 (1998): 105–23.

86. Markos Orpanos, "The Procession of the Holy Spirit According to Certain Later Greek Fathers," 34.

87. Gregory Palamas, *Logos Apodeiktikos* 2.30 (Boris Brobrinsky, *Logoi Apodeiktikoi*, 105).

88. See next chapter.

89. According to Cydones, "He was second to none of his contemporaries in learning . . . recognized by all as an authority [and] quoted far and wide. . . . He praised the wisdom of the Latins in glowing terms, being, as he was, an enthusiastic admirer of Thomas Aquinas's works. . . . Here we were of one mind. In fact, much of what he knew of Thomas he had learned through me." Demetrius Cydones, *Apologia* (Eng. trans.: James Likoudis, *Ending the Byzantine Greek Schism*, 56–57).

90. *Nilus Cabasilas et Theologia s. Thomae de Processione Spiritus Sancti*, ed. Emmanuel Candel (Vatican City: Bibliotheca Apostolica Vaticana, 1945). This treatise was later attacked by Cydones (*Defense of Thomas Aquinas Against Nilus Cabasilas*).

91. Critical edition with French translation: Théophile Kislas, ed., *Sur le Saint-Esprit* (Paris: Les Éditions du Cerf, 2001).

92. Nilus Cabasilas, *Five Discourses against the Conclusions of the Latins on the Matter of the Holy Spirit* 5.6–7 (Théophile Kislas, *Sur le Saint-Esprit*, 379–381).

93. Nilus Cabasilas, *Five Discourses* 5, 13 (Théophile Kislas, *Sur le Saint-Esprit*, 385).

94. "Αὐτὸ δὲ τὸ λέγειν ταύτην μὲν τὴν αἰτίαν ὁ Υἱὸς οὐκ ἔχει τοῦ Πνεύματος, τὴν πρώτην δηλαδή, ἣν καὶ ὁ θεῖος Μάξιμος ἀφαιρεῖ ται τὸν Υἱόν, ἐκείνην δὲ ἔχει, ἣν ἂν Λατῖνοι φαῖεν, οὐκ ᾔδει σαφῶς δύο τοῦ Πνεύματος ἀρχὰς ἀναπλάττουσιν, ἅμα καὶ πόλεμον ἑαυτοῖς ἐπάγοντες ἀρνουμένοις, τὸν Πατέρα καὶ τὸν Υἱόν δύο τοῦ Πνεύματος ἀρχὰς ἀξιουν." Nilus Cabasilas, *Five Discourses* 5.17 (Théophile Kislas, *Sur le Saint-Esprit*, 387).

95. Nilus Cabasilas, *Five Discourses* 5.12 (Théophile Kislas, *Sur le Saint-Esprit*, 385).

96. The *Memoirs* were written by Syropoulus several years after the conclusion of the Council, (ca. 1445) and its anti-unionist tone has led many scholars (especially in the West) to read it with a degree of skepticism. For this older view of Syropoulus's trustworthiness (or lack thereof) see Carl Hefele and Henri Leclercq, *Histoire des conciles*, vol. 7.2 (Paris: Letouzey & Aneé, 1916), 958–59. Although few today hold this position, there is certainly reason to question the overall objectivity of the account. Syropoulus, a staunch anti-unionist, had himself been a signatory to the union. His description of the Council, emphasizing as it does the imperial desire for union (maintained, on occasion, by the emperor's interference in dogmatic disputes), the financial hardships imposed on the Byzantines, and the general homesickness of the

Greek delegates, may in fact be something of an apology for his own actions. However, more recent studies have recognized both the general accuracy of the *Memoirs* and their importance in providing our only "behind-the-scenes" look at the deliberations and attitudes of the delegates themselves. See Joseph Gill, "The Sources of the 'Acta' of the Council of Florence," and "The 'Acta' and the Memoirs of Syropoulus as History," in *Personalities of the Council of Florence* (Oxford: Basil Blackwell, 1964), 131–77; Deno Geanakoplos, "A New Reading of the *Acta*, especially Syropoulus," in Giuseppe Alberigo, ed., *Christian Unity: The Council of Ferrara-Florence 1438/9* (Louvain, Belgium: University Press, 1991), 325–51.

97. See John Barker, *Manuel II Palaeologus (1391–1425); A Study in Late Byzantine Statesmanship* (New Brunswick, N.J.: Rutgers University Press, 1969).

98. Quoted in Edward Gibbon, *The Decline and Fall of the Roman Empire*, vol. 6 (New York: Bigelow, Brown & Co., 1845), 422.

99. Martin reasoned that since Rome was the "mother church," it was only appropriate for the child (i.e., the East) to come to the parent. Syropoulus, *Memoirs* 2.13 (V. Laurent, *Les Mémoires*, 114).

100. "To be paid by the Pope means to recognize his authority over myself. And how shall a hireling slave refuse obedience to his master? Think, also, what state we shall be in if, once in a strange land, we meet with a refusal to pay our expenses or the means of returning home." Syropoulus, *Memoirs* 2.18 (V. Laurent, *Les Mémoires*, 120) (Eng. trans.: Ivan Ostroumoff, *The History of the Council of Florence* [Boston: Holy Transfiguration Monastery, 1971], 18).

101. For Eugene's motives see Joseph Gill, "Pope Eugenius IV," in *Personalities of the Council of Florence*, 35–44; idem, *Eugene IV: Pope of Christian Unity* (Westminster, Md.: Newman Press, 1961).

102. The fathers at Basel initially had the upper hand, as they were originally supported by the Western emperor (Sigismund) and the other secular powers—the very people that the Byzantines needed in their battle against the Turks. Terrified by the threat of another prolonged schism in the Western Church, Emperor Sigismund and the other kings of Europe eventually abandoned their overt support of Basel. Sigismund himself, who might have played a greater role in unifying the Western powers against the growing Turkish threat, died in December 1437 while the Greeks were still en route to Ferrara (his death prompting Emperor John to consider the possibility of abandoning the whole project and returning to Constantinople). See Joachim Steiber, *Pope Eugenius IV, the Council of Basel, and the Secular and Ecclesiastical Authorities in the Empire: The Conflict over Supreme Authority and Power in the Church*, Studies in the History of Christian Thought 13 (Leiden: Brill, 1978).

103. The decision to leave with the papal envoys can be explained, in part, by the mistakes of the conciliarists at Basel. In the preamble to their 1434 decree *Sicut pia mater*, the council declared its intent "to put an end straightaway the recent schism of the Bohemians [i.e., the Hussites] and the ancient one of the dissident Greeks," which the Byzantines immediately took as an insult since it seemingly equated them with a group they knew to be notorious heretics. See *Sicut pia mater. Monumenta Conciliorum Generalium Concilium Basileense Scriptorum: Tomus Secundus* (1873), 752. For the Byzantine reaction see Syropoulus, *Memoirs* 2.37 (V. Laurent, *Les Mémoires*, 142–44). However, the chief reason for the Greeks' choice of the papal fleet was, according to

Joseph Gill, that despite their obvious sympathies with "Latin conciliar theory, they [the Greeks] had no doubt that the head of the Latin Church was the Pope [and that] their tradition of negotiation with the West had been with popes." Joseph Gill, *The Council of Florence* (Cambridge: Cambridge University Press, 1959), 84.

104. Joasaph of Ephesus died soon afterward, so Mark Eugenicus was chosen as both the Antiochene procurator and Metropolitan of Ephesus in his place. Only later, upon the death of Dionysius after the Greeks' arrival in Italy, did Mark become the representative of Jerusalem as well.

105. Syropoulus, *Memoirs* 3.8 (V. Laurent, *Les Mémoires*, 168).

106. Syropoulus, *Memoirs* 3.10 (V. Laurent, *Les Mémoires*, 170). According to Gill, Bessarion was also "thoroughly conversant" with the work of Cabasilas, although he later showed a preference for the more patristically grounded *Epigraphae* of John Beccus. Joseph Gill, "Sincerity of Bessarion the Unionist," 385. In addition to Cabasilas, Eugenicus seems to have collected his own *florilegia* in support of the Greek position. These texts can be found in Ludivico Petit, ed., CF 10.2: *Marci Eugenici, metropolitae Ephesi, opera antiunionistica* (Rome: Pontificium Institutum Orientalium Studiorum, 1977), 34–59.

NOTES TO CHAPTER 8

1. As Yves Congar wrote: "In substance it [the schism] consisted in the acceptance of the situation of non-rapport. . . . Not that the schism is of itself the estrangement . . . it was the acceptance of the estrangement." Yves Congar, *After Nine Hundred Years: The Background of the Schism between the Eastern and Western Churches* (New York: Fordham University Press, 1959), 88–89.

2. There are three main sources for our knowledge about the Council of Ferrara-Florence: the *Acta graeca*, authored in large part by Dorotheus of Mitylene (Joseph Gill, ed., *Quae supersunt Actorum Graecorum Concilii Florentini: Res Ferrariae gestae*, CF 5.1.1 [Rome: Pontifical Oriental Institute, 1953] and idem, *Quae supersunt Actorum Graecorum Concilii Florentini: ResFlorentinae gestae*, CF 5.2.2 [Rome: Pontifical Oriental Institute, 1953]); the account of the Latin consistory, Andrew da Santa Croce, generally referred to as the *Acta latina* (George Hoffman, ed., CF 6: *Andreas de Santacroce, advocatus consistorialis, Acta Latina Concilii Florentini* [Rome: Pontificium Institutum Orientalium Studiorum, 1955]; and the *Memoirs* of Sylvester Syropoulus.

3. Syropoulus, *Memoirs* 4.19 (V. Laurent, ed., *Les Mémoires du Grand Ecclésiarque de l'Église de Constantinople Sylvestre Syropoulos sur le Concile de Florence (1438–1439)*, CF 9 [Rome: Pontifical Oriental Institute, 1971], 216.) Gill questions Syropoulus's accuracy on this point, since the week of preparation in 1438 began not on the eighth of February (when the Venetian feast allegedly took place), but on the seventeenth. See Gill, *Council of Florence*, 99 n. 1. If Syropoulus is correct, it certainly would have reinforced the Byzantine perception (expressed in so many anti-Latin tracts) that Western fasting practices were too lax.

4. Syropoulus, *Memoirs* 4.25 (V. Laurent, *Les Mémoires*, 222–24).

5. For his part, the patriarch believed his relationship to the pope (which he always intended to be familial) would be determined by their age, not by their respective rank within the pentarchy. While in Venice, he confided to one of Eugene's

representatives: "If the pope is older than I am, I will consider him as my father; if my equal in age, I will consider him as my brother; if younger, I will consider him my son." Syropoulus, *Memoirs* 4.31 (V. Laurent, *Les Mémoires*, 230). As a matter of record, Joseph was (by Traversari's guess) almost eighty at the time of the council, while Eugene was only fifty-five.

6. Syropoulus, *Memoirs* 4.33 (V. Laurent, *Les Mémoires*, 232–34) (Eng. trans.: Deno Geanakoplos, "The Council of Florence [1438–1439] and the Problem of Union between the Greek and Latin Churches," in *Constantinople and the West* (Madison: University of Wisconsin Press, 1989), 235.

7. Syropoulus, *Memoirs* 4.46–47 (V. Laurent, *Les Mémoires*, 251–53).

8. See G. R. Evans, "The Council of Florence and the Problem of Ecclesial Identity," in Giuseppe Alberigo, *Christian Unity*, ed., *Christian Unity: The Council of Ferrara-Florence 1438/9* (Louvain, Belgium: University Press, 1991), 177–85.

9. Syropoulus, *Memoirs* 4.46 (V. Laurent, *Les Mémoires*, 250) (Eng. trans.: Deno Geanakoplos, *Byzantium*, 380–81).

10. This was probably done, as Gill suggests, for financial reasons, since the cost of maintaining over 700 Greek delegates was quickly emptying the papal treasury. See Gill, "The Cost of the Council of Florence," in *Personalities of the Council of Florence* (Oxford: Basil Blackwell, 1964), 186–203.

11. Pletho was also present at the Council of Florence and acted as one of the six orators for the Byzantine delegation. Though he was a lay philosopher, his lectures attracted a great deal of interest among the humanists of Florence, although his contributions to the *filioque* debates were of little significance. See Constantine Tsirpanlis, "Byzantine Forerunners of the Italian Renaissance: Plethon, Bessarion, George of Trebizond, John Argyropoulos, Manuel Chrysoloras, Demetrios Cydones, Barlaam of Calabria," *Patristic and Byzantine Review* 15 (1996/7): 23–57; John Monfasani, *Byzantine Scholars in Renaissance Italy: Cardinal Bessarion and Other Émigrés: Selected Essays* (Brookfield, Ver.: Variorum, 1995).

12. See Ludwig Mohler, ed., *Kardinal Bessarion als Theologe, Humanist, und Staatsmann. Funde und Forschungen*, 3 vols. (Paderborn 1923–42; repr.: Aalen: Scientia-Verlag, 1967); Joseph Gill, "Cardinal Bessarion," in *Personalities of the Council of Florence*, 45–54; idem, "The Sincerity of Bessarion the Unionist," *Journal of Theological Studies* 26 (1975): 377–92; idem, "Was Bessarion a Conciliarist or Unionist before the Council of Florence?" in *Orientalia Christiana Analecta* 204 (Rome: Pontificium Institutum Orientalium Studiorum, 1977), 201–19; André Halleux, "Bessarion et le palamisme au concile de Florence," *Irenikon* 62 (1989): 307–32. In fact, the evidence suggests that Bessarion was firmly convinced of the Byzantine position, and his actions during the early stages of the council attest to the strength of these convictions. For example, Bessarion ably defended Mark Eugenicus (whom he referred to as "the holy and most blessed exarch of this holy assembly, the most truly wise and foremost theologian, and our teacher, the Archbishop of Ephesus" [Joseph Gill, *Acta graeca*, 46]) when, early in the proceedings, he came under threat of imperial censure for his imprudent language. Also, it was Bessarion who argued that the Byzantines should directly challenge the Latins on the theology of the *filioque*, believing that "we can say much about the doctrine, and say it well, and need not cower before the Latins. Cabasilas wrote only four pages on the subject of the addition, yet the speeches we

ourselves have made are enough for a book. On the subject of the doctrine he wrote a whole book, and so surely we shall be able to say a great deal." Syropoulus, *Memoirs* 7.12 (V. Laurent, *Les Mémoires*, 362).

13. Eugenicus himself claimed that Bessarion had made himself a servant, paid off with papal gold and cardinal red. Syropoulus, *Memoirs* 9.11 (V. Laurent, *Les Mémoires*, 446).

14. Joseph Gill, "The Sincerity of Bessarion the Unionist," 391. For more on Bessarion and the fathers see Francis X. Murphy, "Bessarion's Patristic Heritage," *Studia Patristica* 23 (1989): 250–55.

15. Views of Mark Eugenicus, like those of Bessarion, have largely divided along denominational lines. For the Orthodox view see Constantine Tsirpanlis, ed., "St. Mark Eugenicus and the Council of Florence," *Patristic and Byzantine Review* 10 (1991): 104–92; idem; *Mark Eugenicus and the Council of Florence: An Historical Re-evaluation of his Personality* (New York: Κεντρον Βυζαντινων Ερευνων, 1979); Alexander Schmemann, "St. Mark of Ephesus and the Theological Conflicts in Byzantium," *St. Vladimir's Seminary Quarterly* 1 (1957): 11–24. A more critical view of Mark's personality and theological acumen can be found in Carl Hefele and Henri Leclercq, *Histoire des conciles*, vol. 7.2 (Paris: Letouzey & Aneé, 1916); Joseph Gill, "Mark Eugenicus, Metropolitan of Ephesus," in *Personalities of the Council of Florence*, 55–64. The most recent, and perhaps most balanced, study of Mark (with a complete review of the primary and secondary literature) is Nicholas Constas, "Mark Eugenicus," in Carmelo Conticello and Vassa Conticello, eds., *La théologie Byzantine et sa tradition*, vol. 2 (Turnhout: Brepols, 2002), 411–75.

16. Joseph Gill, *Acta graeca*, 216 (Eng. trans: Joseph Gill, *The Council of Florence*, 163).

17. Mark, alone among the Byzantines, was unafraid to say that "the Latins are not only schismatics, but heretics," and if previous generations of Greeks had been silent about this statement, they were so only because the Latins were so many in number or because of hopes of converting them. Joseph Gill, *Acta graeca*, 400. Mark's intemperate language angered the unionists, especially the Bishops of Mitylene and Lacedaemon, "who could barely restrain themselves from rushing upon him to tear him to pieces with their teeth and hands." They then threatened to tell the pope so that Mark could receive his just punishment. Syropoulus, *Memoirs* 9.10 (V. Laurent, *Les Mémoires*, 444) (Eng. trans.: Deno Geanakoplos, *Byzantium*, 224).

18. Syropoulus, *Memoirs* 10.15 (V. Laurent, *Les Mémoires*, 496). Pope Eugene later referred to "that wretched Ephesian, spewing out his poisonous thought everywhere. If only the emperor had consented to his being punished as he deserved, in the same way that Constantine permitted the punishment of Arius—that poison of the Church. . . both time and money would not have been wasted." George Hoffman, ed., CF 1.3: *Epistolae Pontificiae ad Concilium Florentinum spectantes cum indicibus ad partes 1–3* (Rome: Pontificium Institutum Orientalium Studiorum, 1946), 17–18 (Eng. trans.: Nicholas Constas, "Mark Eugenicus," in *La théologie Byzantine et sa tradition*, vol. 2, 420).

19. Joseph Gill, *Acta graeca*, 159 (Eng. trans.: Joseph Gill, *Council of Florence*, 155).

20. Joseph Gill, *Acta graeca*, 92–93 (Eng. trans.: Joseph Gill, *Council of Florence*, 151). The Latins' continued reliance upon Aristotle prompted one frustrated Byzantine

to exclaim: "Why Aristotle, Aristotle? Aristotle is no good. . . . What is good? St. Peter, St. Paul, St. Basil, Gregory the Theologian, Chrysostom—not Aristotle, Aristotle!" Syropoulus, *Memoirs* 9.28 (V. Laurent, *Les Mémoires*, 464).

21. Joseph Gill, *Acta graeca*, 207.

22. Cesarini was not being disingenuous. He claimed to have knowledge of an edition of the acts of the fifth, sixth, and seventh councils (brought from Constantinople by Nicholas of Cusa) that also contained the phrase *et ex Filio*, but so badly erased that the words remained visible. See Joseph Gill, *Council of Florence*, 149 n.1. Cusanus himself, although not present for most of the council, played a pivotal role in its development, since many of the ancient manuscripts he had collected in the East (including a copy of Basil's *Adversus Eunomium*) were used by the Latins to support the authenticity of their own codices. Some of the manuscripts he copied had actually been borrowed from Mark Eugenicus of Ephesus, with whom he enjoyed cordial relations. This fact adds weight to the argument that Mark's hostility to the Latins prior to the council has been exaggerated.

23. Syropoulus, *Memoirs* 6.31 (V. Laurent, *Les Mémoires*, 330–32) (Eng. trans.: Ivan Ostroumoff, *The History of the Council of Florence* [Boston: Holy Transfiguration Monastery, 1971], 72).

24. Joseph Gill, *Acta graeca*, 132; Syropoulus, *Memoirs* 6.35 (V. Laurent, *Les Mémoires* 334–36). His purpose, according to Hans-Jürgen Marx, was threefold. "First, [to prove] that the addition [i.e., the *filioque*] was already in the Latin version of the Constantinopolitan Creed by the time of the sixth ecumenical council. Second, the Greeks had known about it. And third, that Maximus had used the Latin addition in his vehement defense against the monothelite polemicists." Hans-Jürgen Marx, *Filioque und Verbot eines anderen Glaubens auf dem Florentinum: zum Pluralismus in dogmatischen Formeln* (Sankt Augustin: Steyler Verlag, 1977), 223. Syropoulus claimed that Andrew's purpose was simply "to prove that the addition was not the cause of the schism, but that it occurred for other reasons." Syropoulus, *Memoirs* 6.35 (V. Laurent, *Les Mémoires* 334).

25. See the rebuke of Nicholas Secundinus. Joseph Gill, *Acta graeca*, 132. Marx believes that "it is very likely the Greeks came to the council with the intention of giving the *Letter to Marinus* of Maximus to the Latins as a formula for union. It would have conceded the orthodoxy of the *filioque* but would have simultaneously allowed dogmatic adherence to the Photian interpretation of the διὰ τοῦ Υἱοῦ formula." Hans-Jürgen Marx, *Filioque und Verbot eines anderen Glaubens auf dem Florentinum* (Sankt Augustin: Steyler Verlag, 1977), 122.

26. Syropoulus, *Memoirs* 6.36 (V. Laurent, *Les Mémoires* 336).

27. Ibid.

28. The emperor did make it clear that the Greeks reserved the right to return to the liceity of the addition, despite the Latins' belief that their point had already been won. Joseph Gill, *Acta graeca*, 224–46.

29. Just as important, the Florentines had offered to assist the pope with his financial obligations to the Byzantine delegates. See Joseph Gill, "The Cost of the Council of Florence," in *Personalities of the Council of Florence*, 186–203. One of the stipulations made by the Greeks for the council's transference was that while they were at Florence, "the payment of their allowances should be direct and not dependant

on his [the pope's] Camera." Ibid, 200. However, the length of the council and the increasing cost of supporting such a large undertaking still made payment irregular, prompting Syropoulus's continued references to the poverty of the Greek delegation.

30. Discussion on purgatory lasted from June 4 to July 17. Public debates on the addition held at Ferrara lasted sixteen sessions, from October 8 to January 10.

31. "Therefore we Greeks began to get irritated, not only the hierarchs, but also all the clerics, the nobles, and the whole assembly, saying: What are we doing speaking and listening to empty words? They will not persuade us, nor we them; for this reason we ought to turn back to our city." Joseph Gill, *Acta graeca*, 217.

32. Ibid., 253; George Hoffman, *Acta latina*, 136. It is not certain which text John cited, since there is a discrepancy in the Greek and Latin *Acta*. It was either John 8:42 (*Ego enim ex Deo processi et veni*) or John 16:28 (*Exivi a Patre et veni in mundum*). However in neither case does the Greek use ἐκπόρευσις or its variants to refer to the Son.

33. Joseph Gill, *Acta graeca*, 254; John of Damascus, *De Fide orthodoxa* 1. 8.

34. Ibid., 255–56.

35. Ibid., 256; Epiphanius, *Ancoratus* 71 (PG 43, 153).

36. Ibid., 257.

37. Ibid., 260.

38. Ibid., 260–61.

39. Ibid., 261–62.

40. Ibid., 271.

41. Ibid., 271.

42. Ibid., 278.

43. Ibid., 279.

44. Ibid., 283.

45. Ibid., 287–88.

46. Ibid., 292.

47. Ibid., 294.

48. Ibid., 287.

49. It should be noted that although the intellectual weakness of the Greek delegation has often been emphasized, especially in the face of the Latin syllogisms (see Joseph Gill, *Council of Florence*, 227–30), Eugenicus believed that up to this point the Byzantines had ably defended the logic of their position. That it was Montenero who demanded a return to the patristic witness may, in fact, testify that the Latins were of the same opinion.

50. Joseph Gill, *Acta graeca*, 262, n. 12 (Eng. trans.: Joseph Gill, *Council of Florence*, 199, n. 1).

51. Ibid., 296.

52. In fact, modern patristic scholarship has proved Eugenicus substantially correct as to his reading of the text, but wrong as to the reason. Although both versions were in circulation, even before the schism, the Greek text appears to have been Basil's own work, the addition in the Latin text apparently being an excerpt of Eunomius's added later. "On this point we can conclude that there was diversity of ancient texts of Basil's *Contra Eunomium*, and that this divergence was not a case of fraudulent manipulation of texts." Bernard Sesboüé, ed., *Basile de Césarée: Contre Eunome,*

146–47, n. 1. See also M. Van Pays, "Quelques remarques à propos d'un texte controversé de Saint Basile au Concile de Florence," *Irenikon* 40 (1967): 6–14.

53. Joseph Gill, *Acta graeca*, 297. Later in the debate Montenero produced another ancient copy provided by Dorotheus of Mitylene that agreed with his own.

54. Ibid., 298–99; Cyril of Alexandria, *Epistula* 39 (PG 77, 181) and *Epistula* 40 (PG 77, 200–201).

55. Ibid., 300–301. According to Mark, Zosimus had sent to the Council of Carthage a purported canon of the Council of Nicea, which he claimed granted the papacy universal jurisdiction as a court of appeal. Montenero protested that Mark had no evidence that Zosimus had done this, and that both Cyril and Athanasius had in fact recognized Rome as a court of appeal against their enemies in the East.

56. He compared this form of argumentation to that employed by the Greeks at Ferrara, who had maintained that "even if the *filioque* were true it should not be added. . . . We did not accept the truth of the proposition, but taking it as a concession as agreed, we use it to prove the truth of the conclusion and that truth is therefore not doubtful but absolute. I am surprised that this has escaped a man of your intelligence." Ibid., 386–87 (Eng. trans.: Joseph Gill, *Council of Florence*, 211).

57. Ibid., 314.

58. Ibid., 314.

59. Ibid., 304–5.

60. Ibid, 345.

61. During the earlier debates on purgatory Mark had refused to answer a similar question posed by Andrew of Rhodes. Syropoulus, *Memoirs* 5, 38 (V. Laurent, *Les Mémoires*, 292). Prior to their departure from Byzantium, John Palaeologus had strictly forbidden mention of Palamas or his theology, most likely to maintain harmony within the delegation, afraid of reintroducing a debate that had torn the empire apart only a century earlier. Although there is no indication, perhaps the emperor was aware that the scholastic teaching on knowledge of the divine essence contradicted Palamas's own views on the subject (See Thomas Aquinas, *Summa Theologiae* Pt.I, Q.12, Art.1). Aquinas's views were later dogmatized in 1336 by Pope Benedict XII: "The saints in heaven . . . have seen and see the divine essence by intuitive vision, and even face to face, with no mediating creature . . . but the divine essence immediately revealing itself plainly, clearly, and openly to them and seeing thus they enjoy the same divine essence." *Benedictus Deus* in Henry Denzinger, ed., *The Sources of Catholic Dogma* (St. Louis: Herder, 1957), 198. It should be noted that this was originally intended not as an attack upon Palamism, but upon certain ideas that had already been condemned by the Archbishop of Paris in the thirteenth century. The final union decree later affirmed, *contra* Palamas, that the blessed "clearly behold the triune God as he is." *Leatentur Caeli* (Norman Tanner, *Decrees of the Ecumenical Councils* [Washington DC: Georgetown University Press, 1990], 528).

62. Joseph Gill, *Acta graeca*, 346.

63. Robert Haddad, "Stations of the *Filioque*," *St. Vladimir's Seminary Quarterly* 46 (2002): 257–58.

64. "All the previous sessions passed in the examination of two or three passages from the fathers. This way of conducting the dispute must not last forever and we have therefore agreed to offer our arguments concretely, extracting them not from spurious

or little known sources, not from doubtful and corrupted places, but from the Holy Scriptures and by all received passages from the fathers. If we continue to dwell upon one and the same subject there will be no end of our refutations of your words and answers." (Joseph Gill, *Acta graeca*, 373 [Eng. trans.: Ivan Ostroumoff, *History of the Council of Florence*, 114–15].)

65. Ibid., 365–66 (Eng. trans.: Ivan Ostroumoff, *History of the Council of Florence*, 108–9).

66. Ibid., 367 (Eng. trans.: Ivan Ostroumoff, *History of the Council of Florence*, 109).

67. Ibid., 368–69; Dionysius, *De divinis nomine* 2 (PG 3, 641), and Athanasius, *Contra Sabellianos* (PG 28, 97).

68. Ibid., 376–77 (Eng. trans.: Ivan Ostroumoff, *History of the Council of Florence*, 111).

69. Ibid., 377; Gregory of Nazianzus, *Oration* 34 (PG 36, 252).

70. Ibid.; Acts of the Council of Ephesus (Mansi 4, 1364).

71. Ibid., 379; Cyril of Alexandria, *Apologeticus contra Thedoretum* (PG 76, 391–452).

72. Ibid., 381; Theodoret, *Epistula* 172 (PG 83, 1484).

73. Ibid., 382 (Eng. trans.: Joseph Gill, *Council of Florence*, 211).

74. Ibid., 390.

75. The emperor asked Montenero for a written copy of his teaching on this matter, presumably as a means of convincing the Greeks of the sincerity and orthodoxy of the Latin position. Ibid., 390–93.

76. Ibid., 392–93.

77. Syropoulus, *Memoirs* 8.12 (V. Laurent, *Les Mémoires*, 400).

78. Ibid.

79. Ibid.

80. Ibid.

81. The *Acta* records that the emperor commanded Mark, along with the other staunch anti-unionist, Metropolitan Anthony of Heraclea, not to appear in order not to prolong the debate (Joseph Gill, *Acta graeca*, 394). Eugenicus himself, in his *Relatio de rebus a se gestis*, says that he was absent because of ill health. Mark of Ephesus, *Relatio de rebus a se gestis* (Ludivico Petit, ed., *Marci Eugenici, metropolitae Ephesi, opera antiunionistica*, CF 10.2 [Rome: Pontifical Oriental Institute, 1977], 138).

82. George Hoffman, *Acta latina*, 198.

83. Ibid., 202–4; Jerome, *Epistola* 141 (PL 22, 1180); Hilary, *De Trinitate* 3.29 (PL 10,69–70); 12.57 (PL 10, 471–72); Ambrose, *De Spiritu Sancto* 1.11 (PL 16, 732); 2.12 (PL 16, 771); 2.15 (PL 16, 739).

84. Ibid., 205–6; Augustine of Hippo, *In Joannis Evangelium Tractatus* 99.6.7 (PL 35, 1889); *De Trinitate* 4.20 (PL 42, 908); 5. 14 (PL 42, 921); 15.25 (PL 42, 1092).

85. Ibid., 206; Hormisdas, *Epistula* 79 (PL 63, 514).

86. Ibid.; *Vita Gregorii Magni* 2.2 (PL 75, 87–88).

87. Ibid. 208.

88. Ibid., 209. Epiphanius, *Ancoratus* (PG 43, 153). For more on Montenero's sources see Alexis Alexakis, "The Greek Patristic *Testimonia* presented at the Council

of Florence (1439) in support of the *Filioque* reconsidered," *Revue des Études Byzantines* 58 (2000),149–65.

89. George Hoffman, *Acta latina*, 210–11; Didymus, *De Spiritu Sancto* 37 (PG 39, 1065–66); Athanasius, *Oratio I contra arianos* 50 (PG 26, 118); *Oratio III contra arianos* 22 (PG 26, 376).

90. Ibid., 214; Cyril of Alexandria, *Epistula* 17 (PG 77, 117).

91. Ibid.; Cyril of Alexandria, *Epistula* 55 (PG 77, 316).

92. Ibid., 214.

93. Ibid., 218.

94. Ibid., 219.

95. Emmanuel Candal, ed., CF 7.2 : *Bessarion Nicaenus, S.R.E. Cardinalis, De Spiritus Sancti processione ad Alexium Lascarin Philanthropinum* (Rome: Pontificium Institutum Orientalium Studiorum, 1961), 40–41 (Eng. trans.: John Erickson, "*Filioque* and the Fathers at the Council of Florence," in *The Challenge of Our Past* [Crestwood, N. Y.: St. Vladimir's Seminary Press, 1991], 159).

96. Joseph Gill, *Acta graeca*, 400.

97. Ibid., 406.

98. This was some time between April 12 and April 15.

99. While both simple and persuasive, Bessarion's arguments were hardly original. In both his selection of texts and content, Bessartion relied heavily on the work of John Beccus. According to Gill, "His [Bessarion's] dependence on Beccus is clear because occasionally he even includes the short phrases by which Beccus linked some of his quotations." Joseph Gill, "The Sincerity of Bessarion the Unionist," 386.

100. Emmanuel Candal, ed., *Bessarion Nicaenus, Oratio dogmatica de unione*, CF 7.1 (Rome: Pontifical Oriental Institute, 1958), 29–30.

101. Ibid.; Basil of Caesarea, *Contra Eunomium* 5 (PG 29, 733).

102. Ibid., 30.

103. Ibid, 37–38.

104. Ibid, 42.

105. Ibid, 43.

106. Ibid.

107. Ibid, 45.

108. Bessarion, *Refutatio Capitum Syllogisticorum Marci Ephesii* (PG 161, 240).

109. For more on Scholarius see Michael Azkoul, "St. George Scholarius and the Latin Theological Tradition," *Patristic and Byzantine Review* 10 (1991): 167–72; C. J. G. Turner, "George-Gennadius Scholarius and the Union of Florence," *Journal of Theological Studies* 18 (1967): 83–103; Joseph Gill, "George Scholarius," in *Personalities of the Council of Florence*, 79–94. A full biography and review of secondary literature is found in Franz Tinnefeld, "George Gennadios Scholarius," in *La théologie Byzantine et sa tradition* 2, 477–549. There remains scholarly debate as to the sincerity of Scholarius's unionist leanings. Some have chosen to interpret *On the Need for Aiding Constantinople* as a plea for an "economic" union (i.e., merely to obtain Western aid against the Turk) while others (including Gill) believe Scholarius was firmly convinced of the Latins' orthodoxy. Scholarius himself, upon assuming the anti-unionist leadership in 1444, had difficulty explaining his advocacy of Florence and exactly what had occurred to him in its aftermath. Perhaps the most convincing argument is put forward by

C. J. G. Turner, who claims that Scholarius embraced Florence as both a "dogmatic" and "economic" union but that for a combination of political, psychological, theological, and personal reasons he slowly began to regret his decision. C. J. G. Turner, "George-Gennadius Scholarius and the Union of Florence," 83–103.

110. George Scholarius, *De pace deque adiuvanda patria adhortatio* (Joseph Gill, ed., CF 8.1: *Orationes Georgii Scholarii in Concilio Florentino habitae* [Rome: Pontificium Institutum Orientalium Studiorum, 1964], 5–20).

111. It should be noted that the emperor, even at this late stage, chose Mark of Ephesus, Dositheos of Monembasia, and Anthony of Heraclea as members of the delegation despite his own desire to consummate the union. These choices would seem to cast further doubt upon Syropoulus's claim that the emperor, having decided on union, forcibly silenced the anti-unionists. Others chosen included Bessarion, Isidore, and Dorotheus of Mytilene.

112. While the addition to the creed had been treated as a separate canonical issue at the council (i.e., whether it was licitly added in the first place), both Mark Eugenicus and the Latins believed that the removal of the *filioque* would also have been a *de facto* admission of its heterodoxy.

113. Syropoulus, *Memoirs* 8.27 (V. Laurent, *Les Mémoires*, 414).

114. Joseph Gill, *Acta graeca*, 412.

115. Syropoulus, *Memoirs* 8.30 (V. Laurent, *Les Mémoires*, 416–18) (Eng. trans.: Joseph Gill, *The Council of Florence*, 248).

116. "We do not accept it because we do not possess the letter in its entirety." Syropoulus, *Memoirs* 8.34 (V. Laurent, *Les Mémoires* 420).

117. Ibid.

118. Syropoulus, *Memoirs* 8.40 (V. Laurent, *Les Mémoires* 426) (Eng. trans.: Joseph Gill, *The Council of Florence*, 250).

119. L. Petit and M. Jugie, eds., *Oeuvres completes* vol. 3 (Paris: Bonne Presse, 1930), 127. During the private discussions, Anthony of Heraclea had also attempted to introduce the *Tomos* as a conciliar witness against the Latin doctrine, but (according to Syropoulus) was prevented from doing so "because the evildoer who was shown to be our enemy [i.e., the emperor's confessor], used all his zeal to prevent us from knowing of this work." Syropoulus, *Memoirs* 9.9 (V. Laurent, *Les Mémoires* 442–44).

120. Syropoulus, *Memoirs* 8.40 (V. Laurent, *Les Mémoires*, 426).

121. Joseph Gill, *Acta graeca*, 418 (Eng. trans.: Joseph Gill, *The Council of Florence*, 252–53).

122. When Cesarini pressed for a definitive statement of faith a few days later, the emperor pleaded: "Of course we ought to have given an explanation of our confession of faith, but the most part of our bishops are in doubt as to what is demanded of them, some through ignorance, others because they cannot reject the doctrine received by the Fathers. . . . I am not the master of the Greek synod, nor do I want to use my authority to force it into any statement." Joseph Gill, *Acta graeca*, 421 (Eng. trans.: Joseph Gill, *The Council of Florence*, 253).

123. "What am I to say? I see division everywhere before my eyes and I wonder what use to you division will be. Still if it shall be, how are the western princes going to look on it? And what grief will you yourselves have; indeed how are you to return home? Union, however, once achieved, both the western princes and all of us will

be greatly rejoiced and will provide generous help for you." Joseph Gill, *Acta graeca*, 424 (Eng. trans.: Joseph Gill, *The Council of Florence*, 254).

124. According to John Erickson, while "Mark's theory of wholesale fabrication is rather farfetched . . . spurious texts did play a certain role in the 'success' of the council, particularly in the way in which the crucial problem of the procession of the Holy Spirit was addressed." John Erickson, "*Filioque* and the Fathers at the Council of Florence," 160.

125. Ludovico Petit, "Marci Ephesii: Relatio de rebus a se in synodo Florentina gestis," *Marci Eugenici opera antiunionistica*, 140 (Eng. trans.: Ivan Ostroumoff, *History of the Council of Florence*, 140).

126. Syropoulus, *Memoirs* 9.7 (V. Laurent, *Les Mémoires* 440–42).

127. Joseph Gill, *Acta graeca*, 401 (Eng. trans.: Joseph Gill, "The Sincerity of Bessarion the Unionist," 387).

128. "Why do you not listen to me? Was it not from my cell that you came out? Was it not I who raised you to the rank of bishop? Why then do you betray me? Why did you not second my opinion? Think you, then, that you can judge better than others about dogmas? I know as well as anybody else what the Fathers taught." Syropoulus, *Memoirs* 9.17 (V. Laurent, *Les Mémoires*, 450–52) (Eng. trans.: Ivan Ostroumoff, *History of the Council of Florence*, 136).

129. Ludovico Petit, "Marci Ephesii: Relatio de rebus a se in synodo Florentina gestis," *Marci Eugenici opera antiunionistica*, 140 (Eng. trans.: Ivan Ostroumoff, *History of the Council of Florence*, 140). The patriarch's own statement read: "I will never change or vary the doctrine handed down from our fathers but will abide in it till my last breath. But since the Latins, not of themselves but from the Holy Scriptures, explain the procession of the Holy Spirit as being from the Son, I agree with them and I give my judgment that this 'through' gives to the Son to be cause of the Holy Spirit. I both unite with them and am in communion with them." Joseph Gill, *Acta graeca* 432; Syropoulus, *Memoirs* 9.19 (V. Laurent, *Les Mémoires*, 452–54) (Eng. trans.: Joseph Gill, *The Council of Florence*, 260).

130. Ibid.

131. Joseph Gill, *Acta graeca*, 438.

132. George Hoffman, *Acta latina*, 254 (Eng. trans.: Joseph Gill, *The Council of Florence*, 265).

133. Joseph Gill, *Acta graeca*, 440.

134. Patriarch Joseph allegedly left a will and last testament that recognized "everything . . . that the Catholic and Apostolic Church of Our Lord Jesus Christ of the elder Rome understands and teaches . . . further the most blessed Father of Fathers and supreme Pontiff and vicar of Our Lord Jesus Christ, the Pope of elder Rome I confess for the security of all." Joseph Gill, *Acta graeca*, 444–45 (Eng. trans.: Joseph Gill, *The Council of Florence*, 267). Gill accepted the authenticity of the will largely on the basis of its mention by Greek sources as early as 1442. However, a stronger case can be made against the will's authenticity, since it is never mentioned by Syropoulus or any of the other Greeks (e.g., Pletho, Eugenicus) in their accounts of the council, nor was it utilized by the Latin or Byzantine delegates during the council's final deliberations. Also the letter is dated June 11, despite the fact the Patriarch clearly died the day before. The will's authenticity aside, the Latins were convinced enough of the

patriarch's commitment to communion to permit him burial, with honors, in the Church of Santa Maria Novella, where he remains to this day. See Joseph Gill, "Joseph II, Patriarch of Constantinople," in *Personalities of the Council of Florence*, 15–34.

135. "The Greeks have already conceded to the Latins more than what is right. The Latins ought to be contented and accomplish the Union of the Churches. But they care very little about peace and only increase the number of their demands. If the Pope will not rest contented with what we have already agreed to, then we have only to hire ships from the Florentines and go home." Syropoulus, *Memoirs* 10.7 (V. Laurent, *Les Mémoires*, 480–82) (Eng. trans.: Ivan Ostroumoff, *History of the Council of Florence*, 150).

136. The statement about papal primacy, for example, while recognizing the ancient prerogatives of the other patriarchates, was a clear declaration of the Roman faith.

> We also define that the holy apostolic see and the Roman pontiff holds the primacy over the whole world and the Roman pontiff is the successor of blessed Peter prince of the apostles, and that he is the true vicar of Christ, the head of the whole church and the father and teacher of all Christians, and to him was committed in blessed Peter the full power of tending, ruling and governing the whole church, as is contained also in the acts of ecumenical councils and in the sacred canons. (*Laetentur Caeli* [Norman Tanner, ed., *Decrees of the Ecumenical Councils* 1, 528]).

137. The compromise was that the pope's name should be listed first, with the words, "with the emperor's consent" immediately following.

138. Joseph Gill, *Acta graeca*, 467.

139. Syropoulus, *Memoirs* 10.16 (V. Laurent, *Les Mémoires* 496–500). A few days later the pope was invited by the emperor to celebrate the liturgy in Greek, but, pleading ignorance of the rite, he asked that some of his representatives might first view the liturgy so that its suitability could be assessed. The emperor, insulted at the suggestion that the Eastern liturgy might somehow be found lacking or inappropriate, immediately withdrew the proposal. Syropoulus, *Memoirs*, 10.17 (V. Laurent, *Les Mémoires*, 500–502).

140. *Laetentur Caeli* (Norman Tanner, *Decrees of the Ecumenical Councils* 1, 526).

141. Syropoulus, *Memoirs* 10.23 (V. Laurent, *Les Mémoires*, 508–10) (Eng. trans.: Ivan Ostroumoff, *History of the Council of Florence*, 159–60).

142. The emperor did tell the pope that appropriate steps would be taken to silence Mark unless he subscribed to the union at some point after his return East. Andrew of Rhodes records that Mark had promised to accept the decrees once an ecumenical patriarch was elected in Constantinople (since the Byzantines also refused the papal request that the election be held in Florence so that a patriarch could be chosen from among the unionist delegates). See Joseph Gill, *The Council of Florence*, 297.

143. Syropoulus, *Memoirs* 11.9 (V. Laurent, *Les Mémoires*, 530).

144. Doukas, *Historia Turco-Byzantina of Doukas*, crit. ed. Vasile Grecu (Bucharest: Editura Academiei Republicii Populare Romîne, 1958), 315. See George Demacopoulos,

"The Popular Reception of the Council of Florence in Constantinople (1439–1453)," *St. Vladimir's Theological Quarterly* 43 (1999): 37–53.

145. Bessarion's contributions to the revival of Greek learning in the West have long been a subject of interest among scholars. Although Bessarion is best remembered for his intellectual and humanitarian legacy, his political activity (e.g., attempting to unite the Western powers for the relief of Constantinople) was also considerable. He was so respected for his achievements that in the conclave of 1455 he was considered by many to be the leading candidate to replace Nicholas V—the reason often given for his failure to become pope is the fact that he maintained his beard in the Greek fashion.

146. Isidore allegedly entered Moscow on March 19 behind a Latin cross, with the anti-unionist monk Symeon in chains before him. Immediately he went to the Church of the Ascension, where he included the pope's name in the commemorations and formally proclaimed the union. Within four days he was in prison on charges of heresy.

147. Georgius Phrantzes, *Chronicon*, ed. E. Bekker, Corpus Scriptorum Historiae Byzantinae (Bonn, 1838), 271–79 (Eng. trans.: Steven Runciman, *The Fall of Constantinople 1453* [Cambridge: Cambridge University Press, 1965], 131).

148. The same author who had berated his fellow delegates for their ignorance and implored them to union in order to save the Great City now wrote:

> Wretched Romans, how you have gone astray! You have rejected the hope of God [and] trusted in the strength of the Franks; you have lost your piety along with your city which is about to be destroyed. Lord have mercy on me. I testify before you that I am innocent of such transgression. Know, wretched citizens, what you are doing. Along with your impending captivity you have forsaken the faith handed down from your fathers and assented to impiety. Woe unto you when you are judged! (Doukas, *Historia Turco-Byzantina of Doukas*, 317 [Eng. trans.: Deno Geanakoplos, *Byzantium*, 388].)

NOTES TO CHAPTER 9

1. See Samuel Powell, *The Trinity in German Thought* (Cambridge: Cambridge University Press, 2001); Simo Knuuttilla, "Luther's Trinitarian Theology and Its Medieval Background," *Studia Theologica* 53 (1999): 3–12; Albrecht Peters, "Die Trinitätslehre in der reformatorischen Christenheit," *Theologische Literaturzeitung* 94 (1969): 561–70; Reiner Jansen, *Studien zu Luthers Trinitätslehre* (Bern, 1976); Joachim Heubach, *Luther und die trinitarische Tradition: Ökumenische und philosophische Perspektiven* (Erlangen, Germany: Martin-Luther-Verlag, 1994).

2. See Ioannes Karmires, 'Ορθοδοξία καί Προτεσταντισμός (Athens, 1937); Ernst Benz, *Die Ostkirche in Lichte der protestantischen Geschictsschribung von der Reformation bis zur Gegenwart* (Munich: Karl Alber, 1952); idem, *Wittenburg und Byzanz: Zur Begegnung und aus Einandersetzung der Reformation und der Östlich-Orthodoxen Kirche* (Marburg, Germany: Fink, 1949).

3. Martin Luther, *Smalcald Articles* I (Eng. trans.: Theodore Tappert, ed., *The Book of Concord: The Confessions of the Evangelical Lutheran* Church [Philadelphia: Fortress Press, 1959], 291).

4. Martin Luther, "Treatise on the Last Words of David," (Eng. trans.: Jaroslav Pelikan, ed., *Luther's Works* 15 [Saint Louis: Concordia Publishing House, 1972], 309–10).

5. The views of Luther (and many of the Reformers) on the uselessness of scholastic metaphysical speculation were summed up by Philip Melanchthon: "We do better to adore the mysteries of deity than to investigate them" (*Die Geheimnisse der Gottheit sollten wir lieber anbeten als sie zu erforschen*).

6. Martin Luther, *The Large Catechism*, trans. Robert Fischer (Philadelphia: Muhlenberg Press, 1959), 59.

7. Martin Luther, "The Small Catechism," in Timothy Lull, ed., *Martin Luther's Basic Theological Writings* (Minneapolis: Fortress Press, 1989), 480.

8. Melanchthon claimed that even "our adversaries approve" the teaching contained in the Augsburg Confession that "there is one undivided divine essence, and that there are nevertheless three distinct and coeternal persons of the same divine essence, Father, Son, and Holy Spirit." Philip Melanchthon, "Apology to the Augsburg Confession," in *The Book of Concord*, 100. For Melanchthon's understanding of the fathers see E. P. Meijering, *Melanchthon and Patristic Thought: The Doctrines of Christ and Grace, the Trinity and the Creation*, Studies in the History of Christian Thought 32 (Leiden: Brill, 1984).

9. It was probably at this time that, with Mysos's help, he began translating the *Augsburg Confession* into Greek.

10. Philip Melanchthon, *Loci Communes*, trans. J. A. O. Preus (St. Louis: Concordia Publishing House, 1992), 29.

11. Ibid., 30.

12. Ibid., 21.

13. Martin Chemnitz, *Loci Theologici*, vol 1, trans. J. A. O. Preus (St. Louis: Concordia Publishing House, 1989), 142.

14. Ibid., 143.

15. Ibid.

16. Ibid., 144.

17. Ibid.

18. Ibid.

19. Martin Chemnitz, Jacob Andreae, and David Chytraeus, "Formula of Concord: Solid Declaration" in *The Book of Concord*, 605.

20. This was especially true of Michael Servetus, who had criticized the doctrine of the Trinity. After his condemnation by the French Inquisition, Servetus fled to Geneva, where he was recognized and arrested after attending one of Calvin's sermons. In 1553 he was tried and sentenced to burn at the stake as a heretic, although Calvin tried to change the mode of death to beheading. In 1554 Calvin justified Servetus's execution in his *Defensio orthodoxae fidei de sacra Trinitate contra prodigiosos errores Michaelis Serveti* (*Defense of Orthodox Faith against the Prodigious Errors of the Spaniard Michael Servetus*), calling him a madman who "promulgated false and thoroughly heretical doctrines." The complete works of Servetus are found in Angel

Alcala, ed., *Miguel Servet: Obras Completas* (Zaragoza, Spain: Prensas Universitarias de Zaragoza, 2003–7). An English translation of his trinitarian writings are found in Michael Servetus, *The Two Treatises of Servetus on the Trinity*, trans. Earl Morse Wilbur (Cambridge, Mass.: Harvard University Press,1932). For more on Servetus see Roland H. Bainton, *Hunted Heretic: The Life and Death of Michael Servetus 1511–1553* (Gloucester, Mass.: Smith, 1978); Marian Hillar, *Michael Servetus: Intellectual Giant, Humanist, and Martyr* (Lanham, Md.: University Press of America, 2002); idem, *The Case of Michael Servetus: The Turning Point in the Struggle for Freedom of Conscience* (Lewiston, N.Y.: Edwin Mellen Press, 1997).

21. John Calvin, *Institutes of the Christian Religion* vol 1, ed. John McNeill, Library of Christian Classics 10 (Philadelphia: Westminster Press, 1960), 143.

22. Ibid.

23. Calvin, like Gregory of Nazianzus, recognized that not everyone was well suited to certain aspects of theological inquiry and that trinitarian speculation was "to certain minds more difficulty and trouble than is expedient," Ibid., 146.

24. Ibid., 538.

25. Ibid., 541.

26. Ibid., 538.

27. Ibid.

28. John Calvin, "French Confession of Faith," in Jaroslav Pelikan and Valerie Hotchkiss, eds., *Creeds and Confessions of Faith in the Christian Tradition* 2 (New Haven, Conn: Yale University Press, 2003), 376–77.

29. For example: *The Belgic Confession* (1561): "We believe and confess that the Holy Ghost proceeds eternally from the Father and the Son . . . neither made nor created, nor begotten, but only proceeding from the two of them," Ibid., 411; *The Second Helvetic Confession* (1566): "The Holy Spirit truly proceeds from them both . . . and is to be worshipped with both," Ibid., 463; *The Thirty-nine Articles of the Church of England* (1571): "The Holy Ghost, proceeding from the Father and the Son, is of one substance, majesty, and glory with the Father and the Son," Ibid., 529; *The Westminster Confession* (1647): "The Father is of none, neither begotten nor proceeding; the Son is eternally begotten of the Father; the Holy Spirit eternally proceeding from the Father and the Son," Ibid., 609.

30. See Dorthea Wendebourg, *Reformation und Orthodoxie: der okumenische Briefwechsel zwischen der Leitung der Württembergischen Kirche und Patriarch Jeremias II. von Konstantinopel in den Jahren 1573–1581* (Göttingen, Germany: Vandenhoeck & Ruprecht, 1986). Eng. trans. of the correspondence is found in George Mastrantonis, *Augsburg and Constantinople: The Correspondence Between the Tübingen Theologians and Patriarch Jeremiah II of Constantinople on the Augsburg Confession* (Brookline, Mass.: Holy Cross Orthodox Press, 1982).

31. George Mastrantonis, *Augsburg and Constantinople*, 32.

32. Ibid., 32–33.

33. Ibid., 103.

34. Ibid., 117.

35. Ibid., 118. The key biblical texts in their argument were John 10:30, 15:26, 16:14, Romans 1:4, and Ephesians 5:25–26.

36. Ibid., 119–20.

37. Ibid., 120.

38. Ibid., 162.

39. Ibid.

40. Ibid., 173.

41. Ibid., 224, 227.

42. Ibid., 225.

43. Ibid., 232.

44. Ibid., 234. It is interesting to note that the Lutherans rejected as "absurd" the notion of procession διὰ τοῦ Υἱοῦ "since for us it is not customary to speak thus"; Ibid., 237.

45. Ibid., 239.

46. Ibid., 290.

47. Ibid., 306.

48. Also anathematized were those who do "not confess that at the Mystery of the Holy Communion the laity must also partake of both kinds," those who say "that our Lord Jesus Christ at the Mystic Supper had unleavened bread [made without yeast], like that of the Jews," those who claim "that the souls of Christians who repented while in the world but failed to perform their penance go to a purgatory of fire when they die," and those who profess "that the Pope is the head of the Church, and not Christ, and that he has authority to admit persons to Paradise with his letters of indulgence or other passports"; MS Codex No. 772 of the Monastery of St. Panteleimon.

49. Ibid.

50. Deno Geanakopolos, "An Overlooked Post-Byzantine Plan for Religious Union with Rome: Maximos Margounios the Cretan Humanist-Bishop and His Latin Library Bequeathed to Mt. Athos," in *Byzantine East and Latin West: Two Worlds of Christendom in the Middle Ages and Renaissance* (Oxford: Blackwell, 1966), 165. See also Giorgio Fedalto, *Massimo Margunio e il suo commento al 'De Trinitate' di S. Agostino (1588)* (Brescia, Italy: Paideia, 1968); idem, *Massimo Margounios e la sua opera per conciliare la sentenza degli Orientali e dei Latini sulla Processione dello Spirito Santo* (Padua, Italy: Tip. del Seminario, 1961).

51. Deno Geanakopolos, "An Overlooked Post-Byzantine Plan for Religious Union with Rome," 171.

52. The Venetians, however, refused to hand him over, claiming that under Venetian law the Orthodox enjoyed the freedom to practice their own faith.

53. Deno Geanakopolos, "An Overlooked Post-Byzantine Plan for Religious Union with Rome," 172.

54. In 1476 Metropolitan Mysail and other hierarchs of the Church of Kiev sent a lengthy letter to Pope Sixtus IV claiming that "there is no difference among Greeks and Latins concerning Christ" and that both are part of "one and the same faith . . . called to live according to their respective traditions." Although Mysail claimed allegiance to the Florentine union, he signed the letter "metropolitan-elect" since his appointment had not yet been confirmed by the Constantinopolitan patriarch, whose jurisdiction over him he continued to recognize.

55. See his *On the Unity of the Church of God under the One Shepherd and on the Greek Separation from that Unity*, in Piotr Skarga, *O jedności Kościoła Bozègo pod jednym pasterzem i o greckiem i ruskiem od tej jedności odstapieniu* (Krakow, 1885).

56. The motives of the Ruthenian hierarchy have long been the subject of debate, and judgment has often been along denominational lines—Roman and Eastern Catholics claiming that they desired only a renewal of the Church, Orthodox Christians maintaining the union was achieved for political ends (i.e., separating the Ukraine from Russian influence). See Josef Macha, *Ecclesiastical Unification: A Theoretical Framework together with Case Studies from the History of Latin-Byzantine Relations*, Orientalia Christiana Analecta 198 (Rome: Pontifical Oriental Institute, 1974); Oscar Halecki, *From Florence to Brest (1439–1596)* (Rome: Sacrum Poloniae Millennium, 1958).

57. *Articles of Union* 1, as cited in Borys Gudziak, *Crisis and Reform: The Kyivan Metropolitanate, the Patriarchate of Constantinople, and the Genesis of the Union of Brest* (Cambridge, Mass.: Harvard University Press, 1998), 264. Other conditions included the retention of their traditional rites (e.g., ringing the bells on Good Friday), keeping a married clergy, freedom from participating in Latin customs (e.g., blessing the Easter fire and processing for Corpus Christi), the right always to have bishops consecrated without mandate from Rome, and "parity of esteem and privilege" between Eastern and Roman clergy.

58. Pope Clement VIII, *Magnus Dominus* in Atanasij Hryhorij Velykyj, *Documenta Unionis Berestensis eiusque auctorum* : (1590–1600) (Rome: Basiliani, 1970), 217–26. Within a few years many of the Eastern Churches in union with Rome would, in fact, insert the *filioque* under pressure to conform to the Latin practice. However, following the Second Vatican Council there was an effort among Eastern Catholics to shed many of the "latinizations" that had crept into their churches, leading to the excision of the *filioque* where it had occurred.

59. See Colin Davey, *Pioneer for Unity: Metrophanes Kritopoulos, 1589–1639, and Relations Between the Orthodox, Roman Catholic and Reformed Churches* (London: British Council of Churches, 1987). Although the Anglican Church had, in large part, embraced the *filioque*, there were, even in the seventeenth century, theologians willing to consider the Greek case. See John Pearson, *An Exposition of the Creed* (London: Bell, 1857), 492–96; Edward Stillingfleet, *A Rational Account of the Grounds of the Protestant Religion* in *Complete Works* (Oxford, 1844).

60. Ioannes Karmires, *Ta dogmatika kai symbolika mnemeia tes orthodoxou katholikes ekklesias* (Graz, Austria: Akademische Druck- und Verlagsanstalt, 1968), 73, as cited in Jaroslav Pelikan, *Credo: Historical and Theological Guide to Creeds and Confessions of Faith in the Christian Tradition* (New Haven, Conn.: Yale University Press, 2003), 421.

61. Metrophanes Kritopoulos, "Confession of Faith," in Jaroslav Pelikan and Valerie Hotchkiss, eds., *Creeds and Confessions of Faith in the Christian Tradition* 1, 479.

62. Ibid.

63. Ibid., 484.

64. Ibid., 485.

65. Ibid., 488.

66. See George Hadjiantoniou, *Protestant Patriarch: The Life of Cyril Lucaris* (Richmond, Va.: John Knox Press, 1961); Gloys Pechler, *Geschichte des Protestantisme in der orientischen Kirche im XVII Jahrhundert order der Patriarch Cyrill Lukaris und seine Zeit* (Munich, 1862); George P. Michaelides, "The Greek Orthodox Position on the Confession of Cyril Lucaris," *Church History* 12 (June 1943): 118–29; J. Mihalcesco, "Les idées calvinistes du patriarche Cyrille Lucaris," *Revue d'hist* (1931): 506–20; Carnegie Samuel Calian, "Patriarch Lucaris's Calvinistic Confession," in *Theology Without Boundaries: Encounters of Eastern Orthodoxy and Western Tradition* (Louisville, Ky.: Westminister/John Knox Press, 1992); Lukas Vischer, "The Legacy of Kyrill Lukaris: A Contribution to the Orthodox-Reformed Dialogue," *Mid-Stream* 25 (1986): 165–83; J. M. Hornus, "Cyrille Lukaris: À propos d'un livre recent," *Proche Orient Chrétien*, Tome 13 (1963).

67. Text found in Jaroslav Pelikan and Valerie Hotchkiss, eds., *Creeds and Confessions of Faith in the Christian Tradition* 1, 549–58.

68. Jaroslav Pelikan, *The Christian Tradition* 2, 282–83. Arguments for and against Lukaris's authorship can be found in George P. Michaelides, "The Greek Orthodox Position on the Confession of Cyril Lucaris," 118–29.

69. Cyril Lukaris, "Confession of Faith," in Jaroslav Pelikan and Valerie Hotchkiss, eds., *Creeds and Confessions of Faith in the Christian Tradition* 1, 551.

70. The patriarch's enemies, including Cyril Kontaris (later Patriarch Cyril II) and the Jesuits, frequently conspired together against him—Kontaris offering the Turks 20,000 thalers, the papacy allegedly giving over 50,000 crowns in exchange for Lukaris's life. Lukaris's body was thrown in the sea, where it was washed ashore and secretly buried by his supporters. Only later, under Patriarch Parthenius, was he granted an honorable burial.

71. For Mogila see William K. Medlin and Christos G. Patrinelis's *Renaissance Influences and Religious Reforms in Russia: Western and Post-Byzantine Impacts on Culture and Education, Sixteenth-Seventeenth Centuries* (Geneva, Switzerland: Librairie Droz, 1971), 124–49; Georges Florovsky, *Ways of Russian Theology*, The Collected Works of George Florovsky vol. 5 (Vaduz, Switzerland: Büchervertriebsanstalt, 1979), 64–78; S. I. Golubev, *Kievskii Mitropolit Petr Mogila i ego spodvizhniki* (Kiev, 1883–1898); Émile Picot, "Pierre Movila (Mogila)," in *Bibliographie hellénique, ou Description raisonnée des ouvrages publiés par des Grecs au dix-septième siècle*, vol. 4, ed. Émile Legrand (Paris, 1896), 104–59; Téofil Ionesco, *La vie et l'œuvre de Pierre Movila, métropolite de Kiev* (Paris, 1944).

72. Kallistos Ware, *The Orthodox Church* (New York: Penguin Press, 1991), 97.

73. "We find the said book to be set in the footsteps of the Church of Christ, and to be agreeable to the holy canons, from which it differs not in any part. . .. We do therefore, with our unanimous and synodical sentence, decree and ordain that every pious and orthodox Christian who is a member of the Eastern and Apostolic Church do attentively, and sedulously, read and receive the said book"; Jaroslav Pelikan and Valerie Hotchkiss, eds., *Creeds and Confessions of Faith in the Christian Tradition* 1, 561.

74. This was the edited version of the text, revised by Meletius Syrigos, who had found Mogila's teaching on the moment of consecration and purgatory too "Roman."

75. Peter Mogila, "Orthodox Confession," in Jaroslav Pelikan and Valerie Hotchkiss, eds., *Creeds and Confessions of Faith in the Christian Tradition* 1, 565.

76. Ibid., 591.

77. Ibid., 592.

78. Patriarch Dositheus, "Confession," in Jaroslav Pelikan and Valerie Hotchkiss, eds., *Creeds and Confessions of Faith in the Christian Tradition* 1, 615. See also J. N. W. B. Robertson, *The Acts and Decrees of the Synod of Jerusalem* (New York: AMS Press, 1969).

79. Jaroslav Pelikan, *Credo*, 422.

80. Philaret of Moscow, "Longer Catechism of the Orthodox, Catholic, Eastern Church," in R. W. Blackmore, *Doctrine of the Russian Church* (London: J. Masters and Co., 1905), 73–74.

81. R. Raikes Bromage, ed., *The Holy Catechism of Nicolas Bulgaris* (London: J. Masters and Co., 1893), 172.

82. Gregory XIII, "Professio fidei Graecis praescripta," in Henry Denzinger, ed., *The Sources of Catholic Dogma* (St. Louis: Herder, 1957), 312.

83. Benedict XIV, *Nuper ad nos*, in Henry Denzinger, ed., *The Sources of Catholic Dogma* (St. Louis: Herder, 1957), 359.

84. Ibid.

85. Benedict XIV, *Etsi Pastoralis*.

86. Benedict XIV, *Allae Sunt*, in Claudia Carlen, ed., *Papal Encyclicals 1740–1878* (New York: Consortium Press, 1981), 65.

87. Ibid.

88. Ibid.

89. Ibid.

90. Ibid., 66. Although the purpose of the encyclical was to discourage the forced latinization of Greek Catholics, this was not because Rome believed in the equality of the Greek and Latin rites. According to the encyclical, "Since the Latin rite is the rite of the holy Roman church and this church is mother and teacher of the other churches, the Latin rite should be preferred to all other rites. It follows that it is not lawful to transfer from the Latin to the Greek rite. . . . Transferrals in the opposite direction are not forbidden as strictly as the former"; ibid., 58.

91. Ibid., 66.

92. It should be noted that Döllinger's personal relationship to the "Old Catholic Church" formed after the Union of Utrecht was never clearly defined. For more see Alfred Plummer, *Conversations with Dr. Döllinger, 1870–1890* (Leuven, Belgium: Leuven University Press, 1985); C.B. Moss, *The Old Catholic Movement: Its Origins and History* (Berkeley, Calif.: Apocryphile Press, 2005); Urs Küry, *Die Altkatholische Kirche. Ihre Geschichte, ihre Lehre, ihr Anliegen* (Stuttgart, Germany: Evangelisches Verlagswerk, 1966).

93. See Heinrich Reusch, *Report of the Union Conferences Held from August 10 to 16, 1875 at Bonn*, trans. Samuel Buel (New York: T. Whittaker, 1876); E. Pusey, *On the Clause "And the Son" in regard to the Eastern Church and the Bonn Conference* (Oxford, 1876); E. Michaud, "L'état de la question du 'Filioque' après la Conférence de Bonn de 1875," *Revue internationale de Théologie* 3 (1895), 89–99; J. J. Overbeck, "The Bonn Conferences, and the *Filioque* Question," *Orthodox Catholic Review* 4 (1875): 217–64; idem, *Die Bonner Unions-Konferenzen* (Halle, Germany,1876).

94. Heinrich Reusch, *Report of the Union Conferences Held from August 10 to 16, 1875 at Bonn*, xxxiii. The revised text, added to the preface, read: "The way in which the

filioque was inserted in the Nicene Creed was illegal, and that, with a view to future peace and unity it is much desired that the whole Church should set itself seriously to consider whether the Creed could possibly be restored to its primitive form without sacrifice of any true doctrine expressed in the present Western form"; in Jaroslav Pelikan and Valerie Hotchkiss, eds., *Creeds and Confessions of Faith in the Christian Tradition* 3, 366.

95. Heinrich Reusch, *Report of the Union Conferences*, 35.

96. William Steven Perry, *The Union Conference at Bonn: A Personal Narrative* (privately published, 1875), 10.

97. Heinrich Reusch, *Report of the Union Conferences*, 115.

98. Ibid., 111.

99. Ibid., 17. Augustine's idea of *principatiter procedere* appeared to the Greeks to be the closest Latin equivalent to ἐκπορεύεσθαι Ibid., 88.

100. Ibid.

101. Ibid., 134.

102. Ibid., 136.

103. The two commissions exchanged three sets of findings over the next decade. Many of these were published in Urs Küry, "Die letzte Antwort der orthodoxen Petersburger Kommission an die altkatholische Rotterdamer Kommission," *Internationale kirchliche Zeitschrift* 58 (1968): 29–47, 81–108. See also Christian Oeyen, "Chronologisch-bibliographischen Übersicht der Unionsverhandlungen zwischen orthodoxer Kirche und altkatholischer Kirche," *Internationale kirchliche Zeitschrift* 57 (1967): 29–51.

104. In 1868 Pope Pius addressed another letter to the Orthodox bishops (*Arcano Divinae Providentiae consilio*), asking for their return to the Catholic fold and participation in the upcoming council.

105. *Encyclical of the Eastern Patriarchs: A Reply to the Epistle of Pope Pius IX*, in Jaroslav Pelikan and Valerie Hotchkiss, eds., *Creeds and Confessions of Faith in the Christian Tradition* 3, 266.

106. Ibid., 268.

107. Ibid., 267.

108. Ibid.

109. Ibid., 269.

110. Ibid., 270–71.

111. Quoted in Theodoret, *Ecclesiastical History* 5.11 (Eng. trans.: NPNF 2.3.140).

112. Ibid.

113. Leo XIII, *Praeclara Gratulationis Publicae* in *Leonis XIII Pontificis Maximi Acta*, vol. 14 (Graz, Austria: Akademische Druck, 1971), 195.

114. Ibid., 201–2.

115. Anthimos VII, *A Reply to the Papal Encyclical of Pope Leo XIII on Reunion*, in Eustathius Metallinos, ed., *Orthodox and Catholic Union* (Seattle: St. Nectarios Press, 1985).

116. Ibid., 2.

117. Ibid., 4.

118. Ibid.

119. Ibid., 5.

120. Basil Bolotov, *"Thesen über das Filioque von einem russischen Theologen,"* Revue *internationale de Théologie* 6 (1898): 681–712. The theses were given an English translation in Yves Congar, *I Believe in the Holy Spirit* 3 (New York: Crossroad Publishing, 1997), 194–95.

121. Yves Congar, *I Believe in the Holy Spirit* 3 (New York: Crossroad Publishing, 1997), 194.

122. Ibid.

123. Ibid.

124. Ibid.

125. Ibid.

126. Ibid., 195.

127. Ibid. Bolotov defined in the article what he understood a *theologoumenon* to be:

> In essence it is also a theological opinion, but only the opinion of those who for every catholic are more than just theologians: they are the theological opinions of the holy fathers of the one undivided church; they are the opinions of those men, among whom are those who are fittingly called "ecumenical doctors." *Theologoumena* I rate highly, but I do not in any case exaggerate their significance, and I think that I "quite sharply" distinguish them from dogmas. The content of a dogma is truth: the content of a *theologoumena* is only what is probable. The realm of a dogma is *necessaria,* the realm of a *theologoumena* is *dubia: In necessariis unitas, in dubiis libertas!"* (Basil Bolotov, *"Thesen* über *das Filioque von einem russischen Theologen,"* 682.)

128. Ibid. Bolotov affirmed "without evasion" that the papacy, not the *filioque,* was responsible for "sundering the communion of the one catholic Church."

129. Kireev was on friendly terms with the Old Catholic theologian Abbé Eugène-Philibert Michaud, with whom he corresponded for many years. See J. H. Morgan, "Early Orthodox—Old Catholic Relations: General Kireeff and Professor Michaud," *The Church Quarterly Review* 152 (1951): 1–10. For Kireev's views see "Erklärungen von Professor Ossinin in München und Bonn (1871 und 1875)" *Revue Internationale de Théologie* 4 (1896): 489–501; idem, "Une replique du Général Kiréeff à M. le Prof. Gousseff sur l'ancien-catholicisme," *Revue Internationale de Théologie* 6 (1898): 124–29; idem, "Zur altkatholischen Frage," *Revue Internationale de Théologie* 5 (1897): 847–50. A good summary of the debate can be found in Maria-Helene Gamillscheg, *Die Kontroverse um das Filioque: Moglichkeiten einer Problemlosung auf Grund der Forschungen und Gespräche der letzten hundert Jahre* (Würzburg, Germany: Augustinus-Verlag, 1996), 85–100. For ecumenical debates in Russia see George Florovsky, "Russian Orthodox Ecumenism in the Nineteenth Century," in *Ecumenism II: The Collected Works of George Florovsky* 14 (Vaduz, Switzerland: Büchervertriebsanstalt, 1989), 110–63.

130. Gusev argued that the positive dogma contained in the creed (i.e., that the Holy Spirit proceeds from the Father) had a negative side as well—that is, if he comes from the Father, then from whom does he not come? If the *filioque* led to an unacceptable answer to this question (and by the illegitimate attribution of causality to someone other than the Father, it does), then the Eastern Church was right to adopt the negative

dogma that he proceeds from the Father alone in order to protect the true faith. See Dimitri Gusev, "Nochmals zur Verständigung: Antwort an Herrn Prof. Gussew an der Akademie zu Kasan," *Revue Internationale de Théologie* 10 (1902): 1–20, 436–46, 447–75.

NOTES TO CHAPTER 10

1. Joachim III, "Patriarchal and Synodical Letter of 1902," in Gennadius Limouris, ed., *Orthodox Visions of Ecumenism: Statements, Messages, and Reports on the Ecumenical Movement 1902–1992* (Geneva: World Council of Churches, 1994), 2–3.

2. Ibid. As to the orthodoxy of the Old Catholic confession (especially on the *filioque*), Joachim wrote:

> Various opinions about it are expressed by our churchmen, both by those who have known them at close quarters and also by those who have studied them at a distance: some of them have decided that on important dogmatic points this confession is still far from perfect Orthodoxy, and others on the contrary consider it not to contain essential differences which would preclude unity of faith and ecclesiastical communion. (Ibid., 3–4)

3. Joachim III, "Response to the Reactions of the Local Orthodox Churches," in Gennadius Limouris, ed., *Orthodox Visions of Ecumenism: Statements, Messages, and Reports on the Ecumenical Movement, 1902–1992* (Geneva: World Council of Churches, 1994), 7.

4. Examples of this close relationship include the establishment of the Fellowship of St. Alban and St. Sergius in 1928. See Nicolas and Militza Zernov, *The Fellowship of St. Alban and St. Sergius: A Historical Memoir* (Oxford, 1979). Historically the most problematic issue between the Orthodox and Anglicans has been the recognition of Anglican orders. Although the Ecumenical Patriarchate recognized in 1922 that Anglican orders "possessed the same validity as those of the Roman, Old Catholic, and Armenian Churches," and similar recognition was given by the Patriarchates of Jerusalem (1923) and Alexandria (1930), in 1948 the Moscow Patriarchate came to the conclusion that Anglican orders were invalid.

5. *The Episcopal and Greek Churches: Report of an Unofficial Conference on Unity between Members of the Episcopal Church in America and His Grace, Meletios Metaxakis, Metropolitan of Athens, and His Advisers. October 26, 1918* (New York: Dept. of Missions and Church Extension of the Episcopal Church, 1920).

6. Ibid.

7. Ibid.

8. Ecumenical Patriarchate, "Unto the Churches of Christ Everywhere" in Gennadius Limouris, ed., *Orthodox Visions of Ecumenism*, 9–11. This is widely acknowledged to be the genesis of the World Council of Churches, which was established in 1948 with the participation of the Ecumenical Patriarchate. The Moscow Patriarchate did not participate, seeing the mission of the WCC to be at odds with "the ideal of Christianity or the aims of the Church of Christ as understood by the Orthodox Church." The Moscow Patriarchate did not become a WCC member until 1961.

298 NOTES TO PAGES 195–196

9. Vasileios Istavridis, *Orthodoxy and Anglicanism in the Twentieth Century* (London: Faith Press for the Anglican and Eastern Churches Association, 1959), 36. In 1925, at the commemoration of the 1600th anniversary of the Council of Nicea, Metropolitan Germanos (the official representative of the Ecumenical Patriarchate) and Patriarch Photius of Alexandria recited the unaltered creed in Westminster Abbey together with the Anglican clergy and faithful. This "constituted an unprecedented event in the history of the Orthodox Church . . . for which the popular Orthodox mind was completely unprepared"; ibid., 44.

10. Resolutions of the 1930 Lambeth Conference 33a.

11. See *Report of the Joint Doctrinal Commission appointed by the Oecumenical Patriarch and the Archbishop of Canterbury for Consultation on the Points of Agreement and Difference between the Anglican and the Eastern Orthodox Churches* (London: S.P.C.K., 1932).

12. Nicholas of Hermopolis, "Report to the Holy Synod of Constantinople of the Church of Alexandria upon the First Session," *The Christian East* (1933): 87–91.

13. Both sides were clear that "this does not require from either communion the acceptance of all doctrinal opinion, sacramental devotion, or liturgical practice characteristic of the other, but implies that each believes the other to hold all the essentials of the Christian Faith." "Statement Agreed between the Representatives of the Old Catholic Churches and the Churches of the Anglican Communion," in Harding Meyer and Lukas Vischer, eds., *Growth in Agreement: Reports and Agreed Statements of Ecumenical Conversations on a World Level* (New York: Paulist Press, 1994), 37.

14. According to Bishop Moog of the Old Catholic Church, the liturgical books in Germany and Austria still contained the *filioque* (albeit in brackets) but it would be deleted in future editions. See "Proceedings of the Conferences between the Old Catholic and Orthodox Churches, held at Bonn, on October 27th and 28th, 1931," *The Christian East* 13 (1932): 91–98.

15. Ibid. According to Kallistos Ware, in spite of the apparent agreement reached at Bonn, "no concrete steps have yet been taken [by the Orthodox] to establish visible unity. From the Orthodox standpoint a complicating factor is the relationship of full communion that has existed since 1931 between the Old Catholics and the Anglicans. Thus the question of Old Catholic/Anglican union cannot be settled in isolation." Kallistos Ware, *The Orthodox Church* (New York: Penguin Press, 1991), 317.

16. See Rowan Williams, *Sergii Bulgakov: Towards a Russian Political Theology* (Edinburgh: T & T Clark, 1999); Paul Valliere, *Modern Russian Theology: Bukharev, Soloviev, Bulgakov* (Grand Rapids, Mich.: Eerdmann's, 2000); Thomas Hopko, "Receiving Fr. Bulgakov," *St. Vladimir's Theological Quarterly* 42 (1998): 373–83; Myroslaw Tataryn, "Sergius Bulgakov: Time for a New Look," *St. Vladimir's Theological Quarterly* 42 (1998): 315–38; Catherine Evtuhov, *The Cross and the Sickle: Sergei Bulgakov and the Fate of Russian Religious Philosophy* (Ithaca, NY.: Cornell University Press, 1997); Nicholas Zernov, *The Russian Religious Renaissance of the Twentieth Century* (New York: Harper and Row, 1963).

17. Sergius Bulgakov, *The Comforter* (Grand Rapids: Eerdmans, 2004), 75.

18. Ibid., 92.

19. Ibid., 127.

20. Ibid.

21. Ibid.

22. Ibid., 132.

23. Ibid., 148.

24. Ibid., 149.

25. Vladimir Lossky, "The Procession of the Holy Spirit in Orthodox Trinitarian Doctrine," 88. This was based on his 1947 Oxford lecture and became his most famous work on the subject. In a series of unpublished lectures, delivered between 1953 and 1956, Lossky developed many of the themes of the earlier work. References to these lectures can be found in Oliver Clément, *Orient-Occident, Deux Passeurs: Vladimir Lossky et Paul Endokimov* (Geneva: Labor et Fides 1985)), 76–89.

26. Ibid., 73.

27. Ibid., 77.

28. Ibid.

29. Ibid., 76.

30. Ibid., 78.

31. Ibid., 90–91.

32. Ibid., 91–92.

33. Ibid., 94.

34. Ibid., 95.

35. Ibid., 96.

36. Aside from Staniloae, Clément, and Brobrinskoy there are Paul Endokimov, *L'Esprit Saint dans la tradition orthodoxe* (Paris: Éditions du Cerf, 1969) and Nikos Nissiotis, "Pneumatologie orthodoxe," in F. J. Leenhard, ed., *Le Saint-Esprit* (Geneva, Labor et Fides, 1963), 85–106.

37. Dimitru Staniloae, *Theology and the Church*, trans. Robert Barringer (Crestwood, N.Y.: St. Vladimir's Seminary Press, 1980), 96.

38. Ibid. See Maximus the Confessor, *Quaestiones ad Thalassium* 13 (Carl Laga and Carlos Steel, eds, *Quaestiones ad Thalassium*, 97).

39. Ibid., 100. Paul Endokimov, meditating upon the Rublev icon, wrote in similar terms about the Holy Spirit: "He is in the middle of the Father and the Son. He is the one who brings about the communion between the two. He is the communion, the love between the Father and the Son. That is clearly shown by the remarkable fact that the movement comes from him. It is in his breath that the Father moves into the Son, that the Son receives his Father and that the word resounds." Paul Endokimov, "L'icone," *La vie spirituelle* 82 (1956): 24.

40. Ibid., 103.

41. On the basis of this understanding, Staniloae recognized the "orthodoxy" of certain reunion formulas then being proposed in the West, including the idea that "the Spirit proceeds from the Father who begets the Son" and "In taking his origin [ἐκπορευόμενον] from the one Father who begets the one Son, the Spirit proceeds [πρόεισι] out of the Father as origin, by his Son." However he "judged it preferable not to use the word 'proceed' for the relation of the Spirit to the Son, since it can give the impression of a confusion of this relation with the procession of the Spirit from the Father." Instead he suggested "terms which have been used by the Eastern fathers" such as "'shines out from' or 'is manifested by.'" Dumitru Staniloae, "The Procession

of the Holy Spirit from the Father and His Relation to the Son as the Basis of Our Deification and Adoption," in Lukas Vischer, ed., *Spirit of God, Spirit of Christ* (London: S.P.C.K., 1981), 177.

42. Dimitru Staniloae, *Theology and the Church*, 104.

43. Dumitru Staniloae, "The Procession of the Holy Spirit from the Father and His Relation to the Son as the Basis of Our Deification and Adoption," 175.

44. Dimitru Staniloae, *Theology and the Church*, 107.

45. Ibid.

46. Oliver Clément, *Essor du christianisme oriental* (Paris: Presses Universitaires de France, 1964), 18. See also "La question du 'filioque' et de la procession du Saint-Esprit," *Messager de l'Exarchat du Patriarche russe en Europe Occidentale* 75–76 (1971): 171–90.

47. Ibid.

48. Ibid.

49. Oliver Clément, *The Roots of Christian Mysticism*, trans. Theodore Berkeley (London: New City, 1993), 72.

50. Oliver Clément, *Byzance et le christianisme* (Paris: Presses Universitaires de France, 1964), 47 (Eng. trans.: Boris Bobrinskoy, *The Mystery of the Trinity*, 290).

51. Ibid.

52. Boris Bobrinskoy, "The Filioque Yesterday and Today," in Lukas Vischer, ed., *Spirit of God, Spirit of Christ*, 142–43.

53. Ibid., 141.

54. See pp. 29–30.

55. Ibid., 145–46.

56. Ibid., 146.

57. For Romanides's views on Augustine and the *filioque* see John Romanides, *The Ancestral Sin*, trans. G. Gabriel (Ridgewood, N.J.: Zephyr Publishing, 1998); idem, *Franks, Romans, Feudalism and Doctrine: The Interplay between Theology and Society* (Brookline, Mass.: Holy Cross, 1981); idem, *An Outline of Orthodox Patristic Dogmatics*, ed. and trans. George Dragas (Rollinsford, N.H.: Orthodox Research Institute, 2004). Because Augustine is sometimes viewed as the protogenitor of the *filioque* and other theological errors (e.g., original sin), his place within the Orthodox Church remains a subject of intense debate. In 2007 Fordham University sponsored a conference on the Orthodox reception of Augustine; the proceedings are found in George Demacopoulos and Aristotle Papanikolaou, eds., *Orthodox Readings of Augustine* (Crestwood: N. Y.: St. Vladimir's Seminary Press, 2008). The introduction of this book offers a brief but insightful history of Augustine's place within Orthodoxy. For a Roman Catholic view see Aidan Nichols, "The Reception of St Augustine and His Work in the Byzantine-Slav Tradition," *Angelicum* 64 (1987): 437–52.

58. Michael Azkoul, *The Influence of Augustine of Hippo on the Orthodox Church*, Texts and Studies in Religion 56 (Lewiston, N.Y.: Edwin Mellen Press, 1990).

59. Joseph Farrell, *God, History, and Dialectic: The Theological Foundations of the Two Europes and Their Cultural Consequences* (Seven Councils Press, 1997).

60. Boris Bobrinskoy, "The Filioque Yesterday and Today," 147.

61. See, for example, Karl Rahner, "Oneness and Threefoldness of God in Discussion with Islam," *Theological Investigations* 18, trans. Edward Quinn (New York:

Crossroad, 1983), 105–21; idem, "Remarks on the Dogmatic Treatise *De Trinitate*," *Theological Investigations* 4, trans. Kevin Smyth (Baltimore: Helicon Press, 1966), 77–102; idem, *The Trinity*, trans. Joseph Donceel (New York: Herder and Herder, 1970).

62. Karl Rahner, *The Trinity*, 22.

63. Ibid., 10–11.

64. Other Orthodox theologians have looked less favorably on Rahner's work, accusing him of oversimplifying and distorting the complex relationship between theology and economy as found in the fathers. John Behr, although crediting Rahner with a renaissance in trinitarian studies, has questioned the usefulness of his *grundaxiom*, writing "It is not enough simply to assert the identity of the 'economic' Trinity and the 'immanent' Trinity, or to emphasize the 'economic' basis of our knowledge of the Trinity. . . . It is doubtful that the distinction, drawn in the manner, between 'immanent' and 'economic' trinitarian theology really corresponds, as is often asserted, to the patristic usage of '*theologia*' and '*economia*'," John Behr, *The Nicene Faith* 1, 7.

65. Zizioulas believes that Rahner admirably captured the biblical and Greek patristic notion that "the unity of God, the one God, and the ontological 'principle' or 'cause' of the being and life of God does not consist in the substance of God but in the hypostasis, that is, the person of the Father." John Zizioulas, *Being as Communion: Studies in Personhood and the Church* (Crestwood, N.Y.: St. Vladimir's Seminary Press, 1985), 40.

66. See also Gregory Havrilak, "Karl Rahner and the Greek Trinity," *St. Vladimir's Theological Quarterly* 34 (1990): 77.

67. De Lubac himself notes that the series had originally been conceived by Rev. Victor Fontoynont as "an instrument of rapprochement with the Orthodox Churches." Henri de Lubac, *At the Service of the Church: Henri de Lubac Reflects on the Circumstances that Occasioned His Writings*, trans. Anne Englund (San Francisco: Ignatius Press, 1993), 94.

68. Eng. trans.: Hans Urs von Balthasar, *Cosmic Liturgy: The Universe According to Maximus the Confessor*, trans. Brian Daley (San Francisco: Ignatius Press, 2003).

69. Reference to this work was already made in the earlier chapter on Maximus. See pp. 82–83.

70. See Juan Miguel Garrigues, *L'Espirit qui dit 'Pere': Le problème du Filioque* (Paris: Tequi, 1981); idem, "Procession et ekporèse du Saint Esprit: discernement de la tradition et reception oecuménique," *Istina* 17 (1972): 345–66; idem, "Le sens de la procession du Saint-Esprit dans la tradition latine du premier millénaire," *Contacts* 3 (1971): 283–309.

71. Juan Miguel Garrigues, "A Roman Catholic View of the Position Now Reached in the Question of the Filioque," in Lukas Vischer, ed., *Spirit of God, Spirit of Christ*, 151.

72. Ibid., 152.

73. Ibid., 160.

74. Juan Miguel Garrigues, *L'Espirit qui dit 'Pere,'* 84 (Eng. trans.: Yves Congar, *I Believe in the Holy Spirit* 3 [New York: Crossroad Publishing Co., 1997], 200).

75. André Halleux, "Orthodoxie et Catholicisme: du personnalisme en pneumatologie," *Revue théologique de Louvain* 6 (1975): 3–30; idem, "Pour un accord

oecuménique sur la procession du Saint-Esprit et l'addition du Filioque au Symbole," *Irénikon* 47 (1975): 170–77. This last article can be found translated and
expanded in "Towards an Ecumenical Agreement on the Procession of the Holy
Spirit and the Addition of the Filioque to the Creed," in Lukas Vischer, ed., *Spirit of
God, Spirit of Christ*, 149–63.

76. André Halleux, "Towards an Ecumenical Agreement on the Procession of the
Holy Spirit and the Addition of the Filioque to the Creed," 184.

77. Although he admired Palamas, Congar found himself "in disagreement with
the concepts that he uses and his metaphysical mode of expression." Yves Congar, *I
Believe in the Holy Spirit* 3, 66. Nevertheless he accepted as a legitimate *theologoumenon*
the orthodoxy of Palamas's writings on the Trinity believing that the essence–energy
distinction need not be antithetical to the Catholic system despite the claims of earlier
Catholic theologians. ibid., 61–71.

78. Ibid., 201.

79. Ibid., 213.

80. Ibid., 203.

81. Ibid., 187.

82. Ibid., 214.

83. Ibid., 206.

84. Ibid., 214. Congar was clear that this action would have to be met by the
Orthodox with a recognition of the *filioque*'s non-heretical nature. See also Yves
Congar, *Diversity and Communion*, trans. John Bowden (Mystic, Conn.: Twenty-third
Publications, 1984), 97–104.

85. Aidan Nichols, *Rome and the Eastern Churches* (Collegeville, Minn.: Michael
Glazier, 1992), 219–20. Nichols was dubious that the Church could adequately put
across the important difference between the theological truth of the *filioque* and its
removal from the creed. The suppression of the *filioque* might also call into question
the authority of the pope and "whether the Roman Church really is, as Irenaeus stated,
that church with which all other churches must concur." ibid.

86. Aidan Nichols, *Light from the East: Authors and Themes in Orthodox Theology*
(London: Sheed and Ward, 1995), 90.

87. Thomas Weinandy, *The Father's Spirit of Sonship: Reconceiving the Trinity*,
(Edinburgh: T. & T. Clark, 1995), 34.

88. Secondary literature on Barth and his influence is extensive. See, for example,
Hans Urs von Balthasar, *The Theology of Karl Barth*, trans. Edward Oakes (San
Francisco: Ignatius Press, 1992); G. C. Berkouwer, *The Triumph of Grace in the Theology
of Karl Barth* (London: Paternoster Press, 1956); Geoffrey W. Bromiley, *An Introduction
to the Theology of Karl Barth* (Edinburg: T & T Clark, 2000); Colin Brown, *Karl Barth
and the Christian Message* (Eugene, Ore: Wipf & Stock Publishers, 1998); *Eberhard
Busch, The Great Passion: An Introduction to Karl Barth* (Grand Rapids, Mich.: Eerdmans,
2005); Trevor Hart, *Regarding Karl Barth* (Downers Grove, Ill.: InterVarsity Press,
2000); George Hunsinger, *How to Read Karl Barth: The Shape of His Theology* (New
York: Oxford University Press, 1993); Eberhard Jüngel, *Karl Barth: A Theological Legacy*
(Edinburgh: Scottish Academic Press, 1987); Bruce L. McCormack, *Karl Barth's
Critically Realistic Dialectical Theology: Its Genesis and Development 1909–1936* (Oxford:
Clarendon Press, 1997); Joseph L Mangina, *Karl Barth: Theologian of Christian Witness.*

Great Theologians Series (Aldershot, UK: Ashgate, 2004); Richard A. Muller, "The Place and Importance of Karl Barth in the Twentieth Century: A Review Essay," *Westminster Theological Journal* 50 (1988): 127–56; S.W. Sykes, ed., *Karl Barth: Centenary Essays* (Cambridge: Cambridge University Press, 1989); Thomas F. Torrance, *Karl Barth: Biblical and Evangelical Theologian* (Edinburgh: T & T Clark, 1990); idem, *Karl Barth: An Introduction to His Early Theology: 1910–1931* (Edinburgh: T & T Clark, 2000); John Webster, ed., *The Cambridge Companion to Karl Barth*. Cambridge Companion to Religion (Cambridge: Cambridge University Press, 1997).

89. Karl Barth, *Church Dogmatics I.1: The Doctrine of the Word of God*, trans. G. W. Bromiley (Edinburgh: T & T Clark, 1975), 473.

90. Ibid., 478. In the *Church Dogmatics* Barth gave a brief history of the debate, alleging that "in this whole affair the battle has really been fought sharply and seriously by the Eastern Church, while the Western Church has on the whole confined itself to the defensive"; Ibid. Among present-day Orthodox, Barth thought Bolotov's solutions "incomparably saner" than those of his colleagues, believing that his position best reflected "the prevailing view in the Eastern Church today"; ibid., 479.

91. Ibid.

92. Ibid.

93. Ibid.

94. Ibid., 480.

95. Ibid., 481.

96. Ibid.

97. Ibid., 482.

98. Ibid., 484.

99. Jürgen Moltmann, "Theological Proposals towards the Resolution of the Filioque Controversy," in Lukas Vischer, ed., *Spirit of God, Spirit of Christ*, 164–73; idem, *The Trinity and the Kingdom*, trans. Margaret Kohl (San Francisco: Harper Collins, 1981), 178–87; idem, *The Spirit of Life: A Universal Affirmation*, trans. Margaret Kohl (Minneapolis: Augsburg Fortress, 1992); Joy Ann McDougall, *Pilgrimage of Love: Moltmann on the Trinity and Christian Life* (Oxford: Oxford University Press, 2005).

100. Jürgen Moltmann, *The Spirit of Life: A Universal Affirmation*, 306.

101. Jürgen Moltmann, *The Trinity and the Kingdom*, 181.

102. Jürgen Moltmann, "Theological Proposals towards the Resolution of the Filioque Controversy," 167.

103. Jürgen Moltmann, *The Trinity and the Kingdom*, 184.

104. Ibid., 185.

105. Ibid., 186.

106. Ibid., 187.

107. See especially Urs Küry, "Die Bedeutung des Filioque-Streites für den Gottesbegriff der abendländischen und der morganländischen Kirche," *Internationale kirchliche Zeitschrift* 33 (1943): 1–19; idem, "Grundsätzlich-theologischen Überlegungen zur Filioque-Frage," *Internationale kirchliche Zeitschrift* 58 (1968): 81–108.

108. "Erklärung der Internationalen Altkatholischen Bischofskonferenz zur Filioque-Frage," in *Internationale kirchliche Zeitschrift* 61 (1971): 69.

109. Ibid., 70.

110. "The Doctrine of God: Agreed Statement Joint Orthodox/Old Catholic Commission (Chambésy, 1975)," in Harding Meyer and Lukas Vischer, eds., *Growth in Agreement*, 395.

111. See H. M. Waddams, *Anglo-Russian Theological Conference: Moscow, July 1956* (London: The Faith Press, 1957).

112. Ibid., 51–52.

113. Ibid., 99.

114. Ibid., 93.

115. Kallistos Ware and Colin Davey, eds., *Anglican-Orthodox Dialogue: The Moscow Statement Agreed by the Anglican-Orthodox Joint Doctrinal Commission 1976* (London: SPCK, 1977), 87–88.

116. Ibid., 63.

117. Ibid., 62.

118. Ibid.

119. "Athens Statement of the Anglican/Orthodox Joint Doctrinal Commission (1978)," in Harding Meyer and Lukas Vischer, eds., *Growth in Agreement*, 50.

120. *Report of the Lambeth Conference 1978* (London: CIO Publishing, 1978), 51–52.

121. *Anglican-Orthodox Dialogue: The Dublin Agreed Statement 1984* (Crestwood, N.Y.: St. Vladimir's Seminary Press, 1997), 26.

122. Ibid., 27.

123. Ibid.

124. "Although the Western tradition has spoken from time to time of the Son as a cause, this language has not met with favour and has fallen into disuse"; Ibid.

125. See Lukas Vischer, ed., *Spirit of God, Spirit of Christ*.

126. Ibid., 4.

127. Ibid., 9.

128. Ibid., 9–10.

129. Ibid., 12.

130. Ibid.

131. Ibid., 13.

132. Ibid.

133. Ibid., 15.

134. Ibid., 15–16.

135. Ibid., 17

136. Ibid., 18.

137. See Stelios Castanos de Médicis, *Athénagoras Ier: l'Apport de L'Orthodoxie à l'Oecuménisme* (Lausanne: Editions l'Age d'Homme, 1968); Demetrius Tsakonas, *A Man Sent by God: A Life of Patriarch Athenagoras of Constantinople*, trans. George Angeloglou (Brookline, Mass.: Holy Cross Orthodox Press, 1977); Aristide Panotis, *Les Pacificateurs: Jean XXIII-Athénagoras-Paul VI-Dimitrios* (Athens: Dragon, 1974); Peter Hebblethwaite, *John XXIII* (London: Chapman, 1984).

138. The many written exchanges between Rome and Constantinople have been collected in the *Tomos Agapis* ("Book of Love"). Eng. trans. in: E. J. Stormon, ed., *Towards the Healing of the Schism: The Sees of Rome and Constantinople*, Ecumenical Documents 3 (New York: Paulist Press, 1987). Rome's commitment to ecumenism,

expressed in the conciliar document *Unitatis Reintegratio*, focused particular attention on the Church's unique relationship to the Orthodox, who, "although separated from us, yet possess true sacraments and above all, by apostolic succession, the priesthood and the Eucharist, whereby they are linked with us in closest intimacy." For this reason the meeting in Jerusalem (the first meeting of a pope and patriarch since the Council of Ferrara-Florence) was considered an important ecumenical moment. Unlike the 1438 meeting of Patriarch Joseph and Pope Eugene, the Roman party never broached the possibility of Athenagoras's kissing the pope's foot, opting instead for a fraternal embrace. In fact, eleven years later in Rome (December 14, 1975), when Metropolitan Meliton (representing Patriarch Dimitrios I) announced the renewal of theological dialogue between the two churches, Paul VI knelt down to kiss *his* foot, proclaiming, "Blessed are the feet of those who bring good news."

139. For a history of these churches in the twentieth century, many of which had entered into communion with Rome at the Synod of Brest in 1596, see Serge Keleher, *Passion and Resurrection: The Greek Catholic Church in Soviet Ukraine 1939–1989* (L'viv, Ukraine: Stauropegion, 1993). In 1946 Josef Stalin arranged for the Eastern Catholic hierarchy to be incorporated into the Orthodox Patriarchate of Moscow at the (pseudo) Synod of L'viv. The Eastern Catholic churches were closed or given over to Orthodox control, and dissenting clergy were either killed, sent to prison, or forced to minister underground. Similar "reunion" synods were held in Transcarpathia (1947), Romania (1948), and Slovakia (1950). In the wake of the revolutions of 1989 and the restoration of religious freedom in the Soviet Union, these Eastern Catholics (many of whom had for decades been nominally "Orthodox") reemerged and demanded the restoration of their churches. Disagreement (sometimes violent) over the ownership of seized church properties forced the Catholic and Orthodox hierarchies to address the issue of Uniatism and the possibility for a peaceful resolution to these tensions. Although the Joint International Commission issued a document in 1993 to address the problem ("Uniatism, Method of Union of the Past, and the Present Search for Full Commun- ion," better known as the "Balamand Statement"), it remains, as of this writing, unresolved. The Moscow Patriarchate continues to accuse the Catholic Church of "proselytizing"—that is, turning Orthodox Christians into Eastern Catholics—which is why Patriarch Alexei II (1990–2008) refused to meet with either Pope John Paul II or Benedict XVI. The establishment of four Catholic dioceses in Russia in 2002 and the decision of the Greek Catholics to move the archbishopric from L'viv to Kiev in the hopes of making it a patriarchate, have only complicated matters further.

140. Eng. trans. found in: "The Greek and Latin Traditions Regarding the Procession of the Holy Spirit," *Catholic International* 7 (1996): 36–43.

141. "The Latin tradition of the Creed confesses that the Spirit "proceeds from the Father *and the Son (filioque)*." The Council of Florence in 1438 explains:

> The Holy Spirit is eternally from Father and Son; He has his nature and subsist- ence at once [*simul*] from the Father and the Son. He proceeds eternally from both as from one principle and through one spiration. . . . And, since the Father has through generation given to the only-begotten Son everything that belongs to the Father, except being Father, the Son has also eternally from the Father, from whom he is eternally born, that the Holy Spirit proceeds from the Son.

At the outset the Eastern tradition expresses the Father's character as first origin of the Spirit. By confessing the Spirit as he "who proceeds from the Father," it affirms that he *comes from* the Father *through* the Son. The Western tradition expresses first the consubstantial communion between Father and Son, by saying that the Spirit proceeds from the Father and the Son [*filioque*]. It says this, "legitimately and with good reason, for the eternal order of the divine persons in their consubstantial communion implies that the Father, as 'the principle without principle,' is the first origin of the Spirit, but also that as Father of the only Son, he is, with the Son, the single principle from which the Holy Spirit proceeds" *Catechism of the Catholic Church* 246, 248.

142. "The Greek and Latin Traditions Regarding the Procession of the Holy Spirit," 39.

143. Ibid.

144. Ibid.

145. Ibid., 40. It is somewhat ironic that, after having rejected the *Letter to Marinus* at Ferrara-Florence as both spurious and ambiguous, the Roman Catholic Church used it as the hermeneutical key to understanding its position in the twentieth century.

146. Ibid.

147. Ibid.

148. Ibid.

149. Ibid.

150. A more critical assessment was offered by Jean-Claude Larchet, "À Propos de la Récente Clarification du Conseil Pontifical pour la Promotion de L'Unité des Chrétiens," *Le Messager orthodoxe* 129 (1997):3–58.

151. John Zizioulas, "One Single Source: An Orthodox Response to the Clarification on the Filioque," http://agrino.org/cyberdesert/zizioulas.htm.

152. Ibid.

153. Ibid.

154. Ibid.

155. Ibid.

156. "The *Filioque*: A Church-Dividing Issue? An Agreed Statement of the North American Orthodox- Catholic Theological Consultation (October 25, 2003)," *St. Vladimir's Theological Quarterly* 48 (2004): 93–123.

157. "When Patriarch Dimitrios I visited Rome on December 7, 1987, and again during the visit of Patriarch Bartholomew I to Rome in June 1995 . . . the Pope and Patriarch proclaimed the Creed in Greek [i.e., without the *filioque*]. Pope John Paul II and Romanian Patriarch Teoctist did the same in Romanian at a papal Mass in Rome on October 13, 2002. The document *Dominus Iesus: On the Unicity and Salvific Universality of Jesus Christ and the Church*, issued by the Congregation for the Doctrine of the Faith on August 6, 2000, begins its theological considerations on the Church's central teaching with the text of the creed of 381, again without the addition of the *filioque*"; ibid., 110–11.

158. Ibid., 112.

159. Ibid., 113.

160. Ibid., 115.

161. Ibid., 116.

162. Ibid., 116–17.

163. Ibid., 117.

164. Ibid., 117–18.

165. Ibid., 118.

166. Ibid., 118–19.

167. Ibid., 119.

168. Ibid., 122.

169. Specifically the Catholic Church was asked to declare as no longer applicable "the condemnation made at the Second Council of Lyons (1274) of those 'who presume to deny that the Holy Spirit proceeds eternally from the Father and the Son'"; ibid.

170. Ibid. This last recommendation would, for example, encourage a Catholic appraisal of the Synod of Blachernae as well as a reevaluation of the ecumenicity of the eighth council (i.e., acknowledging the legitimacy of the 879–80 synod that restored Photius rather than the 869 anti-Photian gathering).

171. Ibid.

172. Ibid., 122–23.

173. Ibid., 123.

Bibliography

ABBREVIATIONS

    ACW = *Ancient Christian Writers*
    ANF = *Ante-Nicene Fathers*
   CCG = *Corpus Christianorum Series Graeca*
   CCL = *Corpus Christianorum Series Latina*
     CF = *Concilium Florentinum: Documenta et Scriptores*
     FC = *Fathers of the Church*
 MGH = *Monumenta Germaniae Historica*
NPNF = *Nicene and Post-Nicene Fathers*
     PG = *Patrologia Graeca*
     PL = *Patrologia Latina*
     SC = *Sources chrétiennes*

Abramowski, L. "Das Bekenntnis des G bei Gregor v. Nyssa u. das Problem seiner Echtheit." *Zeitschrift für Kirchengeschichte* 87 (1976): 145–66.

Acropolites, George. "Λόγος δεύτερος περὶ τῆς ἐκ πατρὸς τοῦ ἁγίου πνεύματος ἐκπορεύσεως." In *Georgii Acropolitae Opera* 2, ed. A. Heisenberg, 45–66. Stuttgart: Teubneri, 1978.

Adonis Viennensis. *Chronicon in Aetates Sex Divisum* (PL 123, 23–138).

Aeneas of Paris, *Liber adversus Graecos* (PL 121, 683–721).

Agnellus, *Epistola ad Armenium de ratione fidei* (PL 68, 381–86).

Alberigo, Giuseppe, ed. *Christian Unity: The Council of Ferrara-Florence 1438/9*. Louvain: University Press, 1991.

Albright, William Foxwell, and C. S. Mann. *The Gospel According to Matthew*. Anchor Bible Series 26. New York: Doubleday, 1971.

Alcuin of York. *Commentaria in sancti Joannis Evangelium* (PL 100, 733–1008).

———— *De Fide sanctae et individuae Trinitatis* (PL 101, 1–58).

————. *Libellus de Processione Spiritus Sancti ad Carolum Magnum* (PL 101, 63–84).

Alexakis, Alexander. *Codex Parisinus Graecus 1115 and Its Archetypes*. Washington D.C.: Dumbarton Oaks Research Library and Collection, 1996.

————. "The Greek Patristic *Testimonia* presented at the Council of Florence (1439) in support of the *Filioque* reconsidered." *Revue des Études Byzantines* 58 (2000): 149–65.

Allen, Pauline, and Bronwen Neil, eds. *The Life of Maximus the Confessor Recension 3*. Early Christian Studies 6. Strathford: St. Pauls, 2003.

Allen, Pauline, ed. *Maximus the Confessor and His Companions: Documents from Exile*. Oxford: Oxford University Press, 2002.

Altaner, Bernard. "Augustinus in der griechischen Kirche bis auf Photius." *Historisches Jahrbuch* 71 (1951): 37–76.

Ambrose of Milan. *De Spiritu Sancto* (PL 16, 731–850).

————. *Theological and Dogmatic Works*. Trans. Roy Deferrari. FC 44. Washington D.C.: Catholic University of America Press, 1963.

Anastasiou, Ioannis. "I tentative de Barlaam Calabro per l'unione delle chiese." In *La Chiesa greca in Italia dall'VIII al XVI secolo: Atti del Convegno storicointerecclesiale*. Vol. II, 663–84. Padua: Editrice Antenore, 1972.

Anastasius Bibliothecarius. *Anastasius ad Ioannem Diaconum* (PL 129, 558–62).

Anatolios, Khaled, ed. *Anthanasius*. The Early Church Fathers. New York: Routledge, 2002.

Andrea, Alfred, ed. *Contemporary Sources for the Fourth Crusade*. Medieval Mediterranean 29. London: Brill Academic Publishers, 2000.

Anglican-Orthodox Dialogue: The Dublin Agreed Statement 1984. Crestwood, N.Y.: St. Vladimir's Seminary Press, 1997.

Angold, Michael. *The Fourth Crusade: Event and Context*. Harlow: Longman, 2003.

Anselm of Canturbury. *Anselm of Canterbury: The Major Works*. Trans. and ed. Brian Davies. Oxford: Oxford University Press, 1998.

————. *Anselmi Opera Omnia*, 6 vols. Trans. and ed. F. S. Schmitt. Edinburgh: T. Nelson and Sons, 1938.

Anselm of Havelberg. *Dialogi* (PL 188, 1139–248).

Aquinas, Thomas. *Contra Errores Graecorum*. In *Ending the Byzantine Greek Schism*, ed. James Likoudis, 125–89. New Hope, Ky.: Catholics United for the Faith, 1992.

————. *On the Power of God*. Trans. English Dominican Fathers. Westminster, Md.: Newman Press, 1932.

————. *Summa Contra Gentiles*. 5 vols. Trans. Charles O'Neil. Notre Dame, Ind.: University of Notre Dame Press, 1975.

————. *Summa Theologica*. 5 vols. Trans. the Fathers of the English Dominican Province, Westminster, Md.: Christian Classics, 1981.

Arunde, A. "El Espíritu Santo en la Exposición de fe de S Gregorio Taumaturgo." *Scripta Teol* 10 (1978): 373–407.

Athanasius. *Athanase D'Alexandrie: Lettres a Sérapion*. SC 15. Joseph Lebron, ed. Paris: Les Éditions, 1947.

Athanasius. *Contra Arianos* (PG 26, 12–527).

(Pseudo) Athanasius. *Contra Sabellianos* (PG 28, 95–122).

Augustine of Hippo, *The Confessions*. Trans. Maria Boulding. The Works of St. Augustine: A Translation for the 21st Century. Brooklyn, N.Y.: New City Press, 1996.

———. *Contra Maximinum* (PL 42, 743–814).

———. *De Trinitate*. 2 vols. Ed. W. J. Mountain. CCL 50–50a. Turnhout, Belgium: Brepols, 1968.

———. *In Joannis Evangelium Tractatus CXXIV*. Ed. D. R. Willems. CCL 36. Turnhout, Belgium: Brepols, 1954.

———. *Letters 156–210*. Trans. Roland Teske. The Works of St. Augustine: A Translation for the 21st Century 2.3. Brooklyn, N.Y.: New City Press, 2005.

———. *On Christian Belief*. Trans. Boniface Ramsey. The Works of St. Augustine: A Translation for the 21st Century. Brooklyn, N.Y.: New City Press, 2005.

———. *Tractates on the Gospel of John 55–111*. Trans. John Rettig. FC 90. Washington D.C.: Catholic University of America Press, 1994.

———. *The Trinity*. Trans. Edmund Hill. The Works of St. Augustine: A Translation for the 21st Century. Brooklyn, N.Y.: New City Press, 1991.

Auxentios, Bishop. "St. Mark of Ephesus: His Person and Liturgical and His Theological Expertise." *Patristic and Byzantine Review* 10 (1991): 159–66.

Avitus of Vienne. *Fragmento libri de divinitate Spiritus Sancti* (PL 59, 385–86).

Azkoul, Michael. "St. George Scholarius and the Latin Theological Tradition." *Patristic and Byzantine Review* 10 (1991): 167–72.

———. *The Influence of Augustine of Hippo on the Orthodox Church*. Texts and Studies in Religion 56. Lewiston, N.Y.: Edwin Mellen Press, 1990.

Backus, Irena ed. *The Reception of the Church Fathers in the West From the Carolingians to the Maurists*, vol. 1. Boston: Brill Academic Publishers, 2001.

Bailleux, Emile. "L'Esprit du Père et du Fils selon saint Augustin." *Revue thomiste* 7 (1977): 5–29.

Balthasar, Hans Urs von. *Cosmic Liturgy: The Universe According to Maximus the Confessor*. Trans. Brian Daley. San Francisco: Ignatius Press, 2003.

Barker, John. *Manuel II Palaeologus (1391–1425); A Study in Late Byzantine Statesmanship*. New Brunswick, N.J.: Rutgers University Press, 1969.

Barlaam of Calabria. *Barlaam Calabro: Opere contro I Latini: introduzione, storia dei testi, edizione critica, traduzione e indici*. 2 vols. Ed. Antonis Fyrigos. Studi e testi 347–48. Vatican City: Bibliotheca Apostolica Vaticana, 1998.

———. *Primatu Ecclesiae Romenae et Processione Spiritus Sancti* (PG 151, 1271–82).

Barrett, C. K. *Epistle to the Romans*, 2nd ed. Black's New Testament Commentaries. London: A& C Black, 1991.

———. *The Gospel According to St. John*. London: SPCK, 1967.

———. *The Holy Spirit in the Gospel Tradition*. New York: Macmillan, 1947.

Bartelink, G. J. M. "Pope Gregory the Great's Knowledge of Greek." In *Gregory the Great: A Symposium*. Notre Dame, Ind.: University of Notre Dame Press, 1995, 117–36.

Barth, Karl. *Church Dogmatics I.1: The Doctrine of the Word of God*. Trans. G. W. Bromiley. Edinburgh: T & T Clark, 1975.

Barvinok, V. *Nikofor Vlemmid I ego sochineniia*. Kiev, 1911.

Basil of Caesarea. *Basile de Césarée: Contre Eunome*. Ed. Bernard Sesboüé. SC 305.
Paris: Les Éditions du Cerf, 1983.

———. *Contra Eunomium*, Liber V (PG 29, 709–74).

———. *Letters 1–185*. FC 13. Trans. Agnes Clare Way. Washington, D.C.: Catholic
University of America Press, 1951.

———. *On the Holy Spirit*. Trans. David Anderson. Crestwood, N.Y.: St. Vladimir's
Seminary Press, 2001.

———. *Traité du Saint-Esprit*. Ed. Benoit Pruche. SC 17. Paris: Les Éditions du Cerf,
1945.

Bayer, Axel. *Spaltung der Christenheit: Das sogenannte Morgenländische Schisma von 1054*.
Cologne: Böhlau Vertag, 2002.

Beccus, John. *Adversus Andronicum Camaterum* (PG 141, 395–612).

———. *De Processione Spiritus sancti* (PG 141, 158–276).

———. *De unione Ecclesiarum veteris et novae Romae* (PG 141, 15–158).

———. *Epigraphae* (PG 141, 613–723).

———. *Letter to Pope John XXI* (PG 141, 943–50).

———. *Refutatio libri Georgii Cyprii* (PG 141, 863–926).

———. *Refutatio libri Photii de processione Spiritus sancti* (PG 141, 725–864).

Bede. *Ecclesiastical History of the English People*. Trans. Judith McClure and Roger
Collins. Oxford: Oxford University Press, 1994.

Beeley, Christopher. *Gregory of Nazianzus on the Trinity and the Knowledge of God*.
Oxford: Oxford University Press, 2008.

Behr, John. *The Formation of Christian Theology 2: The Nicene Faith*, 2 vols. Crestwood,
N.Y.: St. Vladimir's Seminary Press, 2004.

———. *The Mystery of Christ: Life in Death*. Crestwood, N.Y.: St. Vladimir's Seminary
Press, 2006.

———. *The Way to Nicea*. Crestwood, N.Y.: St. Vladimir's Seminary Press, 2001.

Benz, Ernst. *Die Ostkirche in Lichte der protestantischen Geschictsschribung von der
Reformation bis zur Gegenwart*. Munich: Karl Alber, 1952.

———. *Wittenburg und Byzanz: Zur Begegung und aus Einandersetzung der Reformation
und der Östlich-Orthodoxen Kirche*. Marburg: Fink, 1949.

Bernonis. *Libellus de quibusdam Rebus ad Missae Officium Pertinentibus* (PL 142,
1055–80).

Berrouard, M.-F. "La théologie du Saint-Espirit dans les *Tractates*." *Homélies sur
l'Evangile de saint Jean LXXX-CIII*. Bibliothèque Augustinienne 74B. Paris:
Institut d'études augustiniennes, 1998.

Berthold, G. C. "The Church as *Mysterion*: Diversity and Unity According to Maximus
Confessor." *Patristic and Byzantine Review* 6 (1987): 20–29.

———. "Cyril of Alexandria and the *Filioque*." *Studia Patristica* 19 (1989): 143–47.

———. "Did Maximus the Confessor Know Augustine?" *Studia Patristica* 17 (1982):
14–17.

———. "Maximus the Confessor and the *Filioque*." *Studia Patristica* 18 (1983): 113–18.

———, ed. *Maximus the Confessor: Selected Writings*. Classics of Western Spirituality.
Mahwah, N.J.: Paulist Press, 1985.

———. "St. Anselm and the Filioque." In *Faith Seeking Understanding*, ed. George
Berthold, 227–34. Manchester: Saint Anselm College Press, 1991.

Bessarion of Nicea. *Against the Syllogisms of the Monk Maximus Planoudes Concerning the Procession of the Holy Spirit According to the Latins* (PG 161, 309–18).

————. *Refutatio Capitum Syllogisticorum Marci Ephesii* (PG 161, 137–244).

Betz, Hans Dieter. *Galatians: A Commentary on Paul's Letter to the Churches of Galatia.* Hermeneia Series. Minneapolis: Fortress Press, 1979.

Blackmore, R. W. *Doctrine of the Russian Church.* London: J. Masters and Co., 1905.

Blastic, M. W. *Condilectio: Personal Mysticism and Speculative Theology in the Works of Richard of St Victor.* Ann Arbor, Mich.: UMI, 1991.

Blemmydes, Nicephorus. *De Processione Spiritus sancti orationes duae* (PG 142, 553–84).

Bligh, J. "Richard of St Victor's *De Trinitate*: Augustinian or Abelardian?" *Heythrop Journal* 1:2 (1960): 126–31.

Blowers, Paul. *Exegesis and Spiritual Pedagogy in Maximus the Confessor: An Investigation of the Quaestiones ad Thalassium.* Notre Dame, Ind.: University of Notre Dame Press, 1991.

————. "Theology as Integrative, Visionary, Pastoral: The Legacy of Maximus the Confessor." *Pro Ecclesia* 2 (1993): 216–30.

————, and Robert Wilken, eds. *The Cosmic Mystery of Jesus Christ.* Crestwood, N.Y.: St. Vladimir's Seminary Press, 2003.

Bobrinskoy, Boris. *The Mystery of the Trinity: Trinitarian Experience and Vision in the Biblical and Patristic Tradition.* Trans. Anthony Gythiel. Crestwood, N.Y.: St. Vladimir's Seminary Press, 1999.

Boethius. *The Theological Tractates.* Trans. H. F. Stewart and E. K. Rand. Loeb Classical Library. New York: Putnam and Sons, 1926.

Bolotov, Basil. "Thesen über das *Filioque* von einem russischen Theologen." *Revue internationale de Théologie* 6 (1898): 681–712.

Bonaventure. *Breviloquium.* Trans. José de Vinck. The Works of Bonaventure 2. Paterson, N.J.: St. Anthony Guild, 1963.

————. "*Commentaria In Quatuor Libros Sententiarum.*" In *Doctoris Seraphici S. Bonaventurae Opera omnia* 1. Quaracchi, 1882.

Bonner, Gerald. "St. Augustine's Doctrine of the Holy Spirit." *Sobornost* 2 (1960): 51–66.

Borgolte, M. "Papst Leo III, Karl der Große und der Filioque-Strit von Jerusalem." *Byzantia* 10 (1980): 403–27.

Bornkamm, Günther. "Der Paraklet im Johannes-Evangelium," in *Geschichte und Glaube Erster Teil.* Munich: Kaiser, 1968: 68–89.

Bougerol, Jacques Guy. *Introduction à saint Bonaventure.* Paris: Librairie Philosophique J. Vrin, 1988.

Boularand, E. "L'argument patristique au concile de Florence, dans la question de la procession du Saint-Esprit," *Bulletin de literature ecclésiastique* 63 (1962): 161–99.

Boulnois, Marie-Odile. *La paradoxe trinitaire chez Cyrille d'Alexandrie: Herméneutique, analyses philosophiques et argumentation théologique.* Paris: Institut d'Études Augustiniennes, 1994.

Bourassa, François. "Communion du Père et du Fils." *Gregorianum* 48 (1967): 657–707.

————. "Théologie trinitaire chez saint Augustin I-II." *Gregorianum* 58 (1977): 675–775; 59 (1978): 375–412.

Bouyer, Louis. *The Eternal Son: A Theology of the Word of God and Christology.*
    Trans. Simone Inkel and John Laughlin. Huntington, Ind.: Our Sunday Visitor,
    1978.

Bradshaw, David. *Aristotle East and West: Metaphysics and the Division of Christendom.*
    Cambridge: Cambridge University Press, 2004.

Brett, Edward Tracy. *Humbert of Romans: His Life and Views of Thirteenth Century
    Society.* Toronto: Pontifical Institute for Medieval Studies, 1984.

Brock, Sebastian. "Two Sets of Monothelete Questions to the Maximianists." *Orientalia
    Louvaniensia Periodica* 17 (1986): 119–40.

———, ed. "An Early Syriac Life of Maximus the Confessor." *Analecta Bollandiana* 85
    (1967): 285–316.

Bromage, R. Raikes, ed. *The Holy Catechism of Nicolas Bulgaris.* London: J. Masters and
    Co., 1893.

Brown, Raymond. *The Birth of the Messiah.* New York: Doubleday, 1977.

———. "Diverse Views of the Spirit in the New Testament: A Preliminary Contribu-
    tion of Exegesis to Doctrinal Reflection," chapter in *Biblical Exegesis and Church
    Doctrine.* New York: Paulist Press, 1985: 101–13.

———. "Does the New Testament Call Jesus God?" in *Jesus: God and Man.* New York:
    Macmillian Publishing, 1967:1–38.

———. *The Epistles of John.* Anchor Bible Series 30. New York: Doubleday, 1982.

———. *The Gospel According to John XIII–XXI.* Anchor Bible Series 29a. New York:
    Doubleday, 1970.

———. *An Introduction to the New Testament.* New York: Doubleday, 1997.

Bruce, F. F. *The Epistle to the Galatians.* New International Greek New Testament
    Commentary. Grand Rapids, Mich.: Eerdmans, 1982.

Bulgakov, Sergius. *The Comforter.* Trans. Boris Jackim. Grand Rapids, Mich.:
    Eerdmans, 2004.

Bultmann, Rudolf. *The Gospel of John: A Commentary.* Louisville: Westminster John
    Knox Press, 1971.

———. *The Johannine Epistles.* Hermeneia Series. Minneapolis: Fortress Press, 1973.

Burgess, Stanley. *The Holy Spirit: Ancient Christian Traditions.* Peabody, Mass.:
    Hendrickson, 1984.

Burn, A. E. "Some Spanish MSS of the Constantinopolitan Creed." *Journal of Theologi-
    cal Studies* 9 (1908): 301–3.

Byrne, Brendan. *Romans.* Sacra Pagina 6. Collegeville, Minn.: Liturgical Press, 1996.

Cabasilas, Nilus. *Nilus Cabasilas et Theologia s.Thomae de Processione Spiritus Sancti.* Ed.
    Emmanuel Candel. Vatican City: Bibliotheca Apostolica Vaticana, 1945.

———. *Sur le Saint-Esprit.* Ed. Théophile Kislas. Paris: Les Éditions du Cerf, 2001.

Calian, Carnegie Samuel. *Theology Without Boundaries: Encounters of Eastern Orthodoxy
    and Western Tradition.* Louisville: Westminister John Knox Press, 1992.

Calvin, John. *Institutes of the Christian Religion* 2 vols. Ed. John McNeill. Library of
    Christian Classics 10. Philadelphia: Westminster Press, 1960.

Cammelli, Giuseppe. "Demetrio Cidonio al fratello Procoro." *Studi bizantini* 2 (1927):
    49–55.

Campbell, Theodore. "The Doctrine of the Holy Spirit in the Theology of Athanasius."
    Scottish Journal of Theology 27 (1974): 408–43.

Canard, P. "Nicéphore Blemmyde et la mémoire adressé aux envoyés de Grégoire IX (Nicée, 1234)." *Orientalia Christiana Periodica* 25 (1959): 310–25.

Candel, Emmanuel. "El 'Kanon esti theologikos' de Nilo Cabasilas." *Orientalia Christiana Periodica* 23 (1957): 237–66.

―――. "Processus Discussionis de Novissimus in Concilio Florentino." *Orientalia Christiana Periodica* 19 (1953): 303–49.

―――, ed. *Andreas de Escobar, O.S.B., episcopus Megarensis, Tractatus polemico-theologicus de graecis errantibus.* CF 4.1. Rome: Pontifical Oriental Institute, 1952.

―――. *Bessarion Nicaenus, S.R.E. Cardinalis, De Spiritus Sancti processione ad Alexium Lascarin Philanthropinum.* CF 7.2. Rome: Pontifical Oriental Institute, 1961.

―――. *Bessarion Nicaenus, S.R.E. Cardinalis, Oratio dogmatica de unione.* CF 7.1. Rome: Pontifical Oriental Institute, 1958.

―――. *Joannes de Torquemada O.P., Cardinalis Sancti Sixti, Apparatus super Decretum Florentinum Unionis Graecorum.* CF 2.1. Rome: Pontifical Oriental Institute, 1944.

―――. *Joannes de Torquemada O.P., cardinalis sancti Sixti, Oratio Synodalis de primatu.* CF 4.2. Rome: Pontifical Oriental Institute, 1954.

Carlen, Claudia, ed. *Papal Encyclicals 1740–1878.* New York: Consortium Press, 1981.

Cassiodorus. *Explanation of the Psalms* 1. Trans. P. G. Walsh. ACW 51. New York: Paulist Press, 1990.

Cavadini, John. *The Last Christology of the West: Adoptionism in Spain and Gaul 785–820.* Philadelphia: University of Pennsylvania Press, 1993.

―――. "The Sources and Theology of Alcuin's *De Fide Sanctae et Individuae Trinitatis.*" *Traditio* 46 (1991): 123–46.

Cavallera, Ferdinand. "La doctrine de Saint Augustin sur l'Esprit-Saint à propos du 'De Trinitate.'" *Recherches de théologie ancienne et médiévale* 2 (1930): 365–87; 3 (1931): 5–19.

Chadwick, Henry. *East and West: The Making of the Rift in the Church: From Apostolic Times until the Council of Florence.* Oxford: Oxford University Press, 2003.

Chemnitz, Martin. *Loci Theologici,* 2 vols. Trans. J. A. O. Preus. St. Louis: Concordia Publishing House, 1989.

Clapsis, Emmanuel. "The Filioque Question." *Patristic and Byzantine Review* 1 (1982): 127–36.

Clément, Oliver. *Byzance et le christianisme.* Paris: Presses Universitaires de France, 1964.

―――. *Essor du christianisme oriental.* Paris: Presses Universitaires de France, 1964.

―――. "La question du 'filioque' et de la procession du Saint-Esprit." *Messager de lExarchat du Patriarche russe en Europe Occidentale* 75–76 (1971): 171–90.

―――. *Orient-Occident, Deux Passeurs: Vladimir Lossky et Paul Endokimov.* Geneva:Labor et Fides 1985.

―――. *The Roots of Christian Mysticism.* Trans. Theodore Berkeley. London: New City, 1993.

Congar, Yves. *After Nine Hundred Years: The Background of the Schism between the Eastern and Western Churches.* New York: Fordham University Press, 1959.

―――. *Diversity and Communion.* Trans. John Bowden. Mystic, Conn.: Twenty-third Publications, 1984.

———. *I Believe in the Holy Spirit*. Trans. David Smith. New York: Crossroad Publishing Co., 1997.

———. "Le Père, source absolue de la divinité." *Istina* 25 (1980): 237–46.

Conticello, Carmelo, and Vassa Conticello, eds. *La théologie Byzantine et sa tradition*, Vol. II. Turnhout, Belgium: Brepols, 2002.

Contos, L. C. "The Essence-Energies Structure of St. Gregory Palamas with a Brief Examination of Its Patristic Foundations." *Greek Orthodox Theological Review* 12 (1967): 283–94.

Craddock, Fred. *Luke*. Interpretation Commentaries. Louisville: John Knox Press, 1990.

Cross, Richard. *Duns Scotus on God*. London: Ashgate, 2004.

Cullen, Christopher. *Bonaventure*. Oxford: Oxford University Press, 2006.

Cydones, Demetrius. *De Processione Spiritus Sancti adversus Gregorium Palamam* (PG 154, 835–62).

———. *De Processione Spiritus Sancti* (PG 154, 863–958).

Cyril of Alexandria. *Apologeticus contra Thedoretum* (PG 76, 385–452).

———. *Commentariorum in Joannem* (PG 73 and 74, 9–756).

———. *De Adoratione in Spiritu et Veritate* (PG 68, 133–1126).

———. *De Fide sanctae et individuae Trinitatis* (PG 77, 105–22).

———. *Epistula* 39 (PG 77, 181).

———. *Epistula* 40 (PG 77, 200–201).

———. *Letters 51–110*. John McEnerney, ed. FC 77. Washington, D.C.: Catholic University of America Press, 1985.

———. *Thesaurus de sancta et consubstantiali trinitate* (PG 75, 9–656).

Daley, Brian. "Revisting the Filioque: Roots and Branches of an Old Debate." *Pro Ecclesia* 10 (2001): 31–62.

———. "Revisiting the *Filioque*: Contemporary Catholic Approaches." *Pro Ecclesia* 10 (2001): 195–212.

———, ed. *Gregory of Nazianzus*. Early Church Fathers. New York: Routledge, 2006.

Dalmais, Irénée-Henri. "La Vie de Saint Maximus le Confesseur Reconsidérée." *Studia Patristica* 17 (1982): 26–30.

Damaskinos, M. "La disponbilité au Saint Esprit et la fidelité aux origins d' après les Pères grecs." *Istinia* 19 (1974): 49–64.

Damasus. *Tomus Damasi: Confessio fidei* (PL 13, 558–64).

Davey, Colin. *Pioneer for Unity: Metrophanes Kritopoulos, 1589–1639, and Relations Between the Orthodox, Roman Catholic and Reformed Churches*. London: British Council of Churches, 1987.

Davies, Stevan. *Jesus the Healer: Possession, Trance, and the Origins of Christianity*. New York: Continuum Publishing Company, 1995.

Davies, Steven, Daniel Kendall, and Gerald O'Collins, eds. *The Trinity: An Interdisciplinary Symposium on the Trinity*. Oxford: Oxford University Press, 1999.

de Aldama, J. A. *El simbolo Toledano I Su texto, su origin, su posición en la historia de los simbolos*. Rome: Pontificia Universitas Gregoriana, 1934.

de Lubac, Henri. *At the Service of the Church: Henri de Lubac Reflects on the Circumstances that Occasioned His Writings*. Trans. Anne Englund. San Francisco: Ignatius Press, 1993.

de Margerie, Bertrand. *The Christian Trinity in History*. Trans. Edmund Fortman. Still River, Mass.: St. Bede's Publications, 1981.

de Régnon, Théodore. *Etudes de théologie positive sur la Sainte Trinité*. Paris: Retaux, 1892.

de Urbina, Ortiz. "Un codice fiorentino di raccolte patristiche." *Orientalia Christiana Periodica* 4 (1938): 423–40.

de Villehardouin, Geoffrey. "Chronicles of the Fourth Crusade and the Conquest of Constantinople." In *Chronicles of the Crusades*. Trans. and ed. Margaret Shaw. New York: Penguin, 1972.

Declerk, José, ed. *Quaestiones et dubia*. CCG 10. Turnhout, Belgium: Brepols, 1982.

Dejaifve, G. "Diversité dogmatique et unite de la Révélation." *Nouvelle Revue Théologique* 89 (1967): 16–25.

Dekkers, E. "Maxime le Confesseur dans la tradition latine." In *After Chalcedon: Studies in Theology and Church History Offered to Professor Albert Van Roey*, ed. C. Laga, J. A. Munitiz, and L. Van Rompay, 83–97. Leuven: Department Oriëntalistiek, 1985.

Del Colle, Ralph. "Reflections on the *Filioque*." *Journal of Ecumenical Studies* 34 (1997): 202–17.

Demacopoulos George, and Aristotle Papanikolaou, eds. *Orthodox Readings of Augustine*. Crestwood, N.Y.: St. Vladimir's Seminary Press, 2008.

———. "The Popular Reception of the Council of Florence in Constantinople (1439–1453)." *St. Vladimir's Theological Quarterly* 43 (1999): 37–53.

Den Bok, N. *Communicating the Most High: a Systematic Study of Person and Trinity in the Theology of Richard of St. Victor*. Paris: Brepols, 1996.

Dendrinos, Charalambos, Jonathan Harris, and Judith Herrin, eds. *Porphyrogenita: Essays on the History and Literature of Byzantium and the Latin East in Honour of Julian Chrysostomides*. Aldershot: Ashgate, 2003.

Denzinger, Henry, ed. *The Sources of Catholic Dogma*. St. Louis: Herder, 1957.

Devreesse, R. "La Vie de S. Maxime le Confesseur et ses récensions." *Analecta Bollandiana* 46 (1928): 5–49.

Didymus. *De Trinitate*. Hönscheid Jürgen and Ingrid Seiler, eds. Meisenheim: Hain, 1975.

———. *Traité du Saint-Esprit*. SC 386. Louis Doutreleau, ed. Paris: Les Éditions du Cerf, 1992.

Dondaine, Antoine. "Contra Graecos: Premiers écrits polémiques des dominicains d'Orient," *Archivum Fratrum Praedicatorum* 21 (1951): 320–446.

———. "Nicolas de Cotrone et la sources du *Contra errores Graecorum* de Saint Thomas." *Divus Thomas* 29 (1950): 313–40.

Doukas. *Historia Turco-Byzantina of Doukas*. Ed. Vasile Grecu. Bucharest: Editura Academiei Republicii Populare Romiî ne, 1958.

Dragas, George. "The Eighth Ecumenical Council: Constantinople IV (879/880) and the Condemnation of the *Filioque* Addition and Doctrine." *Greek Orthodox Theological Review* 44 (1999): 357–69.

———. "St. Maximus the Confessor and the Christian Life." In *Church and Theology : An Ecclesiastical and Theological Review of the Archbishopric of Thyateira and Great Britain*. ed. Methodios Fougias, 861–84. London: Archbishopric of Thyateira and Great Britain, 1981.

Drecoll, Volker Henning. *Die Entwicklung der Trinitätslehre des Basilius von Cäsarea.* Göttinggen: Vanderhoeck & Ruprecht, 1996.

Dudden, F. Homes. *Gregory the Great: His Place in History and Thought.* 2 vols. London: Longmans, Green, 1905.

Dulles, Avery. "The Filioque: What Is at Stake?" *Concordia Theological Quarterly* 59 (1995): 31–48.

Dunn James D. G. *The Christ and the Spirit 1: Christology.* Grand Rapids, Mich., Eerdmans, 1998.

———. *Christology in the Making: A New Testament Inquiry into the Origins of the Doctrine of the Incarnation.* Grand Rapids, Mich.: Eerdmans, 2003.

———. *The Christ and the Spirit 2: Pneumatology.* Grand Rapids, Mich.: Eerdmans, 1998.

———. *Jesus and the Spirit: A Study in the Religious and Charismatic Experience in the New Testament.* Grand Rapids, Mich.: Eerdmans, 1997.

———. *Romans 1–8.*Word Biblical Commentary 38a. Dallas: Thomas Nelson, 1988.

———. *The Theology of Paul the Apostle.* Grand Rapids, Mich.: Eerdmans, 1998.

Dvornik, Francis. *Byzantium and the Roman Primacy.* New York: Fordham University Press, 1966.

———. *Photian and Byzantine Ecclesiastical Studies.* London: Variorum Reprints, 1974.

———. *The Photian Schism: History and Legend.* Cambridge: Cambridge University Press, 1948.

Efthymiades, Stephanos, ed. *The Life of the Patriarch Tarasios by Ignatios the Deacon.* Brookfield, Vt.: Ashgate, 1998.

Einhard. "Life of Charlemagne." In *Einhard and Notker: Two Lives of Charlemagne.* Trans. Lewis Thorpe. London: Penguin, 1969.

Elliott, Charles. "The Schism and Its Elimination in Humbert of Rome's *Opusculum Tripartitum.*" *Greek Orthodox Theological Review* 34 (1989): 71–83.

Emery, Giles. *The Trinitarian Theology of St. Thomas Aquinas.* Oxford: Oxford University Press, 2007.

———. *Trinity in Aquinas.* Ypsilanti, Mich.: Sapientia Press, 2003.

Endokimov, Paul. *L'Esprit Saint dans la tradition orthodoxe.* Paris: Éditions du Cerf, 1969.

Epiphanius of Salamis. *Ancoratus* (PG 43, 11–236).

———. *Panarion Haer 65–80.* Karl Holl, ed. Die Griechischen Christlichen Schrift Steller der Ersten Jahrhunderte. Berlin: Akademie-Verlag, 1985.

The Episcopal and Greek Churches: Report of an Unofficial Conference on Unity between Members of the Episcopal Church in America and His Grace, Meletios Metaxakis, Metropolitan of Athens, and His Advisers. October 26, 1918. New York: Dept. of Missions and Church Extension of the Episcopal Church, 1920.

Erickson, John. *The Challenge of Our Past.* Crestwood, N.Y.: St. Vladimir's Seminary Press, 1991.

"Erklärung der Internationalen Altkatholischen Bischofskonferenz zur Filioque-Frage." *Internationale kirchliche Zeitschrift* 61 (1971): 65–68.

Etherianus, Hugo. *De haeresibus quas Graeci in Latinos devolvunt, sive quod Spiritus Sanctus ex utroque Patre et Filio procedit* (PL 202, 227–396).

Ethier, A. M. *Le De Trinitate de Richard de Saint-Victor.* Paris: J. Vrin, 1939.

Eucherius of Lyons. *Instructiones ad Salonium* (PL 50, 773–822).

Eustathius of Thessalonika. *L'espugnazione de Thessalonica*. S. Kyriakedes, ed. Palermo, 1961.

Every, George. "Peter Lombard and II Lyons." *Eastern Churches Review* 9 (1977): 85–90.

Farrell, Joseph. *Free Choice in Maximus the Confessor*. South Canaan: St. Tikhon's Seminary Press, 1989.

———. *God, History, and Dialectic: The Theological Foundations of the Two Europes and Their Cultural Consequences*. Seven Councils Press, 1997.

Fatula, Mary Ann. "The Council of Florence and Pluralism in Dogma." *One in Christ* 19 (1983): 14–27.

———. "A Problematic Western Formula." *One in Christ* 17 (1981): 324–34.

Fedalto, Giorgio. *Massimo Margounios e la sua opera per conciliare la sentenza degli Orientali e dei Latini sulla Processione dello Spirito Santo*. Padua: Tip. del Seminario, 1961.

———. *Massimo Margunio e il suo commento al 'De Trinitate' di S. Agostino (1588)*. Brescia: Paideia, 1968.

Fee, Gordon. "Paul and the Trinity: The Experience of Christ and the Spirit for Paul's Understanding of God." In *The Trinity: An Interdisciplinary Symposium on the Trinity* ed. Steven Davies, Daniel Kendall, and Gerald O'Collins. Oxford: Oxford University Press, 1999: 49–72.

———. *Paul, the Spirit and the People of God*. Peabody, Mass.: Hendrickson, 1996.

"The *Filioque*: A Church-Dividing Issue? An Agreed Statement of the North American Orthodox- Catholic Theological Consultation (October 25, 2003)." *St. Vladimir's Theological Quarterly* 48 (2004): 93–123.

Fitzmyer, Joseph. *Acts of the Apostles*. Anchor Bible Series 31. New York: Doubleday, 1998.

———. *Romans*. Anchor Bible Series 33. New York: Doubleday, 1993.

———. "The Ascension of Christ and Pentecost." *Theological Studies* 45 (1984): 409–40.

———. *The Gospel According to Luke I-IX*. Anchor Bible Series 28. New York: Doubleday, 1981.

Flogaus, Reinhard. "Die Theologie des Gregorios Palamas—Hindernis oder Hilfe für die ökumenische Verstandigung?" *Ostkirchlichen Studien* 47 (1998):105–23.

———. "Palamas and Barlaam Revisited: A Reassessment of East and West in the Hesychast Controversy of 14th Century Byzantium." *St. Vladimir's Theological Quarterly* 42 (1998): 1–32.

Florovsky, George. "Russian Orthodox Ecumenism in the Nineteenth Century." In *Ecumenism II: The Collected Works of George Florovsky* 14. Vaduz, Switzerland: Büchervertriebsanstalt, 1989: 110–63.

Fortman, Edmund. *The Triune God: A Historical Study of the Doctrine of the Trinity*. Eugene, Ore.: Wipf and Stock Publishers, 1999.

France, R. T. *The Gospel of Matthew*. New International Commentary on the New Testament. Grand Rapids, Ind.: Eerdmans, 2007.

Franchi, Antonio, ed. *Il Concilio II di Lione (1274) secondo la ordinatio concilii generalis Lugdunensis*. Studi e Testi Francescani 33. Rome: Edizioni Francescane, 1965.

Freeman, Ann, ed. MGH Leges 4 Concilia 2 Suppl. 1: *Opus Caroli regis contra synodum*. Hanover, Germany: Hahnsche Buchhandlung, 1998.

———. *Theodulf of Orleans: Charlemagne's Spokesman Against the Second Council of Nicaea*. Variorum Collected Studies Series, 772. London: Ashgate, 2003.

Fulgentius of Ruspe. *Selcted Works*. Trans. Robert Eno. FC 95. Washington D.C.: Catholic University of America Press, 1997.

Gamillscheg, Maria-Helene. *Die Kontroverse um das Filioque: Moglichkeiten einer Problemlosung auf Grund der Forschungen und Gesprache der letzten hundert Jahre*. Würzburg, Germany: Augustinus-Verlag, 1996.

Garrigues, Juan Miguel. "A la suite de la clarification romaine: le Filioque affranchi du 'filioquisme.'" *Irenikon* 64 (1996): 189–212.

———. "Le Martyre de saint Maxime le Confesseur." *Revue Thomiste* 76 (1976): 410–52.

———. "Le sens de la primauté romaine selon Maxime le Confesseur." *Istina* 21 (1976): 6–24.

———. "Le sens de la procession du Saint-Esprit dans la tradition latine du premier millénaire." *Contacts* 3 (1971): 283–309.

———. *L'Esprit qui dit 'Pere': Le Problème du Filioque*. Paris: Tequi, 1981.

———. *Maxime le Confesseur: La charite, avenir divin de l'homme*. Paris: Beauchesne, 1976.

———. "Procession et ekporèse du Saint Esprit: discernement de la tradition et reception oecuménique." *Istina* 17 (1972): 345–66.

Gay, J. *Les Registres de Nicolas III*. Paris: Bibliothèque des Ecoles Françaises d'Athènes et de Rome, 1904.

Geanakoplos, Deno John. *Byzantine East and Latin West*. New York: Harper and Row, 1966.

———. *Byzantium: Church, Society and Civilization Seen through Contemporary Eyes*. Chicago: University of Chicago Press, 1984.

———. *Constantinople and the West*. Madison: University of Wisconsin Press, 1989.

———. "The Council of Florence (1438–1439) and the Problem of Union between the Greek and Latin Churches." *Church History* 24 (1955): 324–46.

———. "Michael VIII Palaeologus and the Union of Lyons (1274)." *Harvard Theological Review* 46 (1953): 79–90.

———. *Michael Palaeologus and the West*. Cambridge, Mass.: Harvard University Press, 1959.

———. "An Orthodox View of the Councils of Basel (1431–49) and Florence (1438–39) as Paradigm for the Study of Modern Ecumenical Councils." *Greek Orthodox Theological Review* 30 (1985): 311–34.

———. "Some Aspects of the Influence of the Byzantine Maximus the Confessor on the Theology of East and West." *Church History* 38 (1969): 150–63.

Gemeinhardt, Peter. *Filioque-Kontroverse zwischen Ost- und Westkirche im Frühmittelalter*. Berlin: Walter de Gruyter, 2002.

Gennadius of Marseilles. *De ecclesiasticis dogmatibus* (PL 58, 979–1054).

Geoffrey de Villehardouin. "Chronicles of the Fourth Crusade and the Conquest of Constantinople." In *Chronicles of the Crusades*. Trans. Margaret Shaw. New York: Penguin, 1972, 29–162.

Giannelli, Ciro. "Un progetto di Barlaam per l'unione delle chiese." In *Miscellanea Giovanni Mercati 3: Letteratura e storia bizantina*. Studi e Testi 123.Vatican City: Biblioteca apostolica vaticana, 1946.

Giannoni, Carl. *Paulinus II, Patriarch von Aquileia: Ein Beitrag zur Kirchengeschichte Österreichs im Zeitalter Karls des Grossen*. Wien, Austria, 1896.

Gibbon, Edward. *The History of the Decline and Fall of the Roman Empire*. 6 vols. New York: Penguin, 1994.

Gill, Joseph. *Byzantium and the Papacy 1198–1400*. New Brunswick, N.J.: Rutgers University Press, 1979.

———. "The Church Union of Lyons Portrayed in Greek Documents." *Orientalia christiana periodica* 40 (1974): 5–45.

———. *Church Union: Rome and Byzantium 1204–1453*. London: Variorum Reprints, 1979.

———. *The Council of Florence*. Cambridge: Cambridge University Press, 1959.

———. *Eugene IV: Pope of Christian Unity*. Westminster, Md.: Newman Press, 1961.

———. "John Beccus, Patriarch of Constantinople." *Byzantina* 7 (1975): 251–66.

———. *Personalities of the Council of Florence*. Oxford: Basil Blackwell, 1964.

———. "The Sincerity of Bessarion the Unionist." *Journal of Theological Studies* 26 (1975): 377–92.

———. "An Unpublished Letter of Germanos, Patriarch of Constantinople." *Byzantion* 44 (1974): 138–51.

———. "Was Bessarion a Conciliarist or Unionist before the Council of Florence?" In *Collectanea Byzantina*, 201–19. Orientalia Christiana Analecta, 204. Rome: Pontifical Oriental Institute, 1977.

———, ed. *Concilii Florentini descriptio e Ms. venetiano (In hoc appendice titulus voluminis V sic completur: necnon descriptionis cuiusdam eiusdem)*. CF 5.Appendix. Rome: Pontifical Oriental Institute, 1964.

———. *Orationes Georgii Scholarii in Concilio Florentino habitae*. CF 8.1. Rome: Pontifical Oriental Institute, 1964.

———. *Quae supersunt Actorum Graecorum Concilii Florentini : Res Florentinae gestae*. CF 5.2.2. Rome: Pontifical Oriental Institute, 1953.

———. *Quae supersunt Actorum Graecorum Concilii Florentini: Res Ferrariae gestae*. CF 5.1.1. Rome: Pontifical Oriental Institute, 1953.

Glassberger, Nicholas. *Chronica (Analecta franciscana 2. Quarracchi, 1887)*.

Golubovich, G. "Cenni storici su Fra Giovanni Parastron." *Bessarione* 10 (1906): 295ff.

———. "Disputatio Latinorum et Graecorum." *Archivum Franciscanum Historicum* 12 (1919), 428–70.

Gouillard, J. "Michel VIII et Jean Beccos devant l'Union." In *1274: Année charnière. Mutations et continuities*. Paris, CNRS, 1977: 179–90.

Gratieux, A. *A. S. Khomiakov et le Mouvement Slavophile 2*. Paris: Les Éditions du Cerf, 1939.

"The Greek and Latin Traditions Regarding the Procession of the Holy Spirit." *Catholic International* 7 (1996): 36–43.

Green, Joel. *The Gospel of Luke*. New International Commentary on the New Testament. Grand Rapids, Ind.: Eerdmans, 1997.

Grégoire le Grand. *Dialogues 1–3*. Adalbert de Vogüé, ed. SC 260. Paris: Les Éditions du Cerf, 1979.

———. *Forty Gospel Homilies*. Trans. Dom David Hurst. Kalamazoo, Mich., Cistercian Publications, 1990.

———. *Moralia in Iob* (PL 75–76).

———. *Morales sur Job 1–2*. Robert Gillet, ed. SC 32. Paris: Les Éditions du Cerf, 1950.

Gregory of Cyprus. *Apologia pro tomo suo* (PG 142, 251–70).

———. *De Processione Spiritus Sancti* (PG 142, 269–300).

———. *Expositio fidei contra Veccum* (PG 142, 233–46).

Gregory of Nazianzus. *De Vita Sua* (PG 37, 1133–62).

———. *Grégoire de Nazianze: Discours 20–23*. Ed. Justin Mossay. SC 270. Paris: Les Éditions du Cerf, 1980.

———. *Grégoire de Nazianze: Discours 24–25*. SC 284. J. Mossay, ed. Paris: Les Éditions du Cerf, 1981.

———. *Grégoire de Nazianze: Discours 42–43*. Ed. Claudio Moreschini. SC 358. Paris: Les Éditions du Cerf, 1990.

———. *On God and Christ: The Five Theological Orations and Two Letters to Cledonius*. Trans. and ed. Lionel Wickham and Frederick Williams. Crestwood, N.Y.: St. Vladimir's Seminary Press, 2002.

Gregory of Nyssa. *Adversus Eunomium* (PG 45, 243–1122).

———. *De Spiritu Sancto adversus Pneumatomachos Macedonianos* (PG 45, 1301–34).

———. *Gregorii Nysseni opera dogmatica minora*. Vol 3.1. Fridericus Mueller. Gregorii Nysseni Opera. Leiden: Brill, 1958.

Gregory of Tours. *History of the Franks*. Trans. Lewis Thorpe. New York: Penguin, 1976.

Gregory Thaumaturgus. *St. Gregory Thaumaturgus: Life and Works*. Trans. Michael Slusser. Washington, D.C.: Catholic University of America Press, 1998.

Grumel, V. "Le Filioque au concile photien de 879–880 et la témoignage de Michel dAnchialos." *Echos d'Orient* 29 (1930): 257–64.

———. "Nicéphore Blemmyde et la procession du Saint-Esprit." *Revue des sciences philosophiques et théologiques* 18 (1929): 636–56.

———. "S. Thomas et la doctrine des Grecs sur la procession du Saint-Esprit." *Echos d'Orient* 25 (1926): 258–80.

———. "Un ouvrage recent sur Jean Beccos, patriarche de Constantinople." *Echos d'Orient* 24 (1925): 229–37.

Gudziak, Borys. *Crisis and Reform: The Kyivan Metropolitanate, the Patriarchate of Constantinople, and the Genesis of the Union of Brest*. Cambridge, Mass.: Harvard University Press, 1998.

Gusev, Dimitri. "Nochmals zur Verständigung: Antwort an Herrn Prof. Gussew an der Akademie zu Kasan." *Revue Internationale de Théologie* 10 (1902): 1–20, 436–46, 447–75.

Haddad, Robert. "The Stations of the *Filioque*." *St. Vladimir's Seminary Quarterly* 46 (2002): 209–68.

Hadjiantoniou, George. *Protestant Patriarch: The Life of Cyril Lucaris*. Richmond, Va.: John Knox Press, 1961.

Hadrian, *Epistula Adriani Papae ad beatum Carolum Regum* (PL 98, 1247–92).

Haenchen, Ernst. *The Acts of the Apostles: A Commentary.* Philadelphia: Westminster Press, 1971.

Hahn, August. *Bibliothek der Symbole und Glaubensregeln der Alten Kirche.* Hildesheim, Germany: Georg Olms, 1962.

Haight, Roger. *Jesus: Symbol of God.* New York: Orbis Books, 1999.

Halecki, Oscar. *From Florence to Brest (1439–1596).* Rome: Sacrum Poloniae Millennium, 1958.

Hall, Douglas. *The Trinity: An Analysis of St. Thomas Aquinas' Expositio of the De Trinitate of Boethius.* Leiden: Brill, 1992.

Halleux, André. "Bessarion et le palamisme au concile de Florence." *Irenikon* 62 (1989): 307–32.

———. "Cyrille, Théodoret et le *Filioque*." *Revue d'histoire eclésiastique* 74 (1979): 597–625.

———. "Orthodoxie et Catholicisme: du personnalisme en pneumatologie." *Revue théologique de Louvain* 6 (1975): 3–30.

———. "Pour un accord oecuménique sur la procession du Saint-Esprit et l'addition du Filioque au Symbole." *Irénikon* 47 (1975): 170–77.

Hanson, R. P. G. "The Divinity of the Holy Spirit." *Church Quarterly* 1 (1969): 298–306.

Harris, Jonathon. *Byzantium and the Crusades.* New York: Palgrave, 2003.

Harris, Murray. *Jesus as God: The New Testament Use of Theos in Reference to Jesus.* Grand Rapids, Mich.: Baker Academic, 1998.

Harrison, Verna. "Perichoresis in the Greek Fathers." *St. Vladimir's Theological Quarterly* 35 (1991): 53–65.

Haugh, Richard. *Photius and the Carolingians: The Trinitarian Controversy.* Belmont, Mass.: Nordland Publishing Co., 1975.

Havrilak, Gregory. "Karl Rahner and the Greek Trinity." *St. Vladimir's Theological Quarterly* 34 (1990): 61–77.

Hayes, Zachary. "Introduction to Saint Bonaventure's *Disputed Questions on the Mystery of the Trinity.*" In *Works of St. Bonaventure* 3. New York: The Franciscan Institute, 1979.

Heath, R. G. "Western Schism of the Franks and the *Filioque*." *Journal of Ecclesiastical History* 23 (1972): 97–113.

Heinz, Hanspeter. *Trinitarische Begegnungen bei Bonaventura: Fruchtbarkeit einer appropriativen Trinitätstheologie.* Münster, Germany: Aschendorff, 1985.

Heinzer, Felix, and Christoph Schönborn, eds. *Maximus Confessor: Actes du Symposium sur Maxime le Confesseur, Fribourg, 2–5 Septembre 1980.* Fribourg-en-Suisse: Editions Universitarires, 1982.

Hendry, G. S. *The Holy Spirit in Christian Theology.* Philadelphia: Westminster, 1965.

Henry, Paul. "The Adversus Arium of Marius Victorinus, the First Systematic Exposition of the Doctrine of the Trinity." *Journal of Theological Studies* ns1 (1950): 42–55.

———. "On Some Implications of the '*Ex Patre Filioque Tanquam ab Uno Principio.*'" *Eastern Churches Quarterly* 7/Supplementary Issue (1948): 16–31.

Hergenroether, J. *Monumenta graeca ad Photiumeiusque Historia Pertinentia.* Ratisbon, Germany, 1869, 84–138.

Herman, A. "I legati inviati da Leoni IX nel 1054 a Constantinopoli." *Orientalia Christiana Periodica* 8 (1942): 209–18.

Heron, Alasdair. *Studies in the Trinitarian writings of Didymus the Blind, his authorship of the Adversus Eunomium IV–V and the De Trinitate.* Tübingen, Germany: University of Tübingen, 1972.

Heubach, Joachim. *Luther und die trinitarische Tradition: Ökumenische und philosophische Perspektiven.* Erlangen, Germany: Martin-Luther-Verlag, 1994.

Hilary of Poitiers. *The Trinity.* Trans. and edit. Stephen McKenna. FC 25. Washington, D.C.: Catholic University of America Press, 1954.

Hildebrand, Stephen. *The Trinitarian Theology of Basil of Caesarea.* Washington, D.C.: Catholic University of America Press, 2007.

Hoffman, George. "Patriarch Johann Bekkos und die latienisch kultur." *Orientalia Christiana Periodica* 11 (1945): 141–61.

———, ed. *Acta Camerae Apostolicae et civitatum Venetiarum, Ferrariae, Florentinae, Ianuae de Concilio Florentino.* CF 3.1 Rome: Pontifical Oriental Institute, 1950.

———. *Andreas de Santacroce, advocatus consistorialis, Acta Latina Concilii Florentini.* CF 6. Rome: Pontifical Oriental Institute, 1955.

———. *Epistolae Pontificiae ad Concilium Florentinum spectantes cum indicibus ad partes I-III.* CF 1.3. Rome: Pontifical Oriental Institute, 1946.

———. *Epistolae Pontificiae de rebus ante Concilium Florentinum gestis (1418–1438).* CF 1.1. Rome: Pontifical Oriental Institute, 1940.

———. *Epistolae Pontificiae de rebus in Concilio Florentino annis 1438–1439 gestis.* CF 1.2. Rome: Pontifical Oriental Institute, 1944.

———. *Fragmenta protocolli, diaria privata, sermones.* CF 3.2. Rome: Pontifical Oriental Institute, 1951.

———. *Orientalium documenta minora.* CF 3.3. Rome: Pontifical Oriental Institute, 1953.

———, and Emmanuele Candal, eds. *Isidorus Arch. Kioviensis et totius Russiae, Sermones inter Concilium Florentinum conscripti et Card. Iuliani Cesarini Memoria de additione ad symbolum.* CF 10.1. Rome: Pontifical Oriental Institute, 1971.

Hoffman, George, and Ludovico Petit, eds. *De Purgatorio disputationes in Concilio Florentino habitae.* CF 8.2. Rome: Pontifical Oriental Institute, 1969.

Holtzman, W. "Die Unionsverhandlungen zwischen Kaiser Alexios I und Papst Urban II im Jahre 1089." *Byzantinische Zeitschrift* 28 (1928): 38–67.

Hormisdas. *Epistula 79 ad Justinum Augustinum* (PL 63, 512–15).

Hornus, J. M. "Cyrille Lukaris: À propos d'un livre recent." *Proche Orient Chrétien,* Tome 13 (1963).

Hubbard, B. J. *The Matthean Redaction of the Primitive Apostolic Commissioning.* Missoula, Mont.: Scholars Press, 1974.

Hull, J. H. E. *The Holy Spirit in the Acts of the Apostles.* London: Lutterworth, 1967.

Humbert of Romans, *Opusculum tripartitum.* In *Fasciculum rerum expetendarum et fugiendarum* 2. Ed. Ortuin Gratius. London, 1690: 185–229.

Hussey, Edmund. "Palamite Trinitarian Models." *St. Vladimir's Theological Quarterly* 16 (1972):83–89.

———. "The Person-Energy Structure in the Theology of St. Gregory Palamas." *St. Vladimir's Theological Quarterly* 18 (1974): 22–43.

Hussey, J. M. *The Orthodox Church in the Byzantine Empire*. Oxford History of the Christian Church. Oxford: Clarendon Press, 1986.

Hyland, William. "John-Jerome of Prague (1368–1440) and the *Errores Graecorum*: Anatomy of a Polemic against Greek Christians." *Journal of Religious History* 21 (1997): 249–67.

Isidore of Seville. *De Ecclesasticis Officiis*. Trans. Thomas Knoebel. ACW 61. New York: Paulist Press, 2008.

———. *Etymologiae* (PL 82, 9–728).

Istavridis, Vasileios. *Orthodoxy and Anglicanism in the Twentieth Century*. London: Faith Press for the Anglican and Eastern Churches Association, 1959.

Jansen, Reiner. *Studien zu Luthers Trinitätslehre*. Bern, 1976.

Janssens, Bart, ed. *Ambigua ad Thomam una cum Epistula Secunda ad Eundem*. CCG 48. Turnhout, Belgium: Brepols, 2002.

Jeauneau, Edward. "Pseudo-Dionysius, Gregory of Nyssa and Maximus the Confessor in the Works of John Scottus Eriugena." In *Carolingian Essays*, ed. Uta-Renate Blumenthal, 137–49. Washington, D.C.: Catholic University of America Press, 1983.

Jeanneau, Edward, ed. *Ambigua ad Iohannem*. CCG 18. Turnhout, Belgium: Brepols, 1988.

John Cassian. *The Conferences*. Trans. Boniface Ramsey. ACW 57. New York: Paulist Press, 1997.

John of Damascus. *John of Damascus: Writings*. Trans. Frederic Chase. FC 37. Washington, D.C.: Catholic University of America Press, 1958.

———. *Three Treatises on the Divine Images*. Trans. Andrew Louth. Crestwood, N.Y.: St. Vladimir's Seminary Press, 2003.

John Scotus Erigena, *De divisione naturae* (PL 122, 439–1022).

Johnson, Luke Timothy. *Acts of the Apostles*. Sacra Pagina 5. Collegeville, Minn.: Liturgical Press, 1992.

Jordan, Mark. "Theological Exegesis and Aquinas' Treatise 'Against the Greeks.'" *Church History* 56 (1987): 445–56.

Jorgenson, James. "The Debate over Patristic Texts on Purgatory at the Council of Ferrara-Florence." *St. Vladimir's Theological Quarterly* 30 (1986): 309–34.

Juel, Donald. "The Trinity in the New Testament." *Theology Today* 54 (1997): 312–24.

Jugie, Martin. "Démétrius Cydonès et la théologie latine à Byzance." *Echos d'Orient* 31 (1928), 385–402.

———. "Le culte de Photius dans l'Église byzantine." *Revue de l'orient chrétien* 3 (1922–23): 105–22.

———. *Le Schisme Byzantin*. Paris: P. Lethielleux, 1941.

———. "Origine de la controverse sur l'addition du Filioque au Symbole." *Revue des sciences philosophiques et théologiques* 28 (1939): 369–85.

Julianus Pomerius. *De Vita Contemplativa* (PL 59, 415–520).

Kaiser, C. "The Development of the Johannine Motifs in Hilary's Doctrine of the Trinity." *Scottish Journal of Theology* 29 (1976): 237–47.

Kannengieser, Charles. "Athanasius of Alexandria and the Holy Spirit between Nicea I and Constantinople I." *Irish Theological Quarterly* 48 (1981): 166–80.

Karayiannis, Vasilios. *Maxime le Confesseur: Essence et Energies de Dieu.* Paris: Beauchesne, 1993.

Karmires, Ioannes. Ὀρθοδοξία καί Προτεσταντισμός. Athens, 1937.

———. *Ta dogmatika kai symbolika mnemeia tes orthodoxou katholikes ekklesias.* Graz, Austria: Akademische Druck- und Verlagsanstalt, 1968.

Käsemann, Ernst. *Commentary on Romans.* Grand Rapids, Mich.: Eerdmans, 1980.

Keleher, Serge. *Passion and Resurrection: The Greek Catholic Church in Soviet Ukraine 1939–1989.* L'viv, Ukraine: Stauropegion, 1993.

Kelly, J. N. D. *Early Christian Doctrines.* San Francisco: HarperCollins, 1978.

———. *The Athanasian Creed.* London: Adam & Charles Black, 1964.

———. *Early Christian Creeds*, 3rd ed. New York: Longman, 1972.

———. *Jerome: His Life, Writings, and Controversies.* Peabody, Mass.: Hendrickson, 1998.

Kennedy, Kevin. "The Permanence of an Idea: Three Ninth Century Frankish Ecclesiastics and the Authority of the Roman See." In *Aus Kirche und Reich: Studion zu Theologie Politik und Recht im Mittelatter.* Hubert Mordek, ed. Sigmaringen, Germany: J. Thorbecke, 1983, 105–16.

Kireev, Alexander. "Erklärungen von Professor Ossinin in München und Bonn (1871 und 1875)." *Revue Internationale de Théologie* 4 (1896): 489–501.

———. "Une replique du Général Kiréeff à M. le Prof. Gousseff sur l'ancien-catholicisme." *Revue Internationale de Théologie* 6 (1898): 124–29.

———. "Zur altkatholischen Frage." *Revue Internationale de Théologie* 5 (1897): 847–50.

Knowles, David, and Dimitri Obolensky. *The Middle Ages.* The Christian Centuries 2. New York, McGraw Hill, 1968.

Knuuttilla, Simo. "Luther's Trinitarian Theology and Its Medieval Background." *Studia Theologica* 53 (1999): 3–12.

Kolbaba, Tia. "Barlaam the Calabrian. Three treatises on papal primacy, introduction, edition and translation." *Revue des études byzantines* 53 (1995): 41–115.

———. *The Byzantine Lists: Errors of the Latins.* Chicago: University of Illinois Press, 2000.

———. *Inventing Latin Heretics: Byzantines and the Filioque in the Ninth Century.* Kalamazoo, Mich.: Medieval Institute Publications, 2008.

Köstenberger Andreas, and Scott Swain. *Father, Son, and Spirit: The Trinity and John's Gospel.* Downers Grove, Ill.: Intervarsity Press, 2008.

Kösters, Oliver. *Die Trinitätslehre des Epiphanus von Salamis.* Göttingen, Germany: Vanderhoeck & Ruprecht, 2003.

Krajcar, John, ed. *Acta slavica Concilii Florentini. Narrationes et documenta.* CF 11. Rome: Pontifical Oriental Institute, 1976.

Krauthauser, Carl. "The Council of Florence Revisited: The Union Decree in Light of the Clarification." *Diakonia* 29 (1996): 95–107.

Künstle, Karl. *Antipriscilliana.* Freiburg im Breisgau: Herder, Germany, 1905.

Küry, Urs. "Die Bedeutung des Filioque-Streites für den Gottesbegriff der abendländischen und der morganländischen Kirche." *Internationale kirchliche Zeitschrift* 33 (1943): 1–19.

————. "Die letzte Antwort der orthodoxen Petersburger Kommission an die altkatholische Rotterdamer Kommission." *Internationale kirchliche Zeitschrift* 58(1968): 29–47.

————. "Grundsätzlich-theologischen Überlegungen zur Filioque-Frage." *Internationale kirchliche Zeitschrift* 58 (1968): 81–108.

L'Huillier, Peter. *The Church of the Ancient Councils: The Disciplinary Work of the First Four Ecumenical Councils.* Crestwood, N.Y.: St. Vladimir's Seminary Press, 1996.

Ladaria, L. F. *El Espiritu Santo en San Hiliarie de Poitiers.* Madrid: Eapsa, 1977.

Laga, Carl, and Carlos Steel, eds. *Maximi Confessoris Quaestiones ad Thalassium.* CCG 7. Turnhout, Belgium: Brepols, 1980.

————. *Maximi Confessoris Quaestiones ad Thalassium.* CCG 22. Turnhout, Belgium: Brepols, 1990.

Laiou, Angeliki. *Constantinople and the Latins; The Foreign Policy of Andronicus II, 1282–1328.* Cambridge, Mass.: Harvard University Press, 1972.

————, and Roy Parviz Mottahedeh, eds. *The Crusades from the Perspective of Byzantium and the Muslim World.* Washington, D.C.: Dumbarton Oaks, 2001.

Lampe, G. W. H. *The Holy Spirit.* Oxford: SLG Press, 1974.

————. "The Holy Spirit and the Person of Christ," in *Christ, Faith, and History: Cambridge Studies in Christology,* ed. E. G. Sykes and G. E. Clayton. Cambridge: Cambridge University Press, 1972.

Lapidge, M. *Archbishop Theodore, Commemorative Studies on His Life and Influence.* Cambridge: Cambridge University Press, 1995.

Larchet, Jean-Claude. "À Propos de la Récente Clarification du Conseil Pontifical pour la Promotion de L'Unité des Chrétiens." *Le Messager orthodoxe* 129 (1997):3–58.

————. "Ancestral Guilt according to St. Maximus the Confessor: A Bridge between Eastern and Western Conceptions." *Sobornorst* 20 (1998): 26–48.

————. *Maxime le Confesseur, médiateur entre l'Orient et l'Occident.* Paris: Les Éditions du Cerf, 1998.

Laurent, V. "La croisade et la question d'Orient sous le pontificat de Grégoire X." *Revue historique du Sud-Est européen* 22 (1945): 105–37.

————. "Le schisme de Michel Cérulaire." *Echos d'Orient* 31 (1932): 97–110.

————, ed., *Les "Mémoires" du Grand Ecclésiarque de l'Église de Constantinople Sylvestre Syropoulos sur le Concile de Florence (1438–1439).* CF 9. Rome: Pontifical Oriental Institute, 1971.

————, and J. Darrouzès, eds. *Dossier Grec de l'Union de Lyon 1273–1277.* Paris, 1976.

Leo III, *Epistula 15 seu symbolum orthodoxae fidei Leonis papae* (PL 102, 1030–32).

Leo the Great. *Epistle 15 to Turribius, Bishop of Astorga* (PL 54, 677–92).

————. *Letters.* Trans. Edmund Hunt. FC 34.Washington, D.C.: Catholic University Press, 1957.

————. *Sermons.* Ttrans. Jane Patricia Freeland and Agnes Josephine Conway. FC 93. Washington, D.C.: Catholic University Press, 1996.

Leo XIII, *Leonis XIII Pontificis Maximi Acta* vol. 14. Graz, Austria: Akademische Druck, 1971.

Leyser, K. "The Tenth Century in Byzantine-Western Relationships." In Derek Baker, ed., *Relations between East and West in the Middle Ages.* Edinburgh, Edinburgh University Press, 1973.

Lienhard, Joseph. "Augustine and the Filioque." In *Festschrift for Roland Teske* (forthcoming).

Likoudis, James. *Ending the Byzantine Greek Schism*. New Rochelle, N.Y.: Catholics United for the Faith, 1992.

Limouris, Gennadius, ed. *Orthodox Visions of Ecumenism: Statements, Messages, and Reports on the Ecumenical Movement 1902–1992*. Geneva: World Council of Churches, 1994.

Liutprand of Cremona, *Mission to Constantinople: Liutprand of Cremona*. Trans. Lynn Nelson and Melanie Veenbuer Shirk. Lawrence, Kan.: Coronado Press, 1972.

Löffler, Paul. "Die Trinitätslehre des Bischofs Hilarius zwischen Ost und West." ZKG 71 (1960): 26–36.

Logan, A. "Origen and the Development of Trinitarian Theology." In L. Lies, ed., *Origeniana Quarta*. Innsbruck-Vienna: Tyrolia, 1987: 424–29.

Lombard, Peter. *The Sentences Book 1: The Mystery of the Trinity*. Trans.Giulio Silano. MST 42. Toronto: Pontifical Institute for Medieval Studies, 2007.

Longenecker, Richard. *Galatians*.Word Biblical Commentary 41. Dallas: Thomas Nelson, 1990.

Lossky, Vladimir. *The Mystical Theology of the Eastern Church*. Trans. the Fellowship of St. Alban and St. Sergius. Crestwood, N.Y.: St. Vladimir's Seminary Press, 1976.

———. "The Procession of the Holy Spirit in the Orthodox Triadology." *Eastern Churches Quarterly* 7/Supplementary Issue (1948): 31–53.

———. "The Procession of the Holy Spirit in Orthodox Trinitarian Doctrine." In *In the Image and Likeness of God*. Crestwood, N.Y.: St. Vladimir's Seminary Press, 1985.

Louth, Andrew. "Dogma and Spirituality in St. Maximus the Confessor." In *Prayer and Spirituality in the Early Church*, ed. Pauline Allen, 197–208. Queensland: Australian Catholic University, 1998.

———. *Greek East and Latin West: The Church AD 681–1071*. The Church in History 3. Crestwood, N.Y.: St. Vladimir's Seminary Press, 2007.

———. "Recent Research on St. Maximus the Confessor: A Survey." *St. Vladimir's Theological Quarterly* 42 (1998): 67–84.

———. "St. Gregory the Theologian and St. Maximus the Confessor: The Shaping of Tradition." In *Making and Remaking of Christian Doctrine : Essays in Honour of Maurice Wiles*, ed. Sarah Coakley and David Pailin, 117–30. Oxford: Clarendon Press, 1993.

———. "St. Maximus Confessor between East and West." *Studia Patristica* 32 (1997): 332–45.

———, ed. *Maximus the Confessor*. New York: Routledge, 1996.

Lull, Timothy, ed. *Martin Luther's Basic Theological Writings*. Minneapolis: Fortress Press, 1989.

Luther, Martin. *The Large Catechism*. Trans. Robert Fischer. Philadelphia: Muhlenberg Press, 1959.

———. "Treatise on the Last Words of David." In Jaroslav Pelikan, ed., *Luther's Works* 15. Saint Louis: Concordia Publishing House, 1972.

Macha, Josef. *Ecclesiastical Unification: A Theoretical Framework Together with Case Studies from the History of Latin–Byzantine Relations*. Orientalia Christiana Analecta 198. Rome: Pontifical Oriental Institute, 1974.

MacIntyre, J. "The Holy Spirit in Greek Patristic Thought." *Scottish Journal of Theology* 7 (1954): 353–75.

Madden, Thomas. *The Fourth Crusade: Event, Aftermath, and Perceptions*. London: Ashgate, 2008.

Maertens, Thierry. *The Spirit of God in Scripture*. Baltimore: Helicon, 1966.

Malaterra, Goffredo. *Historia Sicula* (PL 149, 1087–1216).

Mango, Cyril. *The Homilies of Photius of Constantinople: English Translation, Introduction, and Commentary*. Cambridge, Mass.: Harvard University Press, 1958.

Mann, C. S. "Pentecost, Spirit, and John." *Theology* 62 (1959): 188–90.

Mann, William. "Anselm on the Trinity." In Brian Davies and Brian Leftow, eds. *Cambridge Companion to Anselm*. Cambridge: Cambridge University Press, 2004, 257–78.

Marius Victorinus, *Theological Treatises on the Trinity*. Trans. Mary Clark. FC 69. Washington, D.C.: Catholic University of America Press, 1981.

Markus, R. A. *Gregory the Great and His World*. Cambridge: Cambridge University Press, 1997.

Marshall, Bruce. "Action and Person: Do Palamas and Aquinas Agree about the Spirit?" *St. Vladimir's Theological Quarterly* 39 (1995): 379–408.

Marshall, I. Howard. *Epistles of John*. New International Commentary on the New Testament. Grand Rapids. Mich.: Eerdmans, 1994.

Martin, Vincent. "Aspects théologiques du 'Filioque.'" *Irénikon* 62 (1989): 36–50.

Marx, Hans-Jürgen. *Filioque und Verbot eines anderen Glaubens auf dem Florentinum: zum Pluralismus in dogmatischen Formeln*. Sankt Augustin, Germany: Steyler Verlag, 1977.

Mastrantonis, George, ed. *Augsburg and Constantinople: The Correspondence Between the Tübingen Theologians and Patriarch Jeremiah II of Constantinople on the Augsburg Confession*. Brookline, Mass.: Holy Cross Orthodox Press, 1982.

Matera, Frank. *Galatians*. Sacra Pagina 9. Collegeville, Minn.: Liturgical Press, 1992.

Maximus the Confessor, *Opusculum* 10 (PG 91, 136).

Mayne, Richard. "East and West in 1054." *Cambridge Historical Journal* 11 (1954): 133–48.

Mccauley, Leo, John Sullivan, Martin McGuire, and Roy J. Deferrari, eds. *Funeral Orations by Saint Gregory Nazianzen and Saint Ambrose*. FC 22. Washington, D.C.: Catholic University of America Press, 1968.

McDougall, Joy Ann. *Pilgrimage of Love: Moltmann on the Trinity and Christian Life*. Oxford: Oxford University Press, 2005.

McGuckin, John. *Saint Gregory of Nazianzus: An Intellectual Biography*. Crestwood, N.Y.: St. Vladimir's Seminary Press, 2001.

Meijer, Johan. *A Successful Reunion Council: A Theological Analysis of the Photian Synod of 879–80*. Thessalonikē, Greece: Patriarchikon Hydrima Paterikōn Meletōn, 1975.

Meijering, E. P. "The Doctrine of the Will and of the Trinity in the Orations of Gregory of Nazianzus." *Nederlands Theologisch Tijdschrift* 27 (1973): 224–34.

———. *Hilary on the Trinity*. Leiden: Brill Academic Press, 1982.

———. *Melanchthon and Patristic Thought: The Doctrines of Christ and Grace, the Trinity and the Creation*. Studies in the History of Christian Thought 32. Leiden: Brill, 1984.

Melanchthon, Philip. *Loci Communes.* Trans. J. A. O. Preus. St. Louis: Concordia
 Publishing House, 1992.

Menzies, R. P. *The Development of Early Christian Pneumatology with Special Reference to
 Luke-Acts.* Sheffield: JSOT Press, 1991.

Mercati, Giovanni. *Notizie di Procoro e Demetrio Cidone Manuele Caleca e Teodoro
 Meliteniota ed altri appunti per la storia della teologia e della letteratura bizantina del
 secolo XIV.* Studi e testi 56. Vatican City: Biblioteca Apostolica Vaticana, 1931.

Metallinos, Eustathius, ed. *Orthodox and Catholic Union.* Seattle: St. Nectarios Press,
 1985.

Metochites, George. *De Processione Spiritus Sancti* (PG 141, 1405–17).

———. *Historia dogmatica* 2, ed. A. Mai. Rome, 1871.

Meyendorff, John. *Byzantine Theology: Historical Trends and Doctrinal Themes.* New
 York: Fordham University Press, 1975.

———. "Byzantium as the Center of Theological thought in the Christian East." In
 Schools of Thought in the Christian Tradition. ed. P Henry. Philadelphia: Fortress
 Press, 1984.

———. *Christ in Eastern Christian Thought.* Crestwood, N.Y.: St. Vladimir's Seminary
 Press, 1987.

———. "Free Will in St. Maximus the Confessor." In *Ecumenical World of Orthodox
 Civilization,* ed. Georges Florovsky, Andrew Blane, and Thomas Bird, 71–75. The
 Hague: Mouton, 1974.

———. *Imperial Unity and Christian Divisions: The Church 450–680 A.D.* The Church in
 History 2. Crestwood, N.Y.: St. Vladimir's Seminary Press, 1989.

———. "La Procession du Saint-Esprit chez les Pères orientaux." *Russie et chrétienté* 2
 (1950): 158–78.

———. *A Study of Gregory Palamas.* Trans. George Lawrence. Crestwood, N.Y.: St.
 Vladimir's Seminary Press, 1998.

———. "Un mauvais théologien de l'unité au quatorzième siècle: Barlaam le Calabrais." In *L'église et les églises, 1054–1954: Etudes et travaux offerts a Dom Lambert
 Baudouin* vol. 2. Chevetogne, Belgium: Éditions de Chevetogne, 1955, 47–64.

———. "Was There an Encounter between East and West at Florence?" In *Rome
 Constantinople and Moscow: Historical and Theological Studies.* Crestwood, N.Y.: St.
 Vladimir's Seminary Press, 1998.

———, and Michael Fahey. *Trinitarian Theology East and West.* Brookline: Holy Cross
 Orthodox Press, 1977.

Meyer, Harding, and Lukas Vischer, eds. *Growth in Agreement: Reports and Agreed
 Statements of Ecumenical Conversations on a World Level.* New York: Paulist Press,
 1994.

Meyer, John. "Clarifying the *Filioque* Formula Using Athanasius' Doctrine of the Spirit
 of Christ." *Communio* 27 (2000): 386–405.

Michaelides, George P. "The Greek Orthodox Position on the Confession of Cyril
 Lucaris." *Church History* 12 (June 1943): 118–29.

Michaud, E. "L'état de la question du '*Filioque*' après la Conférence de Bonn de 1875."
 Revue internationale de Théologie 3 (1895), 89–99.

Michel, Anton, ed. *Humbert und Kerularios: Quellen und Studien zum Schisma des XI.
 Jahrhunderts.* Vol. 2. Paderborn, Germany: Schöningh, 1924.

Mihalcesco, J. "Les idées calvinistes du patriarche Cyrille Lucaris." *Revue d'hist* (1931): 506–20.

Mohler, Ludwig, ed., *Kardinal Bessarion als Theologe, Humanist, und Staatsmann. Funde und Forschungen*, 3 vols. Paderborn, Germany, 1923–42; repr: Aalen, Germany: Scientia- Verlag, 1967.

Moingt, Joseph. "Procession et mission du Saint-Esprit." In *La trinité: livres VIII-XV*. Bibliothèque Augustinienne 16. Paris: Études Augustiniennes, 1991.

———. *Théologie Trinitaire de Tertullien* 3 vols. Aubier, France: Paris: Aubier, 1966.

Moltmann, Jürgen. *The Spirit of Life: A Universal Affirmation*, trans. Margaret Kohl. Minneapolis: AugsburgFortress, 1992.

———. *The Trinity and the Kingdom*, trans. Margaret Kohl. San Francisco: Harper Collins, 1981.

Monfasani, John. *Byzantine Scholars in Renaissance Italy: Cardinal Bessarion and Other Emigres: Selected Essays*. Brookfield, Ver.: Variorum, 1995.

Montague, G. T. *The Holy Spirit: Growth of a Biblical Tradition*. New York: Paulist Press, 1976.

Moorhead, John, ed., *Gregory the Great, The Early Church Fathers*. New York: Routledge, 2005.

Morgan, J. H. "Early Orthodox—Old Catholic Relations: General Kireeff and Professor Michaud." *The Church Quarterly Review* 152 (1951): 1–10.

Morris, G. "L'Origine du symbole d'Athanase." *Revue Bénédictine* 44 (1932): 207–19.

Mühlen, H. "Das Konzil von Florenz (1439) als vorlaufigen Modell eines kommenden Unionskonzils." *Theologie und Glaube* 63 (1973): 184–97.

Mullett, Margaret. *Theophylact of Ochrid: Reading the Letters of a Byzantine Archbishop*. Birmingham Byzantine and Ottoman Monographs 2. London: Variorum, 1997.

Munitiz, J. "A Reappraisal of Blemmydes First Discussion with the Latins." *Byzantino-slavica* 51 (1990): 20–26.

Murphy, Francis X. "Bessarion's Patristic Heritage." *Studia Patristica* 23 (1989): 250–55.

Ngien, Dennis. *Apologetic for Filioque in Medieval Theology*. Waynesboro, Ga.: Paternoster Press, 2005.

Nicetas Choniates. *The Sack of Constantinople*. Trans. D. C. Munro. Translations and Reprints from the Original Sources of European History, Series 1, 3.1. Philadelphia: University of Pennsylvania Press, 1912.

Nicetas of Maroneia. *De Procession Spiritus Sancti* (PG 139, 169–222).

Nicetas of Remesiana. *De Spiritus Sancti Potentia* (PL 52, 853–64).

———. *Explanatio Symboli* (PL 52, 865–74).

Nicholas III. *Epistula 92 Responsa Nicholai ad consulta Bulgarorum* (PL 119, 1012).

———. *Epistula 98 Ad Michaelem Imperatorem* (PL 119, 1016–45).

———. *Epistula 152 Ad Hincmarum et caertos episcopos in regno Caroli constitutos* (PL 119, 1152–61).

Nicholas of Hermopolis. "Report to the Holy Synod of Constantinople of the Church of Alexandria upon the First Session." *The Christian East* (1933): 87–91.

Nichols, Aidan. *Byzantine Gospel: Maximus the Confessor in Modern Scholarship*. Edinburgh: T&T Clark, 1993.

———. *Light from the East: Authors and Themes in Orthodox Theology*. London: Sheed and Ward, 1995.

———. "The Reception of St Augustine and his Work in the Byzantine-Slav Tradition." *Angelicum* 64 (1987): 437–52.

———. *Rome and the Eastern Churches*. Collegeville, Minn.: Liturgical Press, 1992.

Nicol, Donald. "The Byzantine Reaction to the Second Council of Lyons, 1274." In *Councils and Assemblies: Papers Read at the Eighth Summer Meeting and the Ninth WinterMeeting of the Ecclesiastical History Society*, ed. G. J. Cuming and Derek Baker, 113–46. Cambridge: Cambridge University Press, 1971.

———. *Byzantium: Its Ecclesiastical History and Relations with the Western World*. London: Variorum, 1972.

———. "Greeks and the Union of the Churches: The Preliminaries to the Second Council of Lyons, 1261–1274." In *Medieval Studies Presented to Aubrey Gwynn*, ed. John Watt, John Morrall, and Francis X. Martin, 454–80. Dublin: Lochlainn, 1961.

Nissiotis, Nikos. "Pneumatologie orthodoxe." In *Le Saint Esprit*, ed. F. J. Leenhard. Geneva: Labor et Fides, 1963.

Noble, Thomas. "From the *Liber Carolini* to the *Opus Caroli Regis*." *Journal of Medieval Latin* 9 (1999): 131–47.

Nolland, John. *Luke 1–9:20*. Word Biblical Commentary 35a. Dallas: Thomas Nelson, 1989.

Norwich, John Julian. *Byzantium: The Early Centuries, History of Byzantium* 1. London: Viking, 1988.

Novatian. *The Trinity, The Spectacles, Jewish Foods, In Praise of Purity, Letters*. Trans. Russell Desimone. FC 67. Washington, D.C.: Catholic University of America Press, 1972.

Oberdorfer, Bernd. *Filioque, Geschichte und Theologie eines ökumenischen Problems*. Göttingen, Germany: Vandenhoeck & Rupert, 2001.

Obolensky, Dimitri. *The Byzantine Commonwealth: Eastern Europe 500–1453*. London: Weidenfield and Nicolson, 1971.

———. "Theophylact of Ohrid." In *Six Byzantine Portraits*, 34–82. Oxford: Clarendon Press, 1988.

O'Collins, Gerald. *The Tripersonal God: Understanding and Interpreting the Trinity*. New York: Paulist Press, 1999.

Odo of Deuil, *De profectione Ludovici VII in orientem*. Trans. V. Berry. New York: Columbia University Press, 1948.

Oeyen, Christian. "Chronologisch-bibliographischen Übersicht der Unionsverhand-lungen zwischen orthodoxer Kirche und altkatholischer Kirche." *Internationale kirchliche Zeitschrift* 57 (1967): 29–51.

Opusculum Contra Francos. In *Monumenta graeca ad Photium eiusque Historiam Pertinentia*. J Hergenroether, ed. Ratisbon, Germany, 1869.

Origen. *Commentary on the Epistle to the Romans*. Trans T. P. Schek. FC 103–104. Washington, D.C.: Catholic University of America Press, 2001–2002.

———. *Commentary on the Gospel According to St. John Books 1–10*. Trans. Ronald Heine. FC 80. Washington, D.C.: Catholic University of America Press, 1990.

———. *On First Principles*. Trans G. W. Butterworth. New York: Harper and Row, 1973.

Orlandis José, and Domingo Ramos-Lisson. *Die Synoden auf der Iberischen Halbinsel bis zum Einbuch des Islam.*, Paderborn, Germany: F. Schöningh, 1981.

Orphanos, Markos. "Some Points of Mark of Ephesus' Criticism of the *Filioque*." In *Philoxenia*, ed. Anastasios Kallis, 223–32. Münste, Germany: Aschendorff, 1980.

Ostroumoff, Ivan. *The History of the Council of Florence.* Trans. Basil Popoff. Boston: Holy Transfiguration Monastery, 1971.

Overbeck, J. J. "The Bonn Conferences, and the *Filioque* Question." *Orthodox Catholic Review* 4 (1875): 217–64.

———. *Die Bonner Unions-Konferenzen.* Halle, Germany, 1876.

Pachymeres, George. *De Michaele et Andronico Palaeologis libri tredecim* 1. Bonn: Corpus Scriptorum Historiae Byzantinae, 1835.

Painter, John. *1,2, and 3 John.* Sacra Pagina Series 18. Collegeville, Minn.: Liturgical Press, 2002.

Palamas, Gregory. Λόγοὶ Ἀποδεικτικοὶ Δύο. In *Γρηγορίου τοῦ Παλαμᾶ Συγγράμματα.* Vol.1. Ed. Boris Bobrinsky. Thessalonica, Greece, 1962.

Palmer, G. E. H., Philip Sherrard, and Kallistos Ware. *The Philokalia*, vol. 2. London: Faber and Faber, 1981.

Papadakis, Aristeides. "Byzantine Perceptions of the Latin West." *Greek Orthodox Theological Review* 36 (1991): 231–42.

———. *The Christian East and the Rise of the Papacy.* Crestwood, N.Y.: St. Vladimir's Seminary Press, 1994.

———. *Crisis in Byzantium: The Filioque Controversy in the Patriarchate of Gregory II of Cyprus.* Crestwood, N.Y.: St. Vladimir's Seminary Press, 1996.

———. "Ecumenism in the 13th Century: The Byzantine Case." *St. Vladimir's Theological Quarterly* 27 (1983): 207–17.

———. "Gregory of Cyprus and Mark's Report Again." *Greek Orthodox Theological Review* 21 (1976): 147–57.

———. "Late Thirteenth Century Byzantine Theology and Gregory II of Cyprus." In *Byzantine Ecclesiastical Personalities*, ed. N. M. Vaporis, 57–72. Brookline, Mass.: Holy Cross Orthodox Press, 1975.

Papadopoulos, S. "Thomas in Byzanz: Thomas Rezeption und Thomas Kritik in Byzanz zwischen 1354 und 1435." *Theologie und Philosophie* 49 (1974): 274–304.

Papathomopoulos, Manoles, Isabella Tsavari, and Gianpaolo Rigotti, eds. Αὐγουστίνου περὶ Τριάδος βιβλία πεντεκαίδεκα ἅπερ ἐκ τῆς Λατίνων διαλέκτου εἰς τὴν Ἑλλάδα μετήνεγκε Μάξιμος ὁ Πλανούδης. Athens: Kentron Ekdoseos Ergon Hellenon Syngrapheon, 1995.

Pechler, Gloys. *Geschichte des Protestantisme in der orientischen Kirche im XVII Jahrhundert order der Patriarch Cyrill Lukaris und seine Zeit.* Munich, 1862.

Pelikan, Jaroslav. *The Christian Tradition 2: The Spirit of Eastern Christendom.* Chicago: University of Chicago Press, 1974.

———. *The Christian Tradition 3: The Growth of Medieval Theology.* Chicago: University of Chicago Press, 1978.

———. "Council or Father or Scripture: The Concept of Authority in the Theology of Maximus the Confessor." In *Heritage of the Early Church: Essays in Honor of the Very Reverend George Florovsky*, ed. David Neiman and Margaret Schatkin, 277–88. Rome: Pontifical Oriental Institute, 1973.

————. *Credo: Historical and Theological Guide to Creeds and Confessions of Faith in the Christian Tradition*. New Haven, Conn.: Yale University Press, 2003.

————. "The Doctrine of the *Filioque* in Thomas Aquinas and Its Patristic Antecedents." In *St. Thomas Aquinas Commemorative Studies*, 315–36. Toronto: Pontifical Institute of Medieval Studies, 1974.

————. *The Melody of Theology: A Philosophical Dictionary*. Cambridge, Mass.: Harvard University Press, 1988.

———— and Valerie Hotchkiss, eds. *Creeds and Confessions of Faith in the Christian Tradition*, 3 vols. New Haven, Conn.: Yale University Press, 2003.

Peri, Vittorio. "Il Simbolo Epigrafico di S. Leone III nelle Basiliche Romane dei SS. Pietro e Paolo." *Rivista di Archeologia Christiana* 45 (1969): 191–221.

————. *Ricerche sull'editio princeps degli atti greci del Concilio di Firenze*. Città del Vaticano: Biblioteca Apostolica Vaticana, 1975.

Perry, William Steven. *The Union Conference at Bonn: A Personal Narrative*. Privately published, 1875.

Pesch, Rudolf. *Die Apostelgeschichte*. Evangelisch-Katholischer Kommentar zum Neuen Testament. Zürich: Benzinger Verlag, 1986.

Peter Damien. *Contra errorem Graecorum de Processione Spiritus sancti* (PL 145, 633–42).

Peter of Antioch. *Petri Theopoleos totiusque Orientis patriarchae disertatio* (PG 120, 795–815).

Peters, Albrecht. "Die Trinitätslehre in der reformatorischen Christenheit." *Theologische Literaturzeitung* 94 (1969): 561–70.

Peterson, Joan. "Did Gregory the Great Know Greek." In D. Baker, ed. *The Orthodox Churches and the West*. Studies in Church History 13. Oxford: Oxford University Press, 1976, 121–34.

————. "Homo omnino Latinus? The Theological and Cultural Background of Pope Gregory the Great." *Speculum* 62/63 (1987): 529–51.

Petit, Ludovico, ed. *Marci Eugenici, metropolitae Ephesi, opera antiunionistica*. CF 10.2. Rome: Pontifical Oriental Institute, 1977.

Phillips, Jonathan. *The Fourth Crusade and the Sack of Constantinople*. New York: Penguin, 2005.

Photius of Constantinople. *The Mystagogy of the Holy Spirit*. Trans. Holy Transfiguration Monastery. Astoria, N.Y.: Studion Publishers, 1983.

Piétri, Charles. *Roma Christiana* I. Rome, 1976.

Piret, Pierre. *Le Christ et la Trinité selon Maxime le Confesseur*. Paris: Beauchesne, 1983.

Podskalsky, G. *Theologie und Philosophie in Byzanz*. Munich, 1977.

Porsch, F. *Pneuma und Wort*. Frankfurt am Main: J. Knecht, 1974.

Powell, Samuel. *The Trinity in German Thought*. Cambridge: Cambridge University Press, 2001.

Prestige, G. L. *God in Patristic Thought*. London: SPCK, 1952.

"Proceedings of the Conferences between the Old Catholic and Orthodox Churches, held at Bonn, on October 27 and 28, 1931." *The Christian East* 13 (1932): 91–98.

Pseudo-Dionysius. *Pseudo-Dionysius: The Complete Works*. Ed. trans. Colm Luibheid. Mahwah, N.J.: Paulist Press, 1987.

Pusey, E. *On the Clause "And the Son" in Regard to the Eastern Church and the Bonn Conference*. Oxford, 1876.

Quasten, Johannes. *Patrology 3: The Golden Age of Greek Patristic Literature.* Westminster, Md.: Christian Classics, 1990.

Queller, Donald, and Thomas Madden. *The Fourth Crusade: The Conquest of Constantinople.* Philadelphia: University of Pennsylvania Press, 1997.

Rahner, Karl. "Oneness and Threefoldness of God in Discussion with Islam." *Theological Investigations* 18. Trans. Edward Quinn. New York: Crossroad, 1983, 105–21.

———."Remarks on the Dogmatic Treatise *De Trinitate.*" *Theological Investigations* 4. Trans. Kevin Smyth. Baltimore: Helicon Press, 1966, 77–102.

———. *The Trinity.* Trans. Joseph Donceel. New York: Herder and Herder, 1970.

Ratramnus of Corbie, *Contra Graecorum Opposita Romanam Ecclesiam Infamantium* (PL 121, 225–346).

Ratzinger, Joseph. *Introduction to Christianity.* Trans. J. R. Foster. New York:Seabury, 1969.

Reid, Duncan. *Energies of the Spirit: Trinitarian Models in Eastern Orthodox and Western Theology.* Atlanta: Scholars Press, 1997.

Reidinger, Rudolf. "Die Lateranakten von 649, ein Werke der Byzantiner um Maximus Homologetes." *Byzantion* 13 (1985): 517–34.

Report of the Joint Doctrinal Commission appointed by the Oecumenical Patriarch and the Archbishop of Canterbury for Consultation on the Points of Agreement and Difference between the Anglican and the Eastern Orthodox Churches. London: S.P.C.K. 1932.

Report of the Lambeth Conference 1978. London: CIO Publishing, 1978.

Repsonsio Episcoporum Germaniae Wormatiae coadunatorum de Fide Sante Trinitas contra Graecorum Haeresim (PL 119 1201–12).

Reusch, Heinrich. *Report of the Union Conferences Held from August 10 to 16, 1875, at Bonn.* Trans. Samuel Buel. New York: T. Whittaker, 1876.

Richard de Saint-Victor. *La Trinité.* G. Salet, ed. SC 63. Paris: Les Éditions du Cerf, 1959.

Riebe, Alexandra. *Rom in Gemeinschaft mit Konstantinopel: Patriarch Johannes XI. Bekkos als Verteidiger der Kirchenunion von Lyon (1274).* Wiesbaden, Germany: Harrassowitz Verlag, 2005.

Ritter, A. M. *Das Konzil von Konstantinopel und sein Symbol.* Göttingen, Germany: Vandenhoek and Ruprecht, 1965.

Roberg, Burkhard. *Das Zweite Konzil von Lyon.* Paderborn, Germany: Ferdinand Schöningh, 1990.

———. *Die Union zwischen der griechischen und der lateinischen Kirche auf dem II Konzil von Lyon.* Bonner historische Forschungen 24. Bonn, 1964.

Rodulfus Glaber. *Historiarum libri quinque* (PL 142, 611–98).

Rodzianko, V. "*Filioque* in Patristic Thought." *Studia Patristica* 2 (1957): 295–308.

Romanides, John. *The Ancestral Sin.* Trans. G. Gabriel. Ridgewood, N.J.: Zephyr Publishing, 1998.

———. *Franks, Romans, Feudalism and Doctrine: The Interplay between Theology and Society.* Brookline, Mass.: Holy Cross, 1981.

———. *An Outline of Orthodox Patristic Dogmatics.* Ed. and trans. George Dragas. Rollinsford, N.H.: Orthodox Research Institute, 2004.

Rose, Seraphim. *The Place of Blessed Augustine in the Orthodox Church.* Platina, Cal.: St. Herman of Alaska Brotherhood, 1996.

Rosemann, Phillip. *Peter Lombard*. New York: Oxford University Press, 2004.

————. *The Story of a Great Medieval Book: Peter Lombard's "Sentences."* Peterborough, Ontario: Broadview Press, 2007.

Royer, Wilfred. "The Trinity in the Thought of St. Bonaventure : An Eastern Orthodox Perspective." Ph.D. Thesis, Fordham University, 1994.

Runciman, Steven. *The Eastern Schism: A Study of the Papacy and the Eastern Churches during the XIth and XIIth Centuries*. London: Oxford University Press, 1955.

————. *The Fall of Constantinople 1453*. Cambridge: Cambridge University Press, 1965.

————. *A History of the Crusades*, vol. 3: *The Kingdom of Acre and the Later Crusades*. Cambridge: Cambridge University Press, 1951.

Russell, Norman. "Anselm of Havelberg and the Union of the Churches." *Sobornorst* 1 (1979): 19–41.

————. "Palamism and the Circle of Demetrius Cydones." In J. *Chrysostomides, Jonathan Harris, Charalambos Dendrinos, and Judith Herrin*, eds., *Porphyrogenita: Essays on the History and Literature of Byzantium and the Latin East in Honour of Julian Chrysostomides*. London: Ashgate, 2003, 153–74.

Rusticus. *Contra Acephalos Disputatio* (PL 67, 1167–1254).

Sand, Alexander. *Das Evangelium nach Matthäus*. Regensburger Neues Testament. Regensburg, Germany: Verlag Friedrich Pustet, 1986.

Schaberg, J. *The Father, the Son, and the Holy Spirit*. Chico, Cal.: Scholars Press, 1982.

Schmemann, Alexander. "St. Mark of Ephesus and the Theological Conflicts in Byzantium." *St. Vladimir's Seminary Quarterly* 1 (1957): 11–24.

Schnackenburg, Rudolf. *The Gospel According to St. John 3*. Trans. David Smith and G. A. Kon. New York: Crossroad, 1982.

Scholarius, George. *Oeuvres completes*. 7 vols. Ed. L. Petit and M. Jugie. Paris: Bonne Presse, 1928–36.

Schultze, Bernard, ed. *Fantinus Vallareso, archiepiscopus Cretensis, Libellus de ordine generalium conciliorum et unione florentina*. CF 2.2. Rome: Pontifical Oriental Institute, 1944.

Schultze, Bernhard. "Patriarch Gregorios von Cyprem über das Filioque." *Orientalia Christiana Periodica* 51 (1985): 163–87.

————. "Zum Ursprung des Filioque: das Filioque und der römische Primat." *Orientalia Christiana Periodica* 48 (1982): 5–18.

Schweitzer, E. *The Holy Spirit*. Philadelphia: Fortress Press, 1980.

Senior, Donald. *Matthew*. Abbington New Testament Commentaries. Nashville, Tenn.: Abbington Press, 1998.

Setton, Kenneth. *The Papacy and the Levant 1204–1571*, 2 vols. Philadelphia: American Philosophical Society, 1976.

Ševčenko, Ihor. "Intellectual Repercussions of the Council of Florence." *Church History* 24 (1955): 291–323.

Shapland, C. R. B. *The Letters of Saint Athanasius Concerning the Holy Spirit*. London: Epworth Press, 1951.

Sherrard, Philip. *The Greek East and the Latin West: A Study in the Christian Tradition*. Limni, Greece: Denise Harvey & Company, 1992.

Sherwood, Polycarp. *An Annotated Date List of the Works of St. Maximus the Confessor*. Rome: Herder, 1952.

———. *The Earlier Ambugua of St. Maximus the Confessor.* Rome: Herder, 1955.

———. "Exposition and Use of Scripture in St. Maximus the Confessor as Manifest in the *Quaestiones ad Thalassium.*" *Orientalia Christiana Periodica* 24 (1958): 202–7.

———. "Survey of Recent Work on Maximus the Confessor." *Traditio* 20 (1964): 428–37.

———, ed. *St. Maximus the Confessor: The Ascetic Life, the Four Centuries on Charity.* ACW 21. New York: Newman Press, 1955.

Siecienski, A. Edward. "The Authenticity of Maximus the Confessor's *Letter to Marinus*: The Argument from Theological Consistency." *Vigiliae Christianae* 61 (2007): 189–227.

———. "Avoiding the Sin of Ham: Dealing with Errors in the Works of the Fathers." *Studia Patristica* 45, ed. J. Baun, A. Cameron, M. Edwards, and M. Vinzent. Leuven, Belgium: Peeters, 2010: 175–79.

Simon, Reinhard, *Das Filioque bei Thomas von Aquin: Eine Untersuchung zur dogmengeschichtlichen Stellung, theologischen Struktur und ökumenischen Perspektive der thomanischen Gotteslehre.* Berlin: P. Lang, 1994.

Sinkewicz, Robert. "The Doctrine of Knowledge of God in the Early Writings of Barlaam the Calabrian." *Medieval Studies* 44 (1982): 181–242.

———. "A New Interpretation for the First Episode in the Controversy between Barlaam the Calabrian and Gregory Palamas." *Journal of Theological Studies* n.s. 31 (1980): 489–500.

Skylitzes, John. *Synopsis Historion* (PG 122, 367–476).

Smith, Mahlon. *And Taking Bread . . . Cerularius and the Azymite Controversy of 1054.* *Théologie Historique* 47. Paris: Beauchesne, 1978.

Smulders, P. *La Doctrine trinitaire de S. Hilaire de Poitiers.* Rome: Univ. Gregoriana, 1944.

Sole, Claudia. *Jerusalem-Konstantinopel-Rom: Die Vitan des Michael Synkellos und der Brüder Theodorus und Theophanes Graptoi.* Stuttgart, Germany: Steiner, 2001.

Sopko, Andrew. "'Palamism before Palamas' and the Theology of Gregory of Cyprus." *St. Vladimir's Theological Quarterly* 23 (1979): 139–47.

Souarn, R. "Tentatives d'union avec Rome: un patriarche grec catholique au XIIIe siècle." *Echos d'Orient* 3 (1899/1900): 229–37, 351–70.

Speck, Paul. "Die griechischen Quellen zur Bekehrung der Bulgaren und die zwei ersten Briefe des Photios." In *Polupleuros Nous. Miscellanea für Peter Schreiner zu Seinem 60. Geburtstag.* Munich: K. G. Saur, 2005, 342–59.

Staniloae, Dumitru. "The Christology of Saint Maximus the Confessor." *Sourozh* 52 (1993): 10–16.

———. *Theology and the Church.* Trans. Robert Barringer. Crestwood, N.Y.: St. Vladimir's Seminary Press, 1980.

Stead, Julian. "The Meaning of Hypostasis in Some Texts of the Ambigua of Saint Maximus the Confessor." *Patristic and Byzantine Review* 8 (1989): 25–33.

———. "St. Maximus the Confessor and the Unity between the Christian Churches Today." *Patristic and Byzantine Review* 13 (1994): 77–86.

———, ed. *St. Maximus the Confessor: The Church, the Liturgy and the Soul of Man.* Still River, Mass.: St. Bede's Publications, 1982.

Steiber, Joachim. *Pope Eugenius IV, the Council of Basel, and the Secular and Ecclesiastical Authorities in the Empire: The Conflict over Supreme Authority and Power in the Church.* Studies in the History of Christian Thought 13. Leiden: Brill, 1978.

Stormon, E. J. ed. *Towards the Healing of the Schism: The Sees of Rome and Constantino-ple*, Ecumenical Documents 3. New York: Paulist Press, 1987.

Strecker, Georg. *The Johannine Letters*. Hermeneia Series. Trans. Linda Maloney. Minneapolis: Fortress Press, 1996.

Stylianopoulos, Theodore. "An Ecumenical Solution to the *Filioque* Question." *Journal of Ecumenical Studies* 28 (1991): 260–80.

——— and S. Mark Heim, eds. *Spirit of Truth: Ecumenical Perspectives on the Holy Spirit*. Brookline, Mass.: Holy Cross Orthodox Press, 1986.

Swete, H. B. *The Holy Spirit in the New Testament*. Eugene, Ore.: Wipf and Stock Publishers, 1999.

———. *On the History of the Doctrine of the Procession of the Holy Spirit from the Apostolic Age to the Death of Charlemagne*. Eugene, Ore.: Wipf and Stock, 2004.

Tanner, Norman. *Decrees of the Ecumenical Councils. 2 vols*. Washington, D.C.: Georgetown University Press, 1990.

Tappert, Theodore, ed. *The Book of Concord: The Confessions of the Evangelical Lutheran Church*. Philadelphia: Fortress Press, 1959.

Tavard, George. *Trina Deitas: The Controversy between Hincmar and Gottschalk*. Milwaukee: Marquette University Press, 1996.

Tertullian. *Adversus Praxeam* (PL 2, 175–220).

Theodore the Reader. *Ecclesiasticae Historiæ* (PG 86, 165–216).

Theodoret, *Epistula* 171 (PG 83, 1483–86).

Theophanes. *The Chronicle of Theophanes*. Trans. Harry Turtledove. Philadelphia: University of Pennsylvania Press, 1982.

Theophylact of Ohrid. *Liber de iis in quorum Latini incusantur* (PG 126, 222–50).

Thunberg, Lars. *Man and the Cosmos: The Vision of Maximus the Confessor*. Crestwood, N.Y.: St. Vladimir's Seminary Press, 1985.

———. *Microcosm and Mediator: The Theological Anthropology of Maximus the Confessor*. Chicago: Open Court Press, 1995.

Tinnefeld, F. *Jahrbuch der österreichischen Byzantinistik* 39 (1989): 95–127.

Torre, Michael. "St. John Damascene and St. Thomas Aquinas on the Eternal Procession of the Holy Spirit." *St. Vladimir's Theological Quarterly* 38 (1994): 303–27.

Torrell, Jean-Pierre. *St. Thomas Aquinas: The Person and His Work*. Trans. Robert Royal. Washington, D.C.: Catholic University of America Press, 1996.

Tsirpanlis, Constantine. "Byzantine Forerunners of the Italian Renaissance: Plethon, Bessarion, George of Trebizond, John Argyropoulos, Manuel Chrysoloras, Demetrios Cydones, Barlaam of Calabria." *Patristic and Byzantine Review* 15 (1996/7): 23–57.

———. *Mark Eugenicus and the Council of Florence: An Historical Re-evaluation of his Personality*. New York: Κεντρον Βυζαντινων Ερευνων, 1979.

———, ed. "St. Mark Eugenicus and the Council of Florence." *Patristic and Byzantine Review* 10 (1991): 104–92.

Turner, C. J. G. "George-Gennadius Scholarius and the Union of Florence." *Journal of Theological Studies* 18 (1967): 83–103.

Ullman, Wolfgang. "Das Filioque als Problem ökumenischer Theologie." *Kerygma and Dogma* 16 (1970): 58–76.

Ury, M. William. *Trinitarian Personhood: Investigating the Implications of Relational Definition*. Eugene, Ore.: Wipf and Stock Publishers, 2002.

Vaggione, Richard Paul. "'All These Were Honored in Their Generation' : The Problem of Conflicting Patristic Evidence in Photius." *Patristic and Byzantine Review* 2 (1983): 275–83.

Van Pays, M. "Quelques remarques à propos d'un texte controversé de Saint Basile au Concile de Florence." *Irenikon* 40 (1967): 6–14.

van Rossum, Joost. "Athanasius and the *Filioque*: Ad Serapionem 1.20 in Nikephorus Blemmydes and Gregory of Cyprus." *Studia Patristica* 22, ed. Elizabeth Livingstone. Leuven, Belgium: Peeters, 1997: 53–58.

Velykyj, Atanasij Hryhorij. *Documenta Unionis Berestensis eiusque auctorum : (1590–1600)*. Rome: Basiliani, 1970.

Verghess, Paul. "The Monothelete Controversy—A Historical Survey." *Greek Orthodox Theological Review* 20 (1980): 196–211.

Verkhovskoy, Serge. "Procession of the Holy Spirit according to the Orthodox Doctrine of the Trinity." *St. Vladimir's Seminary Quarterly* 2 (1953): 12–26.

Vincent of Lerins, *Commonitorium* (PL 50, 637–86).

Vischer, Lukas. "The Legacy of Kyrill Lukaris: A Contribution to the Orthodox-Reformed Dialogue." *Mid-Stream* 25 (1986): 165–83.

———, ed. *Spirit of God, Spirit of Christ: Ecumenical Reflections on the Filioque Controversy*. London: SPCK, 1981.

Vlasto, A. P. *The Entry of the Slavs into Christendom*. Cambridge: Cambridge University Press, 1970.

Voelker, John. "Marius Victorinus: Early Latin Witness of the Filioque." *Studia Patristica* 46, ed. J. Baun, A. Cameron, M. Edwards, and M. Vinzent. Leuven, Belgium: Peeters, 2010: 125–30.

Waddams, H. M. *Anglo-Russian Theological Conference: Moscow, July 1956*. London: 1957.

Wainwright, Arthur. *The Trinity in the New Testament*. London: SPCK, 1967.

Wallach, Luitpold. "The *Liber Carolini* and Patristics, Latin and Greek: Prolegomena to a Critical Edition." In *The Classical Tradition: Literary and Historical Studies in Honor of Harry Caplan*, Luitpold Wallach, ed. Ithaca, N.Y.: Cornell University Press, 1966.

Ware, Kallistos. "The Debate over Palamism." *Eastern Churches Review* 9 (1977): 45–63.

———. *The Orthodox Church*. New York: Penguin Press, 1991.

———, and Colin Davey, eds., *Anglican-Orthodox Dialogue: The Moscow Statement Agreed by the Anglican-Orthodox Joint Doctrinal Commission 1976*. London: SPCK, 1977.

Warnach, Viktor. "Das Wirken des Hl. Geistes in den Gläubigen nach Paulus" In *Pro Veritate: Ein theologischer Dialog. Festgabe L. Jaeger und W. Stählin*, ed E. Schlink and H. Volk. Münster and Kassel: Aschendorff, 1963.

Weedman, Mark. *The Trinitarian Theology of Hilary of Poitiers*. Supplements to Vigiliae Christianae. Leiden: Brill, 2007.

Weinandy Thomas. "Clarifying the *Filioque*: The Catholic Orthodox Dialogue." *Communio* 33 (1996): 354–73.

———. *The Father's Spirit of Sonship: Reconceiving the Trinity*. Edinburgh: T. & T. Clark, 1995.

————; and Daniel Keating, eds. *The Theology of Cyril of Alexandria: A Critical Apprecia-tion.* New York: T & T Clark, 2003.

Wendebourg, Dorthea. *Reformation und Orthodoxie: der ökumenische Briefwechsel zwischen der Leitung der Württembergischen Kirche und Patriarch Jeremias II. von Konstantinopel in den Jahren 1573–1581.* Göttingen,Germany: Vandenhoeck & Ruprecht, 1986.

Werminghoff, Albert, ed. MGH Concilia 2 Tomos 2 Pars 1: *Concilia Aevi Karolini.* Hanover: Germany: Hahnsche Buchhandlung, 1906.

Wetter, Friedrich. *Die Trinitätslehre des Johannes Duns Scotus.* Münster, Germany: Aschendorff, 1967.

White, Despina Stratoudaki. "Patriarch Photios—A Christian Humanist." *Greek Orthodox Theological Review* 20 (1980): 195–203.

————. *Photius: Patriarch of Constantinople.* Brookline, Mass.: Holy Cross Orthodox Press, 1981.

————. "Saint Photius and the *Filioque* Controversy." *Patristic and Byzantine Review* 2 (1983): 246–50.

————, and Joseph R. Berrigan, eds. *The Patriarch and the Prince: The Letter of Patriarch Photios of Constantinople to Khan Boris of Bulgaria.* Brookline: Holy Cross Orthodox Press, 1982.

Wilkins, Jeremy. "'The Image of the Highest Love': The Trinitarian Analogy in Gregory Palamas's *Capita* 150." *St. Vladimir's Theological Quarterly* 47 (2003): 383–412.

Will, Cornelius. ed. *Acta et scripta quae de controversiis ecclesiae Graecae et Latinae saeculo undecimo composita extant.* Frankfurt, Germany: Minerva, 1963.

Willach, Luitpold. *Diplomatic Studies in Latin and Greek Documents from the Carolingian Age.* Ithaca, N.Y.: Cornell University Press, 1977.

William of Ockham. "Allegationes de potestate imperiali." In H. S. Offer, ed., *Opera Politica* 4. Oxford: Oxford University Press, 1997.

William of Tyre. *A History of Deeds Done beyond the Sea.* Trans. E. Babcock and A. C. Krey. New York: Columbia University Press, 1943.

Willjung, Harold, ed. MGH Concilia Tomus 2, Supplementum 2: *Das Konzil von Aachen 809.* Hanover, Germany: Hahnsche Buchhandlung. 1998.

Wilson, A. N. *The Ground of Union: Deification in Aquinas and Palamas.* New York: Oxford University Press, 1999.

Wolter, H., and H. Holstein, *Lyon I et Lyon II.* Paris: Éditions de l'Orante, 1966.

Yannaras, Christos. "The Distinction Between Essence and Energies and Its Impor-tance for Theology." *St. Vladimir's Theological Quarterly* 19 (1975): 232–45.

Yeago, David. "Jesus of Nazareth and Cosmic Redemption: The Relevance of St. Maximus the Confessor." *Modern Theology* 12 (1996): 163–93.

Zinn, Grover, ed. *Richard of St. Victor: The Book of the Patriarchs, The Mystical Ark, Book Three of the Trinity.* New York: Paulist Press, 1979.

Zizioulas, John. *Being as Communion: Studies in Personhood and the Church.* Crestwood, N.Y.: St. Vladimir's Seminary Press, 1985.

————. "One Single Source: An Orthodox Response to the Clarification on the Filioque." http://agrino.org/cyberdesert/zizioulas.htm.

————. "The Teaching of the Second Ecumenical Council on the Holy Spirit in Historical and Ecumenical Perspective." In *Credo in Spiritum Sanctum: Atti del*

Congresso teologico internazionale di pneumatologia in occasione del 1600 anniversario del I Concilio di Constantinopoli e del 1550 anniversario del Concilio de Efeso: Roma, 22–26 marzo, 1982. Rome: Libreria Editrice Vaticana, 1982.

Zmijewski, Josef. *Die Apostelgeschichte.* Regensburger Neues Testament. Regensburg, Germany: Verlag Friedrich Pustet, 1994.

Zymaris, Philip. "Neoplatonism, the *Filioque* and Photius' Mystagogy." *Greek Orthodox Theological Review* 46 (2001): 345–61.

Index

anti-unionists (*continued*)
  Synod of Blachernae and, 142
  See also unionists
Apologia (Jascites), 136, 137
Apologia pro tomo suo (Gregory II of Cyprus), 142
Apology (Demetrius Cydones), 143–144
apophatic principle, 144–145, 211–212
apostles, descent of Holy Spirit on, 25–26
Apostles' Creed, 68
apostolicity of *filioque*, 67–68
Aquinas, Thomas, 8, 128–131, 197, 268n155, 282n61
argument from relations, 128–129
argument from silence, 127
Arianism, 6, 51–52, 53, 194–195
Arians, 41, 65
Armenian Catholic Church, 185
Armenians, 186
Arn(o) of Salzburg, 98
"Articles for which We Need Guarantees from the Lord Romans. . .", 181–182
Ascoli, Jerome, 136
Athenagoras I (Aristocles Spyrou), 209
Athanasian Creed (*Quicumque Vult*), 8, 68, 105, 174
Athanasius, 37–38, 159, 161
Athens Statement of 1978, 207
Augsburg Confession (trans. Andreae and Crusius), 177
Augustine of Canterbury, 89
Augustine of Hippo, 8, 9, 59–63, 144, 161, 236n52
  awareness of limitations, 63
  ἐκπορεύεσθαι *vs. procedere* and, 83–84
  influence of Hilary on, 53
  influence of Victorinus on, 54–55, 233n17
  Maximus's knowledge of, 245n43
  mutual love theory, 120
Avitus of Vienne, 65
Azkoul, Michael, 200
azymes, 113, 126, 169, 260n42

Baldwin of Flanders, 124–125
Balthasar, Hans Urs von, 13, 201
baptism
  of the Franks, 89
  of Jesus, 19, 25–26, 29
Barlaam of Calabria, 144
Barth, Karl, 204–205
Basil I (emperor), 103, 106
Basil of Caesarea (the Great), 8, 39–40, 46, 57, 156–158, 161, 163
Beccus, John XI, 8, 133, 138–140, 142, 271n36, 272n53

Bede, 88
"Beelzebub controversy," 20
Behr, John, 37, 43, 46
Benedict V (pope), 112
Benedict VIII (pope), 113
Benedict XII (pope), 144
Benedict XIV (pope), 185, 186
Benedict XVI (pope), 62
Berengar I of Friuli, 257n2
Berno of Reichenau, 113
Berthold, George, 48
Bessarion of Nicea, 143, 149, 171, 288n145
  at Council of Ferrara-Florence, 152, 153, 156, 160, 278n12
  as unionist, 8, 162–164, 165, 166, 167
Bible
  New Testament of, 17–31
  Old Testament, 82
  translation of, 59
  use of Scriptures at Council of Florence, 159, 160–161
biblical witness of *filioque* debate, 17–31
  the Apostles, 21–29
  the Synoptics, 18–21
Blemmydes, Nicephorus, 125–126
Bobrinskoy, Boris, 26, 29–30, 48, 199–200
Boethius, 65–66
Bolotov, Boris, 190–191
Bolshevik Revolution, 193
Bolsheviks, 196
Bonaventure, 126–128
Bonn Conferences, 13, 186–188, 195
Book of Revelation, 22
Boris I of the Bulgars (king), 100–101, 253n93
Bouyer, Louis, 18
bread, unleavened. *See* azymes
Breviloquium (Bonaventure), 126
Brown, Raymond, 18, 21, 23, 24, 25
Bulgakov, Sergius, 34, 196–197
Bulgarian church, 100–101
bulls, papal, 114–115, 135, 186
Bultmann, Rudolf, 23, 24, 25
Burn, A. E., 69
Byrne, Brendan, 28
Byzantine Empire
  anti-Latin sentiment of, 124
  forced to use interpolated creed, 125
  liturgy of, 171
  See also Constantinople

Cabasilas, Nilus, 147–148, 150
Caesarius of Arles, 68
calendar, Gregorian, 180
Calvin, John, 176–177
Calvinists, 183

CPSIA information can be obtained
at www.ICGtesting.com
Printed in the USA
BVHW041555220919
558954BV00013B/3/P

9 780199 971862